The computer as medium

Learning in doing: Social, cognitive, and computational perspectives

GENERAL EDITORS: ROY PEA, *Institute for the Learning Sciences*
JOHN SEELY BROWN, *Xerox Palo Alto Research Center*

Many industry training applications, educational applications, and of course information applications such as databases and hypermedia are all attempts to communicate, and yet we really don't know much about the computer as a communicative medium. Bringing together a collection of essays presenting such diverse theoretical approaches as general semiotics, linguistics, communication theory, literary and art criticism, sociology, and history, the editors set out to establish and elaborate the role of computer systems as a sign technology.

The volume is divided into three main parts, each focused on a different field of semiotic inquiry. "Computer-based Signs" discusses the special nature of signs produced by means of computers. "The Rhetoric of Interactive Media" deals with codes of aesthetics and composition for the new "elastic" medium of communication: interactive fiction and hypertext. "Computers in Context" analyzes computer technology in the larger cultural, historical, and organizational contexts.

Scholars in computer science, cognitive science, organization theory, information and media science, semiotics, communication, and linguistics will find this book invaluable, and as current excitement about hypermedia and electronic books continues to grow, a broader audience including computer artists and literary critics will also find it a useful resource.

The computer as medium

PETER BØGH ANDERSEN
BERIT HOLMQVIST
JENS F. JENSEN
Aarhus University
Denmark

CAMBRIDGE
UNIVERSITY PRESS

CAMBRIDGE UNIVERSITY PRESS
Cambridge, New York, Melbourne, Madrid, Cape Town, Singapore, São Paulo

Cambridge University Press
The Edinburgh Building, Cambridge CB2 2RU, UK

Published in the United States of America by Cambridge University Press, New York

www.cambridge.org
Information on this title: www.cambridge.org/9780521419956

First published 1993
This digitally printed first paperback version 2007

A catalogue record for this publication is available from the British Library

Library of Congress Cataloguing in Publication data
The computer as medium / Peter Bøgh Andersen, Berit Holmqvist, Jens F. Jensen.
     p.   cm. – (Learning in doing)
    Includes index.
    ISBN 0-521-41995-6
    1. Computers. 2. Mass media. 3. Interactive media.
  I. Andersen, Peter Bøgh. II. Holmqvist, Berit. III. Jensen, Jens.
F. IV. Series.
QA76.5.C612554 1994
302.23 – dc20

                           93-25898
                                CIP

ISBN-13 978-0-521-41995-6 hardback
ISBN-10 0-521-41995-6 hardback

ISBN-13 978-0-521-03580-4 paperback
ISBN-10 0-521-03580-5 paperback

Contents

Series Foreword

This series for Cambridge University Press is becoming widely known as an international forum for studies of situated learning and cognition.

Innovative contributions from anthropology, cognitive, developmental, and cultural psychology, computer science, education, and social theory are providing theory and research that seeks new ways of understanding the social, historical, and contextual nature of the learning, thinking, and practice emerging from human activity. The empirical settings of these research inquiries range from the classroom to the workplace to the high-technology office to learning in the streets and in other communities of practice.

The situated nature of learning and remembering through activity is a central fact. It may appear obvious that human minds develop in social situations, and that they come to appropriate the tools that culture provides to support and extend their sphere of activity and communicative competencies. But cognitive theories of knowledge representation and learning alone have not provided sufficient insight into these relationships.

This series is born of the conviction that new and exciting interdisciplinary syntheses are underway, as scholars and practitioners from diverse fields seek to develop theory and empirical investigations adequate to characterizing the complex relations of social and mental life, and to understanding successful learning wherever it occurs. The series invites contributions that advance our understanding of these seminal issues.

Preface

Most of the chapters in this book consider computer systems from a specific point of view — as *media* or as *sign systems*. The primary purpose guiding the composition of the book has been to present various theoretical frameworks for working within this perspective.

Computer technology does not lend itself readily to definition. It is made up of many strands and trends, like an optical illusion that changes shape according to the point of view adopted. The central idea of the book is to establish computer systems as media — as intermediate technological agencies that permit communication and as such are used for transmission of information, conversations, requests, entertainment, education, expression of emotional experiences, and so on. Therefore the analogies and metaphors we use for describing and coming to terms with computer systems are not drawn from the domain of machines or tools — as is frequently the case — but from the realm of media (film, theater, television, telephone, books, comics, cartoons, and so on).

But a computer is not just *a* medium in the simple sense of a television set, a radio, a telephone. On the contrary, a computer is an extremely flexible and polymorphous medium. It is a *multi-medium* since the same physical machine can serve as host for a variety of previously independent media-functions: It can simultaneously be an electronic mail system, a word processor, a database, a tool for advanced design, a paint box, a calculator, an electronic book, and a game-machine.

In this view, computers are essentially media for transmitting signals from human senders to human receivers. We are, however, not concerned with any kind of signals, but only with those that stand for something for somebody. At the center of this concern is *the sign*, for *the sign* is exactly something that stands for something for somebody (C.S. Peirce). In other words, signs are signifying constructs.

The "'sign" as a concept has numerous definitions, and this lack of agreement — or better, this copiousness of thoughts — is necessarily reflected in this book, too. Nevertheless, all the sign-concepts share a common core, since all are necessarily preoccupied with three components that must be involved in any construction of meaning: (1) the physical, perceivable sign (*representamen*); (2) the external reality the sign refers to (*object*); and (3) the effect on the mind of the user of the sign (*interpretant*).

The study of signs and the way they function in the production of meaning is called *semiotics* or *semiology*, and this discipline provides the central

1

theoretical foundation of most of the chapters. However, as any other scientific discipline, semiotics has its limits, which is why other approaches are also a part of the book.

Semiotics is based on the assumption that creation and communication of meaning is based on signs and codes. As a method it draws primarily on approaches and terminology from linguistics, and traditionally it has used spoken language as its prime example of a sign system. However, it is not so much in the analysis of spoken language that it has made progress and achieved success over the past decades, as in the study of other sign systems, especially cinema, literature, pictures, television, cultural codes, and advertisements. And now it is the turn of the most recent sign system, — computer systems.

Computer-based technologies possess special features making them particularly interesting objects of study from a semiotic point of view, and, conversely, making semiotics a particularly privileged scientific approach to the study of computers.

As we know, a computer can be described as a machine that processes data on the basis of a set of operating rules, by means of which it generates new data or combinations of data. Thus the computer is a data-processing machine.

But the data produced has to be read as information (if the computer system is to make sense) — that is, to be interpreted as referring to something else by virtue of a social convention, to be read as signs. Therefore computer systems are also sign-producing machines, semiotic systems, semiotic technologies, and as such a central concern for semiotics. At the same time — as pointed out by Peter Bøgh Andersen in Part I — computer-based signs have specific characteristics that set them apart from all other known kinds of signs. For that reason, too, a semiotic study of computers is an urgent task.

Semiotics is traditionally divided into three main fields of study: (1) the sign itself, including the different types of signs and the different ways they enter into the construction and transmission of meaning; (2) the codes or systems that organize the signs, including communication, encoding and decoding of signs; and (3) the culture within which the signs are used.

This book is divided into three main parts that to a certain extent reflect this classical triadic subdivision of semiotic studies, and at the same time describe a centrifugal movement, starting close to the computer and gradually moving outward in larger and larger circles. The three parts can be outlined as follows:

(1) *Computer-based signs,* which discusses the special nature of signs produced by means of computers, with respect to programming as well as to interface design.

(2) *The rhetoric of interactive media,* which deals with codes of aesthetics and composition for the new medium of communication: interactive fiction and hypertext.

(3) *Computers in context,* which analyzes computer-technology and computer-signs in the larger cultural, historical, and organizational context.

The general approach of the three parts can be characterized with reference to the triadic sign-model. In his chapter in Part III, Jens F. Jensen argues that the computer system occupies all three positions in the Peircean sign model: It acts as a *representamen* when we use it to refer to something else — for example, when we read an inventory control system as assertions about the stock of spare parts; it can itself be the *object* of another sign — for example, in user manuals or advertisements; and we use it as an *interpretant*, governing the way we talk about the world, when we describe humans as data-processing automata.

The humanities normally focus on computers as objects and to a lesser degree as representamens. This book, however, differs by dealing with all three positions, and especially by placing the emphasis on analyses of the computer as *representamen* — as a sign-vehicle that forms part of the construction of meaning. Part I presents semiotic analogs to programming and interface design based on the concept of computer-based representamens. Part II discusses aesthetic issues of these representamens. And Part III elucidates all three aspects of the semiotic functions of computer-systems — in particular in their contextual aspects. In this way, we hope to give a more complete and integrated treatment of computer systems than is normally the case in the humanities.

The concepts of media, sign, and interpretation are thus the glue that keeps the majority of the chapters together. Within this basic framework we have tried to present a diverse and rich range of theoretical approaches, ranging from general semiotics, linguistics, communication theory, literary and art criticism, cultural studies, and conversation analysis to sociological and historical approaches. The range of topics is correspondingly broad. It includes technical issues such as machine architecture, programming methods, interface design, aesthetic issues of interactive systems, hypertext composition, theoretical and empirical investigations of computers used as media for communication in organizations, and computer systems seen as cultural constructions.

Compared with Andersen's *A Theory of Computer Semiotics* (Cambridge University Press, 1990), this book thus presents a richer selection of methods and a broader range of topics, which of course makes it less homogenous and systematic. We have, however, tried to make links and bridges between the essays where we have discovered similarities or differences. These connections are sometimes described in footnotes, sometimes in introductions, and sometimes in the form of mini-chapters.

We believe that the methods presented here are relevant for designing and analyzing computer systems, and that their relevance will increase in the years to come. One reason is that computer technology is changing. One of the major changes is described in Jens Christensen's chapter in Part III as a change from data processing to information handling. The emphasis is shifting from the mechanical manufacture of data to the problems of interpreting and using this data, the main problem being the transformation of data into information, or — in semiotic terms — the genesis of computer-based signs that stand for something to somebody.

We think that the human sciences will play an increasingly important role in this development. We already see how linguistics, psychology, sociology, and aesthetics make their ways into journals and curricula previously dominated by natural science, and we hope that our book can contribute to this adjustment of scientific balance.

We do not, however, see the present approaches from the human sciences as competitors to natural science. On the contrary, there are many important issues that are outside the scope of this book, and the relevant goal for the future, therefore, is to make insights from one scientific tradition combine with knowledge couched in terms from another tradition.

We hope that the "openness" of our approach is reflected in the chapters that follow, and that readers will be aware of this as they proceed.

Finally, we wish to thank the Danish Humanistic Research Council and the Nordic Research Academy for supporting a preparatory seminar financially.

Contributors

ANDERSEN, PETER BØGH
Department of Information and Media Science, University of Aarhus. Niels Juelsgade 84, DK-8200 Aarhus N, Denmark.

BANG, JØRGEN
Department of Information and Media Science, University of Aarhus. Niels Juelsgade 84, DK-8200 Aarhus N, Denmark.

BRANDT, PER AAGE
Centre for Semiotic Research, University of Aarhus. Finlandsgade 26, DK-8200 Aarhus N, Denmark.

CHRISTENSEN, JENS
Department of Information and Media Science, University of Aarhus. Niels Juelsgade 84, DK-8200 Aarhus N, Denmark.

HASLE, PER
Department of Information and Media Science, University of Aarhus. Niels Juelsgade 84, DK-8200 Aarhus N, Denmark.

HOLMQVIST, BERIT
Department of Information and Media Science, University of Aarhus. Niels Juelsgade 84, DK-8200 Aarhus N, Denmark.

HOUGAARD, JENS
Department of Scandinavian Languages and Literature, University of Aarhus. Niels Juelsgade 84, DK-8200 Aarhus N, Denmark.

JENSEN, JENS F.
Department of Communication, University of Aalborg. Fr. Bajersvej 7, DK-9220 Aalborg, Denmark.

JENSEN, KLAUS BRUHN
Department of Film, TV, and Communication, University of Copenhagen. Njalsgade 80, DK-2300 Copenhagen, Denmark.

JØRGENSEN, KELD GALL
Ålykkehaven 18. DK-5000 Odense, Denmark.

LAURSEN, BJØRN
Department of Information and Media Science, University of Aarhus. Niels Juelsgade 84, DK-8200 Aarhus N, Denmark.

LIESTØL, GUNNAR
Department of Media and Communication, University of Oslo. PO 1093, Blindern, 0317 Oslo, Norway.

MARKUSSEN, RANDI
Department of Information and Media Science, University of Aarhus. Niels Juelsgade 84, DK-8200 Aarhus N, Denmark.

PIOTROWSKI, DAVID
Institut National de la Langue Française. 44 Avenue de la Libération, C.O. 3310, F-54014 Nancy, France.

QVORTRUP, LARS
The Telematics Project, University of Odense. Campusvej 55, DK-5230 Odense, Denmark.

SORENSEN, ELSEBETH KORSGAARD
UNI•C. Danish Centre for Research and Education. Olof Palmes Allé, DK-8200 Århus N, Denmark.

SØRENSSEN, BJØRN
Department of Drama, Film, and Theatre, University of Trondheim. N-7055 Dragvoll, Norway.

PART I

COMPUTER-BASED SIGNS

Introduction

PETER BØGH ANDERSEN

This part presents semiotic approaches to the design and analysis of computer systems. Theoretically, the five chapters range from classical structuralist methodology to new developments in catastrophe theoretical semantics to Peircean traditions. The programming paradigms include object-oriented programming, functional programming, and logic programming.

The chapters by Peter Bøgh Andersen, David Piotrowski, and Per Hasle establish semiotic frameworks for programming. Per Aage Brandt's chapter is concerned with the new kinds of semioses emerging in human-computer interaction, and Keld Gall Jørgensen discusses computer intelligence from a Peircean point of view.

I compare the approaches and coverage of the five chapters by discussing the problem of meaning and machines. The problem that has engaged philosophers like John Searle and Daniel Dennett is the following: Can computers be said to contain and process meaning, or do they just contain and process empty syntactical expression to which humans assign a content?[1]

The concrete point of departure is the following simple fact: Through keyboard or mouse we can input data into the computer, which responds by writing or drawing on the screen or activating the loudspeaker. The input and output are assigned a meaning and thus form a composite sign. Meaning is produced, but how and by whom?

Fig. 1. Document before dragging.   Fig. 2. Document after dragging.

Example 1. So-called direct manipulation programs often allow the user to use the mouse to "drag" objects around on the screen. As Figure 1 shows, I can move the cursor over the document, press the button, and move the

---

[1] A short summary of this discussion is given in Jens F. Jensen's chapter.

mouse to the folder. The document follows the mouse until I release the button. The result is a shown in Figure 2.

The inputs are signals I create by moving the mouse and pressing its button. The response on the screen is a change of location of the document. The relation between inputs and outputs is meaningful, because I can interpret the whole process as "I move the document". My actions are interpreted as a physical cause of the changes on the screen.

Example 2. The relation between inputs and output can be interpreted quite differently. Consider the following input and output pairs (lines preceded by "?" are typed by me; lines without are written by the system).

```
?- human(socrates).
    yes
?- mortal(socrates).
    yes
?- mortal(zeus).
    no
?-
```

My actions are interpreted as questions, the outputs as answers, and the relation between the two as logical inferences.

Brandt's chapter analyzes these phenomena in a Peircean framework: The stream of alternating inputs and outputs is seen as a representamen the user tries to interpret. The object of the sign is the user's mental images, which in our case could either be "a physical causation" or "a logical inference." Brandt's main concern, however, is the interpretant, the user's "explicative schemes" that insert the images into the gap between user action and system response.

The particular stream of inputs and outputs, interpretable as inferences, in Example 2 is the topic of Gall Jørgensen's chapter. Clearly the programmer intended the user to interpret the pairs as inferences, but are AI and cognitive science right in concluding that machines can think? Jørgensen's chapter discusses this from a Peircean point of view: Assuming that machines can *represent* human thought, can we conclude that the machines also *are* what they represent? Can the map be identified with the landscape? The case of machine intelligence is an old controversy that in my opinion has always suffered from standpoints that were as irreconcilable as they were unfounded. The semiotic approach in Jørgensen's chapter provides a new setting that could replace the ideological deadlock by more rational and sober pros and cons.

In Hasle's and Piotrowski's chapters, we move inside the machine and take a closer look at then "cognitive gap between the initial and terminal instances of the sign" (Brandt's chapter). The gap is of course specified in a program, but users do not see it and are therefore ignorant about how input and output is related technically. Still, they cannot help generating mental images, since humans are compulsory creators of meaning, as implied in Brandt's chapter.

In our two examples, the gaps are filled by very simple pieces of code inside the computer. The document is dragged by the following pseudo code that keeps recording the location of the mouse (OldMl and NewMl) and adds the x and y-displacements (xdiff, ydiff) to the x and y coordinates (targetX, targetY) of the document:

```
on dragobject
  put the MouseLoc into OldMl
  put the x of the target into targetX
  put the y of the target into targetY
  repeat until the mouse is up
   put the MouseLoc into NewMl
   if newML ≠ OldMl then
     put (the x of NewMl - the x of OldMl) into xdiff
     put (the y of NewMl - the y of OldMl) into ydiff
     add xdiff to targetX
     add ydiff to targetY
     set the location of the target to targetX,targetY
     put NewMl into OldMl
   end if
  end repeat
end dragobject
```

Code 1. How to drag an object.

This text interprets the computer as a two-dimensional space where objects are located and change location. The logical example presents a different interpretation. The program is written in Prolog, which interprets data processing as logical inferences. It contains one rule of inference (major premise) and one fact (minor premise):

```
mortal(X) :- human(X).
human(socrates).
```

Code 2. How to reason about Socrates.

The examples show that not only input/output pairs, but also the "hidden" program are interpretable signs. A program expresses a specific interpretation of the machine, the data processing, and the domain of application.

Hasle's chapter deals with logical grammar that is the theoretical basis of logical programming languages like Prolog. An important problem of logical grammar is the treatment of semantics. A standard extensional logic takes terms like *Socrates* to refer to a particular object, whereas predicates like *mortal* are said to refer to sets of objects (all mortal objects). But this gives us problems with expressions like *The President of the United States:* A couple of years ago it meant Reagan, later Bush, and now it means Clinton, so according to the theory, the meaning of the expression has changed in the meantime. But this solution is counterintuitive, since we feel there is a fixed meaning associated to the title that is not affected by a presidential election.

Intensional logic solves the problem by positing an intermediate logical language into which the expression is translated. The translation of *The President of the United States* will be the same under both Bush and Clinton, since the meaning of the phrase is no longer a president, but a device for picking out presidents on the basis of information about the universe of discourse. (Are we in 1980 or 1990? Is it the real world or a fictive world?)

With this revision, answering the question *human(sokrates)* (Is Socrates human?) proceeds in two steps: (1) The question is translated into a device for inspecting different contexts, finding persons called Socrates, and checking whether they are humans. (2) This device is put to work in an actual context, and returns the truth, *yes* or *no*, of the predicate in the chosen world.

The purpose of Hasle's chapter is to place logical grammar in a Peircean semiotic context. Like Brandt, he suggests that the relations between inputs and outputs belong to the Peirce's interpretant category. The two translations are classified as signs; the first one translates *The President of the United States* (representamen) into its intentional representation (object); this object acts as a representamen in a second sign that is given an interpretant specifying the proper context, and points out the president in this context.

However, there is one important difference between Brandt and Hasle: The interpretant now consists of formal rules that can be implemented in a programming language making the interpretant a property of the machine, not the user. In this construction it seems as if the machine can process meaning and reason like at human. So maybe the map *is* identical to the landscape?

Piotrowski's chapter increases our doubts. His background is not Peircean, but Hjelmslevian semiotics. In opposition to Brandt and Gall Jørgensen, Piotrowski focuses on the computational process unfolding between input and output, with the purpose of placing the process in a semiotic structure. In computer science this topic is normally dealt with under the heading of formal semantics of programming languages, so in a sense Piotrowski's project is to construct an operational formal semantics based on glossematics.

The chapter strives to establish a theoretically sound foundation of computer semiotics, not a mere analogy. Therefore it is systematically based on fundamental semiotic concepts, two of which are *form* and *matter*.

The units of form are purely relational and independent of the matter in which they are manifested. For example, we can define vowels as units that can occur alone in a syllable, and consonants as units that require the presence of vowels. This definition can be upheld in spoken (matter = sound) as well as written (matter = paper and ink) language.

Piotrowski shows that a similar form/matter distinction can be established in a computer system and that a level of description exists where a glossematic form analysis is appropriate since relational definitions can be used. For example, functional languages are based on a distinction between operators and terms. In the expression *2+3*, *2* and *3* are terms and *+* is an operator. It turns out that operators can be defined relative to terms in the same way as we defined consonants relative to vowels: The operator presupposes the terms, because we can have terms without operators, but never operators without terms.

The form/matter separation is important in practice, because it makes programs portable. If the programmer separates the machine-dependent features ($\approx$ matter) from the machine-independent features ($\approx$ form), it becomes much easier for him to move a program from an IBM PC to an Apple or Sun machine.

Now, if Piotrowski is right in stipulating a level of abstraction where descriptions of computer systems and semiotic systems coincide, does this not further challenge the point about the map and the landscape made by Gall Jørgensen? Are we not compelled to admit that computers can process meaning?

This is a serious problem that has occupied the minds of better philosophers than I, but I will still venture a proposal. One possible solution is to recognize that both Hasle and Piotrowski deal with a special kind of meaning — namely, formal meaning in which all semantic features are expressed syntactically.

This is not the case in language. Consider for example the smallest unit that can constitute a sentence. On the content plane, this unit is the morpheme, since we can have an utterance like *stop!* On the expression plane, the minimal unit is the syllable. In some cases, these units coincide (as in *stop*), but it is certainly not the general rule. For example, the word *unit* is semantically one morpheme, since it cannot be further decomposed into parts with separate meanings, but it still consists of two syllables, *u-nit,* and can thus be decomposed on the expression plane.

In glossematic terms this means that the content and expression planes of formal languages are isomorphic, but then Occam's razor effectively prevents us from postulating two different planes at all! From a strictly structuralist point of view this again entails that a programming language contain no analog to the content plane of natural language, because the former is mono-planar, the latter bi-planar.

This is the position in Andersen's chapter, which presents an integrated description of both the visible interface and the 'hidden' processes. Like Piotrowski's chapter, it is mainly based on Hjelmslev's glossematics. Its pur-pose is to lay a foundation for practical programming methods based upon the assumption that programming is sign-creation and use of programs is sign-usage, and it consistently views a computer system as the expression plane of a sign system whose content plane is provided by programmers or users. Thus a computer system has no inherent semantics.

The problem with this approach is simply that there is a huge literature on the formal semantics of programming languages that makes perfect sense. If Andersen's approach is right, this ought not to be the case!

Thus the problem is not easily dismissed, and we in fact meet it in other domains — for example, literature. If all the semantics of *Treasure Island* is generated by the reader, then we should expect readings to show no con-stancy since they will only depend upon the reader's background. But they do show constancy. On the other hand, if all the meaning resides in the novel, then every reader ought to produce the same readings. But the history of literary criticism shows that readings change.

Perhaps we should understand the inherent semantics of novels and com-puter systems as mechanisms that delimit the possible readings, but do not completely determine a unique one? The distinction between "preferred readings," "negotiated readings," and "oppositional readings" in Jens F. Jensen's chapter seems relevant here: The "preferred readings" are the "proper" readings intended by the author/designer, the "negotiated read-ings" are local adaptations within the norm, and the "oppositional readings" are consciously subversive and disloyal readings. One could say that the formal semantics discussed by Piotrowski and Hasle belongs to the category of "proper, preferred" readings, whereas the readings treated in Andersen's chapter are of the "negotiated" kind.

A related distinction between free "personal," and bound "impersonal" interpretants is found in Brandt's chapter:

The analysis of personal interaction must therefore distinguish "free" and "bound" interpretants, and accordingly, intelligibility referring to human reality (interpersonal, untechnical)) and to institutional reality (impersonal, technical) as contents of obtained belief.

The question remains, however, why it is so difficult to establish a contract concerning the interpretation of computer systems. Why has computer technology become what Jensen calls a "defining" technology that generate metaphors "we live by." Why does the distinction between map and landscape become blurred? Two characteristics of computer-based signs can help explaining this:

Computer-based signs have a larger "iconic range" than other signs. As argued in Andersen's chapter, computer-based signs possess four main classes of expression features: *permanent, transient, handling,* and *action* features.

Like pictures and texts, they utilize features that do not change in time (for example, the document shape in Figure 1). Like film and video, they also exploit features that do change (for example, the location or 'highlight' of documents in Figure 2). But unlike any other signs, they can be handled by the user and respond in a meaningful way (Code 1 and Code 2).

Pictures can only represent *states* iconically — that is, they can only simulate the visual impressions we get when we remain immobile. Film adds the possibility of iconic representations of the perceptions received by a *moving* body: "tilting and panning," "traveling" camera. But neither medium can create icons of us *interacting* with other minds or bodies, and this is precisely what computer-based signs can do: Their increased iconic range consists in providing icons of our interaction with our environment. AI (Code 2) creates icons of our interaction with other minds, whereas virtual reality takes care of our interaction with three-dimensional space (Code 1).

Computer-based signs can create some of their physical referents. Although normal signs can create social referents (a marriage, an appointment, an academic degree), they certainly cannot create physical referents. Uttering the word "cake" does not produce a strawberry pie. But in an increasingly number of cases, computer-based signs can do this. It is, for example, possible, to draw a physical object in a CAD-program, push a button, wait a few minutes, and then have a metal or plastic replica in one's hand.

This was called a magic a few hundred years ago. No wonder we sometimes mix up the map and the landscape.

1

A semiotic approach to programming

PETER BØGH ANDERSEN

The main aim of this chapter[1] is to argue that semiotics can serve as a theore–tical framework for programming computer systems (on semiotic approaches to systems design, see Rasmussen, 1986; Kaasbøll, 1986; Nadin, 1988; Holmqvist & Bøgh Andersen, 1991; Bøgh Andersen, 1990a; Figge, 1991; Boland, 1991; Stamper, 1992). The reason is that although computers are ma–chines, they are not ordinary machines, assembled with bolts and screws. They are symbolic machines constructed and controlled by means of signs.

The interface of the systems is an obvious example of a computer-based sign, but underneath the interface, in the intestines of the system, we also find signs. The system itself is specified by a program text (a sign since it stands for the set of possible program executions to the programmer). The ac–tual execution involves a compiler or interpreter that directly or indirectly[2] controls the computer by means of the program text, and since the compiler is based on a text standing for the set of permissible program texts, a part of the compiler is a meta-sign that — in some versions — very much resembles ordinary grammar.

If we continue this descent through the different layers of the system, passing through the operating system and the assembly code down to the actual machine code, we will come across signs most of the way down.

There are always texts that must be interpreted as statements or prescrip–tions about some present or future state of the system by a group of profes–sionals.

As we change levels, the concepts signified by the texts change. On the lower levels, the signs are related to the physical parts of the machine, such as *registers* and *storage cells*. As we ascend, the texts are interpreted differ-

---

[1] I wish to thank Randy Trigg for interesting discussions and valuable criticism of this chapter. I am indebted to Kim Halskov Madsen for ideas about connections between object-oriented programming and semiotics.

[2] A compiler does not directly control the execution by means of a text. Rather, it translates the program text into machine executable code, and it is this second text that actually controls the machine.

ently, we move away from a physical interpretation, and new software concepts appear, such as *run-time stacks, heaps,* and *variables.*

A computer system can be seen as a complex network of signs, and every level contains aspects that can be treated semiotically. Since this is the case, semiotics can be the basis of a humanistic computer science playing a role similar to that played by mathematics in standard computer science. The semiotic approach will be complementary, not antagonistic, to the natural science variant, since issues that can be treated systematically in one are typically outside the range of the other. For example, calculations of time and space requirements of algorithms are best done using mathematics, whereas assessments of ease of use of interfaces require a semiotic analysis of meanings expressed by the interface and the users' work language.

The programming paradigm in this chapter is object-oriented programming. Two other chapters in this volume present semiotic approaches to programming: Piotrowski's chapter deals with applicative programming languages, whereas Hasle's chapter is concerned with logic programming.

Sign-oriented programming

The theoretical basis of this chapter is European and American Peircean semiotics. Like Piotrowski (this volume), I prefer European structuralism, in particular Hjelmslev's glossematics, as an aid toward understanding the system itself. However, when it comes to system usage, Peirce seems to offer more helpful concepts. For a Peircean view on programming, the reader is referred to Hasle (this volume). I shall start by introducing Peirce's sign-concept (Figure 1.1). Later I shall add a structuralist version of it.

According to Peirce, a sign is something that stands for something else in some respect to someone. The sign has three aspects:

- A *representamen*: the something that "stands" — a sound, a picture, a gesture, and so on.
- An *object*: the something it stands for. The object can be a physical object *(this horse)* or a class of objects *(horses)*, and it can also be emotions *(anger)* or fictitious things *(unicorn)*
- An *interpretant*: the respect in which the representamen stands to its object. The interpretants can be seen as an interpreter's reaction to the sign. It can be verbal (as when we talk about the pictures in an art museum) or non-verbal (as when we do something in response to a request). The interpretant can itself be a new sign, which in turn can call forth new interpretants, and so on, and so on.

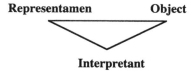

Fig. 1.1. Peirce's sign concept.

In the special case of computer-based signs, a first approximation is as follows: The representamen is the visible and audible part of a program execution, the object is the topic of the system (for example, flights in a flight reservation systems or documents in a filing system), and the interpretant is the speech and actions of the user in response to the execution.

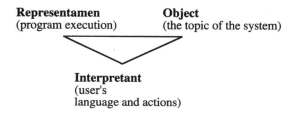

Fig. 1.2. Computer systems as signs

Since we are concerned with programming, we have to enter program texts and programmers into the diagram (Figure 1.2), thereby revealing a small part of the multi-layer sign structure described in the previous section: The representamen of the programmer's level is the program text and the programming aids that surround it, the interpretant is the programmer's speech and actions, and the object is a set of program executions because program texts are about program executions.

But besides being objects for programs, executions are also representamens at the end-user level, so programs are meta-signs describing object signs — namely, the executions interpreted by the end-users (Figure 1.3).

Now, how would programming look, if we adopted this view? There are two main points:

- We will always describe the system, even its most technical aspects, in terms of interpretants produced by a group of users, be they developers, end-users, system administrators, maintenance programmers, teachers, or salesmen. We are concerned with interpreted technology.

- Since program executions are seen as signs, we would like to structure the program text in a way that emphasises sign-formation. Therefore we will write the program using concepts that have traditionally been found useful for describing signs.

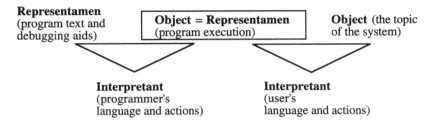

Fig. 1.3. Program structure according to Peirce.

In the next section I shall provide a brief description of simple computer-based signs. However, the main emphasis in the rest of the chapter will be on the structure of composite computer-based signs. Seven concepts have traditionally been useful for describing complex signs: *syntagm, paradigm, subordination, interdependence, constellation, agreement,* and *government.* The concepts all stem from European structuralism, my main inspiration being Louis Hjelmslev (Hjelmslev, 1966, 1971). My dynamic interpretation of the concepts, especially useful for programming, is influenced by René Thom's catastrophe theory (Wildgen 1982, 1985).

Simple signs

Peirce's sign concept works well as a general framework but needs to be supplemented with more operational methods. Therefore I also use concepts and techniques from the European structuralist tradition, in particular Hjelmslev's glossematic version. The Hjelmslevian sign is illustrated in Figure 1.4.

This is mainly a description of a sign *type*, which focuses on social and institutional aspects, whereas the Peircean concept has its point of departure in usage. The structuralist sign has two main planes, the *expression* and the *content* plane, also called the signifier and the signified. Both planes have two aspects, a *substance* and a *form* aspect.

The substance of the sign is a part of the continuum articulated by the form of a sign occurrence. When a sign token is produced in some situation, two continua are articulated: significant distinctions are introduced into the expression continuum — for example, sound in spoken language. And via the *sign function,* these form elements are correlated with semantic form elements, which in turn establish distinctions in the content continuum.

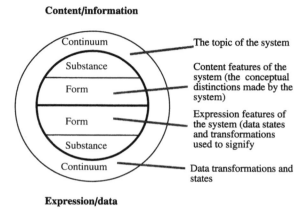

Fig. 1.4. The structuralist sign concept.

The theoretical role of the continuum is solely that of an amorphous mass that can be formed. We cannot say anything about it, since the continuum has already been formed and turned into substance. Nevertheless it helps us define the concept of a computer-based sign since, according to the analysis by Piotrowski in Chapter 2, we can identify the expression continuum of computer-based signs with the storage cells of the computer. If we disregard the program, the only thing that can be said about the cells is that they are different and can be in different states but are able to enter into meaningful relations when structured by a program. Furthermore, like the continuum of the sign concept, they are extremely versatile and able to manifest widely different kinds of meaning-bearing forms: word processors, spread-sheets, databases, and so on.

The cells that control the screen and loudspeaker of the computer are of special interest to us when we analyze the expression continuum of computer-based signs, since expression units need to be perceived in order to constitute a sign. As examples of form elements, we can list the elements of various interface standards: highlighting, button shape, window type, and so on.

As an example of the content plane continuum, consider a flight reservation system: the content continuum includes, among other things, airplanes, engines, passengers, flights, departure and destination location and times.

This continuum can be articulated in many ways. Computer science has developed methods for doing this that in many cases are parallel to semantic analysis in the structuralist tradition. In the following I use the object-oriented design methods in Rumbaugh et al. (1991) as an example of these methods. The flight reservation example is from Kristensen et al. (1991).

The first important decision concerns the boundaries of the system: In object-oriented design, the question is which objects and object classes are relevant. Passengers and seats should probably be objects. Airplanes are also necessary, and most passengers know the concept of a "flight." But what about bus transportation to and from the airport, or hotels owned by the airline company? Do they belong to the system?

The next steps also resemble traditional semantic analysis. We have to assign the objects to a limited set of basic classes: objects (nouns), associations between objects (declarative verbs), attributes of objects (adjectives), and operations on objects (imperative verbs). Thus we chose a particular perspective in the analysis; the perspective is not a natural property of reality but is superimposed on it, due to the language we use:

> .. no part of the world "is a system" as an inherent property. It is a system if we choose a system perspective. *(Kristensen et al, 1991: 234)*

The system perspective is a conceptual "grid" that expresses the basic view on the application area and corresponds to the content form of the Hjelmslevian sign. Designing the grid can involve difficult decisions. For example, should we classify a *reservation* as an operation or is it an object? Counterintuitively, a reservation should probably be considered an object because it contains manipulable properties.

Following sound structuralist methodology, objects are partially defined by means of the relations they mutually enter into: A flight *is accomplished by means of* an airplane, an airplane *contains* seats, a customer can *book* a seat, and so on.

On the basis of this analysis the objects are arranged in a class hierarchy, defined by the classical *genus et differentiae* technique (Eco, 1986: Ch. 2). For example, we may set up a *reservation* class (genus) with two differentiae: date and customer. This class can have two species: a *flight reservation* whose differentiae are flight and seat number, and a *hotel reservation* containing hotel name and room number.

This example also demonstrates why the structuralist tradition should at least be part of a computer semiotics: It is easy to reinterpret computer science methodology in a structuralist framework. We shall examine the Peircean tradition as well later on.

However, the Peircean and Hjelmslevian sign concepts do not map neatly onto each other, although it is possible to indicate loosely some correspondences. Peirce's *representamen* corresponds to Hjelmslev's *expression plane*, while the *object* seems similar to the *content substance*. The interpretant — the most intriguing and elusive concept in Peirce's semiotics — has several aspects: One of its main functions is to relate the representamen to its object, and in this capacity it resembles Hjelmslev's sign function (cf. Hasle's Chapter 4). As mentioned, another feature of the interpretant is its role as "reaction" to the representamen/object association. The reaction can be a sign, as when we talk about a picture we see or have seen, but Peirce is prepared to go even further, so that any thought or action made in response to the sign counts as an interpretant. It is this idea that makes Peirce useful for analyzing computer-based signs. These signs are designed to be used in a work process, and therefore we need concepts that relate signs to non-symbolic work. It seems as if the interpretant concept is well suited for this role.

Distinctive features

The two planes of a sign are composed of smaller units. The smallest expression units in language are the phonemes. We can use them to build syllables, and syllables can in turn be parts of words, which again are parts of tone-groups and utterances. In a similar vein, we must look for the smallest elements with which to build computer-based signs. In the following I shall give a rough outline of the nature of computer-based signs and their methods of combination. The prototypical computer-based sign is made up of three classes of distinctive features[3]:

- A *handling feature* of a computer-based sign, produced by the user, and including key-press, mouse, and joystick movements that cause electrical signals to be sent to the processor.
- A *permanent feature* of a computer-based sign, generated by the computer. It is a property of the sign that remains constant throughout the lifetime of a sign token, serving to identify the sign by contrasting it with other signs. Examples: icons in picture-based systems, or letter sequences in textual systems.
- A *transient feature* of a computer-based sign, generated by the computer, but unlike permanent features, it changes as the sign token is used. It does not contrast as much with other signs, but rather inter-

---

[3] I use the concept distinctive features in the modern loose sense of "any part or property of a sign that contributes to creation of meaning." It sometimes correponds to Hjelmslev's taxeme (the smallest segment of a text), sometimes to his glosseme (a distinctive property of a taxeme).

nally in the same sign, symbolizing the different states of the sign referent. Examples: location, highlight.

In addition we must incorporate the notion of *action* in the definition of the
sign types, since our interpretation of a computer-based sign also depends
upon what it can do to other signs. For example, the fact that the pencil sign
can leave black traces on the paper sign of the screen enables the pencil and
the paper to form a composite, computer-based sign, paraphrased as "I am
painting the paper with the pencil." Similarly, a *sort* command would not be
interpreted as "sorting" if it did not change its object in a specified way.

		+action		-action
		+handling	-handling	
+permanent	+transient	**Interactor**	**Actor**	**Object**
	-transient	**Button**	**Controller**	**Layout**
-permanent			**Ghost**	

Figure 1.5. Classification of computer-based signs. (Note that +*permanent*
+*transient* means that the sign contains both permanent and transient features, not that
the same feature can belong to both classes.)

The classification in Figure 1.5 of computer-based signs is based on two criteria:

- Which features does the sign possess?
- Can the sign perform actions that affect features of other signs?

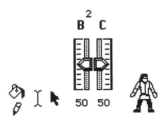

Fig. 1.6. Interactors. Cursors from Canvass™, sliders from Digital Darkroom™,
and the protagonist from the adventure game Dark Castle™.

Interactors are unique to the computer medium: Like pictures they possess
permanent, stable features, and like film they have transient, changing fea-

tures. But unlike any known type of sign, they also possess handling features, enabling the users' own actions to be a part of the semiosis.

The Interactor (Figure 1.6) exploits features from all three dimensions. It is distinguished from the other signs by permanent features — for example, size and icon, and during its lifetime it can change transient properties — for example, location and color, these changes being functionally dependent upon its handling features. In most cases it can perform actions that change transient features of other signs.

Buttons resemble Interactors, but their transient features are rudimentary, consisting of highlighting. *Actors*, lacking handling features, are autonomous processes that cannot be interfered with once started. In a word processor they include operations like sorting, creating a table of contents, or saving the text to disk. In games, actors represent the opponent. *Controllers* lack transient and handling features, but can still act on other signs. Windows are often divided into areas — for example, a tool palette and a work space — whose borders are controllers that change the cursor Interactor. If the cursor is within the palette it becomes an arrow for selecting a tool, while it changes into a tool when moved into the work space. As the name indicates, *objects* are passive items lacking handling and action features. They are typically acted on by means of actors or interactors. Examples are signs for work objects like pictures and texts. *Ghosts* are signs that can neither be seen nor handled, but can still influence other signs. Examples are hidden typographical codes for *new line* and *soft hyphens* in word processors. In games, ghosts can represent hidden traps. Finally, *Layouts* lack all features except permanent ones, being mere decorations. Examples: constant headings in textual systems, and boxes and colors in graphical systems.

It is important to notice that this definition of computer-based signs is not a definition of interface elements, since a semiotic analysis of the form of computer-based signs is orthogonal to the standard distinction between functionality and interface. On the one hand, there are features of the interface that do not belong to form but to substance, since they play no role in the creation of meaning. On the other hand, according to the preceding argument about the pencil sign and the sort-command, certain features of the algorithms that provide the functionality of the system belong to form, since the meaning of the signs depends upon them. For example, the sort-sign incorporates those parts of the sort algorithm that distinguish it from merge-processes. It encompasses what in computer science are called the *invariants* of the sort-process.

Suppose that x and y are elements that can be ordered in a list. Let C(x) be the contents of the elements and let us suppose that an order is defined on the contents also, e.g. an alphabetical order. Let $P(x,y) =_{def} (C(x) < C(y)) \rightarrow$

(x < y) be an ordering principle demanding that the two orders must agree. An important part of the meaning of sorting is that before sorting, at least two elements did not satisfy P, while after sorting, all elements satisfy P. This description captures the essential meaning of "sorting" — its content form distinguishing it from other kinds of processes.

The specific method of sorting, however, belongs to the substance of the sort-sign, since exchanging one method for another does not alter the interpretation of the process, as long as certain properties — for example, speed — stay within critical limits. This last precondition is important: We have a range of algorithms, some quicker than others, that will all be accepted as representing "sorting," but if the critical limits are exceeded, the user will refuse to interpret the process as sorting, and may instead decide that the system is stuck. A continuous range with discontinuous jumps is a basic phenomenon in the emergence of form (morphogenesis); in the last part of the chapter, catastrophe theory is presented as one way of dealing systematically with this phenomenon.

Programming simple signs

I conclude this section with a small programming example. Most of my examples are done quickly in Supercard, so the programs are mainly written in Supertalk. However, for "real" programming, I will use the following Simula-like notation.

A class named A with actions X and Y is described:

```
Class A;
  procedure X;...
  procedure Y;...
end A
```

If A is used as a superclass (genus) of B, so that B (species) inherits properties from A, I write:

```
A class B;
  procedure Z
  procedure W
end B
```

B possesses four procedures: its own (Z and W) and those inherited from A (X and Y). Sending a message to the object named A, requiring it to perform action X, is written A.X.

Peter Bøgh Andersen

The first example (Figure 1.7) is adapted from Supercard's help-system. It shows how to program a simple slider:

Fig. 1.7. The slider interactor.

The black slider can be moved up and down along the scale, and as long as it is moved, the box displays the number selected. The slider is an interactor, displaying all four kinds of features:

- *Handling*: The user can move it.
- *Permanent*: It retains its black triangular shape.
- *Transient*: It changes location.
- *Action*: It writes a number in the box.

To a certain degree, Supertalk (and its cousin Hypertalk) support such an analysis linguistically:

- *Handling*: User messages are a subset of the general message passing system of Supertalk. The system routes messages to the screen object that the user points to with the cursor. For example, if the cursor is on the slider and the mouse button is pressed, the slider receives the *MouseDown* message.
- *Permanent and transient* features: Each object in Supertalk possesses a number of properties that can easily be manipulated. For example, the expression *the property of objectdescriptor* retrieves a property of the object, while *Set property of objectdescriptor to value* changes the property of the object *objectdescriptor* to *value*.
- *Action*: Supertalk provides facilities for associating code (called scripts) with an object or class of objects.

The script of the slider looks like this:

```
on mouseDown
    -- centerLine = x-coordinate of the scale
    -- maxTop = the y-coordinate of the top of the scale
    -- maxBottom = the y-coordinate of the bottom of the scale
    repeat until the mouse is up
        -- read mouse
```

```
    get the mouseloc
    -- store y-value into sliderHeight
    put item 2 of it into sliderHeight
    -- prevent the slider from going outside the scale
    if sliderHeight<maxTop then put maxTop into sliderHeight
    if sliderHeight>maxBottom then put maxBottom into sliderHeight
    -- set the location of the slider to new value
    set the loc of me to centerline,sliderHeight
    -- store the number it points to on the scale into field output
    put 241-sliderHeight into cd fld 'Output'
  end repeat
end mouseDown
```

Code 1. A slider.

This script shows how Supertalk chooses to implement the four features:

- *Handling*: The name of the handler, *MouseDown*, implements its handling feature. The code is executed if the object receives a mousedown
  message from the user.
- *Permanent and transient features:* Its permanent feature, the icon, can
  be selected in the editor, or it can be assigned by the command *set the
  icon of objectdescriptor to iconname*. The icon property is used as a
  permanent feature here, while the location property is a transient feature that is changed in the line *set the loc of me to centerline, slider-
  Height*. The line changes the y-coordinate of the slider to that of the
  mouse, if the mouse is within the range of the scale.
- *Action*: The effect of the slider on the box is implemented as the line
  put 241 - sliderHeight into cd fld 'Output'.

Subordination, interdependence, and constellation

In the following I use an editor for constructing interactive multimedia applications, called *Plays*, as my general example. The editor has the following
main modules:

- The *Editor*, where the objects of the product are created, edited, and
  deleted.
- The *Display*, where the objects are shown and the user interacts. The
  Display is divided into Windows, each of which can show different
  Scenes, but only one at a time.

- The *Object Specification,* where data about each object is stored. Object Specification and Display together constitute a multimedia application. The former stores data, the latter displays it. The two of them are simply called a *Play*.

A typical screen (Figure 1.8) will look like this:

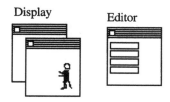

Fig. 1.8. Typical screen layout.

We see two Windows of the Display: They can display still-pictures, animations or real-time video and the reader can interact with them. The Editor is based on form-filling. Entering new values in a slot — for example, a new location for an Actor — will cause the Display to change — for example, by moving the Actor. The Object Specification is not visible, but active.

This structure was designed after several errors, and a natural question to ask is: Why this structure? One consideration is that a module should be able to contract definable relations with other modules. Let me start by giving some examples of these relations. The first examples are *syntagmatic* relations, relations between signs that occur together in the same context — a both-and relation. The pattern *Subject + Verb* is a syntagmatic pattern from language, while *Jacket + Trousers* is a syntagm from the language of clothing.

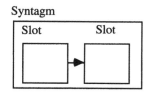

Fig. 1.9. Syntagm and slots.

Since syntagms are composite signs they must have a content; not just any juxtaposition of elements counts as a syntagm. In normal prose, *Jack runs,* is a syntagm, while *colorless green ideas sleep furiously* is not. However, the sentence may well be the masterpiece of Chomsky's Collected Poems, since in this context it will be read in a different way.

I use a slot-and-filler notation for describing syntagms. A syntagm consists of one or more slots, depicted as boxes. Slots can establish different kinds of relations, here shown (Figure 1.9) by arrows connecting the boxes.

Slots are filled with fillers. Fillers can be grouped in *paradigms.*[4] A paradigm is a set of signs that can occur in the same slot but that exclude each other, an either-or relation. For example, the set of *nouns* in verbal language form a paradigm, the set of *trousers* do so in the code of clothing, and *cards* form a paradigm in the Hypercard system.[5] I sometimes indicate the allowed fillers of a slot in the following way (Figure 1.10):

Fig. 1.10. The paradigm of fillers (here nouns) of a slot.

I use three traditional kinds of syntagmatic relations — *subordinations, interdependences,* and *constellations.*[6]

Subordination. The Editor is subordinate to the Play, since it makes no sense for the Editor to occur if there is no Play to edit. If the user sees an Editor, he quite sensibly believes that he can edit. But since he cannot edit if there is no Play, we are really promising him something we cannot fulfil, and according to normal communicative norms we should not do such a thing. Subordination is denoted by a single-headed arrow pointing from subordinate (the modifier) slot to superordinate (the head) slot. Although the Editor is subordinate to the Play, the reverse is not true, since the Play must be able to occur alone as a stand-alone application. A large group of users only read the system but do not edit it.[7]

Interdependence. What about the relationship between Display and Object Specification? It does not make sense to show the Display without

---

[4] In programming languages, the notion of types can be used to implement paradigms. A type declaration in Pascal is a description of a collection of values; a variable is a slot in the run-time stack syntagm, and its type indicates the paradigm from where its fillers can be taken.

[5] Choice of paradigms has hardware implications too. Since members of a paradigm are not present at the same time, only one of them needs to occupy RAM-space. The others can be stored on the disk.

[6] The concepts are from Hjelmslev (1966). However, I deviate in one respect, since I have replaced Hjelmslev's (counter intuitive) term *determination* by *subordination.* Piotrowski's chapter retains Hjelmslev's original term.

[7] See Piotrowski's chapter for a different treatment of the same phenomenon. In his words, we would say that the Editor is an operator that calls its argument, the Play.

Object Specification, since it is the Specification that makes things happen in the Display, and we may safely believe that the user opens the Display to see something interesting. But would it make sense to have the Specification without Display, for example during editing?

It depends on the interpretants that we want to help the user produce. If we want him to be able to form a clear impression of the visual effects of the editing, a representamen only consisting of the verbal command will be of little use, since he will have to imagine the visual effects himself. However, if we create a two-part representamen, *verbal command in Editor + visual change in Display,* the user can immediately see the visual results of his editing and has a better chance of producing the desired interpretant. This again means that the Display and Specification must always occur together, both during reading and editing; we say that they are *interdependent.* Interdependence is denoted by a double-headed arrow connecting the slots.

Constellation. Finally, let us look at the individual Editor forms. In one form, the user can edit the Actors, while another form is used for specifying the Actions. Suppose we have three actors — Adam, Eve, and the Apple — and two actions pulling Adam towards and away from the Apple. The relevant question is: Do we only want to have one Editor form on the screen at a time, or will we need to look simultaneously at an Actor and an Action during editing?

If we adopt the first solution, all Editor forms should constitute a paradigm, but that solution is probably bad, since when we create an Action we specify the shape changes of its Actor, and it would be helpful to be able to see the shapes available to the Actor as we specify them in the Action Editor. But this is only possible if the Actor Editor is open (Figure 1.11).

On the other hand, there could be other cases where it would be possible to edit an Actor or Action in isolation, so they should not form an interdependence; we do not want to have all editors forced upon us if we just want to use one. The relation between the editors should therefore be a *constellation.* In a constellation the signs do not presuppose each other; in our case we may have Actor Editor alone, Actor Editor + Action Editor, and Action Editor alone. Constellation is shown by a line without arrows, or not shown at all.

Different design decisions in Hypercard and Supercard provide a similar example: In Hypercard, the scripts form a paradigm, since we can only edit one at a time, while the editor of Supercard allows us to edit more than one script at a time. Here they form a syntagm, namely a constellation.

These notions can also be used on a more detailed level. The next example, shown in Figure 1.12, is a fragment of the Actor Editor.

The top rectangle displays the object edited (Peter). Three buttons follow: *Create* (creates a new object), *Delete* (deletes the current object), and *Script* (lets the user edit the code associated with the object).

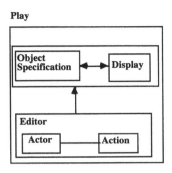

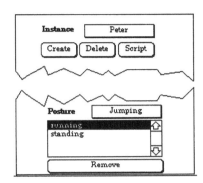

Fig. 1.11. Main module structure. Single arrow head: subordination. Double arrow head: interdependence. No arrow head: constellation.

Fig. 1.12. Fragment of the Actor Editor.

The lower half displays a list of postures that Peter can assume; in the example he can run or stand. A pop-up menu of postures is associated with this list. In Figure 1.12 it displays the last posture selected, namely *jumping*. Selecting an item in the menu adds the selected posture to the object. The *Remove* button removes the selected posture.

These signs cohere in various ways. It is always possible to *Create*, but *Delete*, *Script*, and the posture menu only make sense if there is an object — which is not the case when we work on a new scene and have not yet created any actors. Similarly, *Remove* only makes sense if the posture list exists — that is, if the Actor has at least one posture. These cohesions can be described as subordinations, as shown in Figure 1.13:

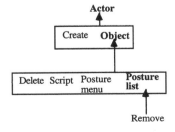

Fig. 1.13. Analysis of the Actor Editor. Boldface: data items, non-bold: operations.

Diagrams like these are helpful when the interface is complex and we want to ensure that only those signs the user can, in fact, use appear in the interface. Programming this is no easy matter, but the diagram helps by abstracting the essentials. If we descend to even lower levels of detail, the same concepts remain useful.

The posture menu is a pop-up menu, so that when it is pressed, a list of available postures appears, and one of them can be selected. The relation between a menu heading and menu items can be classified as a subordination, where the heading is the head and the item list is the modifier, since the heading can occur without the list, whereas the list can only occur together with the heading.

Syntagmatic types: Definition and implementation

To summarize, the three main type of syntagms, *constellations, subordinations,* and *interdependences,* can be defined formally as shown next (on application of the concepts to composition of hypertext systems, see Bøgh Andersen (1990b)):

- In a *constellation,* all slots can be filled or empty.
- In a *subordination,* one slot (often called the *head* or *constant* of the construction) must be filled, while the other slot (the *modifier* or *variable* part of the construction) need not be.
- In an *interdependence,* all slots must be filled.

The formal definitions have analogies in logic, a constellation corresponding to a *disjunction,* a subordination to an *implication,* and an interdependence to an *equivalence.* This similarity is found in the code that implements the relations.

In the case of the multimedia editor, let us assume that user interaction (opening and closing windows) can occur in so many different places (a fixed menu, a button in the editor, or directly from the desktop) and in so many situations that it is impossible to keep track of them. Since the roots of the disturbances are so numerous and varied, it would produce a very messy code if we tried to enforce the equilibrium relations each time a disturbance occurs.

Instead, the code ensuring that the correct syntagmatic relations are obeyed is written in one place[8] and activated by intercepting messages about closing and opening objects. In Supercard, these objects can be projects, windows, cards, buttons, and so on. The code following was actually

---

[8] I shall later present theoretical arguments for this solution.

used for project and window control but is generalized so as to be useful for all kinds of system objects.

```
on subordination head, modifier, governor
  if governor = modifier then
    --user interacts with modifier. Add the head if modifier is
      present.
    if  StillVisible (modifier) then AddObject head
    exit subordination
  end if
  --user interacts with head. Remove the modifier if head is gone.
  if governor = head then
    if not(StillVisible (head)) then RemoveObject modifier
    exit subordination
  end if
end subordination

on interdependence object1, object2, governor
  subordination object1, object2, governor
  subordination object2, object1, governor
end interdependence
```

Code 2. Interdependence and subordination.

Subordination can be implemented as a single implication (*if StillVisible (modifier) then AddObject head + if not(StillVisible (head)) then RemoveObject modifier*), the modifier implying the head. Interdependence is a double subordination, while the members of a constellation establish no implications at all.

Note that a subordination can be satisfied in two ways: If only the modifier but not the head occurs, then we can either close the modifier or we can open the head. Both actions will enforce the constraints, and in order to decide which one is appropriate, we have to take the user's work into account. We do this by letting the action depend on the Object in which the interaction takes place. If the user opens the modifier, then he probably wants that on the screen, and in order to satisfy the subordination, we open the head too. Similarly, if he closes the head, this is what he wants, and in order to satisfy the constraints, we must close the modifier. Therefore the code has "governor," the object interacted with, as its third parameter (the governor concept is explained more fully next.

In our case, we write the handler *Keepwatch* to enforce the syntagmatic relations between *Display*, *Editor,* and *Object Specification.* The Display and Object Specification must establish interdependence, while the interdependence must be the head of a subordination with the Editor as the modifier. This could easily be implemented in a real object-oriented language; however, in the Supertalk code shown here, the head of the subordination is not the interdependence itself, but one of its members:

```
on KeepWatch governor
    subordination Display, Editor, governor
    interdependence Display,ObjectSpec,governor
    unmark
end KeepWatch
```

Code 3. Equilibrium constraints.

Finally, the *KeepWatch* handler must be activated whenever the user introduces a possible disturbance into the equilibrium — which boils down to events where Objects appear and disappear on the screen. If the *Objects* are *Projects*, then the system receives the message *Openproject* during opening, and *Closeproject* during closing. So we just intercept these messages and enforce the equilibrium constraint when these messages occur[9]:

```
on openproject
    keepwatch projectname
end openproject

on closeproject
    keepwatch  projectname
end closeproject
```

Code 4. Activation of equilibrium constraints.

This brings us to the end of the formal definitions of the syntagmatic types. Their semantics can be described as follows (Diderichsen, 1962):

---

[9] A neater solution would be to use the idle message to enforce constraints. The problem with this solution is that many equilibrium constraints will comsume processing time and therefore encumber the user. We have some timing problems left. Suppose we close the Display in Figure 1.8. Then KeepWatch is called, requiring us to close the Object Specification too. So we do that. But this closing-message will call the KeepWatch handler again, requiring us to close the Display, which again..... In order to prevent this kind of recursion we have to mark the objects to be opened or closed and prevent them from influencing the process further.

- In a *constellation,* both parts relate to the context; an individual part can play the same semantic role as the whole construction. In "I saw a big red house," both *big* and *red* relate to *house*, since it makes sense to say "I saw a big house," and "I saw a red house." Menu items in two different menus — for example, *Monaco* in the font menu and *12* in the size menu — form a constellation, both on the screen and in their verbal paraphrase: *I use a monaco 12 point font.*

- In a *subordination*, only the head is in direct contact with other meanings in the text. The modifier does not directly relate to the signs outside the subordination, only to the head by modifying it in some way — for example, by predicating a property of it or restricting its reference. In "I saw a large tree," *large* relates only to *tree*, not to *I* or *saw*, and *large* predicates a property of the tree. In a hierarchical menu, items in the embedded menu are subordinate to items in the embedding menu. For example, in Adobe Photoshop, the *Image* menu contains a *Filter* item that heads a subordinate menu containing *Despecle* and *Blur*. *Blur* is subordinate to *Filter*.

- In an *interdependence*, the effect of the whole cannot be reduced to the effect of one of its parts, so neither of the two parts relates individually to the surrounding text. Only the combination of them does so. Another way of putting it is to say that the meaning attributed to the whole interdependence is not a sum of the individual parts, but an emergent new phenomenon. In "I said he came" *he came* as a whole relates to *said*. It makes no sense to say "I said he" or "I said came". In addition, the meaning of *he came* is a proposition about the world, a meaning that is neither present in *he* nor in *came*.

Constellations express contingent relations — for example, an open enumeration of elements that can be continued: "I saw a house, a car, a train, ..." By contrast to this, *interdependences* express necessary relations, and their parts form a closed set. The relation expressed by "He came" must contain two elements, while that of "He gave the book to me" needs three. We cannot add elements at random as with constellations.

Finally, *subordinations* organize the material in subordinate and superordinate elements. For example, it follows from the definition that only the head of a subordination is active in creating the narrative structure of a text. A good illustration of this is the following two texts that contain exactly the same sentences and differ only in that sentences that are heads in one text are modifiers in the other. The first text is a description:

The policeman, who fired at the robber, was a young Negro. The robber, who fell down and dropped his bag, had squinting eyes and a black beard.

The second is a real narrative:

> The policeman, who was a young Negro, fired at the robber. The robber, who had squinting eyes and a black beard, fell down and dropped his bag.

The formal relations expressed in a program text are a description of the expression plane of the sign — that is, of the means of expression we use in order to tell the user something. A basic requirement of a good program is that the user can produce a content when interpreting the expression; it must have a meaning to the user. If we employ the coding scheme we described, it means, for example, that in a formal subordination, the modifier must also be semantically interpretable as a modification of the head. Expression and content must correspond.

This fits our case: The Play can be interpreted alone, but the Editor cannot. Having an Editor alone is as incomplete as having a sentence "You can edit..." without an object. The semantic relation of Editor to Play is precisely that the Editor can make modifications to the Play.[10]

Similarly, the interdependence between Specification and Display produces new interactive signs with properties that are not present in either of the parts. The Display contains one part of the new signs — their visual properties — while the Specification contributes the ability to act and to be influenced by the reader.

Object design

A basic question of object-oriented programming is which properties and actions make up a particular object. Two main criteria can be used to make this decision (the term *cohesion* denotes the class of subordinations and interdependences):

1. *Functional analysis:* The object's actions depend upon its properties. The properties and actions of an object form the most specific cohesion of all cohesions that can be recorded in the system. This is known as the *encapsulation* principle of object-oriented programming: Only the object itself has access to its own data. No trespassing by strangers!

2. *Semantic analysis:* Objects carry out, are used to carry out, or suffer actions. Thus, if action A is a part of object O, there should be interpre-

---

[10] Most Macintosh programs respect the subordination when opened: Clicking Microsoft Word opens the program *and* an untitled text. However, the text can be closed without closing Word, so we can have a situation where the editor occurs alone. I find this confusing, particularly in connection with the Multifinder that allows you to see work material from other programs. Visually you are led to believe that the menubar of Word can be applied to the drawing of an image processor that happens to be open at the same time.

tants like *O A's (The button sorts the text), I A with O (I draw with the pencil), I A O (I close the window).* This again means that the user should be able to assign case roles[11] like *agent, cause, instrument,* or *direct object* to the object in relation to its actions.

Consider a drawing program with three objects, a pencil, a brush, and a paper. There are two actions that are interpreted differently by the user: *drawing* with a thin black line, and *painting* with a pattern of variable size. There are the following cohesions in the program:

- Both painting and drawing require the paper.
- Drawing also requires the pencil, and painting the brush.

In principle, we could assign the painting and drawing actions to the paper, because they are both subordinate to it:

```
Class paper
  Procedure Draw...
  Procedure Paint...
End paper
```

and then have a piece of code saying

```
Case tool of
  Pencil: APaper.Draw
  Brush: Apaper.Paint
End case
```

However, this analysis violates both of our rules. Rule 1 is violated because the subordination on which we build the analysis is not the most specific one: Although the paper is the head of a subordination whose modifier can be filled with two elements — *drawing* and *painting* — the pencil is the head of a subordination whose modifier contains only one element — *drawing*. This latter cohesion is not explicitly represented in the class-structure.

If we adhere to Rule 1 we would first register specific subordinations between *drawing* and *pencil*, and *painting* and *brush*. These subordinations follow a general pattern, according to which actions are subordinate to tools. But the subordination is only valid if the paper is present; so the subordination (Figure 1.14) between tool and action is itself nested in a larger subordination where the tool-action syntagm fills the modifier slot and the material the head slot:

---

[11] Case is a very old concept for describing the semantic roles of sentence constituents. It was the basis of Latin grammar that used roles like nominative, accusative, and so on, and was later revived by the American linguist Charles Fillmore (Fillmore 1968, 1977) and the French linguist Tesniere.

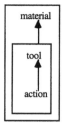

Fig. 1.14. Nested subordination between actions, tools and materials.

One way of implementing this analysis is to set up a general class of tools where a virtual action[12] expresses the general subordination of actions to tools. The subclasses of the tool class — for example, pencil and brush — will then specify the properties of the action that are subordinate to the particular tool:

```
Class tool
  Procedure Action: virtual
End tool

Tool class pencil
  Procedure Action: (definition of drawing)
End pencil

Tool class brush
  Procedure Action: (definition of painting)
End brush
```

This solution also agrees better with Rule 2, since we will naturally create interpretants like *I draw on the paper with the pencil* (where the object is instrument in relation to its actions) or *The pencil draws on the paper* (the object is agent in relation to its actions). The first proposal, where the actions are assigned to the paper, violates Rule 2, since the paper object is locative in relation to its actions. The interpretant of the code *aPaper.draw* is obscure because you have to passivize the verb in order to express the intended meaning: *aPaper is drawn on,* or something like this.

---

[12] A virtual action is an abstract action whose implementation is only fully specified in the subclasses of the class in which the action is declared. Virtual actions are part of the object-oriented programming paradigm and are supported by SIMULA and BETA (Kristensen et al., 1991), for example.

A systematic way of representing the *action - tool - material* dependencies in Figure 1.14 is to use block structure[13]: Tools are components of materials and actions components of tools. First we write a general description of how materials, tools and actions relate:

```
Class material
   Class tool
     Procedure action: virtual
   End tool
End material
```

Then we specialize these classes and implement the virtual action:

```
Material class paper
   Tool class pencil
     Procedure action: (definition of drawing)
   End pencil

   Tool class brush
     Procedure action: (definition of painting)
   End brush
End paper
```

The two criteria need not coincide. In the Dark Castle adventure game we can observe the hero forming the following cohesions:

If he is on a floor (Figure 1.15), he can move left, move right, jump, and throw stones, but he cannot move up and down. Let us call this paradigm of actions P. Thus P = <left, right, jump, throw> enumerates those actions that have the hero as the agent (Figure 1.16) and therefore should belong to him by virtue of Rule 2.

Fig. 1.15. Actions belonging to the floor.

Fig. 1.16. Actions belonging to the hero.

Let us now look at the cohesions mentioned in Rule 1. It turns out that a subparadigm — <left, right> — is closely connected with the floor, since rats

---

[13] I owe this point to Randy Trigg.

and guards can also move left and right on floors, while another sub-paradigm, <jump, throw>, belongs to the hero, since only he but neither rats nor guards can perform them.

Therefore, by Rule 1, <left, right> should belong to the floor-object, while <jump, throw> should go into the hero object, thus giving us the following class structure:

```
Class floor
   procedure left(object);...
   procedure right(object);...
end floor

Class hero
   procedure jump;...
   procedure throw;...
end hero
```

In this case, a functional analysis yields one result (actions *left* and *right* belong to the floor), while considerations of the interpretant yield the opposite result (actions *left* and *right* belong to the hero).

According to functional analysis based on Rule 1, the program text contains two different expressions for similar kinds of actions. Moving left reads *floor.left(hero)*, while jumping reads *hero.jump*.

If instead we place the emphasis on Rule 2, the class hierarchy contains

```
Class hero
   procedure left;...
   procedure right;...
   procedure jump;...
   procedure throw;...
end hero
```

and the program text will read *hero.jump* and *hero.left*.

The question is then: which one is best? In order to answer this, we have to explicate what we mean by a good program text. This is the topic of the next section.

Program texts and executions

The program text is a description of the executions. Since executions are used as signs, the program text is a meta-sign describing an object sign. But what is a good program text?

We have already seen that a Program Text is a meta-sign and that systems design can be interpreted as a kind of semantic analysis. I choose to see the Program Text as analogous with another kind of meta-sign — namely, a Semiotic Analysis, and the Execution as a text to be analyzed (Figure 1.17).

$$\frac{\text{Program text}}{\text{Execution}} \approx \frac{\text{Semiotic Analysis}}{\text{Text}}$$

Fig. 1.17. Basic analogy.

I expect the Program Text to attain goals similar to those of a Semiotic Analysis: to make explicit the intricate mechanisms of meaning production and to emphasize recurrent sign patterns.

However, there is an important difference between a Semiotic Analysis and a Program Text. A normal Semiotic Analysis is subordinate to its text, since the text is there whether or not someone has done an analysis, whereas we have the opposite relation in the case of the computer. Here the Execution is subordinate to Program Text, since Program Texts can exist without Executions, but not vice versa. In the former case the analysis describes an existing Text, in the latter case it produces it.

One important tool in Semiotic Analysis is the *commutation test*. The purpose of the test is to find out which elements take part in the meaning production of the sign — the semiotic *invariants,* the *form* elements — and which elements do not — the semiotic *variants.* If we want to find out which expressive elements are effective in meaning production, we exchange one piece of the expression plane (for example, a sound) of the sign for another piece, and record the changes of meaning.[14]

Comparing [lab] and [lap] tells us that [p] and [b] are pertinent units in English and belong to different phonemes. This has nothing to do with the physical sound properties — it is a purely semiotic phenomenon, and other languages articulate the sound substance differently. For example, in Danish we get a different result, since the two expressions here mean the same, the reason being that the two sounds are variants in syllable final position.

The commutation test can also be performed on program Executions. Consider sequence, for example. In some cases, sequence is an invariant since it carries meaning. The sequence of operations *select text, cut, select text, paste* means *moving text from one place to another,* while *select text, cut, paste, select text* must be interpreted as undoing an error: We select text

---

[14] Texts have many layers of meaning, and the commutation test can be applied on every level. I shall ignore this complication in the following.

and cut it out, then discover that it was the wrong text, put it in back again, and finally select the correct piece of text.

But sequence can also be a variant, since permutation of operations may mean the same. For example, if we type book descriptions into a library system, the sequences *type author + type title + type publisher* describe the same book as *type publisher+ type title + type author*.

The idea is now to use the commutation test as the basic method for program writing, so the general rule is:

> *Main rule:* Program texts should contain only names that denote invariants in the Execution.

A good program text, then, should display the aspects of the Execution that contribute to meaning creation — that is, show commutation.

Since the purpose of a Semiotic Analysis is to make meaning production in a text transparent, we just reverse the analytical procedure and turn it into a constructive one. Let a and b be segments or properties of a sequential computer-based syntagm. Then a and b are said to commute if and only if

- there exist two segments X and Y so that both a and b occur in the context of X and Y (that is, XaY and XbY actually occur as Executions),
- and an interpreter produces an interpretant of XaY that is different from the one XbY gives rise to.

If a and b commute, they are probably[15] invariant form elements and should be given distinct names in the analysis. According to the definition, a and b are variants if either of the following conditions is true:

- They have no common contexts of occurrence (in which case they are called *bound variants*). "Highlight" in the Macintosh interface has three bound variants: inversion, the checkmark, and the bullet. They are bound, since they never occur in the same context: The bullet is used with radio buttons, the checkmark with checkmark buttons, and inversion with normal buttons.[16]

---

[15] The commutation test cannot be applied mechanically; sometimes it gives ambiguous results that require judgement. For example, it needs a certain amount of analysis to decide whether [ng] in [sang], past tense of "sing", should be described as a variant of the phoneme /n/, whether it is best analysed as consisting of two phonemes, /n+g/, or whether it is an independent phoneme.

[16] The reader may well ask: "If they have no common context of occurrence, how can we identify them?" What are the arguments for classifying checkmark and radio buttons as variants of the same class? The problem is well known in for example phonemic analysis where guidelines have been developed. One of the goals of the analysis is to arrive at the simplest possible description, but there is no mechanical way of achieving this. Each solution typically requires pro and con arguments.

- They have common contexts of occurrence, but exchanging a for b does not produce different interpretants (which makes them *free variants*). Some of the Macintosh window types are free variants. They have no special meaning in the Macintosh interface standard and can be changed for aesthetic reasons.

We turn this around and require of a good program text that if it contains two different names P and Q (for example, names of data types, variables, constants, functions, or procedures), then the features a and b in the Execution controlled by these program items must commute. Let us call this the *Rule of Semiotic Relevance.*

In order to apply the rule, the Execution must be manifested by sign tokens. The method will not work on a program text whose Executions are invisible. The reason is that the test presupposes that an interpreter in fact interprets sign tokens, and this is impossible if the sign tokens are invisible. In order to perform the test on a program text, the program text must have a corresponding interface.

The necessity of levels of interfaces

Since most systems contain a user interface[17] — the ordinary text and graphics window for program output — constructing a program level describing this interface presents no problems. But a programmer needs to have other interpretations as well; in particular, he needs to be able to work at a level geared to the implementation of the user interface and the production of the data displayed, "the internal mechanics" of the system.

But what is the relation between the different levels? In general, the idea is that the lower levels implement or manifest the higher levels, so that *the invariant content features of texts at the lower levels are variant expression features of executions at the higher levels.* Take, for example, a piece of code that implements the form elements of the Macintosh interface, *click*, *double-click*, and *drag*. In order to determine whether we have a click or a double-click, we must measure the pause between the mouseup of the first click and the mousedown of the second click. If the pause is longer than a given number — for example, 10 — we have two single clicks; otherwise we have a composite sign called a double-click. The code might contain the following statement:

```
if ticks-oldticks>10 then return 'Pause'
```

---

[17] Exceptions: hidden microcomputers in cars and washing machines.

The condition *ticks-oldticks>10* describes a different implementation level execution than *ticks-oldticks>15*. The first one applies to an execution in which the pause is longer than 10, the latter to one in which it is longer than 15. Since at the moment we are telling a story about variables changing values, we clearly have two different stories and two different interpretants.

But if we analyze the same two executions according to the user interface signs, the difference between 10 and 15 in the definition of a pause is not interpretable at all and certainly does not commute, a pause of 10 meaning one thing, and one of 15 meaning another thing, so 10 and 15 are expression variants at this level.[18]

Since the same program text cannot possibly be a good description of the user interface, its technical implementation, and its functionality, we must design the program text with different levels, each level being a good description of one aspect of execution. This recommendation is very much in line with normal guidelines for good program texts. The characteristic feature of this approach lies in the principles according to which levels are separated. Each level is defined by a particular set of concepts occurring in the program text and by a corresponding set of signs displaying the execution in a particular way. These signs in turn can only be evaluated with respect to a user group's particular tasks in relation to the system. The notion of the "correct" or "real" description of a system makes no sense here.

Let us use the piece of code from before as an example. The sentence

```
if ticks-oldticks>10 then return 'Pause'
```

does not belong to the top-level describing the user interface since it contains a constant 10 that does not describe a feature that commutes at this level of the execution. The code belongs to the level below where we monitor variables. A program text that includes the earlier code in the part that implements the user interface is a bad program text!

Note how the distinction between user and programmer has by now become a matter of degree. Both need to interpret the system; they just interpret different signs and do different things with them. This again makes it natural to envisage a gradual transition from one role to another, corresponding to a gradual transition from a collection of signs interpreted by the end-user to the sign configuration relevant to the programmer. Design of the different system configurations becomes a *pedagogical* task focusing on the *learning opportunities* of the system.

---

[18] However, as we noted in the discussion of the sorting algorithms, the pause will be bounded by critical limits. If these are exceeded, the user will no longer regard himself as "clicking" or "doubleclicking" at all.

Object design revisited

Let us now return to the topic of the design of the floor and hero objects and compare the two texts:

1.   floor.left(hero), hero.jump.
2.   hero.jump, hero.left.

corresponding to the two object designs we discussed previously.

Text 1 introduces a syntactic distinction that text 2 does not have. In *floor.left(hero)* the subject is described as a parameter of a procedure associated with the floor object, while in *hero.jump* the subject of the action is the data object with which the action is associated. If we look at the end-user interface, this syntactic difference does not commute since it is not reflected in the interpretant. Both are paraphrased by means of an *agent verb* structure: *the hero moves left* and *the hero jumps*. Therefore, with respect to the end-user interface 1 is bad and 2 is good.

But as we have just seen, there are other interfaces than the end-user interface — namely, the programmer's interface. The programmer may have technical reasons for placing left and right movement in the floor object and therefore for wanting the difference between the two expressions to commute in his interface. Maybe the programmer interprets the two expressions, not as descriptions of events in the game, but as descriptions of the message-passing of the system where *floor.left(hero)* has a different meaning from *hero.jump*.

We use the principle of multiple interfaces to solve the problem; the Program Text is divided into two sections, one describing the end-user interface, the other one the programmer's interface.

In the first one we would like to be able to write *hero.left* and *hero.jump,* while other considerations might make us want to be able to write *floor.left(hero)*, *hero.jump* in the programmer's interface. This could be achieved by defining *left* and *right* in the hero object as messages sent to the floor at a lower level.

```
Class hero
   procedure left; floor.left(me)
   procedure right; floor.right(me)
   procedure jump;...
   procedure throw;...
end hero
```

In this way we can build up levels of description, each adapted to a particular view of the execution.

Distinctive features of computer-based signs

As mentioned earlier, computer-based signs can be analyzed into groups of distinctive features that can establish relations with other features. I shall start with the simple issue of which signs among the total set should be visible. Traditionally we separate the system into a *functionality* whose specification is hidden from the user and consists of code and data, and the *interface* that we construct to show part of the data produced by the functionality. Related concepts like *model* and *view*[19] also differ in terms of visibility.

In a semiotic approach each part of the system is a sign for somebody, so the default is that *everything should be visible and interpretable while invisibility should be explicitly decided.*

In an object-oriented programming environment this might indicate that the system should contain a library of frequently used classes like lists, queues, stacks, and tables, with methods for displaying their state and operations. Furthermore, any use of a class should automatically display its use, if not vetoed by the programmer. This default invites the programmer to remember that other people than himself will be interpreting his work and should be able to do so. When we write code, we are normally *not* only addressing the machine but also present or future colleagues: programmers in the same project, maintenance programmers, salesmen, users, and so on.

However, we may plan a particular division of labour around the system and decide that particular parts of the system are irrelevant to some groups. But since people change roles in an organisation, they may also wish to change roles with respect to the computer system. I shall return to this point at the end of this section.

Let us again look at the Object Specification of the multimedia editor. This module contains code and data that control the actors in the play and it must occur whenever the Display occurs. However, we can only use that argument with respect to its actions. In fact, displaying code and internal data changes to the viewer of the play spoils the aesthetic experience. During the viewing process we do not want a two-part sign consisting of <data changes, visual change>. Although we want the actions of the Object Specification to occur, we want its visual appearance to be absent. This means that we have to divide the computer-based signs into bundles of features. The syntactic relations need not hold between whole signs; they may only pertain to a feature class — that is, the permanent, transient, handling, or action features described previously.

---

[19] The model and view distinction is systematically supported by the SmallTalk language.

The gist of the preceding discussion is that only the action feature of the Object Specification should be interdependent with the Display (Figure 1.18). The rest of the features should not be present, so that the user watching the play is not forced to see data and data changes, and is not allowed to interact directly with the object specification.

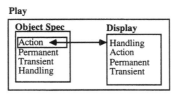

Fig. 1.18. Feature cohesions of the modules.

The individual scenes of the Display provide another example of how the individual features of signs can establish different relations.

In the system, the scenes form a *constellation*, since I want to be able to display two or more concurrent episodes. Furthermore, I decided to group sets of scenes into paradigms, one for each window. A window is thus a slot that can be filled with one scene. In addition, I had to comply with the Macintosh concept that builds on the notion of a *current window*, where only one of the windows is able to receive user-interaction at a time. Therefore, I decided to let the action and handling features of all scenes form a paradigm, only one of which can occur at a given time (Figure 1.19):

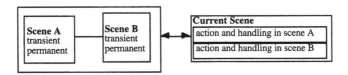

Fig. 1.19. Feature cohesions between scenes. Note that there is only one slot (the Current Scene slot) for action and handling features, so only one window can be active at a time.

Thus, although the transient and permanent features of the scenes form a constellation, their action and handling features form a paradigm from which the single Current Scene slot is filled.[20]

---

[20] This turned out to be a design error, since I should not have lumped the handling and action features together. Although interaction in more than one window is outside the Macintosh standard, displaying actions in several windows is not, and I missed a useful facility in this way.

The analysis of the Actor Editor in Figure 1.13 must also be expanded into an analysis of individual features. As it stands, it says that some operations (Delete, Script, and so on) are subordinate to an object (the object can occur without any operations being performed, while performing operations requires the presence of the object), and that others, such as Create, are not dependent upon it.

In reality, we are only entitled to state that the Handling and Action features of the operation signs are subordinate to the Permanent and Transient features of the object sign. We must prevent the user from triggering the action of an operation button if its data object does not exist.

What we do with the rest of the features is a matter of interface style. One possibility is to let the buttons appear and disappear when the data appears and disappears, thereby making the permanent features of the buttons and fields interdependent. The action and handling features of the buttons are still subordinate to those of the field. The contract with the user is that all visible operation signs can — but of course need not — be used. Other stylistic variants — for example, dimming the operations when they are not available — are better described as *government*, as demonstrated next.

It is worth noticing that the relations described so far reflect particular use situations, either imagined or real. They form an organizational interpretation of the system. For example, when we say that the Editor is subordinate to the Play, we are really thinking of the author's work situation. If we take the user's usage as our context of analysis, we might not even record the existence of the Editor, since the user might just want to watch.

The descriptions can also be made to reflect a history of usage of a particular group. Suppose for example that we have a fourth generation system used on three levels: 1) end-user level, 2) programming by form-filling, and 3) programming by writing code (Figure 1.20). If we take snap-shots of the learning process of a particular user, we might record:

Stage 1. + End-user display - Form-filling - Code writing
Stage 2. + End-user display + Form-filling - Code writing
Stage 3. + End-user display + Form-filling + Code writing

The relationship between the three main modules of the system is subordination.

Using the KeepWatch procedure here could mean that if we open a module its head should be opened at the same time, since we assume that the user has mastered the facilities there, while its subordinate modules should not be opened, but made available to the user as an invitation to explore the system further. Seduction of the reader should not be reserved for novelists; programmers can also use it.

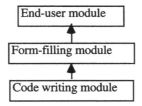

Fig. 1.20. Module subordination in a fourth generation system

This example emphasises an important characteristic of the method presented here: It can provide descriptions of the technical aspects of a system, but it must always do it relative to a particular interpretation or usage. Technology is always interpreted technology.

Concurrent and sequential syntagms

Let us now look a little closer at the scenes. As mentioned, the Display module consists of one or more Windows present simultaneously on the screen. The reason for this requirement is that I want it to be possible to create complex signs using several Windows. For example, I want to be able to narrate two simultaneous events at different locations, or to describe the same event from two different points of view.

Thus we must recognize two kinds of meaningful chains: *concurrent* chains consisting of signs that occur simultaneously, and *sequential* chains whose signs replace each other in time:

- A *sequential chain* is a composite sign consisting of signs that occur after each other at different points in time. Signs in a sequential chain replace each other on the screen and the order in which they do this conveys meaning.
- A *concurrent chain* is a composite sign consisting of signs that occur together at the same point in time. Signs in a concurrent chain occur simultaneously on the screen.

Having established these two kinds of chains, we can define the corresponding notion of patterns, *sequential syntagms* (patterns of sequential chains) and *concurrent syntagms* (patterns of concurrent chains). Therefore our three syntactic relations come in two forms, a sequential form and a concurrent form.

The difference between concurrent and sequential syntagms appears in Hypertext literature, although they have not been given special names. For example, the Notecard tabletop (Trigg, 1988) and the discussion of layout of tabletops (Marshall & Irish, 1989) reflects the conscious use of concurrent syntagms of cards, while the guidelines in Landow (1987) and the guided tours in Trigg (1988) concern the structure of sequential syntagms. Ogawa (1990) presents an elegant 3D-model for editing concurrent and sequential syntagms, which I shall use in the following. According to this, height and breadth depict the concurrent dimension, while depth describes the sequential dimension.

So far, we have only met concurrent relations: For example, there is a concurrent subordination between Editor and Play, while there is concurrent constellation between the individual Windows. However, the components of Windows, the Scenes, form a sequential chain, and their patterns are sequential syntagms (Figure 1.21).

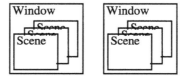

Fig. 1.21. Concurrent syntagm of windows, each containing a sequential syntagm of scenes.

Deciding whether a set of objects should form a sequential or a concurrent chain is an important design decision. In Hypercard, the script windows form a sequential chain, since we can only see one of them at a time, while the Supercard editor allows us to build concurrent chains of script windows. The latter solution is by far the best, since one often needs to compare two scripts and work on them simultaneously.

The hypertext authoring tool Storyspace recognizes the need for both chains when writing and reading Hypertext. The preference menu contains the checkbox "Don't maintain windows." If it is not checked, the system will close the current window when a new one is opened, thereby only allowing sequential reading syntagms; if it is checked, the reader is able to work on several windows at a time — a concurrent syntagm.

If the slots of a sequential chain occur at the same place on the screen, there is a simple *Rule of Correspondence* that systems may obey:

> *Rule of correspondence:* a sequential syntagm is a concurrent paradigm and vice versa.

Thus, the sequential syntagm of scenes of a window form a concurrent paradigm, since they replace each other in the window.[21]

Note, however, that this rule is not a natural law but a contract established between designer and user, and like other aesthetic conventions, its ultimate fate is to be broken by imaginative authors. In an exercise where a class of my students were asked to "computerize" a comic book, many groups used the following pattern (Figure 1.22) to create the equivalent of a filmic scene (a sequence of shots without any changes of time and place):

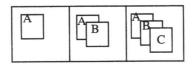

Fig. 1.22. The "solitaire" syntagm.

First they show a frame A, then the next frame B is added, then the next, and so on, as when you play solitaire. In this case, we have a sequential syntagm (in most of the systems an interdependence), but not a concurrent paradigm. Instead we have a concurrent subordination, the later frames being subordinate to the earlier ones. Figure 1.23 shows a sophisticated example, where the earlier frames are dimmed.

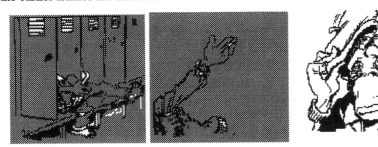

Fig. 1.23. Student use of the "solitaire"-syntagm.

Since the definition of the syntagm is a definition of form, it can be realized in other media too. For example, one group invented a pattern that shows a comic frame for a few seconds, and then plays a sound related to the frame.

---

[21] In his chapter on Hypertext, Liestøl distinguishes between time and space ordering of nodes. A Hypertext browser displays the nodes ordered in space, but a reader will order nodes in time. The "non-linear" space is made linear in the reading process. In the terminology of this chapter, the set of links of a node defines a sequential paradigm of nodes, only one of which can be chosen. The reading path itself is a sequential syntagm.

The pattern is the same: Frame and sound form a sequential interdependence but a concurrent subordination (we can have frame without sound but not sound without frame).

It is important to note that sequence in a sequential chain must function as a sign — that is, it must have a meaning. A sequence that is due to slowness of the system is not a sequence in this semiotic sense. So if a figure is first shown in a vertical position and then in a horizontal position, this is a sequential syntagm, since it means "she is falling." However, if the user can see the updating of the screen, the upper parts being updated before the lower parts, this process is not a sequence, since it has no meaning in the system; it is simply noise.

Programming concurrent and sequential syntagms

As mentioned previously, one way of implementing the *concurrent* subordination between Editor and Play is a routine that continually checks whether the Editor has been opened; if it has, the routine will produce the Play (= Display + Object Specifications).

The Play itself has many examples of *sequential* subordinations — for example, that the entrance of the villain must be followed by his evil servant. The meaning of the sequence might be that the villain is the forceful person who is followed by his serf who is psychologically dependent on him.

Because the two cases are formally similar, we might be tempted to program both in the same manner, but from a semiotic point of view, the two cases are very different: The first kind of sequence has no meaning and should be performed with a minimum of delay, while the second one has definite meaning, and the delay itself could be significant — for example, expressing the willingness with which the servant follows his master. Also, reversing the order from *Show(Villain)* + *Show(Servant)* to *Show(Servant)* + *Show(Villain)* communicates something completely different — for example, that the Servant might try to escape from the Villain, while reversing the order of displaying Editor and Play has no significance.

The example highlights the difference between a "physical" and semiotic description made in "What is a good Program Text." From a physical point of view, we could say that all events in a sequential processor are ordered in a sequence, since the processor can only do one thing at a time. But this fact is irrelevant to a semiotic analysis; since these sequences are used to manifest signs, their role is that of a continuum articulated by the form of the signs. What is important in this situation is that some sequences are made pertinent and significant; they contribute to the creation of meaning and are *invari-*

ants in the semiological sense. Others do not contribute to meaning, just to a particular implementation, and are therefore *variants*.

Since a good program structure is one that emphasises the individual parts' contribution to sign-formation, we distinguish systematically between variants and invariants. In our case this would mean that the processes controlling the concurrent syntagm (where sequence is a variant) should be clearly separated from the processes controlling sequential syntagm (where sequence is an invariant).

If this distinction is promoted to a basic system structure, a system execution will consist of a cycle where two main events happen: First, the sequential syntagm module is executed, and afterward the concurrent syntagm module is activated, reestablishing the concurrent constraints that may have been violated.[22] Thus, the program is seen as states of *equilibrium* that are repeatedly *disturbed* by sequential syntagms and restored by concurrent ones.[23]

The distinction between concurrent and sequential syntagms is not unknown in computer science. In their book on object-oriented modeling and design, Rumbaugh et al. (1991) distinguish between an *object model*, depicting the class hierarchy and component structure of objects, "the possible patterns of objects, attributes, and links that can exist in a system"(p. 84), and a *dynamic model,* describing how the properties and components of objects change over time, "the sequences of events, states, and operations that occur within a system of objects...a pattern that specifies the allowable scenarios that may occur" (p. 112). Clearly, the object model consists of concurrent syntagms while the dynamic model consists of sequential syntagms.

Algorithms as sequential syntagms.

In computer science an algorithm is a method that is guaranteed to solve a particular problem in a finite number of steps. An algorithm is a goal-directed pattern of behaviour that can be broken down into a sequence of separate steps, and is thus a special type of sequential syntagm.

I shall use *binary search* as my general example of an algorithm. The purpose of the algorithm is to determine whether a word W occurs in a list L of words that are already alphabetically ordered. One way of doing this (linear search) is of course to start with the first word and to continue down the list until we encounter a word that alphabetically comes after W. However, with

---

[22] Similar ideas can be found in constraint oriented programming (Freeman-Benson et al., 1990).

[23] This view of basic system operation is inspired by de Saussure's conception of language change (Saussure, 1966: 85, 95, 140).

large lists the search time can be intolerably long — the worst case is identical to the length of the list.

The *binary search method* consists in dividing the list into two halves and asking whether W comes before or after the midpoint. If W comes before it, W must be in the upper half, if W comes after it, W must be in the lower half. We then do the same thing with the now established half, and continue until we have narrowed down the interval to exactly one line or have found the word. This method is faster than linear search with long lists, since the worst case is $\log^2$ of the length of the list.

In the following table we list some examples of how we would tackle different inputs and different lists. In the first example, the list is empty, so the interval is less than 1 and the answer is therefore *false*. In the last example, we first ask whether b comes before or after e. B comes before e, so we select the upper half of the list (a..e) and make a new midpoint — namely, c. Again b is before the midpoint, and the upper interval (a..c) is selected. This time the midpoint is b, we have found the word, and answer *true*.

Input	List:	Method:
c		Interval is one or less. False
c	a, b, c, d	Interval is more than one and word not found. Select lower half. Make new midpoint. Word is found. True
b	a, b, c, d, e, f, g, h, i, j	Interval is more than one and word not found. Select upper half. Make new midpoint. Interval is more than one and word not found. Select upper half. Make new midpoint. Word is found. True

If we analyze protocols like these, we discover underlying regularities that can be conceived as their syntagmatic structure.

First we note that each text ends with either true or false; if it ends with true, the preceding line is "Word is found," while it is "Interval is one or less" if the ending is false. We can say that there is an interdependence between two slots, *EndingCondition* and *Result*, since they always occur together. *EndingCondition* is filled by the paradigm <Word is found, Interval is one or less> while *Result* takes its fillers from <True, False>. Finally, *EndingCondition* governs *Result*. Since the whole behaviour can consist of this interdependence, it must be the head of a subordination whose modifier is the rest of the behavior.

The modifier consists of one or more occurrences — a constellation — of a new interdependence with three slots: *ContinueCondition* (Interval is more than one and word is not found) + *IntervalSelection*(<Select lower half, Select upper half>) + *MidpointSelection* (Make new midpoint).

The three texts can be described by the syntagmatic structure shown in Figure 1.24:

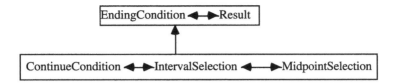

Fig. 1.24. Binary search as sequential syntagms.

From this syntagmatic structure we can immediately construct a program that will generate the behavior:

```
function search myword,mylist
   put firstline(mylist) into lower
   put lastline(mylist) into upper
   put (upper+lower) div 2 into midpoint
   repeat until myword = line midpoint of cd fld mylist or
      (upper-lower † 1)
      -- ContinueCondition
    if myword < line midpoint of cd fld mylist then
       --  IntervalSelection
      put midpoint into upper
    else
       --  IntervalSelection
      put midpoint into lower
    end if
    -- MidpointSelection
    put (upper+lower) div 2 into midpoint
   end repeat
   -- Ending Condition
   -- Result
   return (myword = line midpoint of cd fld mylist)
end search
```

Code 5. Binary search.

Apart from showing how algorithms fit into the framework of this chapter, the example illustrates a special approach to algorithm design. The concept of a syntagm is originally developed as a tool for analyzing human (sign) usage. The behavior is given, and we want to know which principles it follows.

Furthermore, we do not necessarily want to produce formal descriptions of behavior, but are more interested in extracting significant patterns — patterns that tell us something new and interesting about human conduct.

Taking this as our point of departure, we are invited to start algorithm construction with praxis; we try to solve examples of the problem by hand, and continually extract patterns from what we do in order to acquire some insight into the problem. When we feel that we have grasped the essentials, we can begin to turn the syntagmatic structure into the special kind of structure that can be performed by a machine — we formalize it.

This may not be the method programmers are taught at school, but I suspect most programmers do it in praxis. The method is recommended in Rumbaugh et al. (1991) in connection with designing the dynamic model of a system. First, you create various scenarios, representing typical processes. These scenarios are then analyzed; some of the scenarios have certain parts in common but branch off at some point, while others contain repetitions. Finally, the analysis is used to build a dynamic model.

It is possible that the method is more relevant for some programming tasks than for others. For example, it is appropriate for programming those parts of the system that are close to the user. In such cases, we would collect a representative corpus of examples of tasks that the user wants to perform with the system, analyze them in order to find their recurrent syntagmatic patterns, and finally formalize them so that they can be programmed.

In the exercise just described, the students were told to visualize their ideas quickly in spaghetti code, and then stand back, analyze the syntagmatic structures underlying their creation, and use the analysis to structure the code properly. In creative programming I think this is the only feasible method.

Agreement and government: From structure to process

These two concepts (Diderichsen, 1949) are most easily described as relations between paradigms. Recall that a paradigm is a set of signs that can occur in the same slot in a text or picture. *Number* is a paradigm containing two elements, *singular* and *plural*. A noun is either in the singular or in the plural, but it cannot be both at the same time. A noun can be described as a two-slot syntagm, Stem + Number, where each slot can only be filled by items from a particular paradigm: the Stem must be filled by nouns (for example, *car* or *flower*), while the Number must be filled by either *Singular* or *Plural*, manifested as zero or -s.

Sentences normally have more than one occurrence of the number slot. For example, in

This car runs fast

the Number slot occurs three times: in the demonstrative (*this* vs. *these*), in the noun (*car* vs. *cars*) and in the verb (*runs* vs. *run*). The sign structure is reinforced by the constraint that the same element, either Singular or Plural, must occur in all three slots.

Definition of agreement and government

In general, we say that slots in a text *agree* if they take their fillers from the same paradigm, and the same element is required to appear in all of them. If the slots are filled from different paradigms and the choice of an element in one slot requires a particular choice in another slot, we say that there is *government* between the first and the second slot. The standard example is that of German prepositional phrases, where the preposition slot governs the case slot of the noun; for example, if *durch* is chosen, the case must be accusative, while *aus* requires the dative.

In many cases of government and agreement, we feel intuitively that the force of the relation emanates from one of the slots. For example, in *durch die Stadt* it is the preposition *durch* that determines the accusative case of the noun, and not the case that determines the preposition. Similarly, the noun in *this car* is first put in the singular, and this causes us to choose *this* and not *these*.

In traditional grammar, the forceful slot is called the *regens*, and the submissive one the *regendum*. I shall use the English terms *governor* and *governed* (cf. Code 2 earlier). While our three syntactic functions specify whether or not signs occur at all, government and agreement describe constraints between already occurring signs.

In the preceding discussion I have used static versions of the syntagmatic types. For example, a subordination was formally defined to mean that the modifier requires the presence of its head. From this definition we can extract a series of states in which the subordination holds: If *good* is subordinate to *pencil* in *good pencil,* it means that constructions like *a good pencil* and *a pencil* are well-formed states, while *a good* is deviant. This worked very well with the examples I used, since all of them concerned concurrent syntagma where time does not convey meaning.

In the following sections I also use examples where chronological sequence is significant, thereby introducing a dynamic version of the concepts.

Thus, instead of the state-description "good is subordinate to pencil", I use the process phraseology that *good* attracts or is attracted to *pencil*. When an adjective occurs, it attracts or is attracted to a noun (Piotrowski, Chapter 2, that the modifier *calls* the head).

The syntagmatic relations, which describe the patterns of sign occurrence, can be reinterpreted as agreements between the location property of the signs. Using the notion of attraction, we can say that the location property of the modifier, filled with a member of a paradigm of locations, is attracted by the location of the head, so that they become more similar. In the case of Editor and Display, the locations include all possible screen locations (Figure 1.25).

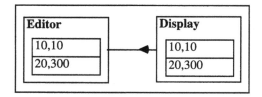

Fig. 1.25. Agreement of location.

The agreement can be understood as a *vector* that pulls the filler of a slot of the "subject" toward the filler of the same slot in the "destination" of the vector. I connect the two components of the agreement by means of an arrow and place an arrowhead near the "subject" of the vector. The direction of the head indicates whether the target is being pulled towards or away from the source. If the destination pulls it, the vector is called an *attractor*; if it repels it, it is called a *repulsor*.

Agreement and government in interface design

As a first example of the usefulness of the concepts of government and agreement, let us look at interface design. I have already mentioned that dependencies between interface signs can be signified by government between their transient features, while their permanent features remain visible constantly. In the Macintosh interface the subordination between an operation and its data can be expressed by "greying" or "disabling" the button when it is not applicable (Figure 1.26).

In the situation on the left, the operation sign has all of its features, whereas in the situation on the right, the handling feature has gone and can no longer be clicked.

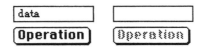

Fig. 1.26. Disabling in the Macintosh interface.

This subordination is expressed by a concurrent government (Figure 1.27) from the *empty/non-empty* paradigm of the data field, and the *enabled/disabled* paradigm of the button[24]:

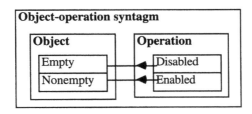

Fig. 1.27. Object-operation government. Arrows point from governed to governor.

An interface specification thus includes a list of syntagms, whose head is a field, whose modifiers are buttons, and whose head governs the modifiers. The code requires a handler like the following:

```
on FieldButtonGovernment fldname, btnnames
  repeat with i = 1 to the number of items of btnnames
    set the disabled of btn (item i of btnnames) to (fld fldname is
        empty)
  end repeat
end FieldButtonGovernment
```

Code 6. Government.

The handler is given a fieldname plus a list of button names — for example, *FieldButtonGovernment myfield, "button1, button2"*. It disables the buttons if the field is empty, but otherwise it enables them. But there are also

---

[24] It is important to note that the features are invariant form features that can be manifested in several variants in different interface standards and even inside the same standard.

dependencies between the fields. A common dependency is a concurrent agreement saying that the governed fields must agree with their governor with regard to "emptiness." If the governor is empty, then so are the governed fields (Figure 1.28).

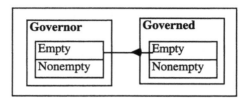

Fig. 1.28. Fieldfield agreement

Suppose, for example, that in entering data for a person, we record that the person has a child and we enter its sex and age. These fields should become empty if we erase the child, since sex and age only have meaning when a child possessing these properties occurs in the form.

In designing complex interfaces I have found it useful to separate government and agreement from the actual user interaction. As before, the interface specification is divided into an *equilibrium* constraint containing all governments and agreements of the interface, and a *disturbance* part executing the operations that the user performs. Each time a disturbance happens, the equilibrium module is activated to enforce its constraints.

Catastrophe theory: A possible theoretical basis[25]

Attraction, equilibrium, disturbance: all these concepts are dynamic concepts and, as such, foreign to the structuralist tradition employed so far. The reason for introducing them is simply that programming specifies the structure of a computational process that is inherently dynamic. We need a theoretical framework that will allow us to combine "thermodynamic" notions with the basic semiotic approach, and it would appear that catastrophe theory developed by the French mathematician René Thom offers a possibility (Petitot 1989, Brandt 1989a, 1989b, 1990a, 1990b, Wildgen 1982, 1985). Wildgen 1985 provides a very thorough and pedagogical introduction for beginners.

---

[25] I am indebted to Per Aage Brandt for helpful discussions on this subject.

As mentioned earlier, a semiotic approach to interactive systems design must incorporate the notion of a substance that is formed. A program text forms (or structures) the substance of machine cells much as the English phonological system forms the substance of sound. European structuralism provides sophisticated techniques for describing form as structure and state, but offers few ideas for understanding the genesis of form (morpho-genesis). By contrast, applying catastrophe theory to semiotic analysis opens up interesting new possibilities for understanding this process.

One of the basic ideas of catastrophe theory comes from analysis of the behavior of certain families of equations called *elementary catastrophes,* one of which is the cusp ($y = x^4 + ax^2 + bx$). For some values of a and b (called the *external control variables*), the curve contains two minima, but if a and b are altered in certain ways, one of the minima disappears. Thus, besides undergoing quantitative changes — for example, by increasing or decreasing minima — the cusp can also be subject to qualitative changes — for example, from having two minima to only having one. The latter change is called a catastrophe, and the hypothesis is that catastrophes can be used as a formalization of the notion of form.

The minima and maxima of the curve in Figure 1.29 can be interpreted as the vectors, minima as attractors, maxima as repulsors:

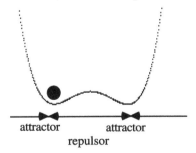

Fig. 1.29. The cusp with attractors and repulsors. The closed circle represents the system.

The easiest way of visualizing this is to think of a pin-ball machine. We interpret the curve as a solid surface, and add a constant gravitational pull downwards. The system whose behavior we want to describe is placed in this topology and is subject to the combined effect of gravity and the resistance of the "curved" surface. If the system is placed at a maximum, its state is unstable and it will roll down one of the slopes. On the other hand, if it is placed at a minimum, it will stay there as its state is stable.

Catastrophe theory distinguishes between two kinds of necessary processes: processes in the internal topology and processes in the external topology. The former processes describe changes that occur in one particular topology — for example, when the system moves toward an attractor. The latter processes describe changes in the topology itself caused by control variables. The former changes are changes of substance, the latter changes of form.

Let us take the cusp family of equations again, $x^4 + ax^2 + bx$, and vary the a and b parameters systematically. If we plot a and b values in a coordinate system, and at each point record the shape of the curve, we get a picture like the one shown in Figure 1.30, called the *external topology:*

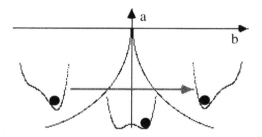

Fig. 1.30. The external topology with snapshots of curve shapes, depending on *a* and *b* values.

In the situation on the left, the object is stable in its minimum. As we increase b, traveling along the grey arrow, a new minimum appears and the old one gradually disappears. When this happens, the object becomes unstable and rolls toward the remaining left minimum. The curved lines in the lower half of the figure represent *catastrophic* points: a and b values where the curve undergoes qualitative changes. If we enter the picture and take a stroll along the arrow, the mathematical landscape in which we travel will look like Figure 1.31. The arrow shows how the object will move, as we advance through the "Twin Valley."

The system will stay in the right valley as long as it exists.[26] However, it will eventually disappear, and as the system becomes unstable, it will roll down into the emerging valley on the left.

Several researchers have suggested a semiotic interpretation of these phenomena. For example, the *system* can be translated as *actants* in the sense found in French structuralism — for example, the hero, the princess, and the

[26] This is true only if we adopt the "perfect delay" convention. Another convention, the "Maxwell convention," makes the object jump when the two minima are equally strong.

villain of the fairy tale. They are the narrative units that perform and suffer the actions of the story. The attractors and repulsors are properties that the actants can assume or places where they can be.

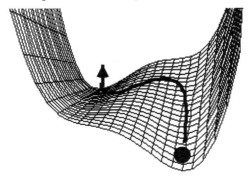

Fig. 1.31. A stroll in the external topology of the cusp-family. We start with a right minimum; as we walk into the picture, a new left minimum gradually appears while the old one disappears.

At the beginning, the princess is at home but is influenced by the villain attractor; she is abducted and imprisoned in his cave. In order for her to get home, the topology has to change. The hero now acts as an attractor, fights the villain, drags her out of the cave, and brings her home (the "Disturbing communication" note in Qvortrup's chapter "Hi-Tech Network Organizations as Self-Referential Systems" presents ideas for a catastrophe theoretical understanding of communication within Luhmann's theory of organisations).

The semiotic structures we see at this level of abstraction seem to apply not only to fairy tales, but also to system executions. We recognize the basic rhetorical figure from previous sections: *disturbances* (changes of the topology defining the equilibrium conditions) followed by adaptations of the actants to the new *equilibrium*.

Let us now reconsider the dynamic interpretation of subordination introduced above. As an example, consider the use of grid-lines in a drawing program. In graphical layout the designer often needs to align the graphical objects he creates. The artist does not need the total freedom of the paper, but wants to place objects along a few lines. Grid-lines work as an equilibrium constraint, placing any moved or newly created object along the nearest gridline.

According to static structuralist theory, we can say that graphical objects (O) are subordinate to the grid-lines (G), since syntagms like G+O and G alone are permissible, while O alone is illegal (Figure 1.32). In a dynamic interpretation we associate with each object O a vector dragging the object toward a gridline; the association of a vector with an object is the dynamic way of realizing the static equilibrium constraint that objects are subordinate to grids. Finally, in catastrophe theory, we shall represent gridlines as minima — sinks attracting the objects. In fact, a grid can be implemented as a simple sine-curve (in mathematical terms, I am moving outside standard catastrophe theory here, since sines do not belong to the family of elementary catastrophes):

Graphical objects

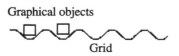
Grid

Fig. 1.32. Non-standard sine-curve
implementing a grid.

Fig. 1.33. A chase

We can generalize from this example and suggest that *a modifier can be defined as an object associated with an attractor that attracts the object to its head or the head to the object.*

Besides the conventional uses described in the preceding sections, this dynamic modifier is also suited for more unconventional and artistic applications. In a picture-based interactive narrative, vectors can be used to construct the basic narrative units. As shown in Figure 1.33, a *chase* can be built of an attractor from pursuer to pursued, and a repulsor from pursued to pursuer. Other applications are described in Chapter 11.

Conclusion

The theoretical assumption of this chapter is that computer systems are sign–systems. I have tried to draw practical consequences of this position by demonstrating how semiotic concepts can guide the programming process. We started with traditional static structuralism, made it dynamic by adding the vector concept, and ended by suggesting catastrophe theory as a theoretical framework for this "dynamized" structuralism.

If we seriously believe that computers are media for communication between humans, we need to develop methods for actually designing and constructing computer systems as sign-systems. I hope the ideas presented here are helpful for this purpose.

Bibliography

ANDERSEN, P. BØGH (1986). Semiotics and informatics: Computers as media. In *Information technology and information use. Towards a unified view of information and information technology,* eds. P.Ingwersen, L.Kajberg, A.Mark Peitersen, 64-97. London: Taylor Graham.

ANDERSEN, P. BØGH (1990a). *A Theory of Computer Semiotics. Semiotic Approaches to Construction and Assessment of Computer Systems.* Cambridge: Cambridge University Press.

ANDERSEN, P. BØGH (1990b). Towards an aesthetics of hypertext systems. A semiotic approach. In *Hypertext: concepts, systems, and applications,* eds. A. Rizk, N. Streitz, J. André, 224-238. Cambridge: Cambridge University Press.

ANDERSEN, P. BØGH (1991a). A semiotic approach to construction and assessment of computer systems. In *Information systems research: Contemporary approaches & emergent traditions,* eds. H.-E. Nissen, H. K. Klein, R. Hirschheim, 465-515. Amsterdam: North Holland.

ANDERSEN, P. BØGH (1991b). Vector spaces as the basic component of interactive systems. Towards a computer semiotics. *VENUS report 8.* Aarhus: Dept. of Information and Media Science, University of Aarhus.

BOLAND, J. R. (1991). Information system use as a hermeneutic process. In *Information systems research: Contemporary approaches and emergent traditions,* eds. H.-E. Nissen, H. K. Klein, R. Hirschheim, 439-458. Amsterdam: North Holland. Amsterdam.

BRANDT, P. AAGE (1989a). Agonistique et analyse dynamique catastrophiste du modal et de l'aspectuel. *Semiotica 77:1/3.*

BRANDT, P. AAGE (1990a). The dynamics of meaning. Three studies of modal semiotics. Copenhagen, unpublished.

BRANDT, P. AAGE (1990b). The dynamics of modality: a catastrophe analysis. *RSSI 9:1-2-3.*

BRØNDMO, H. P., G. DAVENPORT (1989). Creating and Viewing the Elastic Charles — a Hypermedia Journal. In *Hypertext II Conference Proceedings.* York, England.

DIDERICHSEN, P. (1949). Morpheme categories in modern Danish. In *Recherches Structurales,* eds. L. Hjelmslev, 134-155. Copenhagen.

DIDERICHSEN, P. (1962). Elementær Dansk Grammatik [Elementary Danish Grammar]. Copenhagen: Gyldeldal.

ECO, U. (1984). *Semiotics and the philosophy of language.* Bloomington: Indiana University Press.

ECO, U. (1977). *A Theory of Semiotics.* London: Macmillan.

EHN, P., M. KYNG (1991). Cardboard computers: mocking-it-up or hands-on-the-future. In *Design at Work,* eds. J. Greenbaum, M. Kyng, 169-197. Hillsdale: Earlbaum.

FIGGE, U. L. (1991). Computersemiotik. *Zeitschrift für Semiotik 13(3/4),* 321-330.

FILLMORE, CH. J. (1968). *The case for case.* In *Universals in Linguistic Theory,* eds. E.Bach, R.T.Harms, 1-90. London, New York, Sydney, Toronto: Holt, Rinehart and Winston.

FILLMORE, CH. J. (1977). The case for case reopened. In *Syntax and Semantics: 8. Grammatical Relations*, eds. P. Cole, G. M. Sadock, 59-81. New York: Academic Press.

FREEMAN-BENSON, B. N., J. MALONEY, A. BORNING (1990). An Incremental Constraint Solver. *Comm. of the ACM, 33:1:* 54-63.

GREIMAS, A.J. (1970). *Du Sens. Essais Sémiotique.* Paris: Éditions du Seuil.

GREIMAS, A.J. (1966). *Sémantique Structurale.* Paris: Larousse.

HJELMSLEV, L. (1971). *Essais Linguistique.* Paris: Les Éditions de Minuit.

HJELMSLEV, L. (1963). *Prolegomena to a Theory of Language.* Menasha, Winsconsin: The University of Wisconsin Press. Translated from *Omkring Sprogteoriens Grundlæggelse.* University of Copenhagen 1943, reprinted and published by Akademisk Forlag, Copenhagen 1966.

HOLMQVIST, B., P. BØGH ANDERSEN (1991). Language, perspective, and design. In *Design at Work,* eds. J. Greenbaum, M. Kyng, 91-121. Hillsdale, NJ: Earlbaum.

KAASBØLL. J. (1986). Intentional development of professional language through computerization. A case study and some theoretical considerations. Paper for the conference on *System Design for Human Development and Productivity: Participation and Beyond.* Berlin: Humboldt-Universität zu Berlin.

KRISTENSEN, B. B, O. L. MADSEN, B. MØLLER-PEDERSEN, K. NYGAARD (1991). *Object-oriented programming in the BETA programming language.* Aarhus: Dept. of Computer Science, University of Aarhus.

LANDOW, G. P. (1987). Relationally Encoded Links and the Rhetoric of Hypertext. *Hypertext '87 Papers,* 331-343. New York: The ACM.

MARSHALL, C.C., P. M. IRISH (1989). Guided tours and on-line presentations: how authors make existing hypertext intelligible for readers. *Hypertext '89 Proceedings,* 15-26.

NADIN, M. (1988). Interface design: A semiotic paradigm. *Semiotica 69:* 269-302.

OGAWA, R., H. HARADA, A. KAMEKO (1990). Scenario-based hypermedia: A model and a system. In *Hypertext: concepts, systems, and applications,* eds. A. Rizk, N. Streitz, and J. André, 38-51. Cambridge: Cambridge University Press.

OUELLET, P. (1989). *Semiotics, cognition, and artificial intelligence.* Special issue of Semiotica. *Semiotica 77.*

PETITOT, J. (1989). On the linguistic import of catastrophe theory. *Semiotica 74-3/4:* 179-209.

RASMUSSEN, J. (1986). *Information processing and human-machine interaction.* New York: North-Holland.

RUMBAUGH, J. et al. (1991). *Object-oriented modeling and design.* Englewood Cliffs: Prentice-Hall.

SAUSSURE, F. DE (1966). *Course in General Linguistics.* New York: McGraw-Hill.

STAMPER, R. (1992). Signs, organizations, norms and information systems. *Proc. Third Australian Conference on Information Systems.* Dept. of Business Systems, Univ. of Wollongong, Australia.

TRIGG, R. H. (1988). Guided Tours and Tabletops: Tools for Communicating in a Hypertext Environment. *ACM Transactions on Office Systems, 6/4:* 398-141.

WILDGEN, W. (1982). *Catastrophe Theoretic Semantics.* Amsterdan: John
  Benjamins Publ. Comp.
WILDGEN, W. (1985). *Archentypen-semantik.* Tübingen: Gunter Narr Verlag.

2

Structuralism, computation and cognition: The contribution of glossematics

DAVID PIOTROWSKI

This chapter[1] is concerned with the *intrinsic* semiotic nature of a computer. We shall begin by sketching the principles of the computational paradigm of cognitive science in order to establish the cognitive relevance of the computer. Then we shall show that this cognitive relevance is also semiotically relevant by analyzing the glossematic relations, with particular reference to the "constant" concept . Finally, we shall define a "cognitive virtual machine" that specifies (a part of) the semiotic nature of a computational machine.

For nearly 40 years, the methodology of linguistics has been based on an "epistemology of refutation" (Popper, 1959; Milner, 1989). According to this epistemology, a theory is scientific only to the degree that it can be refuted. This claim can be summed up in the following two points:

(1)   The theory must be expressed in unequivocal and calculable terms in order that theoretical descriptions can be submitted to a refutation test.
(2)   The theory must contain operational methods for the refutation of hypotheses.

The framework of computer science satisfies these prerequisites in a coherent way: The general theory of formal languages — the principal foundation of computer science — allows a precise formulation of linguistic descriptions, and at the same level of formal analysis (the logico-algebraic level) it provides a device for evaluating linguistic theories, since the computer can process symbolic data automatically.

This epistemological position has pointed linguistic research in a certain direction: It assigns a test function to the computer system, and it forces linguists to choose a certain kind of formal description.

This direction of research has had detrimental influence on another scientific approach — namely, European structuralism. The epistemology of struc-

[1] I thank Peter Bøgh Andersen for helping with the English version of this chapter.

turalism is based on the axiom that linguistic facts do not consist of stable autonomous data. On this point it differs from the "epistemology of refutation", which posits autonomous and pre-established empirical data that can
be used for evaluating and refuting linguistic theories.

As Saussure remarked:

> language (...) presents this strange and striking characteristic of not presenting
> units in an immediate manner, without any doubt however that they exist (...)
>
> *(Saussure, 1972: 149, our translation)*

The identity and value of the data must be constituted by means of a theoretical framework. In this case we speak of an "epistemology of constitution".

But this second position is much more difficult to implement because it requires a difficult double reflection, both on the primitive concepts that constitute structural objectivity, and on their formal expression. Thus the
"epistemology of refutation" simultaneously necessitates a choice of an operational level of formal description and assigns the function of an experimentation device to the computer. The structural epistemology of constitution did not offer similarly clearcut solutions, and in fact raised more problems
than it could solve, at least in the first half of the twentieth century.

Together with problems of complexity and empirical applicability, this fact
explains why the formalist and the computational research paradigm have
gained the advantage over a scientific tradition of exceptional richness and
depth, a tradition that encompasses the conceptual world of some of the
greatest thinkers within linguistics and semiotics.

Let us now look at the current trends. Current computational linguistics is
based on the epistemology of refutation, and in practice it *uses the computer
as a batch processing system* (a system that takes a text as input and produces certain data — for example another text — as output). It would certainly be false and peremptory to claim that this research paradigm is exhausted, but we must recognize that it has been, and keeps being, confronted
by apparently insurmountable difficulties.

At the same time, we are witnessing a renewal of the structural viewpoint
that overcomes the limitations mentioned: this is evident in the works of R.
Thom, J. Petitot, and P.A. Brandt in morphodynamic structuralism, and in the
research by P. B. Andersen and B. Holmqvist, that renew the traditional
"operational" conception of the computer by developing an "interactive"
conception that put the emphasis on the system's interaction with the user.

This chapter is in line with these recent works and their revival of structural thinking and it assigns another role to the computer than that of a batch
system. Our purpose is to show how the Hjelmslevian position, as expounded in the glossematic theory, forms part of cognitive science. In partic-

ular, we shall attempt to identify the *intrinsic* semiotic structure of a computer. In this way our work may be seen as complementary to investigations of the *external* semiotic structure and behavior of a computer — that is, the structure of the computer as a medium (see Andersen's and Brandt's chapters in this volume).

Our study, which belongs to the symbolic paradigm of cognitive science, falls into two parts. The first part reviews the principles of the symbolic paradigm as they are developed in Z. Pylyshyn's book *Computation and Cognition*. We shall identify the major properties that add a cognitive and semiotic dimension to the computational domain. In the second part we shall illustrate the relevance of glossematics by examining the Hjelmslevian concept of a *"constant"*. We shall first show that the concept of a "constant" gives a cognitive and computational relevance to glossematics. Next we shall show how this concept can assist in the construction of what Pylyshyn calls a "Cognitive Virtual Machine" (CVM) of semiotic processing — a machine that will specify a part of the *intrinsic* semiotic nature of a computer.

Principles of the symbolic paradigm

The cognitive sciences presuppose the existence of behavioral regularities for the description of which we need a *"cognitive vocabulary"* (Pylyshyn, 1984: 2). This cognitive vocabulary must be able to account for "intelligent" behavior that cannot be adequately described in other paradigms — for example, the neuro-biological, behavioral or physical paradigms. The cognitive vocabulary contains such terms as *to identify, to deduce, to decide, to know, to remember, to be informed...* Pylyshyn illustrates the necessity for such a vocabulary by the following scenario:

> A pedestrian is walking along a sidewalk (...) At the same time, a car is travelling rapidly down the street toward the pedestrian (...) The car skids and swerves over to the side of the road, hitting a pole. The pedestrian hesitates, then goes over and looks inside the car (...) He runs to a telephone booth at the corner and dials the numbers 9 and 1.   *(Pylyshyn, 1984: 3)*

It is clear that a physical description of such a scene (in terms of geometrical trajectories, forces, energy, or the rotation of the telephone dial) cannot create cohesion, since they are unable to link the different components in the necessary succession. Behaviorist or neurophysiological descriptions suffer from the same inadequacy. Moreover, such descriptions would not allow all the possible empirical realizations of this scenario to be united under the same regulatory scheme, since such a scheme requires terms from the cognitive vocabulary like "to identify" (the seriousness of the accident), to infer (the need for help), "to remember" (the phone number) and so on.

Thus, cognitive science conforms to the principles of an "epistemology of constitution" that takes a class of facts — a certain empirical diversity — and constitutes them as objects (determines them, grasps and fixes them under a unifying system of concepts and laws). Cognitive science selects the class of intelligent behavior as primitive facts; then — in a "*founding abduction*" (Petitot,1989:180) — it works out a system of determinations, defining the scope of the cognitive system and organizing its empirical diversity.

The terms of the cognitive vocabulary proposed here describe the class of the analyzed phenomena appropriately, at least to a first approximation, but they are still not operational for the cognitive subject. Therefore we need to examine the operations that underlie the actions of the cognitive vocabulary.

First, we must hypothesize a *functional level* of cognitive processing on top of the neuro-biological level that describes the brain as material — as a physical basis for cognitive operations.

Although neurobiological mechanisms do not account adequately for so-called intelligent behavior, they nevertheless constitute its material basis, and even though it is necessary to go beyond them, we must stay in touch with them. In order to do this we will consider the cognitive processes in more abstract terms — in terms of mental states and mental operations. When introduced in this way, the notions of mental states and operations refer to nothing but stable cognitive states, performed in the brain, and the operations on them. This defines the functional level:

> by "functional architecture" I mean those basic information-processing mechanisms
> of the system (...)   *(Pylyshyn, 1984: xvi)*

But in the same way that the biological category cannot capture the regularities of cognitive facts, the functional category turns out to be inadequate for accounting for other behavioral phenomena. This leads Pylyshyn to argue for a third level of description, the *semantic level*, and to introduce the concept of "representation".

First the concept of representation is introduced in order to account for the connection between the environment and the cognitive system. The concept is necessary to answer the question:

> how is it possible for properties of the world to determine behavior when the prop-
> erties are not causally related in the required sense to the functional states of the sys-
> tem...?   *(Pylyshyn, 1984: 26)*

Motivated in this way, the concept of representation is an essential descriptive component for analyzing a very large class of complex forms of interaction between the cognitive subject and its environment. In addition, the notion of representation is necessary in order to account for transitions of mental states controlled by principles or constraints related to the meaning of these states:

> (...) there are certain principles constraining transitions among states individuated in terms of content and (...) these principles do not apply to states individuated by function [of the functional level] alone.   *(Pylyshyn, 1984: 33)*

For instance, it is difficult to explain the relation between a question and its answer without considering the content of the question and the answer or positing a *"principle of rationality"* that requires the content of the answer to satisfy that of the question. In this way the concept of representations defines a fully cognitive system at a higher level. In short, the system of cognitive operations works on three levels:

(1)   The *neurobiological level*, constituting the physical basis of the functional level operations.

(2)   The *functional level,* comprising the primitive operations of symbolic processing that are independent of the representational contents. This second level is concerned with the mechanisms

> [that] make the system run (...) It includes the basic operations (...) for storing and retrieving symbols, comparing them, treating them differently as a function of how they are stored (...) and so on, as well as such basic resources and constraints of the system, as a limited memory.   *(Pylyshyn, 1984: 30)*

(3)   *The semantic level,* concerned with the cognitive processes controlled by the contents of the internal representations. So

> just as physical-level principles provide the causal means whereby symbol level principles (...) can be made to work, so symbol level principles provide the functional mechanisms by which representations are encoded and semantic level principles realised.   *(Pylyshyn, 1984: 132)*

Following Pylyshyn, we shall insist on the lack of isomorphism between the semantic and the functional level:

> Two systems in exactly the same representational state (...) can nonetheless still be functionally distinguished.   *(Pylyshyn, 1984: 31)*

The functional and the semantic levels thus delimit two distinct areas of cognitive processes:

> Generalizations can be captured by referring to the content of representational states that differ from those captured by referring to functional mechanisms.
>   *(Pylyshyn, 1984: 32)*

But when it has been recognized that the content — the meaning of the symbols — is part of the cognitive processes, then the way the semantic values are involved in the mental operation rules acquires theoretical importance. This claim is not obvious, since it is known that the mental operations are embedded in a causal network of neurobiological states :

> (...) the semantics of representations cannot literally cause a system to behave the way it does; only the material form of the representation is causally efficacious [...] When we say that we do something because we desire goal G or because we believe P, we are attributing causality to a representation, though it is not the content that does the causing.   *(Pylyshyn, 1984: 39).*

This point is crucial because at this stage the cognitive processes are governed by the same principles as the computational ones, establishing what Pylyshyn calls *"the relevance of computation "* (Pylyshyn, 1984: 49).

In fact, if the causal chain of mental states is somehow controlled by the semantic content encoded by these states, it is controlled by these states, and its succession of transitions reflects the content of the states:

> What actually do the causing are certain physical properties of the representational state — but in a way that reflects the representational state's content. There is, if you like, a parallel between the behavioral patterns caused by the physical instantiation of the representational states and the patterns captured by referring to the semantic content of these states.   *(Pylyshyn, 1984: 39)*

Here lies the central problem: What are the principles of this parallelism between the meaning and the physical processing? And the answer establishing the "computational paradigm" is:

> (A) What the brain is doing is exactly what computers do when they compute numerical functions; namely, their behavior is caused by the physically instantiated properties of classes of substates that correspond to symbolic codes. These codes reflect all the semantic distinctions necessary to make the behavior correspond to the regularities that are stateable in semantic terms.   *(Pylyshyn, 1984: 39).*

Let us recapitulate:

In order to recognize (to describe and explain) a category of behavioral facts, it has first been necessary to introduce a "cognitive vocabulary" of concepts specific to the domain.

Second, in order to account appropriately for these same behavioral facts, it was necessary to distinguish between two levels of cognitive control: the functional and the semantic. The modes of operation of the semantic level then turned out to have features in common with those of computational mechanisms. This in turn enabled us to use computational mechanisms as an explanatory model of the cognitive phenomena, establishing "the relevance of computation".

We now need to elaborate a recognition (still in the sense of a "description" and of an "explanation") of the cognitive facts that conform to a computational model. We have to refine and strengthen the reasons and the principles for considering the computational category to be explanatorily appropriate. The two other foundations of this appropriateness follow.

(B) Like the cognitive mechanisms, the computational mechanisms are operations of symbolic processing. As Pylyshyn insists:

> The notion of a discrete atomic symbol is the basis of all formal understanding. Indeed, it is the basis of all systems of thought, expression or calculation for which a notation is available.   *(Pylyshyn, 1984: 51)*

Similarly, an appropriate explanation of the workings of a computer also refers to the symbolic level of analysis, and not, for example, to the physical level:

> (...) the record of a particular sequence of physical states tells us nothing about the computational process going on in the machine.   *(Pylyshyn, 1984: 55)*.

This is true for two reasons. First, the same calculatory state can be realized by a large number of different physical states; secondly, very few physical properties are directly connected with the properties of computer's calculatory functions. Thus, the relevant states of a computational process are not physical states but the states of symbolic processing.

(C) Since neither the states of calculatory systems nor the states of cognitive systems can be explained by physical principles, it follows that computational processes as well as the cognitive processes must be considered as "rule-governed processes" and not as processes governed by physical laws:

> One of the most important similarities between cognition and computation (...) is suggested by the observation that the explanation of how a computation (...) proceeds must make reference to what is represented by the various intermediate states of the process just as the explanation of cognitive processes must make reference to the content of the mental states. In other words, the answer to the question "What computation is being performed?" requires a discussion of semantically interpreted computational states.   *(Pylyshyn, 1984: 57-58)*

Thus, we can localize the equivalence between cognitive and the computational structures to the following two properties:

P_1 The cognitive and the computational categories are symbolic categories.

P_2 The cognitive and the computational categories are "operational" categories.

We have already argued for property P_1, and property P_2 emerges from Pylyshyn's general argument that aims to prove that *"computation is a literal model of mental activity"* (Pylyshyn,1984: 43).

As we have seen, the "relevance of computation", hinges fundamentally on the cognitive and computational mechanisms having the same "operational" character (here, "operational" means "processing rules of mental states"). In the next quotation, Pylyshyn emphasises that the operation chain is connected with the meaning of the symbols processed. For example, if we want to explain why a computer prints the symbol 5 after the symbolic chain (PLUS 3 2), it is necessary to refer to the *meaning* of the symbol 5 and the expression (PLUS 3 2):

> The explanation of why the particular numeral "5" is printed out follows from (...) the definition of the symbols, or numerals, as representations of numbers, and from the definition of "PLUS" as representing a certain abstract mathematical operation, [and] it follows that some state of the machine, after reading the expression, will correspond to a state that represents the value of the function and (...) cause the printing of the appropriate answer   *(Pylyshyn, 1984: 58)*.

If we accept that *"the brain is the kind of system that processes [symbolic] codes"* (Pylyshyn, 1984: 40), then the content of the symbolic codes must at least in certain cases be connected with principles of operation that order the transitions and lead towards the resulting state, as in the case of the symbol PLUS in the example given.

The "operational" and symbolic nature of cognitive and computational structures is also pointed out by Winograd (1983). After noting that

> the computer shares with the human mind the ability to manipulate symbols and carry out complex processes that include making decisions on the basis of stored knowledge.   *(Winograd, 1983: 13)*

Winograd emphasises that

> the element in [the computational] model that distinguishes it from non-computational approaches is its focus on the description of processes that explicitly manipulate formal structures. The general idea of a process operating with a knowledge base and acting to generate structures and interact with an environment is central to all areas of computer science, and it is the framework for linguistic description used in the computational paradigm.   *(Winograd, 1983: 16)*

The cognitive virtual machine

In this section we shall specify more precisely to what extent computational structures and cognitive structures can be said to be equivalent, and what kind of equivalence exists between a cognitive and a computational process.

The first possible kind of equivalence is a weak equivalence — the equivalence of the "black box" where two processes are equivalent if their input and their output are identical. Since this operational equivalence reveals nothing about the internal nature of the examined processes, it is rejected by Pylyshyn:

> Clearly, if the computational system is to be viewed as a model of the cognitive process rather than a simulation of cognitive behavior, it must correspond to the mental process in greater detail than is implied by weak equivalence. *(Pylyshyn, 1984: 89)*

However, the other extreme of establishing an equivalence by identifying particular internal states of the computational or cognitive system is cognitively irrelevant:

> It is equally clear that, because computers not only are made of quite different material than brains but, through details of realizing particular operations (for example, certain register-transfer paths or binary mechanisms and bit-shifting operations), differ from the way the brain works.   *(Pylyshyn, 1984: 89)*

So the conclusion is:

> The correspondence between computational models and cognitive processes appears to fall somewhere between these extremes.   *(Pylyshyn, 1984: 89)*

This intermediary level of equivalence, which Pylyshyn calls "strong equivalence", is defined within the framework of an operational semantics: Two processes are equivalent if their translation into the programming language of a virtual machine is the same, if their execution in a virtual machine realizes the same chain of state transitions:

> In my view, two programs can be thought of as strongly equivalent or as different realisations of the same algorithm or the same cognitive process if they can be represented by the same program in some theoretically specified virtual machine.
>   *(Pylyshyn, 1984: 91)*

Adopting this approach, we then need to specify a "cognitive virtual machine" (CVM) that will define an operational equivalence between the cognitive system to be modeled and the computational system that is the model. In practice, the functional architecture of this CVM will be determined by choosing symbolic processing operations (primitive operations, memory organization) at a certain level of computational organization, or "aggregation level" (see the last section):

> The way I address the issue of the appropriate level of comparison between a model and a cognitive process — or the notion of strong equivalence of processes — is to provide a specification of the functional architecture of a «cognitive virtual machine».
>   *(Pylyshyn, 1984: 92).*

However, before proposing a CVM of semiotic processing, we must return to the important concept of "aggregation level" — or "degree of descriptive specification".

The operation modes and the internal states defining the functional architecture of a CVM reflect the nature of the cognitive structures, of the mental organizations. Choosing operations that are too global (too superficial) will prevent us from recognizing and exhaustively modeling cognitive processes, because certain accurate mechanisms will not be able to function. Conversely, choosing operations of too small granularity will introduce artificial functions that are irrelevant from a cognitive point of view.

The architecture of the CVM must satisfy principles that are in fact the Hjelmslevian principles of *exhaustiveness* and *appropriateness* (Hjelmslev, 1969: 11-14). These principles define the upper and lower bounds of the "aggregation level". The principle of exhaustiveness requires that all details of the cognitive processes must be accounted for; in this way, it defines the upper bound of the aggregation level, above which the considered operations are too general. Similarly, the principle of appropriateness defines the lower bound, below which the elementary mechanisms are no longer appropriate with respect to the category of cognitive processes.

In the definition of the present topic, a CVM of semiotic processing, we shall choose a degree of appropriateness (or level of specificity) that allows semiotic representations and operations to be encoded in terms of "manifestation" (in the Hjelmslevian meaning of this term).

At the "aggregation level" chosen, these operations and representations will not be directly connected with the process actually performed in a machine. In fact, the operations and representations of the CVM constitute macroscopic operations and states relative to the specific processes and properties of the machine. In Hjelmslev's terms, the operations and states of the CVM constitute a "cognitive form"; a regulation that, from another point of view, appears as a "substance" to be analyzed, as a "matter" organized by a form that can be identified.

But the decomposition of this substance into a new form by a microscopic examination of the underlying mechanisms takes us beyond the threshold of cognitive relevance. At a certain level of description — the level determined by the principles of appropriateness and exhaustiveness — the decomposition of the operations of the CVM leads to a disintegration of the cognitive category, because the operations that are identified by a new analysis are no longer of a cognitive nature. Rather, they belong to the fields of neurobiological or strictly computational facts.

Thus, the instantiation of a CVM at a certain level of a computational architecture must be carried out without regard to the complex mechanisms that ensure the running of the computer, since these mechanisms belong to another category and their details do not belong to the cognitive approach.

The concept of "constant"

Let us first recall that the structural approach postulates an immanent system of meaning. It is the internal organization of "meaning", in the full generality of this term, that constitutes the object of the structural epistemology. This internal organization determines its constituting elements and ensures their cohesion as a unit. The defining characteristics of structure, cohesion, and immanence are clearly emphasised by Hjelmslev: "*[A structure] is an autonomous entity of internal dependences*" (Hjelmslev, 1971: 28). Cohesion is emphasised through the notion of dependence, immanence through the notion of autonomy and internality.

A more precise determination of a structure will thus require us to specify the different kinds of dependences that establish it. To this end, Hjelmslev introduces three fundamental kinds of dependences: unilateral, bilateral, and reciprocal dependences.

We will speak of a unilateral dependence "when there is between two objects a relation such that one of them necessarily implies the other, but not vice versa". There is a bilateral dependence if "the first term necessarily implies the second and the second necessarily the first". A reciprocal dependence is the relation where "the first term does not necessarily imply the second, nor the second necessarily the first. *(Hjelmslev, 1985: 76-77, our translation).* Technically, these three kinds of dependences are called *determination, interdependence* and *constellation*.

However, these relations do not constitute the primitive notions of Hjelmslevian structural thought since they are defined by means of more general concepts — namely, the concepts of *constant* and *variable*. And these concepts are in turn defined by means of the primitive notions of *presence, necessity,* and *condition* (Hjelmslev, 1969: 35), which belong to the class of undefinable concepts in the glossematic theory and thus constitute the "*categories of structural objectivity*" (Petitot, 1985).

We define determination, interdependence and constellation as follows.[2] First, we shall introduce the notions of a constant and a variable: A *constant* is "a functive [i.e. the pole of a relation] whose presence is a necessary condition for the presence of the functive to which it has function" (here "function" has the general meaning of "relation"), and a *variable* is "a

---

[2] The same concepts are used in Andersen's chapter. The only difference is that Andersen replaces the term "determination" by the more frequently used "subordination." (Peter Bøgh Andersen)

functive whose presence is not a necessary condition for the presence of the functive to which it has function" (Hjelmslev, 1969: 35).

Determination is then defined as a function between a constant and a variable, *interdependence* as a function between two constants, and *constellation* as a function between two variables (Hjelmslev, 1969: 35).

After these definitions, we shall examine the concept of constant in order to show its relevance for the cognitive approach and for the definition of the internal semiotic structure of a computer — the CVM of semiotic processing.

Difficulties

The first difficulty we encounter stems from the fact that the definition of "determination" is ambiguous. The statement *"the presence of A is a necessary condition for the presence of B"* (A is a constant relative to B) can be read in two ways:

(1) The presence of A is a prior, necessary condition for the presence of B.
(2) The presence of B "implies" (with the meaning "calls", "needs") the presence of A.

The first reading is proposed by Jørgensen and Stjernfelt (1987) in their study of the relation of determination (the relation between a constant and a variable). According to the authors, "the only Hjelmslevian relation a little 'consistent' (...) is dependence, which gives to the selected term an ontological primacy over the selecting term [i.e. the variable] and over the relation itself" (Jørgensen and Stjernfelt, 1987: 89).

They continue: "Only determination (...) introduces in the relational network what is called a fork in mathematics, that is to say a point where 'something is happening,' where a choice is made, where we move from the selected term to the selecting term" (Jørgensen and Stjernfelt, 1987: 90).

This reading claims that the constant A — the selected term — must be present in order to enable the presence of B — the selecting term (which is optional in the case of determination). In our opinion, this reading is incorrect; we shall now show why this is so, and argue for the second reading.

The first reading forces us to rank the *"ontological primacy of the selected term over the selecting term and the relation."* It thus presupposes a successive production of objects: First the constant is produced, then the variable. But this is inconsistent with a structural approach that recognizes only networks of relations, not isolated objects. Even if such a successive production is controlled by a dependence, it must be governed by a rule that is external to the semio-linguistic system, for the simple reason that it is not governed by any internal dependence. This contradicts the immanent nature of the notion of structure.

However, the second reading seems to argue for an immanent and strictly relational meaning. On the one hand, saying that *the presence of B implies the presence of A* amounts to saying that there is no B that can be realized independently of A. If both B and A are produced, they are not produced one after the other; rather, an oriented relation is produced of which B and A are only the poles. On the other hand, the dynamics of the production of the object-terms A and B is inherent in the system itself.

Let us examine this more closely. According to Jørgensen and Stjernfelt, we start with the constant A, and then exploit a certain faculty of decision that is external to the semio-linguistic system and that enables us to choose whether or not term B (a variable) should be realized together with A. For example, the nominal category (constant) implies a choice between realizing a term of this category alone or together with a term of the variable category of adjectives. Such a decision requires a double mechanism: first, the choice of the constant, and second, the possibility of an additional variable term.

In general, it will be necessary to contemplate a complex succession of such choices and options. But if we admit that the initial choice of the discourse is controlled by external forces (for example the purpose of producing a certain meaning) that are objectified in the semio-linguistic system, then nothing warrants the claim that the process is the same for the next choice — at least if we follow a structural methodology.

On the other hand, if we accept the second reading of the definition of a constant, where "A is a constant for B" means that "the presence of B implies (calls) the presence of A", then a single choice (a single purpose of meaning) is enough to decide whether the nominal term will occur alone, or whether the complex nominal-adjectival term will appear. In fact, choice of the constant causes it to occur alone, whereas choice of the variable leads to joint occurrence of variable and constant, because the variable term "needs the presence" of the constant.

The second reading, then, eliminates the operation of branching, which presupposes a cause that is external to the semio-linguistic system. The productive mechanism associated with the second reading therefore reduces the role of intentionality of the subject by subordinating it to the linguistic structure. Note that such a subordination is consistent with the Hjelmslevian purpose of discovering the *"constancy"* of language which

> may be projected on the "reality" outside language, of whatever sort that "reality" may be (physical, physiological, psychological, logical, ontological), so that, even in the consideration of that "reality", language as the central point of reference remains

the chief object — and not as a conglomerate, but as an organized totality with linguistic structure as the dominating principle. *(Hjelmslev, 1969: 8).*

In fact, the second reading is very explicitly supported by Hjelmslev, who notes that "it is evident that it is the secondary term which is the calling term and the primary term which is the called term: a primary term can appear without a secondary term, but not inversely" (Hjelmslev,1971: 156). In the same manner, Hjelmslev defines *rection* (which is a determination (Hjelmslev, 1971: 157)) "as a necessary call that explains the necessity to distinguish a calling term and a called term" (Hjelmslev, 1971: 156).

Identification of the structure induced by a constant

The arguments above lead us to assign the role of a "called" term to the constant, and the role of a "calling" term to the variable. But the relational value of the constant and the variable is not fully analyzed yet, since the calling and called terms derive from an *analysis* — that is, they derive from the decomposition of an object submitted to the glossematic method of description. In this kind of analysis, additional relations can be defined:

Both the object under examination and its parts have existence only by virtue of the dependences; the whole of the object under examination can be defined only by their sum total; and each of its parts can be defined only [1] by the dependences joining it to other coordinated parts, [2] to the whole, and [3] to its parts of the next degree, and by the sum of the dependences that these parts of the next degree contract with each other. *(Hjelmslev, 1969: 22-23).*

This is illustrated in Figure 2.1 the following way: The object A is analyzed into two parts A_1 and A_2, and R_1 and R_2 are the relations between A_1 and the whole A, and between A_1 and the coordinated part A_2, respectively .

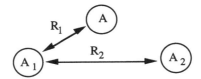

Fig. 2.1. Analysis of unit A_1.

The unit A_1 is then defined

(1)   by its relation R_2 to the coordinated part A_2, according to the first point in the quotation;

(2)   by its relation R_1 to the whole A, according to the second point.

The third point concerns the "inner" dependences of A_1 identified only at a lower level of analysis, so it is sufficient to characterize the unit through its relation to its "parent" unit of the upper level, and its relation to its coordinated "siblings" at its own level.

Thus, the calling term and the called term are defined not only by their reciprocal dependency relationship, but also relatively to the whole construction — that is, to the totality within which they are identified. Consequently, we can identify the calling term with an algebraic "operator" in terms of relation roles.[3]

In the exact relational meaning of the term in the theory of "lambda-calculus" (see Barendregt, 1984; Hindley and Seldin, 1986), an operator is in fact defined by its capacity for acting on an argument and producing a result. An operator is a term calling an argument (a called term) controlling the construction of the resulting term at the level above.

We see that the analysis of the term A into a constant, A_1, and a coordinated term A_2, is entirely consistent with an algebraic characterisation that identifies the term A_2 as an operator (a calling term) and A_1 as an argument (a called term). The precise relational role of A_2 is shown in the following rule:

$$A_2(A_1) \rightarrow A$$

which means that the action of A_2 on A_1 yields the global term A at the upper level.

In conclusion we can say that the preceding analysis of the concept of a constant demonstrates the relevance and appropriateness of the structural point of view in a computational and cognitive framework.

As has been argued, the operational aspect is constitutive of both computation *and* cognition, at least in the symbolic paradigm. And we have just shown that the concept of a constant belongs to an operational aspect: A constant identifies the variable term as an operator. Thus, this fundamental concept of glossematic analysis organizes the semio-linguistic system under an operational aspect, and ascribes a computational and cognitive validity to the structural analysis of glossematics.

In other words, we can claim that there is a close correlation between the organization of the meaning in the computational paradigm of cognitive science and in the Hjelmslevian structural point of view: Each of them considers the relational modalities of meaning under an operational aspect.

---

[3] Andersen's chapter suggests a related but different dynamic interpretation of Hjelmslev's variable concept. (Peter Bøgh Andersen)

We can thus confirm the hypothesis of a strong equivalence between the semiotic structure of meaning and the *internal* computational structure.

Formalizing the relations of interdependence and determination

The concept of a constant introduces an operational specification into the semio-linguistic organization: A constant is established relatively to an operator, which implies the presence of this constant so as to produce a unity of an upper level. However, such a specification is still not adequate, since it only determines the *general* properties of the constants and operators identified in the glossematic analysis of the empirical data.

All terms associated with the constants are operators, and all constants are arguments, but the terms must be further differentiated since they do not all have the same scope of operation. Some operators can be applied only to certain particular arguments, and conversely, certain arguments can only be arguments for specific operators. Obvious examples are nouns and verbs in relation to adjectives and adverbs. The noun is a constant in relation to the adjective, and the verb a constant in relation to the adverb. But although the operator of adjectivation can and must be applied to a noun, it cannot be applied to a verb. Therefore, it is necessary to specify the structural constraints that determine the operator/argument relations characteristic of each constant and its associated term.

The general problem is the following: Let us take a term A that is analyzed into two terms A_1 and A_2, where A_1 is a constant. Let us suppose that the operational feature of A_2 is given (for example, by a lambda-term or an expression of combinatory logic (Piotrowski, 1990). We then have to specify the applicative capacity of A_1 to work on A_2 only. In other words, it will be necessary to "type" A_1 and A_2 in such a manner that the operational capacity of A_2 concerns only A_1.

Such a specification can be formalized in the theory of types. In the most simplified version of this theory (which is sufficient for our purpose since we merely want to call attention to this), we recursively define a class of types on the basis of a countable set of primitive types (for example: α, β, γ...) and of an operation for construction of types, here denoted F:

(i) The primitive types α, β, γ... are types.
(ii) If x and y are types, then Fxy is a type.

The types limit the application operation by means of the rule F_e (F elimination):

$$\frac{X : F\alpha\beta \qquad\qquad Y : \alpha}{(XY) : \beta} \quad [F_e]$$

This rule states that a term X of type $F\alpha\beta$ can be applied to a term Y only if the type of this last term is α. The result (XY) (application of X on Y) is then type β.

Very generally, if a term A of type α is analyzed into a constant A1 of type β and into another term A_2, the latter term will play the role of an operator, and the structural constraint on this role is expressed by a type of the form $F\beta\alpha$. This means that A_2 can be applied only to a term of type β, such as A_1, in order to produce a term of type α, such as A. Now, we will have to determine the identity of β in the two possible cases where:

(1) A_2 is a constant.
(2) A_2 is a variable.

(1) If A_2 is a constant, a difficulty arises: Since A_1 and A_2 are both constants relative to A, they are symmetrical. But in that case, it is impossible to differentiate between them in the relational system, which means that from an immanent point of view, they cannot be distinguished. In fact, Hjelmslev uses this very argument to reject the Boolean dichotomy as a basis for defining semiotic oppositions (Hjelmslev, 1985: 35).

Therefore, we do not assign A_2's identity (the identity of an operator) to A_1, but we give A_1 the identity of being an argument of A_2 whose type specifies:

(1)   that A_1 cannot play the role of an operator — that is, its type is not of the form Fxy,
(2)   that A_1 belongs to a lower level of analysis than A. That is, the type of A_1 is built on the type of A by a unary type operator, here denoted ϕ.

So if the terms A_1 and A_2 result from an analysis of A (whose type is α) as a constant-constant relation, then their types will be: $\phi(\alpha)$ for A_1 and $F[\phi(\alpha)]\alpha$ for A_2.

This type characterization expresses the relational roles of A_1 and A_2 relative to A. In fact, A_2 is an operator that calls an argument and its type specifies that the argument must be of type $[\phi(\alpha)]$ — a term of the same kind as A_1 — and that the result will be of type α, i.e. will belong to the level of A. Similarly, A_1 is specified by the type $[\phi(\alpha)]$ based on type α, which represents the level of analysis immediately below the level of A. Since A_1 cannot play the role of an operator, then *relative* to type α (on which it is constructed), it will require the action of A_2 to pass on to the level of A.

(2) If A_2 is a variable, it means that A_1 can occur alone. For, since A_1 is a constant relative to A_2, it does not require the presence of A_2. Consequently, we must assign it a type that "alone" can perform the "jump" to the upper level of analysis.

In other words, the type of A_1 must be something like a "self-operator" type — a type such that its own execution yields the type of A. To formalize this operator, we will use a particular type system (Piotrowski, 1990) where a particular "pseudo-combinator" denoted "i" is introduced (the term "pseudo-" suggests that it has nearly the same behavior as a combinator in the theory of Combinatory Logic, even if it is not defined exactly like a combinator).

Let us turn our attention to the pseudo-combinator "i". This term denotes a unary type operator whose action on an argument X produces this argument X. More precisely, "i" is defined by the following rule R_i:

$$X : i\alpha$$
$$\text{---------} \quad [R_i]$$
$$X : \alpha$$

This means that if the expression X has the type $i\alpha$, then we can deduce that it can have the type α. Note that the formal system in which the pseudo-combinator "i" is defined does not allow inferences such as:

$$X : F[i\alpha]\beta$$
$$\text{---------------} \quad [R_i]$$
$$X : F[\alpha]\beta$$

With the R_i rule it is possible to formalize the terms that result from an analysis of A in a constant-variable dependence: If the type of A is α, A_1 will be the type $i\alpha$ and A_2 will be the type $F[i\alpha]\alpha$.

By applying the rules F_e and R_i, it will then be possible to execute the two operations:

(1) Application of the operator A_2 on A_1, yielding the result A:	(2) Auto-reduction of A_1 according to the rule R_i:
$A_2 : F[i\alpha]\alpha.$ $A_1 : i\alpha$ $\text{--------------------------------}$ $[F_e]$ $A = A_2(A_1) : \alpha$	$A_1 : i\alpha$ ----------- $[R_i]$ $A_1 : \alpha$

Before we introduce the semiotic specification of the CVM, we shall give some illustrative examples of the previous formalization. Let us take the sentence S: "the little dog sleeps", and let us specify its type as λ, for "lexie" (Hjelmslev, 1971: 68). If we analyze S in terms of constant-constant and constant-variable relations, it will generate the following tree (Figure 2.2), labelled with the relational roles (C for constant and V for variable):

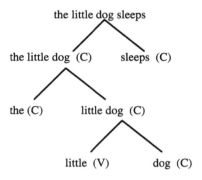

Fig. 2.2 Analysis of "The little dog sleeps"

The different components will be of the following types:

the little dog sleeps : λ
the little dog : $\phi(\lambda)$
sleeps : $F[\phi(\lambda)]\lambda$
little dog : $\phi^2(\lambda)$ $\phi^2(\lambda)$ stands for $\phi(\phi(\lambda))$)
the : $F[\phi^2(\lambda)][\phi(\lambda)]$
dog : $i\phi^2(\lambda)$
little : $F[i\phi^2(\lambda)][\phi^2(\lambda)]$

By the rule F_e, these characterizations allow not only the construction of S, but also the construction of S': "the dog sleeps". Indeed:

$$
\begin{array}{c}
\text{dog}: i\phi^2(\lambda) \\
\rule{3cm}{0.4pt}\ [R_i] \\
\text{the}: F[\phi^2(\lambda)][\phi(\lambda)] \qquad \text{dog}: \phi^2(\lambda) \\
\rule{10cm}{0.4pt}\ [F_e] \\
\text{the dog}: \phi(\lambda) \qquad\qquad\qquad \text{sleeps}: F[\phi(\lambda)]\lambda \\
\rule{12cm}{0.4pt}\ [F_e] \\
\text{the dog sleeps}: \lambda
\end{array}
$$

The Cognitive Virtual Machine

Let us now return to the basic ideas of a virtual cognitive machine of semiotic processing. Recall that this machine defines the computational architecture relevant for the cognitive point of view: The CVM establishes the intrinsic semiotic form of a computer.

Defining a virtual cognitive machine of semiotic processing thus amounts to constituting an organization that implements the notion of semiotic forms at a certain level of description of computational architecture. We will limit ourselves to forms based on constants and their associated constant or variable operator-terms.

We have seen that the operational aspect, via the concept of a constant, makes computational structures appropriate for the semio-linguistic organization. We have also seen that the notion of a constant requires type specification. Therefore we must introduce the equivalent of a type organization into the internal structure of a computer; in this way, we can define the internal computer-semiotic structure more comprehensively.

In particular, we propose that the type structure should be implemented in the computer via a *manifestation* (in the Hjelmslevian sense). This guarantees the semiotic and cognitive relevance of the construction. The key-concepts of a "manifestation" are those of *form*, *substance* and *matter*. Let us describe them briefly.

The *form* is a relational system, an abstract organization of relations determining the units of structural objectivity. The *matter* is an non-ordered class of units without any features other than their individuality: They cannot be mutually differentiated. The *substance* is a manifestation of form in the matter, an instantiation of the abstract semiotic form in the units of matter. The substance is matter ordered by the relational network of the semiotic structure.

It is possible to identify a certain level of organization of a computer that satisfies the glossematic definition of matter. This level is characterised by a certain description of the RAM memory of a computer: The "random access memory" (RAM memory) is seen as a conglomerate of memory-cells that are only specified by their location. All we do is enumerate the cells: "Here is cell number 1, here is number 11, here is number 347". We cannot say that "this cell performs this function in relation to this one". All memory-cells are unique, but they cannot not be characterised in relation to each other, since they share no relation.

The only structure of the set of memory-cells is an *external* structure of location whose relevance is only practical ("cell number 465"). The locations constitute a "presentation" — in the sense of Curry (1974: 20) — just as a letter is the "presentation" of an abstract unit in a formal system, or a sound is a "presentation" of a phoneme. The memory-cells are thus interchangeable, and this is in fact exploited in practice by memory managing software.

In order to instantiate a semiotic form in the matter constituted by a RAM memory, we will have to order the memory-cells according to the structure of the type system. We choose to instantiate the type system by organizing the memory-cells by means of pairs of pointers. This organization will manifest the abstract structure of the type system. The matter so ordered will then constitute the manifestation of the pure form of the semiotic structure. For this reason we will speak of a "semio-computational" substance[4].

When we describe a certain level of the computational system as a matter that can instantiate a semiotic form, we ensure the semiotic relevance of the chosen architecture. At this level, the computational system is devoid of any internal computing structure. Let us note that nothing prevents us from considering the computational system at another level of organization (for example, as Andersen notes in his chapter: machine code, assembler, operating system, application program, user interface) where specific computing modes appear. But these modes are not necessarily relevant for the analysis of the *intrinsic* semiotic form of a computer, even if they can be analyzed according to semiotic principles. What interested us was to identify "computational matter" that constitutes an amorphous computational domain and hence can support a semiotic form.

Construction

We build the semiotic architecture inductively in the same manner as we build the type class of a type system (the implementation was actually done in the C-language that is well suited to defining a system of pointers).

The type system is built on a primitive type (the "lexie"), denoted "λ", which represents the first data of an analysis based on the binary construction operation "F" and the unary operations "ϕ" and "i".

The rules are:

(i) λ is a type,
(ii) if α and β are types, then $F\alpha\beta$ is a type,
(iii) if α is a type, then $\phi(\alpha)$ is a type,
(iv) if α is a type, then $i(\alpha)$ is a type.

In the machine this construction will be implemented as follow:

(i)   We choose a memory-cell for the manifestation of type λ,.
(ii) The operation of F is implemented by a construction of double-cells such that if $[\alpha]$ and $[\beta]$ are two cells of the system representing the types α and β, then the double-cell, whose left pointer is pointing to $[\alpha]$ and the right pointer to $[\beta]$, manifests type $F\alpha\beta$.

---

[4] This conception of a "semio-computational" substance is borrowed by Andersen in his paper in his chapter. (Peter Bøgh Andersen)

(iii)   The operation of φ is implemented by a construction of double-cells
        such that if [α] is a cell representing type α, then type φ(α) will be
        manifested by a double-cell whose left-pointer is pointing to cell [α].
(iv)   The operation of "i" is implemented by a construction of cells such
        that if [α] is a cell representing type α, then type iα will be manifested
        by a double-cell whose right-pointer is pointing to cell [α].

Thus it is possible to describe the architecture of the type system as a network of pointers, with cell [λ] as the anchorage of the network.

Example: A dotted line denotes the left-pointers, and a full line the right-
pointers of a (double)-cell representing a type.

Fig. 2.3. Instantiation of a semiotic form

Fig. 2.3 illustrates the instantiation of a fraction of the semiotic form of the
analysis of the sentence: "the little dog sleeps" shown in Fig. 2.2.

The left part of the illustration displays the type system instantiated in
RAM, the right part the sentence components linked by an arrow to their
type specification. Thus, it does not matter which memory cells instantiate
the types, only the relations represented by the pointers are relevant. The
identity of a type cell is the identity of its position in the network of pointers.

We have now constructed the manifestation of a fraction of a semiotic
form at a certain level of computational organization. This manifestation defines the structure of a cognitive virtual machine of semiotic processing.

Conclusion

In order to establish the intrinsic semiotic nature of a computer, we have primarily attempted to define an operational structure of the computational mechanisms (property P_2 of the computational paradigm previously described) that is appropriate for the operational structure introduced by the glossematic concept of constant. But we have left implicit the basic choices that allow us to establish such an appropriateness: the choice of a logico-algebraic level of analysis. In fact, the correspondence between intrinsic computational structures and semiotic structures arises from the fact that

(1)   the category of computation is a category of symbolic processing (cf. property P_1), and

(2)   the first level of analysis in glossematic methodology is also a symbolic level (Piotrowski, 1990).

However, it has to be admitted that the semio-linguistic form has a fundamentally topological nature. The semio-linguistic identity is a positional identity determined by a network of boundaries, and the glossematic approach, conforming to the principle of appropriateness, makes use of topological notions at the higher levels of its conceptual architecture.

Consequently, even if the logico-algebraic approach developed in this chapter can give some important clues about the semiotical structure of a computer, we must admit that it is limited. In order to apply the precise and more advanced concepts of glossematic theory, it will be necessary to change the level of analysis — to develop a topological and morpho-dynamical view.[5]

Bibliography

ANDERSEN, P. B. (1991). *A semiotic approach to programming. Towards a computer semiotics*, VENUS report 8, Dept. of Information and Media Science, University of Aarhus.

BARENDREGT, H.P. (1984). *The lambda-calculus, its syntax and semantics*, Amsterdam: North-Holland.

BRANDT, P. A. (1989). Agonistique et analyse dynamique catastrophiste du modal et de l'aspectuel, *Semiotica 77:1/3*.

BRANDT, P. A. (1989). The dynamic of modality: a catastrophe analysis. *Recherches Sémiotiques/Semiotic Inquiry 9:1/2/3*.

CURRY, H.B., FEYS, R. (1974). *Combinatory Logic*, Vol. 1. Amsterdam: North-Holland.

---

[5] A similar conclusion is reached in Andersen's chapter that presents a morpho-dynamical interpretation of Hjelmslev's concepts. (Peter Bøgh Andersen)

HINDLEY, J.R., SELDIN, J.P. (1986). *Introduction to combinators and lambda-calculus.* Cambridge: Cambridge University Press.

HJELMSLEV, L. (1969). *Prolegomena to a theory of language.* Madison, University of Wisconsin Press.

HJELMSLEV, L. (1971). *Essais linguistiques.* Paris: Editions de Minuit.

HJELMSLEV, L. (1985). *Nouveaux essais.* Paris: Presses Universitaires de France.

JØRGENSEN, H., STJERNFELT, F. (1987). Substance, substrat, structure. *Langages 86.*

MILNER, J. C.(1989). *Introduction à une science du langage.* Paris: Le Seuil.

PIOTROWSKI, D. (1990). *Structures applicatives et Langage naturel.* Thèse de l'Ecole des Hautes Etudes en Sciences Sociales, Paris, Ecole des Hautes Etudes en Sciences Sociales.

PETITOT, J. (1985). *Morphogénèse du sens.* Paris: Presses Universitaires de France.

PETITOT, J. (1989). On the linguistic import of catastrophe theory. *Semiotica 74: 3/4.*

PYLYSHYN, Z. (1984). *Computation and cognition.: Toward a foundation for cognitive science.* Cambridge, Mass: MIT Press.

POPPER, K. R. (1959). *The logic of scientific discovery.* London: Hutchinson and Co.

SAUSSURE, F. (1972). *Cours de linguistique générale*: Paris: Payot.

WINOGRAD, T. (1983). *Language as a cognitive process.* Massachussets: Addison-Wesley.

3

The shortest way between two points is a good idea. Signs, Peirce, and theorematic machines

KELD GALL JØRGENSEN

The question to what extent a computer can think is an often recurring one that, owing to the quick shift in generations within the computer sciences, continues to be of relevance, although there is no real reason to expect an unequivocal answer. It can, however, be moderated to — to what extent can computers *learn* to think? Were we to bide our time, would it not be possible to make a machine that could stand comparison to human thinking? Or we could choose to ask ourselves: *What* is common to machinal and human reasoning? From which follows the closely related questions: Can computers dream? Can they discover, feel, error, lie, get good ideas? Can they develop or mature? Have they ethics, morals, aesthetic judgement, fantasy, intuition? And, last but not least, can they distinguish between differences that make a difference, and differences that do not?

Regardless of how one chooses to address these interrelated questions, the various answers that will ensue allow us to distinguish on the one hand between the cultural or developmental pessimists, who are convinced that machines are on the verge of a take-over and, on the other, the cultural optimists, whose view is that machines will continue to be but an ancillary instrument for human thought.

From this point we can thus go back in history (an age-old tactic in itself) and examine how previous generations reacted to the encounter with new machines. In his time, N.F.S. Grundtvig (1838) was forced to relate to the steam-machine, and opted for a reasoned humanistic skepticism:

Dare I thus excommunicate Mathematics, outlaw the machinery and denounce industriousness of the English as a colossal proof of spiritlessness; this then would I do, without asking what good it would be; but, as stated, I dare, I may, I can not, but am to the contrary forced to admire the Great-Spirit, which even in the desert can create a paradise, render Mathematics, in itself the most dead and emptiest of all our Knowledges, an incomparable spur for living activity and a lever for what is too heavy for the hands of the united gargantuans. I can rue, and rue truly, that the Great-Spirit of the North does no better and in the Language of the Spirit far greater things

92

than these, rue that the English Industry continually strives after what one names pure reward, without care to the means, enslaved to the Moment, without thought of the Future; but I see clearer each day, that the reason therefore lay as little in Activity as in Freedom, but in a quite other something, that would be far more regrettable if one sat with hands alap and did not a thing with eagerness and zeal.   *(Grundtvig, 1838, x)*

Grundtvig's device could be boiled down to: "Better movement forward than no movement at all", with the necessary addendum: "Better a little more spirit than far too tight (material) bonds." From Grundtvig we could thus leap ahead to the next turn of the century, to the tribute paid the machine by Johannes V. Jensen, who bought himself a motorcycle and toured the world over on the trail of technical genius. From here we could move up through our century, where we would meet in the attitudes of man to machine an admixture of praise, skepticism, and rejection. Let us, though, pause at the modernistic writer Svend Åge Madsen, whose juvenilia includes the science-fiction novel *Den største gåde* (The Greatest Enigma). Here he turns our conceptions of the man-machine relationship on end, presenting a once-upon-a-time when the "Past-Machines", faced with "the Great Machine Plague", created mankind, and precoded us to recreate the computers when the threat of contamination had passed. A charming thought indeed.

The purpose of this chapter is not, however, to examine how writers have at various times related to machines, but how semiotics can contribute to an elucidation of the relationship between human and machine language. First I will look at the founding father of semiotics — the eldest of them (for their number is so great that a paternity suit could easily ensue), Charles Sanders Peirce's (1839-1914) preoccupation with logic-machines. I will then bring down to the sign-level the question of the extent to which a machine can think, where it will become a matter of marking the upper, lower, and other limits of the sign, or of the process of meaning: What is the difference between a signal and a sign? What is the difference between an idea and a sign? These questions, in turn, bring out the importance of taking the materiality of the sign into consideration.

Peirce: Semiotics and logic

Peirce was educated as a chemist, but worked primarily as a physicist whose heart belonged to philosophy and semiotics. If one must identify an interest central to his radically interdisciplinary oevre this would have to be the very nature of scientific method: what reasoning is. And it was in connection precisely to the nature of mathematic reasoning that he held an interest in logic machines. He knew the study of machines by Babbage (cf. Hyman, 1982)

and Jevons (cf. Ketner, 1984), and it is said that he made a sketch — Peirce
would say diagram — of an electronic logic machine (cf. Ketner, 1988, my
source here).

A logic machine is a machine that can produce the pertinent conclusions
from the premises with which it is fed. According to Peirce, the value of the
logic machine lies in its ability to demonstrate to what degree reasoning is a
mechanical process and to which extent further observations are necessary:

> Precisely how much of the business of thinking a machine could possible be made
> to perform, and what part of it must be left to the living mind, is a question not with-
> out conceivable practical importance, the study of it can at any rate not fail to throw
> needed light on the nature of the reasoning process.   *(Peirce, 1887: 165-70)*

It is hardly to be doubted that Peirce was a vitalist, though he would pre-
sumedly not have ever excluded the possibility that, through mechanical avenues, a gradual approximation could be made to the human mind's capacity
to reason:

> Even syllogistic reasoning in its higher varieties as they appear in the logic of rela-
> tives, requires a living act of choice based on discernment, beyond the powers of any
> conceivable machine, and this sufficiently refutes the idea that man is a mere mechani-
> cal automaton endowed with an idle consciousness.   *(Peirce, 1894: 344-45)*

"The logic of relatives" was Peirce's most touted contribution to logic, and
it gradually developed into a comprehensive epistemology or methodology.
Even though he, as the polyhistor he was, also contributed to new breakthroughs within more concrete mathematics and physics, it was never his in-
tent to create formal calculus, but to analyze reason and the nature of reasoning. This analysis along the way turned into a semiotics, which to a high degree he equivocated with logic or, more precisely, with the logic of relations
noted above (cf. Peirce, 1893-1910).

Philosophically, this concerns a phenomenology that differentiates between the various modes of being of phenomena: They can belong to firstness — exist independently of anything else; to secondness — exist in a
dyadic relationship to something of firstness; or they can belong to third-
nesss, being thus a mediating moment between something first and something second.

These are the fundamental *relations* from which all sign processes or
semioses can be observed. And it was this triadic doctrine of categories in
which Peirce founds his semiotic, in that he distinguishes three ways in
which a sign can refer to any object: the relation can be *iconic*, *indexical*, or
symbolic. The iconic signs represent their objects by virtue of a relation of
similarity. They lend their objects firstness. Indexical signs refer to and are
influenced by the objects with which they share one or another quality. Here

we can speak of a relation of contiguity as opposed to that of similarity in the icon. Symbolic signs are bound up with their objects by virtue of a convention, a law, whereby the symbolic sign is itself elevated to a general type or regularity.

Typical examples of icons are *pictures, ideas, metaphors, diagrams*, and *equations*. Typical examples of indices are *tracks, barometers, dials, the polarstar, weathervanes*, and *demonstrative pronouns*. Symbols are first and foremost the majority of words of the natural language (onomatopoeic words can also be considered icons), *sentences, books* and other conventional signs. In actuality, however, many signs will contain more than one of the three possible relations to their object. For example, mathematic formulas and diagrams are icons, even though there is no sensible resemblance between them and their objects, but only an analogy between their respective components. As Peirce indicates (ibid. 105) it can seem strange to designate a mathematic formula an icon, as it would seem better to view it as a complex conventional sign. He maintains, however, a similarity between the primary internal relations of the mathematic formula and those of the object, whereas the more conventional relations at a higher level (for example the symbol-value of the individual signs), being most certainly present, are nonetheless secondary.

What is decisive in turning to the computer debate is first of all Peirce's insistence on the crucial difference between mechanical and living processes. He would view logic machines or computers as diagrams — iconic replications of what is at play whenever humans reason. But, as semioticians revel in saying, "the map is not the landscape," and Peirce insists on this decisive difference. In a letter to J.M. Hantz (quoted in Ketner, 1988: 44-45), he says:

> It is my fate to be supposed an extreme partisan of formal logic, and so I began. But the study of the logic of relations has converted me from that error. *Formal logic centers its whole attention on the least important part of reasoning*, a part so mechanical that it may be performed by machine, and fancies that that is all there is in the mental process. *For my part, I hold that reasoning is the observation of relations, mainly by means of diagrams and the like. It is a living process.* This is the point of view from which I am conducting my instruction in the art of reasoning. I find out and correct all the pupil's bad habits in thinking: I teach him that reasoning is not done by the unaided brain, but needs the cooperation of the eyes and hands. Reasoning, as I make him see, is a kind of experimentation, in which, instead of relying on the intelligible laws of outward nature to bring out the result, we depend upon the equally hidden laws of inward association. I initiate him into the art of this experimentation. I familiarize him with the use of all kinds of diagrams and devices for aiding the imagination. *(emphasis mine, KGJ)*

It is at this point worth taking a closer look at Peirce's argumentation in asking how he determines and qualifies the limits of mechanical reasoning, and by what means this determination distinguishes itself qualitatively from the nature of human thought. What is, for Peirce, the most essential part of reasoning not addressed by formal logic? What is "a living process" and "the hidden laws of inward association?"

In the preceding quotation he says that to reason consists partly in observation, partly in experimentation. Other places, where he treats the nature of logic machines and mathematic models, he assigns human reasoning the further attributes of creativity, serendipity, free choice, valuation, differentiation, and originality.

It could now be objected that modern computer technology has transferred some of these characteristics to the machinal mode, through, among other things, experimentation in neural networks and artificial intelligence, and one could return the volley to Peirce in asking of the *sine qua non* of human reasoning. But this would only be the equivalent of demanding of Peirce that he solve the enigma of existence, and he would be able to reply, modestly, that he is content with dealing with existence, thus leaving the enigmatical to others.

The aporia is in other words irresolvable. Ketner (1988) also asks of the lesson learned from Peirce's distinction between mechanic and living processes, and comes to the conclusion that it is the circumstance whereby mechanical processes build upon deterministic algorithms which sets them apart from living processes. A viewpoint which, rendered in everyday language, says that a machine can only do what it is instructed to do, even when it is informed to do something wholly unexpected, or hardly probable. Peirce makes quite parallel formulations with respect to the machine's range of ability: It "would only do the special kind of things it had been calculated to do" and "it has been contrived to do a certain thing, and it can do nothing else" (quoted in Ketner, 1988: 51).

I shall not discuss further the extent to which the improbabilities of human association can be captured with the aid of micro- and biochips. The probability of predicting the process of association can be rendered so minute that it verges on indeterminism. But is it the difference between deterministic processes and free choice that unequivocally distinguishes machinal from human reasoning?

Ketner finds in Peirce's texts fair support for the hypothesis that determinism is the crucial point. Following immediately after the preceding quote, where Peirce uses the formulation "a living process" Ketner cites another:

But this school is for ever exaggerating the resemblances of psychical and physical phenomena, for ever extentuating their differences. Ribot, for example, often speaks of the "mechanism of association", and even attempts to apply to it the physical distinction of potential and kinetic energy. But looking at that matter without prepossession, or with that of a student of mechanics, the analogy between the process of association and any mechanical motion does not appear to be very close. Both are operations governed by laws, it is true. But the law of mechanics is absolute, prescribing (after two positions are given) the precise point of space where each particle shall be at each instant of time; while the force of association is essentially a gentle one (two ideas that have occurred together have a gentle tendency to suggest one another), and if it were made absolute, ideas would at once be rigidly bound together, and the whole phenomenon of learning, or generalization, which is the essence of association, would be put to death.   *(quoted in Ketner, 1988: 45)*

Based on Peirce's distinction between absolute, mechanic regularities and the more gentle chains of association, Ketner goes on to distinguish *deterministic* from *theorematic* machines. He also terms these latter Peirce-machines, and contrasts them to the deterministic Turing machines. Many non-deterministic machines are to be found, of which the theorematic are seen as a specific group that transcend determinism by introducing various ancillary-hypotheses and premises that lead reasoning onto new avenues. In a letter to William James, Peirce writes:

To the diagram of truth of the Premisses something else has to be added, which is usually a mere May-be and then the conclusion appears. I call this *Theorematic* reasoning because all the more important theorems are of this nature.
                                        (quoted in Ketner, 1988: 49)

The non-descript ancillary-hypothesis, the little May-be, is integrated into Peirce's semiotics via the *interpretant,* which enters as the mediating moment (thirdness) between *sign* (here: the components of the machine), and *object* (here: thought). The inevitable result must then be that in the attitude he adopts to the difference between mechanical and living processes, between deterministic and theorematic reasoning, Peirce insists upon both forms building upon an indissolvable triadic structure. Or, in other words, that consciousness, thought, and logical conclusion cannot be reduced to mechanical categories (action-reaction); even strictly determinist processes build upon *observation,* as Peirce says, which render them replicas and demand valuation or interpretation.

It can be asserted that Ketner makes too big a deal out of determinism. As Nickerson says in an excellent comment on Ketner's article, non-determinism is of no help to us in building a theorematic machine. Instead, he suggests that we focus on the *probability* and *continuity* of the processes:

The real limitation of the Turing machine comes not from the strict determinism of the transition table, but from the finiteness of the number of states. Our computation is not providing us any information that is not already latent in the state table and the input tape.
(Nickerson, 1989: 330)

I am of the opinion that both Ketner and Nickerson make too much out of a resolving of the question of the crucial difference between the machinal and the human *logically* instead, as Peirce suggests, of solving it *semiotically*. For the consequence of equating logic with semiotics must be that focus is directed toward representation. Machines can represent something else, human reasoning, for example, but they can never be identical with it due to the mediating instance — due to the interpretant. On the other hand, no objection can be raised against the attempt to try to set this representation complexus in a scientific and conceptual framework.

I shall in summary fashion present my objections to Ketner's and Nickerson's interpretations of Peirce as two questions: 1) Is there not a difference between mathematic-statistic infinity and *real* infinity, where the former can at best be an iconic resemblance of the latter? 2) Could we not, slightly poetically, assert that the human being lives the solutions to their equalities out, and in this living of them realize a deferred truth-value, and that this residual truth must be internalized in a mathemato-logical calculus *if* the machinal is to capture the essence of human reasoning?

These two objections are obviously interrelated since we are in both cases addressing the difference between a static model and a living process. In all fairness, it must be remarked that Ketner duly attends to Peirce's notion of *self-criticism*. For self-criticism is a specifically human capability of deferred valuation and adjustment of the processes one has internalized, a capacity that the advent of cybernetics has allowed us to partially automatize, but never entirely to replace.

The question to what extent the computer can think can, *summa summarum*, only be defended upon one condition: If humans can think, and if humans are capable of teaching a computer to think, then it is possible, upon the essential reservation, that this demands a *mapping out* of the process, and that this cartographing will, naturally, never be identical with the process, but at most only an image of it. The map is not the landscape.

The upper, lower (and other) limits of the sign

Peirce's contributions to the understanding of the nature of human reasoning were manifold. Aside from the aforementioned fact that he described it in connection with mathematico-logical reasoning, he also supplemented the two primary ways of reasoning, deduction and induction, with a third: *abduction*. Abduction has quite a bit to do with the incidental May-be — the little ancillary hypotheses that Peirce indicated as being the most essential characteristic of the theorematic reasoning. He illustrates the difference between deduction, induction and abduction in the so-called "Famous 1878 bean-bag example":

DEDUCTION
Rule: All the beans from this bag are white.
Case: These beans are from this bag.
Result: These beans are white.

INDUCTION
Case: These beans are from this bag.
Result: These beans are white.
Rule: All the beans from this bag are white.

ABDUCTION
Rule: All the beans from this bag are white.
Result: These beans are white.
Case: These beans are from this bag.

(quoted in Eco and Sebeok, 1983: 8).

This exemplifies how abduction is to be understood as a qualified guess, and it is also Peirce's idea that the fecundity of thought should be increased through abductive reasoning, even if this is effected to the detriment of surety: "But we must conquer the truth by guessing, or not at all" (ibid. 11).

While one can increase the probability of the truth value of inductive reasoning by testing the rule — for example by taking more beans from the sack and verifying that they are white — what characterizes abductive reasoning is that one must posit several parallel arguments for the case. The abductive method has been compared to that of the detective's — viewed as a hypothetical intuitional approach for relieving the phenomena of their truth and coherency. This could also be seen in its near relation to the *modus operandi* of the artist.

Whereas in deduction the relation between premises and conclusion is *necessarily* true, and in induction *probably* true, the abductive conclusion is *possibly* true. These same determinations can be brought down to the sign-level as characteristic of the three prementioned sign-relations — indexical, iconic, and symbolic — in such a way, however, that the iconic and the indexical must be reversed: In the index a *necessary* relationship exists between sign and object, in the icon there is probable connection, and in the symbol a possible one. Let us now look at Peirce's definition of the sign:

A sign, or *representamen*, is something which stands to somebody for something in some respect or capacity. It addresses somebody, that is, creates in the mind of that person an equivalent sign, or perhaps a more developed sign. That sign which it creates I call the interpretant of the first sign. The sign stands for something, its object. It stands for that object, not in all respects, but in reference to a sort of idea, which I have sometimes called the ground of the representamen.   *(Peirce, 1893-1910: 99)*

Peirce's concept of sign is illustrated in Figure 3.1 in its triadic nature in the following manner:

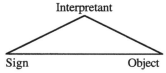

Fig. 3.1. Peirce's sign concept.

The sign as such can now be delimited in relation to the signal by the two determinations Peirce assigns the sign: This supposes in part the presence of an interpretative consciousness "stands to somebody" — which the signal does not (necessarily) do and it relates in part to an idea or "ground."

The first determination is directly understandable, and has, for example, led to the view within the computer-science debate that man and machine can be considered a totality where man, at a higher level, continuously interprets the machine's signals as part in the sign process (cf. Feenberg, 1989; Nadin, 1988). Concerning the second determination, Peirce makes no effort to explain what he means by "ground," but I offer a proposal that connects this with the frame of interpretation toward which he imagines the processes of meaning to intend whenever signs are to be interpreted, and these interpretations in turn are proposed as signs in new interpretations. As Peirce states:

The meaning of a representation can be nothing but a representation. In fact, it is nothing but the representation itself conceived as stripped off irrelevant clothing. But this clothing never can be completely stripped off; it is only changed for something more diaphanous. So there is an infinite regression here. Finally, the interpretant is nothing but another representation to which the torch of truth is handed along; and as representation, it has its intepretant again. Lo another infinite series.

(quoted in Silverman, 1983: 15)

The semiotic materiality of the sign is constituted simply by the possibilities the sign has of entering into different frames of interpretation (cf. Petrilli, 1986: 226), whereas the signal, in contrast, is characterised by a monogamous coupling of content and expression (ibid. 227). However, the signal can, just as all other conceivable phenomena, *become* a sign if it is somehow coded and acknowledged as being part of a cultural collectivity (cf. Eco, 1979: 17). That is, if it constitutes part of an interpretation and an interpretational frame of reference.

In other words, Peirce's sign concept allows for the property that he sees as characteristic of theorematic reasoning but that is lacking in diagrammatic reasoning. This determination, as we have circumscribed it by Peirce's various designations serendipity, free choice, guessing, secondary valuation, differentiation, and originality, enters in already at the sign-level.

Here, however, it is only the sign's semiotic materiality that is at issue, and it must be added that the sign also has other material presuppositions. Susan Petrilli, in her article "The materiality of signs" (1986: 242), summarizes and concludes that the sign's materiality can be presented schematically as Figure 3.2:

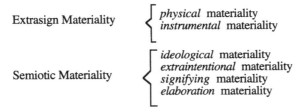

Fig. 3.2. The materiality of a sign.

Since the difference between semiotic and extrasign materiality is our present concern the single modes of materiality will not be treated here. What we saw earlier, and that which constitutes the lower limit of the sign, is that signals presumably have extrasign-materiality but not semiotic materiality. At the other end of the scale the sign must be delimited from *the intention* and the idea in order to explain why a computer cannot have intention and why it cannot come up with a good idea.

It is common within semiotics to define the sign in various interrelated ways. That "signs are everything that can be used to lie" — is one such definition and which directly indicates *intention* as fundamental to the constitution of the sign. The sign stands for or pretends to stand for something else. As mentioned, it enters into several interpretative frameworks and its intention consists in referring some few of these as pertinent and others as impertinent.

A good idea

Concerning the relation of sign to idea Peirce, as noted, says that ideas are examples of icons, where the sign-object relation is founded on similarity. Thus ideas are signs of the first order. In this sense some signs are obviously deposited in even the most primitive of (computational) machines in that the relation of the single components of the machine are iconic representations of other relations: "Principles of design are by nature semiotic" (Nadin, op. cit. 269). When at work, when reasoning, the machine gets neither further good nor bad ideas. In my opinion, this has to do with the crucial difference between an idea proper and what we associate with a *good* idea, a difference that everyday parlance as a rule conceals by permitting the acquisition of an idea to be synonymous with getting a good idea.

What does it mean to get a good idea? To the extent that we were able to map this out it would also be possible to mechanize the process. This is why there must, always, exist an indeterminant moment of surprise in every good idea. To what degree this idea is at all a good idea is usually registered only later, when somebody else catches on to it. The good idea cannot be qualified absolutely as such; we must recognize that what is at play are relations between several thoughts and way of thought whose validity can only be evaluated in relation to a basis, understood as lived experience.

If in this connection we consider man's specific ability to consociate two thoughts simply because they are present, for one or another wholly arbitrary reason, above the threshold of consciousness (cf. Peirce's quote above), then a good idea can be said to be the shortest way between two points. The computer takes the long way. Humans get good ideas.

Bibliography

BATESON, G. (1984). *Ånd og natur.* Copenhagen: Rosinante.
ECO, U. (1979). *A Theory of Semiotics.* Bloomington: Indiana University Press.
ECO, U., T. SEBEOK eds (1983). *The Sign of Three. Dupin Holmes Peirce.* Bloomington: Indiana University Press.
GREIMAS, A.J., J. COURTÉS (1988). *Semiotik. Sprogteoretisk ordbog.* Aarhus: Aarhus Universitetsforlag.
GRUNDTVIG, N.F.S. (1943). Mands Minde 1788-1838. In *Værker i Udvalg,* ed Georg Christensen & Hal Kock, vol. 4.
HOFSTADTER, D.G. (1979). *Gödel, Escher, Bach: an Eternal Golden Braid.* Stanford: The Harvester Press.
FEENBERG, A. (1989). A user's guide to the pragmatics of computer mediated communication. *Semiotica 75(3/4).*
HIMMELSTRUP, J. (1964). *Terminologisk Ordbog til Søren Kierkegaards Samlede Værker.* Copenhagen: Gyldendal.

HYMAN, A. (1982). *Charles Babbage: Pioneer of the Computer.* Princeton: Princeton University Press.

KETNER, K.L. (1984). The early history of computer design. Charles Sanders Peirce and Marquand's logical machines. *The Princeton University Library Chronicle 45*: *188-224.*

KETNER, K.K. (1988). Peirce and Turing: Comparisons and conjectures. *Semiotica 68(1/2).*

MADSEN, S.Å. (1982). *Den største gåde.* Copenhagen: Aschehoug.

NADIN, M. (1988). Interface design: A semiotic paradigm. *Semiotica 69(3/4).*

NICKERSON, J.V. (1989). Circumventing the barriers of computation. *Semiotica 74(3/4): 329-335.*

PEIRCE, C.S. (1887). Logical machines. *The American Journal of Psychology 1: 165-70.*

PEIRCE, C.S. (1955). Logic as Semiotic: The Theory of Signs. In *Philosophical Writings of Peirce,* ed. J. Buchler. New York: Dover (1893-1910).

PEIRCE, C.S. (1894). Spinoza's ethic. *The Nation 59: 344-45.*

PETRILLI, S. (1986). On the materiality of signs. *Semiotica 62(3/4):* 223-45.

SILVERMAN, K. (1983). *The Subject of Semiotics.* New York: Oxford University Press.

4

Logic grammar and the triadic sign relation

PER HASLE

The tradition of analytical semiotics initiated by C. S. Peirce is often thought of as being in some sense contrary to formal logic. This is especially so, when formal logic is associated with the classical correspondence theory of truth as in the project of formal semantics for natural language. However, the perceived opposition between the two traditions has become dubious since the advent of logic grammar, which came mainly from the works of Richard Montague in the late 1960s.

Logic grammar differs from philosophical logic first and foremost by specifying a translation procedure from natural language into formal logic. It is true, of course, that the very idea of representing the meaning of natural language sentences by logical forms has been prominent in philosophical logic and analytical philosophy throughout our century. One particularly famous example is Bertrand Russell's discussion of "definite descriptions" (Russell, 1905), and his suggestion of representing sentences containing definite descriptions by a certain type of logical forms. For instance, the sentence

(1)   "The present King of France is bald"

should be represented as

(2) $\exists!\, x.\, \text{King-of-France}(x) \wedge \text{bald}(x)$

where (2) may be read as "there exists one and only one object, which is king of France, and which is bald." Russell considered the sentence (1) to be false if uttered in our time (or 1905); the transcription of (1) into (2) would serve as a formal explanation of the falsehood of (1). It should be noted, however, that in philosophical logic formal representations are simply *stipulated* for the purposes of whichever discussion is going on. Montague's works, on the other hand, specified a mechanical procedure for translating a suitably limited subset of a natural language into the desired logical representations. The introduction of such a procedure has three major consequences. First, the representations one obtains by using the procedure have a *systematical status*, as opposed to the stipulations of philosophical logic; second, this systematical relation between language and formal logic has made it possible for the first time ever to utilize logic within genuinely linguistic description of language; and third, it has made for a close connection between the project of logic grammar and information technology. It is a straightforward matter to implement the translation algorithm on a computer. When that has been done, one may input linguistic data such as the sentence (1), and the implemented translation algorithm will then yield as output a representation such as (2). Furthermore, it is not too difficult to utilize this kind of output in a logic programming environment, since the formal language of logic grammars is basically of the same type as logic programming languages (although there are certain computational limitations for richer logical languages). Then, natural language input can be utilized in an information system.

These above observations should serve to place logic grammar in a wider context, with a view to philosophy as well as technology. However, the crucial point about the relation of logic grammar to Peircean semiotics stems from the specific manner in which meaning is assigned to logical, respectively linguistic expressions in Montague's logic grammar (or Montague Grammar, as it is also often called). In classical correspondence theory the meaning of for instance a term like "the Queen of Denmark (in 1992)" is taken to be the real-world person Margrethe the Second, who actually *is* the Queen of Denmark. Similarly, the meaning of predicates such as "a student at the University of Cambridge" is supposed to be simply the set of all persons, who actually happen to be students at that university. The meaning of a predicate like "woman" is taken to be all existing women — and so forth. Montague objected to this over-simplified conception of the notion of meaning. Instead he proposed that meanings of linguistic expressions should be construed from the set-theoretic notion of functions. The functions that Montague had in mind are construed from so-called "possible worlds" into concrete objects or sets of objects. (We may take the liberty of interpreting a "possible world" as a given situation or context.) Such functions are called *intensions*. The meaning of an expression such as "the Queen of Denmark" will then be an intension, which in different contexts so to speak points out different persons — namely, in each context the person, who happens to be the queen of Denmark. The basics of Montague's system can in a simplified version be rendered as a triple consisting of

(1)   E, a set of objects (or entities),

(2)   C, a set of contexts (or possible worlds), and

(3)   F, a function, which assigns intensions to linguistic expressions.

Such a system <E,C,F> is called an *interpretation*. In a quite striking manner, this kind of interpretation seems to fit with the triadic sign relation of C. S. Peirce, which will be described next.

So with Montague a sign (or more precisely, a symbol) does not have a meaning, which is given once and for all as in classical correspondence theory. Rather, it has a meaning only relative to an interpretation, which determines for any given situation the object "associated with" the sign. For instance, let us call the intension of "the Queen of Denmark" d; technically speaking, this means that F("the Queen of Denmark") = d. Let $C1$ be the context of "Denmark 1992 A.D.," $C2$ the context of "Denmark 1400 A.D." Then,

$d(C1)$ = Margrethe the Second (the actual person),
$d(C2)$ = Margrethe the First (the historical person).

It should be noted that a context C could just as well be a given fictitious context — for instance, Shakespeare's "Hamlet." In that case we would have

$d(C)$ = Gertrude.

Montague's logic is often called "intensional logic" (IL) because of the crucial rôle of intensions within his system. IL will be described in more detail in the next section.

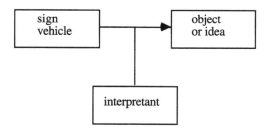

Fig. 4.1. The triadic sign relation.

This very short description already suggests that Montague's use of logic in the description of linguistic meaning is much closer to Peirce's triadic conception of a linguistic sign than is classical correspondence theory. Very briefly, one might say that a sign according to Peirce consists of three parts (or constituents, or aspects): a concrete symbol or *sign vehicle*, for instance the linguistic expression "the Queen of Denmark." an *object* or denotatum, to which the sign vehicle refers (in a given situation), an finally an *interpre-*

tant, which plays a crucial role in linking up the sign vehicle with its denotatum. We may illustrate this conception as shown in Figure 4.1.

Now a sign vehicle can be for instance the sound occurring when the word "woman" is uttered, or the corresponding sequence of symbols from the keyboard on which I am typing, as they appear on this page: woman. The interpretant is that "system of understanding." by which the sign vehicle is related to an object — for instance a set of concrete women, or just the idea of such a set. The triadic sign relation will be more closely described in "The Semiotical Tri-partition of the Study of Language."

When one compares the conception of the triadic sign relation to the structure of IL, it should not be too hard to see that the latter might be regarded as a special case of the former. Indeed, Montague himself saw his own endeavors as being compatible at least with Charles Morris's elaboration of Peircean analytical semiotics (Morris, 1938). In "The Semiotical Tri-partition of the Study of Language" I shall try to relate IL to analytical semiotics in more detail. It may be in order to mention here a general difficulty concerning any discussion of Montague's ideas. Montague himself hardly ever entered into a discussion of the preconditions or the implications of his own work. To a large extent, these must be reconstrued from what Montague actually did do. Rather than theoretically discussing the possibility of describing the semantics of natural language by IL, Montague devoted his energy to the development of fully specified intensional logic grammars, "complete in all details" (his own words). These systems, then, would demonstrate what IL could actually do for the description of natural language semantics. For that reason, Montague's procedure has also been called "arguing by doing."

The questions concerning the relationship between logic grammar and semiotics are in my opinion highly relevant to current endeavors to apply humanistic science to information technology. An investigation into that relationship should be fruitful for establishing a theoretical foundation for describing information technology at all its levels from a humanistic perspective (or at least at all levels from the software engineering level and up to the impact of information technology upon culture). A prima facie argument for the relevance of logic grammar to these endeavors comes from the fact that this discipline obviously combines traditions from the human as well as the natural sciences. For in logic grammar we find an integration of analytical and philosophical methods with constructive technological purposes appertaining to information technology. In my opinion, this integration holds at a completely general level, as I have described it in Hasle (1989). However, it may be worthwhile to draw attention to a particular discipline within logic, where the fusion of analytical and constructive concerns has become espe-

cially obvious, namely *temporal logic* (which also happens to be closely related to intensional logic). One of the main fields of investigation for this
discipline is the logic of temporal expressions and temporal reasoning as
manifest in natural language — for instance, English. To begin with, temporal
logic was developed within an entirely philosophical setting, in an attempt at
clarifying certain logico-linguistic problems, which had been discussed by
Medieval logicians (Galton, 1987; Øhrstrøm and Hasle, 1991b). The founder
of modern symbolic temporal logic was A.N. Prior (1914 - 1969). Prior's work
was motivated by philosophical and language-theoretical questions. In order
to find answers to those questions, or just to be able to state the questions
themselves more precisely, Prior almost single-handedly developed modern
temporal logic in the course of the 1950s and 1960s. Since then, temporal
logic has proved highly useful for such apparently diverse fields as philosophy, logic grammar, and computer science. In computer science, temporal
logic is primarily used for specification and verification of programs — verification being the task of mathematically proving that a program "does what
it is supposed to do" with respect to a given specification. This endeavor is
considered to be one of the most important ones within theoretical computer
science. Temporal logic has also found applications within artificial intelligence, cognitive science, and related areas. The latest development in the
connection between computer science and temporal logic is the introduction
of temporal logic programming languages since the mid-1980s. To sum up,
temporal logic is an active field within computer science at three discernible
levels: theoretical computer science, programming languages, and specific areas of application.

It cannot be denied, of course, that computer scientists have other reasons
for taking an interest in temporal logic than have, for instance, linguists.
However, to my mind the crucial point is that the different uses of temporal
logic should be seen as *different applications of what is essentially one
and the same theoretical subject matter* — this perspective being the contrary of viewing temporal logic in its entirety as a more or less accidental sum
of its different uses within computer science, linguistics, philosophy, and so
on. (different uses which also motivate different formalizations). If we see
temporal logic as suggested here, we can also see that logic may indeed provide a unifying semiotic approach to both analytical and constructive elements within information technology. In the current context, temporal logic
is all the more interesting because Prior explicitly related to Peirce. Within the
framework of his own logic Prior tried to make formally precise some of
Peirce's considerations on determinism, future contingents and what is in our
day called "branching time" (see Øhrstrøm and Hasle, 1991a).

Since this chapter is not meant to be on temporal logic, it is not possible to proceed to describe more closely its various aspects and applications, and the mutual relations among those. These remarks are simply meant to suggest that temporal logic is a most clear-cut example of how analytical and constructive approaches may enter into a synthesis, from which they can be only artificially separated. Most of the issues touched on here are, however, somewhat expanded in (Øhrstrøm and Hasle, 1991a).

Intensional logic

Intensional logic belongs to the semantic component of a logic grammar. The overall layout of a logic grammar is illustrated in Figure 4.2:

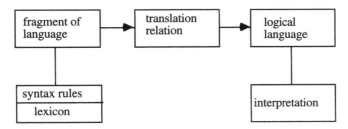

Fig. 4.2. The structure of a logic grammar.

The syntactic component of a logic grammar is not too important in our context, but a brief description may be in order. The syntactic component consists of a lexicon and a set of syntactic rules. The lexicon contains a set of words, each word being listed together with syntactic and morphological information, such as the word class to which the word belongs, inflected forms of the word, and so forth. The syntactic rules describe how the items of the lexicon may be combined to form more complex grammatical units. Take for instance a noun phrase such as "the tall man." which can be formed by combining the article "the" with the modified noun (call it NBAR) "tall man." The NBAR itself has been formed by combining the adjective "tall" with the noun "man." Given a lexicon and a set of syntax rules of a nontrivial size, an infinite number of linguistic expressions can be formed. On the other hand, any existing logic grammar only describes a subset of the language in question, and for this reason the syntactic component is said to define a *fragment* of the language.

Now let us turn our attention to the crucial translation relation. Every syntax rule is mirrored by a translation rule. The translation relation gives us a mechanical procedure for translating linguistic expressions from the fragment of language into logical forms. Since linguistic expressions are often ambiguous, the translation of any given expression is governed by a concrete syntactic analysis of that expression — this is exactly why every syntactic rule is mirrored by a corresponding translation rule. In general, the logical form for a given expression is not a straightforward representation of that expression, but rather a representation of the expression *relative to one of its syntactic analyses*. However, the pair of a linguistic expression and one of its analyses has a unique translation. The syntactic component and the translation rules together specify how the sentence

(1)   "The present King of France is bald"

is translated into, for instance, the logical representation

(2) $\exists! \, x.$ King-of-France$(x) \wedge$ bald(x) .

In Montague's own logic grammar, the logical representations will be expressions in the logical language of IL. Since IL is an extension of classical predicate logic, (2) is also an expression of IL. However, we shall not discuss the language of IL itself. Rather, we shall concentrate on the interpretation, which after all gives us the real semantics of the linguistic expressions translated into IL (logical forms themselves can, however, be said to be semantic representations in the sense that they have a unique interpretation within the semantic component). By means of the structure <E,C,F> meanings are assigned to expressions of IL; in an indirect manner, then, meanings are assigned to syntactically analyzed linguistic expressions, when they have been translated into IL. As an example, let A stand for some linguistic expression from the fragment, and let T be a representation of one of the possible syntactical analyses of A (T is a "parse tree" for A). Now assume that the pair (A,T) translates into the IL-expression B. The function F specifies how to assign a meaning to B, i.e. F(B) is the meaning of B. Then we can also take F(B) to be the meaning of (A,T). To spell it out in detail, F(B) is the meaning of A relative to the syntactic analysis T of A and relative to the given interpretation <E,C,F>.

What kind of meanings, then, are assigned to linguistic expressions? To see this, let us construe a very limited context (possible world) W1, in which all we know are the following facts: three persons exist, a, b, and c, where a and b are men, and c is a woman. We also know that a and b are mortal, whereas c is immortal. This knowledge can be represented by tables 4.1, 4.2, and 4.3. The table for the predicate MAN, for instance, in effect states which persons are men and which aren't in W1 — that is, of whom the predicate is true, and of whom it is false. The number "1" designates *true*, the number "0" designates *false*. So by inspecting the table MAN we find that a and b are men, while c is not a man. Similarly for the other tables. These tables correspond to set-theoretic functions, and in terms of correspondence theory they give us the meaning of the three predicates MAN, WOMAN, and MORTAL. MAN is a predicate within the logical language, and the meaning of MAN w.r.t. W1, (F(MAN))(W1), is exactly that function which "says yes" (or 1) for a and b, and "no" (0) for c. In short, the correspondence-theoretic meaning of MAN (or English "man," where "man" translates into MAN) simply is table 4.1.

MAN		MORTAL		WOMAN	
a	1	a	1	a	0
b	1	b	1	b	0
c	0	c	0	c	1

Table 4.1. Possible world W1.

Nevertheless it is fairly obvious that the table MAN does not really give us the full meaning of the word "man." In real language, such a predicate embodies some sort of "conceptual content," which enables us to use the predicate correctly in different situations — that is, with respect to different possible worlds. To know the meaning of the English word "man" means to possess a linguistic competence, which among other things enables us to decide in different contexts, whether a person of that context actually falls under the concept of being a man — that is, whether the predicate "man" can truthfully be said of that person. And of course the set of men is not really given once and for all, but varies from one context to another. Even proper names may vary in meaning from one context to another.

MAN		MORTAL		WOMAN	
a	1	a	1	a	0
b	0	b	1	b	1
c	1	c	0	c	1

Table 4.2. Possible world W2.

For instance, we may assume that in the context of W1, Kim is the person a, but in some other context W2, Kim is b. So to understand a natural language such as English also means to be able to judge about the truth of a sentence such as "Kim is a man" in a given context. In order to move towards this desirable generalization, let us introduce another possible world W2, specified as shown in Table 4.2.

Given the worlds W1 and W2, and assuming for the sake of argument that no other worlds are known to us, we can now go on to illustrate how intensions are construed by using possible worlds. Specifically, we shall join the tables from W1 and W2 for each predicate. The interpretation function F in a sense does exactly that: it assigns to every predicate, and indeed, every expression of IL, the intensions construed in the same manner as the tables next. We designate the intensions by F(MAN), F(WOMAN), and so on. It should be remembered that intensions are themselves functions — they are functions from possible worlds into another type of functions — namely, the kind of tables that we have already been studying above. The generalised meanings of for instance MAN and KIM — that is, the intensions of MAN and KIM, can now be represented by these tables:

F(MAN):

W1	a	1
	b	1
	c	0
W2	a	1
	b	0
	c	1

F(KIM):

W1	a
W2	b

Table 4.5. Intensions.

The intensions of WOMAN and MORTAL are constructed similarly. At this point, it might well be asked what to do for more complex expressions — for example, "the tall man" or "Kim is a man" — surely it would not be as straightforward to construct tables for such expressions. The answer is that a number of structural rules, which are called *evaluation rules*, permit us to decompose complex expressions down to the point where tables can be specified for their individual parts. One simple example of this is given in the evaluation of "Kim is a man" next.

The word "intension" may be paraphrased into something like "conceptual content." In IL, the conceptual content of a word such as "man" is exactly seen to be that function F(MAN), which permits us in different situations to determine whether a person belongs to the concept or not. However, it must be emphasised that the intensions of IL are but the *mathematical modeling* of the conceptual content of any given linguistic expression. In a broader philosophical or linguistic analysis, one may surely expect a more exhaustive description of conceptual content. An intension in IL is a mathematical abstraction, which reflects the strictly logical aspect of a richer determination of conceptual content. The mathematical representation on the other hand gives a kind of description, which can be manipulated mechanically, a property that clearly holds some advantages, not least with a view to information technology.

It is now possible to show how the sentence "Kim is a man" can be evaluated relative to a given context. That sentence is translated into the logical expression

MAN(KIM).

As mentioned, the semantics contains a number of evaluation rules. I shall state the rule needed for evaluating MAN(KIM) in a way specifically related to that formula, although the rules will of course be stated in a general way in a real logic grammar. Square brackets are inserted for perspicuity:

R1: MAN(KIM) is true relative to a given world w and an interpretation <E,C,F> if and only if F(MAN)(w)[(F(KIM)(w))] = 1.

Taking the world W1 we find (F(KIM)(W1)) = a, and hence

F(MAN)(W1)[(F(KIM)(W1))] = F(MAN)(W1)(a) = 1, that is *true*,

and taking W2 we find

F(MAN)(W2)[(F(KIM)(W2))] = F(MAN)(W2)(b) = 0, that is *false*.

In other words, we fairly soon get down to inspecting the tables in order to determine the truth-value of the sentence. The meaning of the entire sentence — that is, F(MAN(KIM)), is the intension which for any world in our interpretation yields the value 1 or 0.

Since the study of inference is central to logic, I shall conclude this section with a few remarks on that subject. One classical example of valid inference is this syllogism:

> All men are mortal.
> Kim is a man.
> -------------------
> Kim is mortal.

Let us assume that our syntax makes all three sentences unambiguous, and that they translate into the following symbolic version of the syllogism:

> $\forall$x. MAN(x) $\Rightarrow$ MORTAL(x)
> MAN(KIM)
> ------------------------

MORTAL(KIM)

One way of studying inferences is the so-called deductive or syntactic way. It is called syntactic because it essentially consists of a set of rules that refer only to the syntactic structure of the logical expressions — no appeal is made to an underlying interpretation or semantics. From the two premises, one can mechanically derive the consequence. The study of the purely syntactic way to make inferences is called proof-theory.

However, it is also possible to investigate semantically whether an inference is generally valid. To prove the validity of the preceeding syllogism semantically one must prove that the consequence MORTAL(KIM) must necessarily be true in any possible world, wherein the two premises are true — regardless of whatever other facts obtain in any such world. For instance, both premises are true in W1, which can be verified simply by inspecting how W1 was defined; and we can further verify that MORTAL(KIM) is indeed also true in W1. However, the premise "Kim is a man" is not true in W2. In that case it is irrelevant to the validity of the syllogism whether the consequence is true or not. In general, a syllogism or any other valid inference schema only states that *if* the premises are true, *then* so is the consequence. In IL it is possible to undertake a semantic study of the validity of the classical syllogisms as well as inference structures that involve an intensional context-dependency. But space does not permit us to pursue this subject any further here; it is treated in great detail in (Dowty, Wall, and Peters, 1979).

To be true, this exposition of IL does not at all do justice to the richness and expressive power of that system. It is hoped, however, that the central ideas have become sufficiently clear. In IL we find, for one thing, a generalization of the notion of meaning, or conceptual content, and for another thing a certain degree of context-dependency, both of which were outside the scope of classical correspondence theory. The kind of context-dependency discussed so far may certainly seem somewhat unrefined, but it is quite possible to make it more fine-grained within the framework of IL. The contexts or possible worlds may themselves be structured as a number of "pragmatic indices," as we shall see in the next section (if only very briefly). At any rate, Montague Grammar is recognized not merely as a part of semantics, but also as a part of formal pragmatics.

The semiotical tri-partition of the study of language

Semiotics is concerned with the study of signs. Given the triadic structure of signs it seems quite natural, then, that semiotics is partitioned into three subdisciplines, each of which concentrates on one of the three aspects of the sign. One of the great theorists within semiotics, Charles Morris, labeled this tri-partition under the headings of *syntax* (originally *syntactics*), *semantics*, and *pragmatics* (Morris, 1938). Very concisely it can be said that syntax studies the sign vehicles — their syntactic forms and mutual relations, semantics studies the relation between sign vehicles and that to which they refer (the objects or designata), and pragmatics studies the interpretant side of signs.

Rather, Peirce himself made a similar three-ways distinction, but his description of the tri-partition changed in the course of his work. Peirce's distinction was inspired by the tri-partition in the so-called *trivium* of the Middle Ages, which comprised the disciplines *grammar* (approximately syntax), *dialectics* (approximately semantics), and *rhetoric* (approximately pragmatics). As Peirce changed his delineation of each of the corresponding semiotic disciplines, he also changed the terms, he was using for each of them; at the later stage of his work, Peirce called them *speculative grammar*, *critic*, and *methodeutic*, respectively. Since all three aspects of the sign are seen as a unity within semiotics, it should be obvious that the three disciplines are not to be considered as unrelated, but rather as the same study from three different perspectives. Peirce called the unified study of signs *logic*, in a broad sense of the word (at an earlier stage, Peirce used the term "logic" to designate the semantic subdiscipline). However, it is Morris' headings syntax, semantics, and pragmatics, as well as his determination of those, that have become the most well-established way of describing the tri-partition. Especially within the science of linguistics, it is Morris' description of the three disciplines that has proved to have a lasting and heavy impact. Montague himself refers to Morris's tri-partition as a precondition of his own work (see the quotation later).

It is worth noting that the tri-partition has often been used as an argument for isolating semantics from pragmatics. That tendency is evident in the following statement by one of the leading early theorists within IL, David Lewis:

> My proposals will ... not conform to the expectations of those who, in analysing meaning, turn immediately to the psychology and sociology of language users: to intentions, sense-experience, and mental ideas, or to social rules, conventions, and regularities. I distinguish two topics: first, the description of *possible languages or grammars as abstract semantic systems* [my italics] whereby symbols are associated with aspects of the world; and second, the description of the psychological and sociological facts whereby a particular one of these abstract semantic systems is the one used by a person or population. Only confusion comes of mixing these two topics.
>
> *(Lewis, 1976: 7)*

This statement reflects how IL and Morris agree as well as differ on the nature of the relation between semantics and pragmatics. It may be added that Lewis's statement is also representative of Montague's views on the matter. As already mentioned, Montague explicitly referred to Morris's tri-partition as an important precondition of his own work. Since Montague in general did not waste many words on the relation of his work to semiotics or other major theories for that matter, it seems worthwhile to quote him at length on this point:

> The study of language (or *semiosis* or *semiotic*) was partitioned in [Morris 1938] into three branches — syntax, semantics, and pragmatics — that may be characterised as follows. Syntax is concerned solely with relations between linguistic expressions; semantics with relations between expressions and the objects to which they refer; and pragmatics with relations among expressions, the objects to which they refer, and the users or contexts of use of the expressions.   *(Montague, 1976b: 95)*

Montague goes on to observe that by the time of Morris's 1938 monograph, syntax (that is, logical syntax) was a fully developed field, and that the foundations of a fully developed semantics were also present at the time, even though the development itself had not yet been undertaken. But with pragmatics, the case was different:

> Pragmatics, however, was still futuristic at the time of Morris's monograph. It was suggested in [Y. Bar-Hillel: Indexical Expressions. *Mind 63, 1954*] that pragmatics concern itself with what C. S. Peirce had in the last century called *indexical expressions*, that is, words and sentences of which the reference cannot be determined without knowledge of the context of use; examples are the words "I" and "here," as well as sentences involving tenses. Pragmatics did not, however, exhibit any precise technical structure until 1959, when the present author ... initiated considerations [that would lead to such a precise technical structure, namely intensional logic]... It seemed to me desirable that pragmatics should at least initially follow the lead of semantics, which is primarily concerned with the notion of truth ... and hence concern itself also with truth — but with respect not only to an interpretation but also to a context of use.
> *(Montague, 1976b: 95)*

This quotation is, I believe, central to understanding the relationship between IL and analytical semiotics, and I shall come back to it later on.

Within each of the fields of the semiotical study of language one might investigate how IL compares to analytical semiotics. To do so in detail would certainly be illuminating, but here a few observations will have to suffice. Not surprisingly, Morris was aware of some limitations of logical syntax relative to the process of semiosis — which is the process of understanding signs in its entirety:

> ... the formalised languages studied in contemporary logic and mathematics clearly reveal themselves to be *the formal structure of actual and possible languages* [my ital-

ics] of the type used in making statements about things; at point after point they reflect the significant features of language in actual use. The deliberate neglect of the formalist of other features of language, and the way in which language changes, is an aid in isolating a particular object of interest: linguistic structure.   *(Morris, 1938: 21)*

While this quotation does suggest some limits to logical formalization of language, there is at the same time a striking resemblance between Morris's determination of logical syntax as a reflection of "the formal structure of actual and possible languages," and Lewis's description of semantics as the study of "possible languages or grammars as abstract semantic systems." Of course, Morris's statement concerns syntax, and Lewis's semantics; but the basic principle for a formal study seems to be the same, and later progress within formal semantics would seem to warrant the assumption that Morris could today have said the same about semantics.

As long as semantics is understood to be merely a *part* of the complete description of the meaning of linguistic signs, Morris is in agreement with Montague's and Lewis's description of semantics: "Semantics deals with the relation of signs to their designata and so to objects which they may or do denote" (Morris, 1938: 21). Like Lewis, Morris emphasised the point that semantics abstracts from pragmatics, that it is concerned with the semantical dimension of semiosis "prior to the actual use of signs." Nevertheless, some disagreement seems to hover on the horizon. For Morris apparently considered language usage and pragmatic conventions to be the *real* foundation of semantic rules:

> If pragmatical factors have appeared frequently in pages belonging to semantics, it is because the current recognition that syntactics must be supplemented by semantics has not been so commonly extended to the recognition that semantics must in turn be supplemented by pragmatics. It is true that syntactics and semantics, singly and jointly, are capable of a relatively high degree of autonomy. But syntactical and semantical rules are only the verbal formulations within semiotic of what in any concrete case of semiosis are habits of sign usage by actual users of signs. *(Morris, 1938: 29)*

Morris's underlying tenets thus seem to be contrary to Lewis's watertight division between semantics and pragmatics.

The relation between semantics and pragmatics is an essential issue for the relation between semiotics and IL. Morris pointed out that a discussion of the relation between signs and language users *presupposes* knowledge of the relations among signs. Likewise, it presupposes knowledge of the relations of signs to those objects to which they "draw the attention of the interpreters" — that is, the objects which they designate. On the other hand, concrete semantic and syntactic rules are motivated by circumstances which ultimately — one might say, ontologically — belong within pragmatics. But this importance of pragmatics should not lead one into the misconception that language cannot be studied at all in abstraction from the pragmatic factors — or with a well-known slogan, "meaning is use." Morris sharply distanced himself from that point of view, in spite of the fact that he himself considered pragmatics to be the most comprehensive and in a sense most important semiotic discipline:

> A peculiarly intellectualistic justification of dishonesty in the use of signs is to deny that truth has any other component than the pragmatical ... Pragmatism has insisted upon the pragmatical and pragmatic aspects of truth; the perversion of this doctrine into the view that truth has only such aspects is an interesting case of how the results of a scientific analysis may be distorted to lend credibility to quasi-pragmatical statements.   *(Morris, 1938: 40 - 41)*

The relation between analytical semiotics and intensional logic

To my mind, the discussion so far can leave no room for doubting that Montague's intensional logic and Morris's version of analytical semiotics are in deep agreement on important points. In several ways IL makes precise and further develops semantics in the manner called for by Morris in 1938. At the same time, it contains a kind of context-sensitivity, which relates semantics to pragmatics in way which Morris would probably have welcomed. It is the main thesis of this chapter that logic grammar can in general be seen as a special case of analytical semiotics, and hence that logic grammar should have a natural place within a humanistic science based upon semiotics. In my opinion, this is especially true of areas such as information science, computer semiotics, and similar endeavors, because logic unifies analytical activities traditionally belonging to the humanities with constructive and operational activities, which by tradition are characteristic of computer science (and natural science in general).

This is not to deny that possible tensions between analytical semiotics and Montague Grammar do exist. These divergences mainly depend upon two related points: First, how comprehensive is IL's potential for linguistic description; and second, how should the notion of meaning be construed — that is, what is ultimately the basis of meaning, and by implication, what does it really mean to understand a language. In the discussion so far, differences on those points have shone through with respect to three concrete issues:

(a)   how "interpretation" and "interpretant" are defined;
(b)   how pragmatics is defined, and how it is related to semantics;
(c)   a potential disagreement on what "meaning" and "understanding" really are.

Within IL, the interpretation is a well-defined and completely formalized unit; it makes no explicit reference whatsoever to social conventions, psychological effects, and the like. But in semiotics, the interpretant is pragmatically determined:

> Charles S. Peirce ... came to the conclusion that in the end the interpretant of a symbol must reside in a habit and not in the immediate physiological reaction which the sign vehicle evoked or in the attendant images or emotions — a doctrine which prepared the way for the contemporary emphasis on rules of usage. *(Morris, 1938: 31)*

The determination of the interpretant as being dependent upon a habit (or convention) in effect refers us to pragmatics. Nevertheless, no disagreement need arise, if we choose to view the IL interpretant as the purely mathematical modeling of the formal features of such habits. That conception would be entirely compatible with Morris's view that semantical rules must be studied in abstraction from pragmatics, even though they ultimately derive from pragmatical factors. Of course, the interpretant and the interpretation are not identical. What I have been trying to suggest so far is that within IL the interpretation takes on a role akin to the role of the interpretant within semiosis. The conception of the interpretation as a mathematical abstraction of some of the formal features of the interpretant would certainly seem to be an important step towards placing logic grammar as a special case within general semiotical theory.

That conception, however, seems to be contradicted by the way in which Lewis delimited semantics from pragmatics. His definitions seem to suggest an ontological division between the two disciplines and their respective subject matters. In a paradoxical turn of things, this division has led logic grammarians into considering IL to be more comprehensive than the preceeding conception would have it. It is no coincidence that the authoritative work on Montague Semantics (Dowty et al., 1979) called Montague's paradigm "Montague's General Semiotic Program." This heading indicates a conception of Montague's logic grammar as being not merely a special case of the semiotical study of natural language, but rather as being this study in its entirety. The fact that Lewis, Dowty, and others could view Montague's programme in this way must in part be a consequence of a more narrow definition of pragmatics than the one we find with Morris (and Peirce). This more restricted definition came about in a process starting in (Carnap, 1942) and culminating, I believe, in (Bar-Hillel, 1954). Bar-Hillel emphasised that language users are themselves part of the context or possible world within which linguistic signs are being used. The influence of language users upon the object side of signs is limited to the possible changes in denotations. This corresponds to the changes in denotation from one context to another which we saw in the exposition of IL. With Bar-Hillel, pragmatics is limited to the study of these changes, and so broader sociological and psychological aspects are excluded from pragmatics. The overall conception of semiotics is correspondingly curtailed. As far as I can see this is the background against which we must understand Lewis's sharp distinction between semantics on the one side and on the other side the study of preconditions of language use, the effects of language use, and so on. In fairness one should add that while the notion of "possible world" is a bit of a catch-all with Montague, Lewis elaborated that notion such as to be more capable of expressing pragmatic factors. He extended the primitive to comprise eleven "coordinates," including "speaker," "hearer," "previous discourse" and "causal-history." — The fact that Montague in his reference to Morris also calls on Bar-Hillel is another indication that the notion of semiotics has been restricted within IL. And this is something which has to be realized, I believe, if we are to understand one of Montague's most famous and provocative statements:

> There is in my opinion no important theoretical difference between natural languages and the artificial languages of logicians; indeed, I consider it possible to comprehend the syntax and semantics of both kinds of languages within a single natural and mathematically precise theory.   *(Montague, 1976c: 224)*

In the context of this quotation semantics must be understood as comprising formal pragmatics, too. If pragmatics is restricted as described here, Montague's proposition is not as blatantly mistaken as it appears to be prima facie. To the extent that workers within IL acknowledge that only selected parts of pragmatics are treated within this tradition, there is no inherent contradiction between IL and analytical semiotics on this point, either. On the other hand, when leading IL theorists such as Lewis *do* make a sharp ontological division between pragmatics and semantics, then we have the divergence. The reasons for this divergence are to be found in basic differences in metaphysical assumptions current in the two traditions — more precisely, a basic disagreement as to what "meaning" and "understanding" really are.

The early foundation of logic grammar was laid out in the younger Wittgenstein's Tractatus Logico-Philosophicus. There, the understanding of language was described as follows:

> To understand a proposition means to know what is the case, if it is true.
> *(Wittgenstein, 1922/1986: 67)*

Thus the central idea is that the basis of all language understanding is knowledge of the objects to which linguistic expressions refer or may refer. Another very well-known formulation of this principle is the statement that *the meaning of a sentence is identical with the conditions under which the sentence is true*. This conception of language understanding, and by implication, of linguistic meaning, has made a deep mark upon the development of all of logic grammar, including IL. Thomason for one described Montague's work as "a generalization of the *Tractatus* framework" (Thomason, 1976: 41). But within analytical semiotics, understanding and meaning are defined differently:

> To understand a language is to employ only those sign combinations and transformations not prohibited by the usages of the social group in question, to denote objects and situations as do the members of this group, to have the expectations which the others have when certain sign vehicles are employed, and to express one's states as others do — in short, to understand a language or to use it correctly is to follow the rules of usage (syntactical, semantical, and pragmatical) current in the given social community ... Meanings are not to be located as existences at any place in the process of semiosis but are to be characterised in terms of this process as a whole.
>
> *(Morris, 1938: 36, 45)*

Among these two ancestors of IL, Morris and Wittgenstein, we thus find two basically different conceptions of what understanding and meaning ultimately are. Montague obviously was influenced by both of these traditions, but I shall not try to determine his precise position between them. It may be observed, though, that Montague in his reference to Morris stated that at Morris's time of writing, pragmatics was lacking a "precise technical structure." That remark rather suggests that it is Morris's definition of pragmatics which stands in need of revision — that is, that Morris simply did not know the formal developments that were to follow, and which would make it possible to define the role of pragmatics precisely. On the other hand, Montague's remark that "pragmatics ... at least initially [should] follow the lead of semantics" suggests some openness with respect to the future development of pragmatics.

The differences in underlying basic assumptions are certainly interesting and should be kept in mind, but at the same time it is doubtful whether they are all that important with respect to the question of IL's relation to semiotics. To my mind, it has been established with sufficient clarity that IL fits with Morris's framework on a number of important points. For these reasons it is quite possible to view IL as a part of semiotics, while duly acknowledging its limitations with respect to pragmatics.

IL and the process of semiosis

The investigation so far has been related mainly to Morris's version of semiotics, rather than directly to Peirce himself. There are several reasons for this. First, Morris has exerted an influence upon theoretical linguistics that is far more direct and by far exceeds that of Peirce himself. This observation should be qualified, of course, by keeping in mind that it was Peirce who laid out the foundation of Morris's work. But at any rate, it is semiotics first and foremost in Morris's version to which Montague and his successors refer. Second, in actual fact (Morris, 1938) emphasizes the *structure* of sign systems significantly more than the *processes* appertaining to these systems. He certainly does make reference to the process of semiosis, and his thoughts on the structure of signs are compatible with the dynamical theory of semiosis that was at the focus of Peirce's own interest. Nevertheless, Morris himself was in his 1938 monograph mainly concerned with structural aspects. It is true of most of modern linguistics that it is preoccupied with *structure*, and hence that it can be compared with structural aspects of signs much more directly than with processual aspects — and this is especially true of logic grammar (leaving aside some very recent developments in logic grammar, notably that of *dynamic logic*. That field seems to be capable of expressing processual aspects of language understanding much more convincingly than classical as well as intensional logic — see van Benthem, 1991). — Third, the task of relating Peirce's work to IL would also be far more comprehensive. It is well-known that Peirce's theories never achieved a stable and fully systematic form. On the contrary, they underwent constant change with many different positions along the way — positions, that sometimes were even contradictory.

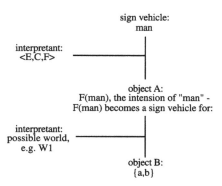

Fig. 4.3. Semiosis as in IL.

In Peirce's work, then, one can find quotations apparently quite incompatible with IL, as well as statements that word by word seem to be entirely in Montague's spirit. In the end, there is to my mind no doubt that the basics of Peirce and Montague are compatible within a general semiotical framework. The many similarities between Morris and Montague should bring home this point, even if in an indirect manner. One can find many analogous points when comparing the work of Montague with central concepts in Peirce's writings. Let me briefly indicate in Figure 4.3 some of the most important of those points.

As I hope to have shown, the interpretation of IL is in its function analogous to the interpretant of semiotics. In fact, that process of interpretation which lies implicitly in IL can be rendered as two adjoined triadic structures (Fig. 4.3).

Let us tentatively determine the interpretative process of signs within IL as a restricted case of semiosis in the Peircean sense. The object A can then be seen as the "immediate object," — that is, the immediate "idea" or conceptual content evoked by the sign vehicle in connection with the interpretant. That object itself takes on the status of a sign vehicle, which gets related to the object {a,b}. The interpretant can in the latter case be identified with some concrete context or possible world — for example, W1 — and in the present case the object {a,b} is precisely the concrete men within that context. The first part of the process seems to be that type of inference structure that Peirce called *abduction*, albeit in a very restricted sense: The assignment of an intension to the sign vehicle corresponds to making a hypothesis concerning what the sign vehicle may "be about," — to what it may refer. The second part of the process may be identified with the Peircean notion of *deduction*, in which a sign (in Figure 4.3, the "upper half" of the structure) becomes related to a "dynamical object" ({a,b}). Now to call this object "dynamical" is not exactly obvious within the framework of IL, and this fact is in my opinion due to a basic problem for the project of logic grammar. In that tradition, semantics is conceived of as studying the relation between linguistic symbols and the real world, but in formal semantics one has to represent the latter also by symbols. There is an ultimate step, which is not captured within IL — namely, that part of the process in which the dynamical object gets related to an "absolute object" in the real world. The process of relating a dynamical object to an absolute object was categorized by Peirce as a type of inference called *induction*. The lack of induction within IL would seem to correspond exactly to those parts of pragmatics left out in the development from Bar-Hillel to Montague, and left out by David Lewis as compared to Morris.

It must be emphasised that Figure 4.3 as well as my relating it to the notions of abduction, deduction, and induction, is not an attempt at establishing a one-to-one translation between concepts of intensional logic and concepts of semiotics. Rather, the goal is to point toward *semiotical definitions of concepts of intensional logic*. Yet this humility on behalf of logic (my own tradition) should not be exaggerated. I have no doubt myself that a more advanced investigation of the relation between modern symbolic logic and semiotics would also lead to a higher level of precision within the conceptual apparatus of semiotics, as well as a more precise understanding of the philosophy of Peirce. Just one example of this is the formal framework laid out by A. N. Prior, which he used for discussing temporal concepts in general as well as a more specific discussion of Peirce's ideas on determinism and statements about the contingent future (Øhrstrøm and Hasle, 1991a). Prior's work has certainly given us a more precise understanding of the problems and relations involved in these matters.

The general perspective, then, should be a further investigation into the relation between semiotics on the one hand and logic grammar on the other (as well as logic in general). In the discussion of Morris I hope to have demonstrated the viability of such a project, and with my remarks here on the relation between IL and the process of semiosis I have tried to suggest a starting point for such a more advanced study.

Conclusion

In a significant recent work, *A Theory of Computer Semiotics* (Andersen, 1990), semiotics is also put forward as a discipline capable of unifying analytical and constructive aspects of information technology. The higher objective is to develop semiotics as a general foundation of a humanistic science, which includes domains traditionally belonging to technical computer science. The line taken by Andersen (1990) is rooted in the tradition of *structuralist* semiotics and its concomitant linguistic science *glossematics*, which was developed not least by Louis Hjelmslev (Hjelmslev, 1943). This tradition does differ from analytical semiotics in important respects, but it is nonetheless clear that the two schools share a lot of common ground beyond being mere namesakes. However, the important topic of their mutual relation cannot be pursued here. With respect to glossematics, that field also has some interesting relations to logic, although this issue is to the best of my knowledge less well researched. One interesting point, however, is the three basic requirements for linguistic description put forth by Hjelmslev:

(1)   Any linguistic description must not contain contradictions (consistency, soundness).
(2)   It must be exhaustive of its subject matter (completeness).
(3)   It must be as simple as possible.

The priorities among these three requirements are as indicated by their enumeration, consistency being the most important property, and so forth. These requirements and priorities are exactly the same as those put forward in formal logic with respect to any logical system. Within mathematical logic, we have precise methods for determining how a given logical system stands to these requirements. But of course, there are systems that cannot be formalized to such an extent that these methods can be applied. The lack of induction and the restriction of the notion of pragmatics within IL should probably be understood in the light of this kind of relative "non-formalisability." On the other hand, it should be advantageous to formalize a theory to the extent that it is possible, also because the formal properties of the theory may then be investigated by such mathematical methods. With respect to glossematics, a formal logical interpretation of the so-called "glossematic functions" has been achieved (Nielsen, 1982), but it is not clear how far this formalization can go — in fact, (Nielsen, 1982) also concedes that glossematics is not "of a logical nature." Accordingly, it would seem, (Andersen, 1990) is fairly critical toward the relevance of logic within computer semiotics (or at least within linguistics, which plays a crucial role in his approach to the field). However, when considering the work of Morris as well as Peirce himself, it is in my opinion beyond reasonable doubt that logic has a natural place within a broader conception of semiotics, which includes the analytical tradition.

One of the differences between analytical semiotics and structuralist semiotics is precisely that the former has been more preoccupied with symbolic logic than the latter. That circumstance may indeed be a special strength of the analytical tradition when related to technical computer science. To be sure, logic is not the only field in which analytical and constructive endeavors are unified, a fact to which the work of (Andersen 1990) itself bears witness. But logic is a particularly striking example of this relationship due to its close connection with some of the most mathematical and technical domains within computer science. Within a semiotical description, logic can be applied at a very low level — a level closely related to the technical aspects of information technology. Both semiotical approaches would then supplement each other. Together they may provide a general scientific framework, within which information technology can be uniformly described at levels ranging from software engineering, via the computer as a medium, and up to the level of cultural analysis.

Acknowledgements

The work described in this chapter was carried out under a grant from the Cognitive Science Research Programme of the Danish Research Council for the Humanities. The unpublished joint Masters's Thesis of (Jespersen and Mark, 1990) has been a source of inspiration for me while trying to get an overview of those aspects of Peirce's work that are most promising for a direct comparison with Montague. In this connection I am also grateful for useful discussions with Hans Roed Mark.

Bibliography

ANDERSEN, P. BØGH (1990). *A Theory of Computer Semiotics*. Cambridge: Cambridge University Press.

BAR-HILLEL, Y. (1954). Indexical Expressions. *Mind 63*, 359 - 379.

BENTHEM, J. van (1991). *Language in Action: Categories, Lambdas and Dynamic Logic*. Amsterdam: North Holland.

CARNAP, R. (1942). *Introduction to Semantics*. Cambridge Massachusetts: Harvard University Press.

DOWTY, D. R., R. WALL, S. PETERS (1979). *Introduction to Montague Semantics*. Dordrecht: D. Reidel.

GALTON, A., ed (1987). *Temporal Logics and Their Applications*. London: Academic Press.

HASLE, P. (1989). Fra sproganalyse til logikprogrammering [From discourse analysis to logic programming]. *Humanistiske Data 3*, 66 - 82.

HASLE, P. (1991). Logic Grammars in Linguistic Description. In *Contrastive Linguistics*, ed. Karen M. and Ole Lauridsen, 105-143. Aarhus: The Aarhus School of Business Studies.

HJELMSLEV, L. (1943). *Omkring sprogteoriens grundlæggelse*. Copenhagen.

JESPERSEN, L. J., H. ROED MARK (1990). *Informatik og semiotik*. Unpublished Masters' Thesis at Department of Communication, Aalborg University.

LEWIS, D. (1976). General Semantics. In *Montague Grammar*, ed B. H. Partee, 1-50. London: Academic Press.

MONTAGUE, R. (1976a). *Formal Philosophy. Selected Papers of Richard Montague*. Edited and with an introduction by Richmond H. Thomason. Yale University Press: New Haven and London.

MONTAGUE, R. (1976b). Pragmatics. In Montague 1976a, 95 - 118.

MONTAGUE, R. (1976c). Universal Grammar. In Montague 1976a, 222 - 246.

MORRIS, C. (1938). *Foundations of the Theory of Signs*. International Encyclopedia of Unified Science, 1-59. Chicago: University of Chicago Press.

NIELSEN, K. HVIDTFELT (1982). A Formal Investigation of Five Glossematic 'Functions.' *Acta Linguistica Hafniensia, 17/ 2*.

PEIRCE, C. S. (1931-1958). *Collected Papers*. Cambridge Massachusetts: Harvard University Press.

RUSSELL, B. (1905). On denoting. *Mind 14*, 479 - 493.

THOMASON, R. H. (1976). Introduction. In Montague 1976a, 1 - 48.

WITTGENSTEIN, L. (1922). *Tractatus Logico-Philosophicus*. Translated from the German by C. K. Ogden and with an introduction by Bertrand Russell. Reprinted in 1986. London: Routledge and Kegan Paul.

ØHRSTRØM, P., P. HASLE (1991a). A. N. Prior's Rediscovery of Tense Logic. In *Abstracts from the 9th International Conference on Logic, Methodology, and Philosophy of Science, Sweden 1991*, 173. Uppsala.

ØHRSTRØM, P., P. HASLE (1991b). Medieval Logic and Natural Language Understanding. In *Natural Language Understanding and Logic Programming III*, eds. C. Brown and G. Koch, 75 - 90. Amsterdam: North Holland.

5

Meaning and the machine: Toward a semiotics of interaction

PER AAGE BRANDT

It is obvious that "symbolic machines" determine a larger and larger part of ordinary life in the kind of social reality we are beginning to experience and to prepare for; it should be just as obvious that this situation calls for a revision of our semiotic "common sense," the kind of conceptual standards with which we meet our compact social challenges. Neither the interpretative semiotics based on the Peircean tradition (such as Eco 1976), nor the structural semiotics of the Saussurean tradition (such as Greimas 1976) — though both are necessary — seem sufficient to follow up the substantial change induced by the on-going implementation of these machines in our "life world," probably for the very simple reason that even these often rather sophisticated semiotic elaborations fail to see what a "symbolic machine" actually is and what it can do. This chapter will be devoted to considerations and theoretical work that may prepare the way for at least a partial updating or restating of some of the fundamental issues involved in this dilemma.

On technical objects and machines

If we consider machines as "technical objects," the semiotic status of this type of objects would be worth considering. I take it to be something like the following. There is a subject actant S and there is a domain of objects D, defined by an intentional relation S-D. S is "doing something" concerning D. The technical object O takes on a specific meaning in this intentional context, if we consider it dynamically: S is "trying" and D is "resisting"; but there is a syntagm SO and a syntagm OD, such that if SO does the trying, OD is no longer resisting. In this sense, O removes or diminishes D's resistance. In modal terms, O transforms a "cannot do" (easily) into a "can do" (easily); it makes a task easier. O has thus a modal meaning in the context S-D. It modifies S's access to D. The mediation SO-OD is "better" than the un-mediated relation S-D.

S may for instance be a person who wants to remove dust from his carpet (D); he could try to do this manually, by picking up dust particles with his fingers, or by shaking the carpet from the open window. The carpet resists, in that it holds back what he wants to remove. He could then take an electric vacuum cleaner and apply it to the carpet; S-D becomes SOD, and SO- is distinct from -OD in this syntagm. OD is more efficient than the unmediated SD.

Non-technical objects, such as aesthetic objects, sometimes have no modal meaning at all. Their meaning is terminal, or existential, for S, and they themselves belong directly to a terminal, existential domain for S. They are absolute values, not relative values. Or they are moralizers for other, more remote tasks of S in more distant domains; this is by far the most frequent case. Most domains are technically determined with respect to other domains, but they can be more or less useful in general terms (the class of distant domains can be open or closed). The *technicality* of O is proportional to the specificity of D (or to the closedness of its D-class). A book can be "very" technical (a users' manual) or "less" technical (an essay of general interest); in practice, the same O has variable technicality for different S-instances, and therefore the whole analysis presupposes collective standard S-instances defined broadly by a culture. Such a standard S is itself a normative complex of wants expressed by paths through a hierarchy of doings in domains, a semantics of values, a technology. Technology is therefore a valid expression of the semantics of a culture.

But a machine is not only a technical object. A book or a knife is not a machine, in the ordinary sense of this term. The technicality of the machine represents its semantic determination; but there is also an ontological determination. In fact, if an O is a machine, there must be an *energetic difference* between the syntagmatic interaction SO and the syntagmatic interaction OD, in the mediation SO-OD. If S wants to inform D of something, and sends a coded message O, this element is not *eo ipso* a machine, whereas it is indeed a technical object. It is simply a means. The energetic situation is essentially the same at the reception and at the sending. S could also send a bomb, programmed to explode at the reception. The encoding and the decoding would no longer belong to the same energetics, and this time it would be a machine. A hammer is not the same thing for a hand and for a nail (despite the mishaps). A pistol relates in different ways to the triggering finger and to the target; there is an energetic transmission crossing the border between ontologically different causal realms. In other words, the interface SO is energetically different from the interface OD in the machine. What is called "mechanical" is the regularity of the transmission from realm to realm (from trigger mechanics to powder chemistry, for instance). In many cases, the "mechanism" of this transmission may be and remain unknown to the user of the machine; he only needs to know and to represent to himself the most important aspects of its regularity. A machine is a divided technical object, a Janus-headed entity, a bivalent function: -O- , manifesting a certain autonomy in its way of linking its two interfaces.

Semiotically, this hidden link between perceived SO-physics and OD-physics makes the machine a signifying object in a specific way. Whereas the ordinary technical object owes its efficiency to the user's motory and mental performance (the knife, the book), so that its meaning is derivable from its S- and D-relevant form (such as "handiness," "fitness," and global "beauty") and from its substantial properties (such as "solidity," "flexibility," "elegance," "economy," and so on), the machine is efficient since it contains an autonomous performance as a substantial property (so that its "reliability" comes much closer to the human meaning of this value). The *interpretation* of a machine, interposed in an intentional act S-D, is therefore necessarily different from the interpretation of the act of using it, and implies a mobilisation of representations containing processual schemes by which the user has to adapt and control his own motory performance, as he must do in human interaction. In other words, there is necessarily a specific instance of *semiosis*, in which the subject has to rely on interpretative representations of what events and instances control inherently the machine's performance and shape his own performance according to these imaginary creations.

The general principle of *interactional semiosis* also accounts for machine interaction, whereas the content of the mobilized interpretative representations is specific in an interesting way. This general principle can be characterized by a simple formula that is related to the Peircean triad. The Sign is temporal in this case, it is the durative representamen perceived by the subject as a process running from the initial SO-syntagm to the terminal OD-syntagm, through an unknown sequence. The Interpretant consists of explicative schemes that bridge this cognitive gap *between the initial and terminal instances* of the Sign, and fill in the syntactic slip. And the semantic result is a believed continuous global sequence (Figure 5.1):

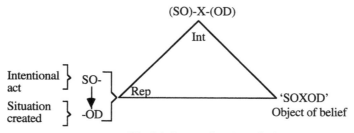

Fig.5.1. Interactional semiosis.

If the object O is a person, and if I am the subject S, then the "reaction" of O affects the domain D, from which I take the motives that orient my intentional act; if a new situation is created in D, my intentions will be reoriented. But this "feedback" D -> S depends on my understanding of how the act "worked" and by what forces or rules it obtained the situational result. A change — which is, in this analysis, a sign — must be intelligible to have any effect on the subject's acts.

Thus "good" intentions can easily create "bad" (unwanted) situations, if the change obtained is not intelligible; any interaction establishes an interpretative context, a semiosis of this kind, because the regulation of the *flow* of SO-acts draws on what is believed to really happen "inside" O. A degenerated semiosis gives rise to "blind" action, discontinuous flows, panic, perplexity, confusion. There is a cognitive demand for interpretative images (X), and they are constructed from certain schemes, with or without specific knowledge of O. A personalized O (an Other Subject) calls for fundamental pragmatic and narrative schemes, which may be independent of the domain they are supposed to operate on — since a Person is basically a rather untechnical object (indeed, this is probably a main source of the very idea of non-technical objects) — but a social, professional "technification" can functionalize it by imposing institutional rules of procedure on X. These rules are impersonal and tend to neutralize the "free" pragmatico-narrative schemes by referring to the domains (as in legal specialization, based on domain-sensitive traditions and the authority of precedents).

The analysis of personal interaction must therefore distinguish "free" and "bound" interpretants, and accordingly, intelligibility referring to human reality (inter-personal, un-technical)) and to institutional reality (impersonal, technical) as contents of obtained belief. This is an important dimension of social phenomenology. We could generalize the distinction and propose the notation Xf vs. Xb (free vs. bound interpretant) as a standard condition of interactional semiosis. Xf would indicate the more intentional part (related to natural patterns of finality), and Xb the more causal or coded (conventional: quasi-causal) part of the interpretant; both components are needed in a global interpretation.

If the object O is a machine, the interpretation follows the same general lines. There is, first, a causal path through the machine, which is a strong interpretative idea, stressing Xb. The SO-syntagm contains a series of acts of control, guiding the work of the machine through a network of bifurcations, guiding a reference unit that "travels" through a bifurcating path, in much the same way as if it were a person running through a physical landscape or a world of branching possibilities. It could be stipulated that the reference unit and its modal path ("necessary" movement, when the path is linear, and "possible," when bifurcating) in the user's imagination, represents his own body projected into the fictive, operative world "inside" the machine. In this sense, *SO as SXb* projects the user's intentional acting into the causal Xb-world, the reference unit being then intentional and the path structure being causal.

These reference units, however, are either discrete volumes or non-discrete flows. The token inserted into a coin-box or a gambling machine is a discrete reference unit, and as such a good representative of the subject body; but the water flowing through a coffee brewer or a central heating plant, or the petrol flowing through a car engine, or the electricity and the signal flowing through a radio, are — surprisingly enough — equally efficient, non-discrete reference units, by means of which the subject makes sense of his own manipulation of the machine. (The car driver thus projects twice: on the global car as a discrete unit, located in the traffic system; and on the gas as a non-discrete unit, located in the combustion system; for the driver, the two worlds seem to be cognitively connected, by a simple category of transmission, *speed*, which relates the spinning of the motor and the rushing of the car.)

Bodies and flows can equally well carry the S-intention into the imaginary O-world by means of projection onto a reference unit, probably because humans identify not only with body-like entities, but also with body-internal flows (such as the air in the lungs, or the proprioceptive feeling of "energy" formerly interpreted as body "spirits" or as a property of the blood, or as "drives"), and with external flows (such as groups and masses in movement). In this elementary, first semiotization of the interactional object which determines the regulatory flow of user operations, a kind of transport model accounts for the minimal user intuition needed; in narrative semiotics (Greimas, 1966: 180), a simple version (Figure 5.2) relates six actants on three axes:

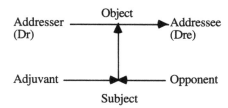

Fig. 5.2. The actant model.

In terms of SXb-syntax, this actantial structure, with its axis of communication (Dr - Dre), its axis of intention (S-O), and its axis of conflict (Adj - Opp), would seem to correspond to a projective icon as in Figure 5.3:

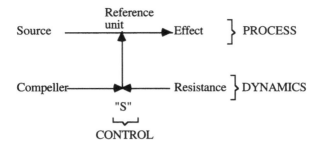

Fig. 5.3. The actant model of interactional semiosis.

A primitive narrative atom like this seems to interpret the "inner," "black box" world of the local process which the user must visualise (iconize) for himself in order to manipulate the machine.

Second, there is a symbolic dimension relating the user-subject to the *designer* of the machine. As a machine is not a piece of pure nature, but rather an arranged disposition that makes use of natural processes and the possible gearing of its energetics for certain *purposes* , the user cannot but feel guided by an already instantiated, implemented intentionality, a designer subject, Sd, inscribed in the arrangements that determines the control offered by the machine. The user "will want to" obtain certain quantities of the effect, and "will want to" avoid certain other effects; the commands available are expressions of this intersubjective, projected "wants" and are read as such by the user-S. The functional connection between the variables of effect and the variables of control is signed by the "author" of the machine, Sd (and concealed in the trademark). The dysfunctions and "eu-functions" of the machine thus modulate a kind of communication between S and Sd. The effect appears as the result of available commands and actual manipulations of them,

E = f(Sd, S)

so that the very functioning of a particular machine expresses a relative harmony (and resignation) in the exchange between S and Sd; an exchange that is also a conflict, in so far as the interests of these subjects are different, in certain respects even opposed (for example, the emphasis on maximal durability, vital to S and lethal to Sd).

This aspect of the "machine meaning" could now be understood as an Xf-interpretative phenomenon, related to the dynamic axis of the actantial model: Sd is *projected* on the opposed instances of Adjuvant and Opponent, and now becomes both a factor of constructive Help and a factor of

Obstruction — a Constructor and an Obstructor — in the perspective of S. Some of his inventions are felt to be truly helpful, others to be impedimental, awkward, harmful, or directly evil. Sd is divided into two opposed actants; this is also fundamentally what happens in direct human communication, a phenomenon that explains the affective ambivalence of intersubjectivity: The Other is helpful and harmful, loveable and dangerous; we must regulate this affective instability to be able to maintain a coherent attitude by symbolic means, such as gestual and verbal politeness. Users of machines always ritualize their commerce with them to some extent, if they integrate them in important operative routines.

The actantialization stresses the bound, physicalistic representation (SXb) on the level of the process axis, but stresses the free, intersubjective, pragmatic representation (SXf) on the level of the conflict axis *of the same interpretative model* . In this full interpretation, the model becomes fully narrative. The resulting belief — SO(XbXf)OD — is therefore both cognitive and pragmatic; it combines inferential intuitions referring to physis and to polis, with causes (forces) and with intentions (rules). It is probable that any complex, concrete-world experience of doing manifests this dynamic character; but the machine experience concentrates it and unfolds it on a strictly local condition: the "box" and its interface.

Symbolic machines

The specificity of computers as symbolic machines adds new determinations to the standard semiotic (causal and symbolic) features of any machine that we have considered. The dialectics of *program* and *data* must first be examined. The SO-sequence inserts initial data into the machine O, and the OD-sequence presents terminal data to D, generally perceived by S; between the initial and the terminal phase, the data are processed by a program, and S can display an interpretative visualisation following the actantial dimensions mentioned earlier; the system interacts with the user — E = f(Sd, S) as before — and S experiences and imagines a process and a dynamics of control which also symbolizes the programmer as a subject (Sd). So far we seem to have an ordinary machine semiotics.

However, there are important differences, which deeply affect the user's semio-phenomenology. The three great semiotic changes are:

(1) The subject controls the running of the program not only by starting and following it, but also by *feeding* it with input; the processing flow is sensitive to the input in quite a different way than, say, a water flow

is sensitive to modifications of its velocity: the "chemics" of the flow itself is modified by the input it receives from S (it memorises).

(2)   The "chemical" transformations of introduced input can be stopped by a bifurcation in the flow, until the user has been "asked" which way to proceed (it gives options).

(3)   But first of all, it "takes" informational *data* , by an inherent tendency to constipation and coagulation which breaks out intermittently and can only be cured by this specific remedy (it makes requests).

By virtue of these major properties, it is impossible for the user-subject to distinguish between the dynamics of interaction — E = f(Sd, S) — and the very object of control, the intentional and the causal aspects of the machine, Xf and Xb in the Interpretant.

In fact, memory, options, and requests are purely interactive properties: both Adjuvants and Opponents have memory; Adjuvants offer facilities, give options (referring to a closed class morphology of "styles"); Opponents ask screening questions, require information (referring to an open class of morphologically defined symbols), punish ignorance (cf. Oedipus and the Sphinx). In order to control or rather to maintain the flow, S has to answer both dynamic instances: to express his wishes, answering the Adjuvant, and to express his knowledge, thereby answering the Opponent. These two types of input constitute the data: *commands* (answers to options), and *information* (answers to requests). Both are absorbed and memorized by the flow. And the decisive feature is precisely that the presentation of options and requests emerges from the flow itself, modified by memory. This flow is *logical*, in a broad sense: it remembers, it asks for orientation, and it asks for information. If the answers are satisfactory, commands work as major premises, information as minor premises, and it presents conclusions — terminal, processed data.

The closed class of commands and the open class of information could even be compared with the distribution of classes in linguistic morphology and semantics (Talmy, 1985); natural logic and linguistic intuition have guided the historical construction of symbolic machines and made them fundamentally compatible with human habits of thought.

The flow and the designer subject necessarily merge in the user's interpretative imagination, since (1) interactive initiatives come from the flow, and (2) these initiatives have intentional meaning by their logical content and efficiency (the production of terminal information). The processing does not have to be highly sophisticated to justify this interpretation. In principle, it is sufficient that initial and terminal informational data differ, and that the latter is more interesting in some way than the former in the same domain (the basic relevance criterion). This is the case where the "chemics" of the flow obey laws — formal manipulations — that humans believe in. Therefore, the available options generally trigger a "style" of manipulation belonging to this category. The great scientific event, which has made the computer possible, is of course the acquisition of a sufficient knowledge of the formal properties of some of these laws, as well as the invention of the silicon chip. Some laws offer more resistance than others; those determining the natural syntax of human language cannot be said to have been acquired yet.

But the user assigns to the computer a sort of semiosis, a "guided, human assisted machine semiosis," by virtue of the previously mentioned fusion of interaction and efficiency. S gives O information (on request) — Representamens — and activates formal processing (by option) — Interpretants — ; and O, the machine, responds by a sort of belief, or conclusion, which is presented to the S. To obtain this, S interacts symbolically with O, answers questions about wishes and knowledge, and keeps "guiding" and "assisting" it in these two ways during the process, until it comes to an intelligent conclusion. The user believes that this symbolic effect is based on a semiosis, comparable to his own. As in human interaction, the idea of a semiosis mentally performed by the other is a leading principle in his own semiosis. The relation is inter-semiotic. If S believes in what O is "saying," he does so believing that there is a belief in O. Instead of an ordinary machine representation (Xb/Xf), which does not project a belief on the machine, because the operations of control are not logical input, the commands must here be interpreted as a kind of major premises, and the information as minor premises, and the processing must be interpreted as an inferential process. Instead of the ordinary machine scheme Xb/Xf, there is a real *semiosis scheme* (Figure 5.4) in the Interpretant of S's semiosis:

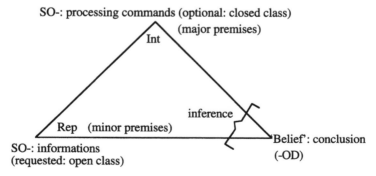

Fig. 5.4. The semiosis scheme of interaction.

The consequence of this semiotization of the flow (by the three features mentioned: memory, options, and requests) is a thorough revision of the actantial model, which is also active in the Interpretant of S's semiosis — namely, as a framework for the idea of interaction allowing S to project himself into the process. The revised version of the actantial model will derive the Adjuvant function (options) and the Opponent function (requests) from the flow; it will let the requests follow from the options, and sometimes inversely, but also let options follow from options, and requests from requests, in memorial circularity. The iconic result is an integrated dynamic, or dialectic, "program-data" model (Figure 5.5):

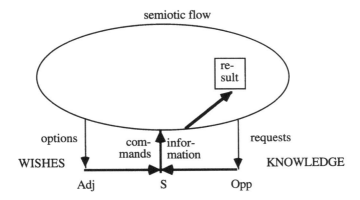

Fig. 5.5. Program-data: actant model.

A circular flow is probably needed in any conception of *belief* as a property of a system; only such a representation can grasp the idea of a memorized, but still changing "plastic" meaning resulting from the application of inherent options to incoming information — a mass of meaning that circulates and determine the treatment of new informations at any moment, itself exposed to growing or shrinking, according to the interactive dialectics of program and data.

So far, we have studied an isolated SOD-semantic situation, where O is a symbolic machine. But in computerized social pragmatics, the domain D often itself contains a set of other S-D relations, each of which unfolds the same machine semiotics *for other subjects* — produced by the same machine. This is the case, when computers are integrated in a network. The intricate circumstance is that alien new data now *inform* the local flow, with the program processing other S"O"-introduced data: This alien input will, second by second, change the content of the semiotic flow, at least of the data-base component of the shared program, so that the processing going on inside the global network is never the same in two local S-D relations or stations, even when they have identical inputs. The shared flow — for example, in a network of bookingoffices — is never literally and substantially identical at two stations, even if the hard core of its flows remains stable and its paths and branchings do not change their qualitative structure; the treatment that the particular data receive is particular and expresses the instantaneous state of the whole network. What is identical is not the content of the flow, but only the flow itself.

This phenomenon changes the pragmatic and symbolic aspect of what the corresponding local semiosis must produce as a meaning ascribed to any process. An inaccessible, collective memory is introduced, and it works in much the same way as what we call History: not as an inert depository, but as a continuous change and growth of the codes that are active in our communication as a mutual "processing." The flow becomes an active, transcendental principle, an instance that carries a kind of general state of belief that cannot be stated explicitly, but only shows its effects in the work that the semiotic flow yields at the separate stations. A particular S, interacting with the network at a station, now knows that some of the conclusions are due to input premises stemming from other stations and others to previous machine conclusions, but he does not know which are close to and which are far from human input; the genetic and epistemic status of a result is indeterminable. Conclusions close to S's beliefs, close to those of other users, and far from anything other than the flow's memorized conclusions, circulate in a semiotic promiscuity comparable to a cultural state of meaning in a human community.

The autonomy of a natural language is based on a similar semantic condition, in so far as the "mechanicized" patterns, metaphors, and associations in the incessant discursive flow behave in exactly the same way. The peculiar authority assigned by language users to conclusions based on such patterns and referring to them probably stems from a dialectic of belief, analogous to and possibly isomorphic with that which the simple computer-semiotic (intersemiosis) disposition already gives rise to and which the network disposition reinforces: The artificial or cultural simulacrum of natural human processing of meaning is *stronger* than the particular original, not only because we believe that artificial or cultural belief is more solid, as such, than the hallucinations of mortal flesh, but also because, being immortal, the *semiotic flow*, whether computational or discursive, embodies the general prerequisite for a particular inference to be *meaningfully* related — by the shared condition of radical difference and the promiscuous contact, the affinity, of symbolic events induced by it — to those of indefinite multitudes of human subjects. If there is a semiosis in the Interpretant of my semiosis, this second order semiosis is also present in other subjects' Interpretants, and this knowledge allows it to act as a general equivalent, a prototype and a norm, for any occurring first order semiosis in the network.

An elementary visualization of such a multi-actantial network model may sum up this outline of a semiotic theory of artificial and natural cultures, as in Figure 5.6:

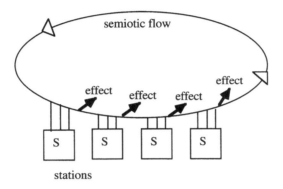

Fig. 5.6. Multi-actantial network.

It would be possible to show that a semiotic community along these lines must be both an epistemic and a passional community (by the actantial functions of wanting and knowing), but that the relationship between the contents (effects) obtained in communication is rather one of analogy, or family resemblance, than one of identity — vagueness is a condition for efficient communicative coherence, and for the kind or mode of identity that is here at stake: the dynamic, semiotic identity as a property of meaning related to continuous, active flows.

Conclusion

Semiotic theory is itself a good example of this communitary condition. Even the strictest adherence to a sub-tradition does not ensure conceptual isomorphism — identity is not in the signified contents, but in the flow relating them. Modifying and mixing the sub-traditions change the options and allow new knowledge or perplexity to be introduced, by which the "same" system comes to behave "differently": it is both closed and open, stable and unstable.

The notion of an entirely closed *code*, in Saussurean semiology, is much too weak to account for the interpretative activity of a semiotic flow. And the notion of communication based on stiff, passive "codes" — illustrated by the "postal" model: sender, receiver, channel, message, code, encoding, decoding — is highly insufficient and inadequate as a semiotic framework for the analysis of interaction. On the other hand, the Peircean notion of Representamen, Sign, must be extended to a temporal configuration, in order to account for the real epistemic input of interpretation; the interpretative patterns have to be de-subjectivized and related objectively to active schemes, which are components of the semiotic flow connecting multiple instances of semiosis. These theoretical operations — here discussed and formulated in a tentative way — modify and combine existing patterns under the pressure of the actual challenge, the symbolic machines; at the same time, they throw new light on classical issues and outline a different theory of general semiotics.

Computer semiotics should thus not be considered a branch of "applied semiotics," still less should it be reduced to a practical exercise; it presents an opportunity to reconsider seriously a whole range of weakly defined entities. First, the concept of technicality, the machine category, and the precarious notion of symbolicity; and second, the overall notions of actant, interaction, and interpretation. In the latter instance, the concept of meaning is deeply affected by these reconsiderations; it appears to survive, however, as does semiotics as such.

Bibliography

ANDERSEN, P. BØGH (1990). *A Theory of Computer Semiotics.* Cambridge: Cambridge University Press.

BRANDT, P. AA. (1992). *La Charpente modale du sens.* Amsterdam: John Benjamins.

ECO, U. (1976). *A Theory of Semiotics.* Bloomington: Indiana University Press.

FIGGE, U. L. (1991). Computersemiotik. *Zeitschrift für Semiotik* **13(3/4)**, 321-330.

GREIMAS, A. J. (1966). *Sémantique structurale. Recherche de méthode.* Paris: Ed. Larousse.

GREIMAS, A. J. (1976). *Sémiotique et sciences sociales.* Paris: Ed. du Seuil.

PEIRCE, C. S. (1982-1986). *Writings of Charles S. Peirce. A Chronological Edition* I-IV, ed. Max H. Fisch et al. Bloomington: Indiana University Press.

SAUSSURE, F. de (1962/1915). *Cours de linguistique générale.* Paris: Ed. Payot.

TALMY, L.(1985). Force Dynamics in Language and Thought. *Parasession on Causatives and Agentivity.* Chicago: Chicago Linguistic Society, University of Chicago.

PART II

THE RHETORIC OF INTERACTIVE MEDIA

Introduction

BERIT HOLMQVIST

During the last twenty years, computer technology has undergone an explosive development. From being a professional challenge to engineers, the computer has developed into a medium among other media in information society — in fact, a super medium that incorporates many other media. Gunnar Liestøl's chapter discusses this fact in the context of academic interactive publishing, and there are many other fields of application.We use e-mail instead of traditional paper-based mail, we enter virtual classrooms instead of taking the train to participate in a weekend course, and our children play computer games together with their friends instead of reading books about cowboys and Indians. Very soon we will exchange the videotape and video recorder for a CD-ROM player connected to our combined television/computer, so that we do not have to passively watch old films but can actively engage in the film making ourselves. But "Powerful media technology is meaningless without content." Unfortunately "In the area of interactive motion video, the embryonic technology is already outrunning creativity" (Larry Press in *Communication of the ACM*. Vol. 32, no 7. 1989: 788).

Expressions like "interactive fiction," "multimedia," and "virtual reality" are becoming familiar. With the new technology we can create simulations of possible and impossible worlds for people to enter and act in, being absorbed and fascinated by. But what kind of worlds? Soldiers can learn how to land an airplane or destroy a tank electronically. A medical student can take a walk inside the human brain. The designer can give form to a glass by means of the computer and an architect construct a whole city. The techniques developed for this kind of purposes are imported by the entertainment business and used to create three-dimensional cartoons or "special effects" in science fiction movies. Unfortunately, not only the techniques but also the aesthetics are imported — the aesthetics of "realism" and "naturalism."

This trend leads to an emphasis on the cosmetic side of the technology; the more natural movements, shapes, and colors, the better and more expensive. The authors in this part of the book regard the demand for creativity as a challenge, because we believe that theories and methods from the humanities will play an important role in the future development of computer systems, and conversely, that confrontation with technology will shake received wisdom and open new avenues of research.

The computer is a new electronic substance waiting to be formed. The new substance put restrictions on the form at the same time as it opens up for new possibilities. We are trying to understand this new substance, find out what its restrictions are, and discover its unique possibilities of aesthetic form. In order to find them we have to explore older media, since new art forms are created through older ones by consciously breaking established norms. This is true of the computer medium too. Therefore computer art should not just be copies or minor variations of older media; it must find its own means of expression. With this point of departure, Holmqvist and Bøgh Andersen give a normative definition of interactive fiction: *interaction* is the basic means of expression of the computer medium, *formalisms* its meter and choreography. The medium should be conceived as a *collage* medium, and interactive systems should be conceived as *inter-textual,* not textual, media. This definition can be taken as the framework for this part of the book.

We do not reject older traditions; on the contrary, we try to exploit them in the development of a new aesthetics. We are not technological optimists waiting for ever more sophisticated technology to come and solve all the problems, but we are optimistic on the account of humanistic research within the field of computer aesthetics. Therefore the chapters in this part are about the aesthetics and rhetoric of older media and the possibilities for adapting them to the computer medium.

A medium that plays an important role in several of the articles is theater. This explains why a chapter on the theater in the eighteenth century is included in a book on computers as media. Jens Hougaard gives a thorough analysis of neo-classical drama, and in many ways provides a historical perspective for the other articles in this part. Hougaard takes as his point of departure a personal astonishment over the fact that an author such as Ludwig Holberg, during his lifetime, wrote in *all the main literary genres*, that he was *enormously prolific* — in under a year he wrote fifteen plays — and that a theater managed to *put a considerable number of them on.*

The explanation of this efficiency is found in the philosophical and aesthetic context Holberg worked in. In the beginning of the eighteenth century the genres were viewed as different modes of cognition, and the attempt to fill them all out was possibly an expression of the writer's progress in age and wisdom. The genres were constituted by a set of rules that were to be followed. There were formal rules, such as the requirement that comedy should be written in prose and tragedy in verse, but also rules for content. Once a genre was chosen, the writer also knew what the basic conflict in the drama should be. In a comedy, for example, it was a conflict about marriage unfolded as a meeting between two families. This basic formal conflict in turn automatically produced a particular gallery of characters. Furthermore, there were rules for subdividing the text into a fixed number of acts, each with a specific function with respect to the conflict to be solved. So the genre solved many technical problems for the author. He just had to fill in the blanks with his real theme. Of course, all this helped Holberg to be as productive as he was, but as Hougaard writes: "We must not forget that he was a very diligent person, for whom every day contained twelve to fourteen hours that were eminently suited to work."

Let us now turn to the efficiency of the theater and the actors. Hougaard mentions a famous actress who, during fifteen years played approximately nine different roles per year. How was that possible? Well, the actors again had the same help from the genres as the author himself, but in addition there were very detailed rules for acting. As Hougaard puts it, the theater of the eighteenth century was "a theater of presentation or display." Realism was not intended. The actors played, in a two dimensional set-up, in the light of tallow candles or oil lamps placed on the stage ramp. The characters were pre-defined by the theory of humoralism: the choleric type, the phlegmatic type, the sanguine type, and the melancholic type. And last but not least, the sign production was strictly formalized for each character. The body of the actor was divided up and there was almost a one-to-one relation between the gestures, facial expressions and general movements, and the content they expressed. So to be a good actor was not to be a great personality, as we are used to think of it today. It was to be as obedient to the rules as possible.

With European industrialism, the conditions were changed, and a new bourgeois art emerged. While in the neo-classical drama the author was a mediator between the "God-given" genres and the play, bourgeois art demanded individualization. The author assumed a dynamic relation to his product and made himself visible in it.

Ironically enough, post-industrial society seems to be recreating the feudal art form. Hougaard compares the feudal neo-classical drama to the mass-produced dramas of our time — soap operas distributed through television and movies. It is as he wants to say to us: "If you are going to exploit the techniques from the eighteenth century drama, make sure you give your products a content more interesting than *Dallas* or *An Officer and a Gentleman.*"

There is a striking resemblance between the neo-classical drama, as presented in Hougaard's paper, and interactive fiction. One characteristic of interactive media is that the balance between the author and the reader shifts and that the size of the narrative controlled by the author shrinks. In interactive media the genres are reintroduced, not as sacred god-given rules, but as profane author-created rules. Instead of enjoying the direct and dynamic relation between writer and product of bourgeois art, the author of interactive fiction must step back and write *programs* that the users execute. So now the author is writing the rules, — creating mini-genres — and the user of the interactive fiction must perform some of the duties of the author apart from still acting as audience. We again have art governed by explicit rules.

Like the stage of neo-classical drama, the screen of the computer is two-dimensional. This puts special demands on the "actors" and the screen display. The main interest in the first chapter by Holmqvist and Andersen (Chapter 6) is in the graphical constraints and possibilities for picture-based fiction on a two dimensional screen, or, in other words, "on how to make scratches in the puritan standard Macintosh Interface." Different techniques for creating atmosphere and economizing the movements of the actors are presented. Furthermore, the authors have consciously chosen a theme for their interactive narrative that would be real challenge against soap opera banality.

Like video games, interactive fiction invites several readings not just one, reading, and each reading should reveal new angles of the subject. The author can achieve this by constructing small narrative pieces that can be combined in many ways, but this causes problems of coherence. Andersen and Holmqvist show how AI techniques can be used as aesthetic techniques for implementing constraints that secure sufficient cohesion to create a substance that the author and reader can form into a narrative. The drama-framework is borrowed from the American interactivist Brenda Laurel, who uses the Aristotelian drama concept. While Laurel uses the Aristotelian concept at a philosophical level, Andersen and Holmqvist pursue the consequences at a more concrete level. Arguing that the substance of an interactive drama is everyday experiences molded by dramatic form, they present descriptions of dramatic form that bear a striking resemblance to Hougaard's account of the candle-lit eighteenth century stage.

Holmqvist takes as her point of departure the traditional metaphors for man-machine interaction (dialogue, tool, mass-medium), discusses the drama-metaphor, and considers the problems each metaphor leads to. She does not reject the drama as a fruitful point of departure for design of interactive media, but discusses the fundamental problem of incorporating the user as a part of the metaphorical sign. She is searching for a new metaphor, and inspired by the philosopher Vilèm Flusser, she introduces the apparatus-metaphor (the camera and its user). The idea is to see the computer as a complex prosthesis for human cognition. The same intention is found in Laursen and Andersen's chapter on a museum system about the Bronze Age. The system is intended to provoke and encourage the user to question his daily life experience of the world and open up for other ways of thinking. Non-realistic drawings are created to display hypotheses about the Bronze Age's perception of the environment.

While Hougaard gives a thorough presentation of one author and the narrative genres of his time, Jørgen Bang describes different narrative models and introduces the idea of spiral composition, a form of composition that is closer to our time and the interactive non-linear computer medium than the neo-classical drama. It is probably one of the most important methods for avoiding the soap opera trap; importing techniques from the neo-classical drama does not force us to import its narrative model too.

The question of linearity and non-linearity is also an important issue in Liestøl's chapter. The chapter is not about interactive fiction, but about academic interactive publishing and hypertext. As many other publications, academic publications presuppose that the context of the subject matter is known to readers, who are often experts in the discipline themselves. What the reader is looking for is new findings or arguments in a well-known context. This fact on the one hand helps avoiding too much redundancy, and on the other hand it puts constraints on the distribution of texts and knowledge. Before the texts are written the researcher has spent much time collecting and documenting knowledge and information, but work is seldom visible in the final publication because of the limitations of paper based technology, although it might contain valuable information for the reader. References and footnotes direct the reader to a context, but as Liestøl writes: "It is not easy for a reader in North America to follow a reference (a virtual link) in the paper he or she reads, if the relevant piece of information is stored in a vault in the basement of a Norwegian museum."

Liestøl argues that hypertext publication and multimedia technology open up much broader access to the research context and thereby for many more perspectives on the subject matter, but he is also aware of the problem with electronic publishing. The rhetorical structure of a text is an important part of its argumentation, and in academic writing, the argumentation is the most important part of the message. In paper-based publication, the author's argumentation is protected by linearity. The characteristic of hypermedia, however, is non-linearity, and the author runs the risk of loosing rhetorical power. Liestøl argues that there must exist a level of intact linearity, representing the author's interpretation of the subject matter: the author's point of view. The interactive freedom of the reader could then be secured via access to a non-linear organization of the author's background material, a freedom to use the same material as a substance to form his own message.

6

Narrative computer systems: The dialectics of emotion and formalism

BERIT HOLMQVIST AND PETER BØGH ANDERSEN

For a long time we were occupied with computers as media in a metaphorical sense, for evaluating such system types as graphical systems, filing systems, or process control systems. In 1989, however, we started to take the media perspective in its literal sense. We wanted to use the computer like a real medium, such as film, television and theater, to create art. Although there are many similarities between other arts and systems design, there is one fundamental difference: Interaction plays an important part in the computer medium, whereas it is absent in other media.

To make our intention clear, we began a project where we used the computer to create interactive fiction. As distinct from more tool-like systems we wanted to define a new class of systems that we called "narrative systems." The characteristic feature of these systems is that their main purpose is communication, so their functionality is almost the same as the interface. Examples are teaching systems, databases, mail systems, and video games. Our purpose was to answer the following questions:

- What kinds of techniques are useful for telling a story where interaction is a fundamental part?
- What kinds of methods are the optimal ones for systems development?
- Could we discover more general narrative techniques that can be used in non-fiction applications, such as data bases and teaching systems.

There is no real tradition for creating fiction with computers other than the one that has developed around computer games. However, it was not a computer game that we wanted to create; it was more like a short story. The attraction of the story was not to be based upon the win/lose paradigm of games, but was to rely on traditional literary techniques for creating excitement and tension.

As far as theory is concerned, we based our work on the European semiotic tradition (Greimas, Bremond, Eco). We used it not only as a general theoretical background, but also as a practical basis for programming. On the technical side, we had access to a Mac II computer with a color screen, plus a black and white scanner, and we used two main tools: Hypercard, a programming environment (which was later replaced by Supercard), and VideoWorks, a system for making and running cartoon films. The basic code was written in the Hypertalk (Supertalk) language from where the cartoon system, running on top of Hypercard, can be controlled. Our intention was to exchange or supplement the cartoons with real videos.

To begin with, we concentrated on the visual aspects of the computer, of which interaction was not the principal aesthetic ingredient. This phase went very smoothly, since we could rely on existing traditions from film and picture aesthetics. However, when we later began to work on the part where interaction was the most important means of expression, we quite simply got stuck. We discovered that this part of the project contained far more practical and theoretical difficulties than we had ever dreamt of. But although what is reported in this chapter might look rather naive and primitive, the experience raised many questions to be answered and ideas to be implemented in our subsequent research.

Generating ideas

When you want to explore the computer in a new field, you need a topic that is fascinating enough and difficult enough to be a real challenge. We agreed that eroticism would be a good choice. We knew from results in other media, where many experiments have been made, that it is very difficult to produce anything interesting in the field. Either it gets too pornographic to create anything but disgust, or too sophisticated to create anything but boredom. We were not convinced that we would be able to create a fascinating, computer-based erotic novel, but we were convinced that the subject poses a real challenge and the right kind of challenge within the specific medium.

To use a computer for this purpose almost sounds absurd — computers are inhuman, controlled by strict formalism, while eroticism is a completely human phenomenon, governed by senses and feelings. It is true that formalization often connotes standardization and inhumanity, but as a matter of fact it can also quite simply mean to *give form*. That is what we did, because that is what is done in all serious arts like poetry, drama, films, and so on. We want to show that *good formalization is a prerequisite for creating good computer-based novels*, just as poetry needs good rhythmic patterns and dance needs good choreography.

The problem with our subject is that it deals more with inner emotions than with outer impressions; it is more about what you feel than about what you see. The only really erotic experience you have is your own. It may be interesting to you, but how do you visualize it and make it exciting to others? We had to find some general abstract ingredients that could be varied when made concrete. Something general and something specific. On the one hand, something that the reader will recognize, and on the other hand, something that is unknown and surprising.

There is one domain, at least, that most people have in common. Dreams. You very seldom remember details from your dreams; what you remember are feelings (of fear, joy, stress, happiness, distortion etc.) These provided us with our general themes. Another typical characteristic is that the scenario and the actors are taken from bits and pieces of daily life and mixed with more fictitious or surrealistic surroundings, like a collage. Yet another ingredient in dreams is that to some degree you can control them yourself. For example, dreams are often interrupted when they are becoming too exciting, dangerous or boring. It is as though unconsciously your cultural self interacts with your unknown self. So computer systems and dreams have one important thing in common: The user/dreamer can interact with the program/dream.

Fig. 6.1. Visual script.

First we needed a script. After having confronted herself with the general aspects of her own sexual dreams and having had them (the aspects) confirmed by others, Berit selected three themes that were to form the basis of the story:

- romance
- aggressiveness
- everyday life

She very soon found out that it was no good starting to tell the story by verbal means only.

In part this had to do with the problem of verbalizing dreams. Dreams are very seldom verbal, they are pictorial. Describing a dream is as difficult as describing one of Picasso's paintings without looking at it. But the choice was also connected with the fact that the computer at that time was an unexplored medium in the field of fiction. We had no "professional language" for describing what we were doing.

Instead of writing a full script Berit made brief notes, which she then explained to Peter.

Woman passive	Woman active
She arrives at the lake	She arrives at the lake
She lies down and falls asleep	She lies down but does not fall asleep
The man arrives at the lake	The man arrives at the lake
He stands still close to the woman	He throws his towel down and undresses
He undresses	
	He walks out into the water
	He swims and walks ashore
	The woman takes his towel
	They stand still and look at each other for a long time
	They move towards each other
He bends down and kisses the woman on the thigh	The woman takes the towel and dries him
The woman draws up her legs but continues to sleep	
She spreads her legs	With mild force she makes him sit down
He "takes" her	She "takes" him
He dresses and leaves on his own	They leave together

Fig. 6.2. Early epic script. The script consists of two possible, independent stories.

It became a close, interactive process, where Berit talked and Peter made drawings at the same time. It turned out that verbal and visual epics together created a constructive process. The fruits of this idea-generating phase were hundreds of sketches and silly ideas (Figure 6.1). Many of them were never used, but it certainly helped us to find out what was viable and what was not.

After many late evening sessions we had our first script. A story with three acts or themes: romance, aggressiveness, and daily life in conjunction with three different settings — at the lake, in the bar, and at home in the suburb.

In short, the story is about a woman who breaks out of her current dreary situation and sets off on a journey in search of a new life. She is seeking a new context. On her travels she passes through different settings, meets different people, and becomes involved in events that she has no control over. She wanders around in a world of deceit and persists in her request for "true" happiness.

At this stage we started to implement small ideas from the first scene. We found out that we had spent a lot of time telling parallel stories, and realized that what we ended up with was a slide show with very few interactive possibilities. See Figure 6. 2. However, it was our intention to make an interactive story, not a slide-show. Our epic script was too boring from an interactive perspective, and giving it a more exciting interaction could not just be a question of allowing the users to choose one or the other fixed sequence of events — they should be able to influence the sequence of events themselves. This means that the ready-made narrative syntagms would have to be much smaller than those described and their possibilities of combination much richer. The events would have to interact with each other so that a choice made early in the sequence of events would have consequences for later events.

We also soon found out that direct manipulation was rather tricky. In some video games, the user identifies with the hero. The user acts in the first person (Hutchins, Holland, Draper, 1986; Laurel, 1986) and manipulates the other people in the game as objects. In an erotic narrative, however, this borders on bad taste; to solve this problem, we invented a helping prop that could take on the role of an interactive sign (see Andersen, 1990). We decided to use the towel in the script, and our epic script was turned into an interactive script that looked like Fig. 6. 3.

The two scripts reveal two points of interest: first, that *scripting and programming should be done in cycles* so that they can influence each other, and not be done in separate phases. The process cannot be broken down into two phases in which the content is determined in the first one, and the form added on in the second one.

Form and content are interdependent, a new form giving rise to a new content. The second point of interest concerns the notion of a "text." A computer-based novel should neither be seen as a single text, nor as a collection of single texts. Rather, its *main message lies between the texts*. A computer-based novel is not a textual object but an inter-textual object. The individual runs of the program should give rise to different meanings.

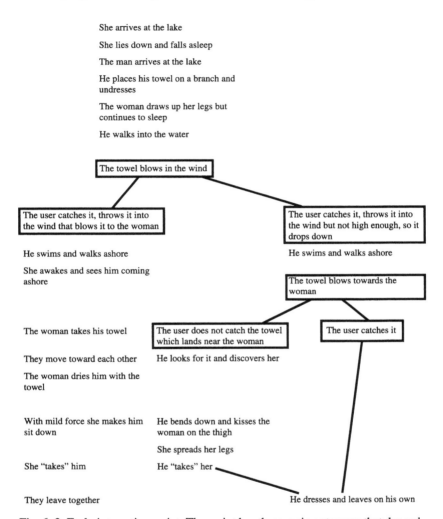

Fig. 6. 3. Early interactive script. The script has three main outcomes that depend upon the reader's actions.

The two scripts exhibit many coherent segments that are related by rhetorical figures. There are parallelism (she arrives at the lake), antithesis (she is awake versus she sleeps) and partial chiasms (she makes him sit down versus he kisses her, she "takes" him versus he "takes" her). The latter figures are related to the general theme of the scene: active versus passive. This theme was later replaced by a more fruitful theme: attraction versus repulsion, which in turn gave rise to the idea of using "vectors" as a basis for programming (see Chapters 1 and 11).

But — as has already been stated — we got stuck, and concentrated our efforts on the visual aspects.

Pictures

The story had to be based on drawings because verbal interaction would create a distance that we wanted to avoid.

First, we discovered that it was no use drawing directly on the screen, which of course was due to the fact that we could only use black and white, not grey-scale or colors. Peter started to make series of paper drawings that were subsequently scanned into the system. The drawings had to be very simple. And they demanded reparation on the screen in any case, because the lines became too thick.

Fig. 6. 4. Lines drawings. Left is the scanned-in raw version. Right is a patched-up version.

Fig. 6. 4 shows the scanned-in raw version together with the corrected version. It is no coincidence that the figure in the original drawing is naked and the final one is dressed. Clothes are too irregular, with too many shadows and delicate lines, to give a good picture when scanned in. The details are merged into one black morass, and you completely lose the feeling of a body. Naked bodies are simpler and more regular, and can later be dressed while keeping the impression of the body intact.

Drawings alone were not enough. By mixing photos with drawings we achieved an interesting contrast of texture: the simple, clean drawings versus the irregular photos. We started to use photos as background for the drawings. The contrast created a desired distance, because pure naturalism does not suit the medium. The medium could not yet achieve the quality of a film or a photograph, and trying to achieve it only emphasized the shortcomings of the medium in this respect, and produced slightly ridiculous results. Since we had already made up our minds about the scenes, we had to search for suitable backgrounds in real life, and when we could not find our motifs, we constructed them by manipulating photos.

Fig. 6. 5. Screen picture produced by manipulating two separate photos.

We needed a tree and a bush, for example, but could not find any with the right distance between them. Therefore, figure 6. 5 is constructed from two separate pictures.

The figure 6. 6 represents the same scene as the script, and shows the effect of having drawn figures in the foreground and using photographs as background. The irregular texture of the background photo stands out clearly when contrasted with the towel on the branch and the woman in the foreground.

Fig. 6. 6. Collage of photos and line drawings.

The effects produced by these simple experiments gave us the idea that the computer should be seen as a collage medium (Figure 6. 6).

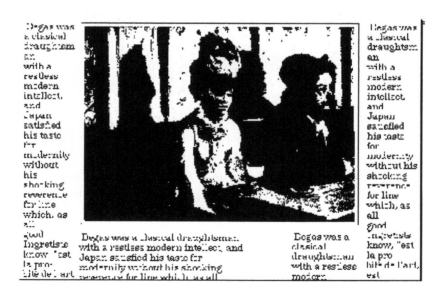

Fig. 6.7. The beginning of the story. The protagonist is imprisoned in the frame of a painting, which itself is enclosed in a computer window.

On the one hand, a scanned-in version of drawings or photos could never compete with the originals, since resolution and control of colors were insufficient. On the other hand, we had the opportunity to put all kinds of pictures into one medium, where they are represented in exactly the same way — namely, as pixels on a screen — and to exploit the contrast between them as an aesthetic effect.

We looked for other graphical possibilities, and began adding paintings from art books and experimenting with variations of the drawing/photo opposition. What would happen if we reversed the situation, so that the background is a drawing while the figures are photos?

The Apple Scanner we used offered some variations of scanning mode. Figure 6. 8 uses "line art," while figure 6. 9 is done with "halftones." The former mode can sometimes produce very nice effects that resemble photo graphics, as Figure 6. 8 shows.

Fig. 6. 8. "Line art" photos. Notice the similarity to photo graphics.

We conclude this section with a real tour-de-force of collage technique. Figure 6. 9, which is a sketch of a background, consists of five layers of pictures. At the bottom is a medieval castle in halftone. In order to create a hazy impression, we placed a transparent light-grey graphic on top of it. In the left-hand corner at the bottom a picture of dancers is then added, but since they are not the main characters they are backgrounded with a grey filter. On the topmost layer the main characters are placed — two halftone photos and one piece of chalk painting in line-art!

Fig. 6. 9. Collage picture. Sketch of decoration composed of medieval pictures, chalk paintings, and photos. The scanning modes are line-art and halftone, and two transparent rasters are used to background pictorial elements.

Scenes

The scene of the computer medium is the screen, and nowadays a computer based scene is often made up of windows. In "normal" programs, windows are used for the following purposes:

- One window displays one object, two windows different objects. A word processor can, for example, display two texts in two different windows.
- Windows can contain different panes, each showing different parts of the same object. If a window shows a text, its panes can display different parts of the text.
- Windows can also be used to show the same object from different perspectives. Then they are said to convey different views. Microsoft Word, which we are using in to write this chapter, can present the same text in an outline view where only headings are shown, in a page view where the page is displayed in natural size, in a print preview, where

one or two pages are shown in small size and the normal view used during writing.

In our story we experimented with both panes and views. The protagonist moves through a landscape, from a wood to a beach (Figure 6. 10). We cannot show this walk naturalistically, so we start with the wood in one window. The protagonist moves out of the window and appears in the next window that displays the beach. It gives the reader the illusion that he is watching a larger landscape through the windows of the screen.

Fig. 6. 10. Two windows show different parts of the same landscape and thereby create the illusion of a space larger than the limited area of the screen. The action in the wood to the right is over, and we should only be reminded of it while the main action occurs on the beach. Therefore the wood is covered with a grey mask.

Multiple windows must be used with care so as not to confuse the reader. We have to show where the main action takes place, so that the reader can focus his attention there. In the theater this is done by means of light, and that is the method we employed in our story. The windows whose action is over are covered by a grey transparent mask, while the action windows are white. Supercard offers good facilities for this. The mask is merely a graphical object whose pattern is grey and whose ink is "or." Figure 6. 10 shows the effect. The action in the wood is over, and the wood-window is therefore darkened by a grey mask.

Figure 6. 10 also shows another use of light — as a means of creating a specific tone or atmosphere. The tone of the beach-window is intended to be dream-like and poetic, and we have tried to achieve this by placing a light grey mask with an "Xor" ink over the background.

Panes can also be used to present simultaneous actions. The next example (Figure 6. 11) presents two parts of the same scene, one in which the male character is drying himself after a swim, and another in which the female character is looking for at place to sleep.

Fig. 6. 11. Two windows showing concurrent actions. The male character comes up from a swim, while the female character lies down to sleep.

In the last part we planned to work with two different views, expressed in different windows that narrated the same course of events, but seen from two different perspectives.

Love poems (and our story is about love) often use metaphors. The loved one is compared with everything from a red rose to nutritious daily bread. But such metaphors only work if we simultaneously think of the real meaning, so that a tension between the two descriptions arises. On the screen, this can be done by having the metaphor (the rose) in one view, while the real person acts in the other, and thereby defining a mapping between events in the two windows. The traditional store of similes has such mappings as "a dew drop on the rose -> a tear in a woman's eye," "the rose withers -> the woman pines away," and so on.

All this is about the content we expressed *in* the windows. However, we also sometimes attributed meaning to the very form of the window. At the beginning, the protagonist is placed as a part of Degas' painting "Absinthe" (see Fig. 6. 7). She wishes to get out of the melancholy picture, to break its confining framework. And she does this, she does indeed move out of the painting, but in order to emphasise her quest for freedom, we also removed the borders around the computer window!

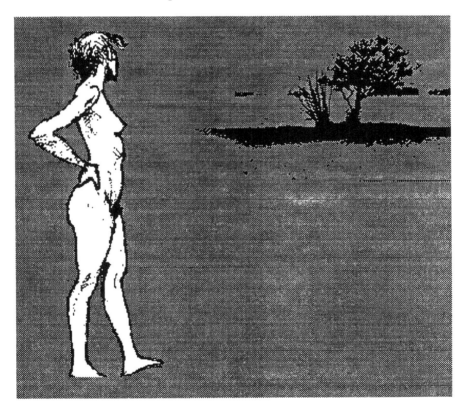

Fig. 6.12. Aesthetic usage of the window frame. The protagonist has literally "broken the frame" of the window. The intended content is freedom, but also lack of community.

This has a strong impact on experienced Macintosh users, who are used to windows with frames and do not expect them to go away (Figure 6.12).

Movement

Our system was primarily a picture story, and we used static as well as animated pictures. Animation is important: The actors must be able to raise their hands in joy, fall on their knees, or bend their heads in sorrow — and adopt all the other postures that are used by actors on the stage. Therefore it must be possible to define different postures of the actor.

If the actor is small and the movement simple, real animation as in a cartoon can be achieved. In our story, we used a butterfly as the narrator that advances the plot, and it was animated just like a conventional cartoon. We used seven pictures that gave a charming impression of a fluttering butterfly.

Fig. 6. 13. Video Works movie run on top of Supercard. Pictures of this size can produce nice animation.

The best result was obtained by running VideoWorks on top of Supercard (Figure 6.13), but this technique has its limitations. When the graphics become larger, the differences between the postures become more pronounced, and the effect is a jerky kind of movement known from video games. Furthermore, the screen begins to blink disagreeably, which is disastrous if you want to create a poetic atmosphere. In addition, this technique is very time-consuming: if more complicated movements than those of a fluttering butterfly are required, a lot of drawings are needed. To make the people in Fig. 6. 11 bend down in a realistic manner would require several days' work.

So we searched for other, easier ways of doing it. Inspired by Will Eisner's excellent book on cartoon drawing (Eisner 1986), we discovered that often only a few distinctive postures are necessary in order to tell a complicated story. If you want to say that someone sits down, it is enough to draw him standing and then sitting — provided, that is, that the drawings are skilfully done.

In Supercard it is easy to make that kind of pseudo-animation (Figure 6. 14). The postures are represented as graphics on a card. At any time, only one graphic is visible, the others are hidden. Animation can be done by hiding and showing different graphics. Spasmodic movements and blinking can be avoided by using two identical cards, of which one is invisible. When the actor assumes a new posture, this posture is first made visible on the invisible card, which is then shown employing the visual effect "dissolve":

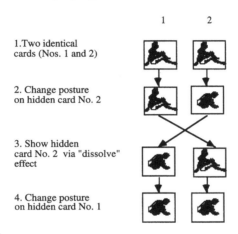

1.Two identical cards (Nos. 1 and 2)

2. Change posture on hidden card No. 2

3. Show hidden card No. 2 via "dissolve" effect

4. Change posture on hidden card No. 1

Fig. 6. 14. "Soft" fading animation of large graphical objects. Two identical cards are used, of which only one is visible. (1) Start. We see only card 1. (2) Hide old posture and show new one on hidden card 2. (3) Show hidden card 2 with dissolve effect. (4) Hide old posture and show new one on hidden card 1.

The result is a poetic, dreamlike "fading" from one posture to another achieving the tone we wanted in our story.

Although the reader may think that this is really dwelling on unnecessary details, that is not the case. If you work seriously with communication and aesthetics, it is important to be able to find the right expression for the content that you want to communicate.

The global narrative structure: The actant role of the reader

An important part in systems development is the writing of a general "logical" system description that describes the general structure of the system without going into details. For "normal" systems development, there are description techniques such as data flows and system models (De Marco, 1978; Jackson, 1983), but they are not suitable for narrative systems, since the system structure of a narrative system is identical to its global narrative structure; a system description for narrative systems should capture the general structure of the narrative. During recent decades, semi-formal models of narratives have been developed within semiotics and literary analysis, and these models seem to be good candidates for system description tools for narrative systems. In the following we show how to use the classical actant model of Propp and Greimas (Greimas, 1966, 1970; Propp, 1958).

In Figure 6. 15 we have six actants: the Subject (the hero) who desires something (the Object, for example, the princess), which someone (the Giver, for example, the king) can give him. He meets animals that test and later help him (Helpers) in his fight against the evil troll (Antagonist) who tries to prevent him from rescuing the princess.

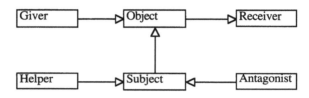

Fig. 6. 15. The actant model.

This model serves as a very abstract description of a fairy-tale. (See also Chapter 5 .)

However, much needs to be specified before we reach the level of the actual text. We have to specify which actors fill the actant roles in the narrative — for example, that the Giver actant is filled with the "king" and the Helper actant with a bird, a snake, and a pig.

Each actant slot can be filled by several actors (bird, snake, and pig are all Helpers), and conversely, one actor can fill more than one actant slot (for example, the youngest son can typically be both Subject (the actor that desires the princess) and Receiver (the actor that marries the princess).

Although there is a certain correspondence between the actants and the actual grammatical roles they fill in the text (the Subject becomes the grammatical subject in certain types of sentences, for example, The youngest son (Subject) slays the troll, the king (Subject) gives his daughter (Object) to the youngest son (Receiver), the actants can fill other grammatical roles than those naturally associated with them. Thus, although the princess fills the Object actant, she can certainly be the grammatical subject of many sentences *(The princess eats the poisoned apple).*

There are various ways of using the actant model as a basis for programming. One method is to implement the actants as object classes, defined by their possible courses of action. The definition of the sphere of action of the Helper in Propp (1975) can be used as an example of what such possibilities will look like:

- Spatial transference of the hero (for example, a flying horse can bring the hero to the castle of the troll).
- Liquidation of misfortune or lack.
- Rescue from pursuit (for example, a bird can divert the attention of the witch pursuing the hero and the princess).
- Solution of difficult tasks.
- Transfiguration of the hero.

The actors — the actual manifestations of the actants — can then be implemented as object instances. There is one important point to be made in this connection. In non-interactive media it makes no sense to place the reader directly in the actant schema, but since our narrative was interactive, we had to assign an actant role to the reader as well.

As already mentioned, the role of Subject must be ruled out since this will create pornography. Therefore, we gave the user the roles of Helper or Antagonist, which in turn means that the interactive actions fall into two main classes: helping somebody to do something or preventing it.

Interactive narrative segments

There is quite a distance between the actant structure and the actual text. One decision that has to be taken concerns the structure of the narrative segments. A narrative segment can be defined as the smallest segment that has a clear beginning and ending and a separate narrative function. C. Bremond (Bremond, 1970) investigated French folk tales and suggested the schema in Figure 6.16 as a possible narrative segment:

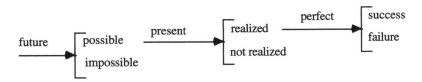

Fig. 6. 16. Basic narrative segment.

First, the event is presented in the future, as possible or impossible (a theft planned, a quest is made possible). If it is possible, then it can either be realized or not realized (the thief starts his evil actions or the hero embarks on the quest), and if realized, it can either succeed or fail (the goods are stolen, the destination of the quest is reached).

In our interpretation, all these sub-segments must be manifested — that is, they are part of actual texts or pictures. The possible misfortune must be signaled by such phrases as Snoopy's "It was a dark and stormy night" or by pictures that create an ominous atmosphere.

Since our aim was to create interactive narrative segments, it was very convenient for us that Bremond had formulated his segments in terms of choices. The reader can then decide whether the future possibility should turn into present reality, and he or she can influence the success or the failure of the action. The difference between ordinary texts and interactive stories is that these choices are latent in texts, but actual possibilities in interactive stories.

This was as far as we got in the first phase of our project. In the next phase we wanted to promote interaction so that it would become the primary ingredient of the story, and we had some general ideas of how it could be done within our framework.

But when we began to translate the ideas into concrete work, it resulted in failure.

One problem mentioned earlier was that "paper contaminates". It is very difficult to write an inherently interactive story on a piece of paper that is inherently non-interactive. We needed a tool that would enable us to work directly with interaction in the authoring process, and we therefore began to construct a story editor. The editor was never used, but the work on it continues.

Another problem was that we were encumbered with an interface whose value as a general story aesthetics was doubtful. The basic concepts in the Macintosh interface is the *hand* (cursor) that can pick up *tools* (palettes, menus) and apply these tools to work *materials* (the main window representing text or drawing paper). But it is very difficult to tell a love story by using a hand, a set of tools, and some working materials! The problem arises because a particular interface type (for example, a direct manipulation interface) is founded on a specific perspective on the roles of user/reader and designer/author and their relation to the interface (See Holmqvist in this volume).

In search of aesthetic norms for narrative systems

In spite of, or rather thanks to, many frustrations, we felt that the project was a marvellous experience; we felt like midwives at the birth of a new art form.

Our story would not in itself be great art but we hoped we could make a product that was so good that people with greater talents than ours would say: "Is this really possible? Well, we can do better!." Our purpose was to help develop an aesthetics of narrative systems, and in fact our efforts were not in vain. They became the point of departure of new exciting experiments, of which the Bronze Age system presented in Chapter 11 is an example.

We will conclude by summarizing the ideas we held about aesthetics at that time because in many respects we think that the ideas are still valid.

What kinds of guidelines can be set up for constructing narrative systems? Before offering some tentative answers, we would like to emphasize that such guidelines will not be psychological laws but aesthetic norms. They are not about the facts of the world, but about how things ought to be done, although they should of course be based on true assumptions about relevant facts. All the norms that we propose rest upon one general norm: *Exploit the specific properties and opportunities of the medium aesthetically.*

Norm: *Formalism* should be the meter and choreography of narrative systems.

Relevant fact: Computer systems must be controlled by formalisms. Computer systems must by necessity be controlled by a program that describes the data processing completely. In this sense the medium is formalistic, but this is not unique to computer systems. On the contrary, formalism is a necessary ingredient of many art forms. Poetry has its meter, dance its choreography, and music its harmonic schemas and rhythm. Art is not an avoidance of formalism, but its utilization as a means of expression.

Norm: The medium should be conceived as a *collage* medium, and naturalism should probably not be attempted.

Relevant fact: It is possible to enter bits and pieces from many different media into a computer, to combine them, and to present them in a uniform way, namely as pixels on the screen. The computer replicas will normally be of poorer quality than the original, but the new opportunities to juxtapose textual and pictorial material from different genres and historical epochs offer exciting aesthetic possibilities that were not present in the originals.

Norm: *Interaction* should be a basic means of expression in narrative systems.

Relevant fact: The computer is the only medium where interaction is possible. Interaction must be a basic ingredient in the composition, and this turned out to be the hardest thing for us to do. During the course of the work we were amazed at how strongly traditional media still influenced our imagination. If we did not take care, we would automatically end up producing an advanced slide-show, where interaction only means that you yourself decide the sequence of the pictures. If this is all that can be achieved, we would prefer a real slide-show. It is larger, has better colors, and is less expensive.

Norm: Narrative systems should be conceived as *inter-textual*, not textual, media.

Relevant fact: If the rhetorical cohesions between the individual runs are not exploited, one might just as well write an ordinary story, save the expensive equipment, and achieve a better result.

Bibliography

ANDERSEN, P. BØGH (1990). *A Theory of Computer Semiotics.* Cambridge: Cambridge University Press.

BREMOND, C. (1970). Morphology of the French folktale. *Semiotica 2*, 247-276.

BREMOND, C. (1973). *Logique du récit.* Paris: Éditions du Seuil.

BREMOND, C. (1966). La logique des possibles narratifs. *Communications 8*, 60-76

DEMARCO, T. (1978). *Structured Analysis and System Specifications.* New York: Yourdon Inc.

EISNER, W. (1986). Comics and Sequential Art.

GREIMAS, A.J (1970). *Du sens. Essais semiotique.* Paris: Editions du Seuil.

GREIMAS, A.J. (1966). *Semantique Structurale.* Paris: Larousse.

HUTCHINS, E.L. HOLLAND, J.D., and NORMAN, D.A (1986). Direct Manipulation Interfaces. In *User centered system design*, eds. D.A. Norman and S.W. Draper. Hillsdale, New Jersey: Lawrence Earlbaum.

JACKSON, M.A. (1983). *System Development.* Englewood Cliffs, New Jersey: Prentice-Hall.

LAUREL, B.K. (1986). Interface as mimesis. In *User centered system design*, eds D.A. Norman and S.W. Draper. Hillsdale, New Jersey: Lawrence Earlbaum.

PROPP, V. (1958). *Morphology of the folktale.* Austin and London: University of Texas Press. Paperback edition 1975.

7

Interactive fiction: Artificial intelligence as a mode of sign production

PETER BØGH ANDERSEN AND BERIT HOLMQVIST

The ideas presented in this chapter[1] grew out of the authors experiences in an earlier attempt to create interactive fiction. In Chapter 6, "Narrative Computer Systems," we describe our struggle with a short story mainly based on pictures. The first part of the story explores the graphical possibilities as means of sign production. However, when we began to work on the next part, where interaction took over as the most important means of expression, we got stuck. There were three interrelated problems:

- The balance between reader and author shifts, since the reader must perform some of the functions previously allotted to the author. Who is responsible for getting a satisfactory experience out of the product? The reader or the author? What is the best balance between the two?
- As a consequence of this, the length of the narrative controlled by the author is shortened, so that the author no longer plans and constructs a 300-page story. Instead, he constructs short narrative pieces that must be combinable in different ways, rather like a construction set. What should these narrative pieces look like?
- How should one compose interactive fiction? We know by tradition how to write a text, but which techniques are suitable for developing a product that is not one, but many texts?

These problems are not special to our project, but are general problems of interactive media, as several researchers in the field have already pointed out. (Yellowlees Douglas, 1990; Moulthrop, 1989; Bolter & Joyce, 1987; Marshall & Irish, 1989). If we define interactive fiction as

a piece of fiction in which the physical movements of the reader are an intended and integrated part of the aesthetic experience by virtue of the fact that they influence the course of events in the fiction,

---

[1] This chapter is an abridged version of a paper from AI & Society 4: 291-313. 1990. With permission from the publisher.

we can immediately see that the problems are inherent in the very notion. The reader is no longer an interpreter of a fixed product, but is in a position to act on it physically and change it.

Maybe the solution is to change our view of the product. Instead of seeing it as a collection of narratives, which the reader can read in different order, we should see the product as a narrative *world*! The reader can act in this world, and it is the author's responsibility to design the world so that using it gives rise to exciting and emotional experiences. Ideas of this kind are suggested by Krueger (1983) who calls it "artificial reality," by Laurel (1986, 1989) and by Smith & Bates (1989), who use the term "synthetic reality."

We do not like the term "reality" since it encourages us to see the product as a simulacrum, as a model that somehow resembles reality. This view of art is very narrow, being associated with the literary schools of realism and naturalism. There are many other aesthetic schools (surrealism, expressionism, modernism, and so on), and in order to make room for these too, we shall use the term *narrative space*.

The term "space" (instead of text or drama) signals that we are not creating a collection of independent texts or plays but rather a space in which the reader can act and experience. The adjective "narrative" reminds us that this space — like other media such as films and books — has but one function: it is a means for the reader to create experiences, emotion and insight, a "machine for generating interpretations" (Eco, 1976).

Now, how do we think of and organize such narrative spaces, when we can no longer place them in a linear sequence of chapters and paragraphs? One way is to envisage it as a space populated by different creatures — which may include human beings. The dispositions and actions of these humans must be described in computational form, and we may look to artificial intelligence for ways of doing it (Laurel, 1989; Smith & Bates, 1989).

Artificial intelligence

Artificial Intelligence (AI) can be defined as:

Machine behavior that gives a human audience the impression that the machine performs cognitive processes similar to human communication, understanding, reasoning, planning, and feeling.

Since its birth, there have been two rather different views on AI, the *ontological* and the *pragmatic* view:

- *The ontological view:* There are non-trivial similarities between the behaviour of machines and human behavior, and studying one of these can teach us something about the other.
- *The pragmatic view:* AI techniques can provide useful and/or exciting interfaces in specific circumstances, but — like all other interface types — they are in principle illusions, created by skilful exploitation of aesthetic techniques.

In our project we adopt the pragmatic view: Computer systems are viewed as a medium analogous with books, films, plays, and pictures, and AI techniques are basically seen as aesthetic techniques for producing particular types of signs that are placed on the scene of the screen in order to convey specific information and emotions to the "reader."

Signs are associations of content (the signified) and expressions (the signifiers). These associations are culturally determined, based on a code that is shared among a group of sign users. Language is one example, pictorial codes another. Computers are also interpreted by means of codes, known as interface standards. The computer-based sign (Figure 7.1) uses sounds (ranging from the beep to human speech), as well as states and systematic changes of screen pixels, as its means of expression:

Expression	Content
The signifier: sound and screen pixels	*The signified: the meaning assigned to sound and pixels*

Fig. 7.1. The computer-based sign.

According to this view, AI provides techniques for specifying roles (not human minds) and staged actions and emotions (not real actions and emotions) that aim at creating *real* experiences and emotions in a *real* human audience.

AI and computer-based signs

Thus, AI is seen as a special type of computer-based sign. The point of doing this is that we are invited to view system components, including AI components, according to their contribution to the total creation of meaning. A system component can only be justified if it itself has a visual expression or exerts perceptible and interpretable influences on the visual expressions of other signs.

This view has methodological consequences. It makes one skeptical about one aspect of the method proposed by Bates (no year) and Smith & Bates (1989) — namely, first to provide the basic machinery of the narrative space and afterward to patch on staging devices. The danger in this method is that it will produce a separation of form and content that runs the risk of creating materials for plots that are either unexciting or cannot be expressed in the computer medium. In our opinion, the method is based on an erroneous conception of staging and content, namely that staging is subordinate to content. If design is based on the sign concept that contains both the signified (the content, the meaning) and the signifier (the staging, the means of expression) as indispensable parts, two sides of the same coin, a different method is preferable, one involving a close dialectic between plotwriting and visualization.

The drama in the pub

The easiest way to illustrate the idea is to give an example. We build the interactive novel by first writing non-interactive episodes in a literary form, then cutting the episode into minimal sign-tokens, and finally defining the sign-types of the tokens by extracting their combinatorial possibilities. The sign-types can then be combined to yield other episodes, and we know that they will yield at least one interesting one — namely, the episode from which they were abstracted. Here is a short piece of our narrative, in which the protagonist, Eve, has entered a pub together with her boyfriend Adam. The names Adam and Eve, Jason and Lea are there for the convenience of the system designers but not known by the "reader."

It was an odd pub I entered. It was very quiet and very dark. There were several guests but they were frozen stiff. It reminded me of the beginning of a modern piece of theatre. You can faintly see the actors on the dark stage but you don't know which roles they are playing. I sat down at a table and waited for the waiter.

While waiting I looked round the room. My eyes slowly got used to the darkness and I started to discern individual people and groups. I could see that there was a bar but there was no bartender. My eyes fell on a pint of beer standing on the counter. Was it for me? Where was the bartender? What if I just walked up there and took the beer? I looked round again. A man and a woman were sitting not far from me both dressed in white and absorbed in each other.

After observing the man for a while, I noticed him moving nervously on the chair. Was it the bartender who had left his post at the bar for a moment? I was thirsty and hoped to be able to hypnotize him back to where he belonged. As if he could feel my eyes burning on his neck, he suddenly extricated himself from the woman and slowly walked towards the bar. I followed him, convinced that I would finally get my beer.

I turned my head and caught sight of the woman who was now left alone at the table. She followed the man with her eyes. They were wide open, but I could not make out if they were expressing yearning or frustration. For a moment my heart was touched. I tried to catch her eyes but she did not see me. She was concentrating on the man, as I had been a few seconds earlier.

Everything grew mysterious. I went up to the bar to order my beer. My beer! The man was not a bartender. He just stood there, leaning against the bar with a pint of beer in his hand. Probably the same one that had been left on the counter because it was not there anymore. Why did he stand there? Had he lost interest in the woman?

Husky laughter from the end of the bar drew my attention. A sinful beauty dressed in black and a huge almost two metre tall man with a black beard stood with their arms around each other, and leaned scornfully towards the counter. The woman half turned against the man in white, the man half turned towards the dark interior of the pub. So that was why the man in white was riveted to the bar! Captured in the field of beauty.

In my mind's eye, I see the image of a spider silently waiting for the innocent fly to be captured in the web. The woman has an unlit cigarette dangling between her lips. The white man looks at the woman and shows her a lighter. The woman gets free from the giant and turns towards the man in white with a provocative smile. For a second I glance at the woman at the table. Her eyes tell a story of despair. I am furious. I want to stop the performance, but the man in white is spellbound, and when the witch raises her hand and strokes his hair, he turns his back on the room and his bride. They embrace each other and I am helpless. A bartender suddenly shows up and places another pint on the bar. I grab it quickly. I want to offer it to the woman in white.

In order to comfort her and divert her attention from the provocative scene, I put the glass on the table in front of her and receive a little smile in return, but I can't catch her eyes. She seems to be in a trance waiting to be awakened. I am standing there and in my mind I stroke her transparent innocence when the shadow of a black cloud falls over the *décolletage* of her white dress. I see the giant rising behind her. He must have come from the inner darkness of the room with evil intentions. The woman is sitting there, quietly, unsuspecting. If she would look at me, I could warn her. She does not. I want to stop the giant and throw myself in between them and force him back. With all my strength I hit him in the stomach, and for a moment he staggers a few steps backwards, but he regains his balance and returns to the woman.

I try again, but this time the villain takes my arm and drags me away from the table. I cannot prevent what is going to happen. He leans over the woman and puts his big hairy hands on her round breasts. She opens her mouth as if to cry out, but her voice is silent. Horrified, she tries to set herself out of his grasp, which is growing tighter and tighter. I cannot bear to look at it. But I cannot get close. I get the idea of drawing the white man's attention to what is happening. When I look towards the bar I can see that it is is to late. The white man is out of control. He is lying on his knees in front of the black woman with his arms around her hips and his head against her bosom. He cannot see her mischievous smile, or feel that the hand on his neck is cold and calculating, not warm and tender. It strikes me that her dalliance with the man has all been part of a plot to make the innocent woman a victim of the evil plans of the giant.

In order to translate these verbal signs into computer-based signs, we simplify them and segment them into seven parts:

When we enter the pub, we can see several people. Eve and Adam, both dressed in white, are sitting at a table, whereas the demonic Lea and Jason are standing by the bar (wearing black, of course). Adam is fidgeting, then he stands up, walks up to the bar, and buys a beer (1). Lea turns toward Adam with an unlit cigarette in her mouth. He lights her cigarette, and she smiles provocatively at him (2). From her table, Eve looks at them with a lost and despairing expression (3). Lea strokes Adam lightly over the chest, and he turns his back on the room (4). In the meantime, Jason has moved down to Eve (5) and, in spite of her resistance, drags her out onto the floor to dance (6). Lea smiles mischievously; her dalliance with Adam has all been a plot to make Eve a victim of Jason's evil plans (7).

Narratives like this are bound together by cohesions on many levels, which can be made visible if we alter the text and note what happens. Sometimes an alteration only produces a different story, and sometimes it transforms it into nonsense. Take, for example, episode (1):

Adam fidgets nervously, then he rises, walks to the bar, and buys a beer.

Many changes of sequence or specific events produce deviant and strange episodes, as for example:

* Adam fidgets nervously, then sits down, walks to the bar, and buys a beer (wrong sequence).
* Adam fidgets nervously, then rises, and walks to the bar, and buys a car (wrong object).

Cohesions like these should be controllable by the author, which again means that they should be represented in the system. This is not because we want to spend all our programming time simulating behavior in a bar; it is because good fiction lives by breaking cohesions like these in *a calculated purposeful* fashion. But in order to do that, the cohesions must be under the author's control. Otherwise, the author has no option but to create narratives that break rules all the time and beyond his control.

Cohesions are found on at least three different levels:

The physical level. Level 1 signs.

The cohesions on the physical level include the contiguities of space, time, and causality. If Adam is to buy a beer at the bar, he must be there, and this he achieves by walking to the bar; but in order to walk, he must get up from his chair. Similarly, in order for him to light Lea's cigarette, she must have an unlit cigarette in her mouth, and he must be close to her. Deviation from these constraints is a deviation from the normal world of the reader, and should therefore be used for an aesthetic purpose only, not forced upon the reader without reason.

AI-techniques for describing purposeful actions can be applied here. Table 7.1 shows four actions specified as *preconditions* that must be satisfied before the action can take place, a *method* for performing the action (which in our case is simply a description of how to move the graphics on the screen and change their shape), and a list of *results* that obtain when the action has been successfully accomplished.[2]

Schemata like these can be used in various ways. A common way of using them is to assign a goal to an actor — for example, to have a beer. The actor selects the action that contain the goal in its result list, and checks its preconditions. If a precondition is not fulfilled, the actor selects a new action (a means) that fulfills the precondition (for example, walking to the bar will fulfill the precondition of being at the bar for the beer-buying action). This may continue until the actor hits upon an action whose preconditions are all fulfilled. Then the constructed plan is executed.

The schemata must be interpreted by the actors, so that one of the results is defined as the goal — the state the actor wants to achieve. For example, *walking to C* is distinguished from *leaving B* in that the first action has *being at C* as its goal, while the latter sees *not being at B* as its goal. Similarly, *buying* and *selling* differ only in that *selling* assumes the goal of the seller (to get a sum of money), while *buying* presents the goal as the acquisition of the commodity.

Table 7.1 illustrates some of the actions behind our short episode.

Table 7.1. *Level 1 signs*

A raises

Preconditions	Method	Results
A is sitting	A changes position to upright	A is standing

A walks to C

Preconditions	Method	Results
A at B	A is moving in the direction of	A not at B
A not at C	C	*A at C*
A is standing		A is standing

---

[2] See Black & Bower (1980) and Meehan (1977) for a treatment of narratives as problem solving.

A buys B from C

Preconditions	Method	Results
A at C	C hands B to A, and A hands	A at C
C has B	money to C	C has money
A has money		*A has B*

A lights a cigaret for B

Preconditions	Method	Results
A has a lighter	A applies lighter to cigaret	A has a lighter
B has a cigaret		B has a cigaret
The cigaret is unlit		*The cigaret is lit*
A is at B		A is at B

These actions translate easily into Prolog statements. For example, the definition of "A walks to C" could be written as

```
walk(A, B, C) :- not(at(A, C)), at(A, B), standing(A),
                 assert(at(A, C)), retract(at(A, B)).
```

The cognitive and social level. Level 2 signs.

But control of the physical cohesions is not enough, since humanly interpreted behaviour is an indispensable ingredient in stories. In our story, the reader and Adam and Eve make a certain interpretation of the actions of Jason and Lea — namely, that Lea is interested in Adam, but this interpretation turns out to be false; their real purpose is to divert Adam and make Eve susceptible to Jason's advances.

We therefore need level 2 signs that interpret level 1 signs and add a new content to them. Thus, whereas the physical signs use screen displays as their expression and denote fictious physical actions, level 2 signs use level 1 signs as their expression, and denote psychological and social relations. Signs with this structure are often called *connotation* signs.

The main theme of the story is the protagonist's search for a context that she feels at home in, so *dissolving* and *establishing* social bonds are important processes. Important states are being *alone* versus being *together*. In the example, a bond is dissolved when Adam abandons Eve, and new bonds are created when Adam contacts Lea.

As shown in Table 7.2, one can abandon someone by walking to a different place, and a man can make contact with a woman by lighting her cigarette.

Table 7.2. *Level 2 signs*

A abandons B

Preconditions	Method	Results
A and B are together	A walks to C	A is alone
C is different from B		B is alone

A contacts B

Preconditions	Method	Results
A is alone	A lights a cigaret for B	A and B are together
B is alone	or	
A is male	A speaks to B	
B is female	or	
	.....	

The schemata show how level 1 signs like *A walks to C* and *A lights a cigarette for B* are part of the method, and thereby of the expression, of the second level 2 signs.

However, not all walks will count as an abandonment, and not just any cigarette lighting as an attempt at contact. The two level 1 signs must be designed in a special way. In the first case, we might show Eve's despairing expression, in the second Lea's provocative smile, in order to provide the extra connotations.

The narrative level. Level 3 signs.

Until now, an episode must obey the constraints of both the physical and the social world. In other words, its signs must be both well-formed level 1 and level 2 signs. But there is more to narration than that. Our story is built around two poles, *harmony* and *disharmony*. The protagonist searches for harmony, of course, but it is not easy to find, and as part of her quest she has to expose herself to experiences, involving the opposite pole: disharmony.

Harmony is characterized by security and normality but runs the risk of being boring; disharmony, on the other hand, is a world of unpredictable events, which may turn out to be dangerous.

The oscillation between harmony and disharmony is the basic theme of the story, but how do we get these abstract concepts to interact with the more concrete happenings on the screen? What kind of system structure can support us?

The answer may be that the basic system structure should be identical to a literary analysis.

In the Narrative Systems project (Chapter 6) we were experimenting with using the actant model; here we are using the so-called semiotic quadrant

(Greimas 1966, 1970) as our basic narrative structure. In the example, the harmony pole is associated with groups of two people of different sex, but of the same color (thus Adam and Eve, dressed in white, are a harmonic group, and so are the black-clad Lea and Jason), while disharmony, its antonym, involves people of different colors (Eve and Jason form a disharmonic couple). In addition, in harmony the normal constraints operate, while disharmony is a carnival where everything can be turned upside down.

According to semiotic narratology, a story can never transfer a protagonist directly from one antonym to the other. There must be "stepping stones"— namely, the negatives of the two poles. We are fairly certain that the negative of harmony should be a vulnerable state where the person is alone, while the negative of disharmony should probably be a state of invulnerability or liberation.

The quadrant defines the global narrative routes of the story. Figure 7.2 shows the popular butterfly route.

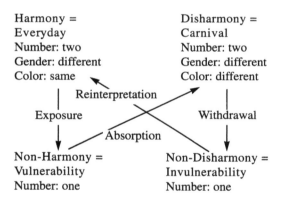

Fig. 7.2. The semiotic square.

The labels of the arrows denote global narrative operations, and in our case, they are level 3 signs that are expressed by level 2 signs.

For example, moving Eve from harmony to vulnerability is called Exposure, which is expressed by the social level 2 episode of Abandoning. Moving her on to the disharmony pole is called Absorption and will be done by a contact-creating act by Jason — namely, his forcing himself upon her against her will. In the continuation of the example, we could have chosen to let the narrator succeed in forcing Jason down to the floor. That would have meant that Eve would again have been alone, this time not abandoned but liberated. This would be Withdrawal to the non-disharmony pole. And Adam could return to the table, take Eve by the hand, and leave the pub together with her, thus bringing us back to the harmony pole.

If we take another look at the episode (Figure 7.3), we can see a complicated three-level sign structure governing the ongoings. The actions must satisfy constraints on all three levels: the physical level, the social level, and the narrative level.

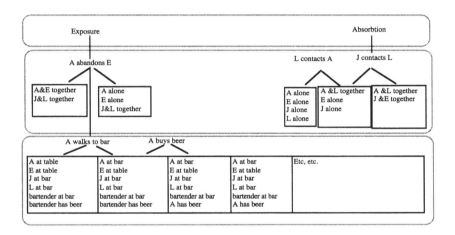

Fig. 7.3. The three-level sign structure of the story.

The story works as follows: If the story is in a state of harmony, then the narrative constraints for displaying an Exposure are satisfied. One possibility is to manifest this as a process where Adam abandons Eve, but this is only possible if they are together at that moment. If not, Exposure could be manifested as, for example, Eve getting rid of the protection she previously had, or by setting out on a dangerous journey.

If the Exposure is realized as an abandonment, again this can be manifested in various ways: One possibility is the one that actually takes place — that Adam walks up to the bar, which again requires the physical condition that Adam and Eve are at the table. Had they not been physically together, the same effect could have been achieved by means of a letter or a phone call.

These constraints define the possible combinations of the narrative signs. Since the narrative is interactive, we cannot know beforehand which state will obtain, so the system must be able to process the constraints in order to determine what will happen next — that is, what type of sign to display next.

AI can provide the substance for artistic form

Let us now try to generalize a little from this example. Art consists in giving form to a substance. The sculptor gives form to his stone, the painter to his colors, the dancer to body movements, and the poet to linguistic material[3]:

> We may define as invention a mode of production whereby the producer of the sign-function chooses a new material continuum not yet segmented for that purpose and proposes a new way of organizing (or giving form to) it in order to map within it the formal pertinent elements of a content-type.   *(Eco 1977: 245)*

What is the substance of a narrative space? We have chosen to let the recognizable features of the readers' everyday life, signified by signs of level 1 and 2, be its substance. These features must be built into narrative space, not because we want to make a model of reality, but because we need some recognizable material, out of which we can give form to an aesthetic experience, much as the sculptor needs a stone and a painter paint and canvas.

This description is based on semiotic, mostly literary, theory, but similar ideas have been proposed from a dramatic point of view by Laurel (1989) who bases her arguments on Aristotle. The substance, consisting of everyday experiences that are molded by dramatic form, corresponds to her *material* cause:

> Material cause: The material cause of a thing is the force exerted on it by what it's made of. So, to pursue the architecture example, the material cause of a building includes stones or concrete or wood, glass, nails, mortar, and whatever else it's made of...the material cause [of drama] is the stuff it's made up of — namely, the sayings and goings of the characters and the affordances of the dramatic situations.
> *(Laurel 1989: 8-9)*

And the form, imposed by the connotative signs, corresponds to her *formal* cause:

> Formal cause: The formal cause of a thing is the force exerted on it by what it's trying to be. ... So in drama, the formal cause of a play is the playwright's notion of what it will be when it's done (which probably includes a notion of genre and style as well as story or plot).   *(Laurel 1989: 8-9)*

We believe that AI techniques could be of use when creating this material for narrative spaces. The restaurant script programmed by Schank & Abelson (1977) seems to be able to account for at least signs of level 1 and 2: It describes the everyday rules one applies subconsciously when dining in a restaurant.

---

[3] Although the idea of giving form to a substance may at first sight seem a strange way of describing programming, some authors, for example, Nygård & Sørgård (1986: 380), have in fact described programming as the imposition of a form (which they call structure) upon a substance (which they call a process).

But there is one further point to make, relating to the form/substance distinction. The substance of narrative spaces differs from the stone manipulated by the sculptor in that it consists of signs. For example, the action of fetching a beer (Figure 7.4) will be constructed out of a sequence of graphics, shown one by one at different locations on the screen.

Expression	Content
Graphics shown at different locations	*Fetching a beer*

Fig. 7.4. Level 1 sign.

The aesthetic sign uses this sign as expression substance for a new sign. The context in which the beer-fetching occurs, the speed with which it occurs, and the way the graphics are drawn can be used to associate a new, specific significance to the action of beer-fetching: In the example, it counts as an act of desertion and betrayal on the part of the man, exposing the female heroine to the dangers of the two daemonic characters (Figure 7.5).

Expression		Content
Expression	Content	*Betrayal, exposure, desertion*
Graphics shown at different locations	*Fetching a beer*	

Fig. 7.5. Level 2 sign.

However, the process through which the connotative sign uses the object sign to signify a new content does not consist in just taking over the object sign as it is. As has already been stated, it involves using the object sign as substance for a new form, and when a substance is used as form, it means that new distinctions are introduced into it.

Viewed merely as an object sign, the beer-fetching episode classifies some properties of the graphic sequence as distinctive form features that must be present in order for the program execution to count as signifying beer-fetching; for example, the initial and final locations of the graphic must be different, since otherwise we would not use the term *fetch*. Also, a beer-graphic — and not a picture showing a car — must be associated with the actor-graphic in the final state, since else it would not be *beer*-fetching. However, the facial expression of the actor, his speed, and much of the context do not constitute distinctive features of form; they are only variants. Faster and slower movements would still signify beer-fetching.

On the other hand, when we use this sign as material for a connotation sign, we introduce new distinctive form-elements into it that were absent in the level 1 sign. Now the context may be significant, or the speed, or the facial expression of the actor.

Apart from molding the lower-level signs in a new way, other things may happen as well: the aesthetic form, may for example,

- Add a new, significant, syntagmatic structure (the three trials of fairy-tales, antithesis, parallelisms).
- Add a new paradigmatic structure (in fairy-tales like Cindarella, the notion of "old" is associated with "bad," since the elder sisters are "bad," while "young" is connected with "good," since the youngest child is always "good" to animals in distress. These couplings do not exist in the language that provides the substance for the fairy-tales — they are added by their aesthetic structure).
- Loosen constraints: Although language separates humans from non-humans so that some verbs can only be used about one of the species, (birds are normally not being able to "talk"), narrative structure can loosen these constraints. In fairy-tales, inanimate things can talk and horses can fly.
- Invert real constraints: Although the peasant in feudal society must remain in his situation in life, he can become a king in the fairy-tales.

Implementation issues

How can these ideas be implemented on a computer? How can the actors, including the user/reader, their movements, goals, and emotions on the one hand, and the aesthetic ideas of the author on the other hand, be made to play together?

Laurel (1989) contains a sketch of a possible program architecture, parts of which we think useful. Our system would contain actors that are programmed to have "normal" reactions, intentions, and feelings. They constantly calculate the next steps they would take in a normal world, but are not allowed to do it immediately. They send their goals and desires to the controlling dramatic episodes, asking: "I want to do this or this or this. Can I?" The episode receives these suggestions; if one can be exploited aesthetically, the actor is allowed to do it. If neither can be used, the episode replies: "No, you cannot have your way. Since this is fiction and you are only an actor, I want you to do this instead."

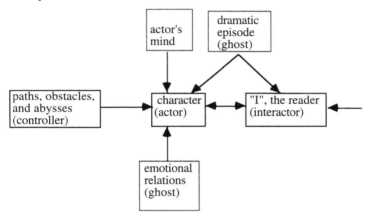

Fig. 7.6. General message-passing in the system.

One suggestion for a system contains the kinds of objects shown in Figure 7.6. In the terminology of Chapter 1 of this volume, there are three visible sign types: *controllers* denoting the parts of the landscape that influence the characters of the play, the characters themselves, implemented as *actors*, and the reader representative, who is, of course, an *interactor*.

In addition to these visible signs, there are three types of *ghost* signs that only reveal their existence by their influence on the visible signs. *The actor's mind* is to be programmed to generate behavior we can interpret as everyday, sensible, goal-directed behaviour, and *the dramatic episode* adds aesthetic requirements to this behaviour, in the manner described. However, in a good narrative the actors do not only have conscious goals and plans, but also subconscious urges, impulses and passions. This is what the *emotional relations* object is used for.

Emotional relations can be expressed by vectors (see Chapters 1 and 11) between people and between people and objects. On the screen display, the vectors are of course invisible, and can only be seen through their effects on man people

Vectors are useful for expressing concepts like ambiguous feelings (positive and negative vector towards the same person) and conscious goals that are hidden from the reader/ user. In our example, the narrator interpreted the situation with Jason and Eve as a dangerous one, wanting to protect Eve. Let us say that Jason is implemented as an interactor and that the user drags him away from Eve. But the reader has misinterpreted the situation, since Eve does not want to be rescued, so she follows and approaches Jason. This can be achieved by a positive vector from Eve to Jason.

The dramatic episode is the third object; it gives dramatic form to the physical and psychological material.

To sum up we can see the actor as being caught in a net of possibly conflicting demands:

- from his conscious plans (be rational; do this in order to achieve that)
- from his emotional relations (avoid or approach someone)
- from the narrative event (be entertaining)
- from the reader (move there or notice this).

It is, of course, no coincidence that the last demand comes at the end. As the reader has probably noticed, there are still parts of the literary version that have not yet been accounted for — namely, the remarks on the author's interpretation of what he experiences in the pub and on what kind of action he takes — for example, *Her eyes tell the story of despair. I am furious. I want to stop the performance. [...] I put the glass on the table in front of her.* In a written text the author can be present, and we use this presence to indicate possible interpretations and possible actions from the part of the reader of our interactive narrative. But since the problem of physical interaction as a meaningful part of the story is not a trivial one, we have to leave it as a dangeling issue for the moment. Some aspects of it, however, will be discussed in Chapter 10 and 11.

Bibliography

ANDERSEN, P. BØGH (1990). *A Theory of Computer Semiotics. Semiotic Approaches to Construction and Assessment of Computer Systems.* Cambridge: Cambridge University Press.

BATES, J. (no year). *Oz Project. Overview and Schedule 1989-1992.* School of Computer Science, Carnegie Mellon University: Pittsburgh.

BLACK, J.B., G.H. BOWER (1980). Story understanding as problem solving. *Poetics* **9**: 223-250.

BOLTER, J. D., M. JOYCE (1987). Hypertext and creative writing. *Hypertext '87 Proceedings.* 41-51. The ACM: New York.

ECO, U. (1976). *A Theory of Semiotics.* Indiana: Indiana University Press

BUXTON, W. (1986). Chunking and phrasing and the design of human-computer dialogues. *Proceedings of the IFIP World Computer Congress.* 59-64. Dublin, Ireland, Sept 1-5, 1986.

FILLMORE, CH. J. (1968). The case for case. In *Universals in Linguistic Theory.* 1-90. eds. E.Bach, R.T.Harms, London, New York, Sydney, Toronto: Holt, Rinehart and Winston.

FILLMORE, CH. J. (1977). The case for case reopened. In *Syntax and Semantics 8. Grammatical Relations.* eds. P. Cole, G. M. Sadock. 59-81. New York: Academic Press.

GREIMAS, A.J. (1966). *Sémantique Structurale.* Paris: Larousse.

GREIMAS, A.J. (1970). *Du Sens. Essais Sémiotique.* Éditions du Seuil: Paris.

JOYCE, M. (1987). *Afternoon.* Jackson, Michigan.

KRUEGER, M.W. (1983). *Artificial Reality.* Reading, Mass: Addison-Wesley.

LAUREL, B.K. (1989). *Interactive fantasy: a dramatic model.* Interactive arts lecture series. Carnegie-Mellon University: Pittsburg.

LAUREL, B.K. (1986). Interface as mimesis. In *User Centered System Design,* eds. D.A. Norman, S.W. Draper 67-86. Hillsdale, New Jersey: Lawrence Earlbaum.

MARSHALL, C.C, P.M. IRISH (1989). Guided tours and on-line presentations: how authors make existing hypertext intelligible for readers. In *Hypertext '89 Proceedings.* The ACM: New York. 15 - 26.

MEEHAN, J.R. (1977). TALE-SPIN, an interactive program that writes stories . In: *5th International Joint Conference on Artificial Intelligence.* 91-98. Cambridge, Mass: MIT.

MOULTHROP, S. (1989). Hypertext and "the Hyperreal." In *Hypertext '89 Proceedings.*259-367. The ACM: New York.

NYGÅRD, K., P. SØRGÅRD (1987). The persepctive concept in informatics. In: (eds.) *Computers and Democracy,* eds. G. Bjerknes et al. 357-379. Avebury: Aldershot.

PROPP, V. (1975). *Morphology of the folktale.* Austin and London.: Univ. of Texas Press:

SCHANK, R., R. ABELSON (1977). *Scripts, Plans, Goals and Understanding.* Hillsdale, New Jersey: Erlbaum..

SMITH, S., J. BATES (1989). *Towards a theory of narrative for interactive fiction.* CMU-CS-89-121. School of Computer Science, Carnegie Mellon University: Pittsburg.

YELLOWLEES DOUGLAS, J. (1990). Is there a reader in this labyrinth? *Paper presented at the conference Computers and Writing III, Edinburgh.*

8

Plays, theaters and the art of acting in the eighteenth century: A formal analysis[1]

JENS HOUGAARD

I

Profound changes have cut us off from the pre-bourgeois cultures. Indeed, the main criteria that are used to define European culture separate us from the culture of earlier periods. Changes set in at the beginning of the bourgeois period that were so radical and have since become so well-established that we often lose sight of the fact that they were the results of a historical development. I am thinking here of the dynamisation of culture that took place in the middle of the eighteenth century as a result of the beginning industrialisation in Europe. Literature, art and philosophy offer countless illustrations of the European time shock.

There were three main effects of this process of dynamization. First, the concept of personality was dynamized. Where previously individuals had been regarded in terms of their absolute relationship to God, they were now also seen in terms of their relationship to themselves. Where previously they had been regarded as members of a community, they were now regarded as separate elements subject to the laws of development. Secondl, society itself came to be regarded as dynamic; where previously it had been analyzed in terms of such concepts as change and modification, it was now understood on the basis of such concepts as transformation and development. And finally, nature came to be regarded as dynamic.

Such changes clearly complicate the way a culture views itself considerably. There is a tendency for cultural and literary critics to regard modern cultural and literary expressions as outpourings of regret that this dynamization took place. They draw attention to the fact that modern culture (culture

---

[1] This essay has been included, partly because its topic is interesting in itself, partly because its description of neo-classical drama bears a striking resemblance to the rhetoric of interactive hypermedia discussed in this part. I have placed a few footnotes referring to the other chapters. (Berit Holmqvist)

since the dynamization processes of the eighteenth century) increasingly employs theories that view the relationship between language and the world as one between separate systems. The redefinition of the relationship between language and reality gained particular momentum after the theoretical, avant-garde insights of the eighteenth century became common currency in the metropolises around the middle of the nineteenth century and found their artistic expression in modernism. The sign systems are described as non-referential, non-mimetic, or something similar. In order to communicate, each sign system must be self-explanatory. Not only literary but all types of communication have to contain their own meta-reflection. The communication must either expound its own codes or operate within closed circuits. These are the conditions of modernity.

The actual dynamization of history at all levels, insofar as a sign system has a referential relationship to the areas undergoing dynamization, prevents it from becoming stable, and its meaning will change at such a pace that it will be difficult for the sign system to take on a permanent, iconographic, stylized meaning. If we talk of gesture and facial expression as visual sign systems, linking them up with a dynamic psychology will prevent them from assuming a definite, general form with a stable meaning, as we know it from the written languages.

With the internationalization of the market for fiction, which the electronic media, in particular, have brought about, the relationship between fiction and the world of experience disintegrates. That is why the means of expression in fiction gravitate towards a stylization that enables the work of fiction to appeal to all markets, irrespective of the cultural context into which the work is being introduced. There is a tendency in the production of fiction for it to develop into an industry with cheap products that, like other industrial products, do not have any individuality. The work of fiction does not approach its subject via the systems of signs or interpretation of one specific culture, but generalizes a culture that is global in nature. The language is standardized into a basic English, which has been purified of the more particular experiences of "dialectal" language or culture.

The bourgeois work of art ceases to exist: The work of art as a finished work is superseded by a serial narrative art that is closer to medieval tales of chivalry or to folk tales than to the bourgeois novel; the relationship between fiction and the dynamic psychology of the personality, as it developed in Europe from the end of the eighteenth century, gives way to a view of characters as types; bourgeois art's concern with the general as interpreted through the concrete is succeeded by abstractions of the great issues such as birth, death, fidelity and so on. There is a discernible movement away from bourgeois art's interest in problems towards a fiction that does not analyze problems but touches on them (or as I have heard it defined polemically: a fiction that scratches the sores instead of healing them); the referentiality of the language, which tends to be undermined by modernity, develops into a stylized referentiality, where one is referred to general human aspects, the great themes, the eternal questions, but it does so within a contraction of meaning around these themes that simultaneously depletes them of concrete historical interpretation; in other words, that "scratches at" the themes instead of offering a "healing" interpretation.

If one views the electronic media against the background of the enlightenment tradition as it developed from the middle of the eighteenth century onward, the above representation of general traits in the development of the production of fiction can be regarded as a story of a decline, in which the enlightenment tradition's hope of freedom is crushed. This type of criticism has been very common since it was first expounded systematically in Jürgen Habermas' s book about structural changes in the bourgeois public. A key concept in this book is expanded so as to attack the movement toward centralisation and the disintegration of the arguing public. Habermas uses the term refeudalisation to describe the tendency toward the destruction of the bourgeoisie's social forms of discussion.

The following is, admittedly, only indirectly concerned with the wider discussion of how public functions develop, both generally and in the fiction of the media, in particular, but it gives an account of a visual "feudal" fiction that developed as a theatrical tradition from the seventeenth century and died out as a system at the beginning of the present century, and of its roots in a feudal view of literature and art.

II

Let us now turn to an author whose work is rather well known, the Danish Molière, Ludvig Holberg, and go on to analyze in more depth a different type of text to the bourgeois kind. There are several introductions to Holberg in English, including my own *The Happy Madness. Ludvig Holberg: The playwright and his time until 1730*, Viking Press, Odense University Press, 1991.

Holberg is an important writer because of the high standard he usually achieves — indeed, a handful of his comedies have never been surpassed. Speaking personally, as a child of the highly productive phase of industrialism, I have always been struck by three things:

1.   He wrote in all the main literary genres.

2.   He was enormously prolific; he wrote fifteen plays, some of them of the highest literary standard, in under a year, thus averaging three weeks per play.

3.   Even though he wrote the plays at a faster rate than the theater in Lille Grønnegade in Copenhagen had time to stage them, it still managed to put on a considerable number of them. How was this possible?

To take the question of genre first. Transgression of the genre boundaries that were the legacy of antiquity was part of the programme of Romanticism. By mixing the genres, the romantics drew attention to the shortcomings of literature on the one hand, while on the other hand highlighting a metaphysical ideal that was both desirable and unattainable. We have inherited this breakdown of the genres from the Romantics. Today, we tend to regard genre as form that can be manipulated.

In the age of Holberg, at the beginning of the eighteenth century, the genres were viewed very differently. They represented modes of cognition that corresponded to different areas of experience and different levels of expression. It was therefore not for purely formal reasons only that Holberg chose to write in different genres; it should rather be seen as an expression of his desire to write at all levels and about all kinds of experience. Far from being just a question of formal experiments, it was also, perhaps primarily, a question of a cognitive ambition. His move from genre to genre can even be regarded as an expression of progress in wisdom and age. There is a line running through his collected works that also appears in the works of the authors of antiquity and in the cultures of antiquity generally.

His first fictitious work was a comic epic poem, and like all epic poems it is concerned with the mythology of the formation of culture; in this particular instance, with the relationship between modern culture, as it existed in early eighteenth century Denmark, and that of antiquity. *Peder Paars* (1719) is the Homer and Virgil of the Holberg canon. It is the key work as far as his view of culture is concerned and the cornerstone of all his works.

At about the same time he published his *Satires* (1719-22), which form his lyrical breakthrough. This is not lyrical poetry in the modern sense of the term, but the lyrical nature poems of the Romantics have come between us and Holberg. It is nevertheless lyrical poetry, insofar as it presents the personal in relation to the social from a subjective viewpoint.

However, it is his plays, or rather a handful of the more than thirty comedies, that assure Holberg his place in world literature. In these plays the lot of the individual within the culture is seen in terms of its relationship to the norm. The plays include a parody of tragedy, which could be regarded as Holberg's contribution to the genre of tragedy, and which is concerned with transgression of the law. Finally, there is *Metamorphoses*, which could be seen as his contribution to a philosophical-lyrical tradition.

This advance through the genres is Holberg's road to wisdom, but at the same time, while transforming himself with the genres he is also reproducing pheno-culturally something that is ethno-cultural, since cultures go through the same stages as individuals (childhood, youth, maturity, old age). One could claim that Holberg reproduces the evolutionary cycle in an individual way, but he does not add anything new to it; he simply repeats in yet another, individual form what many others have done before him. One cannot say that Holberg develops through the genres, but he does make full use of the genres. In following their matrix, he himself is given form. Everything that is a part of himself at the beginning continues to be a part of him; it is just that he becomes more complete. He attains his form, but he does not develop. He does not change as such, but he acquires wisdom and profundity.

This idea that the individual goes through the same stages as the culture as a whole, and that the culture repeats the same course when one cycle comes to an end, though in a new variation, is often found in classical literature. You will no doubt recall Hesiod's division in *Works and Days* or Ovid's exposition of the same idea in *Metamorphoses*, where the ages of gold, silver, bronze, and iron succeed each other as part of a process of decay that repeats itself in an eternal cycle:

> Then sprang up first the golden age, which of itself maintained
> The truth and right of everything unforced and unconstrained.
> There was no fear of punishment, there was no threatening law
> . . .
> And that the silver age came in, more somewhat base than gold,
> More precious yet than freckled brass, immediately the old
> And ancient Spring did Jove abridge, and made thereof anon,
> Four seasons: Winter, Summer, Spring and Autumn off and on:
> . . .
> Next after this succeeded straight, the third and brazen age:
> More hard of nature, somewhat bent to cruel wars and rage.
> But yet not wholly past all grace.
> Of iron is the last
> In no part good and tractable as former ages past.
> For when that of this wicked age once opened was the vein
> Therein all mischief rushed forth: then Faith and Truth were fain
> and honest shame to hide their heads: for whom crept stoutly in,
> Craft, Treason, Violence, Envy, Pride and wicked Lust to win.

The fact that Holberg was able to write fifteen plays, including his masterpieces, in less than a year, an average of about three weeks per play, can undoubtedly partly be attributed to how genre was viewed, but it is also connected with the characteristics particular to comedy as a genre.

III

To paraphrase Aristotle, the leading authority in this field in antiquity as in all later ages on the subjects of tragedy and comedy, in his *Poetics*: Tragedy is about people who are better than the average person, comedy about those who are worse. Tragedy is set among aristocrats, comedy among ordinary citizens. In eighteenth century Denmark, the decision to write comedy or tragedy involved not only a choice as to the type of environment in which the play was to take place but also a stylistic choice. In the eighteenth century, tragedies were written in verse (usually in alexandrines), while comedies were in prose. Important technical decisions had therefore already been resolved for Holberg before he even got down to the actual writing, by virtue of the fact that he had chosen to write comedies. Holberg's comedies illustrate how the genre provides important keys to the form of the literary work.

The above observations have been concerned with the formal requirements of the genre only. But there are also important guidelines with regard to the raw materials and themes of comedies. Thus it is taken for granted in classical comedy that the formal conflict to be resolved (which is not necessarily the conflict of central importance to the play) is a conflict about marriage. The lovers cannot have each other, and the ones who have been contracted to each other do not love each other. The subject matter of a comedy is determined by the genre. The basic conflict has been predetermined, and a number of obstacles are inserted which then make up the actual theme of the play.

In classical comedy, this conflict unfolds naturally enough as a meeting between two families, those of the young man and the young girl. This conflict, however, which in the age of Holberg was merely a formal conflict as far as the playwright was concerned, solves a problem of crucial importance to the author — namely, what the gallery of characters should look like. It emerges as a combination of two families with servants, maids, stable boys, fathers, mothers, and their children, and a few individuals who stand apart from the two families. The purely formal, indeed formalistic basic conflict, on which the author has no intention of giving his views, automatically produces a particular gallery of characters. As we shall see later, this also had some influence on how the plays were performed.

For Holberg, the marriage and its attendant problems merely present him with a peg on which to hang his real theme: the relationship between power and common sense, which have not always been bestowed on the same person. The main character has a flaw that threatens the social order. His titles usually indicate the flaw in question: *Den Stundesløse* (The Busy Man), *Mester Gert Westphaler eller den meget talende Barber* (Master Gert Westphaler or the Talkative Barber), *Den Vægelsindede* (The Weathercock), and so on. But whatever the actual theme, the genre has solved Holberg's technical task. His problem is rather that he has something to say that the genre does not automatically offer him. The poet who has decided to write a comedy has thus, by virtue of that choice, already reached quite an advanced level of detail, but has still far from exhausted the possibilities of the genre.

In classical comedy, the genre also imposes rules as to how the text is to be subdivided. I am thinking here of what anyone who has been anywhere near a Holberg play will have noticed — namely, that the play is divided into five parts, or acts, and that the course of the action is quite closely tied to the existence of five acts. Let me recapitulate here this division, which is so familiar to most that they regard it as a cliché, whereas it is actually a very strong determinant of the curve of action and thereby of the problems and the conclusion. The classical division is as follows:

Act 1   Exposition or background information, in which the themes and elements of the conflict are introduced.

Act 2   The conflict is presented in its concrete form and the conflicting interests are contrasted.

Act 3   The crisis or peripety, which marks the climax of the conflict and prepares the way for the consequences of the crisis.

Act 4   The consequences of the crisis or the turning-point.

Act 5   The catastrophe or resolution, where the conflict is brought to a peaceful conclusion on a new, harmonious basis.

This division may seem trivial in an analytical account of comedy, but not if we observe comedy from the point of view of production. The division itself then becomes the key to a rough structuring of the text so that right from the start it is possible to sort the content into different stages of development and it produces, as a matter of course, a purely mechanical division into five equal parts. While a modern author might have sleepless nights pondering over the arrangement of his material, the arrangement of a classical comedy has been predetermined. The work just writes itself.

One can delve even further into the text. The individual acts are subdivided into scenes by the simple expedient of changing the number of the scene whenever a new character appears on the stage. This only brings partial relief to the extent that the division into scenes corresponds to leaving

out a line or something of a similar nature, but it is not entirely without importance since it determines the course of the process of introduction that needs
to be adopted when new characters are brought into the play: A character is
talked about, he comes onto the stage, he leaves the stage and is maligned af-
terwards. The division into scenes puts the focus on the problem of transition, one of the most difficult problems for the playwright to deal with. Even
so, the division into scenes is only of limited value to the author. There is,
however, another aid at hand.

In the seventeenth century, it became common practice for certain observations in Aristotle's *Poetics* to be interpreted very narrowly, as directions as
to how space and time should be presented in the dramatic genres. These interpretations are encapsulated in what are known today as the rules
concerning the three unities of place, time, and action. These rules could be
regarded as a form of normative madness, but they can also be seen from the
point of view of the productive author. They might appear to be an
unreasonable, feudal form of control on the poetical imagination, but they
could also be regarded as an important, effective instrument that enables the
dramatist to achieve a more assured and quicker result.

As everyone no doubt already knows, the rules state that a drama ought to
be acted out within a period of twenty-four hours (unity of time), in the same
place (unity of place), and should have no subplots that do not have a direct
bearing on the main plot. The consequences of these rules are too comprehensive to be dealt with here, but it is quite clear that all three "unities" are
particularly helpful when it comes to facilitating transitions between the
various scenes as smoothly as possible. They ensure that no individual transition is of a purely fortuitous nature (this means, of course, that they cannot
say anything about chance; but why should they in the eighteenth century?).

Furthermore, each individual scene contains within it useful material that
provides tracks for developing the relationships between the various characters. I have already mentioned the possible existence of a fixed sequence for
the introduction of new characters, which is followed by comments on the
behaviour of the person in question; but an automatic regulation of the
physical aspects of comic acting is also present within the individual scene in
the predetermined (as a rule non-verbal) sequences that are usually known
as *lazzi*, which are handed on from author to author and from actor to actor.
Even at the level of the scene, there is some help available to the author.

I hope that these observations have given some insight into how Holberg
was able to be so productive, while maintaining such an extremely high
standard of work. The rules and norms of the genre facilitated a speedy
structuring of the text. This is true of the different levels in the text and also

of the content (what the text is actually about). Material and theme, gallery of characters, conflict and the course of the conflict, social class and style are all rooted in the requirements of the genre.[2]

All this can only partly explain Holberg's productivity, however. We must not forget that he was a very diligent person, for whom every day contained twelve to fourteen hours that were eminently suited to work.

IV

Let us now consider the surprising fact that the actors attached to the theater in Lille Grønnegade were able, by and large, to keep up with Holberg's pace. In so doing, I will give a closer description of how Holberg's text was translated into a visual form, and look at the rules that governed visual theater work. I shall thus be broadening my perspective so that it includes seventeenth and eighteenth century theater in general, as well as the works of Holberg.

In order to describe the art of acting in the eighteenth century one has to use sources dating from the end of the eighteenth century and the beginning of the nineteenth. Theater historians have found a lot of materials from this period. It was usual for actors to have many roles. In the course of one winter, for example, one individual had thirty-four roles and two chorus parts. The most celebrated of all Romantic actresses, Johanne Louise Heiberg, played 113 roles in fifteen years, an average of approximately nine roles a year. Minor actors could have three or four parts in one play.

This does not explain but provides the background for how it was possible to put on plays at a few days' notice and to put on one or two new plays once or twice a week. This often happened without any rehearsals or with just one, and usually without the benefit of a director.

Eighteenth century theaters were balcony theaters that grew out of the amphitheaters of the sixteenth century (an earlier version was the Teatro Olimpico in Vicenza), where the auditorium was a combination of a gently rising stalls section and closed balconies or boxes, as found in older theaters today. This meant that people from all layers of society could mix in the same room as one audience, without any offense being given to the higher orders, since they were quite separate from the lower ones.

Our information about the acting in these theaters comes partly from extra- and intrapolations of what is known about conditions in France and partly

---

[2] Computer systems are similar to neo-classical drama at a very basic level: Both are governed by explicit rules and use formalized action sequences. Chapter 6 and 7 elaborate this point, and Chapter 10 discusses computer systems as dramas. (Berit Holmqvist)

from our knowledge of the eighteenth century theater. What I shall present here is a somewhat simplified version.

The theater catered for three main genres, each genre having its own special scenery. It is still possible today to find small stages with three sets of scenery in village halls and inns.

Fig. 8. 1. Tragedy setting.

Fig. 8. 2. Comedy setting.

There was one set for tragedies, one for satyric plays, and one for comedies. In strict accordance with the requirements of the genre, tragedies were acted in a temple or palace type of setting with columns (Figure 8. 1). Satyric plays were acted in a rural setting with melancholy shepherds, and comedies were usually set in a public place between two houses (Figure 8. 2).

Fig. 8. 3. Eighteenth century theater

Thus, in comedies, the fact that the plot was concerned with an approaching marriage and thereby also with a future social connection between two families was underlined. The backcloth for comedies was restricted to the deepest but not necessarily the most important stratum of the play. A piece of scenery showing a room in which the marriage negotiations were to take place, as happens in *Den Stundesløse* (The Busy Man), might be added to the street scene.

The eighteenth century theater was what I would call *a theater of presentation or display*, not a theater of illusion. Reality was neither recreated nor purported to be recreated on the stage.[3] The entire theater was lit up with tapers or oil lamps. The dividing line between the space which ought to be the focus of everyone and the space reserved for the spectators was not, as today, the one between the stage and the auditorium, but between the auditorium and the boxes, insofar as the latter could be closed off so that a game of cards, a visit from one's lover or a prostitute, or a meal could be enjoyed there.

Fig. 8. 4 A visit from a prostitute.

The relationship between the spaces in the theater was thus closer to the situation when one watches television than to the one obtaining in the modern theater (Figuress 8. 3 and 8. 4. Note the blind in Figure 8. 4). There were no

---

[3] Chapters 6 and 10 make the same point about computer systems: They should not strive for illusions, but expose themselves as the formal system they are. (Berit Holmqvist)

attempts to create illusion via lighting effects, scenery, or props. In the eighteenth century, furniture and other movable objects were either brought in by the actors or painted onto the flats. That is why it was possible for the actress Madam Schall to make her exit from the stage through a wall and a Turkish sofa, during a performance.

The theater as we know it today originated in modern times at royal courts as a theater of presentation and display, in which princes and nobles saw their lives not so much portrayed as displayed and represented. It is not surprising, therefore, that acting came to be modeled on the aristocratic way of life. The actors and administrators were conscious of this aristocratic background. For example, it is interesting to note that when the three Danish actors Rosing, Preisler, and Saabye traveled to France in 1788, at the expense of the Royal Theater, to study drama and especially the art of acting, only one thing was deemed absolutely essential; they *had to* experience Louis XVI's levee at Versailles. This is the same Rosing who was still maintaining in 1809 that all movements could be learnt from the minuet.

It was thus the gestures, facial expressions, dances, and general movements of the most elevated aristocrats that formed the points of departure for acting. And from a modern point of view, the aristocratic mode of expression was a highly stylized one, its function being that of demonstrating the social status of the speaker in a precise and visible form, but no needs were to be expressed that had not been subjected to social interpretation beforehand. This is a manifestation of a stylization of personal life as something that is always social into something that is social from the outset.[4]

V

From a theoretical point of view, the character of the individual was regarded as stable. It was not until the end of the eighteenth century that the view of character was dynamized by such people as the Swiss theorist Lavater. Before this, theories may have differed but character was not viewed from a perspective that implied development. This view can be traced right back to antiquity.

Humoralism contains a standard description of the four temperaments (Figure 8. 5).

The *choleric* type is described as quarrelsome, obstinate, full of self-esteem, industrious, ambitious, and clear-sighted. His eyes are heroic and fiery, and he has a cheerful appearance and a penetrating voice. He takes long strides when he walks and almost seems to swagger. The *phlegmatic* type is easy-

---

4 Use of standardized postures in computer systems is discussed in Chapter 6. (Berit Holmqvist)

going and indolent, complains bitterly about the slightest thing, is easily lured into unfaithfulness and disloyalty, is short-sighted and slow-witted and seems only to be roused by food and drink. His eyes are soft, watery, and sleepy with no fire in them, his voice is soft and he walks with a dragging gait, knees bent and arms hanging down at the sides.

Fig. 8. 5 The choleric type.   The melancholic type.

The *sanguine* type is sensual, lively, and friendly. He loves praise and tends to be boastful and conceited. He is loquacious and candid, with a cheerful and unsteady gaze. He has a refined voice and walks with short, quick steps. The *melancholic* type yearns for lasting security and fears present dangers. He is profound, lacks wit and cheerfulness, is irresolute and melancholy, close and secretive. In company he is shy, chaste, and modest. He has a slow, steady gaze that burns with a solid, dark fire. His speech and movements are restricted and slow. These are the descriptions of the four temperaments given in Johannes Kämpf's *Von den Temperamenten* (1760).

This view of character can be directly translated into a physiognomy and a pattern of gesticulation that enable the actor to fix his role without rehearsals and without a director. Most important of all is probably the fact that the character is perceived as undynamic, perhaps even as static, and it is clearly assumed that there must be agreement between character, appearance and gesticulation.

VI

This theory about the temperaments surfaces in the eighteenth century view of comedy, with its emphasis on a special type of comedy that we can best approach by seeing how Holberg's comedy was viewed by posterity, and in which the static view of character made the work of both writer and actor much easier.

Toward the end of Holberg's life, his plays lost their appeal. The reasons he himself gave for this provide us with a clue as to the stylization that occurred in eighteenth century humour. What exactly was the boundary that Holbergian comedy had arrived at? Holberg himself was well aware of the fact that one had been reached. In *Epistle 249*, from 1750, he says:

> The very same plays that were performed twenty years ago without provoking any kind of anger, either at court or in the town, now appear to be intolerable to certain people. Perhaps what seems to grate now will be thought harmonious after another 20 years.

But it was a different kind of harmony that came into fashion than the one Holberg had in mind. "Affected gentility has now gone so far that nobody dare call anything by its right name any longer", he says. Holberg's comedy continued to grate in the ears of the genteel for over a century before it became completely respectable again.

Eighteenth century theorists were inclined to interpret comedy as either a purely aesthetic phenomenon or as conduct. In *Afsluttende uvidenskabeligt Efterskrift* (Concluding Unscientific Postscript), Kierkegaard says of humor that it is "the final stage in inner existence before faith" and that "humor rounds off immanence within immanence." To Kierkegaard, therefore, humor is on the highest human plane, and what is most important: humor is the medium through which intensity is able to find expression. The humor that is unable to express intensity of feeling is the immature humor that ignores matters of importance. What is being ignored is the commitment to common human, ethical values.

As late as 1884 Georg Brandes, in his book on Holberg, provides us with an analysis of comedy in which boundary-defining moral comedy disappears. According to him, in *Ulysses of Ithaca* "we become involved in art's joke at its own expense, its own being, in this eternal game with illusion....," and a little later, "But Holberg the literary genius does not adopt the same position as Holberg the moralist."

The same viewpoint is expressed in *Den store Humor* (The Great Humor, 1916) by the Danish philosopher Harald Høffding, who regards humor as an expression of an attitude to life.

The nineteenth century approach to the comic is thus primarily bound up with expressions of intimacy and with a particular form of understanding that provides an outlet for the values of the person who is laughing in sympathy with the ridiculous person or object. This way of looking at comedy does not set up distinctions; on the contrary, there is a constant striving for a harmony that can absorb class differences and discords. It deliberately seeks a serenity in which differences have been resolved or suppressed. Erik

Lunding, the Danish Germanic philologist, has described the bourgeois humanism or biedermeier culture of the nineteenth century as a culture with its roots in the home, especially in the sitting-room. This is where an individual emerges who is primarily a problem for him or herself, and the very circumstance that the individual becomes a relationship is the reason why Holbergian comedy received little attention in the period that followed its heyday. The kind of comedy that makes distinctions and highlights contradictions survived for many years only as folk tradition, outside the mainstream institutions of society. It was not until the bourgeois institutions of the nineteenth century came under attack and under pressure that pre-bourgeois comedy could be reconsidered and re-appropriated.

Let us go one step further and take a look at how the comic element unfolds in neo-classical comedy. Henri Bergson's *Le Rire* (Laughter), which was published as three separate articles in 1899 and then in book form in 1900, is a superb study of comedy. Although it sets out to analyze the general nature of laughter and comedy, this work provides a brilliant analysis of the nature of the comic to be found in neo-classical comedies. This is partly because its examples are taken almost exclusively from the comedies of Molière, partly because, instead of analysing "homeric," "demonic," or "intimate" laughter, Bergson chooses to analyze the laughter that is dependent on fixed social norms; in other words, he analyzes the socially conscious laughter of the bourgeoisie.

The laughter that is unleashed by neo-classical comedy is social laughter in the sense that it presupposes the existence of social norms. It invites both the public and the provokers of their mirth to enter into a social fellowship, but at the same time it rejects whatever deviates from the accepted social norms. Bergson goes so far as to regard feeling as the enemy of laughter.

It is not enough, however, merely to adjust to social norms, the adjustment must be made with a certain flexibility. For we can see clearly enough that Holberg's comic characters are never (or almost never) revolutionaries, who want to bring about the overthrow of society, but people who have been taken over by a particular passion or affectation so that they can no longer function properly and thus pose a threat to the authority of the social norms. According to Bergson comedy begins at the point where social life stiffens into ridiculous, mindless repetition. The life of the person who provokes laughter has become mechanical, and what provokes the laughter is the sight of the expected repetitions in their endless variations. If we accept that feeling is the enemy of neo-classical comedy, then this kind of comedy belongs to an sphere in which our emotions are not moved in the eighteenth century sense of the word.

Let me define this sphere a little more precisely. On the one hand, the ridiculous affectation or inclination must involve a breach of accepted social norms and authority, without this breach being an organically connected part of the whole personality and therefore incurable; it has to be a parasitical passion. On the other hand, the affectation must not consist in a deliberate infringement of the law. For that reason, the comic elements in neo-classical comedy are always visible to the outside world but never to the ridiculous person. Like Olaf Skavlan, the Norwegian literary historian, I would say that neo-classical comedy occupies the territory that lies between the respective spheres of criminal law and moral law.

If we wander into the sphere of criminal law, we approach the tragic, as can be seen in *Jean de France*, and this happens precisely where the affectation in question consumes the whole personality. The attack on the patriarchal order in *Jean de France* is a very serious one, since Jean tries to bring about changes through violence. That is why the defense of the norms is much fiercer than in the other plays and why the play has tragic overtones. It is pointed out time and again that society might find it necessary to protect itself and has the means to do so. At the end of the play Jeronimus swears "that he will not go to bed until he has had [Jean] sent to gaol or to the debtors' prison." In *Jean de France* the intrigue is superseded by watchmen and gallows as a means of bringing about reform of character.

When Holberg writes about his comedies he always stresses the fact that the entertainment is subordinate to the moral purpose, which is that of reforming the spectators. His comedies are attacks on a ruling passion, whether it is ambition, restlessness, extreme talkativeness, or political agitation. Anyone who fails to observe the social norms is condemned not to sympathetic but to merciless laughter that will draw the spectator and the ridiculous character back to the accepted norm. A plot is instigated against the ridiculous character which provokes laughter and calls him to order. In Holberg, laughter is the medium by which those who possess common sense reject madness. The laughter presupposes a definition of the ridiculous that excludes fellowship or intimacy.

The affectation or madness is often expressed in the plays in mechanical behavior in which every single reaction is completely predictable. Human behavior is reduced to mechanical responses to social contacts: The letter of the law is placed above its spirit, book-keeping above love. The social conduct of the madman thus becomes rigid and *his behaviour stiffens into a gesture*. Laughter brings the rigidity back to life.

VII

In the acting tradition, humoralism links up with (especially French) aristocratic, stylized forms and an interpretation of antiquity's manifestation of
feelings in art and philosophy.

In *De oratore* III, 1, 4, Cicero writes, "For nature has given every feeling its
own particular facial expression, its own particular tone of voice and posture." This could be regarded as a working theory of how feelings could be
translated into movements, postures, gestures and facial expressions. The
classical characters established a norm as to how Cicero's law was to be applied in concrete situations.

Fig. 8. 6. Niobe.   Fig. 8. 7. The dying Gaul.

It could be the dying Niobe's physical, gesticulatory, and expressive submission to some incomprehensible, higher force: the distorted, surrendered body,
the uplifted arm and the open face (Figure 8. 6); the dying Gaul: the Gaul
who kills himself and his wife (Figure 8. 7); the terror of the Laokoon group
(Figure. 8. 8).

This interpretation of the relationship between feeling and physical expression cannot, however, be directly translated into a dramatic language. It
must first be passed through various filters. The most important of these,
which I will deal with here, is that the physical expression should be visible
from all angles of a large room. That it should be stylized is not enough, it

should also be capable of being projected to a large number of people, and a certain over-emphasis or even fierceness of expression is required.

Fig. 8. 8. The Laokoon group.

Nor can the technical conditions surrounding theatrical performances be ignored. Before 1818, the Royal Theater was lit by tallow candles, and between then and the advent of gas, it was lit by Argand oil lamps. This meant that, downstage, there had to be a flat arrangement[5] of the set up against the candles. In a theater such as this, making use of the depth of the stage, which is very important in the modern theater, is simply not possible. The flat acting against the candles in itself requires that the face be turned towards the audience, but the aristocratic element in the eighteenth century theater also demands a full face as a mark of respect for a symbolic prince, represented by the audience. It was considered unseemly to turn one's face away from the audience. Toward the end of the eighteenth century there was a debate about the seemliness of not only the half-profile but also the quarter profile. At the beginning of the nineteenth century, Goethe, in Weimar, was one of those who supported the quarter-profile.

The actors went on stage and arranged themselves in a quarter circle in front of the proscenium lighting.

---

[5] Present day computers are also "flat" media, since they only support 2 1/2 dimensions: height, breadth, and a depth only consisting of overlapping perspective. The geometrical perspective of virtual reality is not yet commercially available. (Berit Holmqvist)

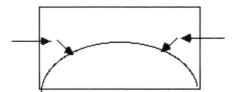

Fig. 8. 9. Entering the stage.

The men usually came on from the royal box side, since they could then draw their swords belligerently, without standing in anyone's light. The women usually came on from the other side. The highest born characters stood in the middle of the stage, and servants or other minor characters could step back a pace from the circle (Figure 8. 9).

Heroes and aristocrats walked with straight knees and backward-leaning bodies, while members of the bourgeoisie in the sentimental dramas of the last part of the eighteenth century walked with bent knees and a forward-leaning, thoughtful body. Aristocrats and heroes stood in position number 4, while the bourgeoisie adopted position number 2. The special kind of obliging attitude that had to be expressed in the sentimental, bourgeois comedies, was called "attendrissement." In this sense, the pattern of movements in ceremonious plays was laid down in advance.

If there is any vestigial surprise that plays could be produced so speedily, it should be noted that movements, positioning, and postures were laid down beforehand, whatever the play. Nor should it be forgotten that actors were highly specialized, both as far as the main genres of tragedy and comedy were concerned and with respect to the roles that these two genres had to offer. There were the heroes and heroines, ingénues, servants, and character parts (both in the Holbergian and in the modern sense of the word). These roles were either played throughout one's acting life or were passed through at various ages.

The codes attached to such features as gait were completely understood by the public. When an actor appeared on the stage, the audience was able to tell, from the gait alone, whether it was a hero or a pseudo-hero. But this was also revealed by general movements and by the way of declaiming, and in case anyone should still have any doubts, the characters, as we saw earlier, were introduced before they appeared (but look, here's Mosjø Jeronimus) and the actors were able to deliver the so-called asides directly to the audience, as when the servants in a Holberg play explain their plans to the audience. Furthermore, the actors and actresses had time to greet their friends and acquaintances in the boxes, which critics frequently complained about.

The body of the actor was divided up in a way that stylized and simplified the acting (once the code had been learnt). So far, I have mentioned the gait, the pattern of movements on the stage, the aristocratic bows and curtseys, but not, as yet, the actual body.

The movements of the head were limited by the demand for full frontal acting. If we take a bird's eye view of the actors, the pattern of movements follows one of the possible courses sketched in Figure 8. 10:

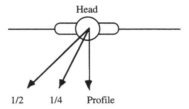

Fig. 8. 10. Movement of the head.

Fig. 8. 11. Tragic = upper part.

Fig. 8. 12. Comical = the lower part .

The body was divided into sections above and below the waist. Under no circumstances were the hands to be dropped below the waist in serious plays.

The boundary that the belt sets between the seemly and the unseemly is a moral boundary that must not be transgressed but, on the same grounds, it also becomes a boundary between the genres, with the seemly and the tragic being associated with the upper part of the body (Fig. 8. 11), the unseemly and comical with the lower part (Fig. 8. 12), See also Fig 8. 13.

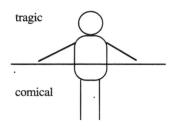

Fig. 8. 13. Tragic and comical.

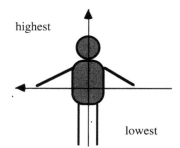

Fig. 8. 14. The four areas of the actor.

There is also a division of the body into a strong right hand side and a weak left-hand side. Thus, there are four areas altogether, from the lower left side to the upper right side (Figure 8. 14).

A corresponding division can be observed in the face. The face, too, is divided up, with the nose as the important boundary, the upper area being the distinguished part and the lower area the unseemly one. In the more elevated, tragic genres, most emphasis is placed on the eyes and the forehead, while the lower parts of the nose and the mouth are largely the preserve of comedy. Even a hero who is *surprised* cannot stand with his mouth wide open, and nothing is more tedious than a pompous clown. Thus, the face has similar divisions to those of the body (Figure 8. 15):

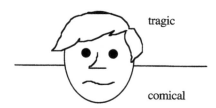

Fig. 8. 15. Tragic and comical parts of face.

In comedy, it is possible to act with the upper part of the face, but as soon as a grimacing or even just a gaping mouth appears, we enter the world of parody.

In the art of acting, mastery of the body is stylized, non-individual, and whether it is tragically elevated or comically anti-aristocratic, it is bound up with the aristocratic way of life. A number of informal movements that seem natural and unobtrusive to us, would therefore not be allowed within the conventions of the classical theater.

All the acting is done in a standing position. Leaning against a chair or putting one's hands in one's pockets is forbidden, women do not put their hands on their stomachs, and it is not acceptable to slap somebody on the back or to tug at his waistcoat buttons. These forms of reference to bodily functions or to intimacy ought not to occur.

Let me give a few examples of this special form of acting that will seem obvious to us in the twentieth century because many of these dramatic expressions have become part of our everyday language: Raised, contracted eyebrows around the root of the nose ("wrinkled brows") mean astonished anger. Wide open eyes indicate astonishment; if they are combined with outstretched, protective arms, it means fear. Hands on the heart mean love. Wrist raised to the forehead means "I am swooning with fear." Eyes raised to heaven mean "God help me." Looking at the ground and pointing an outstretched arm towards it means "You will go to hell." Drawing in air in and speaking out, or just powerful ventilation, means strong emotion ("a heaving bosom"). Outstretched, welcoming arms signify openness, and raised hands, clasped together signify friendliness.

Indeed, the higher the hands, the more powerful the forces appealed to (Figure 8. 11). Outspread fingers signify an unusual degree of excitement.

Fig. 8. 16 The tragi-heroic style of acting meets the comic one.

In Figure 8. 16 the tragi-heroic style of acting meets the comic one: Holberg's *Hexerie eller Blind Allarm* (Witchcraft or False Alarm), V, 1.

VIII

In this chapter, the texts of dramas have been considered from both a formal and a productive point of view. Little has been said about the hermeneutic, the ideological, the political, or the general human aspects.

I hope that it has been established that the writing of every single text takes place on the basis of a number of principles that have nothing at all to do with the individual talent of the author. This individual talent, which in the case of Holberg amounts to genius, is of course a prerequisite.

The making of the text, its originality and its (legal) immunity must be approached quite differently from modern literary texts. Patterns of movements, ways of walking, gestures, and facial expressions are objective expressions of feelings. In the face of these established rules, good actors improvise well, bad actors badly.

The authors of eighteenth century texts did not, however, regard it as their goal or their duty to write something new, but rather to write something that could barely begin to rival the older writings in terms of quality. By older writings they meant the Bible and, in particular, the classical Greek and Roman authors. The work of a writer in the eighteenth century was an eternal and impossible approximation to the unattainable ideal. The neo-classical text has no ambition to represent anything new; on the contrary, it represents something old, although it might do so in a new way. It does not present anything new, but presents something old in a satisfactory or profound way. It does not solve any problems, it lays the old, insoluble paradoxes out to be wondered at anew.[6] To use a metaphor: Where the modern text is a step forward, the neo-classical text is more like small jumps on the spot.

As though by some ironic quirk of history, the formal side of the aesthetic practice of the eighteenth century bears a curious resemblance to the dominant fictional genres of today's media. I shall not develop this idea here, but shall merely point out the similarity of TV series, whose contact with controversial problems is not intended to provoke new answers, let alone solutions, but whose purpose is simply that of touching on the pain spots in the culture, like an old man rubbing his itching leg sores. In the world of fiction, this is refeudalization.

---

[6] Compare this description to the circular dramaturgy recommended for interactive fiction in Chapter 9. (Berit Holmqvist)

9

The meaning of plot and narrative

JØRGEN BANG

The computer was developed as a tool for handling large amounts of informations and for performing complicated calculations. But since the middle of the 1980s, when the personal computer came within the reach of ordinary people, the computer has taken over a wide range of functions, such as word processing, designing, book keeping, information handling, communication, and so on. From being a tool the computer has become a medium.

It is characteristic of other media that they are normally used for both commercial and artistic purposes, in what seems to be some kind of division of labour. On the one hand, the commercial products extend the market and inspire technical innovations for mass production. On the other hand, the artistic productions explore the medium, extend the language used and invent new ways of looking at the world. That is true of the , literature and a modern medium, such as the video. We have advertising and other commercial videos, art videos, and in between we have the music videos. Sometimes they are purely commercial products aiming at promoting a record, but they can also be very artistic productions, where the images are an integrated part of the music.

This dichotomy between entertainment and art is only one dimension of another dichotomy — the one between fact and fiction, or as I prefer to call it, faction — since we are dealing with the presentation of facts in media (mediated facts), not with actual facts. Seen in this perspective of media development, faction will often have the advantages of both "art" and "entertainment." In faction, the innovations developed for commercial and artistic purposes can be used for the presentation of facts in news, information or in education.

In many ways, the computer as a medium can be compared with the video. Both are products of modern technology, both can be used for display of pre-produced products, whether commercial or non-commercial, but both can also be used for self-production. On the entertainment side, computer games are comparable to music videos, but on the artistic side, there are only a few products of computer fiction in existence — and they are in no way compa-

rable to the art videos. One could say that computer art simply does not exist
— at least not in the form of stories.

A further investigation of storytelling and reader response as performed in
other media could be a way of exploring the range of possibilities of computer art.

Stories and storytelling

What is a story and why do we tell stories? These are the basic questions to
ask when dealing with fiction. Twenty years ago, a Danish professor of psychology, Franz From, put forward the following statements in a newspaper
discussion on popular fiction (From, 1973):

> In a strange way, the story is always about you — and if it wasn't, you wouldn't
> want to read it.
>
> (...) no one can create a world on their own and become a human being, it has
> taken thousands of generations. But the pattern to be adopted is found in fiction, in
> the spiritual products of the group. And the pattern is still there: it is in fiction that the
> culture of a people or a group (their specific rules and values) is kept and preserved.
>
> Seen in that perspective, the importance of fiction becomes immense and our need
> for fiction enormous, because we can't live without it.(...). Through fiction we gain
> access to other people's experiences, we become part of the others, and in that way
> we become human beings.

To this broad, cultural, and slightly Jungian perspective one could add an anthropological one, putting the emphasis on the relationship between the
"real" world and the narrated one. It is called "ritual condensation" and
Learch (1976: 37) explains the process as follows:

> By converting ideas. products of the mind (mentifacts) into material objects, "out-
> there", we give them relative permanence, and in that permanent material form we can
> subject them to technical operations which are beyond the capacity of the mind acting
> by itself .

Fiske and Hartley (1978: 90) use this concept and relate it to modern mass
communication, when they talk about the "bardic function" of television:

> The projection of abstract ideas into material form is evident in such social activities
> as religious rituals. But the television medium also performs a similar function, when,
> for example, a programme like *Ironside* converts abstract ideas about individual rela-
> tionships between man and man, men and women, individuals and institutions,
> whites and blacks into concrete dramatic form. It is a ritual condensation of the domi-
> nant criteria for survival in modern complex society.

Telling stories is a way of giving structure to the world. It is a sort of pre-
cognition — pre-epistemological or pre-scientific understanding of one's re-

lationship with other human beings, the surrounding culture, and the outside world.

You may not know the term "sexual harassment," but you can certainly tell the story of how the boss has tried to grab you on several occasions. What you, in fact, are doing is looking backward in time, picking out the relevant situations, arranging them in a line with a beginning and an end and presenting them in a more or less dramatic way. At a later stage knowing the term you may just say: "I have been exposed to sexual harassment at work."

In fact, it was these mechanisms that produced the old mythologies. When people were unable to explain such phenomena of nature as thunder and earthquakes, they had to tell stories about angry giant gods with enormous powers, to bring order into the world — or at least to bring it within a formula, where they could "understand" it and act in it.

The text as a generator of meaning

The hermeneutic philosopher Paul Ricoeur (1981, 1984) has located the metaphor and the narrative as the basic semantic features in storytelling. Metaphor is normally considered to belong to the theory of "figures of discourse" and narrative to the theory of "genres," but according to Ricoeur they are both primarily innovators of meaning-effects at the level of discourse. That is precisely what makes them interesting in this semiotic perspective.

> With metaphor, the innovation lies in the producing of a new semantic pertinence by means of an impertinent attribution: "Nature is a temple where living pillars ..."
>
> With narrative, the semantic innovation lies in the inventing of another work of synthesis — a plot. By means of the plot, goals, causes, and chance are brought together within the temporal unity of a whole and complete action. (*Ricoeur 1984: ix*).

Both metaphor and narrative form a synthesis out of the heterogeneous. The living metaphor brings a new pertinence into the predication. And the feigned plot creates a new congruence in the organization of the events. Through the construction of a new pertinence and a new congruence, fiction is able to create order in an endless universe with no beginning or end. Metaphor enables one to think on themes for which the language or the person speaking has no words. And the plot creates structure out of chaos, it gives meaning to the past and to the future. It is significant that the words story and history have the same etymology — indeed, in Danish it is the same word.

At the same time, this rather "imprecise" way of creating meaning out of an undifferentiated universe creates a certain scope for the "reader" of fiction. Metaphors, in particular, are not very precise — that is why they are used. They leave room for interpretation in the actual meaning production of the reader/receiver. Depending on the plot, the same can be true of narration.

The reader/listener/viewer has to fill in the symbols, the metaphors, the structure and the narrative of the text with his or her own experiences or fantasies. He or she has to perform the text on an "inner" stage like a drama or a piece of music. The text is a scenario, which only comes alive through the active participation of the reader/ listener/viewer.

But at the same time, the receiver is given a role within the fictional universe of the text, provided, of course, that the communication between the text and the reader/listener/viewer is established. The reception takes place on the premises of the text. It is comparable to gambling (Gadamer 1960). As soon as the game begins, it is the game that controls the gamblers, not the other way around. For a time, the gambler gives up his or her consciousness and becomes part of the universe of the game.

On the one hand, the fictional text is as the meaning of the term indicates: feigned, invented — concerned with a non-real world. On the other hand, the fictional text draws on our "inner images," which themselves are complex mixtures of experiences, dreams, yearnings, and hopes that come from our everyday life. Fiction has the power to engage the reader/listener/viewer, to catch his or her attention, to create astonishment, to bring about insight and to establish consciousness. We are dealing with a process of sensuous apprehension, which is taking place via images rather than in rational terms — a process of aesthetic communication.

Through the receiver's integration and interaction with the text, the text is able to create intersubjectivity. The reception is our own, but only to a certain extent. It takes place within a defined universe — if it takes place at all.

Open and closed texts

The story is concrete, person-related, arranged with a beginning and an end, receiver-oriented and genre-conscious. On the one hand, stories are told in order to express common sense experiences in everyday life, which the storyteller either cannot or does not wish to formulate in other terms. On the other hand, stories are "read" in order to reorganize the "world" and expand the consciousness of the reader. When the reader/listener/viewer "invests" his or her experiences and/or images in the text, the process of organization begins. The text comes to resemble a machinery of meaning production.

This process of transformation does not necessarily mean that the text is perceived in the same way by all the recipients. The empirically oriented German psychologist and literary sociologist Norbert Groeben (1980) uses the term "margin of interpretation" as a contrast to the concept of a "super reading" found in Ingarden (1930) and the school of literary criticism known as the New Criticism. He talks about the possibilities of reconstructing the amplitude of the text from the empirical readings of the actual readers. Every text has a certain scope for interpretation, within which the "readings" are neither aberrant, nor incorrect.

From the perspective of semiotics, Umberto Eco (1981) has reached a similar understanding of "reading." But he uses the concept of "possible readings" of the text rather than "actual readings." Wolfgang Iser (1976), from the Konstanz School of German aesthetical receptionists, stresses this internal perspective even further, by referring actual readings to sociology and not to the field of literary theory. He talks about "the implicit reader" as being conceived by the author, to be inside the text.

Eco deals with this essential problem of the relationship between the text and the reception in a more open-minded way using the term "model reader"(1981b: 7):

> To organise a text, its author has to rely upon a series of codes that assign given contents to the expressions he uses. To make his text communicative, the author has to assume that the ensemble of codes he relies upon is the same as that shared by his possible reader. The author has thus to foresee a model of the possible reader (here after Model Reader) supposedly able to deal interpretatively with the expressions in the same way as the author deals generatively with them.

The main point for Eco is to emphasise that a text presupposes its own reader as an inevitable condition both for its ability to communicate and for its own significance. The text is sent for someone to activate it — even if the addressee does not exist in flesh and blood.

At the same time, Eco points to the fact that the codes and competence of the "sender" are not necessarily the same as those of the receiver:

> In the process of communication, a text is frequently interpreted against the background of codes different from those intended by the author. Some authors do not take into account such a possibility. They have in mind an average addressee referred to a given social context. Nobody can say what happens when the actual reader is different from the "average" one. Those texts that obsessively aim at arousing a precise response on the part of more or less precise empirical readers (...) are in fact open to possible "aberrant" decoding. A text so immoderately "open" to every possible interpretation will be called a *closed* one. *(Eco, 1981b: 8)*

Any text will, at the lowest level, explicitly select a possible Model Reader through "the choice (i) of a specific linguistic code, (ii) of a certain literary style, and (iii) of specific specialization-indices" (1981b: 7). The *closed* text will also try to eliminate the scope of interpretation by reducing the amplitude of possible reader positions within the text to a minimum. At the opposite extreme, an *open* text will use its potential as a generator to cooperate with the reader on a common project of meaning production.

> You cannot use the text as you want, but only as the text wants you to use it. An open text, however "open" it be, cannot afford whatever interpretation.
> An open text outlines a "closed" project of its Model Reader as a component of its structural strategy.   *(Eco, 1981b: 9).*

According to Eco the separation of *closed* and *open* texts is not an absolute one. It is a relative differentiation, where one has to talk about more or less "closed" texts and more or less "open" texts.

Modes of storytelling

Traditionally we distinguish between the genre of didactic presentation that belongs to the area of faction and the genres of poetry, drama, and the epic that belong to the area of fiction. But recently we have seen a lot of hybrids — drama-documentaries used for didactic purposes and news told in story form.

Basically the didactic genre aims at a direct relationship with the receiver. The communication takes place on equal terms, though the Sender may address his or her Addressee like a teacher, from a position of greater knowledge, but always taking into account the assumptions of the pupils.

From a similar perspective, poetry as a genre can be characterized as basically Sender-focused and concerned with the expression of the subjective views of the author. The Sender issues the message directly to the audience, but the interaction of the Addressee is only taken into account to a modest degree.

In drama the Sender produces the Message as an act performed in front of the Addressee. Addressing the audience directly is usual only in prologues and epilogues. There is no moderator to translate and interpret the performed action, and each performed episode takes place in real time — at least when we are dealing with live theater, and not with films or television.

One characteristic of the epic genre is the presence of a narrator to facilitate the communication of the "acted" to the reader/listener/viewer. The narrator is encoded by the Sender into the Message and decoded by the Addressee as an integrated feature, not necessarily identical with the author.

The narrator is a translator or interpreter. He or she is the one who advocates the relevance of the story told, but at the same time his or her presence creates a space for reflection upon the "acted" event.

Here we are not dealing with the few occasions where the author (the narrator) directly addresses the audience, as in the opening chapter of each book of Fielding's *Tom Jones.* A Danish novel *Lucky Peer,* by Henrik Pontoppidan adopted for the stage a few years ago, illustrates very clearly what it is all about. In the novel the reader is able to reflect on the life and experiences of Lucky Peer together with the narrator (the author), but in the play he or she, as part of the audience, is only able to identify with the protagonist. It is for the very same reason that Bertolt Brecht introduces an epic element into his anti-Aristotelian drama.

Eco (1981b: 27) distinguishes between plot and "fabula," seeing "fabula" as "the basic story stuff, the logic of actions or the syntax of characters, the time-oriented course of event," whereas the plot is said to be "the story as actually told, along with all its deviations, digressions, flashbacks, and the whole of the verbal devices." In this perspective, plot becomes superior to "fabula", but as far as I can see it also incorporates the narrator and the narrative, not just the narrated. From an analytical point of view, I prefer to see the plot as a combination of "fabula" and "premise" (premise being the morally-oriented statement to be argued by the narrated) for the story told.

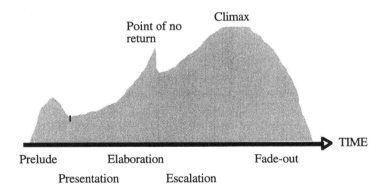

Fig. 9. 1. Linear model of storytelling.

The narrator is not part of the plot. He or she belongs to the level of structure and form, whereas the plot is part of the content, expressing the essential idea of the narrated. In other words, the narrator and narrative are instruments that the author — the Sender — may use in order to present his or her text as a more or less *closed* or *open* one to the "reader" — the Addressee — to "invest in" and communicate with.

Storytelling in Western civilization and especially in modern Western mass communications has been dominated by the linear model presented in Figure 9. 1. The epic slowly builds up a dramatic tension ending in a climax and a fading out.

This model is not necessarily identical with a "closed" text, but very often texts using the linear model end up as rather "closed." The linear structure emphasises a logical, causal universe with a stable system of deixis (I/you/ here/now) and with no direct addressing of the reader to disturb his or her illusion of being in a fictious world. The narrator will often (but not necessarily) be a discreet third person, following close behind the protagonist. He remains in position to comment both on the thoughts and the behaviour of the protagonist. The dominant premise for the story told is that ir should prove something and convince the reader/listener/viewer.

The Danish drama critic Birgitte Hesselaa (1988) calls the linear model a one-dimensional dramaturgy and describes its effects as the authorized dramaturgical intercourse, referring to the similarity between the linear model and the diagram for the male orgasm (Figure 9. 2).

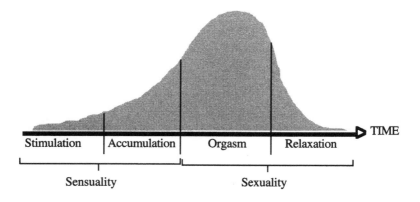

Fig 9. 2. Diagram for the male orgasm.

To emphasis her points, she also quotes a diagram for the female orgasm (Figure 9. 3) and compares it to a wave model (Figure 9. 4, reproduced from Harms Larsen 1990) — also called a circular or spiral model for dramaturgy.

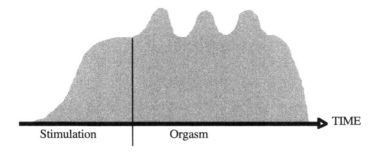

Fig. 9. 3. Diagram for the female orgasm.

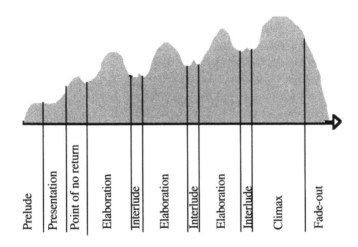

Fig. 9. 4. Wave model of storytelling.

This wave model becomes circular and even turns into a spiral when the episodes are dealing with problems not organized on a line one after the other, but in a recurrent and even escalating manner. Women authors have often used this model and have been accused of not writing dramatically, but the model may also be found in the fine arts and especially in many modern texts.

Circular dramaturgy will often create an alogical final universe with un-stable deixis and with narrated comments directly addressed to the audience, thus constantly reminding the reader/listener/viewer of the fact that she or he is "reading" a text, not participating in a fantastic fictious world. The narrator will often be more sophisticated with a limited perspective, for example, a first-person narrator. The dominant aim of the story will be to test and to analyze a problem.

Modes of reception

Closed and open texts — linear and circular dramaturgy. As argued here, there is a relationship between them, but they are not synonymous — even though both concepts are dealing with reception. As emphasized by Groeben(1980), in his terminology of "amplitude" and "margin of interpretation," and by Eco, in his reference to "the difference in codes by the Sender and the Addressee," the same text can be read in different ways.

A Norwegian investigation into the sociology of readers (Noreng, 1974) has shown that novels considered as fine art, in this case Hamsun's *Hunger* and Moberg's *The Emigrants,* can be read in different ways, primarily according to one's educational background. Readers from the working class, farmers, and fishermen read literature within a historical-sociological framework, whereas middle class readers with a more advanced school education behind them, read within a psychological-individualistic framework. The interpretations they apply to the novels are within the acceptable "margin" or scope, but compared to the "known" intentions of the authors, a historical-sociological interpretation does not apply to Hamsun, but is applicable to Moberg, and the reverse is true with a psychological-individualistic interpretation.

Nevertheless, there will normally be a close relationship between the mode of narration and the structuring of the plot, as indicated above. Closed texts narrated in a linear mode usually offer a "fascinative" mode of reception. According to Bernfeld (1928) fascination is a psychological condition in which the Ego for a time gives up control over the Self. He or she becomes disposed for identification with other characters — for example, in fiction. Or to put it the other way round, "reading" fiction of a persuasive kind places the reader in a state of fascination. The reader becomes absorbed in the universe of the text. When the "reading" stops, the fascination is over and so is the identification with the fictious characters (a secondary identification in Freudian terms).

In contradistinction to fascination, a contemplative mode of reception is created by open texts and circular dramaturgy. Horkheimer & Adorno (1944) refer to the scene of the Odyssey where Ulysses sails past the Sirens tied firmly to the mast of his ship, as the scenario for contemplation. He enjoys his new experiences and his consciousness is filled with them, but he never loses self-control and follows his deep unconscious desires. Contemplation is a mood in which the recipient reflects and reconsiders his or her own achievements and desires in relation to the fictious world presented. Self-control is never at risk. On the contrary, the new aesthetic experiences are seen as an extension of the mind. Any identification takes place at the Freudian primary level (unconscious dream images and fantasies from childhood) and tertiary level (revival of the authorities of our childhood — normally the father figure).

Through the concept of "Verfremdung" Brecht (1957) presents a series of dramatic techniques for achieving contemplation. His basic concern is to avoid fascination. He accuses the audience in the traditional Aristotelian of exchanging a world full of contradictions for one of harmony — not a known one, but one of which they can dream. Instead, Brecht wants to create a in which the social processes are exposed to the audience in such a way that they lose familiarity and become open to intervention. Through "Verfremdung" in character performance, the use of songs to comment on the plot and of an epic storyteller to unite the dramatic episodes, he creates a space for comment and reflection in his dramatic productions. Brecht's ideas for an anti-Aristotelian drama in many ways open up the discussion of linear and circular dramaturgy, but at the same time they also anticipate the later discussions about open and closed texts.

Fiction and interaction

Let me now return to our initial question about computer art and interactive fiction. Computer games have basically the same characteristics as other games and the gamblers react as described earlier, with reference to Gadamer. When the game is on, the gamblers abandon their self-control and become part of the game — the game becomes the active subject. This process is very similar to the secondary identification we meet in the reception of fiction — especially in closed texts narrated in the linear mode. The reader/listener/viewer gives up his or her Ego for a while and starts living through the fictious protagonist.

When computer games are most successful, they are able to combine both the features of the game and those of the identification in fiction. Through simulation, the gambler can identify with a fictious protagonist, which offers tremendous possibilities for the investment of dreams and fantasies within the restricted universe of the game. But to keep up the fascination, the interaction has to be reduced to movements of the joystick or other such simple functions that can be performed almost as reflexes.

Interaction at a more sophisticated level will break the illusions necessary for the mode of fascination. As soon as the choices become more open, the recipient will become reflective and conscious. He or she will be placed in the mode of contemplation. If computer fiction wants to give real opportunities for interaction, the texts have to be open and consequently the narration will become more circular.

Computer fiction ought to accept this limitation and try to explore the possibilities of contemplative art. The computer medium — alone or in cooperation with other media as multi-media — has an enormous potential for creating interactive fiction to explore epistemological problems.

Bibliography

ALLEN, R. C. (1987). Reader-Oriented Criticism and Television, In *Channels of Discourse. Television and Contemporary Criticism*, ed. R.C. Allen. London: Routledge.

BANG, J (1983). Flugten til det "indre" Amerika, [The escape to the inner of America] *Netværk — ord, billeder og handling i kommunikationssamfundet,* Herning: Systime.

BERNFELD, S. (1928). Über Faszination, In *Antiautoritäre Erziehung und Psycholanalyse. Ausgewählte Schriften. Band 1,* Frankfurt/Main: Märtz Verlag, 1969.

BOOTH, W.C. (1961). *The Rhetoric of Fiction,* Chicago: University of Chicago Press.

BRECHT, B. (1957). *Schriften zum Theater.* S.Unseld ed. Frankfurt a. M.: Suhrkamp Verlag. English version in *Brecht on . The Development of an Aesthetic,* ed J. Willett. London: Methuen.

ECO, U. (1976). *A Theory of Semiotics.* Bloomington: Indiana University Press.

ECO, U. (1981). *The Role of the Reader.* London: Hutchinson, (Italian edition 1979).

EGRI, L. (1946). *The Art of Dramatic Writing,* New York: Simon & Schuster (revised an reprinted 1960).

FISH, S. (1980). *Is There a Text in This Class?.* Cambridge, Mass. & London: Harvard University Press.

FISKE, J., J. HARTLEY (1978). *Reading Television.* London & New York: Methuen.

FISKE, J. (1987). *Television Culture.* London: Methuen.

FROM, F. (1973). Om vort behov for historier, [About our need for stories] *Politikens Kronik 23. september, 1973 .* Copenhagen: Dagbladet Politiken.

GADAMER, H-G. (1960). *Wahrheit und Methode,* Tübingen: J.C.B. Mohr (Paul Siebeck). (English edition:*Truth and Method.* New York: Seabury Press, 1975)

GROEBEN, N. (1980). *Rezeptionsforschung als empirische Literaturwissenschaft.* Tübingen: Gunther Narr Verlag.

GOODMAN, N. (1976). *Language of Art: An Approach to a Theory of Symbols.* Indianapolis, Ind.: Hackett.

HESSELAA, B. (1988). "Kan detektiver synge?"[Can detectives sing?], *Kritik 85,* 41-58, Copenhagen: Gyldendal .

HORKHEIMER, M., T. W. ADORNO (1944). *Dialektik der Aufklärung.* Frankfurt am Main: S. Fisher Verlag 1969 (English edition: *Dialectic of Enlightenment,* New York: Herder & Herder, 1972)

INGARDEN, R. (1930). *Das Literarische Kunstwerk.* Tübingen: Max Niemeyer Verlag. (English edition: *The Literary Work of Art.* Evanston, Ill.: Northwestern University Press, 1973).

ISER, W. (1974). *The Implied Reader.* Baltimore Md.: Johns Hopkins University Press.

ISER, W. (1976). *Der Akt des Lesens.* München: Wilhelm Fink Verlag. (English edition: *The Act of Reading: A Theory of Aesthetic Response.* Baltimore Md.: Johns Hopkins University Press).

JAUSS, H. R. (1977). *Ästetiche Erfarung und literarische Hermeneutik 1.* München: Wilhelm Fink Verlag. (English edition: *Aesthetic Experience and Literary Hermeneutics.* Minneapolis: University of Minnesota Press).

LARSEN, P. Harms. (1990) *Faktion — som udtryksmiddel.* Copenhagen: Forlaget Amanda.

LEARCH, E. (1973). *Culture and Communication.* Cambridge: Cambridge University Press.

NORENG, Ø. (1974). *Lesere og lesing. Rapport om Den norske Bokklubbens leser-sosiologiske undersøkelse.* Oslo: Den norske bokklubben.

OLSEN, M. & G. KELSTRUP, eds. (1981). *Værk og læser.* Copenhagen: Borgen/Basis.

RICOEUR, P. (1978). *The Rule of Metaphor.* London: Routledge and Kegan Paul.

RICOEUR, P. (1981). *Hermeneutics and the Human Sciences. Essays on language, action and intertations.* Cambridge & New York: Cambridge University Press.

RICOEUR, P. (1984). *Time and Narrative,* Chigago: The University of Chigago Press.

VALE, E. (1982). *The Technique of Screen & Television Writing.* New York: Simon & Schuster.

10

Face to interface

BERIT HOLMQVIST

In the field of interactive fiction the concept of *interaction* is not just pertinent; it is crucial. An apparently trivial but nonetheless important problem
arises every time we talk about interactive fiction. We do not know what to
call the "user" of the system. It does not feel right to say that one is *using* a
piece of fiction. So we sometimes say *reader* instead. But since we are
mostly working with pictures and even with animation, it might be better to
say *viewer*. But again there is something wrong. A reader and a viewer are
physically passive, while a user of a computer system is active, by definition.

The problem of understanding what happens when people interact with
computer systems is not a new one, nor is it specific to interactive fiction. In
the history of traditional systems development and interface design, the
problem has been tackled by the use of different metaphors. Although these
metaphors have been fruitful within the context of non-fiction systems, they
are part of a dysfunctional metaphorical inheritance that we must, if not get
rid of, then at least try to transform into something workable. When we talk
about interactive media, we are in fact stuck with at least three inherited and
very different metaphors: a *dialogue* partner, a *tool*, and a *media* metaphor.
These three different metaphors are bound up with at least three different
concepts of interaction.

Interaction as dialogue

The dialogue partner perspective stems from verbal communication. Here, interaction means that two or more people participate in the process of creating a discourse. The underlying metaphor for the machine is a human being
participating in a dialogue with the user. It is probably this metaphor which
has given the manipulation of the computer the name man-machine interaction. The metaphor stems from the days when you actually wrote commands
in some kind of restricted language and received verbal answers from the
machine. The metaphor is used to compare the machine to an intelligent or-

ganism. The main point is that you get the illusion of a cooperative process. The user *interacts with* the computer.

Interaction as action

With the Xerox and Macintosh object-oriented design, the linearity of discourse is replaced by the non-linearity of a picture. Instead of writing commands in accordance with explicit syntax rules, you are now manipulating objects on a desk top in a seemingly free order with implicit rules. The word interaction was divorced from its cooperative meaning and the metaphor died. You do not cooperate with a garbage can. Now the underlying metaphor is that of a tool. The direct manipulation style creates an illusion of total control on the part of the user. The user does not interact, he *acts on* the computer.

Interaction as interpretation

A fruitful, analytical tool to evaluate and design user interfaces is to look upon computers as mass media. The perspective derives from literary criticism or mass media research. You disregard the machine as an interactive device and focus instead on the relationship between the systems designer and the user. The former is seen as the creator of a symbolic representation of the world and as a transmitter of messages and the latter as receivers and interpreters of the message. Here, interaction means the mental process of the readers *interpretation* of the author's intended *meaning*.

Since the title of this book is "The Computer as a Medium," one would expect the mass media metaphor to be fundamental. But when trying to achieve an understanding of what interactive media actually are, we shall see that the above-mentioned metaphors are not mutually exclusive, merely different functions of the same phenomenon.

This chapter will discuss this issue, taking the definition of interactive fiction presented in Chapter 7 as its point of departure:

> a piece of fiction in which the physical movements of the reader are an intended and integrated part of the aesthetic experience through their influence on the course of events in the fiction.

Whatever perspective we choose and whatever type of application, even fiction, it always includes a physical process.

Contradictions to be solved

When we focus on the "fiction" side of interactive fiction, the *mass media metaphor* is fundamental of course. As with traditional media, such as films and books, we want to create a piece of art for the "user" to reflect on and be mentally stimulated by. But if "the physical movements of the reader are an intended and integrated part of the aesthetic experience through their influence on the course of events in the fiction," neither the mass media metaphor nor the tool metaphor can provide full understanding of the "interactive" side.

On the one hand, interactive fiction, no matter how interactive it may be, is a piece of mediated art created by somebody with specific intentions for somebody else to interpret and reflect on, so *we don't want the user to have full control over the story*. On the other hand, if the physical movements of the reader should be an integrated part of the story, the direct manipulation style, and thereby the tool metaphor, is almost a prerequisite for interactive fiction, especially if it is based on pictures. *We want the user to have full and direct control over the machine.*

The situation of having full control over the machine but not over the story could, in fact, be compared to the situation in a dialogue. Normally you have "full" control over your means of expression (sounds) related to your intended content (words), but you cannot fully control what effect your action will have on your dialogue partner. You can only guess.

So in interactive fiction, all three metaphors seem to be involved. You manipulate objects on the screen as when using a tool, you interact with the fiction as you would in a dialogue, and you interpret the events as you would in a film or in other traditional media.

In dealing with the narrative system presented in Chapter 6 we worked with the idea of letting the user "drive" the story in three different "gears" corresponding to the three different perspectives. The *editor* gear was based on the tool perspective, and the interaction style was standard Macintosh interaction with a few refinements. The role of the reader was somewhat like an author composing the story (the idea is used in several computer games). The materials he worked on were not fictitious characters, but pieces of paper displaying people he could move around on the scene and whose postures he could change. If he did this successfully he was taken over to the *participant* gear that was based on the dialogue perspective. The reader was a part of the fiction, and his possible courses of action were equal to those of the other actors. He no longer interacted with cardboard drawings, but with (fictitious) characters. The role of the user was that of a *co-actor* who, for instance, could act as the helper or the enemy of the protagonist; if he did this in a meaningful way, he would as a reward enter the *spectator* gear, which was based on the mass media perspective. The user could, in principle, only view the event. Technically, the spectator gear could be realized by a "slide show" of pictures shown in sequence, or by means of a real-time video clip being played on the screen.

This idea grew out of the fact that we realized the necessity of being aware of the different perspectives so as not to get hemmed in by them. But the jump from an analytical insight to a conclusion of construction was too abrupt. We did not solve the problem; on the contrary, in trying to escape it we made it worse. By making the boundaries between the different perspectives concrete, we sharpened them instead of dissolving them.

However, if computer-based serious fiction is to be exciting, we have to bridge the gulf between them. *The naturalness of manipulating a tool must be turned into the naturalness of manipulating the story.*

This means that we cannot be satisfied with pure analogies; we have to develop and adapt the theories and methods of older media to the sphere of the computer. In the traditional media perspective, the result of the mental interaction lies outside the system, in the mind of the user. The user can only influence the content part of the sign. However, behind the very concept of interaction lies the fundamental fact that the user participates in the creation of signs, which means that he influences both the expression and the content part of the sign vehicle.

The drama perspective

With the mass media perspective taken from film and literature, we have the problem of the "dead" interface. The actors in the film are not influenced by the audience, no matter how much they weep or laugh. And in the same way, the author of a novel does not change his mind and offer me another story, if I throw the book away.

A closer analogy might be the theater. In the theater there are real human beings on the stage and real human beings in the audience. A film is the same every night, but a play changes with the mood of the audience and the actors. Living bodies are interacting in the same room. If we extend the theater analogy to involve the user as an actor, we come slightly closer.

The American interactivist Brenda Laurel has most convincingly presented the Aristotelian concept of *drama* as a very productive metaphor for systems design (Laurel, 1986, 1991). The means by which a drama makes representations is signs. The manner in which the signs are produced is enactment (acting out instead of telling or describing). It is possible to generalize the concept of enactment from the actor's manner of producing signs so as also to cover the representation of the user's physical interaction with the system. That means that we turn the user into an actor. But what role can we assign to the user? Well, one place to start is with rhythm.

Rhythm plays a crucial role in all forms of physical interaction (Buxton, 1986), as well as in the interplay between the play and its audience. The rhythm created by the shifts between silence, laughter, and applause interferes with the rhythm of the performance. The role of the audience is that of a back-channel. The feedback is a symptom of the audience's satisfaction or dissatisfaction and therefore creates *indexical* signs.

In computer games the fascination is built on the winner-loser paradigm. And winning means mastering interaction and its rhythm. In many games the mastery of body movements seems to be the superior source of enactment. Interactive rhythm in this respect very much resembles the feed-back function, but we can go one step further and let it be interpretable within the fiction, and exploit tensions between rhythm and content, as we can observe in verse, thus letting rhythm be part of a *symbolizing* activity.

Since there is no standard code for the interpretation of interactive rhythm available, one solution might be to design rhythm as a motivated sign that the reader can interpret by means of his experiences of the real world. We can give the user a point of departure in his own everyday experiences, as that will enable him to give meaning to the events in the story.

For example, if you want to catch a butterfly with your bare hands in the real world, you have to move very quietly and close your hands around it tenderly so that it does not escape and its wings are not hurt. A double click with the mouse will not do. In Chapter 6 we illustrated this idea by programming a butterfly so that it could read the speed of the mouse. If the user is too fast, the butterfly flies away. If he moves the mouse quietly, the butterfly will sit still, but in order to catch it the user has to press the mouse button and hold it down for a while. If he lets go of the mouse button too early the butterfly will escape. Another example is mentioned in Chapter 11, where different degrees of mobility in the Bronze Age landscape can be symbolized by differentiation in the speed with which the surface can be searched. These real life experiences could be used to make the physical interaction a meaningful part of the interactive narrative.

The drama perspective is fruitful in other respects too. It can be a source for the aesthetics of formalisms. In the neo-classical drama represented by Moliére and Holberg we have a most sophisticated system of formalisms (as described in Jens Hougaards article on the theater in the eighteenth century in the present volume). Chapter 7 even suggests theatrical gestures or postures to be a possible substance, on which methods used in artificial intelligence can be used to *form* the performance.

But the Aristotelian concept of drama creates problems in other respects.

Laurel claims that the user of interactive fiction, like the audience of ancient drama, is not interested in seeing what happens backstage but wants to enter a universe and stay within it. One definite requirement for her is first-personness.

> First-personess is most completely realized at the extreme end of each of the interactive variables' continuum: Frequency is continuous: range is infinite: significance is maximal. *(Laurel, 1986: 79)*

But of course there must be constraints, otherwise there will be no drama, but

> Constraints should be applied without shrinking interactive range or significance as experienced by the user. They should limit, not what the user can do, but what the user is likely to think of doing. Context is the most effective medium for presenting such constraints. *(Laurel, 1986: 81)*

This, in fact, is the same philosophy that lies behind the tool perspective. In the tool perspective, there should not be any doubts about what to do, even if the possibilities for action are many.

Creating contexts, then, is seen as the author's means of keeping control over the story. But as long as the author is seen as a kind of demiurge setting the stage (creating context) for actors and users to act on, we cannot move very far from ritualized or habitual behaviour. And that is exactly what we want to do in interactive fiction, if we stick to the characteristics outlined in the introduction to this chapter.

Furthermore, the drama is not sufficient as a point of reference, since the participants in interactive fiction cannot fully be compared to the actors and the audience. The reason is that, even if we equate enactment with rhythm and we design motivated signs to turn the enactment into a symbolizing activity, it does not fully solve the problem that the reader can influence both the content and the expression part of the sign. The user's actions are not just part of the story at the narrative level. By acting *in* the story as the actors do, he acts *on* it at the same time. He produces meta-signs because he is the subject in the meta-narrative concerned with directing the actors and setting the stage. The object he desires is a good story, as does an audience, but he himself is partly responsible for the outcome.

Furthermore, if inter-textuality where meaning arises not *in* certain contexts but *between* them is one of the forces in interactive fiction, as it is claimed in the introduction to this chapter, then context cannot be a good tool for creating restrictions. It might, for example, be very difficult to predict what the user will do when he is confronted with two contradictory contexts. In modern literature there are many examples of experimentation with context. One is *The French Lieutenant's Woman* by John Fowles, where three different views of a certain historical period are presented and inter-mingled; the level on which the story takes place, a fictitious love story; the level on which the author comments on the Victorian age and tries to explain the differences in moral attitudes, natural science and social structure betwe-en the nineteenth and the twentieth centuries; and the level on which he comments on how to write and read a novel. Another is *The Alexandria Quartet* by Lawrence Durrell where the same events in time are presented from the point of view of three different main characters. There is no reason why this type of storytelling could not be a point of departure for interactive fiction.

The idea of the computer as a collage medium, if we adhere once more to one of the norms presented in the introduction, also contradicts the claim that the user should not be able to influence the context. For example, it is by no means self-evident that the relationship between foreground and background should always be the same. Chapter 11 illustrates this idea by sometimes allowing an animal in the landscape to be foreground and at other times allowing the landscape itself to be foreground.

If we want to stay within the world of the theater, it might be a better idea to exchange Aristotle for Brecht. The computer medium encourages a form of story-telling more in line with his reflective tradition and concept of "Verfremdung." Here the audience constantly is forced back to "reality" when absorption is at it's climax. And in fact the changes of context are de-liberately used to create "Verfremdung."

This type of staging is not linear like the classical drama but spiral (cf. Bang in Chapter 9). It does not follow a logical progression of cause and ef-fect, but tries to treat many different aspects of the same problem. It has a plot and a progression in time, but the different layers make one stop the clock and add some new pieces to the interpretation.

If the theater of the eighteenth century (cf. Jens Hougaard in Chapter 8) could be a source of formalization for the denotation of the signs, the spiral composition of the twentieth century might be a source for connotations (cf. Andersen and Holmqvist in Chapter 7). In interactive fiction, this type of staging brings us closer to solving the problem of the balance between the reader and the author on the one hand, and the balance between the actor and the user on the other. And it also strengthens the question mark I placed after the claim that the audience would not be interested in what happens backstage. This is a question that Per Aage Brandt – when writing about the difference between a tool and a machine – turns into the claim that "[...] there is necessarily a specific instance of *semiosis*, in which the subject has to rely on interpretative representations of what events and instances control inherently the machine's performance [..]" (Chapter 5). The user is constantly trying to understand what is happening backstage in order to understand what is going on and what action to take.

Art and cognition

Human cognition is a rather complicated affair that takes place on many interacting "levels." These levels are characterized by different activities. The intra-organic level (organ) that controls our direct senses (sight, hearing, smelling, feeling), the inter-organic level (the body) that controls how we coordinate our different organs to be able to transport ourselves (walk, to jump, to run), the body-object level that controls our manipulation of physical objects (eating food, emptying a garbage can), the inter-body level (the group) that controls our interaction with other living beings (embracing, discussing), and finally the inter-group level that concerns our meta-activities (realising, comprehending) relating to "civilization" (law, literature, religion).[1] The goal of interactive fiction is to incorporate all levels into a composite icon in an aesthetically exciting way.

Art, of course, invites meta-activities, it is its whole essence. But at the same time, different art forms can be seen as icons for percepts linked to different cognitive levels — icons of our being in the world. Thus, a still picture or painting is an icon of our visual perception of the world from a fixed position (sight), a film is an icon of our perception when we move (walking). Peter Bøgh Andersen has extended the media metaphor and given it an interactive dimension by introducing a classification of computer- based signs, among which a particular kind has "handling" as a distinctive feature (Andersen 1990 and Chapter 1). These are Interactive signs, signs that the user can manipulate and change, and a computer system can then be seen as an icon of our physical manipulation of the world around us.

The classification gives us a better understanding of many traditional applications, from word processing to computer games. Peter Bøgh Andersen points out that conventions for relating content to different forms of expression exist within different genres. The problem is that most genres do not climb to the top of the ladder of human cognition, even if some computer games signal their intention of going further than just killing dragons or space ships. Finally, epic drama is an icon for our meta level (reflecting, realizing). The only level that is missing is the inter-body level. Interactive fiction

---

[1] I owe this interpretation to Per Aage Brandt. Cf. also Gardener's theory of multiple intelligences in Chapter 11.

should incorporate that level, too. It is my belief that the notion of dialogue is the missing link.

The dialogue

Normally we reserve the notion of dialogue for face-to-face interaction. What we deal with in interactive fiction is obviously not a *face-to-face* situation, but rather a *face-to-interface* situation. But if we define dialogue as a situation where somebody intentionally performs a (semiotic) act, aiming at somebody else who notices that intention and performs another (semiotic) act in return, it is not really difficult to think of the interaction with the computer system in terms of a dialogue.

Per Aage Brandt claims that "As a machine is not a piece of pure nature, but rather an arranged disposition which makes use of natural processes and the possible gearing of its energetics for certain *purposes*, the user cannot but feel guided by an already instantiated, implemented *intentionality*." (Brandt in Chapter 5). If this claim is true, there is a symbolic dimension relating the user to the designer of the computer system .

The following definition of what happens when people talk to each other *could* be used as a metaphor for what happens when people interact with a computer system.

> In conversation participants use language to interpret to each other the significance of actual and potential events that surround them and to draw consequences for their past and future actions.   *(Labov & Fanshel, 1977: 30)*

In interactive fiction as well as in conversation, the actions presuppose interpretations of previous ones and speculations about subsequent ones. The difference is that in conversation the process usually has consequences for real life actions — the result of conversation lies outside the actual exchange, while in interactive fiction you draw consequences for the actions to be taken in the interaction with the system. This is more like thinking aloud. Joseph Weizenbaum, who created the computer-based psychologist "Eliza," was worried when he discovered that users treated the computer as a human doctor. He thought they believed the computer to be human. I think he underestimated the users. Of course they knew they were talking to a machine, but that made them secure. Without any risk of being misunderstood by an authoritarian doctor, they could reveal their innermost thoughts, as if they were talking to themselves. When you are talking to yourself, you try to objectify your thoughts. You listen to your thoughts in spoken form to try them out or study the result. If you are not satisfied, you can try to reformulate them and study the result again, and so on. The problem with any form of conversation, though, is that you cannot freeze the process. In a computer system, however, this process is visible.

The result of the "conversation" stays within the system and is visible as a process on the screen. So the product is, if not same as the process, an icon of it. This means that the system is not only an icon of the user's interaction with the author of the system (the inter-body level), but is simultaneously an icon of the meta level too. Which, in turn, means that the system is an icon for the user's reflections on, and thoughts about, the overall message.

The apparatus perspective

This last statement forces me to introduce another metaphor, since reintroducing the dialogue-partner perspective does not circumvent the problem that we are dealing with an (interactive) artifact. If we want to retain the dialogue partner perspective, it will have to be incorporated into the composite icon.

Umberto Eco once defined literature as a machine for generating interpretations (Eco, 1977). It is a good metaphor that might be even more applicable to the computer. But there remains the problem of physical interaction. It is not the machine alone that generates interpretation; the user does so, too.

To be able to place the dialogue partner perspective within the realm of interactive fiction, I will compare the computer system to an *apparatus*, the totality of means by which a designated function is performed or a specific task executed. I will regard the system as a camera and its user as a photographer. The reason for choosing the camera is that it incorporates all the cognitive levels in a very concrete sense.

To these levels it is possible to assign different types of prostheses (Eco, 1985): You can use binoculars to see with, a bicycle to move about on, tools such as knives and forks to eat with, and a television set to obtain information about the world from.

In a camera, you use the viewfinder to see with. You do not move your body, as on a bicycle, but different lenses make it possible for you to move closer to or further away from the objects. You press the button to let light onto the film — you manipulate a physical object — and in the end you get a finished photograph, a piece of art that is intended to provide new insights into the world.

And finally, a camera is programmed for special purposes, just like a computer system, so its user enters into a dialogue, in the sense suggested here.

If we return to the three old metaphors, we can describe the difference between them as a question of power. In the tool perspective the power lies in the hands of the user: There are many tools, and Man can choose according to his needs. The tool is a variant and Man the invariant. The worker is superordinate to the tools. In the mass-media perspective the power lies in the hands of the designer. The machine performs the same task irrespective of which worker controls it. The machine is the invariant, the user the variant and subordinated to the machine. In the dialogue partner perspective, however, the power lies in the hands of the interlocutors as a function of a given context. This very much resembles Vilém Flusser's (1983) description of the camera. He argues that the camera is not a tool, but a toy, the photographer not a worker, but a player. A player that plays "against" his toy, not with it. He puts his head into the camera to find out what tricks are hidden there. Flusser claims that this is a new kind of relationship in which man is neither a variant nor an invariant, but that man and apparatus are functionally united. Therefor he wants to call the photographer the functionary of the apparatus.

So the relation between the camera and the functionary can be compared to the relation between the dialogue and the speaker. The camera is not a tool but a toy, and so is a computer used for fiction. The photographer is not playing with his toy, but playing against it. He neither uses it as an extension of his body, like a carpenter with his hammer, nor lets himself be seduced by it's shining surface, like the audience of a classical play. He is actually interested in what happens backstage, as I suggest that the user of interactive fiction should be.

The camera metaphor does not contradict the drama metaphor but combines the notion of enactment with the notion of mental and physical interaction. A photographer does not just mechanically press the button; before doing and while doing so, he does a lot of "acting out." If we look at a photographer in action we se him moving around almost as a hunter with a spear in his hand.

The photographer is hunting for a good picture, and the user of interactive fiction is hunting for a good story. But good pictures do not exist out there, independently of the photographer and the camera. A beautiful sunset does not automatically turn into a good picture when you press the button. If you do not know what kind of toy you have in your hand, the result will probably not be of any interest. This is what Flusser is referring to when he writes that the photographer is playing against the camera. He sees the designer as an *opponent* in Greimas' sense.

At the systems design level, the idea of the user and designer playing "against" each other can be conceptualized as a vector-field, as described in Chapter 1 and 11: "The system is very literally caught in two large force fields: The designer pulls the system in one direction, the user in another" (Chapter 11).

Anyone who has used a camera would agree that "what you see is *not* what you get." As an example, consider the spatial dimension: you take a picture of your beloved daughter from a distance of 2 meters, but when you see the final result, it looks as if she is standing 5 meters away and you can hardly see that she is smiling; furthermore, if you have not been focusing correctly, the flagpole behind her may steal the whole picture. Or take the problem of moving objects: You want to take a picture of your dog at play, but before you have pressed the button, the dog is on its way out of the picture, and what you get is a blurred picture of its waving tail. The examples are endless. In daily life we are surrounded by rapid courses of events, unposed events. The photographer is looking for not yet discovered possibilities within the programme of the camera, trying to produce "impossible" pictures (Flusser, 1983). Therefore, in order to be a good photographer, he has to outwit the "programmer," and in order to be able to do that you have to understand what happens backstage.

Photography has taught us that hidden among the unposed daily life events are moments that, when isolated and taken out of context, give new meanings (Arnheim, 1986). I see this as an ideal for interactive fiction. In order to reach this ideal, we have to place the designer and the user in a communicative relationship. Flusser (1983) makes a comparison between programs and myths, where he describes myths as a ritualization of a prehistoric life-model and programs as a ritualization of a contemporary life-model; contemporary magic. The difference between them is that myths are orally transmitted by authors who are "Gods," — someone who is standing outside the communicative process. Programs are models that are communicated in written form by people that are inside the communicative process (Flusser, 1983).

When Laurel argues that context is the most effective way of creating restrictions, she moves into prehistoric magic. But if for a moment we accept that "God is dead,"we might be able to get a better understanding of what interactive fiction might possibly be. At least it could give us a better understanding of the process as being almost identical with the product. Flusser (1983) describes photographing as an act of communication, and remarks that communication consists of to phases, one in which information is produced and one which store the information. The first one is what we call a dialogue, and the second one what we call a discourse. During a dialogue, different pieces of information are synthesized (process) and the discourse is the phase where the information produced by the dialogue is distributed (product). If we apply this description to interactive fiction the dialogue equals the user's hunting for a good story and the discourse the result of his reading.

With the apparatus as a metaphor we have given the author and the user equal status. They are both seen as functionaries of the artefact. Functionaries that interact via an apparatus.[2]

An author can be regarded as a functionary of the apparatus called "language," since he plays with the symbols within its program (system). In the same way the programmer plays with his programming language. The program is the author's means of expression, the physical interaction is the user's means of expression, and both the program and the physical manipulation are somehow the functionaries' interpretation of the world through the apparatus.

Rudolf Arnheim (1986) puts it in a slightly different but very beautiful way:

> ...the authentically photographic still life is an open segment of a world that continues in all directions beyond the limits of the picture. And the viewer, instead of merely admiring the artist's invention, also acts as an explorer, an indiscreet intruder into the privacy of nature and human activity, curious about the kind of life that has left its traces and searching for telltale clues.   (*Arnheim, 1986:122*)

It looks as if the apparatus metaphor could be useful in our future work on interactive fiction.

Concluding remarks

My intention has not been to solve a very complex problem in the space of a few pages, but to assess past and present experiences in a search for some possible openings for the future. While writing this, I was struck by my own lack of imagination. I experienced an almost neurotic return to unsolved problems in my own little world of computer aesthetics. But as a matter of fact, the liberation from our historical inheritance is not an individual concern, it is a social process that can be seen in many places in the world around us.

Looking up from the computer and out of the windows of my office, I am forced to recognize that life of the drama has moved on since the time of Aristotle and Brecht. There are contemporary performing arts that have already transcended the borders of past and present aesthetics. In a building opposite my office window, an experimental theater group called Exment

---

[2] In Chapter 11 the camera metaphor is made very concrete: the interaction consists in moving a spot (lens) around.

has its studio. And in my hand I have a copy of its "declaration of independence."

I will let a quotation from that declaration close the circle:

Since the beginning of our work, this idea of independence and liberation has been a dominating feature: a departure from the naturalistic theater into the autonomous theater.

In the confrontation between autonomous expressions of art, we think we have found a physical and psychological language of *form*, in which the literary text and the logic of the story are of secondary importance. The form, the colour, the physical space and the movement are the elements that convey meaning in Exment's autonomous theater.

Bibliography

ANDERSEN, P. BØGH (1990). *A Theory of Computer Semiotics*. Cambridge: Cambridge University Press.

ANWARD, J. (1983). *Språkbruk och språkutveckling i skolan*. [Language usage and language development in school]. Lund: Liber.

ARNHEIM, R. (1986). *New Essays on the Pschycholgy of Art*. London: University of California Press.

BENTLEY, E. (1965). *The Life of the Drama..* Edinburgh: Methuen & Co. Paperback version 1969.

ECO, U. (1977). *A Theory of Semiotics*. London and Basingstoke: The Macmillan Press.

ECO, U. (1990/85). *Sugli Specchi e altri saggi*. Milan: Bompinai.

FLUSSER, V. (1983). Für eine Philosophie der Fotografie. In *European Photography*. Andreas Müller-Phole.

LABOV, W & D. FANSHEL (1977). *Theapeutic Discourse*. London: Academic Press.

LAUREL, B. (1986). Interface as Mimesis. In *User Centered System Design: New Perspectives on Human - Computer Interaction*, eds D.A. Norman and S. Draper. Hillsdale, New Jersey: Lawrence Erlbaum.

LAUREL, B. (1991). *Computers as Theater*. Reading, Mass.: Addison-Wesley.

11

Drawing and Programming

BJØRN LAURSEN AND PETER BØGH ANDERSEN

The authors of this chapter were involved in designing and constructing a multimedia system about the Scandinavia Bronze Age (on other ideas for multimedia applications in archaeology, see Chapter 12). The system was an advanced prototype, but near completion enough for us to be able to set it up in the museum and test user reactions. One of us was responsible for the graphics, the other for design and programming.

The system is implemented in Supercard 1.5. The design is complete, but at present the system only contains information about 70 items. It was tested at the local museum for a week. Two observers surveyed the users from an adjoining room; in addition, visitors to the museum guests were asked to fill in a questionnaire, and tape-recorded interviews were made on the spot. The system is in 8-bit color, so the black/white screen dumps in this section give only a partial impression of the real system.

The main system is for browsing and consists of four windows:

(1) A *Map* of Denmark and southern Sweden displaying locations of excavation sites.

(2) An imaginary *Landscape*. A drawing depicting an artist's view of how Bronze Age man might have viewed nature and society.

(3) A *Color Photo* window displaying color photos of archaeological finds.

(4) A *Verbal Information* window, with texts explaining the contents of the landscape and the photo window. The window also contains sound: the written texts are spoken, and the window provides samples of Bronze Age music.

The system contains two smaller subsystems. The *Mystery of the Razor* lets the user participate in solving the mystery of a Bronze Age razor, the idea being to demonstrate archaeological methods of interpretation. The purpose of the *History of Interpretations* is to show how the interpretation of finds depends on the time when the interpretation was made.

Landscape   Map

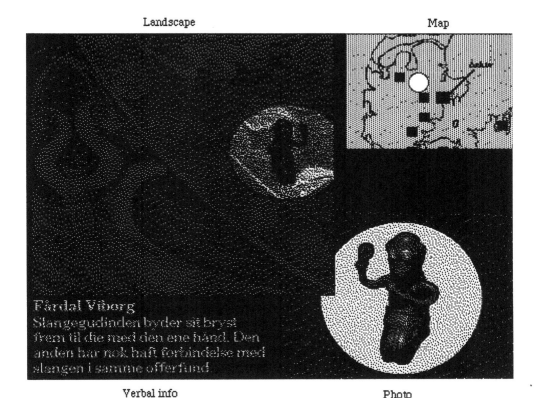

Verbal info   Photo

Fig. 11. 1. Main system consisting of four windows: Landscape, Map, Photo, and
Verbal Info windows.

One of the main points made in this chapter is that programming should *not*
be seen as an a posteriori technical way of implementing already existing
ideas. Most of the ideas in the chapter were generated in a close interplay
between author, artist, and programmer. The input from programming prevents the artist from being confined to paper ("Can we really do this?"),
while the artist prevents the programmer from playing with sophisticated
codes that have no communicative effect.

We have emphasised this point by systematically interspersing artistic
ideas with programming techniques. Furthermore, we have retained our different writing styles. Laursen's is more searching and associative,
Andersen's more matter-of-fact and goal-directed. The stylistic difference
indicates different ways of thinking, both of which are necessary for creating
interactive multimedia.

When the project started, Laursen was very interested in the theory of multiple intelligences advocated by Howard Gardner, and saw multimedia as a means of improving the integration of these intelligences. Multimedia are not a simple prosthesis for one of our senses, they are complex prostheses.

Laursen: A complex prosthesis

Eco refers to mirrors, spectacles, and binoculars as prostheses we trust in everyday life. He defines a prosthesis as any apparatus capable of widening the functional radius of an organ (Eco, 1990:37). It can be productive to think of the creation of a multimedia-system as the building of a complex prosthesis (on the notion of prostheses, see also Chapter 10), a provocative tool for interested individuals.

It operates by complex codes in the computer and activates networks of complex neural codes in the user's competences. It thereby influences many layers in the user's consciousness that react and interact. In this way, a "dialogue" is established between two global network structures, one developed in the user's body during his lifetime, and one constructed in the computer.

In this "dialogue", we experiment with bringing together codes from different layers of these global networks:

We work with the user's present-day perceptual habits, in contrast with the hypothetical configurations of Bronze Age optics, a kinaesthetic code (mouse-handling of the differently behaving objects), auditive codes (decoding various types of sounds), logical codes (why does the view angle change so often?), and linguistic codes (linguistic information).

The signals of these codes are influenced by the global structure formed in the user's mind and by the structure of the computer system that handles many simultaneous functions, depending on what the user is doing at any particular moment.

Gardner has persuasively argued for the following multiple intelligences (Gardner, 1985:73):

- linguistic intelligence
- musical intelligence
- logical-mathematical intelligence
- spatial intelligence
- bodily-kinaesthetic intelligence
- personal intelligence (intra- and interpersonal)

He suggests that the distribution and weight of these aspects of competence are culturally determined:

> Thus, one would expect that, in a traditional agrarian society, interpersonal, bodily-kinaesthetic, and linguistic forms of intelligence would be highlighted in informal educational settings which are largely "on site" and feature considerable observation and imitation. In a society in the early stages of industrialisation, one would anticipate traditional forms of schooling that focus on rote linguistic learning but where logical-mathematical forms of intelligence are beginning to be used. In highly industrialised societies, and in post-industrial society, one would predict a prizing of linguistic, logical-mathematical, and interpersonal forms of intelligence: quite probably, modern secular schools would be yielding to individual computerised instruction. *(Gardner, 1985: 384).*

If we view these competences as interactive ones, we can mix and combine these basic cultural codes in the multi medium, confronting the user with agrarian as well as post-industrial experiences. A multimedia system does not necessarily mirror the post-industrial culture in which it has been created. Critical epistemological elements can widen the hermeneutic space.

By exploiting variations, shifts and rapid fluctuations in the hierarchy of order and dominance of the competences suggested by Gardner, we can let the user enact the spectrum of intelligences characteristic of an agrarian culture, both in order to inform him of this society and to challenge his own contemporary repertoire.

The design of multimedia systems is a new didactic area in the challenge of training competences or intelligences. It opens up new possibilities for working with innovative use of symbols, an activity which many people try to avoid:

> There is in most populations little interest in innovative uses of symbol systems, in departures from the *status quo*. It is given to only a few individuals in most cultures to reach the apogee of symbolic competence and then to move off in unanticipated directions, experimenting with symbol systems, fashioning unusual and innovative symbolic products, perhaps even attempting to devise a new symbol system. *(Gardner 1985: 311)*

Multimedia could enhance innovative thinking by — directly or indirectly — exhibiting the potential dynamic structures in the two global networks mentioned above. The multimedia prosthesis could encourage the user to direct his thoughts along unexpected lines *and get used to it.*

Although we live in a world of change where focusing on *dynamic* aspects is relevant, we face severe didactic paradoxes in curricula that often favour static knowledge, instead of emphasising dynamic and innovative thinking.

Laursen: We only have hypotheses about the perception

It is not easy to find parallels between the global scenario of the Bronze Age and that of the computer. They are completely different. So much so, in fact, that we cannot envisage the differences with any authenticity.

Perceptually we are children of our own time as were the Bronze Age people of theirs. We face two very different epochs of history as well as two very different ways of perceiving the world, so the question we have to ask and put into visual form is:

What kind of perceptual patterns did the Bronze Age population develop, compared to our present ones? What did they pay special attention to? And what characterizes the patterns of perception of our own culture? How do we actually see the world around us?

Can we describe our present culture as perceptually homogeneous, without encountering serious problems? Or would it be more relevant to describe our culture as a highly complex network of people with different jobs, lives, and backgrounds, who on the one hand have developed individual optics to some extent, while on the other hand exploiting a certain number of shared perceptual patterns?

When designing multimedia-systems, it is epistemologically important to establish a clear contract with the user, so that the user is always aware of the fact that whatever visualization appears on the screen, it is to be regarded as a hypothesis: The visualization is always a non-final relevant possibility, but just one among several, as a general rule.

The important point is to establish a visualized scenario that indirectly supports the highly complex edifice of hypotheses in the user's inner scenario — a scenario that has been influenced sensorially by several hypotheses, all showing cognitively relevant, visualized alternatives.

Andersen: Interactive media invite multiple interpretations

These ideas are not unique to our project, but can be found in the works of other writers on interactive media. Interactive media seem to invite a post-modern, non-authoritarian type of teaching and writing.

> The arrival of hypertext is more than an advance in information technology. Seen from the viewpoint of textual theory, hypertext systems appear as the practical implementation of a conceptual movement that coincides with the late phase of modernity. This movement rejects authoritarian, "logo centric" hierarchies of language, whose modes of operation are linear and deductive, and seeks instead systems of discourse that admit a plurality of meanings, where the operative modes are hypotheses and interpretative plays and hierarchies are contingent and local.   *(Moulthrop 1989: 259)*

Similar ideas are put forward by Laurel, Oren and Don (1990), who advocate a conscious use of specific points of view when presenting information.

The possibility of physically manipulating the work of art seems to contradict the idea that there is one right way of writing or painting. If there were, why allow the reader or viewer to generate the other 100 lesser versions?

So the practice of presenting hypotheses, not fixed solutions, seems to accord with a trend within the medium itself. A good example of this is a subsystem called "The History of Interpretations". It is a structured narrative, telling how clothing was interpreted by different generations of archaeologists. In this subsystem, quotations from archaeological books and papers are contrasted with visual information from the time in which they were written.

For example, it is probably no coincidence that a male researcher from the thirties found it difficult to accept that Bronze Age women wore a string skirt with nothing underneath it, while a female researcher in the seventies, when women's lib was a powerful force, stressed the practical, working aspect of the clothing. The system does not explicitly assert that the interpretations were influenced by contemporary society, it merely suggests it by subtly juxtaposing pictures.

Laursen: Facts or hypotheses?

The existence of a large number of hypotheses about life in the Bronze Age do not mean that we have no more than a few facts. We have plenty of discoveries that were made in a landscape that has changed fundamentally over the years. That is one of the main reasons why researchers are often left in a position where the gap in our quantitative and qualitative knowledge are far greater than our actual knowledge. What about Bronze Age language, for example?

After years of brilliant archaeological research, archaeologists can still write volumes about what we do not know but would like to know about the Bronze Age period. Or to put it more succinctly: That may be why the number of unanswered relevant questions has grown remarkably!

Unanswered relevant questions are difficult to deal with. That is why a lot of important questions have not been voiced publicly. Of course, people would prefer to know what life was like rather than what it was not like. That is quite understandable if you consider the primacy of facts in our educational systems. Our traditions have taught us to think in that way. Even so, might it be wise to try to use hypothetical ways of thinking as an integrated part of understanding facts. As mentioned, above, the interactive nature of multimedia is conductive to hypothesis suggestion.

Another asset is their power of visualization, but which kinds of visualizations are relevant? Which kinds of topological spaces can help the user experience the fascination of finding his way into the complex worlds of Bronze Age man?

We are dealing with two different world pictures and must navigate between the world picture of Bronze Age man and that of the user.

The latter is the one that is present when the user meets the computer. Therefore the user's conception of the world must be provoked, not only at the conscious level — but also in its unconscious semantics and logic.

Andersen: The interaction must be a meaningful visual experience

The demand that using the system must provoke not only the conscious but also the unconscious layers of the user's mind presents the poor designer with a difficult job. Since most standard interaction does not meet the requirement, it must be discarded. The interaction itself must be a sign with a meaning closely connected to the main topic of the system: It should make visual the Bronze Age view of nature, illustrate the difference between present and past views, aid exploration and hypothesis generation, and challenge the user's visual habits!

Neither standard menus nor buttons can do this, since they all have meta-signification. They do not denote topics within the contents of the system, but properties of the medium itself. Navigational meanings are typical: A menu denotes an index of pages and selecting an item means go to that page. But the meta-world of turning pages has nothing to do with the contents that Laursen wants to communicate to the user about the relationship between past and present modes of perception.

So we borrowed "spot interaction" from another project (see Holmqvist and Andersen's Chapters 6 and 7). The windows display dark pictures, whose details are difficult to see. Each window contains a spot, a colored transparent circle that the user can move. The details of the picture only become clear when the spots illuminate them. In Figure 11. 2 the user can see the shadows of an axe in the grass (left figure), but it is only when the user moves the spot to the axe that is possible to see the details (right figure).

Fig. 11. 2. The user can examine the large picture by moving the spot.

The advantages of this kind of interaction are as follows:

- Since the system uses colors, the interaction is a visual experience in itself. Good effects can be constructed with the right choice of colors.
- The user experiences the interaction as an exploration of an unknown landscape whose objects are dim and ambiguous but are disambiguated when illuminated.
- The user test showed that the spot metaphor was very easy for users to understand.

Spot-interaction is easy to implement. Here is one way of doing it (Figure 11.3).

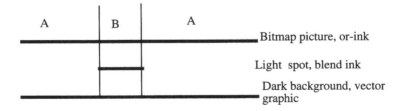

Fig. 11. 3. The spot principle.

You use three layers to create the effect. The bottom layer is a dark monochrome vector graphic, and the top layer is a bitmap-picture with or-ink. The or-ink makes a screen pixel dark if the bitmap-picture or the background is dark. When the background is uniformly dark, the final effect is a dark picture (location A in Figure 11.3). However, where the light spot is interspersed, the uppermost bitmap picture is allowed to keep its white pixels, and therefore stands out clearly within the confines of the spot (location B).

If we look at the individual bits, the process looks like this (Figure 11.3 a):

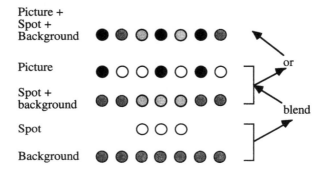

Fig. 11. 3 a. The detailed pixel operations.

Background and Spot combine in such a way that background colors are kept outside the spot, while the spot and background blend and produce a light patch. Now the Picture combines with Spot + Background based on the principle that the darkest wins: black in Picture plus dark from Background produces black, while white in Picture plus dark from Background produces dark, so that outside the spot we see the black pixels from Picture against a dark Background. Inside the spot the same principle applies, only the dark of the background has been blended with the spot, thereby transforming the white pixels of the picture into a light color.

Laursen: Lines and circles. A difficult question

It was not without reason that the Austrian painter Hundertwasser emphasised that we live in the tyranny of the straight line. Computer interfaces are no exception; they also prefer lines and rectangles.

But the Bronze Age period actually preferred a completely different geometrical form: the circle, the two-dimensional sun. The circle seems to dominate large parts of this past universe, judging by the ornamentation on findings. Therefore, this form is given high priority in the largest background in the system, the Landscape window.

The choice of the circle as the central part of the pictures is an attempt to demonstrate to the user that the environment and the spatial conception of Bronze Age man were strongly and spontaneously tied to the sun as the important vital phenomenon.

The Bronze Age conception of space probably differs radically from the one we have today. To us, conceptualizing and experiencing the world around us is, to some extent, a conscious interpretation. But transferring a concept like "conscious interpretation" to the Bronze Age period presupposes that the culture could handle a phenomenon like alternatives, which is by no means certain.

Arguing visually against this epistemological background, we construct the landscape in such a way that it postulates that in the Bronze Age period alternative ways of thinking did not exist; it says that the limits of the surrounding world were not recognised by conscious reflection. The environment was experienced as circular, with the sun as the permanent center. The surrounding world and the conception of the world as a whole were assumed to be the same.

The user cannot cross the edge or border of the landscape when traveling around in the universe. The exact time when the user meets the edge of the picture is an individual matter, but all users will meet it and will hopefully ask the hidden question: How is this whole universe built?

Andersen: Backgrounds can be larger than the window

Computers can handle pictures that are much bigger than the screen.

Large picture

Fig. 11. 4. The Landscape window.

The Landscape window displays part of a large landscape — 60 x 60 cm — placed inside a huge circle. Only small parts of this big picture are visible to the user at any time because the picture is always seen through an 8 x 8 cm window. But the user can move around in the whole picture by moving the spot; when the spot hits the edge of the window, it "pushes" the window in the direction of the movement (Figure 11. 4).

When the user illuminates an object in the landscape, he receives information about it. Technically, the Landscape window is simply a menu, but we have tried to make menu-selection an integrated part of the message that we want to convey to the user. Using the menu will hopefully convey Laursen's ideas of the Bronze Age universe!

Laursen: Visual attractors

If the visual journey in the landscape is to attract the user, the following criteria must be fulfilled:

(1)   *Recognition.* Any visual communication will fail if this aspect is not present, at least in the initial stages of the topological travel; the competence to recognize something is cognitively bound up with the user's stored perceptions made during his life; most of these perceptions are contemporary and are included among the user's perceptual habits. But since we intend to break the user's unconscious perceptual patterns and habits, the topological universe must make visual some

(2)   *perceptual provocations* that make obvious everyday-life experiences less obvious, for example in the way we experience our surroundings'

(3)   *absence* of urban ways of experiencing, which means that the user's spontaneous, unreflected experience of the world is not a suitable path into the closed but semantically fascinating, different and stable universe of the people of the Bronze Age; this assumption gives you the epistemological background for visually constructing the hypothesis of

(4)   *potential Bronze Age optics*, potential Bronze Age perception, or at least suggestions of it as a prerequisite for understanding aspects of how that distant culture perceived the world around it.

After having researched written sources, we decided (though others might choose differently) that it would be relevant to visualize the following spaces as parts of one connected hypothetical mental Bronze Age universe:

Day and night spaces, spaces of seasons, the sun's space. Space of a cattle-breeding culture. The agriculturalist's space. Indoor/outdoor spaces of the village. Spaces of grave mounds and barrows. The fisherman's space (vertical perceptions). The hunter's space (sounds, tracks). Defense space (sounds, views, pointed weapons). Forest space (absence of geography). Moor-land space (fear and danger). Erection Space (sexual instincts). Global connection space.

Andersen: Physical attractors

Visual attractors are well-known in art, but interactive media offer new possibilities for interacting with the user's attention by physically changing the picture. This gives the artist a whole new battery of aesthetic techniques.

In addition to letting the user move the spot or the window, we allow the artist or designer to move it! The actual use of the system is seen as co-operation or competition between viewer and designer, since they are allowed to use the same set of tools.

When the user moves the spot in the Landscape, he may not hit the desired object precisely, so when the user lets go of the spot, the system takes over, inspects the illuminated objects and moves the spot, so that one of them comes into the centre.

Another example is The Mystery of the Razor. This subsystem is a guided tour, the purpose of which is to interpret the engravings of a bronze razor. It presents hypotheses to the user and the user is invited to search the landscape for evidence that can confirm or disprove the hypotheses. Since the landscape is spacious, the system helps by moving the spot to the vicinity of the desired piece of data.

The History of Interpretations is a third example; the user can read whichever interpretation he likes, but since an interpretation is often an answer or an objection to a previous interpretation, the system offers to move the spot, asking if the user has seen the other one or wishes to do so.

Conceptually, all these modes of interaction can be seen as vector fields in the sense described in Chapter 1. The system is very literally caught in two large force fields: The designer pulls the system in one direction, the user in another. Chapter 10 contains a theoretical discussion of this idea.

The space of the day, the season, and the sun

The following sections present concrete ideas for increasing the user's awareness of the difference between perceptual patterns in the present and in the past. Most of the ideas have in fact been implemented, while others are currently being developed.

Laursen: Points of view

The weather is a highly important factor because of the raw material of peasant cultures: the soil. That is why the system suggests that it is important to
pay attention to the weather, to the changing appearance of the sky, because it is highly differentiated. The topological picture shows five different
views of the sky, five different kinds of weather:

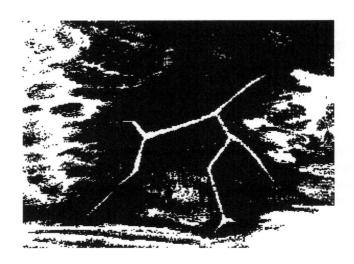

Fig. 11. 5. Thunder and cumulus clouds.

The cumulus clouds signify that the Bronze Age climate was warmer. The
thunder visualizes the remarkable forces of the sky surrounding you outdoors (Figure 11.5).

One of the features we are working on at the moment is information about
the weather: If the user illuminates the cumulus, a voice could give information about the change of climate. If he points at the thunder — or just moves
the window across that area — the system could play recordings of thunder,
lightening and heavy rain.

Multimedia systems make it possible to activate many of the user's senses
simultaneously. Kinesthetically, the user is handling the cursor to make
progress in the system and during this activity he is confronted with important, unusual, visual signals. Figure 11. 6 shows a vertical angle of view.

The fact that something happens when the user moves the window across
the sky makes the process more intensive. Looking vertically toward the
clouds, most urban people become surprisingly aware of their neck muscles
because they do not do it very often. Viewing the sky has a bodily counter-

part, and the multimedia-system may also provoke kinaesthetic details, trying to enrich the user's exploration of life in the Bronze Age.

Fig. 11. 6. Looking upward.

We cannot be sure that the user spontaneously becomes aware of the analogy with Bronze Age experience of the sky, but this single example of an unusual point of view is only one among many aesthetic devices that stimulate the user's interest in examining the surrounding space — the historical as well as the contemporary one.

To give another example, the ordinary user meets the sun in quite an unusual form:

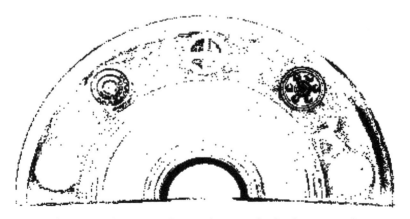

Fig. 11. 7. The sun as a boat, a drum, a wheel, a lur or a carriage.

It is seen pulled by a horse and sailing west in a boat with signs for suns and lures. Possible relationships are visualized and will be made more explicit if the user points at them (Figure 11. 7).

So the drawing simultaneously suggests that Bronze Age people regularly watched the sky and postulates that the user might find meaningful relationships when looking at the lure, the boat and the horse. These elements are not separated from the space of clouds and thunder but are parts of it, as illustrated in Fig. 11. 8:

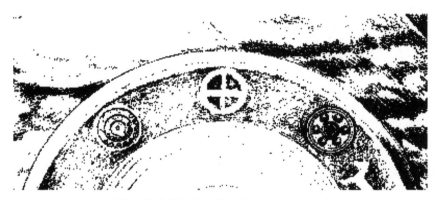

Fig. 11. 8. The "sun" in the space of clouds.

There are 15 visualizations of the sun in the upper half of the large circle. We intend to program the system so that whenever the user points there, other windows will show a picture, a video or a film of the sun. One of these suns is displayed in Figure 11. 9:

Fig. 11. 9. The sun connected to different objects.

The system guides the user toward different experiences of the same theme but at the same time presents a rich, visual variation characterizing the sun as a phenomenon.

The user can meet differences caused by the season, sunrise/sunset, changes caused by atmosphere or clouds, and phenomena not normally part of the everyday experience of the typical user. In this way the differences — which are all recognizable — may have the cognitive effect that after a while the user begins to interpret the signals of the visual variations.

Fig. 11. 10. A "staircase" construction in the sky.

One important intention is, of course, to make the user more sensitive to the environment outside the museum. We postulate that it is important to examine the everyday, contemporary space we live in, a space in which the sky has been reduced to a kind of subsidiary scene.

Figure 11. 10 shows a visualization of one of these visually remarkable phenomena where strong winds have influenced the clouds in a very unusual way with respect to the size and relative locations: The standard-image of a cumulus-sky shows the smaller clouds at the bottom and the bigger ones trailing upward. But it can actually appear quite differently.

As Fig. 11. 10 shows, you may perceive something that looks like a nonlogical "staircase" construction, which seems to allow you to walk from the ground into the sky, especially if you see this phenomenon from the bottom of a hill. We would never think that way in our culture. For good, logical reasons.

And it should be stressed that we did not put this detail into our topology in order to persuade the user to think along these lines. Instead, we are asking the indirect question: How would Bronze Age man have reacted to this phenomenon, which everybody can see every autumn if they are outdoors.

When the user moves around in the landscape, other windows are activated. This gives the designer a lot of different possibilities: to play a video or a sound, give hypothetical interpretations, show pictures or series of pictures or to construct various combinations of these possibilities.

Andersen: Author-generated interpretants

In the actual system we have two windows, the Color Photo and a Verbal Info window, which offer interpretations of what the user sees in the landscape. When the Landscape window displays an object in its (hypothesized) cultural setting, the Color Photo window displays a color photo of the actual find, while the Verbal Info window provides a short verbal explanation in text and sound. We also use music, though mostly for illustration (allowing the user to hear the sounds of the musical instruments of the past) and for atmosphere (playing the "lur" when the user was looking at one of the burial mounds gave the mound an unexpectedly solemn and sinister atmosphere).

But sound can also be used to suggest cultural differences. Sounds of forest animals can be played disproportionately loudly to suggest that Bronze Age man's attention was much more focused on these than ours.

In hypertext, these phenomena will be implemented by means of a link-node structure, but we use the vector inplementation of the traditional linguistic concepts of agreement and government described in Chapter 1. Each window contains three different objects that can enter into agreement: the spot, the area, and the card. The spot has already been introduced and the card is familiar to all users of Hypercard. The Area is simply a polygon defining an area of the card. The agreements can be understood as vectors pulling the subject item towards the destination item. For example, agreement between the Color Photo window and the Spot in the Landscape window can be defined as a vector finding a card in the Color Photo window with the same name as the object illuminated by the spot in the Landscape Window, and pulling it to the front in the Color Photo window.

The vectors are implemented by means of three primitive procedures:

- *AttractCard Cardname, Windowname:* displays a card with name Cardname in window Windowname.
- *AttractArea Areaname, Windowname:* scrolls the window so that area Areaname becomes visible in window Windowname
- *AttractSpot Graphicname, Windowname:* moves the spot of window Windowname to the graphic object Graphicname.

Since the first parameter of the procedures can be names of objects illuminated by the spot, an area name or a card name, this gives us 3 x 3 possible vectors (Table 11. 1).

Table 11. 1.

	Spot	Area	Card
Spot	Move spot in B to object similar to the object illuminated in A	Scroll B to area similar to the object illuminated in A	Show card in B similar to the object illuminated in A
Area	Move spot in B to object similar to the area displayed in A	Scroll B to area similar to the area displayed in A	Show card in B similar to the area displayed in A
Card	Move spot in B to object similar to the card displayed in A	Scroll B to area similar to the card displayed in A	Show card in B similar to the card displayed in A

The nine procedures are constructed by combining the three primitive attractors with three different kinds of arguments, the illuminated *object*, the illuminated *area*, and the current *card*, returned by the functions *getspot, getarea,* and *getcard.* Thus, a *SpotCard* agreement between windows A and B, displaying a card in window B similar to the object illuminated in window A, is implemented by calling the procedure *AttractCard getspot(A), B.*

Each time a user event occurs, agreement-messages are sent to all windows. Each window intercepts the message, and performs its own particular version of the agreement. For example, the large landscape contracts the following agreements with the other windows (Figure 11. 11):

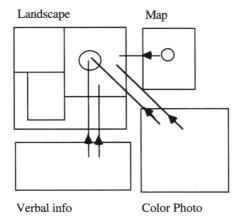

Fig. 11. 11. Verbal Info and Color Photo agree with both spot and area of the Landscape, while the spot of the Map agrees with the area of the Landscape.

Laursen: Signs and non-signs

The potentials of the multi-medium enable the designer to have a semiological discussion with the user: What can be described as a sign — and what cannot? What constituted a sign in the Bronze Age period, but does not now? What constitutes a sign now, but not then? And why?

A fruitful way of answering at least some aspects of these questions is to try to investigate the interests of the cultures involved. Only things of interest find their way into various symbolic systems. If they lose their interest, they will die. But that does not necessarily mean that the particular culture will be conscious of its own priority of interests.

On linguistic consciousness, Gardner comments:

> Like schooling, literacy encourages fresh and, in many ways, more reflective attention to language. In a non-literate society, language tends to be invisible: all that is noticed are the effects of what has been said. In contrast, in a literate society, the individual becomes aware that there are elements like words, that they are combined in certain acceptable ways (grammar), and that these linguistic elements can themselves be referred to (meta-language).   *(Gardner 1985: 359).*

In multimedia we can try to set up possibilities for the user to identify meta-semantic codes in *all symbolic competences* and their *interaction*, which the user is not normally conscious of, body-language being a good example of this.

Because they are so new, multimedia often present unforeseen problems that require solutions. For instance, what happens if the user points to an area without any hidden functions? Will nothing happen then? Of course. The user should be shown different pictures of the sky that do not show the sun. Why? In order to illustrate the preoccupation with the weather that we claim was of fundamental importance in the culture. Therefore, any area that is not a hidden button should be defined as a common weather-button that is met anywhere in the topology in order to stress the dependence on the surrounding material space and in order to use the obvious possibility of allowing the designers to create visually interesting photos, drawings, or videos of the surrounding atmosphere.

Was night an important concept in the Bronze Age? If it was, the sound-signs become interesting: how did Bronze Age people decode night-sounds? Sounds could be linked to the common weather-button, which again may make the user a better listener!

Laursen: Past and present interpretants

There are many signs and tracks in the topology — more than 150. But signs and tracks are ambiguous words. In Figure 11. 12 you find footprints from a roe-deer, a lynx and a hare. To the left are signs of a human trap for catching animals. Pointing at these elements can activate the interpretant windows.

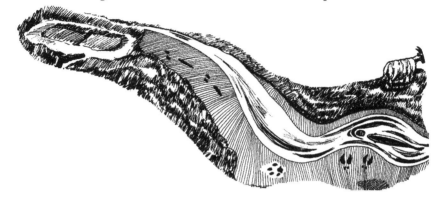

Fig. 11. 12. Different signs in a topology drawn with ink.

The hare, active during the daytime, will be followed by the roe-deer that lives its life at dawn, in the evening and at night. That is why the roe-deer should appear in an interpretant window where the light is fading.

The construction and functions of the trap can be shown by an animation illustrating the interaction between the movements of the animal and the mechanics of the trap. If the user follows the roe-deer footprints vertically upward, the vertical angle of vision leads him to a stone in the river where a salmon is lying in wait, ready to catch food. The fisherman is familiar with that angle and spatial topology, where he often discovers that sort of fish. But most users are accustomed to seeing fish from a different angle — for example in an encyclopedia or in a fish-shop: They see the side and not the back of the fish. In contrast, the sheep slightly higher up in the topology is seen from the overview perspective of a shepherd.

But let us return to the fish in the river for a short while. The interesting thing is that we can actually make significant statements about Bronze Age perception and its typical angles of vision. Authentic pictures of fish from that period have been found on rock engravings and metal works. Here we find both angles: vertical and horizontal.

The horizontal side-view of the fish has been found engraved on a stone that the user may see if he follows the coast-line in the topology (Figure 11.

13). The other one (Figure 11. 14) could be shown in the color photo window if the user points at the salmon. A picture engraved on a fishing-spear interestingly shows fins on both sides of the fish-head, which means that the artist can only have seen the fish-head vertically.

You will also notice some anatomically strange fins on one side of the fish! How do you interpret those phenomena? More than one visual hypothesis may be relevant here. Compare Figures. 11. 13 and fig. 11. 14:

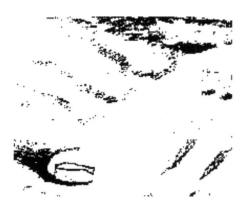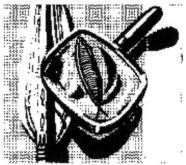

Fig. 11 13. and Fig. 11.14.
Horizontal or vertical view angle on
an object.

Fig. 11. 14 is sketched from a book illustration (but rotated 90 degrees; the book shows the spear horizontally, but that kind of tool or weapon is mostly carried and used vertically) (Jensen 1979). This fish picture indicates that the artist might have been a fisherman or was at least familiar with fishing.

Most Scandinavian types of fish (apart from plaice) lie on one side after being caught, so this view of the fish is a postmortem view (from the fish's point of view, that is!). It comes close to being a pictogram for fish.

That is why the horizontal view is used on the stone: it expresses a general desire for food. However, the vertical spear picture is not focused on fish as food, but mirrors the combat between fish and spear fisher, in which the spear is used as a tool. The angle is used very consciously in the picture since it is a highly significant semantic factor. The intention is to question the user's preconscious fish pictograms and compare them with more unfamiliar but relevant percepts at a conscious level. The vertical angles are not only used for visualizing small fresh-water areas, but also for the larger salt-water areas where the user can catch plaice, cod and garfish, or can gather mussels or amber (Figure 11. 15).

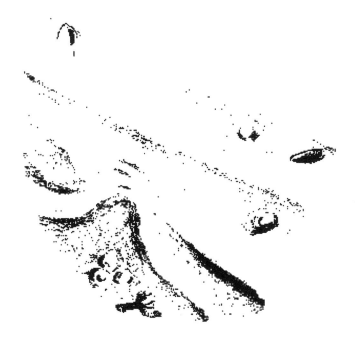

Fig. 11. 15. Sea food and amber.

Sometimes you meet animals during your topological journey (or images that look like animals) or at least signs of their existence. This is an interesting analytical field for decoding the semiosis! Phenomena can be present in various degrees. If animals are present, as some are here, they are not signs (within the fiction, that is), but concrete representations of general phenomena. But when we see a footprint, it is a sign, since it is a hypothetical index of the absent object, the animal.

However, this apprehension of absence might be disturbed by the salmon producing ripples in the surface of the river. Since it can do this it is present. Its movements are the physical force that makes the water move significantly. But although the fish must be present, the user does not see it, so it is also absent.

A trained fisherman, however, rapidly and automatically decodes the movement of the water, to him the fish is almost present. The decoding habits and the degree to which objects are seen as signs at all, characterize any culture. The medium allows us to form hypotheses about a different kind of semiosis and decoding schemes characteristic of a culture that depended upon its environment for its existence.

The perception of the world through experiencing the interpreting topology is visually postulated to be in essence historically determined, a phenomenon that the user can experience in a dialogue with his own present-day perceptual patterns.

Laursen: Large and small, difficult and easy

There are good reasons why we have chosen not to show the complete topological drawing to the user. It is only by activating his visual memory that the user can reconstruct it. In that respect this topology differs from most other visual impressions we come across. We are used to having an overview of a totality, or at least we believe we are. We want an overview and feel uncomfortable in its absence.

Paintings have frames. We cannot focus on all the objects in the plane simultaneously, but most people seem to be unaware of this fact, probably because we are children of a culture that underestimates the cognitive importance of visual perception:

Much of our art tradition has created (and art criticism has analyzed) paintings by focusing on each object equally sharply, a method that our selective perception is unable to follow.

However, a "good picture" manages to focus on all of its objects, without the spectator finding it problematic. He just moves his focal point! That is true. But usually others move it on our behalf: film-, video-, and TV-cameras move our focal point so skilfully that most people forget that they are caught up in the narrow optics of a particular way of decoding and selecting actual surroundings. The more fascinating the product, the more pronounced the tendency. That is the main reason why the user must be kinaesthetically active when he wants to see changes on the computer screen. The user must combine mental and physical competences interactively, because it may draw his attention to what he actually perceives.

Fig. 11. 16 shows the complete topological drawing. The Bronze Age period was a peasant culture. That means that you will find an open type of landscape with cattle. In these areas you will also find the village and the barrows. In the topological drawing, quite a lot of space has also been used to show the sky and the important sun.

The importance of water — fresh and salt — is also pronounced. Although the Bronze Age was a peasant culture, people still seem to have paid a great deal of attention to ships, judging from the art of the period. Dendrologists and botanists have discovered that forests covered a large part of the landscape and that they were very difficult to cross. That is why only one narrow footpath is shown in that part of the drawing.

Fig. 11. 16. The topological drawing and the computer screen.

The picture displays distance (small trees) as well as close-ups (leaves so close that the user feels he is being touched). The point is to give the user an analogical experience of what it would be like to try to cross a forest in those days — and of course to present information about the predominant kinds of trees.

The moor seems to have been a very special place for Bronze Age people. They sacrificed valuable objects there that were never removed or stolen! That seems to indicate low mobility or strong taboos in these dangerous areas.

The priority of the different areas in the drawing is based on an analogy with the predominant types of landscapes in the Bronze Age period. The control over the environment was weak, man did not change the environment in radical ways.

The interpretation of the whole scenario is the task of the user, although its design is based on scientific hypotheses. The topology is a landscape *without a center* where one user is followed by the next, who takes over from the position where the first one left the media. This spatial narrative construction indirectly tells the users that they themselves must form hypotheses.

Being a fiction, the topology does not represent a concrete landscape. But even when you produce that kind of visualizations, you may be surprised during your hard creative work to realise that this analytically well-prepared and at the same time concrete and abstract configuration turns out to resemble some local landscapes that you have actually seen.

Perception and visual memory are basic cognitive qualities of your consciousness.

Andersen: Interactive texture

The combination of kinaesthetic and perceptual effects advocated above can be used to let the user experience the difference between low mobility areas, such as the moor and the forest, and high mobility areas, such as water.

In the Bronze Age, the geography had a very different meaning than nowadays. While we now see water as a hindrance to locomotion, and firm ground as a help, the situation was to some extent the opposite at that time when water united (because of boats) and land divided (because of large forests and moors).

We can let the user experience this through his fingers by making the cursor move differently in different areas. If the spot is on land, it travels slowly, while it goes quickly if it is on sea. Conceptually, we can use the vector-concept again. Moving the spot with the mouse is conceptualized as a strong attractor from spot to mouse, and the texture of the areas is simply another attractor from spot to area. The spot is influenced by two antagonistic vectors, one with the mouse as target, the other with the area as target.

First, I will demonstrate a method for implementing the mouse-vector: When the mouse is pressed on the spot, we measure the spot's coordinates (SpotX, SpotY) and the mouse's coordinates (MouseX, MouseY) (See Figure 11. 17). As long as the user keeps the button down we measure the new coordinates of the mouse (NewMouseX, NewMouseY) and calculate the X-distance (NewMouseX - MouseX) and y-distance (NewMouseY - MouseY) the mouse has moved (Figure 11. 18). Finally, we add these distances to the location of the spot, which makes the spot follow the mouse.

One way of implementing the spot-area vector is to scale the spot-movement: we define a function *MyTexture(areaname)* that returns a number linked to the area representing the texture of the area. If it is between 0 and 1, the spot movement will be slower than the physical mouse movement, signifying that the area is difficult to move in — for example, woodland. If it is larger than 1, the spot will move more quickly, and this could signify water.

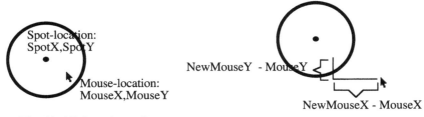

Fig. 11. 17. Locations of spot and mouse.

Fig. 11. 18. Measuring mouse movements.

The following pseudo-code is one way of implementing interactive texture:

```
put the loc of the mouse into MouseX,MouseY
put the loc of the spot into SpotX,SpotY
repeat until the mouse is up
  put the loc of the mouse into NewMouseX,NewMouseY
  put Mytexture(GetArea()) into Texture
  if NewMouseX,NewMouseY ≠ MouseX,MouseY then
    add trunc((NewMouseX - MouseX)*Texture) to SpotX
    add trunc((NewMouseY  - MouseY )*Texture) to SpotY
    set the loc of the spot to  SpotX,SpotY
    put NewMouseX,NewMouseY into MouseX,MouseY
  end if
end repeat
```

Conclusion

Multimedia not only invite integration of different intelligences in the user, they make the same demand of designers. Logical-mathematical intelligence is of course necessary for programming, but it brings forth sterile and boring products without musical and spatial intelligence that possess potentials of how to exploit the opportunities.

In the composition of this chapter, we have tried to demonstrate how the different intelligences can play together. The actual combination of the necessary skills and types of knowledge is a problem. One way of solving it would be to set up groups whose individual members each possess some of the total range of skills. However, this solution still seems somewhat clumsy; imagine a painter who knows how to compose his oil painting, but is so bad at mixing the paint and moving the brush over the canvass that he has to hire a servant to do these things in accordance with his verbal instructions.

The real solution is to invent programming environments and to create a style of programming that artistic people find themselves at home with; in other words, to remove programming from the clutches of logical-mathematical intelligence, and hand it over to musical and spatial intelligence.

Bibliography

ECO, U. (1990/85). *Sugli Specchi e altri saggi*. Milan: Bompinai.

EISNER, E. W. (1988) The Celebration of Thinking. Pi Lambda Theta Lecture. Art as a Tool and Conveyer of Knowledge, pp. 23-40. Stockholm: INSEA-Sweden.

GARDNER, H. (1985/83) *Frames of Mind. The Theory of Multiple Intelligences*. HarperCollins, Basic Books.

JENSEN (1979). Dansk Bronzealder I-II [Danish Bronze age]. Copenhagen: Sesam.

LAKOFF, G. A. (1987). *Women, Fire and Dangerous Things. What Categories Reveal about the Mind*. Chicago: The University of Chicago Press.

LAUREL, B., T. OREN, A. DON (1990). Issues in multimedia interface design: media integration and interface agents. CHI Proceedings, pp. 133-145. The Association of Computing Machinery.

LAURSEN, B. (1990). Drawing and Cognition. VENUS Report no. 6. Aarhus: Dept. of Information and Media Science, University of Aarhus.

LAURSEN, B. (1988). Drawing and creativity reflections on education with visual examples. The INSEA-Sweden Research Pre-Conference. The Valby Institute, Västerrås, Sweden.

MULTHROP, S. (1989). Hypertext and "the Hyperreal." *Hypertext '89 Proceedings*. The Association for Computing Machinery.

12

Hypermedia communication and academic discourse: Some speculations on a future genre

GUNNAR LIESTØL

The written genres of academic communication have evolved and consolidated ever since the founding of Plato's Academy. The conventions, structures, and rhetoric of academic writing and publication have gradually adapted to various technologies and requirements. With the quality of current computer technology, academia is faced with a complex and flexible medium, offering radical extensions to the handling of knowledge and information. It is yet uncertain what consequences this transition will have upon academic communication, but they are likely to be significant.

Experience and knowledge originate after the events, after their objects or entities have appeared and established themselves as subject matters. The title of this chapter suggests a synthesis of hypermedia communication and academic discourse that is in many ways still in its infancy. Consequently the reflections put forward here are speculations prior to the events rather than direct analysis of existing practise. But given the fact that few innovations are radically new or alien to the hosting environment — more a conglomerate of old and new — a certain level of understanding might be deduced in advance. The lack of existing examples of the relationship between this new form of media and established academic convention, unfortunately, means that this chapter can only be exploratory and tentative, and must therefore involve a high level of abstraction. What follows are projections and extrapolations prefacing events to come. The purpose of this is to attempt to identify some possibilities and problems relevant in the evolution of hypermedia.

I will focus on the specific relation between forms of publication in academic discourse and the branch of computer technology known as hypertext or hypermedia.[1] My point of departure is as follows: What will happen

---

[1] Considerable efforts have been invested in defining the central terms: 'Hypertext,' 'Hypermedia,' and 'Multimedia.' Following Ted Nelson's key paper (Nelson, 1965) hypertext only concerns nodes containing verbal text, while hypermedia is the correct term, when nodes also contain, pictures, sound or video (film). But in recent years the institutionalization of hypertext has established 'hypertext' as

to the academic genres, such as the essay, paper, and treatise, and their organization, use, and signification, when implemented and developed in an environment of hypermedia communication? Further, how may genre conventions and structures, developed under centuries of institutional and technological claims, most likely be adapted to such radical change of conditions?

The current computer revolution displays an on-going convergence of cultural tradition and technology, where devices of innovation slowly and painfully enter existing practises and/or create new ones. In general, cultural competence and technological innovations seem to strive for a steady relationship. The necessary balance governing interaction between human proficiency and tools in general, has been emphasised by Engelbart (1963, 1991), who stresses the concept of a human *augmentation system* containing two main subsystems. *Human system* refers to the non-technical skills we have acquired in society and culture. These are language, method, procedures, organization. The *tool system* refers to the collection of technologies such as devices, vehicles, machines, transport, media, and computers. Together with our genetic capabilities, these systems form the augmentation system, which extends the quality and quantity of knowledge work performed by individuals as well as organizations. For any augmentation system to function properly there must be an intimate interaction between its parts. With technological innovation time is needed for cultural competence to develop. If the strategic whole-system approach during rapid development in the tool system is neglected, the augmentation system itself might suffer considerable stress and instability.

In the following I have created a path through these partly unknown intersections of hypermedia and academia. My survey consists of six sections corresponding to the headings of this chapter by relating old discoursal forms to new media strategies. The first section briefly notes the background of the computer medium's current status. The second, third, and fourth sections discuss some technological, economic, and human conditions for an implementation of hypermedia communication in academia, as well as describing current attempts in academic hypermedia. The fifth section outlines the qualities and content of an imagined academic hypermedia publication. In the sixth section it is necessary to elaborate on the different modes of manipulation in a hypermedia message. I conclude with a discussion of the role played by the linear/non-linear dichotomy.

---

the general term (the ACM's bi-annualey Hypertext-conferences), with 'text' as a metaphor for all the different media types. To present my own view of the relationship between these terms I suggest the following equation: Hypertext + Multimedia = Hypermedia, which should be compatible with Nelson's original introduction of the terms.

A medium for other media

Ever since its emergence in electronic-digital form, the computer has been a meeting place of some kind. Like an agora, computer technology and environments have, in their different stages of development, constituted a *place* where persons, disciplines, media, and information have converged and interacted. Starting out as enormous, mainframe computing machines performing arithmetical tasks far beyond individual, manual achievements, the computer has developed into a small, relatively cheap but powerful tool marketed to millions of individual users.

Now not only numbers, but words, drawings, pictures, sound, and video may be digitized, generated, processed, and distributed by means of personal computers. The computer as we know it today has developed into a powerful and complex medium activating and forcing the use of multiple senses and capable of receiving, manipulating, and transmitting all the traditional media types. Different media developed in distinct but overlapping and related institutions and technologies — such as painting, writing, print, photography, telephone, radio, film, television, video — now merge as digitally coded information in the hardware and software of computer terminals. Connected in global networks of end users, the computer medium has constituted itself as a true super- or multi-medium — a medium for other media.

Adding the digital machine's own capabilities of interaction and random access to vast amounts of information, this multimedia vehicle now represents the most technological advanced and complex medium in the joint history of human communication and information technology. Grounded on this infrastructure, we experience the emergence of a post-print, electronic-digital public sphere of only vaguely known structure, function, and consequence.

As these technological innovations spring up and their uses and applications increase and spread to more disciplines of academia, their impact has become subject to critical attention and examination. The multi-functionality of computers currently unites scholars from branches of knowledge as diverse as computer science and literature; biology and linguistics; mathematics and classics. These intersections are often devoted to the further implementation and understanding of computers. Scholars no longer need to restrict their use of computers as a *tool* in their work, but may also use them as means of communication and publication.

Hypermedia communication provides academia with a medium where both reader and writer, user and producer can relate to a flexible, diverse, and complex landscape of texts, that may be accessed and consumed in a variety

of ways, with the consequence of both easing and complicating the process
of communication and exchange.

Information technology in academia

Although commercial computer industries have long targeted both the educational, official, and business markets, it is within and among the universities
and the research and development institutions that we find the most developed and extensive implementations of computer technology. With their existing competence, involvement, and infrastructure, these are the communities
that may most easily develop a full scale digital, multiple media public sphere.

The implementation of hypermedia in academic discourse and communication permits increased speed and flexibility in the way in which information
may be accessed, processed, and manipulated. The product cycle-time of the
major academic commodity, knowledge, may be dramatically decreased by
reducing the time-consuming process of publication, from months and years
to just a matter of days. As a result, delays in exchange of research between
scholars can be reduced and even prevented.

The increasing obstacles in scientific and technological progress was a
main motivation for one of the forefathers of hypermedia, Vannevar Bush. As
an example of failed and delayed communication within the scientific community Bush mentions the publication of Mendel's research on the genetic
code, which had to be rediscovered generations later (Bush, 1945). To solve
the problems of orientation and access to the increasing publications of research, crucial to the continued work and progress of each individual
scholar, Bush presented the idea of the *memex* machine. In lieu of rigid and
hierarchical structure traditionally found in information handling within specialized disciplines, Bush suggested mechanical devices for storage and retrieval of text, images, and sound, imitating and externalizing the associative
structure of the human mind. Bush's visions of a mechanized personal environment supporting scientific knowledge work and discourse is what currently — in a somewhat different (digital) form — is under implementation in
many Western academic environments.

The implementation of hypermedia in academic work has been met with
enthusiasm from several disciplines — for instance, in the study and teaching
of literature where the consequences of its innovative features have been
stressed. It has been argued that hypermedia conveys the potential of being
anti-hierarchical and *democratic*, by obliterating boundaries separating author and reader. The reader may follow not only the final version of a text
but the whole process of textual production in its many phases

(Yankelovitch, Meyrowitz, van Dam, 1985), thereby reducing the authority of the author. In the operations of hypermedia systems there also emerges a *decentralized* structure in which a multi-centred text is constituted by the readers ability to determine freely the order in which the elements of the text should be consumed (Delany, Landow, 1991).

Hypermedia used in specific situations of communication offer new relationships in the exchange of information and knowledge. Since hypermedia systems do not contain or convey a predetermined structure, but present themselves to the reader as a dynamic and flexible pattern of texts, consumption is not governed by enclosed rules in the traditional manner of print technology. In hypermedia communication, the receiver may choose an individual reading of the message, thus creating readings governed by codes of the receiving context, but always within the constraints provided by the software and hardware in use, and, of course, by conventions of genre. In this view hypermedia might offer anti-authoritarian sets of textual strategies capable of undermining domination in the relation between text and reader.

However, current traffic on university electronic networks is dominated by written text, with input constrained by bandwith and the digital keys on the keyboard. Integrations of other media types into network communication systems are under rapid development (Bassetti, Pagani, and Smyth, 1991; Dybvik and Lie, 1992), but still physical media for storage and distribution (CD- technology) offer easier unification of different media types.

Existing academic hypermedia

A distinction between hypermedia systems as *resources* and *environments* has already become evident (Delany and Landow, 1991: 32). A resource is a large collection of read-only texts, either a plain reference work like the *Grolier* encyclopaedia (1990) or *Perseus* (1992), which is a multimedia database of classical ancient Greek texts with maps, drawings, and photographs that are published, mass-produced, and distributed in the CD-ROM medium (Crane and Mylonas, 1991). In *Perseus* users may read, view, copy, and annotate the stored information. However, the information on the disk cannot be expanded, as new material can only be added in the next edition.

The hypermedia *environment* on the other hand, is not constrained by read-only technology. It is an open and individual system where readers and writers share the same electronic environment and users may contribute with their own texts and link them in various ways to the documents already in the system. The hypermedia *environment*, then, becomes an ever-growing and changing body of interconnected electronic texts. In these relations the concept of context gains new significance — texts no longer appear in isolation and nor are they displaced from relevant and related contexts.

The reader/writer then, experiences any text as a part of a flexible whole instantly accessible at any time in the process of use and from any point in the system. *Intermedia*, developed at Brown University, is on of the most advanced example of an hypermedia environment and has primarily been used for the study of literature (Landow, 1989). But the Intermedia environment is also a limited system. It is a limited context because it is not easily accessible to users outside the local net, though extensions have been prototyped (Jackson and Yankelovich, 1991).

The significant difference between a resource and an environment — in other words, between *Perseus* and *Intermedia* — is the function of the authors and readers. Users of *Perseus* also move within an "environment,"but a fixed one, only flexible to the extent that readers may choose their order of consumption within the constraints laid down by the producer/editor, whether by choice of software/hardware or by selection of information and structure. A resource is a publication — a collection of different data types made available for different kinds of use. *Intermedia* on the other hand, is a hypertext used in teaching, study, and research, containing written material from both students and teachers. Short single-node essays produced by students and teachers with links to surrounding and related texts dominate this environment. In *Intermedia* the reader is also the potential writer as the user is allowed to change between the positions of consumption and production. In contrast, *Perseus* can be placed more in a traditional process of communication. The producers select and combine a message that is distributed to a target audience of individual users. The *Intermedia* system or any environment in it, considered as a whole, is not in the same way a situation of communication; it is more a place one enters to find suitable positions and connections for reading and writing texts.

Both *Perseus* and *Intermedia* can be accurately characterized as hypermedia, but it is useful to ask to what extent may they be described as *hypermedia communication*. I use hypermedia communication to refer to the exchange of messages between individuals or groups (similar to books), where the individual message contains hypermedia features. In the case of *Perseus* and the environments in *Intermedia* it does not make sense to ask "What do they (the producers) mean by this" or "What is the message here." However, these are questions we always ask ourselves when involved in academic discourse. As academic communicators and consumers we constantly search for the meaning and signification of the messages we receive in the form of lectures, papers, and treatises.

My concern here is how the hypermedia features may be implemented in the genres of academic discourse, thus forming academic hypermedia messages, where the hypermedia qualities form a constituent part of the message and the potential information and meaning conveyed by that message. Such use of hypermedia communication in academic discourse has so far been very limited.[2] What is common to these few attempts is the relative dominance of linear structure despite the claimed non-linearity of hypermedia. It must here be added that the case is quite different with hypertext fiction, where non-linearity in the spatial organization of text nodes is clearly dominant.[3]

Electronic publishing (of hypertext and hypermedia) is currently modeled on and subordinated to the conception of the printed book. The relative open-ended environment and individual authoring of *Intermedia* is still to be united with the form of publication found in the resource tradition. The total open information environment of the digital world, where every bit of information is instantly available to anybody who is interested (Nelson, 1989), is still theory.

The academic market

Ever since the beginning of academia, writing and publication of books have been one of the core academic practices. Through writing it is possible for knowledge and information to exceed the limits of time and space. Radical and extensive changes came with Gutenberg and printing technology. But also in the pre-print age of hand-written documents copied by manual labour, academic productivity was measured by the output of texts made available to readers. Despite its idealism of truth-seeking, freedom, and independence, academia is first and foremost an industry of knowledge with the university as its main factory. In this community, which has knowledge as a product and commodity, it necessarily follows that the agents of such a market need to demonstrate their ownership and possession in relation to products. The structure of these relations between producer and product, scholar and knowledge, author and text, is partly expressed under the laws

---

[2] Probably the first thesis on hypertext was also written in the very hypertext system that was designed and implemented as part of the project (Trigg, 1983). The electronic version featured annotations, comments, alternative writings and alternative organizations (personal communication with Trigg 1992). In Intermedia one finds a hypermedia thesis on the novels of Graham Swifts (Fishman, 1989), the thesis consists of more than sixty nodes, including text documents and digitized photographs. The thesiselements are linked both internally between each other and externally to other documents in the environment. Academic books published in the traditional print format also have started to appear in parallel electronic hypertext versions (Bolter, 1991).

[3] See the provoking hypertext 'novels' published by Eastgate Systems Ltd., Michael Joyce: *Afternoon* and Stuart Moulthrop: *Victory Garden*.

of copyright and licensing. The system of production and reification of knowledge constrains and creates a specific form of publication, exemplified in any book written by an individual author, demonstrating property.[4]

In the concept of an open hypermedia environment, every user of a personal computer connected to the global university network can participate in the digital public sphere, reading, viewing, writing, and quoting any document of any media type(s). It is not likely that such an open environment will have any influence on the mainstream production of academic messages in the near future. This does not mean that the concept of "constructive hypertext" (Joyce, 1988) is imaginary. But for a long time it may only exists as avant-garde practices on the margins of writing culture, as in hypertext fiction.

In Ted Nelson's open system vision of global hypertext, copyright is guaranteed by recording every bit copied from the original document. Although this may be technically possible, it is doubtful that the current mode of production will allow a radical redefinintion of the individual text as a product and object. If the knowledge commodity, in the form of electronic texts only should be available on-line, the text will loose its appearance as a concrete sensible object unambiguously pointing at its origin, the author-producer. There is also reason to believe that the publishing industry will work hard to keep its position as a distributor of knowledge. Electronic media like television and video have not been able to change that position. Publishers have already taken a step into electronic publishing with their interest in CD-ROM technology (*Perseus*, for example, is published and distributed by Yale University Press).[5]

Since our (western) economic system seems to outlast every challenge from non-market economies, it is likely that the reification of knowledge existing in the age of the printed book will survive the transference to electronic, interactive media and thus favor publishing units and genres compatible with this tradition. Great upheavals may indeed occur in the tool system and cause changes in the augmentation system as a whole, but there are constraining forces in the socio-economic environment and in the traditions of the human system that for a long time may absorb and neutralize the radical potentials of technological innovations.

Thus, what we may see emerge (which already exists as a possibility), in addition to the resource publications, educational material, and reference

[4] In oral cultures, on the other hand, we may find units of knowledge and wisdom, like myths and fairytales, where ownership is not proclaimed and the texts exist as common property.
[5] In this perspective it is likely that a growing competition between publishing and telecommunication will emerge; but over time they might converge and become less individually defined.

works, is publishing of *individual* research work based in CD-technology. A CD-ROM format conserves the needed objectification, and it is a fixed stable unit in time and space; it is non-manipulative and secure to store. A CD-disk and package may also display the author and publishers name, and be sold in bookstores, by mail order, or be distributed over networks. At the same time, the storage capacity has the potential of containing isolated environments many times the size of for instance *Intermedia*. (600 megabytes = 250,000 pages = 15,000 color photographs = 1 hour compressed video, or any combination of these. In comparison, the *Intermedia* environment is altogether about 40 megabytes).

Currently CD's are used to record as many primary (verbal) texts as possible on each disk — like encyclopaedias. These are texts that otherwise would have or have emerged in print. Instead, what may develop is that one might stick to just *one* primary text, and then *include* information and media types traditionally *excluded* from printed publications.

Speculations on academic hypermedia publication

Behind and outside any published academic work there exists a vast and diverse environment of information, material, and activities that is both relevant and necessary to the constitution of the published text. The direct significance of such an extra-textual environment depends on the academic disciplines. In philosophy the subject matter of the text as the discursive presentation of concepts may not be distinguished from the textual presentation itself. The philosophic text, in full in analytic philosophy, formal logic, or other abstract "pure" disciplines, is not directly based on or referring to an excluded environment for it is not primarily a representation of something else. But in most other fields of study, from archaeology and theories of literature and film to chemistry, biology, and medicine, the subject matter or the object of which the written verbal message is a report, has its existence "outside" in the surrounding environment. Such an environment or context is as equally important as the written representation itself.

The academic publications of the paper or thesis are necessarily detached and isolated from their context, basically because it is not practical to include all information relevant to the argument/statement of the message. In many situations of academic communication it is not necessary to include as much relevant information as possible. The readers and members of different disciplines are often so familiar with traditions, theories, and concepts that only minimal textual allusions are required to evoke the necessary association and context for the reader. It is basically in the empirical sciences that the inclusion/exclusion dichotomy is decisive, where information is excluded due to the nature of the information marker, which is of a kind not compatible with the print medium.

This process of *inclusion* and *exclusion* (of gatekeeping) the author's decisions as to what comes in and what stays out, obviously, is central to how an argument is constructed and supported and to what extent the referent (the subject matter as a complex whole) is adequately represented. In research, the "true" relation between text and context is supposedly guaranteed by ethics in the author's sincere obligation to be "true to the facts." Reductionism in academic publishing is inevitable as the text presented may not map or copy the referent in a one to one ratio, but, due to the potential of semiotic freedom in language, the subject matter may to a large extent and for most practical purposes be adequately represented.[6]

A paper published in a scientific journal, be it in medicine, biology, sociology, or archaeology, is only the tip of the iceberg: the chosen top-level out of a large body of knowledge and information. This can be illustrated by a paper in archaeology presenting new knowledge based on, among other topics, an excavation. Prior to the publication a lot of activities, knowledge, work, and documentation have taken place. Artifacts have been found; samplings of soil and coal have been collected; topographic and profile drawings conserving the information of the natural and cultural matrices; archive reports and other unanalyzed documentation; photographs; video, and so on. Together with this specific information the published paper relates to other research and publications in the same and related domains. Given the verbal hegemony in academic discourse and limitations in the print medium, only a fraction of this information necessary and relevant to the argument surfaces in the final printed product. Footnotes and references direct the readers to context, but in real life very little of that context is available practically to the reader/researcher. It is not so easy for a reader in North America to follow a reference (a virtual link) in the paper he or she reads, if the relevant piece of information is stored in a vault in the basement of a Norwegian museum! It may be a big enough problem to find the right book in your local university library. The absence of context in academic publishing may therefore play an important and somewhat underestimated part in the constitution of distributed knowledge.

If the same academic paper on archaeology were to be published and distributed by the medium of CD-ROM (or similar), one could include almost *all* information relevant in constituting this knowledge. (Almost "all" informa-

---

[6] I am discussing the quality and quantity of information available to the reader/user when facing the message. The act of interpretation is not under consideration here.

tion because context also has limits, bordering on other environments without any specific significance to the primary text other than being part of the general environment.) In addition, information constrained by media types not presentable in print — time-based media such as video and audio — could be included. Grounded in the techniques of reference already developed in the medium of print, such as footnotes, quotations, paraphrase, allusion, bibliography, and so on, hypertextual features may link the different information elements in a manner that would provide access for specific needs and purposes of individual readers. It is not difficult to imagine how beneficial it would be for the reader if he or she, while reading the paper, could follow links to underlying material in text, graphic, or video format, and thereby instantly establish a contextual perspective in relating to the analysis presented in the paper. Our archaeologist, or any scientist working with material data of diverse forms, may also include software in the published collection, thereby giving the reader access to the dynamic process of manipulation, selection, combination, and method that transforms "raw" data into neat visual displays of figures and graphics. Illustrations like this, as well as statistics in general, have persuasive qualities with powerful rhetorical effect on the receiver. Such impact would be perhaps greater if the reader could have access to the criteria selected by the author for generating these statistics-based graphics. A reader could then choose other criteria based on his or her individual and maybe opposing approach to the subject matter, and thus generate graphical representations contradicting the published version, and thereby interfering with the author's argument and rhetorical solutions. This possibility of both combining and differentiating individual interpretations from material data could establish a new situation for academic discussion and dispute.

Software for generating simulations based on the available data is of great interest to archaeology, where reconstruction of a long lost past is the main quest. In a CD-ROM publication, software simulating for instance pre-historic economies based on interpretations of the available information could be included, thereby creating a dynamic relation between the authors individual interpretation and the underlying data.

Another discipline that could take advantage of hypermedia communication is media studies. In film and television analysis, the text may not be represented like quotes as in literary criticism. Film or television clips are either represented by still pictures or paraphrased in verbal form. Such a transformational process of representation evidently has bearings upon the context and support for the statements dominant in the text. This is significant when we consider the instrumentalist view of scientific language as transparent and unproblematic. In a hypermedia environment it would be possible to include the film text of study and to integrate it with the verbal analysis. This opens up for an analytical practice that displaces the dominance of verbal text over audio-visual analogue media, and thereby creates a genre the French film director Juan Luc Goddard calls "true analysis of film and television" (Coy, 1990), where presentation and subject matter are united in the same medium, and where the moving images to some extent will be set free from the constraints of linguistic hegemony.

In communication, any text has at least two contexts, that of the sender and that of the receiver. Messages in academic communication not only refer to their originating environments but are also directed against destinations, the reading audience and the constraints and laws of the academic marketplace. The text's mediation between specialized fields of research and the academic community must function satisfactorily in the contexts of both source, medium and destination. The hypermedia message is an extended message, in that it may include its source environment and present itself as a flexible multi-structured text. Consequently, the conditions and structures of encoding and decoding these messages are different. The increased complexity of the hypermedia message creates a different relationship between text and subject. The debate of open and closed texts, preferred readings, and the relationship between dominant ideology and reading subject may here gain new significance.[7]

These new qualities of academic hypermedia publishing may support a less manipulative and more contextualized discourse and thereby reduce ideological domination and other oppressive functions of knowledge production in society, and in particular the academic discourse community. But the necessary organization of hypermedia packages remains to be discussed by proponents and users of hypermedia. We need to ask how they should be structured to serve both the needs of sender and receiver, author and reader, and the whole communication system inside and between academic disciplines. In order to do this we need to look more closely at the characteristics of hypermedia communication and the structure of the hypermedia message.

Manipulating message material

Manipulation of message material has traditionally either been unconventional (forgery of documents) or displaced by copying (quotations).

---

[7] The discussion of decoding messages, especially popular culture texts, (see Eco, 1981; Hall, 1980) is relevant here. Even fixed stable texts/messages may be subject to a variety of decodings and readings, depending on the codes activated in the act of consumption and generation of meaning. It follows that when a stable and fixed signifier may give rise to multiple readings and meanings, a flexible signifier will increase this ratio radically.

In an early version prior to Shakespeare's *Hamlet*, Saxo Grammaticus tells the story of prince Amleth who on his trip to England gets to know the deadly plan of his fellow companions. They were carrying "... a letter graven in wood — a kind of writing material frequent in old times; this letter enjoined the king of the Britons to put to death the youth who was sent to him. (...) Amleth found the letter, and read the instructions therein. Whereupon he erased all the writing on the surface, substituted fresh characters, and so, changing the purport of the instructions, shifted his own doom upon his companions." (Hoy, 1963: 129). Amleth's whittling on the rune stick manipulated the information in the message and consequently saved his life.

Forgery of documents is a major crime, although we easily accept Amleth's action. Manipulation of message material in the cases of text and photographs, has been frequently in use in totalitarian states, where re-writing of history, erasing names from historical documentation, and removing discredited individuals from photographs have been a common procedure. Although active message manipulation is strictly forbidden, we all practice passive manipulation of messages, by turning the radio off in the middle of a program, switching from one TV channel to another, stopping the video player, taping parts of a program, half-listening to a conversation, and many other situations, where we as receiving subjects are free to refuse to consume messages and parts of them, or to exclude them altogether.

The history of media and communication seems to have one stable feature: Despite the many uses and misuses and the different readings and consumptions of messages, a joint characteristic is that the original message remains unchanged *in the process of communication*. The stability of the message is therefore a presupposition of communication. The receiver ceases to exist as such if he or she starts to cut and paste the materiality of the message, or to leave elements out or to rearrange the order. Such manipulation, before or while consuming the message, violates and abolishes that specific act of communication.

Instances of manipulation are also present in forms of discourse other than academic discourse: In literary studies the quotation of a text in an analysis is a manipulation of message material, but quotations are copies and are not themselves the original. The original message remains as a guarantee and reminder of the order of the original text/narrative, which just has been violated by the detachment of the quote.[8]

---

[8] The relevance of the concept 'intertextuality' comes to mind here, and its implications for hypermedia are obvious. But at the moment my aim is just to show the basic quality of material manipulation in hypermedia messages, for that purpose it is sufficient to use the simple example of the quote.

In discussing the potential in hypermedia for text manipulation we need to distinguish between different modes of manipulating the message. Subjective manipulation is constrained by the changing actions and positions of the reading subject in relation to the text. Objective manipulation, on the other hand, in addition to subjective manipulation, also rearranges the message material.

In all receiving of messages the reading subject is free to combine and relate the information and thereby create different meanings according to different ways of relating to the text. But this is only a manipulation at the subjective level and of the relationship between information and meaning, where the message material remains constant and untouched. Alternatively, we have the manipulation of the message material, where the user rearranges the actual order of the message's appearance at the level of the information marker. Nowhere in the history of human communication has there existed a type of message, for use in everyday life and for specialized professional purposes, where the main characteristics have been manipulation and rearrangement, and where the user/receiver is expected and encouraged to actively acknowledge and explore these features. In hypermedia communication this is exactly the case.

In the system of hypermedia communication there are two phases of selection and combination. This amounts to a double process of editing. The sender selects and combines the elements that constitute the hypermedia message as a whole, where each of these operations represents constraints in the process of communication: the selection-act of exclusion and inclusion, and the combination-act concerning the structures of connections (linking). The second process of editing is the reader's selection and combination of elements in the message, constituting the order in which to consume the non-linearly stored information. Here the stored information in the message is articulated and realized as a linear montage, constituting one out of many possible readings. The theories and traditions of montage (and collage), where equal elements may produce different meanings dependent of various ways of editing are of great relevance to hypermedia studies.

Construction of meaning is a function of the codes governing the message and the context of the subject. These are constraining levels in the decoding of a text. The more complex the environment of the receiver and the more complex the codes of the message, the more ambiguous the possible decoding becomes. Hypermedia communication is primarily characterized by the manipulation of message material, which creates increased freedom of decoding. Consequently, in the hypermedia message, where the information marker may be changed by reorganization, the patterns of information change accordingly, thus generating increased variety and diversity. This clearly creates an even more complex meaning production in the text-subject relation. Hypermedia communication, then, offers the possibility of greater semiotic freedom than in any other communication forms where the information marker itself remains stable and unchanged.

While text manipulation and semiotic freedom are welcomed features of hypermedia, the potential for ambiguity is obvious (the term "semiotic freedom" is taken from Wilden, 1987). Hypermedia provides us with a powerful medium of communication, but its messages must entail constraints providing the necessary efficiency in conveying specific meanings from sender to receiver. Different concepts of linearity play an important part in establishing these constraints.

Academic discourse and concepts of linearity

Non-linearity has been put forward as the central quality of hypermedia. In order to appreciate this quality it is useful to first examine what is meant by linearity. Linearity is an organizing principle of great importance in human communication. Consider the following joke, quoted from Wilden (1987: 250):

> Mr Abraham, driven to desperation by the endless delays of a tailor who was making him a pair of trousers, finally cried: "Tailor, in the name of heaven, it has already taken you six *weeks* !"
> "So?"
> "So, you ask! Six weeks for a pair of pants? *Riboyne Shel O'lem* ! God in heaven! It took God only six days to create the *universe* !"
> "*Nu* ," shrugged the tailor, "look at it..."

This little anecdote consists of four elements each containing a speech act in the dialogue, punctuated in terms of layout by line shift and tabulation. The order of these elements is not accidental. The rules and conventions for writing and reading guarantees that the elements are consumed in the correct and intended order. The three first elements are a gradual preparation for the effect of the punch line. Linear organization of this joke is absolutely crucial to its success and existence as a joke. The punch line receives its power from its position in the story and the way it relates to the information preceding it. The punch line has retroactive effects on the proceeding information and changes the meanings of the previous events, now being re-read in a new context (Wilden, 1987: 250).

The same goes for crime stories. There is a memorable closing scene from the 1982 "film noir" *Body Heat* (directed by Lawrence Kasdan). The imprisoned hero receives a high school photograph revealing the true identity of the woman he loved, trusted, and killed for. Given the picture, both the antagonist and the viewer rewind to the preceding events in a new context and all the scenes turns out to mean something quite different from what has previously been assumed. This re-reading of old information in a new context is possible because of the way the information is organized narratively. Many feel tempted to read the last pages in a novel of suspense, but doing so certainly changes and destroys the intention of the message (I am not discussing intentionality as an aesthetic concept here). These examples also show the power and effect of subjective manipulation where message material remains unchanged, and *because* it remains stable.

In the written version of the joke the necessary linear order of consumption is governed by rules contained in the conventions of reading (and layout). In the film, the linear organization is governed by the cinematic apparatus, by the sequence of frames and the numbered film rolls ready for display in the projection room. In telling the joke orally the speaker must remember the right order of the elements. In the pre-print age and for the purpose of remembering the correct (the most efficient) structure of a speech, mnemonics (artificial memory) was developed (Yates, 1966). The technique of mnemonics involves imagining walking through a building with levels and rooms, and memorizing places and images representing topics and parts in the speech. When the speaker gives a speech, the order of things to utter is structured by the memory of walking through this imaginary building. A spatial metaphor thus represents and supports the order of a temporal sequence. It is the path of walking that guarantees the right linear order of topics and gives the speech structure, not the composition of the building. This linear structure is again the guarantee for the persuasive effects of the speech.

Fixed orders of sequences are dominant and necessary in the history of writing, from literature and philosophy to essays, novels, and poetry. The order of representation in Hegel's *Phenomenology of the Mind* is a necessary and integrated aspect of his philosophical method. And Edgar Allan Poe in his essay *The Philosophy of Composition* explaining the writing of the "The Raven," focuses on "the construction of the effect" as the principle of organisation. He describes his efforts with composition as proceeding "...step by step, to its completion with the precision and rigid consequence of a mathematical problem." (Poe, 1983: 1081).

Obviously not every genre of communication and art relies on linear structure in this simple form. In epic literature the linearity of telling (discourse) is supplemented and makes possible another level, the structure of what is told (story). The dichotomy story/discourse is used by Seymour Chatman (1983), but basically derived from Gerard Genette's story/narrative (1982). Most narratives do not display identical order between story and discourse (narrative). Instead, an *asynchrone* relationship is constructed between the chronology of events in the fictional universe and the order in which these events are referred to in the text. In *Body Heat* the photograph of the heroine in the high school album, although at the end of the movie (the discourse line), refers to events early in the storyline. Thus a presentation, linear at the level of message material (the signifier), may mediate or present and make possible a non-linear structure at the level of information and meaning (the signified). One might therefore say that linearity constrains and makes non-linearity possible.

The genres of academic discourse do not escape rhetorical and narrative devices — they are constructed by them and simultaneously construct them. Scientific language and writing in the positivistic way of thinking has been considered pure, concise, and unproblematic, a position extensively criticized by the Rhetoric of Inquiry tradition (Simons, 1990). The dominant structure in most academic writing basically follows the general narrative model of quest: The hero, the researcher/author, desires and seeks an object, knowledge of the truth. This is the story level of an academic paper, while at the level of discourse we find the "line of argument," the order in which the information, data, and argument are presented for the purpose of obtaining the most persuasive effects. To mediate knowledge of some subject matter, the author must apply, consciously or not, the main techniques of rhetoric. And rhetoric, when exercized, needs a linear ordering of the message elements. Thus, most academic writing, like the quoted joke, requires linearity to obtain the intended effects. It is important here also to remember the strict linear sequencing we find in scientific conduct, in the stringent rule-governed procedure of the hypothetical-deductive method, often recognized at the core of academic writing.

While domination of linear organization is accepted in traditional media representations, hypermedia is primarily characterized by providing non-linear (or non-sequential) structures. For our archaeologist to get his or her message through — that is, an interpretation of the subject matter — it is necessary that parts or levels of the hypermedia message remain linear. This means that the text conveying the author's individual interpretation must exist at a different level of organization in the message, a level where linearity dominates non-linear structure; which again does not exclude extended linking from the paper to the rest of the message. But the order of parts in the paper must exist as a non-changeable entity, representing the individual interpretation of the author, unavoidable if the whole hypermedia message shall function for specific purposes of communication.

To further understand the distinction between linearity and non-linearity in hypermedia communication, the conceptions and representations of time and space need to be considered. Non-linearity in time is imaginary; it is a fundamental contradiction of terms and necessarily impossible. *Time is linear* — at least the time that is required to produce and consume hypermedia texts. Reading, writing, and the consumption of text in general are linear phenomena. They are sequential and chronological and conditioned by the ordering of time. But their positions as stored in space are organized as a non-linear pattern. Once a word is read it is chosen and taken out of its non-linear, paradigmatic context and positioned as a sequence in the linear syntagm, which is conditioned by time. However discontinued or fragmented the consumption of a hypermedia message might be, it always, at one level, turns out to be linear. Like Ariadne's thread, it might be tangled, but it conserves its basic and significant quality of being one long line. When consuming hypermedia texts, each of the options represents access to the complex structure as a whole, but non-linearity only exists as positions in space — different alternatives of which we may only choose *one at a time*. By the act of choosing and by selecting the next node to consume, we involve the dimension of time. So the moment we reach into the non-linearity of hypermedia, we *reduce* non-linearity to linearity. This position is inevitable: we always find ourselves at the intersection of time and space, and it frames all our actions. We might here refer to Kant and state that time is a form of representations a priori: a transcendental form of representation existing at another level of reality than representations and objects in time, including hypermedia nodes and links.

Concluding remarks

When using hypermedia communication in academic discourse it is necessary to obtain efficiency in the exchange of understanding. When a scholar publishes research material and its analysis, it is absolutely necessary that his or her interpretation and generated knowledge is adequately communicated. Order and organization, characterized as linear, are major constraints in obtaining proper encoding and decoding. In our example from archaeology, the strictly linear structure of the paper positioned at the top-level in the message as a whole, in addition to being the voice and signature of the individual author, functions as a guide into the material, but then becomes a guide through which authority can be challenged. If hypermedia features are to prove relevant in the exchange of academic knowledge, linear structure must be an important element in the composition and structure of the hypermedia message. We have seen that linearity is a major principle of organization in the communication between defined senders and receivers. The traditions of writing and other forms of media require an extensive use of linear ordering, from the act of consumption to the material organisation of the message.

I have discussed the possible convergence of academic traditions of exchange and the implementation of hypermedia technology in an archaeological environment. More broadly, hypermedia communication provides academic discourse with radically new and interrelated qualities. With increased flexibility and options, it is tempting to let loose all possible features and abandon the structures which for so long have constrained and limited expression and communication in the age of print. But if these new means of *communication* and representation are to serve any central purpose in academic exchange, they must to some extent develop out of the traditions and conventions that constitute our knowledge work and frame the way information is exchanged. The development of hypermedia literacy and competence in the human system must have an absolute priority.

To communicate by means of media is not a practice totally determined by the characteristics of the medium; the use and the social apparatus that operates and articulates messages are equally important. The emergence of technology supporting hypermedia communication implies radical changes in the tool system, but this potential can only be exploited within the constraints of the human system. Although the human system and the tool system are interdependent, they are not "equals" — it is the former that makes the latter possible. Qualities in the tool system will only be realized and taken advantage of to the extent that the human system provides competence for proper handling.

While the use of print technology in academia may be characterized by domination of verbal text, separation of text and context, and fixed message structures, hypermedia communication offers *integration* of media, *inclusion* of context, and *interaction* with each individual user. Integration and inclusion is not the problem. The problem is *interactivity* and the role played by "non-linear" structure and the user's ability to manipulate message material. We have seen that linearity at one level is our basic form of perception, and at another the organizing principle of message-composition in academic systems of communication. Non-linear orientation and consumption of hypermedia messages in academic communication is a valuable attribute of the hypermediated text, but must be related to linearity. The quality of the linear/non-linear relationship depends upon the purpose of communication. When the sender's point of view is stressed, linear structure must dominate non-linear organization. However, if the sender is basically making collections of information available for consumption (like *Grolier* or even *Perseus*), the point of view is reduced to each individually authored text and each single node. Linearity makes a hypermedia message as *one* unit more redundant, while non-linear organization *decomposes* the message as a whole and *delegates* redundancy to the individual nodes in the system.

If academic discourse is to benefit from random access retrieval of information, the integration of more information and multiplication of media types, the problem of linear versus non-linear organization must be recognized. The solution lies not in reciprocal exclusion, but rather in a combination of both linear and non-linear arrangements; subsequently, serious considerations must be given to the distinction between levels of linearity and non-linearity in the hypermedia message.

Bibliography

BASSETTI, O., PAGANI, D., M. SMYTH (1991). Applications Navigator. Using Hypertext to Support Effective Scientific Information Exchange. In *Proc. ACM Hypertext '91 Conf.* San Antonio, TX, Dec 15-18, 1991, 411-416.

BOLTER; J. D. (1991) *Writing Space. The Hypertext.* Cambridge: Eastgate Systems, Inc.

BUSH, V. (1945). As We May Think. *Atlantic Monthly, 176*, 101-108. Reprinted in *CD ROM: The New Papyrus*, Microsoft Press 1986.

CHATMAN, G. (1983). *Story and Discourse. Narrative Structure in Fiction and Film.* London: Cornell University Press.

COY, W. (1990). Film als Buch: Hyperdokumente zur Filmanalyse. In *Hypertext und Hypermedia,* eds. Gloor, P. A. and N. A. Streitz. Springer Verlag, 278-286.

CRANE, G. (1992) (Ed.). *Persus.* Baltimore: Yale University Press.

CRANE, G., E. MYLONAS (1991). Ancient Materials, Modern Media: Shaping the Study of Classics with Hypertext. In *Hypermedia and Literary Studies,* eds. P. Delany and G. P. Landow, pp. 205-220. Cambr., Mass: M.I.T. Press.

DELANY, P., LANDOW, G. P. (1991). Hypertext, Hypermedia and Literary Studies: The State of the Art. In *Hypermedia and Literary Studies,* eds P. Delany and G. P. Landow, pp. 3-52. Cambr., Mass: M.I.T. Press.

DYBVIK, P. E., H. W. LIE (1992). *Multipost — an adaptive multimedia information interchange system.* Internal Note, Norwegian Telecom Research.

ECO, U. (1980). Towards a semiotic enquiry into the television message. In *Communications Studies: An Introductory Reader*, eds. Corner and Hawthorne, pp. 131-50. London.

ENGELBART, D. C. (1963). A Conceptual Framework for the Augmentation of Man's Intellect. In *Vistas in Information Handling*, eds. Hoverton and Weeks. Washington, D.C.

ENGELBART, D. C. (1991). *Bootstrapping Organizations into the 21st Century. A Strategic Framework.* Bootstrap Institute, Doc# 132803.

FISHMAN, B. J. (1989) *The Works of Graham Swift: A Hypertext Thesis.* Honors Thesis, Brown University, 1989.

The Electronic Encyclopedia on CD ROM. Grolier 1990, New York.

GENETTE, G. (1982). *Narrative Discourse. An Essay in Method*. New York: Cornell University Press.

HALL, S. (1980). Encoding/Decoding. In *Culture, Media and Language*, eds. S. Hall, D. Hobson, A. Lowe, and P. Willis. London.

HOY, C. (1963). (ed.) *Hamlet. An authoritative text, Intellectual backgrounds, Extracts from the sources, Essays in criticism*. Norton. New York.

JACKSON, S., N. YANKELOVICH (1991). InterMail: A Prototype Hypermedia Mail System. In *Proc. ACM Hypertext '91 Conf*. San Antonio, TX, Dec 15-18, 1991, pp. 405-410.

JOYCE, M. (1988). Siren shapes: Exploratory and constructive hypertexts. *Academic Computing, 3 (4),* 10-14, 37-42.

JOYCE, M. (1987). *Afternoon, a story*. Cambridge: Eastgate Systems, Inc.

MOULTHROP, S. (1991). *Victory Garden*. Cambridge: Eastgate Systems, Inc.

NELSON, T. H. (1965). A Filestructure for the Complex, the Changing and the Indeterminate. In *Proc. Association for Computing Machinery*.

NELSON, T. H. (1989). *Literary Machines 89.1*. Sausalito, CA: Mindful Press.

NIELSEN, J. (1990). *Hypertext and Hypermedia*. San Diego: Academic Press.

LANDOW, G.P, (1989). Hypertext in literary education, criticism, and scholarship. *Computers and the Humanities 23,* 173-198.

POES, E. A. (1983). *The Unabridged Edgar Allan Poe*. Philadelphia: Running Press. ("The Philosophy of Composition" was first published in 1846.)

SIMONS, H. W. (1990) (Ed.). *The Rhetorical Turn. Invention and persuasion in the conduct of inquiry*. Chicago and London: University of Chicago Press.

WILDEN, A. (1987). *The Rules Are No Game. The strategy of communication*. Routledge & Kegan Paul, London & New York.

YANKELOVITCH, N., N. MEYROWITZ, A. VAN DAM (1985) Reading and writing the electronic book, *IEEE Computer 18*, 10.

YATES, F. (1966). *The Art of Memory,* London.

PART III

COMPUTERS IN CONTEXT

Introduction

JENS F. JENSEN

While Part I of this volume presents semiotic approaches to design and analysis of computer systems, focusing on the internal workings of the machine and the computer-based signs, and Part II deals with interactive composition and aesthetic form, especially the aesthetics and rhetoric of interactive fiction, focusing on man-machine interaction, interface-design and the concept of interactivity, Part III is devoted to the analysis of *computers in context*. In taking up computers in this perspective, we are seeking to discuss a set of issues on yet another level of concern — those wider social, cultural, historical, and organizational conditions and circumstances within which computers and the use of computers are located and made meaningful. The term *context* thus serves to direct attention, on the one hand to the conditioning forces and frames that constitute and regulate the production, circulation and use of computer technology, and on the other hand to the social and cultural situation or environment that computer technology by the same production, circulation, and use affects and sets its mark on.

Computer technology undoubtedly plays an increasingly important role in culture and society. On the basis of large-scale developments in micro-electronics and software design during the past decades, computer technology has established itself as the dominating social technology for communication, storage, processing, and production of data, information, and meaning. What this *means,* however, has not yet been established. There seems to be a broad agreement that Western societies are at present witnessing a so-called "computer" or "information revolution" and that information and computer technologies will radically change our society and culture, remodel our ways of living, reshape work and leisure — and not least, redefine human experience, thought, and knowledge, and thereby inevitably reconstruct the conceptual framework for understanding the world around us. Yet, how computer technology performs these tremendous effects, and how computer technology itself develops, is rarely analyzed. Computers and their contextual effects are simply taken for granted, when they should be taken to bits and pieces.

It is partly the aim of this collection to draw attention to these aspects of computer technology. All the chapters deal with issues related to the contextual meaning of computers — that is, they all in very different ways, try to analyze how computers are inscribed in contextual settings and how contextual settings are inscribed in computers and activities connected to computers. The topics are varied and include: computer advertisements, hypertext, computer-mediated communication, computers in the workplace, the history of computers, and computer culture. And the complex of theoretical disciplines put into play and the types of analytical approaches adopted are similarly multitudinous, covering discourse analysis, communication theory, systems theory, historical approaches, structuration theory, cultural studies — and last but not least, media studies and semiotics.

In the opening chapter "Computer culture: The meaning of technology and the technology of meaning. A triadic essay on the semiotics of technology," Jens F. Jensen sets out to construct a coherent theoretical and analytical framework for the study of technology in a cultural context, using computer and information technology (*the technology of meaning*) as an exemplary technological field. It is argued that if one conceptualizes "culture" as the structures and processes through which a given society organizes its experiences and relations and gives meaning to its "world," then studying technology from a cultural studies approach will consequently mean studying how technologies form part of the structures and processes through which meanings and sign-systems are created — studying technology as part of semiotic systems (*the meaning of technology*). As a result, the study of technology-as-culture becomes a branch of semiotics. The chapter thus at the same time lays the foundations for — what is here introduced as — a *semiotics of technology*.

If one, as in this case, chooses to understand the semiotic structures and processes, through which meaning is created, in terms of C.S. Peirce's triadic sign-concept, it becomes evident that technologies can occupy three different semiotic positions or have three different semiotic functions: as *(i) representamen* (as an actual sign), as *(ii) object*, and as *(iii) interpretant* (positions and functions, which are briefly outlined later as well as more thoroughly in the following chapter). Thus by simultaneously taking as its point of departure the most basic semiotic mechanism (the sign-relation) *and* in the broadest conceivable context (the cultural context), the chapter at the same time provides the overall framework, within which the other chapters in this part are placed.

(i) First, computer-technology can itself, as a physical, perceptible manifestation, take on the nature of *representamen* (or actual sign vehicle) that refers to or "stands for" something else by virtue of a socially conventionalised code. For besides being material entities, computers are symbolic entities as well. A tentative suggestion might be that technologies increasingly seem

to constitute central, symbolic elements in the meaning-producing practices of high-technological cultures. Thus, a technology can, simply by being appropriated by a given culture, come to function as an emblem, symbol — as a sign — of the cultural identity, subcultural affiliation, official "image," technological competence and performance, and so on, of the social group or the individual. In other words, technologies as signs have become an important factor in the way in which (technologically based) social groups and individuals are making sense of themselves and the world, thereby creating their culture. That technology takes on this kind of sign function is perhaps especially palpable and evident in the realm of marketing and advertising. However, the computer is not only a meaningful sign as a physically manifest technology, it also functions literally as a *media* technology, as a vehicle for transmitting signs and texts that in a similar way "stand for" something else, represent something other than themselves. In this way, too, computer technologies can be considered as signs: sign-conveying media that give rise to various media-based organizations, communities, and (sub)cultures. In the present part of the anthology, this field of study is represented by three contributions:

In "One person, one computer. The social construction of the personal computer," Klaus Bruhn Jensen — taking computer advertisements, selected from American magazines over a period of ten years as his point of departure — analyzes the representation and social construction of the computer in advertising discourse, and points to what he calls its "semiotic" and "symbolic diffusion." Whereas Bruhn Jensen's chapter concentrates on the marketing and distribution of computers at the moment of circulation, the following two chapters direct their attention to issues related to the use of computers at the moment of consumption, or more exactly to computer-mediated communication systems in the context of social organization and communication, respectively.

In "Hi-tech network organizations as self-referential systems," Lars Qvortrup introduces a theory for understanding the new organizations and *social networks*, whose organizational interaction and communication are based exclusively on computer-mediated information and communication technologies — the so-called hi-tech network organizations — primarily drawing on Niklas Luhmann's systems theory with its concepts of social and organisational systems as "self-referential" systems. And in the following mini-chapter "Disturbing communication," Peter Bøgh Andersen, with a point of departure in catastrophe theory, points out how these concepts drawn from systems theory can be applied more concretely to communication analysis.

In "Dialogues in networks," computer-mediated communication systems are again the object of study, when Elsebeth Korsgaard Sorensen with an empirical, linguistic approach studies the interaction in a concrete computer-mediated communication system. Among other things, she describes how the electronic organization, independent of time and space, manifests itself in a number of characteristic traits in the electronic dialogue.

(ii) Second, besides being a sign vehicle, computer technology can take on the nature of the *object*, since technologies are obviously not only symbolic but also material entities. In this position, technology functions as "artifacts" or "phenomena" that exist objectively in an external referential reality beyond the world of language and signs, but exactly for that reason they are "objects" that one can speak or think *about*, that one can de*signate* or de*scribe*.

Thus technology becomes the object of another sign — namely, the object that signs *stand for* and culture tries to make sense of and ascribe meaning to. "Objects" that as such have their own (technological) history, their functions as cultural artifacts in everyday life, their impacts as social forces on other levels of society, as, for example, culture, history, politics, economy, organizations, institutions, and so on.

This analytical approach is represented by Jens Christensen's "Historical trends in computer and information technology" that offers a historical outline of the development of computer technology and computer industry from the end of the 1940s to the present. A study that far from being the isolated "internal" technological history one is so often confronted with, is a study of the contextual process that pays due attention to the wider historical and economic environment in which technology is developing. In Peter Bøgh Andersen's short postscript to this chapter, "The history of computer-based signs," Christensen's historical account is related to the chapters that are based on semiotics — making historical viewpoints relevant for semiotic ones and vice versa.

The other chapter that exemplifies this approach also has a historical angle — Randi Markussen's "A historical perspective on work practices and technology — the case of the National Labor Inspection Service," which, as the title suggests, is a case-based analysis of the relationship between a concrete field of work and new information technology.

(iii) And third, besides acting as sign vehicle and object, computer technology can take on the role of *interpretant*, governing the way we talk and think about the world. In other words, technology can be the agency by means of which something other is understood insofar as technologies constitute interpreting figures, metaphors — signs — that conceptualize, structure, or explain a given part of the reality. According to a dominant branch of

contemporary linguistic and cognitive science, such metaphors, through which one thing is understood in terms of another thing, are the very basis of the human conceptual system, the very processes through which cognitive and cultural meaning is produced. To make another tentative suggestion: In the continuous process of comprehending, speaking about, and ascribing meaning to the world, concepts and metaphors from the world of technology, not least from the domains of the computer, EDP technology, and cybernetics, play an increasingly dominant role, even in relation to our understanding of areas that do not, strictly speaking, belong to the domain of technology. Technology and the computer thus appear to supply an increasing number of the concepts and metaphors through which the "present" attempts to understand itself and the world in the continuous sense-making process that is culture.

Since the world is always, in this way, metaphorically constructed, it is, of course, also possible to establish some kind of oppositional analytical reading strategy: to attempt to understand the world through concrete figures. It is this kind of "allegorical" mode of reading — where something is read through something else — that culture analysts such as Walter Benjamin and later Fredric Jameson have excelled in, seeking to uncover deep-lying cultural traits allegorically through the reading of concrete cultural manifestations. This kind of reading-and-interpreting method can be found in "Hypertext: From modern utopia to postmodern dystopia?" in which Bjørn Sørenssen — inspired, among others, by Jameson — via a reading of the concrete computer phenomenon "hypertext" uncovers a large number of the central traits of the underlying opposition between "modernism" and "postmodernism," and in this way both contributes to the wider cultural analysis of the hypertext phenomenon and to the analysis of the currently much discussed historic break between "modern" and "postmodern."

13

Computer culture: The meaning of technology and the technology of meaning. A triadic essay on the semiotics of technology

Computer technology is a *meaning*ful technology, a technology that, in line with the considerable social resources that have been expended on technological innovation and automation in recent decades, has come to play an increasingly meaningful role in a high-technology society. Thus, as early as 1983, the computer had become so meaningful that *Time* (1/3/83) awarded it the prize normally given to the man or woman of the year. So, computer technology is meaningful, full of meanings. What the computer actually *means*, however, to our society, our culture and our consciousness, has not yet been evaluated.

It is this field of mediation, linking technology and the process of meaning, linking computers and culture, that is the subject of this chapter. The main focus is on the title *Computer culture* while, conversely, the subtitle *The meaning of technology and the technology of meaning* is intended as a kind of puzzle picture that changes its meaning, according to the point of view one adopts: On the one hand, *The meaning of technology* is designed to show, as indicated earlier, that we are dealing with an extremely important and meaningful technology: information technology or computer technology, which is precisely a technology that is charged with meaning. On the other hand, *The meaning of technology* is supposed to imply a humanistic and culturo-analytical approach to technology, an approach that places the emphasis on terms such as meaning, systems of meaning, and the production of meaning, and that primarily addresses the question of the actual, cultural meaning of technology, in the sense of the meaning-creating processes and structures that technology forms part of, and the various cultural concepts that attempt to create meaning through technology. The term, *the technology of meaning*, is meant to show, on the one hand, that the technology in question is one that processes meaning — the computer, which has been defined precisely as a "symbol-manipulating" machine, a machine that processes, stores, and transmits data, information, symbols. On the other hand, *the technology of meaning* is intended to emphasize that we are at the same time dealing with the very mechanisms of the construction of meaning, the apparatus of meaning, "semiotic technology" — the mechanisms and processes through which meaning is created in society. Like a puzzle picture it is hoped that the subtitle *The meaning of technology and the technology of meaning* will reflect all these changing meanings.

The aim of the chapter is thus to discuss possible approaches through which technologies can be studied from a culturo-analytical point of view, to study the cultural construction of technology, to survey technologies-as-culture, and more specifically, to construct a coherent theoretical, methodological and analytical approach to technology and culture, a common, scientific language that can encompass both culture and technology and that is thus also capable of capturing sensitively how these are related to each other.

We must start, however, by defining such basic concepts as "culture," "technology," and "technology-as-culture."

The concept of "culture"

"Culture" has traditionally been defined as, respectively, "works of art," "states of mind," or "whole ways of life" by the schools of thought that formerly dominated the study of culture. But these are conceptualizations that in practice frequently turned out to be — as far as the first one is concerned — far too specific, and — as far as the two others are concerned — much too general. The concept of "culture" that is used here has instead been borrowed from a more recent tradition within contemporary cultural studies.

"Culture" may here be defined as Raymond Williams's *"signifying system* through which necessarily ... a social order is communicated, reproduced, experienced and explored" (Williams, 1981: 13); or as Umberto Eco's "way in which a given society organises the world which it perceives, analyses and transforms" (Eco, 1975: 15); or finally, it can be defined more generally and all-embracingly as the structures and processes by means of which a social community organizes its experiences, relationships, and actions — thereby giving meaning to the world and "itself." In other words, "culture" is the way we think and speak *about* the world, and in this way create the world *about* us.

Cultural science: "The semiotics of culture"

If this definition of culture is used, what kind of science and precisely what theories, methods, and conceptual apparatus would be able to cover the study of "cultural phenomena"?

One possible answer, building on Umberto Eco, among others, might be expressed as follows: Do we accept that "culture" is the way in which a given social consensus has chosen to understand, explain, and organize the world? And do we accept that the structures and processes through which a society organizes its perception of the world are sign structures and sign processes? If so, it will also be obvious that the units that make up culture are sign units; that they are of a semiotic nature; or, as Eco puts it, "cultural structures (the way in which a given society organises the world which it perceives, analyses and transforms) are semiotic structures and therefore systems of units each of which can stand for another" (Eco, 1975: 15). In other words, it is by means of such a system of *signifiers* tied to a system of *signifieds* that "a given culture "thinks" and communicates the undifferentiated continuum which is the world" (Eco, 1975: 15). In principle, it is the very same point that Julia Kristeva emphasises when she writes that the "specifically semiotic *discovery*" that has emerged through the study of myths, rituals, moral codes, art, ideologies, and so on as sign systems, is:

> that the *law* governing, or, if one prefers, the *major constraint* affecting any social practice lies in the fact that it signifies; i.e., that it is articulated *like* a language. Every social practice, as well as being the object of external (economic, political, etc.) determinants, is also determined by a set of signifying rules, by virtue of the fact that there is present an order of language; that this language has a double articulation (signifier/signified); that this duality stands in an arbitrary relation to the referent; and that all social functioning is marked by the split between referent and symbolic and by the shift from signified to signifier coextensive with it.
>
> One may say, then, that what semiotics has discovered is the fact that there is a general social law, that this law is the symbolic dimension which is given in language, and that every social practice offers a specific expression of that law.
>
> (*Kristeva, 1975: 47*)

Thus "culture" as social practice is theoretically subject to the same semiotic rules and logic that apply to structures of signs and language. The laws of culture are the laws of communication and meaning. In the final analysis, "cultural logic" is a "semiotic logic," which is why it is not only possible, but also *necessary* to study culture, the basic mechanisms of culture — indeed, cultural life in its entirety — as semiotic phenomena, as semiotic practices. In other words, we must regard cultural structures as an enormous complex of sign systems.

As the science that studies sign systems and meaning systems and how these systems are socially constructed, semiotics is therefore also the science that studies culture. Or to put it more strongly: semiotics is the science — the set of theories, methods, and concepts — that makes it possible for culture to be studied directly, on its own terms: in its essential nature as a realized signifying system. As Eco points out, *"Culture can be studied completely under a semiotic profile"* (Eco, 1976: 28). In short, semiotics is *the* science of culture: cultural science.

Or conversely, if one wishes to define a common trait in semiotic theory, to identify a single goal for the discipline, one might say, with Eco, that semiotics "tend to concern itself with all cultural phenomena" (Eco, 1975: 11). Semiotic projects are therefore concerned with the study of all kinds of cultural phenomena, with *the whole of culture*, understood as realized systems of meaning. In this sense, the discipline thus becomes an extremely comprehensive and far-reaching science that, in the final analysis, could be claimed to assimilate and replace culture analysis and the general theory of culture. It is a semiotics whose main object can perhaps best be identified as "a "logic of culture." Which is — in different words — precisely what ... Saussure and Peirce wanted," as Eco puts it in an article that even has the title, "Looking for a Logic of Culture" (Eco, 1975: 17).

This is also the reason why this science, as suggested in the present context, should be called "the semiotics of culture."

The concept of "technology"

After establishing a definition of "culture" and noting some of its consequences for the study of culture, the next questions that present themselves are how should technology be viewed in a cultural context; how does one define technology-as-culture; how can technology be perceived in a culturo-semiotic perspective? In the first instance, the answers to these questions may be formulated negatively (cf. Dahlberg et al., 1989: 47 ff.).

Studying technology in a culturo-analytical perspective means that technologies must not merely be regarded as isolated techno-systems that, in principle, can be described in their own terms — in purely technical terms, as is often the case in technico-scientific research. For although technologies are, of course, technical systems, they are more than just that. They are an integrated part of a larger cultural system, and this being so, they must be seen as elements of this wider cultural context — in terms of their incorporation into the system determined by the cultural context.

Furthermore, studying technology in a culturo-analytical perspective means that technologies are not only seen as relatively autonomous "variables" with more or less observable "effects" on society and culture, "effects" that can be completely and exhaustively described in purely sociological terms, as is not infrequently the case in the social sciences, for example. For although technologies do, of course, have "effects," do have an "influence" on society and culture, they should primarily be seen as social and cultural entities: socially and culturally produced, socially and culturally distributed, and socially and culturally consumed.

Finally, studying technology in a culturo-analytical perspective means that technologies are not viewed as mere "artifacts," as they quite often are within the research traditions of both social sciences and the humanities. For although technologies are to some extent "artifacts" — concrete, material objects — they are at the same time much more than that. In the words of Alfred Gell:

> ...technology not only consists of the artefacts which are employed as tools, but also includes the sum total of the kinds of knowledge which make possible the invention, making and use of tools ... Technology, in the widest sense, is those forms of social relationships which make it socially necessary to produce, distribute and consume goods and services using "technical" processes.   (*Gell, 1988: 6*)

And understood in this way — as an integrated element of a larger, cultural system; as a socially produced, distributed and consumed entity; as a complex of technological knowledge; as social relations and social practices, and so on — "technology" is also, of course, made accessible as a relevant object of study for the semiotics of culture.

Technology-as-culture: The semiotics of technology

But how exactly, in more concrete terms, can one study technology-as-culture? The following brief, provisional answer might be given to this question: If, as we suggested earlier, one chooses to regard "culture" as the structures and processes through which a given society organizes its experiences, relations, and actions, thereby giving meaning to its "world," then studying technology-as-culture will consequently mean that one studies the various ways in which technologies form part of the structures and processes that create sense and meaning; that one studies how technologies form part of the way in which a society acts in and thinks and speaks about the world — and thus in the cultural construction of the world *about* one. The study of technology-as-culture implies, in other words, that one studies *the meaning of technology*, that one studies technology as a *realized signifying system*, that one studies technology-as-semiotics.

The term "technological culture," in this context, should be taken to mean a component in the total culture of a given society — namely, the meanings, values and activities that define that society's relationships with technologies in the immediate environment of the society in question and with technologies that directly or indirectly affect that environment. Defining the term in this way implies that "technological culture" should be regarded as an integrated, embedded, subordinate element within the total culture of the society, for technologies only become functional in and integrated into a social group insofar as they give meaning, insofar as they mean something, within the framework of the given total culture of that group. "Technological culture" can therefore only be analysed and understood in the context of the total culture (cf. Dahlberg et al.: 47 ff.).

This definition of the study of "technology-as-culture" as the study of technology as part of semiotic systems can be taken at a completely literal, very basic level. Here, it may be useful to take as our starting-point the definitions employed in the semiotics of Charles Sanders Peirce.[1]

According to Peirce, every process of meaning has a basic, triadic structure, in the sense that the precondition for the creation of meaning — the sign — constitutes a relation between three semiotic entities. The Peircean definition of a sign[2] can be briefly summarized as follows: A sign is "a (first) thing" that stands for "a second thing" by virtue of "a third thing." Or in a more expanded form: The sign consists of: (i) the representamen ("a First"), which is the physically manifest, perceivable sign — the entity that *represents*; (ii) the object ("a Second"), which is the item or phenomenon in "external reality" that the representamen refers to — the entity that *is represented*; and (iii) the interpretant ("a Third"), which is the "interpretation," "code" or "other sign" that deciphers and explains the representamen by linking it with the object; in other words, the element that establishes a relationship between the entity that represents and the one that is represented. The actual sign is then finally constituted as a relationship between these three entities. It is this triadic relationship, this active, processual function between repre-

---

[1] For an introduction to C.S. Peirce's 'logic of relations,' semiotics and sign model see Gall Jørgensen's chapter 3.

[2] 'A sign, or *representamen*, is something which stands to somebody for something in some respect or capacity. It addresses somebody, that is, creates in the mind of that person an equivalent sign, or perhaps a more developed sign. That sign which it creates I call the *interpretant* of the first sign. The sign stands for something, its *object*. It stands for that object, not in all respects, but in reference to a sort of idea ...' (Peirce, 1931-58: 2.228). Or: 'A *Sign*, or *Representamen*, is a First which stands in such a genuine triadic relation to a Second, called its *Object*, as to be capable of determining a Third, called its *Interpretant*, to assume the same triadic relation to its Object in which it stands itself to the same Object' (Peirce, 1931-58: 2.274).

sentamen, object and interpretant that Peirce calls *semiosis*. The triadic sign-model can be depicted graphically as in figure 13.1.

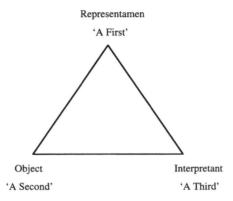

Fig. 13.1. Peirce's triadic sign-model.

If the study of technology as culture means studying how technologies form part of the processes and structures through which meaning is created, and if one chooses to understand the relationship of meaning in terms of Peirce's triadic sign-concept, it immediately becomes clear that technologies can potentially occupy three different positions in the process of meaning — that is, technologies can theoretically have three different semiotic functions: as *(i) the representamen*, as *(ii) the object*, and as *(iii) the interpretant*. Let us take the second position first.

(ii) The most direct, most obvious position that technology can occupy is that of *object*, as the object *about* which one *speaks*; the phenomenon *about* which one *thinks*; the reality one attempts to designate, to describe, to comprehend. Technology here adopts the position of "the second thing" — namely, as something other than the signs (understood as the representamen, "the first thing") that attempt to designate, describe, comprehend it. In this position, technology thus has the status of object or phenomenon in an external reality that is beyond the world of the language and the signs, where the relationship of representation is established solely on the basis of "the third thing": a cultural code that links the representamen with the object. Technology, in other words, assumes the position of "the second thing" that "the first thing" can stand for, by virtue of "a third thing." It is a semiotic function that — if we follow Peirce — could be called *technology as object*.

(i) Technology can also itself occupy the position of sign, in the sense of *representamen*. In other words, technology can itself, as a physically manifest and perceptible object, take on the nature of a sign vehicle that refers to

or represents "a second thing," which is something other than technology itself as a physically manifest object, where this referential function is established as a result of "a third thing": a cultural code, a social convention, an inscribed meaning. In other words, technology here occupies the position of "the first thing" that stands for the "the second thing" by virtue of "a third thing." A semiotic function that could be called: technology as a sign; or to follow Peirce, *technology as representamen*.

(iii) Finally, technology can occupy the position of *interpretant* — it can be that by means of which "the second thing" is understood, namely insofar as technologies constitute patterns of interpretation, metaphors, figures of thought — in short: signs — that clarify, interpret, and explain a given representation by relating it to a given object. It is, of course, possible for this technological interpretant to function as an interpreting figure for a part reality that does not, strictly speaking, have anything to do with technology. In such a context, technology occupies the position of "the third thing" through which "the first thing" can be understood as referring to "the second thing"; a semiotic function that could be called technology as an interpreting figure, or with Peirce, *technology as interpretant*.

Of these three possible semiotic functions that technology can adopt in the process of meaning, the latter two in particular appear to have been overlooked, even though both seem to be extremely important to our understanding of the cultural significance of technology in the so-called "information society" or in the so-called "computer age." What will be suggested, therefore, in the present context is a semiotic discipline, capable of dealing with all three aspects of the cultural significance and semiotic functions of technology. It is a science that can deal with technology as an object, but that is capable of doing so in a way that reflects the semiotic logic playing a part in all attempts to understand and to describe, and a science that is simultaneously capable of studying technology as a sign or representamen and as interpretant.

This science should be called *semiotics of technology* and it should be seen as *a specific semiotics* — in Umberto Eco's sense — since it "is, or aims at being, the "grammar" of a particular sign system, and proves to be successful insofar as it describes a given field of communicative phenomena as ruled by a system of signification" (Eco, 1984: 5). But it will at the same time be classified under *a general semiotics*, which it will both draw on and contribute to, just as it will constitute an important branch of the general humanistic — in this instance, especially culturo-analytical — approach to the study of technologies.

The basic outline of a semiotics of technology of this kind will be briefly sketched next, structured on the three main components involved: *(i)* tech-

nology as representamen, (ii) technology as object, and *(iii) technology as interpretant.* The sketch will consist of an exposition of and critical commentary on some of the available scientific literature on the individual areas, as the central concerns and conceptual apparatus of the science will be established. As has already been mentioned, computer and information technology will be used as an exemplary technological field.

(i) Technology as representamen. Or: The computer — a cultural sign

If the study of technology-as-culture involves studying how technologies form part of the structures and processes via which meaning is culturally constructed, and if the structures and processes by which meaning is constructed are thought of as triadic relationships between representamen, object, and interpretant, then technology may primarily be thought of as a representamen, as an actual *sign.* In other words, technology as a physically manifest, perceptible element takes on the function of a sign vehicle ("a first thing") that stands for or refers to "a second thing" ("something other" than the actual technology) by virtue of a culturally conventionalised system of signification ("a third thing"). In order to understand and explain this aspect of the semiotic functions of technology — an aspect that is especially concerned with communication and signification — it might be worth looking for support in communication theories based on semiotics. One possible link might be Stuart Hall's "Encoding/decoding," where Hall attempts to sketch a semiotic communication model of this kind.

"Encoding/decoding"

Hall takes the traditional view of the communication process in mass-communication studies as his negative point of departure, as he directs critical attention toward this tradition's simple "linear" view of communication, the "sender/message/receiver" model, its focus on "message exchange" and its consequent failure to differentiate between "the different moments as a complex structure of relations" (Hall, 1980: 128). He suggests that instead the process of communication should be thought of as homologous with Marx's analysis of the production of goods — that is, in terms of "a structure produced and sustained through the articulation of linked but distinctive moments — production, circulation ... consumption, reproduction" (p.128). This is a structure that is, on the one hand, made up of a series of mutually dependent practices, but in which every component, on the other hand, has its own specific conditions of existence, forms and modalities. But it is also a structure where the object of these practices is, of course, no longer goods — as in Marx — but "meanings and messages in the form of sign-vehicles ... organised, like any form of communication or language, through the operation of codes within the syntagmatic chain of a discourse" (p.128); in other words, texts. In this transcribed form — as a *communication model* — the structure can be represented graphically as shown in figure 13.2.

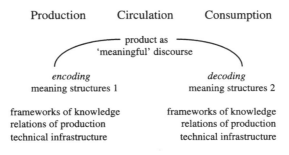

Production   Circulation   Consumption

product as
'meaningful' discourse

encoding
meaning structures 1

frameworks of knowledge
relations of production
technical infrastructure

decoding
meaning structures 2

frameworks of knowledge
relations of production
technical infrastructure

Fig. 13.2. Hall's model of encoding/decoding

The model might be interpreted as follows:

(i) The "product" — the text, is produced in the production moment, a moment that Hall calls *encoding* understood as the translation of the message — here "meaning structures 1" — into a sign vehicle in accordance with the rules of the given code. And as in the production of goods, the production of texts too, as social practice, is based on and conditioned by a number of contextual aspects that Hall calls "frameworks of knowledge," "relations of production," and "technical infrastructure."

(ii) In the circulation moment, a moment called "product as "meaningful" discourse," the "product" — the encoded message or text — is conveyed to the potential recipients. The significant aspect of this moment is thus the realisation of the message in a discursive form that is relatively autonomous of sender and receiver and whose dominant principle lies in the formal rules of discourse and language.

(iii) In the consumption moment the "product," the text, is finally consumed or used. Hall calls this moment *decoding* since before the text can be used and the circuit thus be completed, the discursive form of the message must again be decoded in accordance with the rules of the given code — that is, retranslated into social practice, consciousness, meaning — here called "meaning structures 2." If the decoded meaning is not articulated in social practice and thereby translated into appropriate, meaningful discourse, there can be no consumption. If nobody gets any meaning out of the text, *if it does not mean anything to anybody*, it remains meaningless, it produces no "effect," it makes no sense. The consumption of texts is thus also a form of production or reproduction — namely, a construction of meaning, a production of sense. And as in the encoding of texts for production, the decoding for consumption as a social practice is conditioned by a number of contextual aspects, such as "frameworks of knowledge," "relations of production," and "technical infrastructure."

Neither encoding nor decoding can therefore be defined in simple behaviorist terms. On the contrary, the central, significant characteristic of this model could be said to be the introduction of the semiotic paradigm at both ends of the chain of communication, and moreover in a form that implicitly seems to tie in with Peirce's semiotics, with his concept of the interpretant as the interpreting, decoding element and with his theory of the creation of meaning as *semiosis*.

The strengths of this model for understanding the process of communication are, according to Hall, first that it clarifies how the continuous circuit of production-distribution-(re)production is maintained via "a "passage of forms"" (p.128). Second, it emphasises that encoding, discursive form, and decoding constitute a set of jointly and separately necessary and significant, but simultaneously differentiated and autonomous moments in the total process of communication. And third, that it "highlights the specificity of the forms in which the product of the process "appears" in each moment" (p.128).

While all three moments are thus necessary for the circuit as a whole, no single moment can, on its own, completely guarantee or determine the others. On the contrary, the individual moments, since they each have their own specific forms, modalities, and conditions of existence, can cause breaks or disturbances in the continuous "passage of forms" on which the process of communication depends. *Encoding* and *decoding* are thus certainly related, as elements in the process of communication, but that does not mean that they automatically correspond perfectly, with the latter being a necessary consequence of the first. For example, if the codes that form the basis of encoding and decoding, respectively, are not completely identical, the encoding and decoding will not be symmetrical. What are called "meaning structures 1" and "meaning structures 2" in figure 13.2, therefore, do not necessarily constitute a "direct identity"; on the contrary, depending on the degree of deviation in the code, they will demonstrate different degrees of variance. The relationship between what are normally called "understanding" and "misunderstanding" in communicative exchanges will here be a function of this symmetry/asymmetry in the relationship between *encoding* and *decoding*.

Since *encoding* cannot determine or guarantee the realized *decoding* in any direct way, and since there is consequently no "necessary correspondence" between *encoding* and *decoding*, the relationship between the two moments can take on different forms. Here, Hall identifies three systematic, possible combinations of this relationship, or to be more precise, he operates with a model of three hypothetical positions, from which the decoding of a discursive form can be constructed in relation to its encoding:

(i) First, we may find a decoding position that takes the meaning "full and straight, and decodes the message in terms of the reference code in which it has been encoded" (p.136). In this case, there is thus perfect symmetry between the encoding and the decoding, which is why it also becomes "the ideal-typical case of "perfectly transparent communication"" (p.136). Hall describes this decoding position as "preferred readings," "preferred codes," "preferred meanings," in the sense that they are the readings, codes, and meanings that have been pre-ferred — singled out beforehand, privileged *a priori, despite the fact* that they can never be completely pre-scribed or pre-determined.

(ii) Second, there may be a decoding position that by and large accepts and takes over the codes of the encoding position but which reserves the right to perform negotiating, rejecting or even directly oppositional decodings adapted to "local conditions." That is why this type of decoding would also seem to be "a mixture of adaptive and oppositional elements" (p.137). Hall describes this decoding position as "negotiated readings," "negotiated codes," "negotiated meanings" because the readings, codes, and meanings of the decoding are in a state of continuous "negotiation" with the discursive form that the encoder has constructed.

(iii) And third, we may envisage a decoding position that recognizes and is able to deal with the "preferred codes" of the encoding, but that deliberately chooses to decode the discursive form according to some kind of diametrically opposite code. Hall writes, "it is possible for a viewer perfectly to understand both the literal and the connotative inflection given by a discourse but to decode the message in a *globally* contrary way" (p.137-8). A decoding position that Hall therefore describes as "oppositional readings," "oppositional codes," or "oppositional meanings."

Whereas Hall's project can thus be read as a transference of the structural "production-circulation-consumption" model *from* the analysis of goods *to* the domain of the sign-borne communication — by means of which the model is consequently semiotised — ascribed a dimension of meaning — it is here the reverse operation that will be suggested and tried out: that of conveying Hall's structural model *from* the world of the communication *back to* the world of the objects, though not to the domain of the production of goods but to the domain of technology (this does not appear to be an unreasonable operation, in view of the fact that technologies often share the characteristics of goods), where the dimension of meaning that Hall ascribes to the model — the semiotised form of the model — is retained in the re-transcription. For technologies, too, can contain meanings and can act as signs. If technologies are to be produced, distributed, and consumed, they must necessarily have a meaning, be meaningful. They must mean something — to somebody.

It is precisely this aspect of the semiotic function of technology that is implied when Murdock et al. (1988) note that computers are "complex commodities embodying particular mixes of exchange value, use values and *sign value*" and that, accordingly, the market for them is divided into "the economic, the social and *the symbolic*" (1988: 3, my emphasis). And furthermore:

> Like all goods, home computers carry social meanings which help to make "visible and stable the categories of culture" ... As a consequence their use values are inextricably bound up with their sign values. As well as promoting particular applications and promising particular kinds of pleasures and benefits, the marketing and promotion strategies pursued by the home computer industry actively incorporate and re-work certain cultural and ideological themes directing potential users to read the micro as sign in particular ways ... To fully understand patterns of adoption then, we need to explore the ways in which people locate themselves in the thicket of signs that surrounds home micros, and negotiate the symbolic barriers to participation which they erect. The symbolic dimension is also important in understanding variations in use since promotional discourses also offer a range of user roles and identities...
> *(Murdock et al., 1988: 4)*

This kind of technological re-transcription of the semiotised model will be attempted next, while following the structuring into production, circulation, and consumption and drawing on existing trends toward a theoretical movement of this type.[3]

Technologies as textuality

(i) Production: In production, the technology is designed, constructed, and produced. And every technological construction also contains certain intentions on the part of the designer, the constructor and the producer; a planned

---

[3] The next section of the chapter leans especially on Dalhberg et al., 1989 and Morley and Silverstone, 1989 and 1990.

functionality and because of this an inbuilt — and thus, in the technology, an inherent — structure (of meaning) that, as such, delineates the possible fields of actually realisable applications and the contexts in which they may be used; a production of a particular, meaningful, discursive (technological) form that follows certain codified rules and is conditioned by a variety of contextual factors; and — as far as the constructed, technological object is concerned — comparative autonomy in relation to both constructor and user.

If one takes this argument just a little bit further, one can claim — with Dahlberg et al. (1989) — that technologies in principle are textual, that they, in themselves, can be thought of as texts, either in O'Sullivan et al.'s sense of "a signifying structure composed of *signs* and *codes*" that has "a physical existence of its own, independent of its *sender* or *receiver*" (1983: 238), or in Ducrot and Todorov's sense of "connotative system(s) ... defined by (their) autonomy and closure" (cited from Dahlberg et al., 1989: 59).

Technology is *designed* in production, and the etymological origin of the word de-*sign* is to be found in the Latin word *signum*, which means sign, form, mark. In production, therefore, technology is in a sense signified, described, *inscribed*. It is always produced with a set of instructions — pertaining to function, processing, use — and these instructions too are de-signed, in-scribed in the actual technology (cf. Dahlberg et al.: 59). In the immanent structure of technology, particular models of consumption situations are in this way also in-scribed, certain applications anti-cipated, certain pre-scriptions laid down, with regard to potential consumption. Anti-cipated user-receptions, pre-ferred consumption codes, and pre-scribed meaningful applications that — as can be seen — operate in exactly the same way as Hall's concepts of preferred readings, preferred codes, preferred meanings. Read in this way, technologies are inscriptions, complex systems of signs and codes, realized signifying systems. Or to use terms that echo the preceding: In production, technology is encoded as a particular, meaningful, discursive form, in accordance with the rules of a given code.

All these structures of meaning encoded in the design of the production moment aim at unambiguity, clarity, precision, and are thus an attempt to achieve closure, finality (Dahlberg et al.: 59-60). This is true both as far as specification of function is concerned — namely, the fact that technology is constructed to be used in particular ways with a particular purpose, and as far as reference to a particular group of potential consumers is concerned, as defined by their particular (technological) discourse, knowledge, competence, performance, and so on (*even though* concrete technologies can, of course, *despite* this tentative closure, generate a multitude of different meanings and uses in practice, depending on the decoding of the actual recipient, cf. section (iii) *Consumption*). In this way, the concept of intention is also highlighted. For although the concept of the sender-intention is in many ways problematic for a semiotic interpretation of communication, since this component is difficult to capture and describe, intentionality, as such, cannot really be altogether rejected. For communicating — and communicating with "intentional signs" as it is in fact called by Eco (cf. 1976: 17-19) — must always necessarily involve a *wish to say something* and thus an intention to communicate. This kind of intention-horizon also plays a role in the production of technology. For technologies are not created in the absence of specific — explicit or implied — intentions in the designers, constructors and producers of the given technology. This aspect of the production of technology corresponds thus to speaking or writing: It is an attempt to gain attention, an appeal to a particular group of recipients, a guide to a particular code-use, a pointing out of a particular meaning or function in reading or use, an attempt at closure (Dahlberg et al.: 59).

Whether encoded in accordance with the rules of a given code in a meaningful, discursive form; as a structure inscribed with particular preferred meanings, preferred codes, preferred uses; as a system that has a physical existence of its own and comparative autonomy in relation to both sender and receiver; as a deliberate effort to attract attention and an attempt at closure — in all these aspects, technologies can thus be regarded as textual, *as texts*, and in all these aspects, the production of technologies is to be understood as the device that Hall calls encoding.

(ii) Circulation: In circulation, technology is distributed on the market to potential recipients or consumers. It is distributed as a "product," as a realized, discursive form that is relatively independent of producer and consumer and is chiefly governed by the formal rules of the discourse. In pursuing the proposed text-metaphor, support can now be found in the text-system developed by John Fiske, among others. In *Television Culture*, he points out that textual phenomena, in connection with media technologies, can assume qualitatively different forms, which can be divided into three categories: *(i) primary texts*, *(ii) secondary texts*, and *(iii) tertiary texts* (Fiske, 1987).

(i) *Primary texts* are defined here as the actual texts of the media — the physically manifest texts, proffered by the media, as constituted by their formal qualities. In the medium of television, these are primarily represented by television programs, in the medium of the computer by the formal qualities in both hardware and software (the "program texts" of the computer medium). (ii) *Secondary texts* are defined as the *other texts*, which explicitly and directly refer to the primary text. In the medium of television, this takes the form of, for example, studio publicity, mention of actual television programs in the printed media, and television reviews. And in the medium of the computer they are expressed, for example, in manuals, advertisements for information technology, reviews and discussions of computer products in trade journals, scientific analyses of computer technologies, and so on. (iii)

Finally, *tertiary texts* are defined as the texts that are produced by the actual consumers of the media, during and in connection with the given consumption of the media, where the texts often help create common cultural perceptions of the meaning and function of phenomena from technological media, as exemplified in the medium of television by the viewers' verbal and non-verbal communication and interaction while watching television, conversations about programs that have been watched, readers' letters about television programs, and so on. How this type of text develops in connection with the medium of the computer is discussed later, since tertiary texts do not belong to the circulation moment, which is what we are concerned with here, but to the consumption moment.

Seen in terms of this new conceptual equality and in relation to the text metaphor used here, technologies may be said to be textual at the circulation stage, in at least two ways. First, the technology circulates as a product — as a physically manifest form that is comparatively independent of both the producer-encoder and the consumer-decoder, just as it has the nature of an encoded structure of meaning, a realization as "a meaningful discourse," mainly governed by the formal rules of the given "technological discourse." As a product in the circulation moment, technology thus takes on the characteristics of the text in these aspects. It becomes what Fiske terms a *primary text*.

Second — and perhaps more interestingly — technology becomes textually (re)constructed in the market at the circulation stage. In all sales displays, marketing, advertising campaigns, and in the treatment of technology in trade journals, news media, and scientific journals there is also a social and cultural construction of technology, a tentative establishment of technology's "actual," "correct," "proper" social meaning, function, and use; a construction of its "public image," its culturally legitimate, sanctioned meaning. In the text-metaphor complex, therefore, technology is re-written in the circulation, in the sense that advertisements and marketing in principle attempt to a-scribe to technology a set of (new) meanings. So at that stage, too, technology may be seen as meaning-bearing text, where the ascribing of meaning takes place in what Fiske calls *secondary texts*.

The meanings that are ascribed to technology in this way in the distribution-moment need not, of course, be exactly the same as the meanings constructed in production. In this area, following the example of Roland Barthes, among others, one might talk of *the rhetoric of technology*. For the construction of technology in the market is primarily rhetorical (Dahlberg et al.:

62 ff.), in the sense that technologies are not simply — are often not even primarily — marketed as machines defined solely in terms of their technical functionality and performance, but often also as a particular idea, life style, image, social status, particular attitude to the world, relationship to a (technological) subculture, promise of a stake in the future, and so on. And here it is done specifically by means of rhetoric, the "adorned statement" or the "convincing argument," which attempts to construct an appealing, co-herent, convincing system of meaning around technology: a text. It is a text that often strives toward "closure" in the sense of a stabilization of the meanings via the removal of inconsistencies, problems, and negative valori-sations. These are tentative, textual closures that do not necessarily have to be real, but that can be regarded as purely rhetorical operations — as a kind of "false closures" — whose only meaning lies in the world of advertising (Dahlberg et al.: 62 ff.).

To give an example: The term "user-friendliness" does not originate, as one might think, in scientific interface research or in design literature but in the world of advertising, where its use has also been most widespread. Here, however, the term does not cover a particular concept or strategy in interface design but rather the absence of the same. Norman and Draper write, "like the phrase "to be frank", it [i.e. "the term user friendly," JFJ] tends nowa-days to be applied only to things to which its application is in fact dubious ... In practice it most often refers to verbose or chatty interfaces with many long prompts, messages and menus" (Norman and Draper, 1986: 496). In a histori-cal situation where computer technology to the lay user, and thus also to the wider, general culture, carried such meanings as inaccessibility, complexity, technicality, expert domain, and so on, the function of the term "user friendly" was, in other words, that of deproblematizing, demystifying, and detechnifying technology and thereby restabilizing the product's cultural meaning. This operation was primarily of a rhetorical nature and took place particularly in the sphere of advertising — without it necessarily having any consequences for production and design. The term "user-friendliness" thus attempts, via a kind of "false textual closure" to sell a still relatively inacces-sible technology to a culture alienated from the computer.

In the circulation moment too, therefore, it is possible to perceive tech-nologies as texts or as the moment Hall calls "product as "meaningful" dis-course."[4]

---

[4] This side of the semiotics of technology — the cultural construction of technology through the *secondary texts* of the circulation moment — is discussed in, among others, Leslie Haddon's 'The Home Computer: The Making of a Consumer Electronic' (1988), Murdock et al.'s 'Home Computers: The Social Construction of a Complex Commodity' (1988), and Stuart Jay Kaplan's 'Visual Metaphors in the Representation of Communication Technology' (1990). In the present part

(iii) *Consumption*: Finally, in consumption technology is used and consumed. This consumption necessarily takes the form of the realization of
technology in social practices. If the technology is not articulated in such
social practices and thereby adopted by the culture as a technology, no consumption takes place. The circuit is not completed and the technology will
consequently not have any "effect" and "meaning" (in this moment).

To pursue the text-metaphor further: Adopting and using a technology
corresponds in principle to decoding the discursive (technological) form in
accordance with the rules of the given code, to retranslate the technology
into social practice, since the technology is simultaneously "read" and
"(re)inscribed." Seen from the perspective of consumption the two moments
described earlier — the meaning acquired in production and in circulation —
can only provide a set of potential, possible applications and meanings here.
If a technology is to be accepted by a given culture, however, and not rejected as though it were a foreign body, the technology must first and foremost have meaning for, must make sense to, that particular, concrete culture
(Dahlberg et al.: 57 ff.).

These cultural meanings are, of course, bought and to some extent arrive
together with the technologies as the series of potential meanings that have
been encoded into the technologies in the production moment and added to
the technologies by the *secondary texts* of the circulation moment. But they
are never simply accepted and taken over passively. On the contrary, the
technologies are only made meaningful in practice via the way in which they
are used, misused, defined, redefined, transformed, refined, innovated by the
given culture, subculture, or individual. To buy and make use of a technology is thus never simply a question of taking it over and "consuming" it,
since the actual consumers do not slavishly collect the encoded inscriptions,
they do not follow the pre-scriptions to the letter. On the other hand, it is not
a question, either, of reconstructing the meanings from scratch, of inscribing
(something on) the technology as if it were a *tabula rasa* (Dahlberg et al.:
59). On the contrary, technologies are "read" or "misread," "translated,"
"interpreted" or "mis-interpreted," all active processes in which the user selects, realizes, and elaborates particular meanings from the total reservoir of
available meanings.

The meaning of technology — for the consuming culture — may here be
said to have been realized or constructed only when the decoded, discursive
form has been articulated in social practice. The realized meaning and function will, on the one hand, be defined by the concrete, cultural context of the

---

of this anthology this field of study is represented by Klaus Bruhn Jensen's chapter, 'One Person,
One Computer. The Social Construction of the Personal Computer.'

decoding, as composed of social relations, knowledge, technological competence, and so on; and on the other hand, it will be defined by the degree of
"closure" or "opening" in the given technological text. And as far as the
latter is concerned, computer technologies, in particular, increasingly carry
within them opportunities for "writing" as well as for "reading" — also in a
more *literal* sense (Dahlberg et al.: 59) — namely, in the opportunity for different degrees of interactivity and therefore also for a degree of participation
in the (consumer) design of the technology. Seen against the backdrop of
most other technologies, computer-based technologies are thus usually comparatively "open texts" that give the decoding moment a relatively large
amount of freedom.

The textuality of technologies in the consumption moment is not only directed at the purely functional use; it goes much further than that. For in
adopting a given technology, one is also adopting a highly laden symbolic-
semiotic entity; and this mainly symbolic aspect of technologies seems to be
playing an increasingly significant role in the meaning-creating practices of
high-technological cultures and subcultures. Technologies can thus, solely
by virtue of their appropriation, use, and presentation in given (sub)cultures,
come to function as emblems, as symbols — de facto: as signs — of the
(sub)cultural identity, position, image, self-perception, and world picture, social status, property rights, user competence, performance, "techno-cultural
capital,"[5] and so on. Technologies as signs, in other words, have become an
important element in the way in which social groups and individuals in tech-
nologically-based societies "are making (common) sense of the world" and
thereby constitute their culture.

The term "technological appropriation"[6] will in this context refer to the
process by which cultures and subcultures assimilate technologies
(functionally as well as symbolically), and by which the technologies are
classified in accordance with the culture's existing systems of meaning
(identities, subjectivities, competences, performativities, images of the surrounding world, common goals, and so on) *and also* reflect back on these —
finding their place in the culture, their cultural meaning in this dual process.
There are numerous ways in which technologies are appropriated by cultures, of course, but they may usefully be systematized and conceptualized
according to Hall's three systematic possibilities, in which the decoding of a
discursive form can be constructed with reference to its encoding.

---

[5] This term has been appropriated from Bourdieu's (1984) term 'culture capital.'
[6] This concept has affinity to Dahlberg et al.'s concept of 'domestication' (1989: 24-25), but is not
founded on the family and the household as the basic unit for the consumption of technology and
therefore has a more general meaning.

(i) First, technologies may be appropriated in accordance with the codes of use and meanings that have been inscribed in the production and circulation stages, where the meanings of the decoding are completely symmetrical with the *preferred* meanings in the encoding. Hall refers to such cases as *preferred readings, codes*, or *meanings*. In this largely technological context, I suggest we use the term *preferred uses*. Since computer technologies are usually extremely flexible, comprehensive, complex technologies, it is probable that only a minority of the uses of technology in the different (sub)cultures — and here, perhaps, primarily in the professional, expert-based culture — could be included in this category.

(ii) Second, technologies may be appropriated in such a way that in general they accept and take over the codes of uses and meanings that are constructed in the production and circulation stages, but also in a way so that in certain specific, subordinate areas they create their own divergent or even oppositional meanings defined by the actual context. In such cases, the technology is thus decoded via a mixture of identical and oppositional codes, where certain meanings are accepted and others contradicted, depending on their encoding, and where the decoder-recipient therefore finds him/herself in a continuously negotiating position in relation to the discursive form constructed in the encoding. Hall writes here of *negotiated readings, codes*, or *meanings*, and when referring to the appropriation of technology, one might correspondingly talk of *negotiated uses*. Since computer technology, as mentioned earlier, is characterized by a comparatively high degree of flexibility and textual "openness" — and because of that also by a low level of determination in the relationship between encoder and decoder — a large part of the *general* cultural use of the computer can presumably be placed in this category.

(iii) Finally, technology may be appropriated in such a way that although there is complete insight into and mastery of *the preferred uses* some kind of alternative or opposing use is nevertheless deliberately chosen. When this happens the decoding of technology into social practice thus occurs according to a code that is oppositional to the encoding. Hall refers here to *oppositional readings, codes*, or *meanings*; the parallel technological term would be *oppositional uses*. Typical examples of such *oppositional uses* in the computer world are, of course, such phenomena as hackers and crackers. For within these subcultures there is a use of technologies that, on the one hand, involves complete mastery and knowledge of *the preferred uses* but that, on the other hand, indicates the deliberate choice of an often diametrically opposite code of use. *Oppositional uses* that conflict with the encoder-producer's code and aims and often with professional codes of ethics, the law, social consensus, and so on.

What becomes clear in this retranscription of the semiotised communication model to the domain of technology is that production, distribution, and consumption of technology similarly constitute a set of mutually bound and individually distinct and necessary moments, where every moment — on the other hand — has relative autonomy by virtue of its own specific forms and conditions of existence, and — most important — it also becomes clear that no moment can therefore automatically determine or guarantee the next one. The meanings and codes of use that are read into technology in one moment do not, therefore, have any necessary correspondence with those that are read out or rewritten in another; on the contrary, the technology can be interpreted and used according to completely diverging codes.

This phenomenon is in principle identical with what has been analyzed elsewhere under such headings as the *double life* of technology. David Nobel writes: "technology leads a double life, one which conforms to the intentions of designers and interests of power and another which contradicts them — proceeding behind the backs of their architects to yield unintended consequences and unintended possibilities ... Technologies rarely fulfill the fantasies of their creators" (cited from Pfaffenberger 1988b: 42). The *double life* of technology thus simply refers to the lack of determined correspondence between the individual moments in the continuous circuit of production-circulation-consumption and to the indecisiveness, contradictory nature, and textual "openness" of individual technologies that make possible the realization of many different meanings and uses in different cultural contexts.

The cultural use and meaning of a new technology is therefore never given solely by virtue of its invention and construction. Its actual consumption will always be encumbered with a high degree of uncertainty. There are therefore no simple determinisms between technological innovation and cultural change, either, although this type of conclusion is often made in scientific analyses, not least in popular scientific accounts (the numerous predictions about the cultural consequences of computer technology are obvious examples). For not only is the cultural appropriation of technology always undetermined until it has been actually realized in social practice, but the same technology can be made the object of many different uses by different subcultures and individuals. This indicates that a technology's actual cultural meaning can only be determined via concrete, empirical studies. The model thus has methodological implications in the consumption moment that would seem to require a commitment to empirical, (media-)ethnographic and reception-oriented research.

If we now return to Fiske's triadic text-classification system as presented earlier, it is also within this consumption moment that one may locate what are called *tertiary texts* in this system, defined as the texts that are produced by the users of the medium themselves during or in connection with the use of the medium in question and that, according to Fiske, serve primarily to create common cultural interpretations of the meaning and function of media-technological phenomena. In the medium of the computer, these *tertiary texts* can take the form of verbal and non-verbal communication by computer users while using the computer; user-communication via computer mediated systems of communication; user discussions, small talk, jokes, and so on, that attempt to create common sense of the function and meaning of given computer technologies; letters to the editor and questions in computer trade journals; information supplied by users of new information technology to researchers of computer use and computer culture, and so on. These *tertiary texts* are the ones that constitute the primary empirical materials for ethnographically-oriented user and media studies. They constitute what Kats and Liebes have called the "ethno-semiological data" (Fiske, 1985: 124). And studying these texts is the (only) concrete means of acquiring insight into how given cultures appropriate and create meaning from given technologies, including, among other things, how the primary and secondary texts circulate and are interpreted in their intertextual relations in the user culture, and not least, how they are interpreted in different ways by different readers in different (sub)cultures.[7]

The technology of meaning

However, in contrast to common technologies such as refrigerators, lawn mowers, cars, power drills, toasters, microwave ovens, or the like, which as physically manifest technological artifacts carry meanings and for that reason can be regarded as signs, information and communication technologies — and among these computers — in addition carry a second set of meanings. For exactly as *media*, as *media-technologies*, and as *media-hardware* they function as vehicles for the transmission of another text: a program, a "content," software — signs that "stand for" something else, refer to something other than themselves and thus in a similar way convey meanings (the two sets of meanings — the technologies as texts and the texts carried by the technologies — naturally being to a certain degree interdependent). In this way, too, computer technologies can be considered as signs and texts.

---

[7] There are several extensive analyses within this dimension of the semiotics of technology — the appropriation, the use, and the cultural meanings of computers in the moment of consumption — for example, Haddon (1988); Pfaffenberger (1988b); Dahlberg et al. (1989); Murdock et al. (1988); Turkle (1984); Venkatesh and Vitalari (1984); Holmqvist (1989) and Holmqvist and Andersen (1991). In the present section, this field of study is represented by Lars Qvortrup's chapter 'Hi-tech network organizations as self-referential systems' and Elsebeth Korsgaard Sørensen's chapter 'Dialogues in networks.'

And a semiotics of technology will naturally not least be interested in computers and information technologies on this more specific level. Furthermore, computer-based technologies as media possess special characteristics making them particularly interesting, privileged objects of study from a technology-semiotic point of view. And this has something to do with the computer both as a *technological form* and as a *cultural form*.

Unlike most earlier technologies, which were defined by the direct processing of human beings' concrete, material conditions of existence, and as such formed a direct part of mankind's processing metabolism with nature, the computer is a radically different kind of technology. For the computer does not process "nature" in the sense of material, physical entities; it only processes immaterial, non-physical entities: symbols, data, information — signs. This can be observed in the computer both in its capacity as a *technological form* and in its capacity as a *cultural form*.

As *technological form* the computer can, in principle, be described as a machine that can read, delete, and write symbols in a series of memory cells on the basis of a list of operating rules, by means of which it can also generate new symbols or combinations of symbols. "Actually, the three basic sign operations of *substitution*, *insertion* and *omission* cover the entire gamut of operations the computer performs" (Nadin, 1988: 280), operations that are all, quite plainly, basic semiotic operations. The computer is thus simply a "symbol-processing" system, whose distinguishing feature is "automatic symbol-processing" — that is, parts of the actual manipulation of symbols *may* occur automatically without direct human intervention. To sum up then, as *technological form* the computer is a data-processing automaton.

As a *cultural form* — as a realized signifying system — the computer can, in principle, be described as a complicated representation system consisting of two main components: a program that is a representation of a given problem-solving procedure encoded in a language that can operate the machine; and data — which the machine operates on — that are correspondingly representations of the problem-solving field, encoded in a language that the machine can process. Both program and input and output data in the cultural context are signs that refer to something else via conventional codes. As *cultural form*, therefore, the computer is quite simply a sign-processing machine.

In both its technological and cultural capacities, the computer should thus primarily be thought of as a data-processing automaton, a symbol-manipulating machine, a sign-processing instrument: a *technology of meaning*; and therefore as a semiotic technology *par excellence*, which for that reason alone will be a central concern for a technology-semiotics. Research in this field has developed in two main directions:

First, there is media-oriented research that regards the computer as a medium or tool that is based on, processes, and produces signs. Here the interest is therefore directed at *computer semiotics* understood as the semiotics of the (computer) medium-text. The most important contribution to this burgeoning area of research is Andersen (1990), while lesser works are represented by, for example, Nadin (1988).

This direction again — at least tendentially — subdivides into two subdisciplines: a discipline that is mainly concerned with the semiotic aspects of the computer medium's "internal text" — the program text, the system-architecture, the relationship between logic and semiotics in connection with program languages and so on;[8] and a second discipline mainly interested in the computer-medium's "external text": the *interface*. For if the *interface* is seen as "the boundary" that simultaneously functions as the "dividing line" and the "point of contact" between two separate systems (man and machine) — two systems that are mutually more or less completely separate and thus unable to interfere with each other, but which at the same time are expected to act in concert with each other, to interact — then it becomes clear that the *interface* must necessarily always be of a semiotic nature; that it must consist of signs where "one thing stands for another thing." Or as Nadin expresses it: "If there is a science of interface (computer interface or any other kind), then this science is semiotics" (1988: 272). This branch of research will thus primarily be interested in such areas as communication, rhetoric, aesthetics, text theory, narrative theories, picture analysis, and so on.[9]

And second, there is a direction oriented toward culture analysis that sees the computer as a technological artifact and as a *particular* technological artifact that has a *particular* "effect" on culture, simply because it is a "technology of meaning." This needs further explanation. If "culture" is perceived as the processes through which a social community organizes and interprets its experiences and thereby makes sense of the world and itself, it will immediately become obvious that the culture as a "system of meaning" is not a set of given, permanent, stable elements but, on the contrary, a process in which the interpretations and meanings must be constantly (re)produced and (re)distributed — in order to create meaning. The language and the media thus come to play a crucial role in the social and cultural processes, since they themselves constitute the component, the form in which this cultural production of meaning takes place. The new information and computer media in particular, as they gradually become the leading, basic

---

[8] Many of the chapters in the first part of this anthology belong here.

[9] Most of the chapters in the second part of this anthology are examples of this field of study.

social technology for the communication, storage, manipulation, and production of data, information, and meaning, come to constitute a strategically important nodal point in the social information networks and in the meaning-generating, cultural processes; for these technologies constitute the actual *mainframe* and *modus* in which the cultural structures of meaning are generated and distributed.

The field between computer and information technologies, on the one hand, and the cultural process, on the other, are thus ascribed an especially significant position in the dynamics through which the social structures sustain themselves in the continuous process of the production, reproduction and circulation of meaning, a position that furthermore seems to become even more central, when viewed in a forward-looking perspective. The relationship between computer technologies and culture must therefore necessarily be one of the most central, urgent questions to be addressed by contemporary cultural studies in the so-called "information society" or in the so-called "computer age."[10]

(ii) Technology as object. Or: The computer — a cultural artifact

As well as having the ability to take on the nature of *representamen*, of actual signs, where as "a first thing" they can stand for "a second thing" by virtue of "a third thing" (a cultural code), technologies can also, of course, be the *object* that the signs stand for. For technologies are clearly not only symbolic but material units, too. In this position, the technology has the function of the object that is *spoken about*, the phenomenon one *thinks about*, the reality one attempts to de-*sign*ate, to de-*scribe*, to comprehend, in the sense of the external, referential reality beyond the world of the language and the signs, from which an attempt is made to derive meaning. In other words, the technology has the position here of "a second thing" — of "something other" than the signs that attempt to denote it — which "a first thing" (the signs) stands for by virtue of "a third thing" (a conventionalized code that connects the representamen with the object); a semiotic function that in Peircean terms will be *technology as object*.

The great majority of cases where technologies form part of *semiosis* and thus participate as a component in the cultural creation of signs probably relate to this object-function. This applies both to everyday cultural attempts to create "common sense" out of technological phenomena, via classifications, designations, and constantly negotiating conversations, and to more

---

[10] Analyses that fall within this field can be found in Lyotard (1984), Heim (1987), and Poster (1990), among others.

scientific dealings with technology (but characteristically enough, often without any thought that mention, that comprehension and description always form part of a designating, meaningful process, and always function within a semiotic structure). Within the technical-scientific disciplines, for instance in the form of the description of technology as a "technical object" and as an "isolated techno-system," and within various social sciences, for example in the form of the description of technology as concrete occurrences in a given society, plus as a factor — a more or less "independent variable" that has "effects" at other social, political, economic, and cultural levels; in all these places, it is technology as an object that one seeks to describe and comprehend.

Technology as a cultural artifact

In the humanities and in cultural disciplines, too, it has primarily been technology as an object, rather than technology as a symbolic entity, that has dominated technological studies (where these have existed at all): technology seen as an artifact that has its objective existence in the physical world, and that therefore has its own (technological) history, its function as a cultural artifact in everyday culture, its impact on society, culture, and so on.

The key problem in this kind of "technology and culture" studies is undoubtedly the question of the causal relationship between the two components that constitute the field of research: whether technology carries its own immanent values, by means of which it influences and changes the surrounding culture? Or whether, conversely, technology is primarily influenced and formed by the culture within which it is constructed and used? This question has given rise to a subdivision in the research field, which can be implemented as three directions: (i) *technological determinism*, (ii) *technological somnambulism*, and (iii) *determined technology*.

(i) Technological determinism may here be characterized as the view that technology has both its own immanent values and its own autonomy and self-generating development and that it therefore comes to constitute a kind of first cause — *ultima causa* — which makes all other things (history, society, culture, and so on) "effects" (cf. Williams, 1974: 127). To quote Pfaffenberger, technology is thus given the role of "a powerful and autonomous agent that dictates the patterns of human social and cultural life" (1988a: 239), a view of technology whose most notable expression may be found, for example, in McLuhan (1962, 1964, 1967) and Ellul (1973).

(ii) Technological somnambulism, on the other hand, may be characterized as the view that "the human relationship to technology is simply "too

obvious to merit serious reflection". This relationship consists merely of "making", which is of interest only to engineers and technicians, and "use", which amounts only to an "occasional, innocuous, [and] nonstructuring occurrence" (Pfaffenberger 1988a: 238, citing Winner, 1986). According to this view, technology is neither "good" nor "bad" in itself, but socially, morally, and ethically "value-neutral," where "the effects" will be solely dependent on who is controlling the technology and in what connection it is being used, which is why, generally speaking, it is irrelevant to undertake specialist studies of "technology and culture."

Finally, the last view, *(iii) determined technology* (besides the fact that it has a certain affinity with *(ii)*), may be characterized as a kind of mirror-image of *(i)*, expressed as the idea that technology and the way it develops are always a completely predictable and therefore also controllable set of "effects" of — usually — economic, political, social "causes," which as such are subject to the full rational will and control of human beings, a position that therefore sometimes is called "voluntarism."

These one-dimensional, mono-causal or somnambulatory views of the relationship between technology and culture/society are not only of historical interest, although one might think so from the way in which they have been presented here. On the contrary, they seem to have been given a new lease of life recently, not least in connections relating to information and computer technology. *Technological determinism* is thus often an implicit premise in the many contemporary theories about the so-called "information society," the "post-industrial society," the "computer society," the "technological society," and so on (cf. Bell, 1973). *Determined technology* correspondingly, is often an unformulated presupposition in the tradition for "technology assessment" that is currently developing and for the aroused expectations that have been connected with it (cf. again Bell, 1973). Also, these views — and it can be no more than postulated here — still to a large extent constitute the unreflective basis of many actual studies of "technology and culture."

Naturally, a semiotics of culture-and-technology of the kind outlined here must insist on a radically different reading of the relationship between technology and culture. For on the one hand, technology is regarded as a phenomenon that is physical, social, and symbolic, while on the other hand, cultural practice is seen as constitutive — essentially involved in all forms of social activity (including technological ones). Consequently, possible "influences" between technology and culture should rather be seen as influences *from one social practice to another*. Pfaffenberger, who introduces comparable ideas, writes:

Any study of technology's "impact" is in consequence the study of a complex, intercausal relationship between one form of social behaviour and another. There is no question of finding a nice, neat causal arrow that points from an independent variable to a dependent one, for the causal arrows run both ways (or every which way)...

(Pfaffenberger, 1988a: 244)

Understood in terms of these conditions, a semiotics of technology will also concern itself with technology as an artifact in the culture — with its function as a cultural item or *object* — just as it will be interested in the complex interplay between technology and other social practices. This can take place with many different emphases: on the historical, the sociological, the economic aspect, and so on. It can also take place in many different contexts: the intercausal relationship between work or occupational culture and new information technology; between new domestic technologies and the everyday culture of the family; between computer technologies and the new social structure etc. In short, a technology-semiotics will study how technologies are created and function as objects in the culture and how, as cultural objects, they form part of the other realized systems of meaning that are the culture.[11]

A semiotics of technology will furthermore study these phenomena in a non-naive way, with a continuous, critical awareness that technology is part of *semiosis* in this function, too. For although technology here has the formal status of object in an external, referential reality, any *talk of*, any *thought of*, any attempt to *comprehend, define,* and *describe* the technology will always, inevitably, place it as "the second thing" to which "the first thing" refers via "a third thing"; in other words, place it in a sign process, in a semiotic structure — in *semiosis*. This relationship between sign and referential object is never "direct," "inevitable," or "unproblematic." Julia Kristeva teaches us this when she writes that the linguistic system "stands in an arbitrary relation to the referent," and that all social activity is "marked by the split between referent and symbolic" (1975: 47). The relation between sign and thing is thus never given and never pure. It is not immaterial, for example, whether one culturally defines the computer as "a medium," "a tool," "a system," "a machine," or as "an electronic brain." The chosen conceptual metaphor will always have profound consequences for how one constructs and uses computer systems in the given (sub)culture (cf. Andersen, 1986). Nor is it immaterial whether, from a cultural point of view, one chooses to conceptualize the contemporary social formation as an "information society," a "post-industrial society," a "computer society," a "leisure society,"

---

[11] This analytical approach is represented in this part by Jens Christensen's chapter 'Historical trends in computer and information technology' and by Randi Markussen's 'A historical perspective on work practices and technology — the case of the National Labour Inspection Service.'

a "consumer society," or a "crisis and unemployment society." The chosen concept will always profoundly influence one's social capacity to understand and react to given phenomena — from general, political decision-making processes to ordinary, everyday practice. A semiotics of technology, unlike many other sciences concerned with technology, will be able to participate in critical reflection on this very defining process, through which we understand and describe technologies, and will thus also carry elements that are of a meta-scientific, epistemological nature.

(iii) Technology as interpretant. Or: Culture — in the sign of the computer

As well as being able to take on the nature of *sign*, since via a culturally conventionalized signifying system as "a first thing" they can stand for "a second thing," and as well as being able to take on the nature of *object*, where they themselves hold the position of the referential reality that the signs represent, technologies can also have a third function: as a kind of interpreting figure, a matrix of understanding or a metaphor for the thoughts about and descriptions of a part of the external reality, which is not necessarily located within the domain of technology. Thus, as in its function as *sign*, in this third function, too, technology takes on a symbolic nature. But while technology as *sign* is symbolic and meaningful on a concrete level, as "a first thing" that directly refers to "a second thing," technology is symbolic and meaningful in this third function on a more indirect level, by ascribing structure and meaning to a part of reality that lies outside technology itself: by being "a third thing" by virtue of which "a first thing" can be understood as referring to "a second thing."

This recognition of technology — especially, in this case, computer technology — as a cultural entity that not only has a direct function in the material world, but also has its indirect activity in the symbolic world, is far from new. Thus, as early as 1966, Ulric Neisser in an essay was able to point to two quite separate functions in computer technology, two functions that were highlighted in the very title of his essay, "Computers as tools and as metaphors." The computing machine, Neisser wrote,

> serves us not only as an instrument, but as a metaphor: as a way of conceptualizing man and society. The notions that the brain is like a computer, that man is like a machine, that society is like a feedback system, all reflect the impacts of cybernetics on our idea of human nature.   (*Neisser, 1966: 72*)

Similarly, David E. Wright has pointed out that apart from their social and historical context, technologies can also be viewed in their symbolic context, something that can be measured by "the extent to which technology has changed our perceptions of ourselves and our world" and in "the influence of technology on the meaning and ends of human experience" (1979: 7). This manifests itself, for example, in the fact that: "We have come more and more to conceive, describe, and judge ourselves in technical metaphors and terminology. The brain becomes a computer, the heart a pump, friends and colleagues provide valuable "feedback." To mistreat someone is to "screw" them, a word which is also one of many mechanistic terms for sexual intercourse" (p.9).

But these are just random examples. More extensive, influential works on this particular aspect of the relationship between computer technology and the cultural process of the construction of meaning can, for example, be found in Sherry Turkle's *The Second Self: Computers and the Human Spirit* (1984) and in David Bolter's *Turing's Man. Western Culture in the Computer Age* (1984). At the same time, the previously mentioned analyses of the more indirect, symbolic functions of computer technology represent two diametrically opposed views of where and how meaning is created, a divergence of opinions that can be used as an illustrative point of departure for further considerations.

"An object-to-think-with"

In *The Second Self: Computers and the Human Spirit*, Sherry Turkle sets out to analyze the relationship between the computer and culture. The most significant cultural effects of the computer are here found to be not so much linked to material and social practice as to the plane of intellect and consciousness. "Technology catalyses changes not only in what we do but in how we think. It changes people's awareness of themselves, of one another, of their relationship with the world" (1984: 3). The central question that Turkle is attempting to answer is thus: "How do ideas born within the technical communities around computation find their way out to the culture beyond?" (p.11).

Through her ambitious, ethnographical inspired empirical study of different environments having a direct relationship to modern computer technology, Turkle provides comprehensive documentation of the computer's influence on and formation of consciousness and culture. According to the results of the study, the most important cultural influence of the computer is not only that it anthropomorphizes the machine, but also, conversely, that the computer serves "as a projective screen for other concerns" (p.334), that it functions as "an object-to-think-with." In other words, experience with the machine offers models, metaphors, and frames of reference for human thought and conception about reality, history, sociality, and such basic conceptual categories as "time," "space," and so on. Turkle sums it up like this: "A relationship with a computer can influence people's conceptions of themselves, their jobs, their relationships with other people, and with their ways of thinking about social processes. It can be the basis for new aesthetic values, new rituals, new philosophy, new cultural forms" (p.168). Turkle thus *twists* the traditional, dominant problem complex concerning computers, as promoted by the "artificial intelligence" paradigm: "...experts argue about whether or not computers will ever become true "artificial intelligences", themselves capable of autonomous, humanlike thought. But irrespective of the future of machine intelligence, computers are affecting how today's children think ..." (p.6). Which is why the most relevant and interesting question one can ask about the expanding computer culture is not AI's "Will machines think like people?" (p.15), but whether the machine has not already supplied "a new paradigm for thinking about people, thought and reality" (p.277).

In keeping with her point of departure in psychology, Turkle pays most attention to the level of personal consciousness. Instead of focusing on the "computer as object," she focuses on the "subjective computer" (p.3) — on the machine as an integral part of social life and psychological development. Instead of focusing on the computer as an "analytical" machine (p.3), she focuses on the computer as a "psychological machine" (p.6) — on the machine as an influence on the way people see themselves and on the human psyche. And instead of focusing on the "technical nature" of the computer, she focuses on its "second nature" (p.3) — on its nature as a "suggestive machine," as an "evocative object" (p.3), as a "reflective" and "projective" medium (p.6) that provokes new thoughts, feelings and fascinations.

To Turkle, what is of most importance and significance is that the computer, as a seemingly "thinking machine," an "intellectual technology," has an especially strong impact on our idea of the intellect, the subject, human nature: "For me, one of the most important cultural effects of the computer presence is that the machines are entering into our thinking about ourselves" (p.15). Concretely, for example, in the shape of "a new model of mind as machine" (p.11), "the idea of ... personality as program" (p.160) and computation as model of the self, and in situations where computer-users learn how to make programs themselves, the possibility of creating their own program-worlds, in which they can work, have experiences and live, can even lead to these users entering into "a new relationship with the computer, one in which they begin to experience it as a kind of second self" (p.89). Hence the title of the book.

In this way, Turkle elucidates how the traits embedded in this particular technological form — at the individual, psychological level — have a formative influence on people who are directly confronted by the new "computer experience." But it is also part of Turkle's thesis — albeit less well documented — that the specific forms of consciousness, ways of thinking, "systems of meaning" that are generated by computer experience in the individual computer environments later diffuse and assimilate into the culture as a whole, especially as the computer becomes a more widespread, socially central form of technology. Computer technology and computer experience are thus thought to serve as catalysts for new forms and structures of experience, modes of perception, mentalities, aesthetic sensibilities, linguistic discourses, and so on in the total culture.

What remains unclear in Turkle's account, however, is exactly *where* the origin of meaning is to be located. On the one hand, she maintains that computer technology *in itself* possesses the necessary qualities and powers to posit given meanings, to "provoke strong feelings" and exert a certain "holding power," where the meaning thus seems to be inherent in the technology. On the other hand, she maintains that the computer functions more as "a projection of part of the self, a mirror of the mind" (p.5). In other words, that in principle, it functions in the same way as a Rorschach inkblot: "The Rorschach provides ambiguous images onto which different forms can be projected. The computer too takes on many shapes and meanings ... as with the Rorschach, what people make of the computer speaks of their larger concerns, speaks of who they are as individual personalities" (p.5). Here meaning is seen as a psychological construct that can be ascribed to the individual consciousness, and technology only serves as a projection screen. In her analyses, Turkle seems more inclined toward the latter view — in line with traditional psychological thought generally. However, the question of precisely which mechanisms the process of meaning is subject to, how meaning is produced, circulated, and reproduced, and how the computer can culturally take on the nature of "an object-to-think-with" remain somewhat obscure and unanalyzed in Turkle.

"Defining technology"

David Bolter — the author of *Turing's Man. Western Culture in the Computer Age* — also sets out to analyze "the cultural impact of the computer" (1984: 190). This is not defined, either, as the computer's "immediate economic and political impact" (p.4), and even less as its technical structure and mode of functioning or as its "programming" (p.4). On the contrary, it is defined here as "a change in the way men and women in the electronic age think about themselves and the world around them" (p.4). What the analysis thus explicitly focuses on is the computer's function as a model for thought and perception in other areas. As in Turkle, the most important cultural significance of technology is assumed to be not its direct impact on the material or social context, but its more indirect influence as a model for thought and as a figure of interpretation in a symbolic context. And as in Turkle, there is a kind of twisting of the debate that has long been on the AI agenda: "It seems to me that the whole debate has turned the question around: the issue is not whether the computer can be made to think like a human, but whether humans can and will take on the qualities of digital computers. For that ... is the fundamental promise and threat of the computer age" (p.190).

Bolter's key phrase here is "defining technologies," characterized by himself as the technologies that in given historical periods function as overlapping "thought models," "analogies," or "metaphors," in terms of which other areas of reality are perceived. In other words, "defining technologies" are historical technologies that provide "an attractive window through which thinkers can view both their physical and metaphysical worlds" (p.10), technologies "that caught the interest of contemporary thinkers" (p.16) — philosophers, scientists, poets — and are used "to aid their flights of imagination" (p.16), and which therefore, for the whole epoch, come to function as a species of figures of thought "that help to shape its cultural outlook" (p.16). Bolter himself sums up the term at a central point as follows: "A defining technology develops links, metaphorical or otherwise, with a culture's science, philosophy, or literature; it is always available to serve as a metaphor, example, model, or symbol. A defining technology resembles a magnifying glass, which collects and focuses seemingly disparate ideas in a culture into one bright, sometimes piercing ray" (p.11). In short, "a defining technology" is a *"principal technological metaphor"* (p.40, my emphasis).

The precise qualities that turn a given technology into a "defining technology" are not specified in Bolter's account, however. On the one hand, he maintains that: "All techniques and devices have the potential to become defining technologies because all to some degree redefine our relationship to nature" (p.10). On the other hand, he states in the next sentence that "only a few devices or crafts in any age deserve to be called defining technologies" (p.10-11). In practice, Bolter only identifies four such "defining technologies" in their respective ages: the drop spindle and the potter's wheel in ancient Greece; the mechanical clock in medieval Europe; the steam engine in the nineteenth and early twentieth centuries; and last but not least, the computer in the present age. It is precisely the computer that is identified as "the defining technology and principal technological metaphor of our time" (p.40), which thereby becomes "the Computer Age," just as it is the analysis of the computer as a "defining technology" that forms the core of Bolter's book.

The title — *Turing's Man* — refers to the English mathematician and logician A.M. Turing, who made the theoretical-symbolic sketch for the logical machine, for obvious reasons called "the Turing Machine," which was the forerunner of the computer. He was also one of the first people to prophesy that in the foreseeable future — mythically set at the year 2000 — the computer would be capable of imitating human intelligence. It is from this whole technological, perceptual complex that the book derives its title.

> By promising (or threatening) to replace man, the computer is giving us a new definition of man, as an "information processor," and of nature, as "information to be processed."
> I call those who accept this view of man and nature Turing's men ... We are all liable to become Turing's men, if our work with the computer is intimate and prolonged and we come *to think and speak in terms suggested by the machine* ...
> Turing's man is the most complete integration of humanity and technology, of artificer and artefact, in the history of the Western cultures. With him the tendency, implicit in all eras, *to think "through" one's contemporary technology* is carried to an extreme...
>
> (*Bolter, 1984: 13, my emphasis*)

Throughout the book, via sample studies of central concepts in philosophy and science, seen in a historical perspective, Bolter amply documents how the computer has come to function as the "defining technology" of our age, by supplying metaphors through which we can acquire understanding of many other spheres, thereby forming new perceptions of, for example, mathematics, logic, time, space, language, memory and creativity, and so on.

What Bolter is especially concerned with is how the computer in the present cultural age has come to serve as a metaphor and model for human intelligence. For Turing's Man, "the computer reflects, indeed imitates, the crucial human capacity of rational thinking. Here is the essence of Turing's belief in artificial intelligence. By making a machine think as a man, man recreates himself, defines himself as a machine" (p.13). There is a tendency to equate the human brain with the computer and to employ the language of electronic processors to describe other areas of objects, which Bolter observes in biologists, psychologists, linguists, and *computer scientists*, especially of course those working in the field of AI, a tendency that is most pronounced when the Turingian Men (of science) "no longer claim to be explaining the brain in terms provided by the computer; instead, they say that human brains and computers are two examples of "thinking systems"" (p.42). For the researcher in AI, the computer as a metaphor of the human brain is thus already a "dead metaphor." For him, "the computer and the brain differ only in the unimportant respect that one is made of electronic components and the other of biological ones. Both think. By taking the metaphor to its extreme, proponents of artificial intelligence illustrate with utmost clarity a way of thinking shared by all of Turing's men" (p.208-9).

In identifying the primary, cultural significance of computer technology in the fact that it defines the conceptual frameworks for understanding other areas, since experience with the machine provides models, frames of reference and metaphors for the idea of the world and consciousness, Bolter thus comes very close to Turkle's way of thinking, except that where Turkle focuses mainly on the individual-psychological level, Bolter has much broader interests, oriented more toward history of ideas and culture analysis.

However, Bolter remains silent on the questions of *what* precisely qualifies a technology — taking computer technology as a contemporary example — to be a "defining technology," and *how* these operations of meaning, by which "a second thing" is understood in terms of technology, are established and function. On the threshold of the symbolic he falters, although he vaguely suggests that "there must be something in the nature of the technology itself, so that its shape, its materials, its modes of operation appeal to the mind as well as to the hand of their age" (p.11). Here he seems to incline to the view that meanings are inherent in technologies, that the technologies, as it were, project their meanings onto the culture and onto consciousness. This is backed up by his consistent use of such terms as "technology defines," and so on.

Where Turkle inclines mainly to the view that meaning is created in the individual psyche and is then projected out onto a technology that serves as a projection screen, Bolter inclines to the view that it is the technologies themselves that produce the meaning, which is then projected onto the common perceptual world of the given culture. The two analysts of computer culture thus occupy two diametrically opposite positions to the question of how meaning is produced, since they point to different poles as the origin of meaning — consciousness and technology, respectively. Still, neither analyst attempts to qualify these considerations about the relationship between technology and culture by placing them within a more coherent theory of meaning and the construction of meaning.

Metaphors we live by

However, in order to understand how technologies as semiotic items can form part of the processes of the creation of meaning, and especially in order to understand how technologies can take on the function of interpretant in the triadic sign process, such a general theory of meaning and of the construction of meaning is essential: a coherent theory of the cognitive and cultural processes through which a society structures, understands, and makes sense of its world. From their background in cognitive semantics, linguistics, and anthropological studies, George Lakoff and Mark Johnson (1980) have produced a model for the production of meaning or, in their own words, a "theory of the human conceptual system" (p.106), which takes the concept of "metaphor" as its central point of departure. This is a theory that one might usefully employ, at least as a starting point, when considering this question.

Lakoff and Johnson's main thesis is that the metaphor should not, as is usually assumed, be regarded as an isolated linguistic feature or as purely external, stylistic ornamentation, mainly to be found in poetry and prose fiction. They think that, on the contrary, the metaphor should be regarded as the very basis of the human conceptual system; in short, the basis for the way in which we understand, think, and speak is assumed ultimately to be metaphorical. The metaphor is itself the interpreting framework for the organization of information about the world and for the creation of meaning out of experience. This is why the concept of "metaphor" is also the key to understanding how meaning is created.

What is central to the logic of the metaphor is that one defines one thing in terms of another thing; that one structures one type of situation in terms of another type; and that one conceptualizes one domain of experience in terms of another. Or, in the words of Lakoff and Johnson: *"The essence of metaphor is understanding and experiencing one kind of thing in terms of another"* (p.5), notably, as it says further on, "understanding one thing in terms of something else *of a different kind*" (p.170), so that one term — the metaphor — appears instead of another term, or one sign interprets another sign in such a way that *"one thing"* comes to represent *"another thing."* For Lakoff and Johnson, therefore, the metaphor becomes an elementary mental operation for the creation of meaning that has close affinities with Peirce's view of the sign-relation as *"one thing"* that stands for *"a second thing"* (by virtue of *"a third thing"*).

According to Lakoff and Johnson, what typically happens is that one conceptualizes the less well-defined experience in terms of the more well-defined, the abstract in terms of the concrete, the uninterpretable in terms of the interpretable. And the mechanism of the metaphor is rather like that of an optical instrument, partly focusing on and accentuating certain elements in the area to be comprehended, partly toning down or perhaps even hiding other elements, and finally, always projecting *more* from the area of the metaphor onto the new area that is to be understood. Its function here, via a kind of interpreting framework, is to organize information and experience into a systematic, coherent whole that can create order and meaning out of the world around us. If, in this particular connection, one chooses to view "technology" as "the incarnation of a systematic set of rules," it will also be possible to view the metaphor as a kind of technology — namely, as a systematic set of rules for the construction of meaning, an elementary mental and cultural mechanism for the production of sense. The metaphor should therefore be regarded as a kind of *technology of meaning*.

When the reality of a given culture is defined like this in metaphorical terms, changes of metaphor can also change what appears to be real for that culture. Or to put it more strongly, since it is metaphors that construct social reality, the metaphors are also real for that culture. To quote Lakoff and Johnson: "What is real for an individual as a member of a culture is a product both of his social reality and of the way in which that shapes his experience of the physical world. Since much of our social reality is understood in metaphorical terms, and since our conception of the physical world is partly metaphorical, metaphor plays a very significant role in determining what is real for us" (p.146). The way in which we experience the world is thus fundamentally metaphorical in nature. Lakoff and Johnson actually called their book from 1980 *Metaphors we live by*.

But it is only a short step from saying that the metaphor structures and creates order in the way the world is perceived to saying that the metaphor *creates*, *produces*, *constructs* this picture of the surrounding world. One could go one step further and, like Eco, maintain that the metaphor not only constitutes an organization of signifiers that serve to designate a signified object, it also designates instructions for the *construction* of the signified (cf. Porush, 1985: 15). The metaphor thus *creates* our picture of reality. And since this picture of reality is our only point of access to reality, the metaphor also creates our reality.

Thus, according to Lakoff and Johnson, the way in which people think and understand always follows the formula that one thing is understood in terms of something else. And the third semiotic function of technology in the cultural process of the creation of meaning could be thought, in principle, to operate according to the same logic: One particular part of reality is understood in terms of "something else," by virtue, that is, of a particular *other* figure of interpretation, representation, or metaphor, where the interpreting metaphor in this instance is derived from the domain of technology. Thus, particular — in themselves "non-technological" — areas of reality are captured in the metaphor of a given technology, for example computer technology. Or conversely, that given technologies, such as computer technology, act as the metaphor by means of which "something else" can be understood (in Lakoff and Johnsons terms), or as the mediating "third" interpretant element, by virtue of which "a first thing" can stand for "a second thing" (to use Peirce's terms).

Where Turkle points out that at an individual, psychological level, the computer can act as "an object-to-think-with" and employs such significant formulations as "experiences with computers become reference points for thinking and talking about other things" (1984: 6), and where Bolter points to the fact that at a general, cultural level, technologies can act as "defining technologies" that are literally defined as "a new metaphor" (1984: 10) or as a "principal technological metaphor" (p.40) that functions as "a model for our thinking about" (p.101), where something is therefore understood "in terms of" (p.10) something else; there Lakoff and Johnson maintain that the metaphor is a general cognitive, cultural mechanism for creating meaning out of the world and ourselves, just as Peirce established long ago that cognitive, cultural, interpretant structures of this kind are the very basis of meaning, the very precondition for *semiosis*.

Turkle's idea of "an object-to-think-with" and Bolter's concept of "defining technologies" thus have close affinities with both Lakoff and Johnson's metaphor concept and with Peirce's and Eco's interpretant-based sign concept. Or to be more precise, Turkle's and Bolter's analyses of the cultural impact of (computer) technology and their respective central concepts can be regarded as concrete manifestations or special cases of the more general concepts and theories about meaning and the creation of meaning mentioned earlier — namely, in those special cases where technologies occupy the position of metaphors or interpretants for something else. Neither Turkle nor Bolter explicitly makes any connections with these theoretical references, however, and still less do they express themselves in cognitive-semantic or culturo-semiotic terms.

But alongside these affinities there are also significant differences that are presumably bound up with the lack of theoretical ties. As pointed out earlier, Turkle generally inclines toward the view that meaning is a more or less direct product of the individual psychology, which is simply projected onto a technology that takes on the nature of a projection screen, while Bolter inclines toward the opposite view that meaning is inherent in the technology and that it more or less directly "defines" the individual and cultural ideas of a given age. In both cases, the discussion focuses exclusively on the functions, impact, and consequences of technology: on *the meaning of technology*.

Both Turkle and Bolter err, however, when they believe that it is exclusively a question of *the meaning of technology*, for *the technology of mean-*

ing is at least of equal importance. It is not only the inherent structure of meaning in technology that is the issue, or its qualities as an object of projection, but also the way in which meaning is created and communicated; in other words, the basic cognitive, cultural mechanisms, via which meaning is produced and communicated in a society. If *the meaning of technology* is analyzed in isolation, without an adequate theory of *the technology of meaning*, it will not be possible to understand or explain how technologies can play a part in the fundamental, human practice of meaning. Even *the meaning of technology* will then come to seem like an unexplained, magical property, a mysterious power as in Turkle's quasi-mythological concept of the computer's self-containing "holding power" and in Bolter's idea of technology's "defining," agenda-setting, cultural power.

Lakoff and Johnson's cognitive semantics and the semiotics of culture based on Peirce and Eco here constitute different — though not mutually exclusive or incompatible — suggestions for this kind of general theory of the creation of meaning, on the basis of which it might be possible to explain how technologies can become "defining technologies" and how the computer can become "an object-to-think-with" in a culture. A semiotics of technology, as outlined, will be characterized precisely by its capacity to analyze both *the meaning of technology* and *the technology of meaning*.

Culture — in the sign of the computer

If we choose to see technology from a culturo-semiotic point of view, thereby committing ourselves to taking the symbolic aspect seriously, then this implies, among other things, that the cultural significance of a technology cannot be evaluated solely at a purely physical level, but must also be evaluated at a symbolic level. The cultural impact, position, and advance of a given technology cannot be measured on its concrete, material existence and distribution alone, but must also be measured in terms of its symbolic existence and distribution — that is, according to the extent to which metaphors derived from the technology in question play a part in the way that culture defines itself and its surroundings. Looked at in this way, technology, the machine, and especially the computer seem to be extremely meaningful — pregnant with meaning — in the present age, for all areas of contemporary, Western culture have witnessed an unequivocal advance of technology and the machine as metaphors. To use Wright's formulation, technology and the machine have become "the central symbol of our age, in whose image we define ourselves and in whose language we often describe our metabolic and social functions" (1979: 7).

Consequently, figures and patterns from the world of technology have come to play an increasingly dominant role in the continuing process of speaking about, understanding, and ascribing meaning to the world. And the computer, the EDP technologies, and cybernetics seem to provide many of the concepts and metaphors, through which the present age attempts to make sense of the world and itself, the very process of creating meaning that is "culture." An increasing number of phenomena and domains, which in *reality* have nothing whatsoever to do with computer technology are thus conceptualized by using the computer as a model, not only in ordinary, everyday usage of meaning and *common sense*-consciousness, but also within philosophy and science:

• Social scientists, economists, and analysts of culture have increasingly come to see contemporary society and the present age in the image of technology and the computer, as is reflected in such terms as *The Technological Society* (Ellul, 1973); *High-Tech Society* (Forester, 1987); *The Technetronic Society* (Brzezinski, 1982); *The Age of Information or Communication* or *The Electronic Age* (McLuhan, 1964); *The Cybernetic Age* (Weiner, 1954); *The Computer Age* (Dertouzos and Moses, 1980) and in more non-committal expressions such as *the information society the media society, the computer society,* and so on.

• Molecular biologists and researchers into genetics, with inspiration from and in the metaphor of the computer and datamatics, have attempted to understand the genetic materials and the DNA molecule in terms of programs, genetic codes, and biological information stored in DNA.

• Some linguists have long regarded language as a machine.

• Some structuralists have regarded the different areas and discourses of culture as such and such a number of self-determined apparatuses: the apparatus of film, the apparatus of literature, the apparatus of the myth, and so on.

• Some behaviorists and branches of psychology have long viewed the human being in terms of the machine.

• Researchers of cognition have constructed a whole science around the "the brain-is-a-computer" metaphor — that is, around the hypothesis that the human brain and human consciousness can theoretically be thought of on the model of the computer, as a system that manipulates symbols, a machine that processes information.

• And AI researchers have done the opposite; constructed an entire branch of *computer science* around the "the computer-is-a-brain" metaphor — that is, on the basic assumption that the computer can be regarded as analogous to the human brain, as an "intelligent," thinking, reasoning machine.

Technology — especially computer technology — thus seems to be omnipotent and ubiquitous as a symbolic entity. The computer has become the central metaphor of our age, in whose image we try to understand other phenomena and domains. The computer is the sign of the times, the overlapping, dominant master-metaphor of the present age. And contemporary culture is a culture that attempts to see itself in the image of the computer. A culture — in the sign of the computer.

If what anthropological research has revealed is correct — that the key to the opening of a culture's perceptual world, to deciphering the code for a culture's cognition and knowledge, and the mapping of the hidden vectors in the cosmology of that culture, is often to be found in the overlapping master-metaphors through which the culture has chosen to see its world and reality (cf. Porush, 1985: xi) — then the computer must be extremely *meaningful*, the very master-key to insight into contemporary culture. And meaningful in a way that reaches out far beyond the purely physical spread and use of the computer and beyond its more or less directly observable social and political implications. A significance that must necessarily transform the computer and information technology into a much more central, urgent area for contemporary culture analysis than has previously been the case.[12]

Concluding remarks

In everyday life as in scientific descriptions, these three different semiotic functions of technology are, of course, interwoven in complex, almost indissoluble forms. Differentiating between the technology's functions as representamen, object, and interpretant is thus a purely analytical, not an empirical phenomenon. However, this does not detract from the relevance of the distinction. For it is this analytical differentiation that constitutes the necessary precondition for an unraveling and thus for a scientific description of these complex forms, where technologies empirically take part in semiosis. What a semiotics of technology will study, therefore, is not only the individual, semiotic functions in isolation, but also the very different, very complex combinations into which they actually enter, and in which they form different superpositional interference phenomena.

A corresponding difficulty appears at another level: There is a general tendency to regard and treat *technology* as though it were a monolith (cf. Wright, 1979: 13), thereby lending support to the idea that all technology, in

---

[12] This kind of study — in the form of a 'allegorical mode of reading,' where deep-lying cultural traits are uncovered allegorically through the reading of concrete cultural manifestations — where 'something is read through something else' (cf. 'Introduction') — is in this part of this book represented by Bjørn Sørenssen's 'Hypertext: From modern utopia to postmodern dystopia?'

principle, has the same nature and the same meaning. This tendency can also — because of limitations imposed by time and space — be observed in this essay. It is therefore necessary to point out that technologies can, of course, differ widely from one another, as can their cultural meanings. A technology-semiotics will thus not primarily study *technology* in all its abstractness and generality; rather, it will study specific, concrete technologies — such as, for example, computer technology (which, in turn, consists of many different technologies) — in their different, given cultures.

And finally, technology is becoming increasingly important for culture. Alone of all human inventions, it has succeeded in redefining and recreating entire human environments, even to such an extent that we perhaps no longer live *with* technology but *in* it, as several writers (Wright, 1979: 15; Porush, 1985: 7 ff.; Frentz and Rushing, 1989: 71) have already noted, with a strange mixture of horror and joy. So technology is meaningful. Full of meaning. And just as most other meaningful social practices in recent decades have received their own semiotics — film-semiotics, visual communication, mass communication, text theory and plot structure, musical codes, cultural codes and codes of taste, social semiotics, marketing and semiotics, indeed, even zoosemiotics, medical semiotics and biosemiotics — so it should now also be possible to establish a semiotics of technology. A semiotics that — in Eco's sense — will be a *specific semiotics*, that attempts to chart out "the "grammar" of a particular sign system" — of technology as a sign system, but that at the same time will be classified under, will draw on and contribute to a *general semiotics*. A semiotics that will therefore be capable of studying both *the meaning of technology* and *the technology of meaning*.

Bibliography

ANDERSEN, P.B. (1986). Semiotics and Informatics: Computers as Media. In *Information Technology and Information Use. Towards a Unified View of Information and Information Technology*, eds. Ingversen, P., Kajberg, L., Peitersen, A.M. London: Taylor Graham.

ANDERSEN, P.B. (1990). *A Theory of Computer Semiotics. Semiotic Approaches to Construction and Assessment of Computer Systems*. Cambridge: Cambridge University Press.

BELL, D. (1973). *The Coming of the Post-Industrial Society. A Venture in Social Forecasting*. New York: Basic Books.

BENJAMIN, W. (1955). *Illuminations*, ed. Arendt, H. London: Collins/Fontana Books.

BOLTER, J.D. (1984). *Turing's Man. Western Culture in the Computer Age*. London: Duckworth.

334   *Jens F. Jensen*

BOURDIEU, P. (1984). *Distinction: A social critique of the social judgement of taste.* London: Routledge.
BRZEZINSKI, Z. (1982). *Between Two Ages: America's Role in the Technetronic Era.* Greenwood.
CAYFORD, J. (1987). *Computer Media. Living & Working with Computers.* London: Commedia.
DAHLBERG, A., LIVINGSTONE, S., MORLEY, D., SILVERSTONE, R. (1989). *Families, technologies and consumption: The household and information and communication technologies.* Paper presented to the ESRC Programme on Information and Communication Technologies Conference, Brunel University, May 17.-19. 1989.
DERTOUZOS, M.L., MOSES, J. (1980). *The Computer Age. A Twenty Year View.* Cambridge, Mass.: The MIT Press.
DUNN, T. (1986). The evolution of cultural studies. In *Introduction to Contemporary Cultural Studies*, ed. Punter, D. London: Longman.
ECO, U. (1975). Looking for a Logic of Culture. In *The Tell-Tale Sign*, ed. Sebeok, T.A. Lisse/Netherlands: The Peter de Ridder Press.
ECO, U. (1976). *A Theory of Semiotics.* Bloomington: Indiana University Press.
ECO, U. (1984). *Semiotics and the Philosophy of Language.* London: The Macmillan Press.
ELLUL, J. (1973). *The Technological Society.* New York: Knopf.
FISKE, J. (1990). *Introduction to Communication Studies.* London: Routledge.
FISKE, J. (1987). *Television Culture.* London: Methuen.
FORESTER, T. ed. (1980). *The Microelectronics Revolution.* Oxford: Basil Blackwell.
FORESTER, T. (1987). *High-Tech Society. The Story of the Information Technology Revolution.* Oxford: Basil Blackwell.
FRENTZ, T., RUSHING, J.H. (1989). The Frankenstein Myth in Contemporary Cinema. In *Critical Studies in Mass Communication*, 6.
GELL, A. (1988). Technology as Magic. In *Anthropology Today*, Vol. 4. 2.
HADDON, L. (1988). The Home Computer: The Making of a Consumer Electronic. In *Science as culture 2*. London: Free Association Books.
HALL, S. (1980). Encoding/decoding. In *Culture, Media, Language*, eds. Hall, S., Hobson, D., Lowe, A., Willis, P. London: Hutchinson.
HALL, S. (1981). Cultural studies: two paradigms. In *Culture, Ideology and Social Process. A Reader*, eds. Bennet, T. et al. Batsford Academic and Educational Press.
HEIM, M. (1987). *Electric language: A philosophical study of word processing.* New Haven: Yale University Press.
HODGE, R., KRESS, G. (1988). *Social Semiotics.* Cambridge: Polity Press.
HOLMQVIST, B. (1989). Work-language and perspective. In *Scandinavian Journal of Information Systems* 1.
HOLMQVIST, B., ANDERSEN, P.B. (1991). Language, perspective, and design. In *Design at Work*, eds. Greenbaum, J., Kyng, M. Hillsdale: Earlbaum.
JAMESON, F. (1984). Postmodernism, or The Cultural Logic of Late Capitalism. In *New Left Review*, no. 146.

JENSEN, J.F. (1990). Formatering af forskningsfeltet: Computer-Kultur & Computer-Semiotik (Formatting the field: Computer culture & computer semiotics). In: *Computer-Kultur, Computer-Medier, Computer-Semiotik* (Computer culture, computer media, computer semiotics), ed. J.F. Jensen. Aalborg: Nordisk SommerUniversiet.

JENSEN, J.F. (1990). Computermedier. Computeren som medie, kommunikation og mediekultur (Computer Media. The computer as media, communication and media culture). In: *Computer-Kultur, Computer-Medier, Computer-Semiotik* (Computer culture, computer media, computer semiotics), ed. J.F. Jensen. Aalborg: Nordisk SommerUniversitet.

JOUET, J., PROULX, S. (1988). *Social Uses of Microcomputers.* Report from IAMCR conference in Barcelona 1988.

KAPLAN, S.J. (1990). Visual Metaphors in the Representation of Communication Technology. In *Critical Studies in Mass Communication*, 7.

KNEE, C. (1985). The Hidden Curriculum of the Computer. In *Compulsive Technology. Computers as Culture*, eds. Solomonides, T., Levidow, L. London: Free Association Books.

KRISTEVA, J. (1975). The system and the speaking subject. In *The Tell-Tale Sign*, ed. Sebeok, T.A. Lisse/Netherlands: The Peter de Ridder Press.

LAKOFF, G., JOHNSON, M. (1980). *Metaphors we live by.* Chicago: University of Chicago Press.

LINN, P. (1985). Microcomputers in Education: Living and Dead Labour. In *Compulsive Technology. Computers as Culture*, eds. Solomonides, T., Levidow, L. London: Free Association Books.

LYOTARD, J.-F. (1984). *The Postmodern Condition: A Report on Knowledge.* Minneapolis: University of Minnesota Press.

McLUHAN, M. (1962). *The Gutenberg Galaxy. The Making of the Typographic Man.* London: Routledge & Kegan Paul.

McLUHAN, M. (1964). *Understanding Media. The Extensions of Man.* New York: McGraw Hill.

McLUHAN, M. (1967). *The Medium is the Massage.* London: Allen Lane, Penguin Press.

MORLEY, D., SILVERSTONE, R. (1989). *Domestic communication — technologies and meanings.* Paper from Centre for Research into Innovation, Culture and Technology. Brunel University.

MORLEY, D., SILVERSTONE, R. (1990). Domestic communication — technologies and meanings. In *Media, Culture and Society*, Vol. 12. London: Sage.

MUMFORD, L. (1934). *Technics and Civilisation.* New York: Harcourt Brace.

MUMFORD, L. (1964). *The Myth of The Machine. The Pentagon of Power.* New York: Harcourt Brace.

MURDOCK, G., HARTMANN, P., GRAY, P. (1988). *Home Computers: The Social Construction of a Complex Commodity.* Paper from Centre for Mass Communication Research, University of Leicester.

NADIN, M. (1988). Interface design: A semiotic paradigm. In *Semiotica* 69, 3/4.

NAISBITT, J. (1982). *Megatrends.* London: Macdonald.

NEISSER, U. (1966). Computers as tools and as metaphors. In *The Social Impact of Cybernetics*, ed. Dechert, C.R. London: University of Notre Dame Press.

NORA, S., MINC, A. (1980). *The Computerization of Society*. Cambridge, Mass: The MIT press.

NORMAN, D.A., DRAPER, S.W. (1986). *User Centered System Design. New Perspectives on Human-Computer Interaction*. Hillsdale, New Jersey: Lawrence Erlbaum Associates.

O'SULLIVAN, T., HARTLEY, J., SAUNDERS, D., FISKE, J. (1983). *Key Concepts in Communication*. London: Methuen.

PEIRCE, C.S. (1931-58). *Collected Papers*. Cambridge, Mass.: Harvard University Press.

PFAFFENBERGER, B. (1988a). Fetishised Objects and humanised Nature: Towards an Anthropology of Technology. In *Man: The Journal of the Royal Anthropological Institute*, 23.

PFAFFENBERGER, B. (1988b). The social meaning of the personal computer: Or, why the personal computer revolution was no revolution. In *Anthropological Quarterly*, 61.

PORUSH, D. (1985). *The Soft Machine. Cybernetic Fiction*. New York: Methuen.

POSTER, M. (1990). *The Mode of Information. Poststructuralism and Social Context*. Cambridge: Polity Press.

POSTMAN, N. (1986). *Amusing Ourselves to Death*. London: William Heinemann.

SEBEOK, T.A. ed. (1975). *The Tell-Tale Sign. A Survey of Semiotics*. Lisse/Netherlands: The Peter de Ridder Press.

SOLOMONIDES, T., LEVIDOW, L. eds. (1985). *Compulsive technology. Computers as culture*. London: Free Associaton Books.

TOFFLER, A. (1981). *The Third Wave*. London: Pan.

TURKLE, S. (1984). *The Second Self. Computers and the human Spirit*. London: Granada.

VENKATESH, A., VITALARI, N. (1984). Households and Technology. The Case of Home Computers — Some Conceptual and Theoretical Issues. In *Marketing to the Changing Household: Management and Research Perspectives*, eds. Roberts, M.L., Wortzel, L.H. Cambridge, Mass.: Ballinger Publishing Company.

WEINER, N. (1954). *The Human Use of Human Beings*. Boston: Houghton Mifflin.

WILLIAMS, R. (1974). *Television. Technology and Cultural Form*. New York: Schocken Books.

WILLIAMS, R. (1983). *Culture*. Fontana.

WINNER, L. (1986) Technology as forms of life. In *The whale and the reactor: A search for limits in an age of high technology*. Chicago: Chicago University Press.

WRIGHT, D.E. (1979). Promethean Legacy: Ambivalent Relation Between Man and His Tools. In *Technology in American Culture*.

14

One person, one computer: The social construction of the personal computer

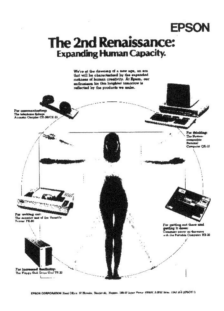

Fig. 14.1. "Expanding human capacity".

To understand the dominating role played by technics in modern civilization, one must explore in detail the preliminary period of ideological and social preparation. Not merely must one explain the existence of the new mechanical instruments: one must explain the culture that was ready to use them and profit by them so extensively. For note this: mechanization and regimentation are not new phenomena in history: what is new is the fact that these functions have been projected and embodied in organized forms which dominate every aspect of our existence. Other civilizations reached a high degree of technical proficiency without, apparently, being profoundly influenced by the methods and aims of technics. All the critical instruments of modern technology — the clock, the printing press, the water-mill, the magnetic compass, the loom, the lathe, gunpowder, paper, to say nothing of mathematics and chemistry and mechanics — existed in other cultures. The Chinese, the Arabs, the Greeks, long before the Northern European, had taken most of the first steps toward the machine. And although the great engineering works of the Cretans, the Egyptians, and the Romans were carried out mainly on an empirical basis, these peoples plainly had an abundance of technical skill at their command. They had machines; but they did not develop "the machine."   *(Mumford, 1934: 4)*

In his classic study of the mechanization of modern societies, *Technics and Civilization* (1934), Lewis Mumford raised issues that remain relevant for, but largely unaddressed by communication research. One fundamental issue is how new technologies are assimilated to specific political, economic, and cultural practices in a particular historical context, thus developing into resources with a characteristic social form. In the area of information and communication technology, the process of assimilation has gone further than in most other areas of social life. It is evident that two generations after Mumford's study, the mass media have become integrated into everyday life to the extent of being in some respects constitutive of social reality. Increasingly, the audience-public can be said to live *inside* "the machine" of mass media, in a qualitatively new form of media environment.

The social implications of this development have, to a degree, been examined from the perspective of media institutions and other infrastructures, frequently with the assumption that an information society is emerging (Nora and Minc, 1980; Porat, 1977; Toffler, 1980). However, the perspective of the audience-public on the many issues relating to that political and cultural change has been given less attention. This chapter outlines a framework for examining the social construction of communication technologies, and presents findings from a study of the introduction and reception of the personal computer in the United States.

Drawing on historical research about the rise of literacy and the development of new genres of communication, I suggest a definition of the social contexts of media use as *media environments*. The contexts of media use set the historical conditions for cultural practices in a way that is broadly analogous to the limiting function of the natural environment for economic enterprise. The introduction of new media as social resources entails a reconstruction of the total media environment, as a new division of labor among the media is negotiated. Simultaneously, "new" media rely on "old" media to present, position, and legitimate an unfamiliar technology to the public acting as consumers and citizens. The empirical findings from a study of computer advertisements in American general-interest magazines over a ten-year period suggest the importance of the symbolic representation of this new medium during the process of its diffusion. Of particular salience in this process has been the intertextuality of the contemporary media environment —

the references in one medium to another medium, genre, or discourse. For communication theory, the findings thus highlight the need to develop a perspective on mass communication that is both historical and discursive, social and semiotic. A medium is frequently the message of another medium.

Media in and on history

Early film audiences reportedly were frightened by the representation of a train approaching on the screen. Today, audiences are said to zip, zap, and graze the television medium, seeking ever greater stimulation and fascination. It is plausible that media recipients, while drawing on decoding skills developed for older media, are continually socialized to the tasks of new media environments (Jensen, in press).

Previous studies on the development of literacy have concluded that a system of writing generally constitutes a cultural resource with important social consequences (Goody, 1987; Goody and Watt, 1963; Innis, 1972; Havelock, 1963; Lowe, 1982; Scribner and Cole, 1981; Thomas, 1989). In the sciences, alphabetic writing, in contrast to oral forms of intercourse, may ensure a systematic and cumulative form of analysis. In politics, literacy makes possible a complex governmental system by providing a resource for organization and communication across time and space. In contrast to the technological schematism of McLuhan (1962; 1964), later work has noted how the modes of communication are shaped not just by the media, but as importantly by their social and contextual uses (see also Ong, 1982). As shown by Eisenstein (1979), it was the scribal culture of the medieval monasteries, as related by Umberto Eco in *The Name of the Rose* (1981), rather than an oral culture, which was transformed by the printing press from the mid-fifteenth century. By putting an end to the monopoly of the Church on the dissemination and legitimation of knowledge, print technology became instrumental in the cultural revolutions summed up as Renaissance and Reformation.

Current developments, perhaps equally fundamental, may entail a reconstruction of the contexts of media reception. It is not only the *private* domain that has become a new form of media environment as television has brought social issues and the "backstage" behavior (Meyrowitz, 1985) of other people into the home in a seemingly unmediated way. Also in *public* life, the total availability of mass communication particularly in urban areas has resulted in a saturation of much of social time and space with cultural products — from billboard advertising and print media read in transit, to television and recorded music in the shopping center and the workplace. If, traditionally, cultural activities have served as a time-out from everyday life, the merging of mass communication with the everyday may be producing a next-to-constant time-in — a specifically modern set of media environments.

Intertextuality

One key feature of contemporary media environments is intertextuality, defined as the structured interrelations between otherwise distinct texts, genres, and media. Originating in Julia Kristeva's structuralist theory of texts, intertextuality may be understood as "a use of language that calls up a vast reserve of echoes from similar texts, similar phrasings, remarks, situations, characters" (Coward and Ellis, 1977: 51). The intertextual aspect of discourse appears especially prominent in mass communication, because the mass media in various ways feed on each other's content. Accordingly, whatever "effect" one medium or discourse may produce is in principle reinforced by intertextuality.

Two main forms of intertextuality can be distinguished. *Thematic* intertextuality refers to narrative elements that are reiterated in other texts. A characteristic example would be recurring literary figures, such as the theme of Oedipus or the legend of Faust in Western arts. More important in this context is *structural* intertextuality, which refers to the configuration of texts in relation to each other as part of a particular mode or purpose of communication. A familiar example is the sequential structure of television programming, comprising also commercials and pre-announcements. Another variety of structural intertextuality is advertising and criticism about new cinema releases in print media and broadcasting. Such recycling of cultural symbols through the media carries major implications for the history and social impact of mass communication, which are only beginning to be examined by research (Bennett and Woollacott, 1987; Pearson and Uricchio, 1991).

An overlooked form of intertextuality is the portrayal of one medium in other media. In particular, mass media serve as vehicles for introducing new communication technologies for general consumption. If consumers are to spend a significant amount of money on a new medium, they must perceive it as relevant or meaningful to their specific social context. Without meaning, no effects. Without symbols, no diffusion.

Symbolic diffusion

The terminology of symbolic diffusion is employed here to specify what is traditionally referred to as the social construction of reality (Berger and Luckmann, 1966). Within the general process of everyday interaction that serves to construct a shared, intersubjective reality and to posit its agents as social subjects, symbolic diffusion refers the specific process by which new cultural resources are disseminated and appropriated. At issue, then, is not merely the marketing question of who acquires what device, from which manufacturer, resulting in what degree of satisfaction, but the cultural question of how the technology is represented to users and non-users alike.

Earlier research has examined the diffusion of various technological innovations and, to some degree, their social consequences. While Rogers (1983) offers a general framework of such inquiry, analyses of the spread of the personal computer (Dutton, Rogers, and Jun, 1987) and earlier studies of the telephone (Pool, 1977) have offered necessary baseline information on the spread of these technologies to different user groups. The development of videotex and its apparent failure as a general service democratizing information, has been examined in several studies (see, for example, Branscomb, 1988; Charon, 1988; Noll, 1985). And computer games, being one of the most widely used genres of computer communication, have been described both in a historical perspective (Haddon, 1988) and as a discursive form similar to earlier forms of story-telling (Skirrow, 1986). Still, little attention has been given to the further significance of these and other communication technologies in the perspective of social or cultural history (but see Rogers and Larsen, 1984; also Schudson, 1991).

Recently, a number of studies have begun to examine the implications of the personal computer for the general audience-public, with Turkle (1984) representing an early and methodologically innovative approach to the cultural significance of the computer as perceived by different user groups. Within a different, philosophical approach to computing, Heim (1987) has analyzed the possible impact of word processing on people's sense of language — the Word — as a means of expression, communication, and ultimately communion. The development of hypertext systems as a phase in the history of literacy has been examined by Bolter (1991). Furthermore, Roszak (1986) has offered a critical assessment of the promises to the public that are implied by the notion of an information society, as symbolized by the personal computer. Finally, a few studies have documented the values and meanings that have been associated with the personal computer during the course of its introduction (Pfaffenberger, 1988) and more generally the visual representation of new communication technologies in media discourses (Kaplan, 1990). So far, however, little research has examined the representation of the personal computer in other mass media and hence its symbolic diffusion.

The symbolic diffusion of the personal computer is of special interest for a critical evaluation of the current state of the information society. The promise that technologies such as the personal computer can help to democratize politics and culture, may lead the audience-public to accept the substantial, direct and indirect costs of introducing a new technological infrastructure in society. In this scenario, the personal computer represents a point of access to the greatly enhanced networks of knowledge and communication at the local, national, as well as international levels. Advertising for computers during the 1980s did indeed rely, in part, on a theme of democracy through technology. An illustrative example is found in advertisements from the Apple company that refer to the twin principles of one person, one vote, and "one person, one computer" (*Newsweek*, Special Election Issue, November/December 1984). The personal computer, then, offers both a symbol and a touchstone of the information society.

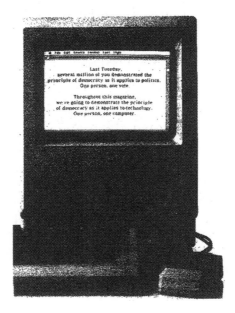

Fig. 14.2. "One person, one vote".

Methodology

The empirical study examined a sample of computer advertisements from *Time* and *Newsweek* covering the period 1977-88. These general-interest news magazines were selected for analysis because, in the United States, they are perhaps the closest approximation to a national press (Gans, 1979:

xi). In addition to choosing media that reach a wide segment of the American public, one aim of the analysis was to explore the discursive forms employed by an "old" print medium to represent a "new" electronic and increasingly visual medium to prospective users. Print media remain an important, but somewhat overlooked constituent of contemporary media environments.

All issues of *Newsweek* and *Time* from the years 1977, 1981, 1984, and 1988 were included in the analysis. These years may be taken as strategic junctures in the life of the personal computer. Taking the introduction of the Apple II in 1977 as the point of departure, the analysis centers on the period starting four years later in 1981 (the year of the introduction of the IBM PC) and ending in 1984 (the introduction of the Macintosh), while adding another year sample taken four years later in 1988. The main advantage of the sample is that it facilitates a characterization of the long waves of symbolic diffusion, which might be lost in other forms of sampling — for example, a selection of magazines from a few weeks in each consecutive year of the entire period. The present sample, further, makes possible a discourse analysis of each advertisement with reference to its context of other media discourses, including various thematic advertising campaigns during a particular period.

The criteria for selecting the advertisements served to identify any advertising for computer products or services as well as commercial messages on behalf of computer companies, such as corporate or image advertising. The purpose of this rather wide-ranging sample was to make possible a comparative analysis of the representation of, for example, the home user versus the business user and of the personal computer versus other types of computing. This called for inclusion of advertising for computer games as well as for whole computer systems aimed at business. The criteria called for exclusion, on the other hand, of computer products or services that were advertised as one element of a company's line of products within one advertisement. Among other things, this would exclude communication systems that comprise elements of computing, such as telephony. These aspects of telecommunications and computing, while relevant for a comprehensive analysis of the symbolic diffusion of informatics and telematics, fell outside the scope of this study. Moreover, advertisements placed by non-computer companies, even when referring to computers as an element of their service to customers, were excluded. Finally, printers referred to as "typewriters" rather than "word processors" or similar items interfacing with a "computer" were excluded from the sample.

The intersubjectivity of the selections made by the primary researcher according to these criteria was verified by another analyst with reference to one whole issue of either *Newsweek* or *Time* from each of the four years (two issues of each magazine). Only one case in which an advertisement had been excluded by the primary researcher was disputed, while none of the ads included was questioned by the secondary analyst.

This procedure, of course, is standard in social-scientific communication research, and it offers a valuable check at the level of selecting particular types of media content. However, when it comes to describing and interpreting the discursive forms through which symbolic diffusion is accomplished, a similar procedure of coding the advertisements by a pre-defined set of categories is insufficient. For the purpose of studying how cultural and political significance is ascribed to technology, one must analyze media contents as discourses.

Discourses of advertising

Recent communication studies have developed discourse analysis as a systematic tool for qualitative research on the content and reception of mass communication (for surveys, see Jensen, 1987; Van Dijk, 1991). Unlike formal content analysis, which employs independent coders and decontextualized categories of analysis as part of a quantitative design, discourse analysis serves to establish the meaning of linguistic and visual elements in their discursive context. Hence, measures of contextual meaning are given priority over measures of recurrence. Counts of particular discursive structures are seldom meaningful since the explanatory value of the analytical categories appears only from specimen analyses.

The approach entails a detailed procedure of verbal and visual analysis, which may combine qualitative and quantitative modes of inquiry. First, the discourse analysis of magazine advertising is taken as the basis for assigning advertisements to a further set of categories of theoretical interpretation. These categories serve to produce a quantitative characterization of the sample of advertisements as a whole. Second, the discourse analysis is qualitative or exploratory, in the sense that it makes possible a further interpretation of key themes in the advertising discourses concerning the social uses of the personal computer. The empirical study thus also reflects on methodological issues of how qualitative and quantitative modes of inquiry may complement each other within a theoretical framework of symbolic diffusion (see also Jensen and Jankowski, 1991).

Concretely, the verbal and visual analysis of advertisements focused on three discursive categories: *actors* (the participants in events represented in advertising); *coherence* (the structure of the advertising discourse, including the functional relations between linguistic statements and images); and *implications* (assumptions serving as implicit premises of an argument or narrative). Most details of the discourse analysis cannot be reported within the scope of this chapter. The section on findings presents, first, the aggregated categorization of computer advertisements that resulted from the discourse analysis, and, second, a more detailed examination of the advertising discourses with respect to their implications concerning the social uses of the personal computer. To illustrate the nature of the discourse approach, a brief exemplary analysis will now be given of the well-known television commercial introducing the Macintosh during the Super Bowl of 1984 (see also Berger, 1989).

The commercial introduces several sets of *actors* who are in conflict, and who are contrasted with each other through their visual representation as well as their actions. Seated in a murky hall before a giant television screen showing some form of Big Brother, a congregation of skinhead zombies dressed in grey are the audience of a propagandistic political speech. Intercut with this scene, the viewer sees a young female athlete, dressed in bright colors and carrying a large hammer, who is apparently approaching the hall while being pursued by helmeted, faceless police. An important narrative device in the overall structure of the commercial is its *coherence,* particularly as established through the intercutting of scenes. This aspect of coherence serves to emphasise the several dichotomies that are acted out in the commercial as the confrontation reaches its climax. Arriving at the hall, the athlete hurls the hammer at the screen, which explodes. Among the *implications* that may thus be activated in the audience are various intertextual structures, aesthetic forms, and myths. Most obviously, an intertextual relation is established to George Orwell's *1984*, which is made explicit in the final text informing viewers that, because Apple is introducing the Macintosh, 1984 will not be like *1984*. Furthermore, the visual and narrative universe of the commercial may recall for viewers *Blade Runner* and other films by Ridley Scott, who also directed the commercial, suggesting the kind of future that the Macintosh can help them to avoid. Finally, the promise may be that, unlike the Big Brother and Goliath of computers (IBM), David (Apple) will empower the individual in the information society of 1984 and beyond, through a truly personal computer.

Findings

The discourse analysis of the sample of computer advertisements from *Time* and *Newsweek* provided the foundation for a categorization of the advertising discourses with reference to a traditional model of communication. Both in the social sciences and the humanities, questions about the communication process — who / says what / to whom / in which context / through which channel and code / with what effect — tend to structure the process of inquiry. While Lasswell (1948) asks about effects in a concrete, material or *social* sense, Jakobson (1960) and other humanistic studies pose their questions with regard to *discursive* impact, meaning, or implications. The discursive mode of inquiry, then, focuses on the actual discourse of communication, examining its structure and the conditions of understanding, while reserving judgement about its further impact on individuals or cultures.

Adopting a discursive approach to computer advertising, the study framed one set of questions to the data in terms of the basic communication model: Who proffers what to whom, in which context, through which channel and code, and with what implications? Special attention is given to the questions of what types of computer products are proffered to which user groups and, above all, with what implications regarding the social uses of the personal computer. These questions are especially important for understanding the process of symbolic diffusion and social construction of new technologies. Several of the other questions call for further historical and discursive analysis, and fall outside the scope of the present study. "In Which Context" addresses the place of the personal computer in social and cultural history, and awaits further work in media history. "Through Which Channel" suggests the need for further work on differences between media as they serve to construct technologies socially as consumer products, while "Through Which Code" points to a great many unresolved issues of communication theory, particularly the specificity of visual and verbal signs and their configuration in advertising and other genres of mass communication.

Who

Although the senders or addressers of communication are defined, in part, by the criteria for selecting the advertisements, there are several noteworthy aspects of the computer companies that are the implied senders of the advertising discourses. First of all, while the advertising is mainly that of individual companies, some advertisements are also designed to build the legitimacy of the computer sector as a whole. This appears to be the case especially with advertising from IBM, even if some other companies refer to the services of the computer to mankind or society in general. An example of such image advertising is a recurring item from IBM showing a line-up of suspects including a computer, asserting that "The computer didn't do it" (*Newsweek* (N), October 12, 1981; *Time* (T), September 21, 1981). The further argument is that even though computers can be misused, they cannot "commit crimes."

Presumably, action with social consequences is the prerogative, not of anonymous technologies, but of human individuals.

Moreover, some advertisements refer to the singularity of a company and its approach to business, rather than its products and services. From 1977 onward, advertising from Wang argues that this company is "hungrier than IBM" (T, 2/28/77). Similar references to a general competitive spirit abound in the sample. Another example is a reference to three businessmen who made their (computer) company the greatest (business) success in history (T, 3/12/84; 3/26/84). Survival and success in market terms may thus serve as an indicator of quality also in terms of the technology or service offered.

Finally, some advertisements associate a sense of community with computer companies. In some cases, the vocabulary suggests that just as the company is responsive to customer needs ("We listen"), its computers are "compatible" with users and speak their "language." In other cases, advertisements appeal to the concept of family as experienced both in the workplace and the home. Computers may furnish a means of contact to various "families," and they may defend the larger family of the nation from external threats, notably Japan. Computers, like other communication technologies, may represent avenues to community.

What

The findings concerning the particular aspects of computing that were advertised during the four years of the study, are summarized in Tables 14.1a and 14.1b. For ease of reference, the tables also list the total number of advertisements for each year in each magazine.

The most noticeable development is the overall growth in the volume of computer advertisements in the first part of the period, followed by an equally marked decline between 1984 and 1988. This trend applies to both *Time* and *Newsweek*. However, the yearly number of items in *Time* is about twice the number in *Newsweek*. This may be explained by differences in the educational, occupational, and income characteristics of readers, which suggest that readers of *Time* are more likely to be in a position to decide to purchase a computer either for a business or for home use (Gans, 1979: 222). In addition, *Time* may be perceived as catering more to the business market, partly because of its relatively more conservative editorial line.

More interestingly, the figures suggest a process of symbolic diffusion gaining momentum from the late 1970s, climaxing in the early to mid-1980s, and subsiding in the late 1980s. This is consistent with the development of the industry reaching a climax and crisis around 1984, with the Apple company as a case in point (Sculley, 1987: chs. 8-9).

Table 14.1a. *Newsweek:* The What of Computer Advertising

	1977	1981	1984	1988
No. of items	11	48	155	70
Hardware	-	-	15	16
Software	-	-	27	-
No distinction	11	48	113	54
(Hereof word processing)	4	12	-	11

Table 14.1b. *Time:* The What of Computer Advertising

	1977	1981	1984	1988
No. of items	33	92	245	130
Hardware	-	1	27	19
Software	-	1	65	34
No distinction	33	90	153	77
(Hereof word processing)	6	27	-	9

The distinction between hardware and software appears to have been established in advertising discourse between 1981 and 1984, even if the majority of the advertisements from 1984 still do not refer exclusively to one or the other. This may be interpreted as a sign that by the mid-1980s the audience-public could be considered familiar with the basic elements of computer technology. This interpretation is supported by the fact that, despite the overall decline in advertising volume from 1984 to 1988, in *Time* the proportion of advertising making the distinction between hardware and software, relative to advertisements without this distinction, was higher in 1988 than 1984, thus suggesting a continued trend toward differentiation. The picture is complicated, however, by the total absence of software advertisements in *Newsweek* during 1988, which calls for further research.

Perhaps the most interesting suggestion of the two tables arises from the figures concerning word processing. The analysis noted whenever reference was made to the designated use of computers for word processing. The findings for both 1977 and 1981 show references to word processing in both magazines without a distinction being made between hardware and software. By 1984, as total volume increases and the hardware-software distinction appears, the references to word processing disappear from both magazines. In 1988, the references have re-appeared despite the decrease in volume. This implies that around the top of the curve of its introduction, the personal computer was constructed in advertising discourse as a "general machine" with various social uses, including but not restricted to word processing. By contrast, 1988 may have witnessed an attempt by companies to reclaim part of their market after the concept of the general machine apparently had failed.

To whom

A number of related conclusions are suggested by the representation of computer users in the advertisements. These findings are summarized in Tables 14.2a and 14.2b, again listing the volume of advertising.

It should be noted that the term *public* refers to the general public as affected by computers and addressed by advertising as citizens. In discourse terms, the public is addressed grammatically as an Afficative element, being affected by computers. The term *home* refers to the private user, who is potentially an Agentive using the computer for various purposes in the home context, but also as part of other social and cultural activities. *Youth* includes children and teenagers.

The first conclusion with respect to user groups is that while the number of advertisements addressed respectively to business and private users rises and falls in accordance with the general curve of symbolic diffusion already noted, the most noteworthy figure documents the growth of advertising in both magazines which is addressed to *any* prospective computer customer, irrespective of context and uses, between 1981 and 1984. This is consistent with the conclusion that the personal computer was constructed socially as a "general machine" that could be assimilated to different uses in different sectors. The development of a home market, while significant, may have been less important, also in social and cultural terms, than the development of a market across user groups and sectors of application.

Second, of the advertisements directed specifically at the home market, a significant portion makes reference to children and youth. An important argument for introducing the personal computer into the home, as discussed further later on, has been that these groups need a computer to get ahead, or stay ahead, in the educational system and later in the job market. So-called computer literacy arguably will become a pre-condition for successful participation in many areas of social life in the information society.

Table 14.2a. *Newsweek:* Computer Advertising To Whom

	1977	1981	1984	1988
No. of items	11	48	155	70
Business	5	31	60	20
(Hereof small)	-	11	1	3
Public	6	5	2	6
Home	-	12	27	8
(Hereof youth)	-	7	19	2
No distinction	-	-	66	36

Table 14.2b. *Time:* Computer Advertising To Whom

	1977	1981	1984	1988
No. of items	33	92	245	130
Business	22	71	11	58
(Hereof small)	10	22	5	14
Public	11	7	6	7
Home	-	14	26	16
(Hereof youth)	-	3	20	12
No distinction	-	-	102	49

Third, a relatively large portion of the advertising addressed to companies makes reference to small business. Even though it was to be expected that small businesses will need small computers, the many references particularly in *Time* suggest that, in order to market small computers at all, advertising is relying on a familiar theme of a general American business ideology — namely, that small is where a business starts, not where it ends. A personal computer may become a resource for building and expanding one's own business.

Fourth and finally, the number of image advertisements directed at the general public remains at the same low level throughout the period. As is the case also with the other figures in the tables, there are no major differences between *Time* and *Newsweek* in this respect. The occasional example of such advertisements may serve to bolster the image of the computer and the companies in the eyes of the audience-public. However, the low figure also suggests that if, indeed, advertising has a general impact on the public's perception of and action vis-à-vis computers, this impact must be traced, above all, to the discourses of actual sales advertising. The entire sample of advertisements carries a variety of implications, finally, regarding the social uses of the personal computer.

With what implications

The presence of particular implications in the sample during each of the four years of the study is noted and discussed here. Rather than counting the *recurrence* of implications during each year, the discourse analysis served to identify the *occurrence* of social, political, and cultural implications at different times. The methodological assumption underlying this approach was that it is the presence or absence of implications in a specific context that may suggest the rise and fall of themes in the process of symbolic diffusion. Hence, whereas the preceding sections on "What" and "To Whom" have presented quantitative measures based on the discourse analysis, this section examines and interprets the qualitative categories of the discourse analysis only. (Again, differences between *Time* and *Newsweek* are negligible, and will not be commented on.)

1977. Two sets of implications can be singled out during the first year of the study. In advertisements addressed to the general *public*, computers are presented as a new technology serving the public interest. Computers can help companies and organizations to give consumers better service and to make production more efficient. More generally, information, as administered through computers, is seen as a resource enabling mankind to manage material resources better as world population continues to increase. The common theme, which becomes explicit in some advertisements, is that of "the information age." It is summarized in an advertisement from IBM, featuring various examples of how this company is "helping put information to work for people" (T, 11/21/77).

The second set of implications is found in advertising addressed to *business*. Not surprisingly, computers are presented as a means to business success: "In other words, results" (T, 4/18/77). More specifically, the means is presented as individual solutions and state of the art equipment. By contrast, low cost is referred to infrequently, and is not a prominent sales argument or theme.

The advertisements further reflect an awareness that computers must somehow be compatible with people and their work routines. This implication is developed as a key theme in advertising to all user groups during later years, but is found during 1977 in a preliminary form addressed to business. The theme of user friendliness is commonly found in references to companies and machines mastering more than one "language," such as a representative of one computer company speaking both English and "medical" (T, 5/2/77). But, also for the operator of the machine, compatibility is key: "Alice your bookkeeper," on being introduced to a new computer system, initially thinks that her bosses have "flipped out," but she quickly learns how accessible that particular system is and becomes "Alice your computer operator" (T, 11/21/77). At the same time, questions of job satisfaction are seen from the perspective of (male) management, as suggested by references to "your" people.

1981. An important implication in the first advertisements directed at the *home* market is that computers are now accessible for everybody. The Atari company, for example, advertises "computers for people" and proposes to "bring the computer age home." Furthermore, a distinction is introduced between games and other uses of the personal computer, implying that different social uses of the computer may be more or less worthy and legitimate. Thus, the producer of one video game emphasizes that it offers not only "the excitement of a game," but also "the mind of a computer" (T, 11/2/81). More generally, the range of possible uses of a computer by ordinary people is emphasised, most clearly perhaps in advertising for the IBM PC that refers to both work, learning, and pleasure. In addition to programming and word processing, the personal computer is presented as a resource for planning your budget, keeping an eye on your calories, and tapping into data banks. The assumption that personal computers have become a staple of the home and family life, is summed up in a headline from IBM: "Dad, can I use the IBM computer tonight?" (N, 11/23/81). However, during 1981 the personal computer was not yet constructed as an indispensable resource for the education of youth, even if learning was presented as one application.

The implications in advertising addressed to the general *public* remain relatively unaffected as the role of computing in other sectors grows. Computers help people and make for efficient production — for example, by saving energy. The computer's helping function is given a new dimension in an IBM advertisement reporting that some computers now have a general "Help" button explaining the system to users (T, 10/5/81). Another development in computer advertising overall is the increasing use, compared to 1977, of slogans about the social consequences of computers. Digital: "We change the way the world thinks." Wang: "Making the world more productive." Such advertising discourse is addressed, in part, to the public as citizens, and it may contribute to the agenda for public debate about computers and hence to symbolic diffusion.

As for *business* users, the implications are in keeping with those noted for 1977. Computer companies offer state of the art service and equipment that is accessible in the user's own "language." There are some additional indications that because computers are now used in a variety of job functions, flexibility increasingly must be presented as a quality of the systems advertised. As mentioned in the section "To Whom," the spread of computers to small businesses is also a prominent theme. Moreover, with reference to intensifying competition, some advertisements during 1981 emphasise that computers are a necessary instrument in order to remain on top of things and accordingly make the right decisions. One advertisement even makes the argument that a particular computer "works for less than the minimum wage" (T, 8/17/81). The right computer can help you avoid "your business running you," and in the process it may give a sense of "freedom" (T, 6/22/81). A sense of intensified competition may also have made itself felt in the computer business, since several companies refer both to the complexity of making a decision to buy a computer system and to the need to explore the uniqueness of *their* system. Under the heading of "How do you explain something that's never existed before?,' one advertisement suggests that it may be as difficult to explain this particular office system as it was for a cave man to explain the concept of the wheel to his fellow cave men (T, 6/8/81).

1984. At the height of the symbolic diffusion of the personal computer, 1984 was the first year when some advertising in the sample was directed to *all users*, carrying implications about its general nature. One common implication is that in the future, everybody will use personal computers; the question is which type. The Apple company made this point in its campaign for the Macintosh, arguing that this machine is for 'the rest of us' who cannot or do not want to use more complicated personal computers. And, in addition to the qualities of accessibility and flexibility noted earlier, new possibilities arguably are offered to new users by portable computers and more sophisticated software.

Two aspects of the social uses of the personal computer stand out in advertising from 1984. First, the computer is associated with success in a society that is constantly under transformation. One computer is offered to "Today's Upward Mobile Society" (T, 1/2/84). The underlying assumption is made explicit in one advertisement for diskettes: "Somebody has to be better than everybody else" (T, 8/13/84).

The other major implication has to do, not with success within current society, but with a possible transformation of society. One product is presented as "The most dangerous computer in the world," possibly leading to "a social revolution," because it decentralizes authority and empowers individuals to transcend time and space. This vision of a different future is associated in the text with Thomas Jefferson (T, 7/2/84). A similar, more elaborate concept of (more) democracy through technology was developed by the Apple company in their Macintosh campaign during the presidential election in late 1984: "One person, one vote. One person, one computer" (N, November/December 84).

Other uses of the personal computer as part of a social change and emancipation arise from new types of software that "multiply thought" (T, 7/16/84), the production of an underground newsletter (T, 12/10/84), and the application of the personal computer as a means of communication with the entire world. The "Era 2" communications software is depicted as a means of plugging a keyboard directly into the Earth (T, 3/12/84). In this scenario, the Orwell of *1984* is proven wrong (T, 1/2/84), and the right computer system will give us "the future without the shock" (T, 4/9/84). How that scenario relates to the other set of implications concerning personal success, is elaborated next.

The implications associated with the *home* user are similar in most respects to those noted for 1981. The personal computer has a variety of uses for the whole family, and as such it is a way for the family, in the terminology of IBM's Chaplin campaign, to plug into "modern times." (Interestingly, another company appropriates the Chaplin figure and suggests that IBM "could make a tramp out of anyone" (T, 5/7/84).) Whereas adults can now take work home, the home use of the personal computer is depicted primarily as the road to educational success for the children, including preparation for college. This theme is articulated in a variety of ways throughout the sample for 1984, so that a personal computer is constructed as a necessary resource in any form of education, also with reference to equal opportunities for ethnic minorities (T, 10/1/84). The Apple company, for example, suggests that because ordinary children are kept away from computers at school by "bully nerds," every child needs an "Apple" after school (T, 9/17/84).

The advertising addressed to the general *public* again refers to the computer working in the public interest, for example, by processing medical information and by bringing computing power inexpensively to the children who need it most. And readers are reminded that since it is in everybody's interest to keep information secure, "there are rules for driving a computer, too" (T, 2/6/84). The public interest, incidentally, is defined as the American interest when a computer chip is said to be a way of meeting Japan's challenge.

Finally, also for *business* users, the implications remain largely unchanged. If computer systems are up-to-date and flexible, they will enable all levels of a business, large or small, to work together toward success. Furthermore, an employee is said to be able to "save" his/her boss by suggesting the right software (T, 9/24/84). Pricing remains a minor consideration, even though a few companies introduce low prices as a sales argument. Humor is used, in part, to poke fun at decision-makers who still cannot make up their mind to buy a computer (now, of course, the solution to their worries is here, T, 6/4/84). And a database program is advertised as exactly what "a big-time executive" like Santa Claus needs to keep an eye on everybody world-wide (N, 4/30/84).

1988. It is significant that the theme of social revolution has disappeared from the advertising discourses by 1988, while the theme of success remains a major implication of advertisements addressed to *all users*. Success is measured in terms of achievement, power, and survival, as suggested by the text of two advertisements: The company behind a flexible system argues that "survival belongs not merely to the fittest, but to those who remain fittest, longest" (N, 10/17/88). And, the producer of a portable computer states that "you can never be too powerful or too thin" (N, 5/16/88).The disappearance of the theme of social revolution will be interpreted and discussed in the conclusion.

Furthermore, some advertising now takes an aggressive approach to marketing by implying that anybody who does not (own and) use a computer is unreasonably backward. One advertisement, showing a very old typewriter, asks in the headline, "Just how simple do word processors have to get before you begin using one?" (N, 2/29/88). Using a computer may have become a prerequisite for being a part of the good society of the information society.

A few specific social uses of computing first appear in the 1988 sample. The personal computer is associated with the work routines of the yuppie, who may use it to transcend time and space: One product is meant "for people whose minds are at work even when their bodies aren't" (T, 7/25/88). And another computer terminal is presented as the monitor on which the (presumably male) reader will meet women when applying to a computerized dating service in AD. 2025 (N, 11/14/88). Moreover, the increasing use of the personal computer for graphic and other visual representation has become a major sales argument. Graphics may help users, for example, to do away with dull presentations. One advertisement even exclaims, with a touch of irony, but nevertheless stressing the visual potential of the personal computer: "Move over, Michelangelo" (T, 4/11/88).

In advertising addressed to the *home* market, educational uses of the personal computer continue to be a major implication. A simple "pre-computer" is advertised as a way to "turn on a mind" (N, 11/7/88). However, the intensive campaign of 1984, suggesting that a computer is a necessary condition of education at any level, had subsided by 1988. Instead, it may have been assumed that the theme of computing as an educational resource had already been established, at least among important segments of the likely market for personal computers. Given this assumption, advertising could focus on additional reasons for acquiring a computer, such as its simplicity ("it works on common sense" (N, 5/23/88)), and its rapidly decreasing price. Several companies including IBM now refer to low prices as the main sales argument in some advertisements.

In image advertising to the general *public*, computers are said to produce benefits for society and profits for companies, especially as accessible and applicable systems become more widespread. Throughout the period studied, then, the advertising discourses make no distinction between the public interest and the interests of American business. Apple, for example, asserts that other companies have begun to copy their general concept of joining "human nature and common sense" and that "American business is reaping the benefits" (T, 11/14/88). Computer simulation can also help society avoid "white elephants" (T, 3/21/88). In the area of news and information, similarly, the computer is seen to be serving the public interest: Under the heading of "Once again the world is flat," *Time* runs a campaign offering an educational version of the magazine on diskette. In the very general terms of another campaign, a company is said to "bring us all together," in one case with reference to black and white groups in the context of the NAACP (National Association for the Advancement of Colored People) (T, 10/31/88). Yet, this notion of cooperation is never linked to specific political ends and means, such as computing as a means of social revolution.

In *business* sector advertising, finally, the flexibility of the personal computer and its contribution to efficient production remain key themes. There are many references to the compatibility of different items, both hardware and software, within a total system of administration and communication. This is the innovative means to a familiar end: success and growth. One advertisement suggests that even if individual enterprise is necessary to start a business, expansion requires the right technology: "Your brains built the business. Ours can expand it" (T, 4/4/88). A key requirement toward this end is control, especially because of the complexity of contemporary business organisations. One company reassures the business reader that with its computer in hand, "being out of town no longer means being out of control" (N, 4/18/88). Interestingly, the issue of control applies across several different levels of social organization, from the level of one company to an entire industry and ultimately the nation in a world context. Control and leadership at one level may help to ensure leadership one level up. One advertisement suggests that the technology of that particular company has made an important contribution to "the world-wide competitiveness of American manufacturing," which is only natural, because "we're both leaders" (T, 5/16/88). What is good for computer companies, may be good for America.

Conclusion

In summary, the discourse analysis and the categorization of magazine advertising support the conclusion that the personal computer was constructed socially as a "general machine" with diverse social uses for many different user groups within the prospect of an emerging information society. The process of diffusion reached a climax and crisis around 1984. It is significant that, increasingly, the same sales advertising was addressed to all user groups and, further, that the image of companies also was built primarily through sales advertising.

The implications or themes that were identified in the discourse analysis, initially refer to the computer both as an increasingly accessible service for the general public, sometimes with explicit reference to the notion of the information society, and as a source of business profits. The public interest is presented as equal to the interests of business in general and American business in particular. In the course of the period examined, the information society becomes an implicit premise of the advertisements, which instead begin to detail the specific uses of the personal computer by individuals, especially its status as an indispensable resource for education and information, as opposed to games and other entertainment genres.

One of the most interesting implications is posed by the rise and fall of the theme of social revolution. Whereas the themes of individual success and social revolution appeared side by side during 1984, only the more conventional theme in the context of American culture — namely individual success — was found during 1988. This may be interpreted to mean that during a phase of introduction, new communication technologies come to represent a social imagination that normally remains unarticulated in media discourses. Symbolic diffusion, accordingly, can be seen as a process of projecting social utopias that may resonate with the audience-public onto new technologies. These utopias may be the positive counterpart of the dystopias envisioned by the moral panics to which new media traditionally also give rise. When the first phase of introduction is over, or when the promise of utopia is seen not to materialize in social practice or in the experience of the audience-public, advertising and similar discourses may re-emphasise more conventional, consensual themes, depending of course on other developments in the given social and historical context. Nevertheless, such utopias remain a source of appeal and fascination that may be tapped during later phases of diffusion.

Even though almost a decade has passed since *Time* chose, not a Person of the Year, but the computer as the Machine of the Year (T, 1/3/83), the question of whether the computer may become a general machine for everybody to use, still produces magazine cover stories (*Business Week,* September 10 1990).

This chapter has presented a study of the social construction of the personal computer in advertising discourses. The empirical findings have substantiated the importance of studying also the symbolic or semiotic aspects of the diffusion of new communication technologies. The methodological approach, furthermore, has pointed to the specific relevance of discourse analysis as a means of integrating qualitative and quantitative modes of inquiry regarding media. In particular, more research on the personal computer as a medium is called for from the perspective of discourse analysis and semiotics (see also Andersen, 1990). Finally, the theoretical framework, focusing on media environments that are characterized by intertextuality, has suggested the need to examine the interaction and the division of labor between media in a specific historical and cultural context. Since one important site of the interaction between media is the audience, further empirical research on media environments should include not just media discourses, but also the reception and social uses of new media. The symbolic diffusion of new media ultimately is enacted by the audience- public in everyday contexts of communication and social action.

Acknowledgments

Research for this chapter was conducted, in part, during 1988-89, when the author was a Fellow of the American Council of Learned Societies at the Annenberg School of Communications, University of Southern California, USA. He wishes to acknowledge the assistance of the ACLS and of Bill Dutton and Everett Rogers at Annenberg. Special thanks are due to the staff of the Documentation Center at the United States Embassy, Copenhagen, Denmark.

Bibliography

ANDERSEN, P.BØGH. (1990). *A Theory of Computer Semiotics*. Cambridge: Cambridge University Press.

BENNETT, T., WOOLLACOTT, J. (1987). *Bond and Beyond*. London: Methuen.

BERGER, A. (1989). 1984 — The Commercial. In *Political Culture and Public Opinion* (pp. 175-86), ed. A. Berger. New Brunswick, NJ: Transaction Publishers.

BERGER, T., LUCKMANN, T. (1966). *The Social Construction of Reality.* London: Allen Lane.

BOLTER, J. (1991). *Writing Space.* Hillsdale, NJ: Lawrence Erlbaum Associates.

BRANSCOMB, A. (1988). Videotext: Global Progress and Comparative Policies. *Journal of Communication, 38,* 50-59.

CHARON, J. (1988). Videotex: From Interaction to Communication. *Media, Culture & Society, 9,* 301-332.

COWARD, R., ELLIS, J. (1977). *Language and Materialism.* London: Routledge Kegan Paul.

DUTTON, W., ROGERS, E., JUN, S. (1987). Diffusion and Social Impacts of Personal Computers. *Communication Research, 14,* 219-50.

ECO, U. (1981). *The Name of the Rose.* London: Picador.

EISENSTEIN, E. (1979). *The Printing Press as an Agent of Change.* London: Cambridge University Press.

GANS, H. (1979). *Deciding What's News.* New York: Vintage.

GOODY, J. (1987). *The Interface Between the Written and the Oral.* Cambridge: Cambridge University Press.

GOODY, J., WATT, I. (1963). The Consequences of Literacy. *Comparative Studies in Society and History, 5,* 304-45.

HADDON, S. (1988). Electronic and Computer Games. *Screen, 29,* 52-73.

HAVELOCK, E. (1963). *Preface to Plato.* Oxford: Blackwell.

HEIM, M. (1987). *Electric Language.* New Haven: Yale University Press.

INNIS, H. (1972). *Empire and Communications.* Toronto: University of Toronto Press.

JAKOBSON, R. (1960). Linguistics and Poetics. In *Selected Writings* (Vol. 3, pp. 18-51), ed. S. Rudy. The Hague: Mouton, 1981.

JENSEN, K.B. (1987). News as Ideology: Economic Statistics and Political Ritual in Television Network News. *Journal of Communication, 37,* 8-27.

JENSEN, K.B. (in press). Print Cultures and Visual Cultures: A Critical Introduction to Research on New Media Environments. In *Approaches to Mass Communication,* ed. J. Stappers. London: Sage.

JENSEN, K.B., JANKOWSKI, N.W. eds. (1991). *A Handbook of Qualitative Methodologies for Mass Communication Research.* London: Routledge.

KAPLAN, S. (1990). Visual Metaphors in the Representation of Communication Technology. *Critical Studies in Mass Communication, 7,* 37-47.

LASSWELL, H. (1948). The Structure and Function of Communication in Society. In *Reader in Public Opinion and Communication* (pp. 178-90), eds. B. Berelson, M. Janovitz (1966), Glencoe, IL: The Free Press.

LOWE, D. (1982). *History of Bourgeois Perception.* Chicago: University of Chicago Press.

MCLUHAN, M. (1962). *The Gutenberg Galaxy.* Toronto: University of Toronto Press.

MCLUHAN, M. (1964). *Understanding Media.* New York: McGraw-Hill.

MEYROWITZ, J. (1985). *No Sense of Place.* New York: Oxford University Press.

MUMFORD, L. (1934). *Technics and Civilization.* London: Routledge.

NOLL, A.M. (1985). Videotex: Anatomy of a Failure. *Information & Management, 9,* 99-109.

NORA, S., MINC, A. (1980). *The Computerization of Society.* Cambridge, MA: MIT Press.

ONG, W. (1982). *Orality and Literacy.* London: Methuen.

PEARSON, R., URICCHIO, W. eds. (1991). *The Many Lives of the Batman.* London: British Film Institute.

PFAFFENBERGER, B. (1988). The Social Meaning of the Personal Computer: Or, Why the Personal Computer Revolution Was No Revolution. *Anthropological Quarterly, 61,* 39-47.

POOL, I. ed. (1977). *The Social Impact of the Telephone.* Cambridge, MA: MIT Press.

PORAT, M. (1977). *The Information Economy: Definition and Measurement.* Washington, D.C.: Government Printing Office.

ROGERS, E. (1983). *Diffusion of Innovations* (3rd Ed.). New York: The Free Press.

ROGERS, E., LARSEN, J. (1984). *Silicon Valley Fever.* New York: Basic Books.

ROSZAK, T. (1986). *The Cult of Information.* New York: Pantheon.

SCHUDSON, M. (1991). Historical Approaches to Communication Studies. In *A Handbook of Qualitative Methodologies for Mass Communication Research* (pp. 175-189), eds. K.B. Jensen, N.W. Jankowski. London: Routledge.

SCRIBNER, S., COLE, M. (1981). *The Psychology of Literacy.* Cambridge, MA: Harvard University Press.

SCULLEY, J. (1987). *Odyssey: Pepsi to Apple.* Glasgow: Fontana.

SKIRROW, G. (1986). Hellivision: An Analysis of Video Games. In *High Theory/Low Culture* (pp. 115-142), ed. C. MacCabe. New York: St. Martin's Press.

THOMAS, R. (1989). *Oral Tradition and Written Record in Classical Athens.* Cambridge: Cambridge University Press.

TOFFLER, A. (1980). *The Third Wave.* New York: Bantam.

TURKLE, S. (1984). *The Second Self.* New York: Simon & Schuster.

VAN DIJK, T. (1991). The Interdisciplinary Study of News as Discorse. In *A Handbook of Qualitative Methodologies for Mass Communication Research (pp. 108-120).* eds. K.B. Jensen, N.W. Jankowski. London: Routledge.

15

Hi-tech network organizations as self-referential systems

LARS QVORTRUP

With new information and communication technologies, new organizational forms are becoming of increasing importance. Particularly, new forms of organisations — so-called "Hi-Tech Network Organizations" — have emerged. The concept of Hi-Tech Organizations is not well defined, but covers such phenomena as telework ("elusive offices"), distance training ("network colleges" and "virtual classrooms"), computer conferencing systems ("network meetings"), "soft cities," "intelligent buildings," "electronic libraries" — organizational or social networks in which people don't interact or work together physically, in an office, a building, or a classroom. However, they still are part of a common organization (a company, a class, an association), but their organizational interaction is based on computers and telecommunication.

Simultaneously, a new paradigm for social theory in general and, specifically, for organizational communication theory has been launched: social and organizational systems are conceptualized as so-called "self-referential" systems — self-producing and self-reflective systems. Often this approach uses the label of organizations as "autopoietical systems", being inspired by the Chilean biologists H. Maturana and F. Varela (1980), and in Europe the dominating approach, explicitly "transforming" the autopoetical concept from biology to social theory, has been elaborated by the German social philosopher Niklas Luhmann (cf. particularly Luhmann 1984 and 1990).

It is my hypothesis that the concept of self-referentiality is particularly fruitful for understanding the new Hi-Tech Network Organizations. In the following I will

- Exemplify the concept of "Hi-Tech Network Organizations"
- Demonstrate the shortcomings of traditional organizational information and communication analysis based on data flow theories
- Apply the theory of self-referentiality to the new forms of Hi-Tech organizations

- Relate the concept of self-referentialityto the traditional theories of so-
cial reproduction
- Finally, present a number of critical remarks, primarily inspired by the
German social philosopher Jürgen Habermas. (cf. particularly
Habermas, 1987)

Hi-tech network organizations

In the "good old days" teaching was related to a classroom. Work was related to a place of work. Lending and reading books was associated with the
library building. Cities were agglomerations of buildings and people. But today, these connections are disappearing. Within the field of teaching one
talks about the "virtual classroom." Within the field of work an emerging
concept is the "elusive office" (Huws, Korte, and Robinson, 1990). Cities
and buildings are conceptualized as "soft cities" and "intelligent buildings." And more than ten years ago Daniel Bell foresaw "the end of the
Alexandrian library" (Bell,, 1979). Let me exemplify the tendency by elabo-
rating a bit on the development of telework theory (the following is based
on Qvortrup, in press).

Within the theory of telework one can specify three organizational phases
(phases should not be understood literally, but rather as ideal types in the
sense of Max Weber) and three corresponding definitions of telework.

The first phase is characterized by an early fragmentation of traditional
centralised organizations. The corresponding definition of telework is to
work at home instead of in a central office, thus substituting telecommunication for the twice-daily commute to and from work. The adequate term is:
Telecommuting.

The second phase is characterised by a dispersion of traditional organizations. New, decentralized satellite offices and local work centers are established in addition to the electronic homework. Still, however, the dominance
of the centre is not challenged. The adequate term is: *Teleworking*.

Finally, the third phase is characterized by a diffusion of traditional organisations. New specialized service organizations are being established, individuals work as advisors and consultants for changing companies, traditional
office work is replaced by work based on computer conferencing networks
etc. The adequate term is: *Networking*.

Regarding "networking," already in 1983 Turoff and Hiltz argued (cf.
Huws, Korte, and Robinson, 1990: 32; see also Hiltz, 1984) that current office
technologies make the concepts of centralization and decentralization out-
moded, substituting a structure based on fluid networks by means of which

teleworkers — or rather, they would say, knowledge workers — become members of ad hoc groupings formed around particular projects. These groupings — or "on-line communities," as they have later on been coined by Hiltz — are not restricted by time or space, but are only based on the specific knowledge project that relate a number of project participants. Here, fragmentation and dispersion are supplemented by a radical *diffusion* of traditional organizational structures.

The most well-known example of "networking" in "on-line communities" is provided by computerized conferencing systems used by groups of scientists working within the same research speciality. Typically such systems provide *message systems* that enable members to send private communications to individuals or groups on a topic of discussion, *conferences* that build up a permanent transcript on a topic of discussion, and *notebooks* where text processing features may be used to work on jointly authored reports (Hiltz, 1984).

Based on such examples, Hiltz totally changes the definition of an office. "Usually," she writes, "one thinks of it as a place, with desks and telephones and typewriters. In thinking about the office of the future, one must instead think of it as a communications space, created by the merger of computers and telecommunications," According to Hiltz these computer mediated communication networks "...can best be thought of as a new kind of social system, in which the familiar social processes in the workplace and the organisation become subtly altered by electronically mediated interactive processes, creating new kinds of "on-line communities"." (Hiltz, 1984: xv, 30).

Recently, Huws, Korte, and Robinson have accepted the same kind of definition. Looking into the future, they believe "...that the traditional concept of the workplace as a fixed geographical space will be replaced by more abstract notions of the working context as a set of relationships, a network, an intellectual space." (Huws, Korte, and Robinson, 1990,: 208). This "network office" is coined: *The Elusive Office.*

More generally speaking, the concept of "network organization" covers what Nilles et al. call the "diffused" organization (cf. also Laing, 1991). Individual employees or specialized service organizations work for a number of different companies, from home or from local work centres like "intelligent buildings," "shared facility centers" or "community teleservice centers." The actual organization is not just less hierarchical, it is based on "ad hocracy," new networks being continuously built and changed. This means that such organizations are characterized by horizontal communication, and that they depend on dispersed information. Actually, the single "thing" or "activity" keeping together such organizations, is communication. One cannot locate them in space, and to a certain degree not even in time, since much of the interaction is asynchronous.

In network organizations, each "node" may typically belong to a large number of "organizations." Such organizations need flexible workforces, with people with high qualifications going in and out of a number of work groups. Also, complex inter-organizational networks are needed, with small groups of people working with and for each other.

Typically, the single networker will be a specialist problem solver, often working as a consultant, working on a contractual basis for several different organisations. Typically, such networkers ask for flexible work arrangements. They will not work full-time in a central office, nor full-time at home, but they want work settings to be adapted to work contents, thus being able to do concentrated writing and reading at home, working, reading, and communicating while traveling, and group work, brain-storming, and meetings in the office or on computer conferencing systems etc. In particular, such networkers will not work on distance in the traditional sense — as home-based teleworkers. But they like to bring work with them and to take work home from office, partly in order to combine meetings in the office with creative and concentrated work in isolation, partly in order to have their longer work days combined with family life (cf. Jensen and Storgaard, 1991). Also, they want to combine work and training — or rather: they cannot really tell the difference. In much information work, personal, informal training, and work is integrated, and one switches continuously from the training mode to the work mode (cf. personal communication from Stan Harms).

Hi-tech organizations and the importance of communication

One important result of the growing influence of information technologies in organizations and in society is that communication has become a basic concept in organizational theory. "Now that we are entering an age with a completely new technological base drawing on microelectronics, new organisational principles are likely to become of increasing importance", writes Gareth Morgan. "In the larger term, it is possible to see organizations becoming synonymous with their information systems, since microprocessing facilities create the possibility of organizing without having an organization in physical terms." (Morgan, 1986: 38, 84)

In parallel, and — in all probability — as a consequence, a new scientific discipline has emerged: Organizational Communication. The first comprehensive review of the literature was available in 1972 in Redding's *Communication Within the Organisation* (Redding, 1972), and looking back Redding has realised that the label of "organizational communication" did not achieve general use until the late 1960s (Redding, 1985). A well-known (information technological) pioneer is H. A. Simon. Not only did he in his classic treatise *Administrative Behaviour* (1945) discuss "organization communications" systems. He also posited the "decisional premise" as the basic unit of organizational functioning, thus defining organizational communication as "any process whereby decisional premises are transmitted from one member of an organization to another" (Simon, 1945: 154, cf. Redding 1985 p. 18). Still, no common theoretical basis has been developed, partly due to the fact that organizational communication course work and research program are offered in such diverse academic departments as business administration, psychology, sociology, speech, rhetorics, and communication. In 1987 the first comprehensive *Handbook of Organizational Communication* was published (Jablin et al., 1987), in which the authors lament that researchers fail to articulate the theoretical frameworks underlying their work. In an introductory chapter, four approaches are adopted: the mechanistic, psychological, interpretative-symbolic, and systems-interaction perspectives (Krone, Jablin, and Putnam, 1987: 19).

Structured analysis and the mathematical theory of communication

According to Karl E. Weick, to an outsider, analyses of organizational communication may look like plumbing diagrams for an old Scottish castle (Weick, 1987: 97). Even though a number of different diagram standards have been developed, normally computerized organizations are presented as systems of bubbles in which data are processed, boxes in which they are filed, and vectors connecting the bubbles and boxes with data flows. Such an analytical diagram is called a "Data Flow Diagram", and the analytical process is called "Structured Analysis."

One of the pioneers of contemporary structured analysis is Tom DeMarco (DeMarco, 1979) (the following is based on Qvortrup, 1992). According to DeMarco the basic object of structured analysis is data flows, not social relations. In his text book, *Structured Analysis and System Specification,* it is several times emphasized that the interaction processes of an organization should be seen from the "viewpoint of the data" and not from the point of view of the users or the organization (DeMarco, 1979: 27, 28, 48f). In reality, structured analysis presupposes that any organization can, without loss of information, be reduced to a complicated structure of data flows.

One of the implications of this approach is that one does not distinguish between those organizational procedures that can be automated and those that cannot. A data flow diagram is "neutral" as to whether the data flows are processed by humans or by machines, and according to the approach there is no fundamental difference between a social organization and a totally automated organization. This, again, implies that an organization is conceptualized as a functional device. Phenomena such as "organizational consensus," "social routines," "unwritten social scripts," or "organisational culture" do not exist within the structured analysis tradition, and Simon's focus on decisional premises seems to have been forgotten.

The conceptual background for Structured Analysis can be found in Claude E. Shannon's mathematical information theory. His "information theory" was presented in 1948 in his article "The Mathematical Theory of Communication" (in Shannon and Weaver, 1964). Later, Shannon himself summarized his theory in his much-quoted contribution to *Encyclopaedia Britannica*. The starting point is a simple communication model with an information source sending "raw information" via a transmitter and a receiver to a recipient. Here we have the metaphor of data flowing from point to point.

But what is actually "information"? "Information is interpreted in its broadest sense to include the messages occurring in any of the standard communication mediums (...) and even the signals appearing in the nerve networks of animals and man", Shannon wrote in the Encyclopaedia. "A basic idea in communication theory is that information can be treated very much like a physical quantity such as mass or energy," he continued. "The formula for the amount of information is identical in form with equations representing entropy in statistical mechanics, and suggests that there may be deep-lying connections between thermodynamics and information theory." (Shannon, 1972: 246B, 247)

When, today, the interchange of information in organizational communications theory is conceptualized as flows of data, then this method is nothing but the practical application of Shannon's concept of information as a physical quantity, and the implications of structured analysis are Shannon's implications that human communication is analogous to the "interaction" of information machines.

The consequence of regarding information technology as a subset of traditional technology is not only that "information" appears to be the physical output of an information machine; a further consequence is that the cognitive products or social organisms that are manipulated by I.T. seem to be the objects of I.T. in a similar way that *nature* and its products have been regarded as the object of traditional technology: social organizms and cognitive products and processes are conceptualized as if they belonged to the natural world.

In keeping with this approach, the aim of analysis is *reduction:* only if we *reduce* social organisms and cognitive products and processes to their seemingly underlying deterministic regularities, we can construct efficient information machinery. "It is my thesis," Shannon's close colleague Norbert Wiener wrote, "that the operation of the living individual and the operation of some of the new communication machines are precisely parallel. (...) In a certain sense, all communication systems terminate in machines, but the ordinary communication systems of language terminate in the rather special sort of machine known as a human being." (Wiener, 1950: 15, 88)

Pragmatic interactionism

In structured analysis the analytical viewpoint is the viewpoint of the data. Consequently, technical communication systems constitute the *general* system, and human beings, social organizations, and society are considered to be variants — special sorts — of the basic technical system. Similarly, the mathematical information and communication theory is considered to be the general theory, only being specified by organizational and human communication theories at a more concrete level. However, if one wants to support the development and implementation of user-friendly information technologically based organizational systems rather than to legitimize the technical determination of human interaction, the starting point must be organizational communication as human interaction.

According to the "interpretative approach" to organizational communication (Putnam, 1983; Putnam, 1985; Putnam and Scott Poole, 1987) the basic concepts are not functional concepts like data flows etc., but conflict, bargaining, and consensus — the basic elements of Simon's decisional process. Any organizational process is a process starting in a state of conflict and then through bargaining developing into a state of consensus, or into a new state of conflict. The driving force is individual persons' interests and motives, and the fundamental tool is human communication. Consequently, such processes must be analyzed through communication analysis and through interpretivism, thus identifying the underlying motives. This means that every organizational communication act is both communication (referring to data) and communication *about* communication (referring to the other person's implicit or explicit motives) — a pragmatic action (cf. Watzlawick, Beavin, and Jackson, 1967). The theory of organizational bargaining may thus be coined "pragmatic interactionism," With reference to computerized organizations, computers and telecommunications networks should provide not only adequate information, but should also allow the users to express their own interests and to interpret the other person's motives.

Organizational communication and self-referentiality

However, I still miss a general theoretical framework for the interpretative organizational communications analyses. The latter certainly point in the right direction, and they have provided us with lots of important knowledge, but they have not constituted a theoretical basis. Here, Niklas Luhmann's theory of self-referentiality (cf. particularly Luhmann, 1984, and Luhmann, 1990) seems to be a challenging and rewarding possibility.

Luhmann's starting point is Talcott Parson's concept of "double contingency": that A's expectations depend on B and vice versa (cf. Luhmann, 1976: 508). This concept is closely related to Watzlawick et al.'s previously mentioned dictum about communication that while we communicate, we also communicate about our communication (cf. Watzlawick, Beavin, and Jackson, 1967). Any human interaction is based on a fundamental uncertainty of the other speaker's values, and any human interaction is devoted not only to the communication of information, but also to the reproduction of shared meanings.

To reproduce a set of shared meanings is to refer to a set of values that has been produced within a mutual process: *self-referentiality*. This is a process that is necessary in any human organization, but it is extraordinarily evident in network organizations: Here, the organization is not represented as a building, or a set of shared facilities, an office community etc. Here, shared meanings must be reproduced through the organizational communication processes, facilitated by the information technological devices.

The theory of self-referential hi-tech organizations is still in its infancy. Even so, in the following sections I will summarize some of the basic concepts that undoubtedly will prove important in the years to come: They are, among others, self-referentiality, the holographic principle, symbolization, complexity, and organizational communication as self-maintenance and perturbation.

Self-referentiality

Self-referentiality means that the organization has the ability to refer to itself. First, the organization has an identity. Second, not only can this identity be referred to by each single node in the organization, but the identity must be represented in the single node (this may be called the "holographic principle": each element contains a picture of the whole organization). Third, this identity is actually reproduced by all the single nodes in a collective process. Thus there must be "something" that stands for the organization, some sort of identity that can be represented in symbolic form. This "something" must be distributed within the organization and represented locally. There must be good communication facilities in order for the local nodes to negotiate their mutual identity. And the identity must be highly flexible in order to be continuously modified.

Self-referentiality (or autopoiesis) is of course a basic concept for network organizations, because these organizations *have* to be self-organized and self-reproductive, rather than being organized by some central or external power or management node. Niklas Luhmann offers the following definition: "A system can be called self-referential, when the system itself constitutes its elements as functional entities, and when it in all relations between these elements allows for a reference to this self-constitution and thus continuously reproduces the self-constitution." (Luhmann, 1984: 59, my translation).[1]

Self-constitution

One consequence of this definition is that self-referential systems at the level of the self-referential organization are *closed* systems. They constitute themselves through themselves and not through anything else. In particular, this means that an organization is not constituted by the environment, but by itself. The organization uses the environment only in so far as the environment can support the self-constitution of the organization. If the organization is constituted by the environment, strictly speaking it has lost its status as organisation.[2]

Identity and symbolization

Identity can be defined as the relationship between system and the outside world. On the one hand there is no communication outside the communication system called "society." This system is the only one that uses this type of operation, and consequently it is necessarily closed. For other social systems it is different. Precisely because social systems exist in a context of simi-

---

[1] This definition is very close to Humberto Maturana's definition of living systems: 'A living system is a system if molecules, whose interactions create a network which produces the same molecules that constitute the network and hereby define the boundaries of the system.' This definition was presented by Maturana as a seminar in Denmark in 1986; here it is quoted from Søren Brier (1987), p. 85ff.

[2] A similar idea regarding marketing has recently been presented by Lars Thøger Christensen (1991).

lar systems it is urgently important for each single organization to define its specific way of operation and its specific identity. In particular, this is of course a problem for network organizations, because they cannot identify themselves geographically or physically (being in the same building, and so on).

But what does a social system do in its internal communication in order to maintain identity? It establishes a difference, a difference between itself and its environment, and a difference that can be used for answering the question: Do I belong to system A or to system B, or — in other words — to this particular system or to its environment — to some other system?

This difference must be of a general nature. It is a difference that can be used for many specific nodes in the system. Such general difference can be called a symbol. The symbol is the tool for measuring whether I as a sub-system belong to the symbolizing system. Luhmann defines symbolization by saying, that "by symbolization (...) is meant the process in which a highly complex situation of interaction can be expressed in a simplified manner and thus can be experienced as a unity." (Luhmann, 1975: 32)

Complexity

Now, why is local representation of identity and organizational structure so vital for the organization and for the single nodes? The answer can be found in the concept of *complexity*. The precondition for successful interaction between two nodes — or between a single node and an organization, or a single node and the environment, or between two organizations or sub-organizations — is that they match each other as to their level of complexity. A node representing a low level of complexity cannot successfully communicate with a node representing a high level of complexity. Why not? Because external complexity can only be reduced — and thus understood — if the internal system of complexity reduction is on the same level of complexity as the external system.

Communication as self-maintenance and perturbation

That organizations are closed in the self-referential sense does not, however, mean that a self-referential system is isolated in relation to the outside world. On the contrary: Communication is the basic activity within and among network organizations. This is the only activity that keeps them together as organisations, partly by maintaining internal relations, partly by confirming external differences. Their single elements are not "together" in space, and perhaps not even in time. But they communicate.

According to Luhmann, this is the case for social systems in general: "For a theory of autopoietic systems, only communication is a serious candidate for the position of the elementary units of the basic self-referential process of social systems." (Luhmann, 1990: 6) In particular, communication is the precondition for self-maintenance. "Communication is an evolutionary potential for building up systems that are able to maintain closure under the condition of openness." (Luhmann, 1990: 13)

In a more fundamental sense, however, communication may be looked at as *perturbation*. First, we don't always communicate in order to maintain ourselves as individuals or organizational systems. Sometimes we communicate in order to change something: the psychological dispositions of another person, or the organizational dispositions of another social system.

But second, and more fundamentally speaking, when two systems communicate, and when those two systems are not structurally identical, in principle *any* transmission of meaning is perturbation or systemic interference — disturbances of one self-referential system on the other system. Even, strictly speaking, internal self-maintenance oriented communication is perturbation between organizational elements, because it is the distribution of a specific symbolic pattern, the acceptance of which is defined as creation of identity.[3]

This has important impacts on the concept of communication as compared with the mathematical theory of information. Organizations don't react on external stimuli, but on themselves. They don't receive "information" in the sense of bits sent into a container; but they registrate "perturbations" — "disturbances" in relation to their own self-referential system. If the organization changes as a result of the communication process, it doesn't respond in the sense of stimulus-response processes. But it *adapts* itself to the incoming influence in order to maintain its own organizational existence. In particular, this means that only a well-developed self-referential system has a high ability of making contacts to the context. The higher the level of self-referentiability, the higher the level of complexity in the context to which the system can establish contacts.

Still, it may be fruitful to distinguish between self-maintenance oriented communication and perturbation-oriented communication. One may say that any communicative process is a "fight" between perturbation and maintenance.

---

[3]This is closely related to René Thom's 'catastrophe theory.' Cf. Peter Bøgh Andersen's remarks in chapter 1.

Education

One example is *education:* Good educational results don't depend *primarily* on the amount or quality of knowledge transfer. Nor is it a matter of adaptation — the ability of the learning system to copy the structure of the teaching system. No, the basic problem is that the learning system must be at a high level of self-referentiability in order to interact with a highly complicated teaching system. This is partly an individual matter; but partly it is a matter of classroom environment; very often the rate of success of distance training is not primarily dependent on the quality of communication, but on the *quality of self-referentiability of the learning environment.* The same goes for interaction between social organizations. The outcome depends on the level of "structural ability" of the two systems.

Here, an alternative to the old communication model is provided. In the traditional model communication depended on the capacity of the *channel* between sender and receiver. Now, we have to look at the structural dispositions of the interacting systems. Furthermore, the aim of communication is not to transfer a certain amount of information; the aim is to interfere with or to influence the structure of the system with which one communicates.

Control and boundary maintenance

Another consequence is the concept of control. Unilateral control is not possible. Of course there can be differences of influence, hierarchies, nonsymmetries, but no single entity of a system can control the other entities without being controlled itself (or: itself to being part of the control system). Control is not a concept of information and feedback between entities, but rather a concept of self-reproduction of a system. This is particularly evident in network organizations.

The point of departure for any systems theoretical analysis is the difference between system and the external world. Without a difference to the external world, self-referentiality wouldn't exist. In this respect, boundary maintenance is system maintenance. It must however be emphazised that a boundary isn't equal to a break of relations, and it cannot be claimed that internal interdependency is higher than interdependencies between system and the external world.

While this problem didn't really appear in relation to old-fashioned fixed, hierarchical and physically well-defined organizations, or simply was presented as information control, gate-keeping, and so on, it suddenly presents itself as a major problem in network organizations. We know that there *is* a system and an outside world. But where are the boundaries? And how are they expressed and maintained?

Here, the answer provided by the theory of self-referential systems seems to be very adequate: That *self-reproductivity is equal to boundary maintenance.*

From organizational hierarchies to system differentiation

It is necessary to further develop the theory of system differentiation. Traditionally, there have been tendencies to describe system differentiation as hierarchy, but today this no longer is adequate. Hierarchy is just one specific example of differentiation, and other types of seemingly more chaotic differentiations have become possible. Again, of course the example of networking organizations is illustrative. Even though it is difficult to identify hierarchies, we still know that differentiations are maintained through more subtle mechanisms.

The concept of "system entity"

In addition to the difference between a system and its outside world it is necessary to make a difference between entity and relation. Traditionally, "entities" have been defined in two different ways, either as an *analytical* concept (implying that entities don't exist in reality, but only as they are defined in the analysis, like "apples" and "bananas" in mathematics), or as an *ontological* concept (implying that entities have a natural and universal existence — a materialistic existence ex ante). For a network organization this isn't adequate: What is, for example, an "office"? In interrelated network organizations an office in *one* organization may be a single node, but in *another* organization the same "office" may be the headquarter, or a sub-office, and so on.

What is the solution? First, "an entity" may be defined as that node in a system that functions as a unit and that need not be further partitioned in relation to the system, even though it, in itself, is a highly complex system. Second, entities are only entities for the systems that use them as units, and they are only entities through these systems. This means that systems at a higher level may be of lower complexity than systems at a lower level.

The concept of "conditionality"

To the concept of *relation* between elements we have to add the concept of "conditionality." Systems cannot be reduced to "relations between entities." The relation between relations is in itself conditioned by general laws. W. Ross Ashby writes: "The hard core of the concept (organization) is, in my opinion, that of "conditionality." As soon as the relation between two entities A and B becomes conditional on C's value or state then a necessary component of "organization" is present. Thus the theory of organization is partly co-extensive with the theory of functions of more than one variable." (Ashby, 1968: 108)

Again referring to the example of network organizations one may say that there are relations between many entities that do not belong to the same organisation. But what, then, makes an organization an organization? Not anything technical or physical/geographical. According to Luhmann the answer is that if relations between entities are *conditioned* by something different from these entities, then they belong to an organization. It seems that this concept of "conditionality" is closely related to the traditional, but not very well defined concept of "organizational culture."

Philosophical background

The emerging network organizations represent a challenge to traditional organizational theory. These new organizations cannot be conceptualized as deterministic systems ruled by a bureaucrat or president through a hierarchical system. They must be based on self-organizational principles, and the system must be run by its own elements.

Here, a discussion rooted in European social philosophy is re-actualized: Is society a mechanical top-down system or is it a political bottom-up system? And, if it actually *is* a bottom-up system, then how is social order possible. How come that society, in spite of conflicting interests, different backgrounds and experiences, conflicts and negotiations, exists as a coherent system?

Society as mechanical system

Traditionally, organizations have been understood as either deterministic systems based on some kind of universal logic (organizations as machines), or as voluntaristic systems based on human choice (organizations as politics). This tendency can be traced back to 1700 Europe (the following is based on

Qvortrup, 1988: 160ff). The French philosopher Antoine N. Condorcet (1743-94) in his book *Esquisse d'un tableau historique des progrès de l'esprit humain* (1793) emphasized that human progress is rooted in an unending fight against nature, depending on human beings' superior intelligence and their ability to discipline themselves. Thus an absolute barrier was constructed between nature and human beings, indicating that human beings individually and within social organizations are representing a non-natural logic, and that progress dependent on the disciplined use and refinement of this logic. Already in 1758, the French Economist François Quesnay (1694-1774) presented a theory of the economical systems that represented one such non-natural logic (see for example, Isaac Ilych Rubin, 1979), and simultaneously Frederick the Great of Prussia, who ruled from 1740 to 1786, introduced reforms in order to develop the army into an efficient mechanical organization (Morgan, 1986: 24). In the beginning of the next century, Auguste Comte (1798-1857) developed a theory for human relations: the theory regarding human and social relations, sociology. His aim was to identify and explain human relations in order to achieve the highest possible progress — to elaborate a "positive way of thinking" with a "...basic ability in a natural way to systematize the healthy concept of order and progress." (Comte, 1844)[4]

However, it was not until the early twentieth century that such ideas were synthesized into a theory of organization and management. One major contribution to this theory was made by German sociologist Max Weber (1864-1920), who defined "bureaucracy" as a form of organization that emphasizes precision, speed, clarity, regularity, reliability, and efficiency achieved through the creation of a fixed division of tasks, hierarchical supervision, and detailed rules and regulations (Morgan, 1986: 24f).

During this century this theory has been transformed into a set of seemingly "neutral" tools for analysis and management, leading into current structured analysis. This contribution was made by a group of management theorists and practitioners in North America and Europe who set the basis for what is now known as "classical management theory" and "scientific management" (Morgan, 1986: 25). Closely related to these organization and management theories, the theory of "Management Information Systems" (MIS) was developed in order to provide managers with detailed information about the organization necessary to implement controls and to give organizational feedback.

---

[4] The project was presented in six volumes *Cours de philosophie positive*, Paris 1830-42. It was summarized in *Discours préliminaire sur l'esprit positif*, Paris 1844, from where I quote.

Society as political system

Already in 1700 Europe the mechanical approach of social systems was confronted by a political approach, emphasising that society and its social organizations are produced by human beings based on their individual needs, their
freedom of choice, and their ability to influence others and to build coali-
tions. Here, Jean-Jacques Rousseau's (1712-78) theory of the social contract
is of course absolutely central (cf. Qvortrup, 1984: 118ff). "If the general will
is to be clearly expressed," writes Rousseau, "it is imperative that there
should be no sectional associations in the state, and that every citizen should
make up his own mind for himself" (Rousseau, 1968 (1762): 73). And, earlier
in the book, he argues that "Sovereignty, being nothing other than the exercise of the general will (...) cannot be represented by anyone but itself —
power may be delegated, but the will cannot be." (Rousseau, 1968 (1762):
69)

With the new network organizations this theory becomes a dominating
one, simply because it is based on the daily life experience that organizations
are the result of human interaction. Somehow, organizational systems are political systems, and politics stems from a diversity of interests, organizational
processes being identical with day-to-day bargaining, power struggles, and
so on.

The modern dilemma

Which one is right: the "mechanical" or "determinist" approach, or the
"political" or "voluntaristic" approach? This discussion is as old as the theories and approaches themselves. Recently, Jürgen Habermas has tried to
combine the approaches, seemingly bridging the dilemma. He emphasizes
that modern society is divided into two worlds: The System World and the
Life World (cf. Habermas, 1981).

The System World is the world of private enterprises and of public under-
takings as well. The criteria of function are cost-benefit ratios or efficiency as
a quantitative term. The products of the system world are commodities,
goods, and services in a wide sense including public human services. The
Life World is the world of human beings in their private families and in their
social communities. Here, the criteria of function are social acceptability of effectiveness. The products of the social life world are personal strength, soli-
darity, and social consensus. However, according to Habermas the two
worlds don't exist in separate parts of the social world. They rather represent

different logics that are always represented in some kind of compositum mixtum in any social organization.[5]

Self-referentiality: An answer to the modern dilemma

Basically, modern, civilized society is based on a social contract among its citizens — *based on its own elements* instead of being based on God or an Emperor as an external authority. Still, however, society and social organizations are coherent systems, and the problem arises, how something that is made up of free citizens with individual experiences and interests can be based on itself? How is society possible? This has been the crux of modern social philosophy, resulting in never ending discussions between "determinists" and "voluntarists." The autopoietical paradigm cuts through this dilemma by basing itself in the precondition that modern society is a self-reproductive and self-reflective system.[6]

Discussion

The answer to the dilemma of modern social philosophy is that modern society is a self-referential system. But the cost of the gains may be the loss of the human subject.

The decline of modern subject-philosophy

But *does* this human subject still exist? To many philosophers, the answer is *no.* "Even those," says Habermas critically, "who, following Lukács, fasten-

---

[5] This differentiation may be phenomenologically correct, but it doesn't solve the theoretical problem that modern society is constituted by functionally differentiated subsystems and that it is impossible to specify any of these systems as the 'true' or 'correct' or 'basic' system either for providing a basis for analysis or an ethical platform. 'Even if a new type of difference develops, i.e., the difference between functionally differentiated systems and the protest against functional differentiation or, to speak with Habermas, the difference between systems and the life-world, it is impossible to decide from which of the two perspectives society could be described comprehensively or, at least, representatively. In historical comparison, a characteristic feature of modern society is thus the loss of natural representation (...). The totality of society is never fully present and cannot be realized as a totality.' Luhmann (1990) p. 125. This is an expression of the inherent paradox in analyzing modern society (analyzing a social system, the analyzer himself being an element of this system, and even claiming on the one hand that the analytical result represents the system in totality, on the other hand emphasizing that the system is combined of non-identical sub-systems, *and* that the observer is representing one of these sub-systems). This paradox has recently been identified in the concept of 'Cybernetics of cybernetics' or 'second order cybernetics', cf. von Foerster (1979) pp. 5ff. See also Steier and Smith (in press), and Steier (1991)

[6] 'Since the end of the sixteenth century, the idea of self-maintenance has been used to displace teleological reasoning and to reintroduce teleology by the argument that the maintenance of the system is the goal of the system or the function of its structures and operations.' Niklas Luhmann (1990) p. 11.

ed upon the concept of reification came to agree more and more with their opponents in their description; they were increasingly impressed with the impotence of subjects in relation to the feedback processes of self-regulating systems, over which they could have no influence." (Habermas, 1987: 353)

This was the situation of for example, French structuralist Michel Foucault, and consequently, in his later works, he replaced the model of domination based on repression (thus building on Marx and Freud) by a model of a complex system of power strategies. According to Habermas, "these power strategies intersect one another, succeed one another; they are distinguished according to the type of their discourse formation and the degree of their intensity; *but they cannot be judged under the aspect of their validity."* (Habermas, 1987: 127)

For decades, this trend in the social-theoretical diagnosis has been heading towards the point that systems functionalism makes into its own point: It allows the subjects themselves to degenerate into systems. It tacitly sets a seal on "the end of the individual."

In sociology, Baudrillard (1983a) draws the consequence by replacing the concept of repression by the concept of *simulation*. Nothing is "real"; everything is a simulation of a simulation of a simulation.[7]

In philosophy (or philosophical systems theory), Niklas Luhmann draws a similar consequence. He simply presupposes (and thus accepts) that the human subject as a unique entity has disappeared and has degenerated into a system of the same kind as any other (social) system. Consequently, personal and social systems form environments for one another. But he does so in a very sophisticated way: His version of systems functionalism takes up the heritage of the philosophy of the subject; it simply replaces the self-relating subject with a self-relating system, a system that relates to itself and which produces its own "meaning" or "social contract." "The world-constituting accomplishments of a transcendental subject that has lost its status apart from and above the world (...) are re-conceptualized as the accomplishments of a system that operates in a meaningful, self-relating way and is capable of forming internal representations of its environment. The fiction-creating productivity of a life-enhancing self-maintenance by subjects, for which the difference between truth and illusion has lost its meaning, is reconceptualized as the self-maintenance of a system that makes use of meaning, a self-mainte-

---

[7] Actually, the system of simulations creates new problems, just because modern democracy depends on *differences* – on citizens being different from their social system. If these differences disappear, then the system collapses or 'implodes.' One such category of the indifferent citizens is the category of the silent masses or silent majorities. Today, *they* (and not the critical minorities) are the problem of the system (cf. Jean Baudrillard, 1983b).

nance that masters the complexity of the environment and increases its own complexity." (Habermas, 1987: 421)

From metaphysics to metabiology

In many ways, Habermas accepts or even admires the achievements of Luhmann: "The models derived from intelligent performances and tailored to organic life come a lot closer to the socio-cultural form of life than classical mechanics. As Luhmann's astonishing job of translation demonstrates, this language can be so flexibly adapted and expanded that it yields novel, not merely objectivating but objectivistic descriptions even of subtle phenomena of the lifeworld." (Habermas, 1987: 385)

Ultimately, however, Habermas cannot accept Luhmann's approach. It may be phenomenologically impressive, but for moral philosophical reasons it must be rejected. It may be more sophisticated than traditional systems theory; yet, it represents the same kind of anti-humanism, Habermas says. I will exemplify this critique.

As can be understood, Habermas doesn't accept Luhmann's "transformation" of the concept of autopoiesis from biology to social science. On the contrary, in a critical paper on Luhmann's general theory of society[8] he concludes that Luhmann's systems theory effects a shift in thought from *metaphysics* to *meta-biology:* "However the expression "metaphysics" may have chanced to arise, one could attribute to it the meaning of a thinking that proceeds from the "for us" of physical appearances and asks what lies behind them. Then we can use the term "metabiological" for a thinking that starts from the "for itself" of organic life and goes behind it — the cybernetically described, basic phenomenon of the self-maintenance of self-relating systems in the face of hyper-complex environments." (p. 372)

This is then the ultimate difference between Habermas and Luhmann: that Habermas insists on the traditional subject-philosophy claiming the existence of a metaphysically thinking subject being outside the boarders of any social system, a subject that has a "for us" relationship to its social world, because this subject is defined *an sich,* in and for itself. The human subject is not reducible to its environment.[9]

---

[8] Jürgen Habermas: 'Excursus on Luhmann's Appropriation of the Philosophy of the Subject through Systems Theory,' in Habermas 1987, pp. 368-385.

[9] If such a subject existed, how would it be able to describe a world of which it is not an integrated part? This is then not a solution to, but just another expression of the problem represented by the above-mentioned second order cybernetics.

But doesn't Luhmann give an answer to this problem? Yes, he does, but according to Habermas his answer is not satisfactory. The system's relation to itself *is* modeled after that of the classical subject in the sense that systems in Luhmann's theory cannot relate to anything else without relating to themselves and reflexively ascertaining themselves. "Nevertheless," Habermas adds, "the "self" of the *system* is distinguished from that of the *subject* because it does not consolidate into the "I" of the apperceptive "I think" that, according to Kant's formulation has to be able to accompany all my representations." (p. 369)

In a very explicit way, Luhmann confirms this point. In reality, he says, there is no reason for maintaining the subject-philosophy paradigm. But if, for some reason, one would like to save the subject terminology, then one could say that "a consciousness is a subject in the world besides which there are other types of subjects, first of all social systems." Or one could say: "Psychological and social systems are the subjects of the world. (...) In any case such expressions ("Thesen", says Luhmann) explode the Cartesian differentiation of subject and object. (...) The selfreferential subject and the self-referential object are thought of as isomorphic structures — like "reason" and "the thing in itself" by Kant." (Luhmann, 1984: 595)[10]

Habermas concludes: In Luhmann's theory of self-referential systems "...subject-centered reason is replaced by systems rationality. As a result, the critique of reason carried out as a critique of metaphysics and a critique of power (...) is deprived of its object. To the degree that systems theory does not merely make its specific disciplinary contribution within the system of sciences (like the systems theory within biology, LQ), but also penetrates the lifeworld with its claim to universality (like Luhmann's social theory, LQ), it replaces metaphysical background convictions with metabiological ones." (Habermas, 1987: 385)

Thus, finally, the discussion between Habermas and Luhmann is a discussion of the nature of our (post-)modern society. Does the critical subject still exist, or is it integrated in feedback processes of self-regulating systems, over which it has no influence? Within the context of this chapter, I only intended to present this discussion, concluding that Luhmann has provided us with a set of concepts that allows us to analyse phenomena within modern (or post-modern) network organizations which could not be understood within the paradigm of traditional organizational communication theory. There is still an enormous, but promising job ahead of us to further develop the analytical

---

[10] In his *Essays on Self-Reference,* Luhmann adds that Habermas' critique '...raises the question of whether there can be a nonparadoxical concept. Habermas claims that the new paradigm of communicative understanding avoids problems of paradox, but how can self-reference be restricted so as to avoid paradoxes.' (1990, p. 142).

potentialities of this paradigm, while not forgetting to reflect its epistemological implications.

Acknowledgments

I would like to thank L. S. Harms and his colleagues at Department of Communication, University of Hawaii at Manoa, Andrew Calabrese and his colleagues at Department of Communication, Purdue University, Thomas L. McPhail, Department of Communication, University of Missouri-St. Louis, and Frederick Steier, Center for Cybernetic Studies in Complex Systems, Old Dominion University, for their comments on an earlier version of this chapter.

Reference List

ASHBY, W. R. (1968). Principles of the Self-Organizing System. In *Modern Systems Research for the Behavioural Scientist,* ed. Buckley, W. Chicago.

BAUDRILLARD, J. (1983a). *Simulations.* New York: Semiotext(e).

BAUDRILLARD, J. (1983b). *In the Shadow of the Silent Majorities.* New York: Semiotext(e).

BELL, D. (1979). The Social Framework of the Information Society, in *The Computer Age: A Twenty-Year Perspective,* eds. Dertouzos, M. L. and Moses, J. Massachusetts: The MIT Press, Cambridge.

BRIER, S. (1987). Naturvidenskab, humaniora og erkendelsesteori. In *Kritik* vol. 79/80. Copenhagen.

CHRISTENSEN, L. T. (1991). The Marketing Culture: The Communication of Organizational Identity in a Culture without Foundation. Paper submitted to the International Conference on "Organizational Culture", Copenhagen, June 26.-28.

COMTE, A. (1830-42) *Cours de philosophie positive.* Paris.

COMTE, A. (1844). *Discours préliminaire sur l'esprit positif.* Paris.

DEMARCO, T. (1979). *Structured Analysis and System Specification.* Englewood Cliffs: Yourdon Press.

VON FOERSTER, H. (1979). Cybernetics of Cybernetics. In *Communication and Control in Society.* Krippendorff, K. New York.

HABERMAS, J. (1981). *Theorie des kommunikativen Handelns.* Frankfurt a. M.: Suhrkamp Verlag.

HABERMAS, J. (1987) *The Philosophical Discourse of Modernity. Twelve Lectures.* Massachusetts: The MIT Press, Cambridge.

HILTZ, S. R. (1984). *Online Communities. A Case Study of the Office of the Future.* Norwood, New Jersey: Ablex Publishing Corporation.

HUWS, U., KORTE, W.B., ROBINSON, S. (1990). *Telework: Towards the Elusive Office.* Chichester: John Wiley.

JABLIN, F. M., PUTNAM, L. L., ROBERTS, K. H., PORTER, L. W. eds. (1987). *Handbook of Organizational Communication. An Interdisciplinary Perspective.* Newbury Park: Sage Publications.

JENSEN, O. M., STORGAARD, K. Information Technology and Ways of Life. In *Danish Experiments,* New Social Science Monographs, eds. Cronborg, T., Duelund, P., Jensen. O. M., Qvortrup, L. Copenhagen.

KRONE, K. J., JABLIN, F. M., PUTNAM, L. L. (1987). Communication Theory and Organizational Communication: Multiple Perspectives. In *Handbook of Organizational Communication. An Interdisciplinary Perspective,* eds. Jablin, F. M., Putnam, L. L., Roberts, K. H., Porter, L. W. Newbury Park: Sage Publications.

LAING, A. (1991). Changing Business: Post-Fordism and the Workplace. London: DEGW.

LUHMANN, N. (1975). *Macht.* Stuttgart.

LUHMANN, N. (1976). Generalized Media and the Problem of Contingency. In *Explorations in General Theory in Social Science 1-2, Essays in Honor of Talcott Parsons,* eds. Loubster, J. J. et al. New York.

LUHMANN, N. (1984). *Soziale Systeme. Grundriss einer allgemeinen Theory.* Frankfurt a. M.: Suhrkamp Verlag.

LUHMANN, N. (1990). *Essays on Self-Reference.* New York: Columbia University Press.

MATURANA, H., VARELA, F. (1980). *Autopoiesis and Cognition,* D. Dordrecht: Reidel Publishing Company.

MORGAN, G. (1986). *Images of Organization.* Beverly Hills: Sage Publications.

PUTNAM, L. (1983). The Interpretive Perspective: An Alternative to Functionalism. In *Communication and Organizations: An Interpretive Approach,* eds. Putnam, L., Pacanowsky, M. Beverly Hills: Sage Publishing Company.

PUTNAM, L. L. (1985). Bargaining as Organizational Communication. In *Organizational Communication: Traditional Themes and New Directions,* eds. McPhee, R. D., Tompkins, P. K. Beverly Hills: Sage Publications.

PUTNAM, L. L., SCOTT POOLE, M. (1987). Conflict and Negotiation. In *Handbook of Organizational Communication. An Interdisciplinary Perspective,* eds. Jablin, F. M., Putnam, L. L., Roberts, K. H., Porter, L. W. Newbury Park: Sage Publications.

QVORTRUP, L. (1984). *The Social Significance of Telematics.* Amsterdam/Philadelphia: John Benjamins Publishing Company.

QVORTRUP, L. (1988). *Det levende eller det døde samfund* (The Living or the Dead Society). Copenhagen: Blytmanns Forlag.

QVORTRUP, L. (1992). Telematics and Organizational Communication: Trends in Organizational Communications Theories. In *Telematics and Work,* eds. Andriessen, J. H., Roe, R. A. London: Lawrence Erlbaum Associates.

QVORTRUP, L. (in press). Telework: Visions, Definitions, Realities, Barriers. In *Handbook on Cities and New Technologies.* Paris: OECD and Urba 2000.

REDDING, W. C. (1972). *Communication Within the Organization: An Interpretative Review of Theory and Research.* New York: Industrial Communication Council.

REDDING, W. C. (1985). Stumbling Toward Identity: The Emergence of Organizational Communication as a Field of Study. In *Organizational Communication: Theoretical Themes and New Directions,* eds. McPhee, R. D., Tompkins, P. K. Beverly Hills: Sage Publications.

ROUSSEAU, J.-J. (1968). *Du contrat social ou principe du droit politique,* (1762), here quoted from the English translation *The Social Contract.* London : Penguin Books.

RUBIN, I. I. (1979). *A History of Economic Thought* (1929).London: Ink Links.

SHANNON, C. E., WEAVER, W. (1964). *The Mathematical Theory of Communication* (1948). Urbana: University of Illinois Press.

SHANNON, C. E. (1972). Information Theory. In *Encyclopædia Britannica, Volume 12.* Chicago et al.:William Benton, Publisher.

SIMON, H. A. (1945). *Administrative Behavior.* New York: Free Press.

WATZLAWICK, P. J., BEAVIN, J., JACKSON, D. (1967). *Pragmatics of Human Communication.* New York: Norton.

STEIER, F. ed. (1991) *Research and Reflexivity.* London: Sage Publications.

STEIER, F., SMITH, K. K. (in press). The Cybernetics of Cybernetics and the Organization of Organization, in: *Organization — Communication. Emerging Perspectives,* Volume III, ed. Thayer, L. Norwood, NJ: Ablex.

WEICK, K. E. (1987). "Theorizing About Organizational Communication." In *Handbook of Organizational Communication. An Interdisciplinary Perspective,* eds. Jablin, F. M., Putnam, L. L., Roberts, K. H., Porter, L. W. Newbury Park: Sage Publications.

WIENER, N. (1950). *The Human Use of Human Beings. Cybernetics and Society.* Boston: Houghton Mifflin Company.

Comment: Disturbing communication

PETER BØGH ANDERSEN

The standard communication model analyses communication into five main elements: A *sender* encodes a *message* into a *signal*, transmits the signal through a noisy *channel* that may distort parts of the signal before it arrives at the *receiver* who decodes the signal and hopefully retrieves the original message.

In semiotic terms we can translate signal by *expression/signifier* and message by *content/signified*. The assumption is that the signified "glue" to the signifier; although it is the signifier that gets transmitted, the signified rides along with it and can be unpacked at the end of the transmission line.

When applied to actual communication, this assumption turns out to be inadequate. The actual interpretation of the "signal" seems to rely more on the context of communication than on the signal received, so the idea of "decoding the signified" explains very little in actual conversations.

Qvortrup's chapter on organization theory replaces the five standard elements by new concepts, two of which are *perturbation* and *self-maintenance*. The purpose of this note is to suggest how they can be applied more concretely to communication analysis with a point of departure in catastrophe theory (CT) (see "A Semiotic Approach to Programming").

Let me start with a conversation from a real workplace[1]:

> S: They are short of people at Cheque Control. Can anyone go over there? *(Do I have the right to redistribute one of you two to the cheque control now?)*
> A: I was there last week *(You have no right to order me. According to the planned system for work circulation, the same person is not obliged to sit on the cheque control for two successive weeks)*
> B: I have to be at the dentist at eleven o'clock *(Ordering me does not make sense. I shall not be present since I am to go to the dentist, which is within my rights)*
> S: But in the afternoon they have a part-timer coming.
> B: Well, I'll go then.

A and B are workers and S is their boss. The boss tries to persuade one of them to move over to another department, Cheque Control, because they are short of people there. The conversation is work distribution, aiming at dividing a task or set of tasks among a group of people.

---

[1] B. Holmqvist: *The Postal Giro as language environment.* University of Stockholm, 1986, p. 80.

384

The italicized parts are a paraphrase expressing contents that are implicit in the original wording, but are understood by the participants because of their knowledge of the rules governing work distribution. The implicit content comes from the world of negotiations and agreements and includes contents such as /right/, /order/, /sense/.

Before the conversation starts, A and B are in an *equilibrium* state, doing their work in their home department. S *disturbs* their equilibrium by suggesting the possibility that one of them moves to Cheque Control. Both try to place obstacles between themselves and their future path to Cheque Control: A was there last week and B is going to the dentist. But S removes the obstacle by arguing that they have a part-timer coming, so B has to go. The conversation ends in a new equilibrium state.

The conversation exemplifies Qvortup's points. The first thing to note is that most of the meaning resides in the context as the paraphrase clearly shows. In CT we would go on stipulating an internal topology in which the two workers are placed. In this case, the topology is simply the plant. The workers are subject to forces in this topology. When conversation starts, they are in an equilibrium — they are placed in a minimum where the potential is lowest (Figure 15.1).

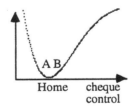

Fig. 15.1. Stable situation in home department.

S's request changes this topology, so that A and B are now placed in an unstable position (Figure 15.2).

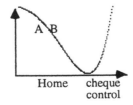

Fig. 15.2. Boss's move creates an unstable situation.

386   *Peter Bøgh Andersen*

If nothing is done, they will slide down to Cheque Control. Their counter-moves change the topology by setting up a hindrance, while of course still retaining the danger of being transferred (Figure 15.3).

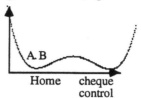

Fig. 15.3. Workers' countermove restores equilibrium.

The main communicative function of this conversation is *directive*. The example shows that directives work by changing the topology of the internal space, causing its inhabitants to occupy new positions.

The next example is the beginning of a problem-solving conversation, whose main function is *representative*. One of the workers has discovered an error in the documents she is working with, and wants to find out whether the customer or she herself has made the error.

A: Lena, this one is 143 crowns out.
B: It shouldn't be out, should it?
A: Nope.
B: Well, then you/ well, then you/ You aren't out by that amount anywhere else, are you?
A: Not in the batch I've been working with.

The purpose of the conversation is to establish the truth of sentences such as "I made the error" vs. "The customer made the error."

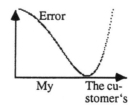

Fig. 15.4. "Error" about to combine with "The customer."

Establishing truth is a process that takes time. It consists in asking questions about the document and possibly in inspecting them again. In opposition to directives that keep Word constant and approach World to Word, representatives keep World constant, and approach Word to it. Representatives try to "come closer to the truth."

In this case, the internal topology is not World, but Word; the changes of the internal topology are not caused by Word but by World. Figure 15.4 in fact is a syntax: The x-axis is a semantic field, and the actant is a noun seeking a genitive. In the directive above, the x-axis is physical plant space, and the actant a worker.

The grammar in Figure 15.4 is special in that its rules of formation are interwoven with dynamic processes in the World referred to by the sentences. If the topology of Figure 15.4 is not changed, the word "error" will slide down to the phrase "The customer's" and produce the phrase "The customer's error." World changes the internal topology of the syntactic space; Word is disturbed, and seeks a new equilibrium.

In the present case, World can be changed by inspecting it again, bringing new facts to the light. In other cases, World changes its physical properties. For example, a document could become unreadable or it could disappear. But World can also change as a result of a directive: For example, B transfers herself to Cheque Control, and this World change disturbs a colleague's topology of Word: "Where is Marita? Oh, she just went to Cheque Control." (See Figure 15.5.)

Correspondingly, the change of Word can easily act as a disturbance of the World. For example, if Word settles in "Customer's error," the worker is supposed to execute a particular action.

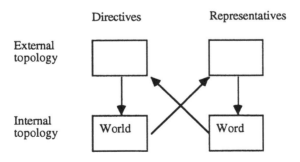

Fig. 15.5. Directives and representatives.

In this way we close the circle: World provides the external control variables for representatives; the internal syntactic space is disturbed and seeks a new equilibrium; the new equilibrium acts as external control variables for World that seeks a new equilibrium, and so on, and so on.

This model of communication possess some of the properties we want: Small perturbation from World or Word in the external topology can cause large qualitative changes in the internal topologies. In fact, this is precisely what Catastrophe Theory is about.

16

Dialogues in networks

ELSEBETH KORSGAARD SORENSEN

Through the technological invention and utilization of computer mediated communication systems (CMC systems) in the domain of human linguistic interaction, the organization of electronic communities across time and space has been made possible. The choice to establish interactive communities exclusively on the basis of shared interest, background or task, has become available. Computer mediated communication systems, providing facilities for this human communication independent of time and place, represent a large and challenging interactive potential, as they entirely overcome many of the practical problems associated with the establishment of a traditional face-to-face communication.

Although the linguistic interaction practised in this type of electronic environment has already been stated generally to be posited somewhere between writing and speech, it is clear that it is not sufficient — or even correct — to characterize this communication, enabled by CMC systems, barely as "a written communication, facilitated electronically." Such a characteristic does not identify the overall nature and conditions involved in this totally new type of linguistic interaction. Viewing communication as a multi-semiotic process (a process that uses a combination of various possible ways — verbal and non-verbal — of establishing meaning in a communication situation), and being aware that the communication of concern here is a process taking place using only one type of all the types of communication involved in the general multi-semiotic communicative process, it seems relevant to discuss and enlighten more thoroughly the various aspects and characteristics involved in the specific type of communication, unfolding itself in a conferencing system.

The objective of this chapter is, through an adequate linguistic approach and frame of reference, to make a comparison with the two main types of communication already familiar, spoken language and written language, in order to move further toward a characteristic of what I perceive to be a qualitatively new type of communication, characterized by its own set of features. A comparison with several other forms of communication (for example, telephone communication, and so on) constitutes a relevant alternative. However, I shall leave that as a possibility to pursue in the future.

For general information, the first section presents a broad characteristic of the technology of concern. The second section contains a presentation of the theoretical perspective behind the analysis of electronic dialogues, while the overall aim of the third section, the main section of the chapter, is to move closer, using illustrating examples of dialogues, toward capturing the communicative nature and potential of computer conferencing systems and describing some of the implications of organizing human interaction electronically, and independently of time and space. The fourth section forms the forum for some final comments and thoughts associated with "the new interactive reality."

Computer conferencing systems: Media for linguistic interaction

This section aims at giving a presentation of conferencing systems and their most important features, not only those forming the conditions and constraints with respect to the possibilities of action, but also aspects of a more abstract character.

A computer conferencing system is one specific type of the range of software, providing possibilities for computer mediated communication. In other words, a technology providing facilities for networking through the organisation of "on-line communities." Conferencing systems are made not only to facilitate and to provide support for communication between individuals and groups of people, but in particular to do so *across time and space*. Tony Kaye describes the software and this side of its characteristics as follows: "A computer mediated communication system allows individuals and groups of people to carry on discussions and conversations over a computer network regardless of time and place constraints, via messages keyed in to microcomputers connected by telephone to a central computer." (Kaye, 1985)

The utilization of a conferencing system is based — as already mentioned — on a principle of *asynchrony* (independence of time and space between the communicating parties). This is realized through an "electronic infrastructure" that allows a relatively large computer, on which the conferencing system is installed, to store, organize, and distribute all contributions and personal letters. Ideally, the computer is running 24 hours per day all year round, so the communication can take place continuously. When a user with the right software on his terminal or work station connects (via telecommunication lines) to the conferencing system, the system distributes the relevant contributions and letters and presents them to the user as "news."

Viewed in quantitative terms with respect to the interlocutors involved, the different types of communication possibilities offered by these systems, are:

- one-to-one
- one-to-many
- many-to-many

All conferencing systems comprise both a conferencing part for handling the many-to-many communication and a mail part for the one-to-one and one-to-many communication. In the *conferencing* part it is possible for a group of people to carry out complex interactions: to create, to store, to access, and to search messages/moves of past interaction, without having to pay attention to time or place constraints. The responsibility for setting up, structuring, and guiding a conference lies with the owner/the creator (also called "the moderator") of a conference. Different conferences containing various topics can be held simultaneously.

The *mail* part of a conferencing system is a complementary feature of the conferencing part, in the sense that it provides electronic delivery of letters (one-to-one or one-to-many). An individual writes a letter/message to another person. The message gets stored and received by the recipient. It is usually the user himself, who has to deal with the storing, organization, or deletion of the mail messages.

Independence in relation to *time* and *space* is a powerful defining feature in relation to the conditions for and the frame within which an interaction between two people or a group of people may be carried out. The individual participants can at *any convenient time* enter an *imaginary place* in the system. This "place" (or "room") may be built and created more or less successfully by the interface.

Most conferencing systems include also the following features for supporting and facilitating communicative actions:

- A directory of all users.
- A directory of conferences, perhaps with a brief description of each conference.
- An editor for composing text messages.
- Facilities for transferring files between the conferencing software and a personal computer.

Computer conferencing systems grew out of a need for communication among a group of people who are dispersed. The software was originally developed with the intention of satisfying governmental needs for communication, in order to deal with national and international crises (CITE Report NO. 91). Today, conferencing systems are applied in several work areas where there is a need for group communication. In particular, the potential of the systems is utilized where people need to communicate over large geographic distances. Conferencing systems are applied in industrial and commercial corporations, as well as government organizations and research institutes. Likewise, the software is used not only in the area of distance education (for example, to support interaction between both students and teachers and among students), but also an increasing number of traditional teaching institutions around the world are incorporating computer conferencing into education and training activities.

Theoretical linguistic perspective: Games and language games

This section departs from the understanding that linguistic interaction is a fundamentally social process between humans. The content of the section leans on Kerstin Eklundh's suggestions for a concrete interpretation of Wittgenstein's notion of language games. It points out important features of human interaction (games) in a general sense, as well as the more specific properties of those games, which are especially associated with the use of language.

As it stands, computer conferencing systems constitute the concrete existential basis for the linguistic domain that forms the focus of my interest. Computers and computer systems are technological inventions, based on the fundamental dualistic understanding within the natural sciences, that it is possible to make objective models of the world in which the original relations (the relations in the "real world") are objectively maintained and mirrored.

Ontologically and theoretically viewed, Wittgenstein's theory of language games constitutes a creative "tool" for approaching the dynamic social phenomenon of discourse. The theory of language games implies that a sign has no meaning in itself, but it is assigned meaning in association with a language game; the meaning is given in the way it is used in the language game. Thus, the language game theory is very general and comprises central aspects and properties of social action.

Language is fundamentally a social phenomenon. If linguistic interaction is to be viewed in the light of language games, one important implication is that an utterance must be interpreted in inextricable association with the activity in which it is used. A general notion of game is one point of departure for analyzing social interpretation and perception. It gives rise to the following conclusions:

- Interaction is rule-governed.

- When we interact, we base our action on inferences (of the nature of the ongoing activity).
- We build up expectations during the course of interaction, which are based on our knowledge of various kind of activities and their rules.

Through these notions some essential features are transmitted of the way in which we perceive social events and how our interpretation of an event influences our choice on how to act: "*To act* in a social setting is to follow rules (and sometimes, to violate rules). A *game* is the general structure, delimited by such rules, in which social action occurs. *The frame* of a game is the set of circumstances through which its actions are interpreted." (Eklundh, 1983)

Humans continuously make inferences about the nature of the ongoing activity and about the other player's intentions. The inferences are sometimes mistaken or incomplete, which complicates the understanding of the sender's intentions. The goal of the game itself is defined indirectly from the type of games in which it may potentially occur.

Finally, a notion of games creates a set of expectations in the mind of the players. If the players do not act according to the required rules of the game, the game gets interrupted. Because the expectations are not satisfied, the resumed game gets interpreted accordingly.

The general process of linguistic communication may be viewed as taking place within a wide semiotic system (if we distinguish semiotic sign categories along the dimension of the area of the various possible ways of communicating information). Which parts of this general system are activated and used in a particular case of communication depends entirely on the type of social game.

In order to reach a characterization of the type of social games, which are especially associated with the use of language (language games), Kerstin Eklundh assumes three semiotically different types of sender activities possible within a communicative act:

1. *Indication*: The sender transmits information, or is available for interpretation (for example, the act of unintended yawning, which may be interpreted — maybe wrongly — regardless of the intention of the sender).

2. *Display*: The sender intentionally displays behavior — the smallest level of initiative required for a game to be classified as a *communicative act* (for example, body language, or intended yawning).

3. *Signaling*: The behavior is intentional and, furthermore, the sender has the intention that the receiver should realize this and also what the intention is (*verbal communication*).

The character of a language game is connected to the third type of sender activity. Kerstin Eklundh provides the following definition of a language game: "A language game, on the other hand, is a communicative game where the rules require that the participants _signal behavior_. The actions in a language game have a symbolic quality, and the symbols involved, taken as a whole, are tied to the game by means of a set of conventions (the conventions of a language)." (Eklundh, 1983). "The convention of a language" is intended to be understood as the set of language games that an individual has acquired during socialization and language use.

Viewing the concept of games in relation to social interaction makes it clear that "_a language game_ is realized as a sequence of actions by participants" (Kerstin Eklundh, 1983). This means that in some sense a "player" in the game knows what to do when another player has acted. The actions are subject to specific rules, and the players in the game possess knowledge of the rules of the game. Finally, the theory of language games indicates that the knowledge of the rules in the game is not explicit in the sense of awareness in the players. For example, in the language game of question-answer, most people are not aware which characteristics constitute an answer to a question. However, they are able to distinguish an answer from a non-answer. The knowledge involved is a knowledge of how to play the game.

Kerstin Eklundh argues that describing a sequence of utterances in terms of games is equivalent to assigning structure to it. In particular the linguistic interaction process (the dialogue) can be understood as successive _openings_ and _closings_ of language games at different levels, where some games, _subgames_, are "embedded" (Goffman, 1971) in and controlled by others. Each game opened creates a set of _expectations_ about the continuation of the game. The important role of these expectations is clarified and described in this way: "The utterances that are made are interpreted according to such expectations, so that depending on the game in which a certain utterance is made, the utterance will get a different interpretation." (Eklundh, 1983)

In the following I list some additional important terms (based on Kerstin Eklundh, 1983), which may be useful in analyzing human communication from the perspective of language games:

- _Initiative_: The initiating party in a language game "defines" the new situation and the roles of the participants. If the participants accept the roles, they should act in agreement with the rules of the game.
- _Intention_: The assumed intention of the initiator of a game/subgame, related to the shared knowledge of the goal of the game.

- *Mutualness/reciprocity*: The shared knowledge, which is potentially assumed or referred to, of the ongoing activity at any point in the linguistic interaction and at any level.
- *Responsibility*: The responsibility of the initiator of a game to take an interest in other contributions, and to make sure that the game is carried to an end.
- *Expectation*: The concept of game implies that a dialogue process is a dynamic process, continuously creating new expectations. The participants are expected to act according to certain rules. The expectations which are still relevant in connection to an interrupted game, will be the ones valid when the game is resumed.
- *Frame*: Each game applies in a certain frame (the set of circumstances in which the game can be applied).
- *Move*: An action, specified by the rules of the game (typically an action which is expected by the participants in the game).
- *Closure*: The game is brought to an end according to rules (without any violations of the rules and without having created new expectations of a continuing act).
- *Repair*: Violations of rules causing the game to fail may be followed by repairs.

As a language game cannot be characterized in an absolute or complete manner, it is sometimes difficult to decide exactly which type of game is taking place (which game is going on is also subject to interpretation). Misinterpretation of the type of language game is a frequent cause of misunderstandings in dialogues.

The elements of Kerstin Eklundh's interpretation of the Theory of Language Games that have been reviewed here constitute an attractive basis for looking at linguistic interaction in comparison to other frameworks: 1) there are no restrictions on the levels available in the analysis, 2) it comprises the important elements of discourse (initiative, reciprocity, and intention), and 3) in agreement with a general theory of social action and comprehension, it supports the view that linguistic dialogues can only be interpreted as part of a social context.

Dialogues in networks

The language game theory, described in the previous section, has constituted the fundamental approach in my analysis of electronic dialogues. In order to establish more closely the features and mechanisms that constitute the language games permitted by conferencing systems, this section deals with the

actual analysis and goes through illustrating examples of electronic dialogues. The results of the analysis are classified and discussed in relation to
certain outspoken areas, which I find to be in focus in electronic dialogues.

The investigated material, which constitutes the body of the analysis, consists of electronic dialogues, retrieved and extracted from conferences run on
COSY — a conferencing system in use at The Open University in England.
The selected conferences and topics are representative of several types of
conferences and conference topics, with various degrees of formality, that I
have studied. It should be noted that the investigated material covers only
electronic dialogues from the conferencing part of a conferencing system —
the area supporting many-to-many interaction, and does not include electronic dialogues from the mail part — the area providing support for one-to-
one or one-to-many communication. Bearing this limitation in mind, I still believe that the two variants of asynchronous interaction have a large proportion of their features in common.

The header of the moves in COSY contains the following information: 1)
the name of the conference, 2) the name of the topic, 3) the sequential number of the move, 4) the COSY-ID of the author, 5) the number of characters
in the move, 6) the date and time of the move. Moreover, the header contains
information about the relation of the move to other moves in the dialogic
structure, assigned by the system (on the initiative of the user). To protect
the identity of the people involved in the dialogues, the names of the conferences, the topics, and the interlocutors are removed. The names are substituted in such a way that allows the structure (assigned by the system) of the
dialogues and the relations between the interlocutors of the various moves
to be maintained.

Some of the observed basic trends and features of electronic dialogues,
which the analysis has proved to be distinctive, fall within the following
themes:

- the time dynamic in the interaction
- compensational behavior
- the independence of time and space

The time dynamic in the interaction

The aim of this subsection is to give an idea of the role that the time dimension in the asynchronous interaction plays in determining the character of
the linguistic dialogue in conferencing systems. Through typical examples of
dialogues and moves I discuss general tendencies in the relationship be-

tween certain linguistic features of the interactive moves and the asynchrony in time of the interaction. However, in order to fully illustrate the mechanism in question, it is necessary first to reach a characteristic of the prototypical cases of respectively spoken and written interaction (face-to-face dialogue versus letter writing).

The general prototypical case of spoken linguistic interaction is one where a speaker tries to influence a listener in order to make him (or them) perceive, understand, feel, or do something, which the speaker has in mind — in other words: the case of a *face-to-face spoken dialogue*. The semiotic communicative elements involved are of both verbal and non-verbal character.

A very basic feature of the prototypical case of spoken communication (a dialogue) is its "actual" or synchronic character: The communication takes place in a *shared time* and *shared space*. Partly due to this, the communicative action/dialogue is closely interrelated with the actual context, which consists partly of various kinds of shared background knowledge between speaker and listener, and partly of the physical and social conditions, in which the communication is embedded. Furthermore, in contrast to writing, spoken interaction is a *dialogic* process.

Another important, basic feature in spoken dialogue is the *inextricable dependency on the context*, in which the dynamic process unfolds itself. First, the spoken communication is only one aspect of the total semiotic communication that takes place in the case of spoken dialogue. Non-verbal behavior accompanies (supplements or contradicts) the verbal behavior. Thus, the verbal messages are often *more implicit* than for example in writing. Dependency on the context especially implies, that dialogues/utterances must be considered in terms of the activity in which they are used. Moreover, speech communication is also very likely in itself to appear less explicit and insufficient for interpretation, due to the dependency on *other semiotic elements*, like gestures, facial expressions, tones of voice, and so on: "After all, the use of an utterance in a normal situation involving face-to-face interaction is not an isolated speech act; it is part of a *comprehensive communicative act* which comprises the use of both verbal means (speech) and non-verbal means (gesticulation etc.). The message is conveyed, or shown, in several ways simultaneously, and the role played by spoken language cannot be properly understood without taking into consideration the whole communicative act." (Linell, 1982). Viewing spoken dialogues as part of the general system of social interpretation and perception (see the second section on games/language games), I shall draw the following conclusions about the characteristics of *a face-to-face dialogue:*

- A spoken dialogue takes place *with synchrony in time and space.*

- A spoken dialogue is *dynamic*.
- A spoken dialogue is *transient*.
- A spoken dialogue is *inter-active behavior* (dialogic).
- A spoken dialogue is *implicit*.
- A spoken dialogue is *multi-semiotic*.
- The production and interpretation of the moves in a spoken dialogue are *dependent on background knowledge*.
- For the structure of a spoken dialogue, *feedback is fundamental*.
- A spoken dialogue is fundamentally *embedded in the immediate context*.
- A spoken dialogue often *involves primary and secondary inferences*.
- A spoken dialogue *involves interactional and propositional coherence*.
- A spoken dialogue is subject to and constructed by *a principle of gear-dynamic* (a mechanism, where a subgame is initiated in order to explicitly define an implied presupposition made by the other interlocutor. This causes the dialogue to slow down — to shift into a lower gear.
- A spoken dialogue is *analytically* composed.

Unlike spoken dialogue, the general communicative situation of the prototypical case of *written dialogue* letter writing, is one where the sender's text production and the receiver's interpretation of the text take place as independent processes, separated in both time and place. In other words: In typical written communication there is *no shared time* and *no shared space* between the writer and the reader and as such between the creation and interpretation of the text. As a result, a written message lacks an immediate context. In fact, the writer's ability to decenter from the immediate context and to place the text in a "wider" shared context of more abstract character is decisive in order for the reader to be able to decode the text. As the semiotic communicative elements used in written communication in comparison to spoken dialogue do not involve non-verbal behavior, but are reduced to making use of written signs, the interpretation of the reader rests upon the writer's *product*, whereas the process of production itself is inaccessible and unimportant.

Contrary to the situation of spoken dialogue, where the speaker in the communicative act makes use of both verbal and non-verbal elements to direct the listener's thoughts and feelings, the producer of a written text can only communicate via the written language, and as such he does not have the same immediate "control" over the reader. Written language is usually produced by a single individual in isolation, without any constraints and pressures derived from a social encounter. In other words: The process of writing is a *monologic* process.

As in the discussion of spoken dialogue, it is possible to draw various conclusions concerning the characteristics of a the prototypical case of *written dialogue*:

- A written dialogue takes place without synchrony in time and space.
- A written dialogue is static.
- A written dialogue is permanent.
- A written dialogue is intra-active behavior (monologic).
- A written dialogue is explicit.
- A written dialogue is mono-semiotic.
- The production and interpretation of the moves in a written dialogue may be dependent on background knowledge.
- The structure of a written dialogue feedback is not fundamental.
- A written dialogue has no dependency on the immediate context.
- A written dialogue may involve primary and secondary inferences.
- A written dialogue is rarely influenced by the dynamic principle of interactional and propositional coherence.
- The constitution of a written dialogue does not imply a principle of gear-dynamic.
- Written dialogue is synthetically composed.

The differences, arrived at here, between the prototypical cases of spoken (face-to-face dialogue) and written interaction (letter writing), are very obvious — the features related to the process of the interaction itself (in other words, features that are partly affected by time and space), and those that confine the way in which the language is composed appear contradictory. However, although there is a clear difference between spoken and written communication, it should be added that this is not necessarily always the case. There are certain genres of spoken language that have their counterparts in written language, and vice versa. Finally, it should also be kept in mind that language is a historically dynamic phenomenon, which is continuously subject to transition.

One existing mechanism in the investigated electronic interactions, established by the analysis, is a dynamic relationship between the level of "interactivity" and the linguistic character of the interaction. Although the significance of social and organizational factors, like roles (for example, moderator of conference, teacher of course, and so on) and levels of formality or "loyalty" toward the traditional style of writing in the electronic dialogues should not be underestimated, it seems to be a clear trend, linguistically viewed, that there is a dynamic relationship between the time frequency of the interactive moves on the one hand, and the level of context dependency of the linguistic character of the moves, on the other.

The following dialogue (Example I) is an example of a dialogue where the extension in time between moves is very short.

Example I

1

xxx/yyy #1, <A>, 204 chars, 21-Apr-90 23:15
There is/are comment(s) on this message.

TITLE: Welcome to the "pub"
Looks like I am the first and only one here. Bit dry at the moment. Could
be a bit wetter in the CB at MK on Monday when I meet a lot of friends F2F
for the first time.
<A>

2

xxx/yyy #2, <B>, 31 chars, 21-Apr-90 23:18
This is a comment to message 1
There is/are comment(s) on this message.

Where is the CB in MK?
<B>

3

xxx/yyy #3, <A>, 361 chars, 21-Apr-90 23:19
This is a comment to message 2
There is/are comment(s) on this message.

Don't know myself yet. It translates as the Cellar Bar and presumably
is somewhere in Fortress Walton. I am (hopefully reliably) informed that
I will be collected from MK station in a BX16 (whatever that is).
Watch this space. It could get interesting, cos I am actually supposed
to be flying in from Holland to go to the computer exhibition at the NEC.
<A>

4

xxx/yyy #4, <C>, 103 chars, 21-Apr-90 23:47
This is a comment to message 3
There are additional comments to message 3.

We've told them to get extra stock in, <A>! And your chariot will be
just a phone call away...
<C>

The purpose of the language game, initiated in message 1, is purely social.
The intention is to start a communication that serves to establish a contact
between the communicating parties. Structurally, the responding move, message 2, does not contain any explicit feedback, but jumps directly to initiate a
new game, which on the surface looks like an intrinsic subgame (a game occurring in the case of wrongly assumed presuppositions) in relation to move
1. It appears as an intrinsic referential subgame, which serves the purpose of
clarifying and making explicit the wrongly presupposed assumption ("CB")
with respect to the shared background knowledge.

Another interpretation, however, is possible. Bearing in mind that the only
purpose or intention of the initiating move 1 is phatic, which implies that the
writer's only expectation is to establish social relations (and not to get any
reactions to the content of his initiative), the bare appearance of another
move in the game fulfils the expectation created by move 1 and represents
semantically a full response. The structural lack of a feedback or response in
move 2 may be an indication of the fact, that B has understood the rules and
purpose of the initiating game, and as such move 2 may by said to represent
both an implicit feedback, accepting the phatic idea of the initiative, and a
new initiative at the same level as the first game.

The expectation, created by move 2, becomes satisfied through the first
two utterances in move 3. Via the rest of the utterances in move 3, the interlocutor partly again supports the social/phatic aspect of the communication,
and partly contributes toward enhancing the area of shared knowledge.

Also move 4 seems intended to support the social/phatic aspects of the
communication. The interlocutor of move 4 perceives in move 3 as the most
essential (though indirect) information, the insecurity and uncertainty in relation to the discussed event, and tries to respond to that, using humor and
wit in the discoursive elements (which also supports the social/phatic intention of the whole game).

Interactively, the moves of the game are made within very small time intervals. The interaction has taken place dialogically, and almost as closely as
possible to the synchrony of spoken interaction. The interactivity manifests
itself more through speech-like remarks than in pieces or blocks of monolog-
ically composed text, similar to those common to the prototypical case of
written interaction.

The way in which the language is formed and used in the remarks is generally very speech-like. In move 1, the imaginary room forming the regi or
background against which the fragments of sentences should be understood,

is created by the title. As no context/frame for the interaction has yet been established (move 1 is the first move, not only in the game, but also in the whole topic of the conference), this element is pertinent for the understanding of the rather implicit and speech-like remarks, which form the move. Almost all the utterances of move 1 lack the personal pronoun "I," and as such they appear more like a train of internal thoughts rather than utterances intended to communicate some information. This "personal investment" also emphasises the social/phatic intention of the move.

As mentioned already, move 2 is structured as the opener of a reference-identification subgame, which appears due to presupposed shared knowledge. The intention is to clarify a certain object (the "CB" at MK). The move is formed like a short speech-like question. This type of subgame, which causes a gear change in the dialogue to a lower level, is not a frequent phenomenon in the electronic interaction. This may have something to do with the sometimes slow interchange of messages, in comparison to that of spoken dialogue. A reference-identification subgame is easy and fast to deal with in face-to-face meetings, but appears to be rather a slow matter in electronic dialogues. This is partly because it occupies the same time and level of attention among participants as the main games, since there are no situationally founded semiotic ways (for example, non-verbal signals) of expressing regulating behavior (for example, tone of voice, facial expression, body gestures, and so on), which could help toward separating different levels of importance in the dialogue. The following single move from an electronic dialogue illustrates how a potential subgame is avoided by predicting behavior ("yes I do get the odd one or two" and "Oh, sorry, you mean we already have one?"):

Example II

========

xxx/yyy #24, <D>, 177 chars, 24-Apr-90 22:08
There is/are comment(s) on this message.

TITLE: Open Day...

Now for an idea (yes I do get the odd one or two), How about a CoSy-tent?
Oh, sorry, you mean we already have one? Was that the beer tent you said?

<D>.

To deal with subgames in electronic dialogues is a time consuming and slow process, and it tends to be avoided — either by (as illustated in Example I) the initiating interlocutor predicting and responding ("Oh, sorry, you mean ....") to the potential subgame himself (by making presuppostitions explicit), or by the responding interlocutor avoiding to initiate subgames and instead responding using inferences based on probability ("Presumably <I> is thinking in terms of ......").

Example III

```
zzz/qqq #37, <E>, 412 chars, 26-Oct-88 14:33
This is a comment to message 36
There is/are comment(s) on this message.
There are additional comments to message 36.

---------------------------
```

Presumably <I> is thinking in terms of a book selling for
$55 US dollars? Thats beginning to approach a days conference fees!
In terms of proportion of salary for US and UK based academics,
what does this mean? I would guess of the back of my enevelope that
a #30 stg book really costs a Briton the same as a $100 US book
would cost an American.

Any comments/refutations from the economists amongst us?

<E>

In general, subgames (for example, repair games, reference-identification games, and so on) seem to occur rarely in electronic dialogues. A subgame implies a shift of the language game into a lower gear. The gear shift mechanism is an important dialogic feature, which is very valuable in various types of spoken interaction. In particular, in pedagogical design situations, it may be important to realise that high gear utterances, which often have highly embedded structures with many latent subgames (many presuppositions), put much more strain on a listener, than a low gear variant (with a low level of embedding) of the same interaction type, where many subgames are processed one by one.

In Example I, move 3 shows that A has realized that B may be a new participant. Consequently, he obviously tries to adapt his use of language to the situation by expressing himself much more explicitly and more according to the convention of written text (hardly any lack of subjects and verbs). Still, a little reminder derived from the feeling of speech-like interaction sneaks in ("cos"). The first two sentences of move 3 constitute a full response to the reference-identification subgame, initiated by move 2. They represent a form of feedback in a wide sense, as they fulfill all the expectations created by move 2, without implying any closure of the subdialogue. Contrary to that, the remaining utterances of move 3 add new information, providing possibilities for a continuation of the dialogue. The information is of both phatic and emotive character insofar as it conveys the uncertainty of the interlocutor, and it serves as a contribution toward building up a shared context .

The "comforting words" of move 4 appear as a response to the phatic and emotive part of move 3 by reassuring an easy access to help if things go wrong. The language used in move 4 is implicit (for example, "them" and "stock") and in construction very similar to that of spoken dialogue — the position of the name at the end of the first utterance ("We've told them to get extra stock in, <A>"). It is clear that the interaction between the interlocutors A and C is marked by a shared background knowledge.

The features discussed in relation to Example I are typical for electronic dialogues with little time interval between the moves. The messages are short and speech-like and are constructed in a very implicit and context dependent way. This is possible as a shared context (at least for two of the interlocutors) is established already in move 1. For the third interlocutor that is not the case, as he does not possess enough background knowledge in order to fully interpret the information made very implicitly in move 1. Consequently, in an attempt to eventually come to share the background knowledge, he initiates a subgame (a latent subgame, which through the use of presuppositions is contained in move 1).

Example IV is an example of a dialogue with a break along the time dimension. It shows how a break in interactivity (a long time period between moves) has an impact on the issue of shared context.

The first part of move 2 in Example IV also serves the purpose of re-creating or resuming the "old" and "lost" background, which was the shared context and background for move 1, and on which the interlocutor of move 2 intends to make a move.

Example IV

1

========================

xxx/rrr #15, <F>, 107 chars, 21-May-90 15:20
This is a comment to message 14
There is/are comment(s) on this message.

If you don't mind living in a mad house, you are welcome to my settee!

<F>

Ps, I live 5 mins from the OU.

2

===

xxx/rrr #30, <G>, 356 chars, 11-Jun-90 23:57
There is/are comment(s) on this message.

TITLE: SOFA

A while ago, I seem to remember a sofa being offered by <F>. I
didn't take up the offer at the time as I thought <H> was
going to do so. As she isn't, is <F's> sofa still available?
I wouls e-mail you <F>, but I can't work out which of all the
aaa's you are. I have a camp bed I could bring as an
alternative. I am very clean and quiet!
<G>

3

===

xxx/rrr #31, <F>, 408 chars, 12-Jun-90 15:37
This is a comment to message 30

Hi <G>, the offer of a sofa is still going — in fact you may even
get a room (maybe not a bed though!!). If you want to e-mail re
details my user name is either aaa (for cosy) or bbb
(for work). You may need the camp bed as one of my sons sleeps
in a cabin bed and the other has a mattress on the floor. (They
should be away at their dad's that weekend so you won't have to
share!!!!!)

<F>

The first move of Example IV functions as a response to a previous move in
an interaction that was carried out over a very short time period. It appears
with linguistic features similar to those of spoken interaction. Move 2 is an
opener of a question-answer language game, which needs the now "lost"
context of move 1. Linguistically, we can observe tendencies as in Example I
in the way in which the move is constructed. The first half of move 2 mainly
shares features equivalent to those of traditional written interaction. The sentences are formed in a complete way, providing (together with the title) the
pre-orientation required to understand the "real" context-dependent move,
which is constituted by the rest of the message. Correspondingly, the second
part of move 2 also displays a noticeable shift in the style of the language.
The sentences are composed in a more speech-like manner ("I would e-mail
you, <F>"), and they all start with the subject and verb. In other words, the
sentences of the second half of move 2 are much more analytically composed
(like speech) than, for example, the first sentence, which displays a more syn-
thetical structure (like writing). The extended use of "I" in short sentences

seems to indicate the more involved interactive part of the message, whereas a prerequisite for the description of the context in the beginning of the move is detached reflection.

The first part of move 3 constitutes a pure feedback, which signals reception and satisfies the expectation created by move 2. The second part of the move contains additional information, which serves to further develop the shared knowledge as well as to provide a ground for a potential continuation of the game. Consequently, the general use of language in move 4 is rather explicit, and lies somewhere between speech and writing. The first part of the move, which forms the feedback, is a bit more speech-like than the rest. Similarly, the time interval in relation to move 2 shows a correspondingly intermediate value.

The examples of Examples I and IV have demonstrated a clear tendency in the material of electronic dialogues that I have been investigating. Although the significance of social and organizational factors, like roles (for example, moderator of conference, teacher of course, and so on) and levels of formality or "loyalty" toward the traditional style of writing in the electronic dialogues should not be underestimated, it seems to be a clear trend, linguistically viewed, that there is a dynamic relationship between the time frequency of the interactive moves on the one hand, and the level of context dependency of the linguistic character of the moves, on the other. Language games work towards termination. If a context (or frame) is already established, this stimulates the dialogue to a frequent exchange of moves. If too much time elapses between the exchanges, the context first has to be built or rebuilt. In the latter case, it slows down the efficiency of the information exchange.

In other words, the higher "interactivity" in the interaction, the higher level of shared context and background knowledge between interlocutors; or alternatively: the more the "interactivity" moves toward "synchrony" in the interaction (toward the situation of face-to-face meetings), the more shared "presence" in the style of the linguistic moves between the interlocutors.

Figure 16.1 illustrates the dynamic principle of interactivity in conferencing systems, indicating spoken and written interaction as representing the two contrasts of language use. The dynamic nature of the language used in conferencing systems is demonstrated by the flexibility with which it adapts to the frequency of exchanges. In other words, the higher the "speed" in the exchange of messages, the more the character and features of the linguistic interaction resemble the prototypical spoken interaction and language. Likewise, when the exchange of messages occur at longer intervals in time, the character of the interaction and use of language will resemble the prototypical written interaction.

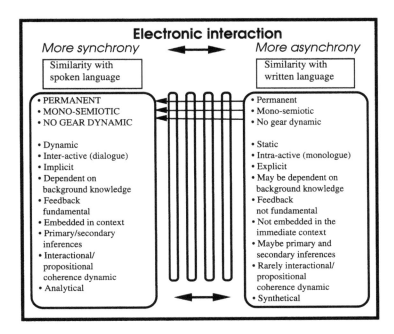

Fig. 16.1. The asynchronic principle of time in electronic dialogues

Although this appears as a general dynamic principle of the electronic inter-action, there seem to be certain permanent properties of the electronic inter-action that are not susceptible to this principle (Figure 16.1). First, the inter-action — despite a high level of interactivity — will never, as is the case with spoken dialogues, be transient. Due to the possibility for retrieval, this per-manence usually characterizing written dialogue has become a characteristic of the electronic interaction. Another invariant feature is the mono-semiotic constraint. Regardless of the level of interactivity, this will always be (at the present time) a condition of the electronic interaction. A third constant fea-ture, which the electronic dialogue seems to have taken over from written in-teraction, is the lack of a tendency to practise gear change in the interaction.

One part of the "ontological" foundation for the existence of conferen-cing systems is asynchrony in space. Viewing this in the light of the previ-ously mentioned dynamic principle, it implies that although the interactive situation moves very close to synchrony in time, a synchrony in space with all its implications and dialogical support (for example, shared situation, multi-semiotic communication, and so on) is not approached. In fact, even if a hy-pothetical total synchrony in time could be obtained, the situation of available linguistic and interactional features would not really differ, as a total synchrony in time would not imply a "new interactive reality." This is partly because it does not happen together with synchrony in space (it will still be mono-semiotic), and partly because the system in principle would treat any synchronous event asynchronously.

Compensational behavior

This subsection enlightens the mono-semiotic condition of the interaction in electronic dialogues, and points out consequences — some of which manifest themselves in compensational behavior. However, to put the whole phenomenon of electronic communication into perspective, I give an introductory account of the various verbal and non-verbal signs generally involved in the different communicative processes.

Communication between humans may be viewed as a process, which takes place within the frame of a wide semiotic system, representing the whole paradigm of possible ways of communicating information, that can be activated in human interaction. In a particular interaction, sometimes only one type of signs is used; in other cases of communicative acts, several types of signs complement each other, some of which may be more pertinent than others from the perspective of reaching a full understanding of the communicative act. The communication through this system of signs can be divided into verbal communication and non-verbal communication.

Verbal communication is understood as that part of a communicative process, that is manifested via linguistic signs, using words or combination of words — for example, spoken language.

Within *non-verbal communication* it is common to distinguish between paralinguistic communication and extralinguistic communication. *Paralinguistic communication* is the term used to denote the communication of non-verbal signs (for example, sound, facial expressions and gestures), which synchronously accompanies spoken verbal communication. *Extralinguistic communication* is communication using non-verbal signs of both auditive and visual nature (for example, sound, sneezes, burps, breathlessness, facial expressions, skin color, dressing) and is independent of any spoken verbal communication.

The verbal and non-verbal signs (or combinations of signs) usually take care of different types of communication. Generally speaking, the verbal signs are especially appropriate and useful for describing, explaining, and argumenting, whereas the most important function of the non-verbal signs is to communicate feelings, states of mind (for example, love, anger, irritation, happiness, sorrow, resignation, tiredness), and attitudes in relation to the communication partner (for example, superiority, inferiority, dominance and submission, contempt, sarcasm, friendship, enmity, and so on).

Several of the elements normally contained in non-verbal communication are pertinent to the interpretation of spoken linguistic communication. Pragmatically, non-verbal behaviour seems to entail not only the expression of social identity, personal traits, and psychological states, but also the signalling of reactions that stimulate the communication partner to react (Scherer and Giles, 1979). In addition, it is fairly well established, that: "(...) the course of a conversation is strongly influenced by the participants' inferences and attributions as to the social identity, personality disposition, and respective psychological states of their partners." (Van Dijk, 1985).

Semantically viewed, the most important role of non-verbal communication seems to be associated with signifying referents directly (for example, the hitchhiker's thumb), or it serves as a regulator in terms of amplifying (for example, energetic gestures, loud voice), contradicting (for example, contradictory face expressions during a phone-call), or modifying (for example, humorous/ironic flavors) the verbally communicated idea.

Also, from a dialogical point of view, non-verbal communication serves important functions, in particular, in asserting the existing relationship between participants in the conversation: "Non-verbal signs such as seating patterns, body posture, and voice quality may reflect the relationship of the interactants in terms of both an attraction-sympathy dimension and a power-dominance dimension (Mehrabian, 1969, 1972). The relative congruence of the sympathy and status cues in the non-verbal behaviour of the conversation partners reflects the degree to which there is a shared definition of the situation in terms of the course of the conversation." (Van Dijk, 1985).

In practice, most non-verbal behaviour is multi-functional in the sense that it serves more than one of the functions mentioned above (for example, a certain body gesture may indicate both a topic change or a speaker turn, intended by the speaker, and it may express a personal feature or/and emotional state).

Many cases of non-verbal communication are natural and inborn responses (for example, laughter, weeping). Although humans are conscious about this phenomenon and to a certain extent are able to control and regulate it, non-verbal communication is often more "reliable" than verbal communication in the sense that it is more difficult in the former than in the latter to simulate feelings and opinions.

Non-verbal communication is fundamental to us in the sense that we cannot avoid communicating non-verbally. This is always the case when it comes to extralinguistic types of non-verbal communication. Moreover, the previously mentioned paralinguistic non-verbal communication usually plays an important accompanying role in any spoken linguistic communication.

An experience shared by many users of conferencing systems is that the interaction type seems more similar to the prototypical case of spoken dialogue than to traditional written interaction. As we have seen, the character of the language use in language games with high interactivity supports this view. Also the choice of metaphors, which have named these systems, emphasises this aspect of the interaction. Nevertheless, the interaction is not a face-to-face interaction, and it does not share the same conditions as that of spoken dialogue. The only semiotic sign through which the interaction of an electronic dialogue can manifest itself is the written word.

As mentioned earlier, the so called paralinguistic semiotic signs synchronously accompany the verbal signs in spoken interaction. Their most important function is to communicate feelings, states of mind, and attitudes to the communication partner. In particular, non-verbal signs seem to entail the expression of social identity, personal traits, and psychological states. In general, these non-verbal signs often appear to be critical for a correct interpretation of an interactive move in spoken interaction. Consequently, as electronic interaction is mono-semiotic (taking place only through writing), it stimulates compensational behavior that is intended to communicate and support exactly those aspects of face-to-face communication that are normally taken care of by accompanying para-linguistic signs.

That the lacking possibility for communicating feelings, states of mind and attitudes to a communication partner is an obstacle that is complex to deal with in the electronic interaction is beyond any doubt. As the electronic interaction in conferencing systems is mono-semiotic, the only immediate possibility for communicating any of these elements in an electronic language game and thereby stimulating a stronger social connection between participants is a "translation" of the issue into those written symbols that are offered by the system/computer.

The following independent moves of dialogues illustrate some of the substitutes for non-verbal behavior that are intended to compensate for the lack of possibilities for multi-semiotic interaction. Examples V and VI illustrate what could be classified as a traditional translation of the state of mind of the interlocutor: example V: "(laugh)"), and example VI: "(gingerly)."

Example V

zzz/qqq #61, <J>, 169 chars, 19-Nov-88 19:39

TITLE: title
(Laugh) no, "cmcde" is cluttered ambiguity,

not cool ambiguity...

Cool ambiguity is found in sunglasses, Ode to Billie Joe, and "the rest is silence"....

Example VI

===========

xxx/yyy #55, <K>, 828 chars, 12-Aug-90 19:54
This is a comment to message 48
There is/are comment(s) on this message.
There are additional comments to message 48.

Tone (OUCH!)

Just read your comment to <L's> reply and have to say that I agree with both of you on this one.

I my typos increase it's because after reading mess. 48 my fingers are bandaged up and it is playing hell with my typing.

<K> (gingerly)
For I read if

The interlocutors of both examples have been through a process of conscious detached reflection in order to be able to translate these states of mind into descriptive language — first the process of analyzing the actual feeling, and then the process of translation into the right choice of words.

Example VI also provides a case ("(OUCH)"), which is a "traditional" linguistic translation of a feeling that in spoken dialogue is dependent on audible perception. In this case, additionally, the typographical features of the written signs have been activated to illustrate the strength of the sound in order to communicate that the move that stimulated the response in Example VI was too long and exhausting to read.

The next two examples (example VII: "HATE," "WHY," "KNOW," and example VIII: "YES <O> SEE YOU IN") illustrate a similar idea. However, in these cases the typographical features of the written language are not used directly to convey states of mind or feelings, but to "imitate" the intonation of the spoken dialogue. Indirectly, on an abstract level, one may talk about strong feelings, but directly the capital letters are used to add emphasis, illustrating the intonation. In Example VII it is clear that the possibilities for expression through the capital letters have not been felt sufficient, as the interlocutor has additionally made use of the strength of repetitive linguistic behaviour to convey his enthusiasm.

Example VII

===

zzz/qqq #50, <M>, 361 chars, 6-Nov-88 17:39
This is a comment to message 48
There are additional comments to message 48.

I HATE spells HATE indexing, but I can do it and have a fair amount of
experience. So if OU's not got a tame (paid!) indexer, I'll do it — just
give me advance earning and more than ten minutes to do the actual work.
(I'd also need to know rough length required of course.)

God, WHY did I not keep quiet? I KNOW I could have got a review copy
anyway.

<M>

Example VIII

===

xxx/rrr #58, <N>, 152 chars, 29-Jun-90 13:45
This is a comment to message 55

YES <O> SEE YOU IN the bar if I can find it.

<N> {{8-)
ps the signature is @reasonably@ self-descriptive. IE curly shoulder lemgth hair & glasses.

Example VIII also presents another type of compensational behavior. The
available signs on the computer keyboard are used creatively to compose an
iconografical sign, whose communication is entirely based upon visual perception and interpretation ("{{8-)" in example VIII is the picture of a happy
face with glasses). The same type of compensational communicative behaviour is present in example IX (":-)" is a happy face).

Example IX

===

xxx/yyy #2, <K>, 86 chars, 10-Aug-90 19:46
This is a comment to message 1
There is/are comment(s) on this message.
There are additional comments to message 1.

Isn't that just like a Scot jumping in before anyone else gets a
chance :-)

<K>

In Example IX (":-)"), the iconic information is pertinent to the interpretation. The visual information appears to be a rational choice, as the use of traditional descriptive language would be a rather laborious and time consuming alternative.

The compensational behavior in these examples clearly demonstrates a certain need for alternative communicating features, other than just those the written language can offer. There seems to be a need for investing "presence" and personal aspects into the interaction, — a need that may be caused by a combination of partly the often large distances (where chances for "in between face-to-face encounters" are limited), and partly the limitations imposed on the interaction as a consequence of the mono-semiotic condition.

In principle, all of these illustrated cases of compensational behavior can be translated into traditional written descriptions. However, doing so would imply a general delay and inertia in the communication process, which would not only be rather frustrating to deal with, but also remove all the spontaneity of the interaction (and, after all, it is the social, interactive aspect of conferencing systems that stimulates the communication). The compensating iconografical/indexical behavior can be viewed as a new and innovative element in the practice of writing that has appeared concurrently — in our culture — with the increasing importance of communication based on pictures or combinations of pictures and text. As for iconic/indexical signs, they may be easier and more direct to interpret, as they do not require a process of translation in the same sense as a written description, but are understood more directly through the impression they make on the senses. On this background, they may represent a more adequate "tool" for expressing exactly the areas of communication that are normally (in spoken dialogue) not covered by verbal communication (for example, feelings, states of minds, attitudes, and so on).

The independence of time and space

The aim of this subsection is to illustrate and discuss certain features of the interaction that may be caused mainly by the independence of time and space.

An electronic interaction appears like a complex mixture of distance and closeness. The feeling of distance may not only be related to the "real" geographical distance between interlocutors as much as to the impossibility of overcoming the asynchronous condition. Although the feeling of distance may vary quantitatively, an element of distance will always be present (of course, also reinforced by the lack of regulating non-verbal behavior). It is conceivable that this condition supports the regularly occurring lack of commitment to respond, which is usually perceived as being related to the size and number of questions posed in one move. Similar behavior is also common in face-to-face dialogues. There, however, it does not appear as a problem, as it gets regulated through repair games/subgames, which are easily and smoothly dealt with in spoken interaction. Still, it is worthwhile noticing the contradiction between this tendency and the ability to retrieve moves (the possibility for "refreshing" earlier moves, and thus realizing the expectations, still unfulfilled, of the language game).

The feeling of closeness may derive partly from the fact that it is always the choice of the interlocutor to "be close" or participate, if he wishes, as participants are always provided with a free choice to respond to or initiate a language game. Also, the metaphor supporting the idea of a shared room for the interaction, may help toward the feeling of closeness.

The following dialogue (X) illustrates how the phatic part of an opener has been viewed as essential and what response it has stimulated. This is once more an indication of the importance of the social aspect in the interaction. The question-opener of move 1 is ignored in the reaction in move 2.

Example X

1

---

xxx/ccc #7, <P>, 383 chars, 28-Mar-90 11:19
There is/are comment(s) on this message.

TITLE: hello fro,m Paris
I am now with <R> and his students in Paris, who will,
I hope; be taking pzart in this conference once they have leqrnt
how to use cosy
ps you will see errors in this message = this is one of the
problems of IT standardisation — keyboards are different in
different countries: what qre the imlicqtions for european
integrqtion of IT industries

2

---

xxx/ccc #8, <U>, 498 chars, 28-Mar-90 12:16
This is a comment to message 7.
There is/are comment(s) on this message.
There are additional comments to message 7.

Greetings, <P>

Good to see you on line from Paris. Yes, there are errors
in your message. I guess you were taking great care to type
accurately. This is not a serious problem as it is quite
easy top decipher your meaning. I believe that text can
accomodate much more serious degradation before meaning is
lost though, I guess the loss is progressive.

These kinds of textual errors could be compounded by problems
in using 8bit ASCII to accomodate foreign language accents,
I suppose.

<U>

The asynchronic conditions of electronic interactions imply a certain liberation from some of the social pressures that normally occur in spoken dialogues. As mentioned before, electronic communication accommodates individual time schedules. The social mechanisms utilized in face-to-face encounters (power, roles, and so on) seem to be less imposing, which gives more
room for the interlocutor to interact more freely on conditions mainly imposed by the system. For various idiosyncratic reasons (psychological, and so
on) an interlocutor in a face-to-face dialogue may for example feel appre-
hensive to express his views, or he may need more time to consider precisely
what he wants to comment. The electronic dialogue implies a freedom to
choose between interacting spontaneously in a similar way to spoken dialogue, or interacting in a way, which allows for reflection and consideration as
in the written style. This is a feature that gives room for a wide range of types
of personalities. On the one hand, communicating asynchronously and
mono-semiotically in written language is likely to balance out some of these
social and psychological effects (for example, lack of abilities to think and
answer fast, dominance from certain participants, and so on). On the other
hand, compared to spoken dialogue, an electronic written communication
puts new demands on the participants in terms of skills, not only with respect
to form, but also concerning the ability to explicitly express thoughts
through writing.

Furthermore, the asynchrony of time and space also makes available to the
interlocutor another communicative property with social implications: The interlocutor always has access to the conversational floor (he does not need to
obey the discursive constraints of a face-to-face situation) and he is always
in charge of the interactive situation (decides when to speak and when to listen). Thus, the problem of turn taking is absent. There are no normative rules
and requests for maintaining a balance between when to "make space for
oneself" and when to "make space for the others." In this respect the elec-

tronic setting does not support the outbreak of quarrels. Of course in the electronic world it is possible to be rude in the use of language, but — as the interactive situation in electronic dialogues does not impose any rules for social behavior (like those involved in a traditional face-to-face encounter) — it is not possible to create disagreements on the meta-linguistic level in a discussion. In other words: To create arguments rooted in the interaction itself (for example, to interrupt, to shout loud and as a consequence cause another interlocutor not to be heard, and so on).

As discussed earlier, the linguistic interaction in a conferencing system is mono-semiotic in as far as the communication is established entirely through writing. This has various general implications. As in traditional letter writing, it provides the interlocutors in a dialogue with a possibility for *controlling identity*: "When writing, it is easier to choose a tone and attitude than it is in speech, dress and gesture. The social subject is profoundly modified by the generalization of such highly controlled forms of self-presentation. The written "I" is not the same "I" who appears in face-to-face encounters. This new "I" has increased its distance from the world and itself." (Feenberg, 19889.

The interlocutor has a possibility for deciding upon the image that he wishes to convey. The written subject (the "I") does not necessarily convey the same identity as the subject (the "I") of a face-to-face encounter. The transmitted written "I" may be a non-interactive "I," arrived at through personal detached reflection and modification. In addition, electronic dialogues also open up the possibility for a less committed behavior in relation to the interaction. It is easier — and more "accepted" — to avoid or delay a reaction electronically than in face-to-face encounters.

A final consequence to be pointed out here, which is related to the independence of the interaction from time and space, is an issue mostly affecting the receiving situation of the interlocutor. As production and comprehension of messages occur at different times and independently of each other, a move is never topical, viewed in relation to the mind of the author. The more time elapses, the more distant the subject. Considering the discussed mechanism between time intervals, the establishment of context/frame and the degree of explicitness in the language use, this is a potential source of interpretative problems, as the responding interlocutor has no chance of predicting the length of time that will elapse before his answer gets read (in other words: How does a responding interlocutor communicate with the "appropriate level" of presuppositions?).

Final discussion

This final section provides comments and thoughts on the new interactive potential embedded in this particular type of software, which enables establishment of on-line communities in organizations, independent of time and space. Some thoughts are given to the inherent conflict in electronic communication: the qualitative difference in nature between the computer system and the domain for which it is being utilized (human linguistic interaction).

It seems clear to me that a relatively frequent and regular interactivity in the electronic communication always will prove to be most successful. The analysis indicates that it will be this type of usage that challenges the potential of the systems. From a philosophical perspective, if we accept the point of view that an individual has "primary access to the world" through pragmatic involved action rather than detached, objectified reflection (even though such a view may go against the idea of the purpose of a conferencing system) and that language games are social activities or "intersubjective practice" (Pelle Ehn, 1988), then it is conceivable that a very low frequency of interactivity (as it, among other things, implies reflection on the reconstruction of context/frame) may have a negative impact in terms of lowering the quality and success of the communicative tasks for which the system is utilized.

A inherent conflict in electronic communication is the qualitative difference in nature between the computer system and the domain for which it is being utilized. The computer system is fundamentally based on the principle of formalisation. In contrast to this stands the domain for which the system is being used, linguistic interaction — a fundamentally social phenomenon, carried out dynamically between human beings. In dealing with electronic human-human interaction in electronic communication systems, we are trying to "merge" the formalized world of the computer and the dynamic, unpredictable, and involved domain of human linguistic interaction. This is a very complex task. A problematic example of a combination of these two domains, which visualizes this conflict, has been demonstrated with "The Coordinator" (Winograd and Flores), a communication system designed on a fundamental principle of reflection on the function of every planned communicative act. Among other things, this design did not allow for the growth of the dynamic and social elements in an interaction. To be forced to reflect on the function of one's action before carrying it out is likely to remove all possibilities for spontaneity, stimulation of phatic behavior and high "interactivity." Nevertheless, it seems fundamental that when we are dealing with the world of the computer and computer systems, we are also dealing with an "ontological" request to formalize. The usual controversial points to discuss in this respect will be "how" to do it and "to what extent."

In this chapter I have, pragmatically through analysis, pointed out some important consequences of the asynchronic conditions of time and space. I shall leave it as a challenge to pursue in the future to what extent the conflictive combination of on the one hand, the formal nature of the computer system, and on the other, the dynamic domain of linguistic interaction, contributes to these consequences. It is conceivable that the mixture of human interaction and machine interaction can give rise to complex discussions within this framework. An example where the integration of these two types of interaction arise and presents itself as one communicative unit (when an interlocutor is "listening"/reading) is provided next:

Example XI

```
zzz/qqq #37, <E>, 412 chars, 26-Oct-88 14:33
This is a comment to message 36
There is/are comment(s) on this message.
There are additional comments to message 36.

--------------------------

Presumably <I> is thinking in terms of a book selling for
$55 US dollars? Thats beginning to approach a days conference fees!
.............
<E>
```

The "receiving" interlocutor is presented not only with the semantic content of another interlocutor's move, but also with the structural context of the dialogue (the formalized structure, assigned by the system/system designer). The structural formalized context of the dialogue is intended to "express" in some way the semantic context of the dialogue (by retrieving the relevant moves, it is possible to recall the semantic context). As we have seen, however, this structural formalization does not replace the need of the interlocutors in the human-human interaction for linguistically and interactively rebuilding the semantic context.

From a concrete pragmatical perspective, it seems clear that it is important to comprehend the nature of this new type of linguistic interaction and reconsider its specific potential in relation to the domain in which it is intended to be utilized. In this respect, the amount of phatic behavior in electronic dialogues may suggest a fundamental potential of conferencing systems for maintaining social relations between people who are geographically dispersed. As, for example, stated by Tony Kaye, when describing the social potential of conferencing systems utilized in the area of distance education: "CMC can become for distance learners the electronic equivalent of the bar, the lounge, the cafeteria, the many other sites of social exchange which play such an important role in on-campus life." (Kaye, 1988).

One useful pragmatical advice is that regardless of the type of communicative task for which the system is being used, it is important to "nourish" the spontaneous dynamic interaction (to allow for free, phatic behavior). This strategy does not, however, provide any theoretical solution to the basic conflict.

In my view, a computer conferencing system provides possibilities for a new type of human interaction. This interaction is susceptible to a dynamic principle related to time, and has general characteristics that resemble the features of, respectively, spoken and written interaction. Although the interaction appears as if it was spoken and shares a high degree of the features of spoken dialogue (due to an often high interactivity), it also contains certain permanent properties, typical of written interaction, that are not subject to the same dynamic principle of time. Finally, the interactional behaviour in electronic dialogues also demonstrates transcendence in as far as it incorporates features that are new in relation to both spoken and written interaction: communication through a combination of written text and pictures.

Using a more abstract frame of reference, the new type of linguistic interaction may also be viewed as representing a movement toward using the written word in an "ontologically" different manner than it is traditionally being used. The result is an interaction that possesses some of the most distinctive and pertinent features of spoken interaction: dynamism and interactivity. Whereas the reflective property of traditional written behavior corresponds to the rationalistic tradition and to the idea of dualism, this request for reflection may in written electronic interaction be transcended and become "intersubjective practice." Instead of using the written word in a detached manner, the new type of communication offers the choice of assimilating exactly those fundamentally social, cooperative, and interactive aspects that are essential to human existence.

Bibliography

ANWARD, J. (1983). *Språkbruk och språkutveckling i skolan.* Lund: Liber Förlag.

ANDERSEN, P. B. (1986). Semiotics and Informatics: Computers as Media, in *Information, Technology, and Information Use. Towards a Unified View of Information and Information Technology*, eds. P. Ingwersen, L. Kajberg, A. M. Peitersen. London:Taylor Graham.

ANDERSEN, P. B. (1988). Arbejde og tegn. Nogle resultater fra et forskningsprojekt om EDB-systemer, arbejde og sprog. *Kultur og Klasse*, nr. 61, pp 51-70. København.

ANDERSEN, P. B.,WILLE, N. E. (1986). Kommunikation og EDB. Om sprog-brugsanalysens relevans for analyse, udvikling og vurdering af EDB-systemer. *MedieKultur* no. 2, pp 45-69. Aalborg.

COULTHARD, M. (1977). *An Introduction to Discourse Analysis*. London: Longman.

DIJK, T. A. van ed. (1985). *Handbook of Discourse Analysis*. Volume 2. Dimensions of Discourse. London: Academic Press.

EHN, P. (1988). *Work-Oriented Design of Computer Artifacts*. Stockholm: Arbetslivscentrum.

EKLUNDH, K. S. (983). *The Notion of Language Game — A Natural Unit of Dialogue and Discourse*. Linköping 1: SIC 5, University of Linköping, Dept. of Communication Studies.

EKLUNDH, K. S. (1986). *Dialogue Processes in Computer-Mediated Communication. A Study of Letters in the COM System*. Malmö: Liber Förlag AB.

FEENBERG, A. (1989). The Written World. In *Mindweave*, ed. by Robin Mason and Anthony Kaye. Oxford: Pergamon Press.

FLORES, F., GRAVES, M., HARTFILD, B., WINOGRAD, T. (1988). *Computer Systems and the Design of Organizational Interaction*. ACM Transactions on Office Information Systems, Vol. 6, no. 2, pp 153-172.

FLORES, F., WINOGRAD, T. (1986). *Understanding Computers and Cognition*. A New Foundation for Design. Norwood, New Jersey: Ablex Corporation.

GOFFMAN, E. (1971). *Relations in Public. Microstudies of the Public Order*. Harmondsworth: Penguin Books.

GRADDOL, D. (1989). Some CMC Discourse Properties and their Educational Significance. In *Mindweave*, eds. Robin Mason and Anthony Kaye. Oxford: Pergamon Press.

HILTZ, S. R. (1984). *Online Communities. A Case Study of the Office of the Future*. New Jersey: Ablex Publishing Corporation. Norwood.

KAYE, A. (1989). Computer-Mediated Communication and Distance Education. In *Mindweave*, ed. Robin Mason, Anthony Kaye. Oxford: Pergamon Press.

KAYE, A., HARASIM, L., MASON, R. (1988). *Computer Conferencing in the Academic Environment*. CITE Report No. 91. Centre for Information Technology in Education. Milton Keynes: The Open University.

KOEFOED, O. (1981). *Noget om semiotik. En indføring i de semiotiske beskriv-elsesmetoder*. København: Romansk Institut, Københavns Universitet.

LINELL, P. (1978). *Människans språk. En orientering om språk, tänkande och kommunikation*. Lund: Liber Förlag.

LINELL, P. (1982). *The Written Language Bias in Linguistics*. Linköping: SIC 2, University of Linköping, Studies in Communication.

LYTTKENS, L. (1982). *Människors möten: En undersökning af samspelets natur*. Bodafors: Doxa.

RICOEUR, P. (1978). *The rule of metaphor. Multi-disciplinary studies of the creation of meaning in language*. London: Routledge & Kegan Paul.

SACKS, H., SCHEGLOFF, E. A. (1973). Opening up Closings. *Semiotica* no. VIII, pp 289-327. The Hague: Mouton.

SORENSEN, E. K. (1990). *A Comparative Evaluation of CMC Systems*. Aarhus: Jutland Open University.
WITTGENSTEIN, L. (1974). *Philosophical Investigations*. Oxford: Basil Blackwell.

17

Historical trends in computer and information technology

JENS CHRISTENSEN

It has been truly said that the computer is the most economically important technological innovation of this century. No other piece of technology has expanded in a way comparable to that of the computer. A vast computer industry has emerged, and what is perhaps even more important, since the 1980s applied computer technology has spread so widely throughout the worlds of business, public administration, science, and so on. that an economy of information seems to be substituting the industrial economy. "Information" also indicates the tremendous changes that have taken place in computing technology and applied technology since computing started in the 1940s. What began as the history of computing is now being transformed into the history of information technology and information society. It is no wonder that the historian and the social and economic analyst of modern technology are experiencing difficulties in coping with this huge and expanding field of research.[1]

Until the 1980s, the American computer industry dominated the international development of the computer, and IBM surpassed any other company to such a degree that everybody else was reduced to followers of the leader. The 1980s saw changes in this pattern, however. European and particularly Japanese industry rose to equal the Americans in many fields of technology,

---

[1] The history of the computer has mainly been dealt with from a technical point of view, with the emphasis on the early periods, as can be seen in the articles of the journal *Annals of the History of Computing*. This is also true for the book of Ralston/Reilly, eds., *Encyclopedia of Computer Science and Engineering*, 1983, which in many ways is a brilliant resumé of computer development until the early 1980s, and it also applies to general historical surveys of computers, like Augarten *Bit by Bit*, 1984. Only recently have broader and more present perspectives been applied to the development of the computer and ofinformation technology. In the following, *references* are only given to important literature of a general kind, which in turn contains references to more detailed studies.

The *approach* applied to the history of computer and information technology in this context is meant to combine the often used way of deviding computer history into generations (Augarten , 1984), mainly based on components, and broader perspectives, like the one focusing on the character of changing constraints opposing and pushing computer development (Friedman, 1989), with the approach of economic and political movers of the world. The text is organized around two perspectives, namely that of the producers and that of applied technology.

while industry and applications were being radically changed all over the place. This trend has continued into the 1990s. But in many ways the Americans and IBM is still in the lead technologically and economically, which makes the U.S. computer industry, and IBM in particular, a natural starting point and focus for an outline of the history of the computer.

The making of the computer in the 1940s and 1950s: The American military mover

The computer grew out of the Second World War and the following Cold War (the subject is dealt with generally by Augarten, 1984: 99-164. Digital Computers: History: 535-544. Sobel, 1981: 95-115. Flamm, 1988: 29-46. Metropolis/Howlett/Rota, eds, 1980). The war made each of the belligerent nations form a so-called *"military-industrial complex"* of close relations between state and industry to fulfil the objects of war. The strategic importance of high technology based on industrial and scientific-technical strength should prove a crucial lesson for the post-war period. The American military-industrial complex was not dissolved after the war, being the foundation of an emerging global Pax Americana, and neither was the complex of the other new superpower, the Soviet Union.

When the Cold War broke out in the late 1940s, two opposing regimes and systems started an ever-growing arms race, based on their respective military-industrial complexes. The computer turned out to be the most important and most complicated part of this high-tech and electronically-inspired arms race. So far, the computers of the Soviet Union have remained mainly within the fields of the military-industrial complex, and they have stayed in the dark, as well. On the American side, however, the military-funded computers eventually gave rise to a U. S. led computer industry to revolutionize the world of technology and economy. That is why the history of computer technology until lately may be considered primarily an American affair.

In the late war years, small groups of scientists and engineers in most of the belligerent countries were working on the problems of design and construction of what was to become the computer. The most influential line of development took place at the Moore School of Electrical Engineering at the University of Pennsylvania in the United States. In 1943 a team led by Mauchley and Eckert started on an army contract to build a machine for ballistic calculations. This work led to the making of ENIAC, which was completed by the end of the year 1945. ENIAC turned out to be not just a dedicated machine for calculations. It was really a general-purpose device, programmed by changing interconnected plugs.

While ENIAC was being constructed, a group of people, including Eckert, Mauchley, Goldstine, and von Neumann, began to meet to develop the conceptual design of the stored-program computer known as EDVAC. The stored-program computer was developed to get rid of the time consuming and inflexible way of programming of ENIAC. EDVAC was made on an army contract, too.

The concept of EDVAC and the stored-program computer was first clearly described in papers by *von Neumann* in 1945-46. To the general idea of the computer as a system consisting of a central processor and memory as well as some peripheral input-output equipment meant to manipulate data by means of programming, von Neumann added at least two important concepts — the concept of the stored program and that of the program counter. Accordingly, instead of the wiring of ENIAC, programming of the computer and computing were matters of logical principles, allowing for more powerful and smaller machines. Basically the present computer is founded on the same principles as those designed by von Neumann in the mid 1940s. That is why it is still called the von Neumann computer.

ENIAC was built to do ballistic calculations, but not being finished before the end of the war it was also used otherwise, for computing some of the complex problems concerning the building of the H-bomb, and in working on it for years ENIAC stood the test and paved the way for the computer. EDVAC was contracted to do the same kind of calculations as ENIAC. The completion was delayed for years, however, due to the dissolution of the Moore School computer group. But experiences from the EDVAC project spread through the people involved, by circulating papers, and by having discussions with other research teams and government representatives, which led to the appearance of the first *international computer science environment*. Accordingly, in 1950 a number of industrial countries had the brain power needed to build a computer, but it would prove crucial to the future of computer technology that the United States alone had the money and the needs required to increase computer power (discounting the Russians).

Whirlwind, SAGE, and Stretch

The original design by von Neumann was just the beginning. There was still a long way to go in the making of the modern computer. Three military financed projects brought the computer technology past its infancy and led the way toward a commercial future: The Whirlwind project of the late 1940s and early 1950s, followed by SAGE, the world's biggest computer project of the 1950s, and the Stretch project of the late 1950s and the early 1960s.[2]

Since 1945, a group led by Jay Forrester at MIT had worked on a military project for designing and building a computer for flight simulation. In 1947, Forrester's group had designed a high-speed electronic digital computer capable of operating in real-time named the *Whirlwind*. The Whirlwind computer called for another important invention. Its internal memory, based on electrostatic tubes, was unreliable and very costly. A better form of memory was needed, and in 1949 Forrester came up with the idea of the magnetic-core memory. It took four years to put the idea into practice, but the effect on performance was startling: speeding up processing and reducing maintenance time considerably. And for the next two decades, computers were generally based on magnetic-core memory.

In the meantime, the Soviet Union exploded an atom bomb in 1949 and was found to have developed long-range bombers capable of reaching the United States. In 1950 the U.S. government decided on a multi-billion dollar project to upgrade the existing defense batteries and develop a comprehensive computerised network for North America. The Air Force asked MIT to establish a research center to design and supervise the construction of such a network. MIT was promised all the money it needed. The Whirlwind computer, the world's only real-time computer, became the basis of the new so-called *SAGE* computer and technology.

The SAGE computers built in the years to come did not only constitute the largest computing centre of the 1950s. It was also a center of technological development that decisively pushed the computer toward its breakthrough. Apart from real-time computing it produced multiprocessing, computer networks and interactive monitors. It was the first computer to use magnetic-core memories as well as 16 bit and 32 bit computers, plus back-up computing and fault-tolerant systems. SAGE was a matter of system building, huge system building. That may be its most important contribution to the American computer industry. SAGE taught the computer industry to design and build large, interconnected, real-time data-processing systems. In this way SAGE paved the way for the modern computer system.

Stretch was the name of a high-speed computer built between 1956 and 1961 by IBM for the Atomic Energy Commission. Stretch was intended to reflect the most advanced technology and knowledge of the time. Transistors were substituted for vacuum tubes, it used parallel processing,

---

[2] The best and most detailed investigation of the technical development from punched-card machines to computers of the second generation is probably the one presented in Bashe et al., 1986. For further references see Augarten , 1984, pp. 195-223. Flamm, 1987, pp. 53-58, 86-95. Molina 1989, pp. 36-62. The Whirlwind is thoroughly treated in Redmond/Smith, 1980.

and it had a very high-performance disk drive, advanced peripherals, and so on. Being the most powerful computer of its time the Stretch project contributed substantially to the making of the new computer architecture, components, and manufacturing techniques of the second and third generation of computers — thereby "stretching" the gains of the two preceding projects.

Fortran and Cobol

The early computers were difficult to program, being based on machine code and with the programmer fiddling directly with the wiring (Augarten, 1984: 210-217. A short survey is given in Software History: 1353-1359. Detailed treatments are found in Sammet, 1969, in Wexelblatt, ed, 1981, and in Bashe et al., 1986: 315-371). So-called *"assembly languages"* or "symbolic languages" were developed to increase productivity. The time for programming and for processing the calculations in those days was somewhat reduced by substituting symbols for binary codes, translated automatically into machine code by internal programs called "assemblers."

The programmers still had to spend a lot of time writing all the subroutines of indexing, floating point operations, handling input and output, and so on. And since computers spent most of their time carrying out such subroutines, data processing was slowed down, too. Consequently, the computer system of the early 1950s had two major bottlenecks: programming and the architecture of the machine. Leading programmers and scientists of IBM, Remington Rand, and MIT, the three centers of early computing, began working on the idea of *"automatic" programming*, as it was called. If indexing, floating-point, and input/output operations could be performed automatically by computers, both the programmers and the machines would be freed from the most time-consuming parts of the computing of those days.

During most of the 1950s, small groups of leading programmers and scientists worked still more intensively on turning the idea of automatic programming into practice. What came out of it were *the compiler and the high-level language*. IBM took the lead in these matters, and kept it. In 1957, IBM launched the world's first real compiler and high-level language called "Fortran" (Formula Translation) made for the 704, and distributed to every 704 installation. Some of IBM's big customers had actually been represented in the groups developing what was to become Fortran. Soon, Fortran compilers were developed for other IBM computers and by license from IBM for competing machines, too. It became the first software standard of the world, and through revised editions it has remained an international standard for scientific computing up to the present.

For business applications, for which Fortran was not well suited, other languages were developed soon after, "Cobol" being the most widely used. Cobol was developed in the late 1950s by a group of American computer manufacturers and big users organized under the Department of Defense. Standards were made for Fortran and Cobol by the American Standard Bureau. For decades, these two languages were to dominate the world of programming and the compiler, leading to true operating systems.

The computer industry

In 1951, Univac delivered its first Univac I to the U. S. Census Bureau for handling the data of the national census of 1950, introducing the age of commercial data processing (Fisher/Mckie/Mancke, 1983: 3-98; Flamm, 1988: 80-94, 105-127; Sobel, 1981: 138-184; Molina, 1989: 36-60). UNIVAC was designed by Eckert and Mauchley, whose company had been taken over by Remington Rand. It was based on their experience from ENIAC, especially from EDVAC.

However, the typical computer of the early 1950s was a large machine ordered by some American military department for the purpose of doing huge calculations. In 1952 IBM, the biggest data-processing company in the world, was chosen as contractor to build the SAGE computers. Consequently, IBM benefited from all the technological inventions of the SAGE project. The experience gained from this project and from its enormously expanded R&D department in computers undoubtedly convinced the IBM management that the company had to make computers the commercial foundation of the future. Accordingly, IBM turned the technological benefits that stemmed from the SAGE project, including a new computer architecture and new methods of programming, into commercial computers and computer systems.

In 1953, IBM delivered its first 701 meant for scientific computing and in 1955 its first 702 for commercial data processing, followed shortly afterward by 704 and 705. Like Univac II and other Remington machines the IBM 704 and 705 were developed to contain the new magnetic core memory. All these so-called *first-generation* computers used vacuum tube components, but they varied as to storage medium, trying to find the most reliable and cheapest one. From the mid 1950s practically all computers of the first generation, and from the late 1950s, of the second generation, based on transistors, used magnetic core storage memory.

In the late 1950s, IBM and its competitors began to introduce their *second generation* and transistorized commercial computers. Based on the technological experiences of SAGE and Stretch, IBM delivered its new 7000 series of large machines to replace the 704 and 705, and a new 1400 series of smaller machines in stead of the popular 650. The 1401, in particular, became very widely distributed and several thousand were installed through out the 1960s. The new high-speed printer and disk drive and a multiplied processing speed, due to the new transistor components, transformed the computers of the second generation into more coherent systems, smaller in size and more usable.

New *competitors* appeared on the scene during the second generation of computers, IBM being by then the dominant company of an emerging new industry. Remington Rand and Sperry, which merged under the name of Sperry Rand, had lost ground but was still number two. Control Data was a newcomer, building very advanced computers. Burroughs and NCR, producers of accounting machines, cash registers, and so on, took up producing computers for their traditional customers. Burroughs and NCR did not switch to computers as completely and as determinedly as IBM, and they entered the market around 1960 when IBM was delivering its successful second generation of computers. Since the *computer market* was still rather *limited*, however, newcomers and older converts did not establish any big computer companies.

Applications

In the *first half of the 1950s*, about twenty computers were built, and with very few exceptions they were made for *military purposes*, mainly doing scientific and engineering calculations.[3] The processing of business data, however, took over in the second half of the 1950s and in the early 1960s.

Apart from advanced machines such as SAGE, whose technology did not become widespread until the third generation of computers, the typical computer of the 1950s was made to do simple arithmetical operations in large numbers. Therefore, the *first business activities* to be computerized were highly structured, administrative routines on a large scale, which had already been partially mechanized. The simple computer technology of those days did not allow for systems to do more than just reproduce existing routines and activities. Only huge organizations doing large-scale operations could hope to make any savings in cost from the very expensive computers of the

---

[3] Friedman, 1989, pp. 81-88. Digital Computers: History, pp. 535-544, passim. For SABRE, the first real-time business system for airline reservations, developed from the mid fifties until the mid sixties, see Bashe et al., 1986, pp. 516-522. For user groups, see Bashe et al., 1986, pp. 347-349, 364-366, and also Computer User Groups, pp. 375-376. To deal properly with applications would call for research into user organizations involved, surpassing the scope of this chapter.

fifties. Another reason for the introduction of computers was the increasing number of transactions that went beyond the limits of electro-mechanical technology. Large insurance companies, banks, government agencies, defence industries, and so on pioneered data processing.

The first business applications were batch systems, which had no direct user interface to the computer. Central data processing (DP) departments were established in large organizations, computerizing office activities, such as accounting, payroll, invoice billing, and so on. The advanced and extremely costly computer systems of SAGE had to wait a decade or more for business applications.

Like the early computer industry, applied computer technology of the 1950s was dominated by the Americans. Big corporations and government agencies formed imposing user partners from the start. For example in 1955, while preparing for the 704 to follow the 701, users of the machine united to secure a better assembler than the one proposed by IBM. They formed a user-group called Share, probably the first of its kind, consisting of the following users: the National Security Agency, the Atomic Energy Commission, 8 aerospace companies (Boeing, Hughes etc.), three industrial corporations (GE, GM and Standard Oil) — and IBM. A similar user-group called Guide was formed just a few months later of IBM users of commercial computers (702 and 705). While Share was mainly aimed at research and development communities, Guide had a broader appeal to large business establishments such as banks, insurance companies, department stores, and so on.

The breakthrough of the computer in the 1960s and 1970s. The world according to IBM

Around 1960, vacuum tubes gave way to transistors and a new generation of machines appeared. A few years later it was followed by a third generation of components, the integrated circuit, which revolutionized the computer technology (Augarten, 1984: 225-251. Flamm, 1987: 51-75. Molina, 1989: 39-98. A general history of the component is presented in Braun/MacDonald, 1982).

The transistor was invented in 1947 at The Bell Labs. It spread to the electronic industry, first in connection with hearing aids in 1953 and with transistor radios in 1954. In 1956 the scientists at MIT and IBM, who were working on SAGE, started developing a transistorized computer to replace the huge vacuum-tube machines of SAGE. While the invention and application of the transistor were taking place, an even more promising technology was emerging for the making of electronic components — that of the semiconductor *integrated circuit*. It meant a much more miniaturized solution. And that was precisely what the American Defence Department was looking for and spending millions of dollars on developing, when space technology, from the late 1950s, became part of the arms race between the United States and the Soviet Union. Consequently, the need for miniaturized electronic circuits increased. Around 1960, the first integrated circuits appeared, but until the mid-1960s they were too expensive to be used in computers outside NASA or any military and highly advanced field.

The strategic importance of computer technology was further stressed by The Defence Advanced Research Projects Agency (DARPA), which has funded and supported basic and applied research in math and computers since 1960, dealing with *innovative fields* such as timesharing, networks, artificial intelligence, advanced microelectronics, computer architecture, and graphics.

But generally speaking, the 1960s brought an end to the total military dominance of computer technology of the 1950s. The economic *importance of military demands diminished* in the 1970s, and apart from a temporary revival in the 1980s, through the Strategic Defense Initiative, to build a space-based ballistic missile defence (the so-called "star wars" program) — note the parallel to SAGE of the 1950s — it never regained the crucial position it had in the 1950s. The 1960s saw the beginning of a new era of mass production and use of computer technology, a true breakthrough in computer technology.

The computer industry

In the early 1960s, IBM had become "the sun" of the computer world, with a number of smaller competing companies circling around it like "moons," trying to adapt to and take advantage of any opportunity given by IBM. However, the computer still played only a minor role in the American economy as a whole. To put the computer into the heart of the economy, radical steps had to be taken. At the beginning of the 1960s, the IBM leadership also realized that during this decade the newly launched second generation of transistorized computers would be superseded by a new generation of computers based on the integrated circuit component. If IBM wanted to keep on dominating the computer industry, it had to plan according to these prognoses, otherwise it might very well end up as just one company among several others, like the Univac of Sperry Rand.

In December 1961, a special committee called SPREAD (The Systems Programming, Research, Engineering, and Development Committee), representing all major parts of the corporation, issued a report that recommended a new product line, later to be known as the *system/360* (Fisher/McKie/Mancke, 1983: 101-142; Sobel, 1981: 208-232; Flamm,1988: 96-102). The report recommended a completely new family of computers based on the best applicable technology. The management accepted the plan, although it was unimaginably risky and costly.

Considerable improvements in price/performance by the 360, compared with the second generation computers, would demand some kind of circuit technology to replace transistors. After much debate it was decided not to go all the way to integrated circuits (IC), but to stop at a hybrid called Solid Logic Technology (SLT). The ICs were at that point about to be used in the NASA space program. They were still rather expensive, and insufficiently developed and adjusted for automatic production to make them as cheap as was desirable. The SLT met all the objectives: higher performance, reduced size, it required less space power and cooling and was much more reliable — all able to be produced at a reduced cost.

The SLT could be adapted for automatic production. Substantial investments in automatic manufacturing tools and techniques allowed for an increase in performance and a reduction in prices. A remarkable rise in productivity was generally obtained by a widespread use of automation. Standardization, compatibility, and modularity allowed for that.

Better components are just one element in increased performance. Faster and consequently more complex systems are of no use unless there is an equivalent improvement in computer architecture. First of all, IBM had to automate as much as possible of the management of resources provided by the system, such as on-line, multi-terminal, real-time, and multiprogramming applications in order to make sure that the user would benefit from the computer's total processing power. Therefore IBM developed a set of operating systems, the OS/360 being the most complex and ambitious of these. The OS/360 was a generalization of "every aspect of operating systems known at the time." It was delayed because of its complexity, while the other, more specific and less complex operating systems of the 360 worked right from the start in 1964. Printers, terminals, disk drives, and other new peripherals allowed for better and faster performance, while modularity and compatibility made it possible to combine "a wide variety of peripheral equipment ... in a very wide range of configurations," thus paving the way for large transaction systems (Fisher et al., 1983: 118-119).

The IBM management decided to design and fabricate all parts of the new system by themselves. Huge new factories were built and its workforce was increased by thousands. The making of the system/360 meant a total and world-wide involvement on the part of IBM. It was turned into one of the first truly transnational corporations in the world, dividing development and manufacturing between American and European centres and controlled by general plans and standards for design and production. "By the mid-1960s, all aspects of IBM's operations were geared toward a single international market, with research and development, component production, and systems assembly allocated among different units around the globe, based on relative costs and the availability of specialised resources in different geographical locations" (Flamm, 1988: 101). IBM competitors followed suit, and the U. S. computer industry generally shifted toward international markets.

Designing and producing the system/360 constituted the greatest project ever launched by a private company. It is said to have cost IBM 5 billion dollars in 1960s prices (approximately 50 billion dollars in present day prices), indicating the extreme risks taken by the company. IBM was rewarded for its courage, however, since the system/360 was probably the most successful product to have been marketed in the history of capitalism. It completely revolutionized the computer industry, as it did the use of computers. The 360 started the mass production and the massive use of computer power in all the main sectors of Western economy; and in the late 1960s, it was followed by institutionalized computer science and education in every industrial country.

Aggressive salesmanship, based on its technological and economic leadership, made IBM set the agenda for this breakthrough in computer technology. Probably no other economic sector has ever been and will ever be so total dominated by one single corporation, as the computer industry and the computer world were by IBM in the 1960s and 1970s. The system/360 became the standard system for IBM, as it did for the world. Competing companies would have to find niches for survival and growth where IBM left room for such competition. What Ford did to the automobile industry in the early twentieth century, IBM managed to do to the computer industry half a century later.

IBM "remained in heaven" for about five years, after introducing the system/360 in the mid-1960s (Fisher/McKie/Mancke, 1983: 143-449; Sobel, 1981: 233-253; Flamm, 1988: 102-133). But by the end of the decade, IBM was beginning to feel "the effects of obsolescence and of *competitive pressures*: pricing actions and product line enhancements and improvements from system manufacturers; rapid introductions of "plug-compatible" peripheral equipment ... ; and the activities of leasing companies.." (Fisher et al., 1983: 366). In the early 1970s, the revenues of IBM's competitors grew substantially more than those of IBM. Increasing user concern about high costs, including the one expressed by the largest customer of all, the federal government, led to increased price competition.

IBM had placed itself in the mainstream of commercial mainframe computer markets, based on central systems for big business, public administration, science, and so on, but left the two areas of "microcomputers" and "supercomputers" open for capable competitors to grasp. System manufacturers trying to meet IBM in the mainstream, such as Burroughs, Sperry, and Honeywell, were only left minor shares of the market. Specialization made more sense as a better market strategy. And the successful American competitors turned out to be those companies that focused on "supercomputers" like Control Data in the 1960s and Cray Research in the 1970s, or "microcomputers" like Digital Equipment Corporation, which expanded rapidly in the late 1970s.

Plug-compatible manufacturers made up the third group of competitors, such as Amdahl in 1970, which tried to exploit the weaknesses of IBM or the competitive potentials of the new system/360 and its follower 370. Leasing companies, purchasing the equipment in the open market and offering computer systems at reduced prices, also appeared on the market, along with service bureaus, which offered batch services or on-line access to a central computer by way of time-sharing. Even software companies were set up, but on a small scale, since software production was dominated by system manufacturers or by the computer departments of the user organizations until the 1980s.

IBM, having spent several years preparing to meet the competition, marketed its new *system/370* in 1970. Processor and main memory were made with the new monolithic semiconductor technology. Followed by improved peripherals, it offered a price/performance improvement by a factor of three compared with the 360. As a result, improvements mainly came from new and better component technology. It was also important that the operating systems of the 370 were supplied with the new virtual memory capability, available from 1972, which automatically took care of the "overhead" of memory allocation. In the following years IBM marketed among other things the famous high-performance Winchester disk drive, new mass storage systems, and terminals. The terminals could perform input and output and some storage and processing functions, but were still far from being able to do the distributed data processing of the microcomputer of the late 1970s." All in all, the architecture of the system/370 did not differ in principle from the system/360. The new generation of integrated circuits led the way, allowing for considerable improvements in performance, and they were followed by necessary changes of organizing internal memory and of peripherals to make the potentials of computer power come true.

The system/370 did not revolutionize the computer industry and applied technology as did the system/360. IBM felt the consequences of *growing competition* and the recession of the 1970s in its basic markets. The essential main-frame business had reached a stage of maturation, leaving expansion to the periphery. Component technology and computer performance changed faster than ever, and Intel's marketing of the microprocessor in the early 1970s ushered in a fourth and revolutionary new generation of computer technology. In the mid 1970s IBM management realized the growing potentials and needs for distributed data processing, based on larger systems and storage on the one hand, and intelligent end-user adapted terminals on the other. For the first time in the history of IBM and of the computer, "alternative solutions" to the traditional large and central systems appeared as something real. It took the rest of the decade for the IBM management to take appropriate action.

In the second half of the 1970s, pressed by competitors, IBM kept on rapidly improving the price/performance of its product line by introducing new processors, storage, and input-output equipment, and by supplying its systems with more refined operating systems and a growing number of application programs. In the late 1970s, IBM announced new computer systems such as the 8100, based on its new advanced 64K chip technology and with operating systems offering distributed data processing, data base management and communications. But these new facilities and the increasing performance of computer systems were still based on IBM's traditional idea of computing through central mainframe systems. Furthermore, IBM products of the 1970s lost the compatibility of the system/360. IBM tried to solve the problems via the Systems Network Architecture of the mid seventies, but it made no real difference. The new line of products of the late 1970s was only the first real step towards truly distributed data processing. IBM did not easily change its basic strategy.

IBM was still the leader, but the innovator of the 1960s had moved into a mature state, waiting for new technologies to prove themselves in the market before striking out into the fields of economic growth. It is also part of the story that IBM had turned into some kind of "super tanker." having great difficulties in changing the course of large mainframe systems that governed all the structures and thinking of this huge corporation. It was only at a late stage that IBM turned to distributed data processing and microcomputers — also pressed by rising competitors abroad.

Europe

After World War II, all industrialized countries formed research groups to explore the new computer technology. The natural way of doing this was to build a computer of their own, and so they did. Compared to the United States, every other national economy in the world was still very weak throughout the 1940s and 1950s. Only the large American defense market had the tremendous resources and demands that were needed to push computer research and technology from its origins in the 1940s to its break through in the 1960s. Outside the United States no real attempt was made to develop a national computer industry, although each country constructed computers of its own, mainly for scientific purposes. A new world-wide "industrial revolution" in the 1960s, including the IBM-led computer revolution, changed the whole picture, however. Governments and leading industrialists of every nation joined forces to meet the American challenge and threat of total economic and technological rule of the world economy. The computer proved to be more than just a tool for war. It promised economic growth and huge profits for the industrialized economies of Europe and Japan, and as they gained substantial economic strength they wanted to make their way toward world economic leadership.

Britain, France, Germany — all tried to make a national computer champion (Flamm 1988: 134-171; *Annals of the History of Computing*, no. 4, 1989, and no. 1, 1990, are special issues on computer development in Europe). However, no European projects had much success in the 1960s and 1970s, however, and never really succeeded in crossing their respective national boundaries. To fill the technological gap, European companies were forced to import American computer and electronics technology, and to some degree transfer scientific knowledge to universities, although the Europeans were much better off in science than in technology. Accordingly, in these decades the largest computer company in every West European country was IBM, which made its way into all kinds of applied technology, into computer science and into education.

Japan

While the European countries failed to build a computer industry of their own that was capable of meeting the American challenge, Japan succeeded in doing so (Flamm, 1988: 172-202; Fransman, 1990: 13-97). How come? Like the Europeans, the Japanese had no large program of defense investment to support computer technology. Economic growth and a growing awareness of the commercial and strategic importance of computer technology made the Japanese government follow the European policy of supporting computer development in the mid-1960s. Unlike the Europeans, however, the Japanese never bet on one "national champion" to stand up against IBM on the home market. Instead, government support was given to a small group of strong and highly competitive companies. Based on a systematic importation of advanced American technology, the Japanese government helped to push Fujitsu, NEC, Hitachi, and others to the same level of micro-technology as the Americans by the late 1970s. Internationally, the leading Japanese companies had built up economic networks in Europe and even in the United States, to fight off the threatening monopoly of IBM and the world-wide dominance of American companies.

The strategy of Fujitsu, Hitachi, and the others was to build IBM-compatible computers of superior price performance. Superior performance required a technological edge, gained through advanced semiconductor technology. By means of a state-supported program for developing very large-scale integrated circuit chips in the second half of the 1970s, Japanese companies were brought to the frontiers of advanced semiconductor technology and the market for IBM-compatible computers by the beginning of the 1980s.

Applications

Throughout the 1960s, commercial systems were established in most *large administrative departments* of the Western world, based on large central mainframe computers. In science as well as in business, basic calculations and the transactions of large corporations and agencies in the 1960s were computerized, followed by many medium-sized organizations in the 1970s. It was a matter of automating certain specific functions, only indicating at the end of the period the potentials of integrated computing. Targeting the automated factory or office had to wait for the next decade.

In software, the spin-off effects of the SAGE project were probably as great as those in hardware (Flamm, 1988: 89-90; Flamm, 1987: 121-122). The complex structures of these systems paved the way for the *first real-time business transaction systems* of the sixties. In 1964, the airline reservation system SABRE, made by IBM, was operational and pioneered commercial real-time transaction processing systems. However, complex real-time transaction systems represented the advanced parts of computer applications in the 1960s and 1970s, being limited to a few large user organizations. It had to wait for the distributed data processing, databases, and data communications of the 1980s to make it a common thing. Only in the 1970s were batch systems gradually replaced by real-time systems.

The computers of the period witnessed an enormous increase in price/performance, but the *software* produced to make this potential come true *lagged behind*, however (Friedman, 1989: 101-137; Samogyi/Galliers,

1987: 30-37). Rising costs of system development, implementation, and maintenance threatened to swallow up most of the productivity advances in hardware. The computer industry, the user organizations, and the computer society of education and science had to develop tools in order to gain control of this huge and important sector of the economy. The general recession of the world economy from the early 1970s likewise contributed to the concern about the growing costs and poor productivity gains in software.

The software crisis was caused by another set of problems, too. Highly structured data operations may be easily reproduced in computer systems. If one goes beyond that level, however, one will most probably be restricted by social activities that are not structured for data processing, or be resisted by people unwilling to be part of a computer system. The extent of such obstacles was probably greater than imagined. One does not easily change the structures and processes of organizations, let alone those of whole societies. And in the technologically dominated minds of the computer world, the scope of this set of problems was hardly recognized. Generally speaking, the processing of data and information, including management procedures within organizations of the 1960s and '70s were still based on principles of the pre-computer era. Being a general technology dealing with data- and information processes, the computer and computer systems could only expand considerably by making the structures and processes of society adapt to the formalizing needs of computer logic.

First, one had to develop the computer tools for doing so, however. Applications spread throughout the 1970s, but that decade should first and foremost be viewed as a forerunner, preparing the way for the present age. Therefore, in developing the computer applications of the 1970s, much *effort* was made *to solve the so-called software crisis* by trying to produce more useful computers used by more users.

The breakthrough in commercial mass computing in the 1960s created new and big problems in user organizations. The computer systems did reduce the number of clerical workers, but the reduction was often more than offset by the high cost of necessary hardware and highly-paid data processing professionals. The maintenance of systems unexpectedly turned out to be a large cost factor. And user dissatisfaction was growing because of distant and inflexible systems requiring a long time for changes, and with data departments apparently unable to satisfy user needs. Furthermore, when computer systems replaced manual operations, job qualifications and relations within organizations changed. The trial-and-error methods of systems developments concentrated on the processing of computers and did not consider any organizational effects of computer systems. Ill-defined specifications lacking documentation, and the want of an overall logic and control of large systems, only made things worse. Finally, the limitations of batch systems became apparent when compared with the needs of business. The systems processed and produced historical rather than current information. And the incoherent systems resulted in fragmented data of little information value. The computer systems were made to process data, being unable to separate data from the basic processes of computing. Data processing was not meant to produce information.

Generally speaking, management had lost control of a rapidly expanding computer world. Expansion outgrew any expectations, and management lacked experience in dealing with the problems of this new technology. Gaining control and integrating computer technology into the general trend of automation and economic growth therefore dominated the efforts in the 1970s of the computer industry, science and education, and important user organizations. The computer had to be more useful, more productive, more profitable, and to conquer still more ground, for the benefit of the producers as well as the users.

Structures of control and analytical methods were needed in software engineering. Most large programs had no true control structure or any overall logic, and were often badly documented. Furthermore, large software projects lacked an adequate organization. Consequently, theoreticians of computer science and engineering started working on concepts and methods to reduce program complexity. The only way to make people capable of dealing with complexity was by breaking it down into more simple parts that could be combined according to some logic structure. From the beginnings of the 1970s, *structuring and modularity* became of primary and growing importance to programming and to systems development, which made systems development, tests, maintenance, fault finding, and corrections easier to do, and thereby reducing costs.

Many obstacles slowed down the process of obtaining control of computer systems and computer people, and of securing cost-savings. There was a shortage of qualified, experienced personal, and the level of turnover was high. Furthermore, the top management's understanding of the computer world was still poor, and they were unwilling to make computer systems and DP departments a genuine part of the general strategy of the organizations. The general economic recession of the 1970s, and the confusion it caused in the political-economic systems of the Western world, were other factors to be considered.

After some years of confusion, management more determinedly targeted the goal of making the computer more useful. A growing capability in central data processing was insufficient to ensure a successful future of the computer. Data processing had to be distributed to users and had to be value-added, thereby turning data into information. The need for accurate information brought about such a new way of thinking and practice, and that the need was growing was underlined by companies changing to on-line processing during the 1970s. Data should be easily processed and easily accessible. This interest in *data* as a fundamental resource of information gradually increased throughout the 1970s. Theories and methods were developed to deal with the problems of organising and storing data, and databases and database management systems appeared.

Whole new types of software showed up toward the end of the 1970s to help organize the mass of data that fed the information systems: databases, data dictionaries, and database management systems. And with respect to computer staff, new specialized jobs such as those of database designer, data analyst, and data administrator appeared alongside the general trend of specialized systems development and programming. The 1970s saw the beginnings of radical change in applied computer technology. It was left for the 1980s to make it come true.

Information technology takes over in the 1980s: A general technology of the world

The late 1970s and early 1980s saw the beginning of a new period in the history of computer technology (Sobel, 1981: 279-346; Fisher/McKie/Mancke, 1983: 409-449; Flamm, 1988: 235-258; Friedman, 1989: 231-238.). The computer spread into all kinds of social contexts and totally changed industry and applications.

IBM was the leading producer of mainframe systems, which in the 1970s constituted by far the largest share of the computer market. However, in the second half of the decade the market for large systems stagnated, while the "supercomputer" and particularly the "microcomputer" markets grew. The Japanese semiconductor offensive in the 1970s led to a dramatic improvement of computer capacities, which made the microcomputer a realistic alternative to mainframes and obtainable for new and minor companies. By the turn of the decade Japanese companies were about to take over the leadership in the production of chips, and other companies, mostly of American origin, profited from the new lucrative markets at the high and low end of computers. IBM had to react and go for these expanding markets, first and foremost the promising market of microcomputers.

In 1981 IBM delivered its first *PC*. In the first half of the 1980s the IBM-PC enjoyed mass sales, and the company succeeded in regaining the initiative in the computer market, by conquering a quarter of this expanding market. In the early 1990s IBM's share of the microcomputer market has not surpassed the level it had reached ten years earlier. Japanese, European, and American competitors had grown sufficiently strong to control three-quarters of the fastest growing and most promising computer market in the world. The relative strength of the mainframe market of the 1970s had been just the reverse. Nevertheless, the IBM operating system set the standard for PCs, as IBM continued to dominate the mainframe market. Also in mainframes, however, IBM felt the growing competition, stemming from stronger and more internationally operating competitor companies and from the changing character of computer technology.

In the mid-1980s, the PC boom was followed by a drop in sales and profits. Besides suffering from the normal economic reactions of a satiated market, the PCs of those days also suffered from a serious "disease" — that of disappointing the expectations of users. For lack of business software, the PC turned out to be more of a toy for children than a tool for business, although it diffused computer knowledge and inspired new applications. Furthermore, the PC was not as easily used and integrated into existing systems and organizations as the computer industry would have liked it to be. Moving from central systems, doing certain specific functions, onto a combination of central and decentralized systems, which spread into all the activities of a company, appeared to be a more complex and qualitative change of things than expected. However, several new trends in the growing computer industry were working on finding ways of removing these obstacles to further expansion.

Apple's Macintosh of 1984 created a minor revolution in microcomputing. (Apple is dealt with by Rose, 1989. The general development of still stronger American IBM competitors is dealt with in Mobley/McKeown, 1989, and McKenna, 1989.) By expanding the operating system, Apple supplied the user with a much better interface of easily learnt symbols, operated by a "mouse" that was common to all types of Macintosh. Furthermore, the Macintosh system was based on the idea of software compatibility, allowing the user to move from one piece of software to another. The early Macintosh computers suffered from the same deficiencies as the first IBM-PCs, however, lacking business software to carry out their splendid intentions. And finally, the Macintosh operating system was incompatible with the dominating PC DOS standard. The only way out of these unfulfilled potentials was to create sufficient software to make the Macintosh attractive to the world of business. And Apple succeeded, helped by the world of education and research, which were highly susceptible to the advantages of this promising microcomputer. In the late 1980s and the early 1990s, the Macintosh computers were perhaps even more successful than the first IBM-PCs a decade before.

The Apple success encouraged all the other computer companies to try still harder to reproduce the superior technology of the Macintosh. But as yet they have not succeeded completely in doing so.

At the beginning of the 1980s, a true revolution was happening in *data communications* (Crandall/Flamm (eds), 1989: 13-61; Forrester, 1987: 81-130; the European perspectives are found in Locksley (ed), 1990). A rapid expansion in distributed data processing was unlikely to be of much use without proper networks and operating systems suitable for data interchange. Furthermore, PCs turned out to be much more useful when combined in networks. At company level, millions of so-called Local Area Networks (LAN) were installed throughout the world during the 1980s, creating a new and large field of industry and knowledge. Cross-company and cross-country electronic communications also appeared. In the 1970s and particularly in the 1980s, the telephone companies switched from an analog to a digital technology. Surpassing the boundaries of the company became much easier. This process was encouraged by allowing competition into the monopoly-like world of telephone companies. The making of a world-wide satellite system, allowing for long distance transmission of any kind of communication, be it television, pictures, writings, or speech, underlined the radical change of data communications in the 1980s. An electronic infrastructure was emerging, bringing information and communication technology together. And in the industrial world the computer companies and the communication companies, including such giants as IBM and ATT, started to converge in order to compete in the same expanding markets. Computer and communication technology moved toward a converging information technology.

Linking computers into local and even national and world-wide communication systems would hardly have been possible with the *operating systems* of the 1970s (Flamm: 242-246; the making of the IBM SAA is described in Killem, 1988). They were not suited to distributed data processing, databases, and data communications. Multi-user systems called for specific networks and multi-facilities, including basic multiprogramming, multiprocessing, and multitasking. IBM and other computer companies developed operating systems to include these new complex structures. It was a gradual process, supporting large systems and PCs separately and stepwise, followed by a trend of convergence from the late 1980s. DOS, the most widely used operating system for PCs, developed by Microsoft for IBM in 1981, did not support LAN until its version 3, and it never could do any multitasking nor advanced memory management. Its successor, OS/2 of the early 1990s, contained most of these modern facilities, including a graphic user interface to meet the challenge of Macintosh. It did not allow for CPU sharing, however, like the successful UNIX operating system of ATT. Unlike traditional proprietary operating systems, UNIX was of a more general kind and relatively easy to move from one system to another. Since the mid 1980s, efforts to make UNIX a de facto standard of operating systems have increased, although being rejected by IBM and others.

The world of *standards* is changing, however (Flamm, 1988: 242-246). The concept of compatibility within a firm's entire product line was brought successfully into the computer industry and the computer market by the system/360 in the 1960s. It also made IBM computers a de facto standard for all computers and operating systems, although many companies tried to go for themselves. To make a standard a company had to be big, and no one was nearly as big as IBM. But increasing competition and a growing market also forced IBM to market still more products in the 1970s, and thus to deviate from its former policy of compatibility within its own product line. The IBM-PC of 1981 followed this trend of company incompatibility. Although the IBM PC DOS managed to become some kind of world standard for PCs, data communications and the PC expansion as well as growing user knowledge and demands pressed for open systems standards.

Since the late 1980s, world-wide non-IBM companies, governments, and big industrial corporations outside the computer industry have joined forces in various ways to pave the way for general standards and to break down the proprietary system led by IBM. A generally accepted Open System Interconnection (OSI) standard for hardware and a non-proprietary UNIX-like standard for software would truly weaken the position of IBM, opening the way to more free competition, but also to more applications of computers. As we move further into the 1990s, IBM seems to have accepted, at least in part, the changing tide, where a single company no longer has the power to run on its own an ubiquitous industry as that of the computer, opening up for general standards concerning hardware, but still rejecting open software standards.

This general move toward non-proprietary standards, in many ways directed against IBM, and the changing nature of the world computer industry have been accompanied by another new trend — that of cooperation and *alliances*.[4] The huge and increasing costs and efforts needed for developing new technologies have made companies join in industry-wide ventures, such as semiconductors, taking advantage of complementary strengths in research and marketing and reducing the problems of national barriers. Without

---

[4] Flamm, 1988, pp. 246-247. Flamm1987, pp. 153-206, for European and American reactions. Hayashi, 1989 for American-Japanese relations. The Americans' concern about their dwindling technological leadership is seen in OTA, 1985, presenting an evaluation of the American level and efforts of R & D in information technology. Dertouzos et al., 1989, deals with the general declining position of the American industry.

abandoning competition, former competitors are brought into alliances, crossing the three economically leading regions of the United States, Western Europe and Japan. Even IBM has adopted the policy of alliances. Close cooperation with Intel in the production of chips and Microsoft in the making of DOS-PC was later followed by alliances with European and Japanese companies, and in 1991 a strategic alliance with the most successful microcomputer company in the world, the American Apple company. Both IBM and Apple run proprietary operating systems, Apple being strong in its user interface and software compatibility, IBM in mass production and sales as well as in large projects. They have formed a large group to design and produce the computer to run the market of the late 1990s, including all the novelties of operating systems, user interfaces, and the new multimedia concept of combining video and computer.

Many of these alliances and the whole idea of cooperation on strategically important projects received government support, as did the efforts to create general standards. Since the Second World War the American military strength had been based on enormous investments in electronics and computers. In the 1970s the cooperative alliance between big corporations and the government was launched to put Japan into a leading position within microelectronics.

The Japanese offensive in strategically important fields of computer technology was intensified in the early 1980s by the so-called *"fifth generation project"* (Fransman, 1990: 193-242; Forrester, 1987: 41-46; for a broader perspective, see Sobel, 1986, and Hayashi, 1989). It contained three parts: first, very large scale integrated circuit chips; second, a new and much more advanced computer architecture making the computer a tool for information production, not just data processing; third, a "natural" and easier interaction between man and machine. This plan, accompanied by a similar project of telecommunications to fulfil the vision of the information society, fueled an international, technological race between Japan, Western Europe, and the USA. Information technology was declared a technology of crucial economic importance by the combined efforts of government and industry to increase basic and applied research in the field. Nurtured by national interests, this race for knowledge accelerated the development of information technology, but at the same time it forced the leading corporations of the world to enter into international strategic alliances. The fifth generation project as such has not yet been fulfilled.

Furthermore, the computer industry was being changed by an expanding *software industry*.[5] Emerging in the 1970s, software houses grew in size in the following decade, making software for hardware and system producers, and applications for user companies. Software production increased in the second half of the 1980s, supplying software for the insatiable PC market. In a broader context, the breakthrough of internal automation of company activities followed by automating data communications for external relations led to an expansion in software production. This software explosion, spreading computer applications to every main social activity, gave rise to two new trends. In the late 1980s, user and producer pressure caused the many different and often incoherent applications to become increasingly standardized. They were all meant to do the same functions, so why not turn them into a few industrially produced software packages. Eventually, the software industry met the fate of all emerging industries — automation and concentration. Furthermore, it changed objectives, going more and more from making software products toward consulting and planning as to which software and hardware products on the market would be most suited to meet the needs of the user organizations.

Growing applications of computers in user organizations, the automation of basic processes, and the increasing importance of external relations and data communications all contributed to a final new economic trend. During the 1980s internal *computer departments* of large corporations were often turned into software and systems *producers of their own*.[6] In the late 1980s and early 1990s, these new companies, closely knitted to the mother company, had in many industries taken over the market for applications software. To secure their positions they normally made alliances with strategically important producers of hardware, operating systems, and complex network software. Perhaps more than anything else, this recent development of user organisations moving into computer technology production, highlighted the ubiquitous presence and strategic importance of a computer technology being transformed into a more complex and widespread information technology.

---

[5] Recent developments in the software industry have not been properly dealt with, so one has to pick out the trends from many different sources, short notices in the literature on systems development, like Friedman, 1989, p. 281, 341 et passim, and on computer companies, like McKenna, 1989, passim. Flamm, 1987 and 1988, pretty much ignores the software industry in dealing with international competition and government industry relations. An analysis of Business Week, Datamation and Computerworld since the mid 1980s would document and elaborate on present trends.
[6] This recent trend lacks sound documentation, too. A proper investigation would have to be based on an analysis of internal developments within user organizations and their respective economic sectors.

Applications

At he beginning of the 1980s there was a growing backlog of maintaining old systems and of developing new systems (Samogyi/Galliers, 1987: 37-40. Friedman, 1989: 239-243, 271-305). It was a software backlog of probably even larger dimensions, considering the "invisible" and undocumented needs of users not wanting to join a growing queue. The massive spreading of the PC had enormous consequences on applications.

Having waited years for systems to meet their requirements *users* started buying their own computers, independently of data departments. A growing familiarity with these microcomputers began to change the attitudes of both users and management. The gap between the low-cost hardware of PCs and the huge and costly demands in manpower for the development and mainte-nance of large computer systems was openly revealed. Consequently, at-tacks were made from all directions to reduce the costs of professional sys-tem development and maintenance. It also became obvious that the micros would not really be of much use unless they were interconnected. So telecommunication came to the forefront, and the digital convergence of so far separate technologies strongly supported the idea and growth of au-tomation and information technology.

For systems developers the results turned out to be revolutionary. The in-creasingly self-confident user now had the tools and the knowledge to de-mand more involvement in the development of systems. End user computing appeared, promoting the idea that systems are the property of users and not of data departments and it was acknowledged that one cannot make useful systems unless users take an active part in their development.

It also became clear that the potential of new computers and the new in-formation technology could only be realized by a substantial *reduction in manual activities of systems development*. Solutions were found in different ways. Ready-made application systems were marketed in large numbers, cre-ating a whole new business. Tools for systems development, supporting end-user computing such as prototyping, formed another solution. So-called fourth generation languages emerged to support systems development of professionals as well as non professionals. And facilities were developed for extracting information from databases and for formatting reports etc. Systems development and data departments were increasingly confronted by the tough realities of industrialization and automation, when management sys-tematically tried to make the computer a general tool for economic growth.

Furthermore, DP departments had to face the *competition* of an external software business expanding greatly throughout the decade. End users provided with PCs and software houses joined forces to undermine the

monopoly of DP departments. Consequently, the technological revolution of
the 1980s brought applied information technology from the backroom,
dealing with matters of efficiency, to the forefront of the company. The
ubiquitous computer and its technological "relatives" had broken down the
traditional boundaries of data departments and computer professionals.
Information technology moved into the world of business strategy.

The PC made no revolution all by itself, neither did trends toward automating systems development, nor an emerging software industry. It all implied
major changes of basic computer systems and of organizations. Establishing
true *databases* (DB) and *database management systems* (DBMS) proved to
be the crucial turning point. From the late 1970s and throughout the 1980s
practically all large organizations of the Western world and Japan switched
over completely to distributed data processing and information handling.
Such a change took more than just converting the old files and databases
into the complex software of modern DB. Modern DB and DBMS were
meant to be tools for information handling, concerning all the activities of the
company. Consequently, a reorganization was needed. Technological integration through automation and networks formed one part of the change,
turning bureaucracies into more flexible organisations. It was accompanied
by an increasing importance and complexity of computer systems, making
them tools for management. The breakthrough of modern DB and DBMS,
along with automation and networks, was the necessary precondition to
make the potentials of the PC come true. Likewise, suitable software for the
PC was needed. It was only from the mid- 1980s that both premises began to
be fulfilled.

From DP departments and computer systems management reactions to
changes in technology and applications came piecemeal, however. When
PCs spread to most offices, so-called *"information centers"* were often
formed outside the data departments to support the many new users (Owen,
1986: 59-68). On the other hand, a growing number of electronic technologies and applications called for a general planning for the whole organization. As a result, the head of the computer department was often elevated to
the *strategic management* group, and the DP department was renamed
Information Systems (IS) department.

With independent information centers supporting ordinary users at the
bottom of the hierarchy, and the head of the DP department mingling with
senior management at the top, the computer department might easily fall
apart. Furthermore the DP department was undermined by the users taking
over systems development and computer applications. And who was supposed to handle all the new technologies of office automation and telecommunications that were outside the field of traditional computer professionals?

So strategic planning for information technology was no simple job. Neither top management, the organization, nor the computer department were geared to this new role. It called for a reorganization and for new perspectives on information technology to be made an integrated part of business strategy. The computer was not just a tool for automating certain company routines. It promised much more if one made it a tool for management to improve competitiveness and flexibility. This would not only stress the importance of coherent information flows, but perhaps even more it would stress the value of the information coming out of the electronic media. The picture of professional information handling was broadened considerably.

A new perspective and a new discipline called *"Information Resources Management"* (IRM) appeared (Burk/Horton, 1988: 1-38). But what does information resources actually mean? To computer professionals, IRM means the management of computerized information systems. To information professionals coming from the fields of librarianship and applied business science, an information resource is not necessarily a matter of technology. It is the knowledge and the business potential that count. On the one hand, these differences of opinion reflect opposing interests between different groups that all want to be in charge of information handling. On the other hand, they mirror a stage of transition in the development of economy and technology. What does the word information actually mean? Is it a matter of technology, meaning computer supported information systems, or does it mean the information and knowledge of the world and the environments of business that are led into the information flows and systems of the company and used for decision making? So far, business and science give no definite answer to that question, waiting for real world clarifications.

Another new discipline called *"Information Management"* might indicate a more strategic attitude toward the handling of information (Marchand/Horton, 1986: 115-140, represents the knowledge perspective, while Earl, 1989, presents the technology view). And so it does. Despite some differences of opinion — computer professionals on the one hand, and non-computer information professionals on the other — there seems to be an increasing trend toward stressing the importance of knowledge as the basis for understanding and managing the information resources of organisations. This is a trend that corresponds to the trend for users taking over the command of technology and the development of a more holistic view of organizations. The coming of information management is based on the growing importance of external relations and of computer applications that deal with the external environments of organizations.

Still, one needs expertise on the running and changing of complex systems and technologies of the company. Now, where does that leave *the computer department*? In small and medium sized companies and public institutions, IS departments will probably disappear. They already have in large numbers. Networks of PCs and enterprises of facilities management are taking over, combining computer knowledge and knowledge of the specific field of business. In large companies and public administrations, the huge and often old computer departments do not simply disappear. Part of it is integrated into the structure of the business organisation. Most of the former computer department is turned into a profit center, or simply into a business unit of its own struggling on the premises of the market. This has been increasingly the case since the second half of the 1980s.

The previous divide between producers and users of computer technology is being substituted more and more by a convergence, as the computer has turned into an ubiquitous information technology. Economically, it is based on the important discovery that information is more than a matter of technology. Like any raw material it may be processed, adding extra value to be sold in the market. We might even generalize this point of view to include all goods produced: it is the cost and value of the knowledge put into the product that count. If this is so, we may be about to enter an *information economy* (Marchand/Horton, 1986: 1-27, and Marchand, 1990: 23-32). Many indications support this view, and it might turn out to be the ruling trend of the 1990s.

Conclusion

From weapons of war in the 1950s, via IBM's mass-produced large systems of the 1960s and 1970s, onto the ubiquitous tool of the 1980s and 1990s, the computer has captured the industrial economies of the world. Led by IBM, the Americans held the lead until the 1980s, when Japan, followed by the EEC countries, began to rival the American world leadership. Huge R&D costs underlined the strategic importance of the computer, originally fueled by the Cold War, and then by the industrial growth of the 1960s, making it a general technology and way of regaining economic recovery in the 1980s and 1990s. Computers mean business. A tool for a rationalized industrial economy has been turned into a weapon for growth. It might even lead toward a new so-called "information economy," making information and knowledge the basic object of business. The breakthroughs of distributed data-processing, of data communications, and of a converged information technology, based on automated processes of work in an electronic infrastructure heading for world-wide integration, have all prepared the way for an information economy. But it takes time, even in a rapidly changing world economy, to reorganize the basic elements of the total economy and its institutions. Radical revaluations are on the way, however, and a growing integration and competition in world economy might speed up the processes of change.

Bibliography

ACADEMY OF MANAGEMENT REVIEW (1985-1991).

AIRLINES RESERVATIONS SYSTEMS: A LESSON FROM HISTORY (1988). In *Journal of MIS Quarterly*, 1988: 353-370.

ANGELL, I. O., S. SMITHSON (1991). *Information Systems Management..* London: MacMillan.

ANNALS OF THE HISTORY OF COMPUTING (1979-1991).

ASLIB PROCEEDINGS (1985-1991).

ASPRAY, W. (1988). An Annotated Bibliography of Secondary Sources on the History of Software, in *Annals of the History of Computing 3/4*: 291-343.

ASPREY, W., D. BEAVER. (1986). Marketing the Monster: Advertising Computer Technology, in *Annals of the History of Computing 2*,127-143

AUGARTEN, S. (1984). *Bit by Bit*. New York: Ticknor & Fields.

BASHE, C. J., et al. (1986). *IBM's Early Computers*. Cambridge, Mass.: The MIT Press.

BRAUN, E., S. MACDONALD (1982). *Revolution in Miniature*, 2nd Ed. Cambridge: Cambridge University Press.

BURK, C. F., F. W. HORTON (1988). *InfoMap*. New York: Prentice Hall

BUSINESS WEEK (1985-1991).

COLLIER, M., ed. (1988). *Telecommunications for Information Management and Transfer*. Aldershot, England: Gower.

COMPUTER INDUSTRY (1983). In A. Ralston, E. D. Reilly *Encyclopedia of Computer Science and Engineering*, 2nd. Ed., 333-355.

COMPUTER USER GROUPS (1983). In A. Ralston, E. D. Reilly *Encyclopedia of Computer Science and Engineering*, 375-376.

COMPUTERWORLD (1985-1991).

CRANDALL, R. W., K. FLAMM, eds. (1989). *Changing the Rules. Technological Change, International Competition and Regulations in Communications*. New York: The Brookings Institution.

DATAMATION (1985-1991).

DERTOUZOS, M. L., et al. *(1989). Made in America. Regaining the Productive Edge*. Cambridge, Mass.: The MIT Press.

DIGITAL COMPUTERS: A HISTORY (1983). In A. Ralston, E. D. Reilly *Encyclopedia of Computer Science and Engineering*, 2nd. Ed., 532-554.

DOSI, G., et al. (1988). *Technical Change and Economic Theory*. London: Pinter.

DRUCKER, P. E. (1986). *The Frontiers of Management*. New York: Truman Talley Books.

DRUCKER, P. E. (1988). The Coming of the New Organization, *Harvard Business Review*, 45-53.

EARL, M. J. (1989). *Management Strategies for Information Technology*. New York: Prentice Hall.

ELECTRONICS (1985-1991).

FINKELSTEIN, J. (ed.) (1989). *Windows on a New World*. London: Greenwood Press.

FISHER, F. M., J. W. MCKIE, R. B. MANCKE (1983). *IBM and the Data Processing Industry*. New York: Praeger.

FLAMM, K. (1987). *Targeting the Computer*. New York: The Brookings Institution.

FLAMM, K. (1988). *Creating the Computer*. New York: The Brookings Institution.

FORRESTER, T., ed. (1985) *The Information Technology Revolution*. Oxford: Basil Blackwell.

FORRESTER, T., ed. (1987). *High-Tech Society*. Oxford: Basil Blackwell.

FRANSMAN, M. (1990). *The Market and Beyond. Cooperation and Competition in Information Technology in the Japanese System*. Cambridge: Cambridge University Press.

FREEMAN, F. C. (1982). *The Economics of Industrial Innovation*, 2nd Ed. London: Pinter.

FRIEDMAN, A. L. (1989). *Computer Systems Development*. New York: Wiley.

GOLDBERG, G. A., ed. (1988). *A History of Personal Workstations*. Reading, Mass.: ACM Press.

HARVARD BUSINESS REVIEW (1985-1991).

HAYASHI, K. (1989). *The U.S. — Japanese Economic Relations*. New York: N.Y. Univ. Press.

HOROWITZ, E. (ed.) (1983). *Programming Languages: A Grand Tour*. Berlin: Springer-Verlag.

HUBER, G. P. (1990). A Theory of the Effects of Advanced Information Technologies on Organizational Design, Intelligence, and Decision Making. *Academy of Management Review 1*, 47-71.

IBM JOURNAL OF RESEARCH AND DEVELOPMENT (1981). Vol. 25.

INTERNATIONAL JOURNAL OF INFORMATION MANAGEMENT (1985-1991).

JOURNAL OF ECONOMIC LITERATURE (1985-1991).

KAPLINSKY, K. (1984). *Automation*. Harlow: Longman.

KAWASAKI, G. (1990). *The Macintosh Way*. New York: Harper Perennial.

KILLEM, M. (1988). *IBM: The Making of the Common View*. Boston: Harcourt Brace.

LANGLOIS, R. N, et al. (1988). *Microelectronics: An Industry in Transition*. Winchester: Unwin Hyman.

LOCKSLEY, G., ed. (1990). *The Single Internal European Market and the Information and Communication Technologies*. Oxford: Belhaven Press.

MADDISON, A. (1989). *The World Economy in the Twentieth Century*. Paris: OECD.

MARCHAND, D. A. (1990). Infotrends: A 1990's Outlook on Strategic Information Management. *Information Management Review*, 23-32.

MARCHAND, D. A., F. W. HORTON (1986). *Infotrends*. New York: Wiley.

MCKENNA, R. (1989). *Who's Afraid of Big Blue? How Companies are Challenging IBM — and Winning.* Cambridge, Mass.: Addison-Wesley.

METROPOLIS, N., et al., eds. (1980). *A History of Computing in the Twentieth Century.* New York: Academic Press.

MOBLEY, L., K. MCKEOWN (1989). *Beyond IBM.* New York: McGraw-Hill.

MOLINA, A. H. (1989). *The Social Basis of the Microelectronics Revolution.* Edinburgh: E. University Press.

NASH, S. G., ed. (1988). *A History of Scientific Computation.* Cambridge, Mass.: Addison-Wesley.

NEWFELD, M. D., M. CORNEY (1986). Database History: From Dinosaurs to Compact Discs.*Journal of The American Society for Informations Sciences 37*, 183-190.

OLAISEN, J. (1990). *Information Management as the Main Component in the Strategy for the 90's in Scandinavian Airlines systems (SAS).* Oslo, Norway: Business School.

OTA (1985). *Information Technology R & D: Critical Trends and Issues.* New York: Pergamon Press.

OWEN, D. E. (1986). SMR Forum: Information Systems Organizations, in *Sloan Management Review 3*, 59-68.

RALSTON, A., E. D. REILLY (1983). *Encyclopedia of Computer Science and Engineering*, 2nd. Ed. New York: Von Nostrand Reinhold.

REDMOND, K. C., T. M. SMITH (1980). *The Whirlwind. A History of a Pioneer Computer.* Bedford, Mass.: Digital Press.

RIFKIn, G., G. HARRER (1988). *The Ultimate Entrepreneur: The History of Ken Olsen and DEC.* Chicago: Contemporary Books.

ROSE, F. (1989). *West of Eden: The End of Innocence of Apple Computer.* New York: Viking.

SAMMET, J. (1969). *Programming Languages: History and Fundamentals.* New York: Prentice Hall.

SMITH, R. E. (1989). A Historical Overview of Computer Architecture. *Annals of the History of Computing 10,* 277-303.

SOBEL, R. (1981). *IBM. Colussos in Transition.* New York: Truman Talley Books.

SOBEL, R. (1986). *IBM vs. Japan*, 1986. New York: Stein and Day.

SOFTWARE HISTORY (1983). In A. Ralston, E. D. Reilly, *Encyclopedia of Computer Science and Engineering*, 2nd. Ed., 1353-1359.

SOMOGYI, E. K., R. D. GALLIERS (1987). Applied Information Technology: From Data Processing to Strategic Information Systems. *Journal of Information Technology 1,* 30-41.

WEXELBLATT, R., ed. (1981). *A History of Programming Languages.* New York: Academic Press.

WILDES, K. L., N. A. LINDGREN (1986). *A Century of Electrical Engineering and Computer Science at MIT 1882-1982.* Cambridge, Mass.: The MIT Press.

WISEMAN, C. (1988). *Strategic Information Systems.* Homewood, Ill.: Irwin.

The history of computer-based signs

PETER BØGH ANDERSEN

The purpose of this short note is to relate Christensen's historical account to the papers based on semiotic theory — making historical viewpoints relevant for semiotic ones and vice versa.

From a semiotic point of view, Christensen tells the story about the genesis of modern electronic signs: the coming of age of computer-based signs. Most — but not all — of the papers treat this sign-type as a synchronous phenomenon, but Christensen's paper shows that computer-based signs like all other signs has a "language history".

The point of departure in this note is the Peircean interpretation of computer based signs reproduced in Fig. 17.1.

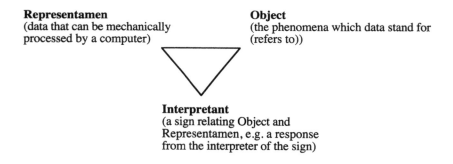

Representamen
(data that can be mechanically processed by a computer)

Object
(the phenomena which data stand for (refers to))

Interpretant
(a sign relating Object and Representamen, e.g. a response from the interpreter of the sign)

Fig. 17.1. Computer based signs in Peirce's framework.

Signs must exist physically (the representamen), they must stand for something other than themselves (their object), and the relation between representamen and object must be related by laws and conventions and cause reactions in the interpreter. In addition, signs must be communicable, and they must be used by a social group of people for managing and co-ordinating the affairs of daily life.

In their infancy in the 40s, the computer-based signs lacked most of these properties, and in fact could hardly be classified as signs at all.

Programming moves away from hardware changing the object of computer based signs

Invention of higher programming languages, beginning with the construction of assemblers, causes the *object* of program texts to change from the physical machine to the domain of application. The object of the assembler code below is the machine: registers, numbers — and the code itself ("jmp mloop" means that the program should return to the line named "mloop"):

```
mloop:movr    1,1 snc
       movr    0,0 skp
       addzr   2,0
       inc     3,3 szr
       jmp     mloop
```

In opposition to this, the next text, written in object-oriented notation, is interpretable as a description of the application domain of the program, a bank account:

```
class account
  owner: ref(person)
  amount: integer;
  procedure deposit...
  procedure withdraw...
end account
```

Whereas older programs referred to storage cells and registers, modern programs can be read as assertions about wages, addresses, and positions. This was achieved by creating layers of signs in the systems. The lower levels are still about the machine, but the higher levels concern the application domain. Higher levels are translated into lower levels.

Thus, the layers we can identify from a synchronous perspective have a diachronous explanation. They are like geological sediments, the upper ones being younger than the lower ones (Figure 17.2).

The historical process is often one of *accumulation*: although the older layers are modified, they are still present. Users of software know this process as *backward compatibility*: new versions of a piece of software must of course offer new facilities, but in addition it must be able to handle the data produced by the older versions (similar relations between synchrony and diachrony have in fact been hypothesised in the domain of language. See

D.W. Lightfoot: *Principles of Diachronic Syntax*. Cambridge University Press, Cambridge, 1979).

level

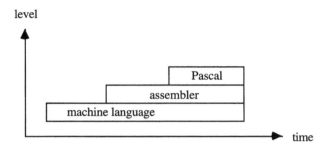

Fig. 17.2. Machine levels are deposited in a historical process.

This very concretely demonstrates that the historical perspective described in Christensen's paper is necessary in order to understand the synchronous state of the technology.

From data production to information handling

By *data* is meant a formalised representamen of such nature that is can be communicated and transformed by means of a mechanical process. By *information* is meant the human interpretation of data, based on a convention. Thus, information in this sense seems to encompass the *object* as well as the *interpretant* of the sign.

In the beginning, much effort was spent on designing the algorithms for producing the *representamen*, and less energy devoted to ensure that users were able to produce the relevant interpretants. Christensen argues that business needs knowledge, but that data in itself does not give knowledge. The growing emphasis on *object* and *interpretant* means that the systems are required to "be about" relevant issues, and that the computer-based signs must elicit relevant responses in their context of use. However, awareness of this issue first emerged in the mid-80s.

Interactive use replaces batch-processing. The handling features

The advent of interactive systems was caused by the need for new updated information.

Early batch systems had a clean division between Input, Process, and Output. Input and Output were seen as passive manipulable objects that were transformed by an active, immutable program — a machine that consumes and produce data in the same manner as factory consuming meat and producing canned beef. Users only saw the paper output, but with real-time, interactive systems the physical *handling* of the system became a decisive factor in the interpretative process.

In modern object-oriented programming, the basic division of a system is not between passive data opposed to an active algorithm; the basic building blocks are now *objects* consisting of cohering data and operations that can be handled by other objects or by users.

In terms of the typology in Andersen's paper, the typical component of a system became the *Interactor* that consists of four main features: (1) permanent, stable features, (2) transient, changeable features, (3) action features enabling the sign to influence itself and other signs, and (4) handling features enabling the user to influence the sign.

Only when this happens, does the computer based sign acquire its special characteristics that set it apart from all other known kinds of signs. Hypertext, discussed in the papers by Liestøl and Sørensen, is a good example of this transition; although prophesied by Vannevar Bush as early in 1945, hypertext first appeared for the public in the 80s. Hypertext can be described as a computer-based version of paper that can only live in an electronic environment, adding handling and action features to the passive paper. The handling features of hypertext, known as "navigation", is one of the key issues in hypertext design and the main reason for bothering with hypertext at all.

Invention of data-communication and local net

Like all other signs, computer-based signs need to be physically communicated in order to reach their interpreters, but the digital messages had to stay within their plastic shells until the beginning of the 80s. Only with the advent of digital telephone networks and local area networks, did the computer-based signs come of age and were given the same travelling opportunities as their older relatives. Before that, computer-based signs were half-caste signs that had to be converted to other media, e.g. paper or tape, before being able to enter a communicative process. Sorensen's paper presents a study of communication in computer networks.

Information technology becomes a general communication and management tool

This is probably one of the most important and difficult phases in the maturation of the computer-based sign a phase that only began in the 80s and has not ended yet.

Basically, sign systems are social phenomena, and computer-based signs first achieve the status of a true sign-system when they become embedded into an organisation and are extensively used for practical daily communication and co-ordination. Since communication is an important part of organisations, change of communication means change of the organisation, as emphasised by Christensen. On the other hand, once in use, computer-based signs may give rise to new forms of organisations like the "hi-tech networks" described in Qvortrups paper. As suggested in Brandt's paper, multi-user systems connected through networks could cause new kinds of semiotic systems to emerge, a kind of collective memory in an organisation, a flow of information that seems to exist and change independently of the individual users.

18

A historical perspective on work practices and technology

RANDI MARKUSSEN

The concept of modernization does not mean the implementation of universal values in democratic institutions, but it does mean the implementation of sophisticated new technologies.   *(Heller, 1985: 146)*

Ongoing processes of change and restructuring of work are becoming a dominant reality in most organizations, often linked to the introduction of technology. While researchers in system development and design are becoming increasingly aware of the importance of the social context for the design of information technology, the subject is rarely seen in its historical perspectives. When participating in a research project on participatory design at a local district of the National Labor Inspection Service in Denmark (NLIS), we became interested in a historical perspective on the processes of change that were taking place within this institution (Bødker et al. 1991).

The work of the NLIS seems fascinating and significant to us in several ways. Not only are we ourselves analyzing work practices at the NLIS, but the institution itself is generally concerned with the interrelations of work and technology. The range of its activities is to a large degree defined by the Work Environment Laws. The laws, however, not only define the range of the NLIS's work, they also bear witness to a public understanding of work environments. In the words of Ricoeur they represent "a horizon of expectation" concerning work environment (Ricoeur, 1985: 207). In this respect the NLIS's domain is symptomatic of work and work practices in general at a social level.

Through conversations and meetings with members of the local district, and by following the inspectors on site visits, we became increasingly aware of the complexity and tensions involved in their work. We came to realize that a sign-oriented perspective is not merely a theoretical stance, but has historically become more and more characteristic of the actual work practices themselves.

L Hirschhorn argues that a sign-oriented and interpretive perspective is becoming more dominant in work practices, and it plays a key role in his view of post-industrial worksettings and the information society (Hirschhorn, 1984). He claims that an interpretive perspective is integral to production processes and the use of cybernetic or automated systems.

> Operators live in a world of signals and signs rather than objects and materials. They observe production processes through information channels that translate unseen events into data. But signals must be interpreted: they only represent the production process. Indeed, workers do not observe separate controls as separate bits of information to be integrated into a theory of what is going on. Rather, they bring a pattern of awareness to the task so that looking and integrating are simultaneous. Thus the interpretation and the observation of signals codetermine one another. *(Hirschhorn 1984: 83)*

The interpretive dimensions of work become critical when second order work is the dominant reality. We presume that an interpretive perspective is just as significant for work practices at the NLIS, due both to technological changes and to a growing social complexity. These processes radicalize questions of how we understand the social context that technology forms part of, and how we acknowledge the complexity and interpretive dimensions of worksettings.

In this chapter we shall explore these questions by using a historical perspective on the NLIS in Denmark. The aim is to establish an understanding of this specific organization, and at the same time to outline a historical approach in order to reveal some significant dynamics and complexities in bureaucracies today.

Our analysis is based on materials collected as one of the initial steps in our research project, and includes conversations with the people at the workplace, written records, and other publicly accessible sources. We do not intend to give a comprehensive historical account of the institution. Our approach is shaped by our interest in the design and use of computer-based information systems and inspired by A. Giddens' theory of structuration, both in terms of the main concepts of the theory and in terms of his analysis of modern societies that forms part of his theory (Giddens 1984).

Basic concepts in structuration theory

Structuration theory concentrates on the production and reproduction of society by the social agents themselves, thus providing an ontology of the constitutive potentials of social life (Cohen 1987: 279). The theory points to both the practical and the discursive consciousness embodied in human action and involved in the recursive ordering of social practices. What he calls the reflexive monitoring of action is understood as a continuous process that is integral to the competence of agents.

In stressing the importance of practical consciousness and situated actions, Giddens draws on the insights of various action theories, among others the ethnomethodological tradition. Within this school of sociology, much light has been thrown on the competences of people involved in different work practices and on the systematic aspects of everyday practices (Suchman, 1987, Heritage, 1987). With agency and the duality of structure as fundamental concepts in structuration theory, however, Giddens goes further in emphasising the historical and institutional dimensions of human conduct. The term agency refers to people's capability of doing things, their power to intervene in a course of events or state of affairs, and their power to act differently in any sequence of conduct (Giddens, 1984: 9).

The aspects of social practices that refer to how people exercise their power, are called rules and resources by Giddens. Resources are seen as bases of power on which people draw in order to influence the course of interaction with others. Giddens distinguishes analytically between two categories of resources: authoritative and allocative. Authoritative resources are in Giddens' words, "non-material resources involved in the generation of power, deriving from the capability of harnessing the activities of human beings." They result from the dominion of some actors over others. Allocative resources are "material resources involved in the generation of power, including the natural environment and physical artifacts." They derive from human dominion over nature (Giddens, 1984: 373). As by rules, Giddens refers to social life as inherently rule-governed and based on procedures of action. He distinguishes between intensive rules that are tacit, informal, and weakly sanctioned — rules of language, for instance — but fundamental in the structuring of everyday life, and shallow rules that are discursive, formalized and strongly sanctioned. The latter should not be understood as rules of greater importance, though. Formulated rules, such as laws are codified interpretations of rules rather than rules as such. They are sanctioned by society precisely because they refer to conflictual areas (Giddens, 1984: 17).

The concept of rules and resources is fundamental to Giddens' reframing of the concept of structure: "Structure, as recursively organized sets of rules and resources, is out of time and space, save in its instantiations and coordinations as memory traces, and is marked by an "absence of the subject." The social systems in which structure is recursively implicated, on the contrary, comprise the situated activities of human agents, reproduced across time and space. Analyzing the structuration of social systems means studying the modes in which such systems, grounded in the knowledgeable activities of situated actors who draw upon rules and resources in the diversity of action contexts, are produced and reproduced in interaction (Giddens, 1984:25). He offers the following table as an illustration of the dimensions of the duality of structure:

structure	signification	domination	legitimation
modality	interpretative scheme	facility	norm
interaction	communication	power	sanction

Giddens thus identifies three analytically separable dimensions of structure — signification, domination, and legitimation — and three equivalent dimensions of interaction — communication, power, and sanction. Dimensions of structure and dimensions of interaction are mediated by three modalities — interpretive schemes, facilities, and norms. Actors draw on these modalities in interaction, while at the same time mediating the structural properties of social systems.

As stated by Cohen the ontological flexibility of structuration theory lays open to substantial inquiry all questions regarding specific systemic patterns and the degree to which systems are stable, organized, and permeable. The only basic distinction that is drawn is the distinction between social integration and system integration. Social integration concerns reciprocities of practices on the level of face-to-face interaction, whereas system integration refers to reciprocal relations between those who are physically absent (Cohen, 1987: 297f).

In class societies this distinction and the interrelations between the modes of integration are of great significance. Absence in space no longer hinders system coordination. To quote Giddens: "The distinctive structural principle of the class societies of modern capitalism is to be found in the disembedding, yet interconnecting, of state and economic institutions. The tremendous economic power generated by the harnessing of allocative resources to a generic tendency towards technical improvement is matched by an enormous expansion in the administrative "reach" of the state. Surveillance — the coding of information relevant to the administration of subject populations, plus their direct supervision by officials and administrators of all sorts — becomes a key mechanism furthering a breaking away of system from social integration" (Giddens, 1984:183).

The importance Giddens attaches to modern means of communication in these processes is of particular interest to us. They permit a degree of contextuality to be generated by agents who are not physically present, allowing for a greater time/space distanciation. This was made possible by the invention of writing and the development of printing and mass literacy, and the invention of electronic media of communication. They not only expand the possibilities for information storage and control, but their diffusion in society has also a significant influence on our sense of historicity and change. Giddens suggests that it stimulates the reflexive monitoring of actions and reflexive self-regulation within organizations. In modern societies, understanding the conditions of system reproduction tends to become part of the conditions of system reproduction as such (Giddens, 1984:191). He claims that information storage in its broadest sense can be viewed as a "thread that ties together the various sorts of allocative and authoritative resources in reproduced structures of domination" (Giddens, 1984: 262).

The history and the field of activity of the NLIS should thus be seen within the overall structures of signification that constitute the symbolic orders and modes of discourse in society. In Denmark as in other Scandinavian countries, the significance of the historical development of the welfare state should be kept in mind. The tradition for class corporation and the existence of numerous statutory institutions, whose governing bodies include representatives of both employers and employees have an impact on society itself and on the expectations that people in general have of state agencies (Lash and Urry, 1987: 232).

The theoretical concepts of Giddens' theory of structuration and his outline of an analysis of modern societies seem to us useful in trying to understand the conditions and dynamics of change within a bureaucratic setting like the NLIS and the part played by computerized information technology.

In the following we shall give a description of the NLIS, primarily at the institutional level. We view the institution as a set of specific discourses concerning objectives, as well as reproduced rules and resources, which together reflect the structural properties of this bureaucracy. With this perspective in mind, we shall take a closer look at the activities in one local district. Our main concern is with organizational changes and the possibilities for computer-based information technologies.

From workers' protection to work environment

Until the 1960's, work environments in the sense we talk about them today were rarely a topic, either in public and political debates or among the parties of the labor market. Workers' protection, however, was a well-known discourse, intimately linked to the emerging dynamics of capitalism. The classic example is still Marx's analysis in "Capital," which show how the exploitation of the English working class threatened its survival and called for a political regulation of working hours and conditions, thereby indicating the role of the emerging modern state.

The discourse of protection is also characteristic of the earliest laws in Denmark in this area. It still dominates their revisions until the 1970s. The actions that could be taken within the law were limited to the regulation of working hours and protection against machine-related accidents. Health issues were thought of in terms of sanitary demands about cleanliness, light, air, and the like. The domain, socially identified as workers' protection, was closely linked with the new mode of production that only covered factory work, trade, and industries, whereas other areas were subject to traditional authority structures.

Hirschhorn distinguishes between different "production paradigms" based on different ways of exploiting allocative resources, to use Giddens' formulation (Hirschhorn, 1984). One is the paradigm of mechanisation, rooted in the challenges inherent in exploiting the possibilities of mechanical design both technically and socially. The other is the emerging paradigm of automation, primarily rooted in experiments within industries, such as petrochemical production, and offering new possibilities for flexibility and integration in terms of new technological ways of handling control.

As stated earlier, work of second order becomes significant within the production sphere, and challenges the mechanical understanding of work and technology. This distinction is interesting to us insofar as it reflects the distinction between the old discourse of workers' protection and the emerging discourse of work environment.

We take the signification of the conditions of work, as reflected in the changing discourse from the idea of workers' protection to the idea of work environments, to be based on the changing technological, social, and ecological practices of work. The laws manifesting this understanding are of course the result of complicated political and social processes, which are not discussed here. As stated by Giddens, a law should be conceived as a codified interpretation of rules rather than rules as such. Laws are strongly sanctioned exactly because they are an attempt to mediate between different aspects of the social practices they deal with.

We focus on the discourse of the Work Environment Law in order to examine what kind of understanding of the domain it represents, what it tells us about the current awareness of work and work practices, what actions are possible within that understanding, and how this shapes the work practices of the NLIS.

The Work Environment Law

In 1975, a Work Environment law was passed in Denmark after eight years of official inquiry into the matter. In contrast to earlier laws, this law covered all kinds of wage labor. The work environment became a topic that concerned all groups in the labor market, not only specific groups in exposed positions. The aim of the law was explicitly stated in a preamble to the first chapter. It was to provide

"a secure and healthy work environment, in accordance with the technical and social developments in society", and to provide "the basis for which firms themselves may solve security and health-issues with guidance from the parties of the labour market and guidance and supervision from the National Labour Inspection Service." *(Law of Work Environment 1975)*

In the remarks following the presentation of the law, the concept of a secure and healthy work environment was defined in terms of general health. It was not only supposed to deal with work accidents and occupational diseases, but was also to include other physical ailments as well as psychological strains, with a view to their long-term effects. As the term "environment" indicates, it was to be handled within a systemic framework and not only as mono-causal relations between certain causes and their consequences. An ergonomic understanding of work was explicitly called for.

The phrase "in accordance with the technical and social developments in society" was in the remarks interpreted as a call for a further democratization of the sphere of working life, in line with an ongoing democratization of public and private life in general. In our view, however, the phrase is interesting in that it explicitly demonstrates an awareness of temporality, a modern awareness of social development as ongoing change and possible improvement, closely linked to the implementation of new technologies. Furthermore, the law is a framework law, mainly stating certain general conditions, but leaving it to the Minister of Work together with the NLIS and several other institutions to fill in the law by regulations and codes. Democracy is viewed just as much as the means as the ends for those endeavors, as a mode of regulation among others, and perhaps for very good reasons. As the awareness of temporality indicates, rationalization seems to imply a demand for a growing flexibility both in terms of time and delegation of power, a call for effectiveness as much as efficiency, in order to cope with immediate adjustment, leaving less space for formal authoritarian hierarchies when they do not meet those demands.

The second paragraph of the preamble demonstrates this further with its call for the parties in the labor market to settle problems locally. It emphasizes a collaborative attitude at all levels of the many kinds of institutions within the field. In fact, one of the most significant innovations in the law was the establishment of several new collaborative institutions, together with a suggested transformation of those already existing. Several chapters in the law define their aims and activities.

The discourse of work environment indicates other modes of regulation than a classical bureaucratic model by suggesting participant models of regulation and models of expert knowledge on many levels in order to cope with the growing complexity within this area of conflicts. From a Weberian point of view, this might be said to indicate other modes of regulation, but still within the structural principles of a bureaucracy. Questions of balancing means and ends become more evident than following formal, hierarchic rules, and open up for systematic approaches to solving problems and making decisions. This is still done within a rational framework, however, in the sense that expert knowledge and science-based investigations of work strains and working conditions are becoming more prominent. The law also states the formal rights and obligations of the parties involved, and the conditions for involving criminal liability. It still acknowledges the employers' ultimate right to direct and divide the work, however, and thus leaves the formal responsibility to them.

In our opinion, the law constitutes the possibility for a growing bureaucratization of the area, because of a desire to cope with its contradictory nature and in order for the institutions to make themselves legitimate. In our view, Weber's insights into the paradoxical relationship between bureaucracy and democracy should not be overlooked, even though modernization processes in bureaucracies at least at the political level are often referred to as de-bureaucratization. Public institutions have to account for their practice in order to make themselves legitimate, especially at times when the state and the state agencies are under political pressure. This aspect becomes even more evident, when one considers the potential for accounting, inherent in computer-based information technologies. The paradoxes might also reflect the ambiguous meaning of democracy both as a specific representative system, operating primarily at the level of system integration, and as a term for direct involvement, operating at the level of social integration.

From another point of view, however, the changing mode of regulation indicates a different understanding of the authoritative resources, in that it implies a change in the structural properties of the domain, which are potentially at variance with the structural principles of bureaucracies. As mentioned earlier, Giddens considers authoritative resources to be just as important as allocative resources as means of generating power. In this respect the law might be said to enforce a reflective monitoring and self-regulation as part of many work processes. One of the inspectors pointed this out to us during a visit to the construction area. He explained that workers might ask how strong the wind was likely to blow, before they stopped working with cranes. His response was that the law leaves the judgment very much up to them.

Such a discretionary principle leads to reflective monitoring on the part of the workers. In our view the law puts new images of authority and of handling power at play, both in terms of the discretionary principle and the call for cooperation as the predominant attitude. It highlights an aspect of authority that we believe is intimately connected with the concept, but now becomes more evident, the ambiguous nature of exercising both care and control (Ericsons, Schultz, 1982, Sennett, 1980).

Since the law refers to all kinds of labor, the changing discourse suggests a change in work practices within many areas and in some respects it brings about certain changes. But the discourse is of course of specific interest for the understanding of the objectives and the organisational changes within the NLIS.

The objectives of the NLIS according to the law

The law stated that the NLIS would consist of the headquarters, named the Directorate and located in Copenhagen, a National Institute of Occupational Health also located in the capital, and 15 local Labor Inspection Districts throughout the country. The objectives of the institution were to be:

- To instruct and guide firms, trade safety councils, parties of the labour market and the public about issues relating to the work environment.
- To assist the department of employment in devising rules, codes, and regulations.
- To issue regulations in accordance with the employment minister's specifications.
- To keep the public informed about technical and social developments in order to improve security and health in the work environment.
- To deal with plans for work processes, workplaces, technical aids, and so on, as well as materials, and to issue permissions in accordance with the law and the administrative regulations.
- To ensure that the law and the regulations are kept.

The regionalization of the institution as a whole indicates the various areas of competence that the institution possesses and the many social levels that they refer to, and therefore reflects the differentiation of society. If we apply some of the concepts from the theory of structuration, we may see the

Directorate as the place where areas of competence concerning rules and regulations both in a strictly legal sense and in a technical and social sense are located. The director and the senior management are also to be found here. The National Institute of Occupational Health is the center for scientific knowledge about work and work environment in order to supply the other parts of the institution, other institutions within this domain, and the public with scientific results and information. The local districts, on the other hand, have knowledge and experience about what is actually going on in factories, firms, and other workplaces in practice.

The different aspects of competence "learn" from each other and refer to each other via both social and system integration. The interrelationship between social and system integration becomes a key factor in making the organization work in accordance with the objectives specified in the Law of Work Environment. The way in which the institution reproduces authoritative resources and interprets the objectives becomes a major consideration.

The formal authority delegated to the institution consists in the right to inspect every plant or workplace within the reach of the law, without a court order. The inspectors have no power to force an entry, however, but they have the right to call in the police, if necessarily. Legal proceedings and prosecution are referred to the general court system. The law does not encourage the NLIS to take initiatives concerning legal proceedings, as it is not mentioned as one of the objectives. This implies that the other objectives are considered more important.

The law indicates that new images of authority are at play. The discourse of work environment with its more holistic approach to the domain, implies a need for other kinds of competence and expertise than technical knowledge. Until 1975, the inspectors were engineers or other technically educated people. Now people with other educational backgrounds are employed as inspectors, both as construction workmen to make special efforts towards construction enterprises, and as professional and semi-professional groups. Chemical engineers were needed in order to tackle problems concerning the increasing use of more sophisticated scientifically based products. People with degrees in health-related subjects — for example, psychologists, physiotherapists and other therapists, nurses — were needed in order to handle the extended concept of a secure and healthy work environment.

The changing educational and professional profile of the institution also indicates that ideas of guidance, of prevention, and a therapeutic attitude become more evident as part of inspection, and require new ways of handling the authority. As stated by the law, part of the objective was to assist the plants, enterprises, and worksettings in helping themselves, to support the Health and Safety Committees at the workplaces in their efforts to monitor and regulate the working conditions. The institution was supposed to give guidance and advice both about those aspects and about explaining the rights and obligations within the law, and at the same time to work toward the implementation and observance of the rules.

The concept of the work environment thus suggests a systemic approach, where balancing different perspectives becomes an important part of the work at all levels of the institution. This tendency is captured in the distinction between problem setting and problem solving that D.A. Schoen has made a strong case for (Schoen, 1987). Within the discourse of workers' protection, the objective of the work could be understood as applying general rules to relatively simple cases. Within the systemic approach of the Work Environment Law, it becomes important how the institution and its members identify problems and interpret the objectives. It demands a reflective attitude, as emphasized by Schoen.

These qualities become significant in the daily practices of the inspectors, when they inspect work settings and plants. But they also refer to other levels of the institution. How should the local districts organize themselves in order to succeed in integrating the various professional competences, for instance? And how is the headquarters supposed to organise itself and carry out a policy that reflects those qualities? In other words, how do they construct the object of their work and form a policy of integration in their daily practice?

Politics of integration — an institutional perspective

The law came into force in 1978. The need for a profound change in the institution was generally recognised. At the end of the 1970s and the beginning of the 1980s the resources delegated to the institution increased substantially. The staff of the institution grew at all the levels, and people with the previously mentioned educational backgrounds were employed. Throughout the 1980s, the administrative and organizational practices of the institution were in fact constantly changing in order to cope with new demands and adjust to political conditions. The changing political climate in the 1980s with a general attack on the welfare state and growing unemployment also influenced the conditions of the NLIS.

There has been a growing pressure of legitimacy on the institution to make it account for the results of its work, and since the middle of the 1980s it has been affected by financial cutbacks, which has resulted in a considerable reduction in staff. The "horizon of expectation" evoked by the law and investigations and discussions of work and working conditions in the 1970s might be said to have faded. However, this does not affect the basic conditions of the law in terms of the changing technological, social, and ecological work practices, though it does make the efforts of putting the law into practice more difficult and less effective. The most significant policies of integration deal with the organizational level and the general policy level of the institution. We will briefly outline the main traits of this policy.

Decentralization — redistribution of knowledge and integration

The law challenged the classical bureaucracy of the institution, often understood as a mechanical mode of organization (Morgan, 1986: 19ff). A movement towards decentralization was encouraged in order to change the organization's functional division of work. The idea was to bring relevant knowledge and place decisions closer to the people involved.

Several tasks that used to be performed by the Directorate were delegated to the districts. These included inquiries into fields with an established practice, prosecuting cases, and having access to documents. Even though the NLIS has no specific right to legal proceedings, in practice it has an important influence on what cases are prosecuted (Rosberg, 1981: 85). The idea was that a decentralization of legal proceedings would create a better cooperation between the NLIS, the prosecution, and the law courts, and create a better understanding of the policy of the NLIS within the local communities. In the 1980s legal advisers were transferred from the Directorate to the local districts.

In 1988, a general law concerning public administration was passed in order to give citizens a better insight into the administration and make the administration more "client"-oriented by providing better information. It meant that in case the inspectors give an order, they have to state explicitly which section of the law they are referring to. Legal knowledge thus becomes important at a very early stage of a case, and the demands on the practice of documentation and accounting increased. When the inspectors "set the problems" out in the field, they have to reflect very specifically on sections of the law.

One of the inspectors made this clear to us by using different metaphors of authority. He invoked the metaphor of a lonely sheriff, pictured in numerous movies of the Wild West. Strong and lonely, he exercises his authority autonomously, using his own judgment, inspecting whichever plant and work setting he prefers, giving orders at random to symbolize his power. Now this attitude has become inappropriate. The inspectors have to take their actions and their consequences into consideration much more consciously. They have to consider the general policy of the institution and use the various instruments deliberately either to guide or to give an order. In giving an order, they have to consider how to document the case both technically and legally, and they must even take the odds of succeeding at court into account. In the local districts, this has meant a growing need for coordinating the different competences and for cooperation between groups of professionals. Work methods such as meetings and project work are some of the means that have become widely used, which indicates a changing pattern in the authoritative resources within the organization.

In terms of structuration theory, decentralization was a means of strengthening the social integration of the institution in the local communities. But it also implied a growing effort on the part of the Directorate to consider the strategy of the work practices in order to enforce integration at the system level. The idea was to "professionalize" the inspections and ensure uniform practices all over the country.

Each year the Directorate makes a working plan, outlining specific objectives and areas of special effort. One of the objectives is to ensure a uniform practice all over the country and make specific problems known to the public. They plan various campaigns that will take place in all districts at the same time, focusing on problems in specific areas — conditions of children's and young people's work, cancer and work, for instance. Seen from the districts, this central planning might imply a loss of autonomy in the planning of activities at the local level. On the other hand, decentralization also makes the headquarters more dependent on the local districts in the creation of a general policy of the institution.

Quality assurance and client orientation — strategic management and politics of information

At the end of the 1980s the management presented a plan for a radical restructuring of the organization "The Labor Inspection Service of the 1990s." The idea of decentralization was further developed, transferring more of the staff from the Directorate to the districts and making the organisation "client-oriented." At the Directorate, the offices were reorganized to match the structure of the Trade Safety Councils. At the same time they enforced a reorganization of the work in the local districts that resembles this structure.

Quality assurance programs formed another part of the restructuring. The senior management set out several objectives in order to ensure the quality

of the services of the NLIS. Among the objectives were a quicker case process, legal information, public security, and uniformity of inspection.

The criteria set up to account for these objectives included specific time
limits for the processing of cases, counting the percentage of the working
hours the inspectors spend out in the field, and counting the numbers of orders by setting up operational criteria for the different branches. The initiatives aim at establishing strategic standards to enhance the services, at making them comparable all over the country, and at accounting for the work of
the institution, both in terms of planning instruments and in terms of control.

The goals involve standards of efficiency, and clearly reflect an economy
of time. The idea is to rationalize the work of the institution even further. The
reinvestment and the decentralization of information technology are considered to play an important part in this.

Even though decentralization was a keyword in the 1980s, it now becomes clear that most of the computeried information systems only reflect
this in terms of providing the headquarters with information in order to coordinate, control, and handle decentralization. Many of the systems are primarily designed to satisfy the headquarters' accounting demands. They help
to account for the activity of the districts in terms of time spent on campaigns, time spent "in the field," the decrease or increase in accident rates,
the number of given orders, and the number of cases brought before the
court.

An EDP office at the headquarters has until now been in charge of the
planning, implementation, and operation of computerized information systems. Increasingly, minicomputers are installed in the districts, where some of
the staff are being trained as EDP instructors. The management intends to introduce local networks and computer work stations not only for the secre-
taries, but also for other groups in the districts, including the inspectors.

How this decentralization of the use of information technology is actually
taking place and how it is going to reflect the strategic management set up
by the senior management become important questions when considering
the introduction of the technology at the local level of the organization.

Politics of integration — the local district's perspective

Under the headquarters' auspices, the local districts are asked to implement
both a new working structure in terms of "client-oriented" cross-disciplinary
groups, work stations, and a local network, as well as the policy of quality
ensuring. Even though people in the districts are used to coping with
change and uncertainties, this is a profound upheaval that affects many as-

pects of their work. Seen from the perspective of the design of computer systems, however, it presents an opportunity to reflect on these processes and discuss possibilities of computer support for the working groups.

Group structure and authoritative resources

The restructuring of the work consists in establishing four groups, corresponding to the groups at the Directorate and matching the structure of the Trade Security Councils. The groups are intended to work rather autonomously, and each group comprises both people with different professional backgrounds and office workers.

In reorganizing the work, the members of the groups have to bring new perspectives to their tasks, and they have to establish a way of cooperating. When we participated in group meetings, it became clear to us how the members of the groups drew on different authoritative resources in their work, reflecting the knowledge and the perspectives of their different tasks.

The images of authority, invoked by the inspectors — the image of the sheriff and the image of the therapist — reflect the inspectors' changing experiences. They spend one third of their time "out in the field," gaining knowledge of how plants, enterprises, and work settings actually function. In turning perceptions of work environments into appraisals of work practices, they interpret events by "bringing a pattern of awareness to the task, simultaneously watching and integrating" — to paraphrase the quote from Hirschhorn in the introduction. They meet primarily demands from human beings, facing the realities of work and working conditions at problematic work places. In order to "set the problem" as formerly described, they become more and more dependent on the ability to document and keep track of papers, tasks that used to be of secondary importance to them. Their primary tasks in many ways comprise the rationale of the local district, and consequently much authority is assigned to their perspectives.

The office workers do not invoke the same colorful images to describe their work. They have traditionally been removed from meeting people "out in the field." Their authority has been based on the bureaucratic aspects of the district's work that, seen from the perspective of the inspectors, have been of secondary importance. For them the information and documentation systems are fundamental as well as the discipline in working with them. No less than the inspectors they in their work "bring a pattern of awareness to the task, simultaneously watching and integrating." They have played an important role in mediating the demands from the headquarters and the inspection work. Due to the former division of labor and their lack of concrete experience "out in the field," they may experience difficulties in establishing a general view and a framework within which to interpret the information.

In the beginning, the restructuring and the introduction of computers were seen as a possibility for office workers to be relieved of routine tasks such as, for instance, typing the same information several times, due to a lack in integration of information systems. They got the chance to take on new tasks, and get closer to the core of the work practices, grounded in inspecting. The introduction of computers renders some of their former tasks superfluous. Gradually, however, it becomes clear to the group that restructuring also implies a change in the work of the inspectors as they are supposed to use word processing and get in closer touch with the bureaucratic aspects.

In order for the cross-disciplinary groups to carry out their work, each member has to be concerned with perspectives, formerly distributed among different groups — inspectors with different professional backgrounds, legal advisers, office workers, and the local management. In order for this to happen, their shared ability to handle and draw on the bureaucratic and the technological resources plays a central role. In order to understand the "the horizon of expectations" that members of the groups bring to the discussions of further use of information technology and the resources they are ready to invoke in becoming familiar with the technology, it is important to understand the changing pattern of social and system integration that the technology forms part of.

Quality assurance, politics of information, and authoritative resources

"Client" orientation is a major concern in restructuring the work of the organisation. Seen from the perspective of the local districts, however, this is an ambiguous statement. In their view, they have always been in touch with clients, experiencing close contact with local enterprises and worksettings, and the local partners of the labour market.

Furthermore, the quality assurance programme mostly reflects efficiency demands. It follows the traditional attitude of using primarily quantitative measures to account for the local districts' work. Locally, they are faced with well known dilemmas of service work (Berger and Offe 1981). They experience a paradox in the sense that when the forms of their work seem to be most concretely accounted for and quantitatively measured, in fact they are most symbolic. Quantitative measures are rather superficial from their point of view. They do not measure the effectiveness of their work, which is integral to the therapeutic practice, inherent in the work environment law. In their view, an order is easily given. There is much more to support and enhance the local health and security work at plants and worksettings.

Client orientation on part of the headquarters thus seems to mean something distinctively different from the meaning, grounded in the district's traditional practices We suggest that this should be seen in the perspective of strategic management, closely linked to the quality assurance programme.

The strategic management invokes an inspection practice that observes a general average view and standards within different branches, in order to guarantee a uniform and thus professional practice. To the inspectors, however, each plant and each work setting is unique. Their general view is based on their rich experience of work and work practices, and reflects the specific contexts of each plant or work setting. Their authoritative resources have been developed in line with the law's systemic understanding with a concern for prevention and support. In order to develop their abilities to set problems and reflect in action they are dependent on various competences and a cooperative attitude. The authority of the sheriff, being absorbed in his own power, has become problematic. In their view, to enhance a professional attitude, they need a shared understanding of their practice, based on their own rich and concrete experience.

They do not interpret the work group structure as just a means to client orientation in terms of a smooth and quick case treatment, a means to adjust to pressures from outside. They think of it as a possibility to enhance a shared understanding and general view of their work in order for them to identify their own objectives and standards.

When the work group that we observed discussed these matters, they did not reject the standards and the strategic attitude set up by management. They are well aware that they have to mediate these objectives in their own practice. They discussed to what extent the information gathered by the senior management, could support their daily work in terms of a relevant feed back. But they are only to some degree resources for the district's daily work practices, even when by means of information technology they are made more easily available to them. They realize that they also need other means to develop and support a shared understanding, instruments that reflect the concrete and qualitative aspects of their practice.

The discussions in the work group and their struggle to come to terms with how to mediate the demands from the senior management and identify their own objectives and understanding of their work seem to us important for the design of information technology. The possibility of designing technology that reflects and supports their perspectives becomes a critical challenge.

Conclusion

We have tried to show how the Work Environment Law that was passed in the 1970s reflects a new understanding of work and work practices in society. More specifically, we have analysed how it sets the agenda for the NLIS and its work, which in itself reflects this new understanding. The law represents a change in the structural properties of the bureaucracy. By stressing cooperation and participation and a need for prevention and therapeutic competences, it suggests different ways of handling power and control and a new understanding of authoritative resources. This means that interpretative and reflective monitoring becomes a significant part of the structural properties.

In carrying out this work in practice, the organization itself has experienced a constantly change. This has been seen as a movement toward decentralization, a redistribution of knowledge within the organization in order to place decisions closer to the people involved. It has opened up for new work methods, new patterns of communication and interdependency in order to enable people to cope with those demands and the interdisciplinary competences within the organization. But it has also meant a growing importance of accountability in terms of legitimacy, planning, and control. Changing patterns of social and system integration might be said to reveal how understanding conditions of system reproduction tends to become part of the system reproduction as such (Giddens, 1984: 191). The senior management is increasingly concerned with strategic planning and the politics of information. We find that the information systems within the organization primarily have reflected decentralization in terms of providing headquarters with information in order to coordinate, control, and handle the decentralization. In considering a further use of information technology in the local districts, the interrelations between work methods, patterns of communication, and the authoritative resources in the local districts, and the need for accountability and strategic planning, become a major concern. By applying a historical perspective, we have tried to show how the immediate social context of the members in the local district that we are in touch with is embedded within structural properties of great importance in considering perspectives on technology and their work. Interpretation thus becomes integral in the design of information technology.

Acknowledgments

I wish to thanks the people at National Labor Inspection Service and the members of the research group: Susanne Bødker, Ellen Christiansen, Pelle

Ehn, Preben Mogensen and Randy Trigg. Special thanks to Ellen, with whom I originally planned to write this chapter, and to Randy for useful comments on earlier drafts. Also thanks to Joan Greenbaum, Lucy Suchmann, and the editors for helpful comments.

Bibliography

BERGER, U., OFFE, C. (1981). Das Rationalisierungsdilemma der Angestelltenarbeit. In *Angestellte im europäischen Vergleich,* ed. J. Kocka, pp.39. Gøttingen: Vandenhoeck & Ruprecht.

BØDKER, S. et al. (1991). Computers in Context — Report from the AT-project in progress. *Proceedings of the NES/ SAM Conference,* Ebeltoft, Denmark 1991.

CHRISTIANSEN, E. (1988). *Den realistiske vision. Kundskabsudvikling og systemudvikling.* (The Realistic Vision. Working Knowledge and Systems Development) Aalborg: University of Aalborg.

COHEN, I. J. (1987). Structuration Theory and Social Praxis. In *Social Theory Today*, ed. Giddens, A., Turner, J. Oxford: Polity Press.

ENGESTRØM, Y. (1990). *Learning, working, and imagining.* Helsinki: Orienta-Konsultit.

ERICKSON, F., SCHULTZ, J. (1982). *The Counselor as Gatekeeper.* New York, NY: Academic Press.

GIDDENS, A. (1984). *The Constitution of Society* . Cambridge: Polity Press.

HELLER, A. (1985).*The Power of Shame.* London: Routledge & Kegan Paul.

HERITAGE, J. (1984). *Garfinkel and Ethnomethodology.* Cambridge: Polity Press.

HIRSHHORN, L. (1984). *Beyond Mechanization.* Cambridge, Massachusetts: MIT Press.

LASH, S., URRY, J. (1987).*The End of Organized Capitalism.* Cambridge: Polity Press.

LAW OF WORK ENVIRONMENT. Law No.681 of December 23, 1975.

MARX, K. (1967). *Capital.* New York: International Publishers.

MOGENSEN, P. (1992). Towards a Prototyping Approach in Systems Development In *Scandinavian Journal of Information Systems*, vol.4. Aalborg.

MORGAN, G. (1986). *Images of Organization* . California: Sage Publications.

MUMFORD, L. (1963). *Technics and Civilization.* New York: Harcourt Brace Jovanovich.

RICOEUR, P. (1985). *Time and narrative.* Vol. 3. Chicago: University of Chicago Press.

RIEPER, O. (1985). *Styring af arbejdsmiljøet — regel eller deltager.* Copenhagen: Erhvervsøkonomisk Forlag.

ROSBERG, B. (1981). *Ansvar og straf i arbejdsmiljøloven.* Copenhagen: Juristforbundets Forlag.

SCHOEN, D.A. (1990). *Educating the Reflective Practitioner.* San Francisco: Jossey-Bass Publishers.

SENNETT, R. (1981). *Authority.* New York: Random House.

SUCHMAN, L. (1987). *Plans and situated actions*. New York: Cambridge University Press.

19

Hypertext: From modern utopia to postmodern dystopia?

BJØRN SØRENSSEN

When Vannevar Bush, in his 1945 article *As We May Think*, presented his vision of the *Memex*, the proposed information retrieval system that later served as an inspiration for Ted Nelson's *Hypertext* concept, this vision was clearly and necessarily rooted in *modernity* as it appeared, unchallenged, at the end of World War II.

Bush held the view that science, having been in the service of destructive forces for the duration of the war, now was able to return to its main objective — to secure progress of mankind. It was to this end that he proposed the *Memex* system:

Presumably man's spirit should be elevated if he can better review his shady past and analyse more completely and objectively his present problems. He has built a civilization so complex that he needs to mechanise his records more fully if he is to push his experiment to its logical conclusion and not merely become bogged down part way there by overtaxing his limited memory (Bush 1945: 108).

This utopian modern optimism elicited by Bush, was considerably tempered by the time Ted Nelson's *Computer Lib* appeared in 1974, a book that clearly places Nelson within the social critical tradition of the American intellectual left in the 1960s. His critical stance was augmented by the ecological awareness of the 1970s expressed through journals like *Co-Evolution Quarterly* and *The Whole Earth Catalogue*, and it is no coincidence that the editor of these two publications, Stewart Brand, wrote the introduction to the 1987 edition of *Computer Lib*. Nevertheless, Nelson's plea in 1974 for the necessity of "understanding computers" is closely linked to the Enlightenment paradigm, as the possible answer to the environmental threats to human society:

Humanity may end with a bang (thermonuclear exchanges or just desultory firings until we're all poisoned or sterile), or a whimper (universal starvation), or , I would

anticipate, some spastic combination of the two, and all within the (possible) lifetime
of the average reader.

...as the problems increase and move toward our heartland, it'll be blamed on envi-
ronmentalists and on the news media, till bang.

Or maybe not. Just maybe.

But we've all got to ... look for holes or strategies. If computer modelling systems
doing this kind of work are made widely enough available, perhaps some precocious
gradeschooler or owlish hobbyist will find some way out that the others haven't hit
on.   (*Nelson* 1987a: 177)

This dramatic conclusion to the 1974 text belies the prevalent enthusiasm of
Computer Lib, and may be viewed as a "politically correct" afterthought.
The rest of Nelson's book presents a firmly consistent belief in modern man's
capability to control and influence his destiny with the help of computers
("You can and must understand computers NOW"), and the 1974/87
"companion" book, *Dream Machines,* prophesies a pivotal role for hypertextual computer design in this respect.

1984 has come and gone and a good many of Nelson's predictions in
Computer Lib and *Dream Machines* have come true, especially those pertaining to technological development. Another striking aspect of this book
today is a consistent argumentation that clearly places Nelson on one side of
an ongoing debate between modernism and postmodernism.

Critical modernism has during the last decade been challenged by various
versions of *postmodern* theory, from writers, artists, and theoreticians who all
express either doubts about or outright rejection of the central pillars of
modernity. In this critical discourse the distinction between modernism and
modernity has become increasingly important in order to avoid confusion
with the old modernist/antimodernist debates, *modernity* being identified
with the general direction of philosophical and social thought of the
Enlightenment.

MTV, a media phenomenon universally proclaimed as "postmodernist,"
announces a daily series of new music videos under the heading
Postmodern, lending further credibility to the view that "postmodern" in
today's everyday language has taken over many of the meanings "modern"
contained in the everyday usage yesterday, with the music video as a major
metaphor. The word now connotes the transitory, the ephemeral, the fragmented, the multifaceted, as well as leaning strongly to a hedonist philosophy.

As for the word "postmodernism" itself, it is, as Fredric Jameson has
pointed out, with its multitude of meanings and uses symptomatic for postmodern thought — "the sheer enumeration of changes and modifications."
(Jameson, 1991). Jameson comments on his 1984 article on postmodernism,

The Cultural Logic of Late Capitalism, by pointing out that the main change in the general view on postmodernism as a phenomenon in 1984 and 1989 was that in the latter year it was nearly impossible, on principle grounds, to *avoid* using the word "postmodern."

Postmodern traits of hypertext. Example: *Hyperland*

In 1990 The BBC produced a television program that presented and demonstrated the potentiality of hypertext as a harbinger of *nonlinear television*. In the program, Douglas Adams (author of *The Hitchhiker's Guide to the Galaxy)* is transported into the near future where he is confronted with a "fully customizable," on-line, humanoid guide through the world of non-linearity.

Adams is presented with a control panel of *micons,* or icons containing small loops of digitized video. These micons represent hypertext nodes, and pointing at a micon, or a part of it, will take him to that hypertext node. Thus the following sequence is initiated:

By pointing at a micon representing Vannevar Bush, a video sequence consisting of archive film and explanatory soundtrack appears, giving information on Bush and the article presenting the *Memex*-idea. This micon is titled *Atlantic Monthly*. At the touch of the word *Atlantic*, several new micons pop up on a background of a rolling ocean with titles like *Oceanography, Live Feed, Literature,* and *Shipping* .

The *Live Feed* micon then takes the user to a concurrent video image from the weather satellite MarSat West in orbit over the Southern Atlantic. Over this image then two more micons representing submersible observation stations in the Atlantic, and a touch on one of these takes the astounded Adams to a live video of dolphins curiously looking at the camera.

From here, a touch on the "Return" icon on the screen, again brings up the five micons of the *Atlantic* menu. The *Literature* micon brings up the images and names of Melville, Coleridge, Conrad, C.S. Forrester, and Hemingway, the appearance of each micon accompanied by selected lines from the works of these authors read aloud on the soundtrack. By touching *Coleridge*, a micon representing *The Rime of the Ancient Mariner* appears over a portrait of Coleridge, accompanied by further micons related to this author. Another touch, this time on *More works*, brings up a new series of choices, among those *Kubla Khan*. After choosing this poem, it is read while the text scrolls in "Star Wars" fashion over the screen. Pointing at any word in the text will stop the text and lead to an explanation of some sorts. Moving our fingers over the phrase "widening chasm," we are informed that this may be viewed as a "metaphor for the female sexual organ," a touch on the word "dulcimer" opens up for a discourse on mediaeval music, as well as a treatise on rhombic shapes, and in the middle of all this, up pops the micon with Ted Nelson's continually shaking head. Why? Because the on-line hypertext system for organizing literature that Nelson has been working on for almost two decades is called — "had to be called," as Nelson puts it — *XANADU.*

I will use this example to illustrate how the hypertext idea is marked by a series of contradictions typical of the modern/postmodern controversy. Although it may be contended that the chosen example is a hypothetical one, and an example of dubious hypertextual design at that, there is no doubt that it represents a very real simulation, based on the current state of the art in the field of hypermedia. Furthermore, the obvious design "faults" in the program are very helpful in illustrating inherent problems in the hypertextual presentation.

Hypertext in the modern/postmodern controversy: The "checklist" of Ihab Hassan

In his article *Concepts of Postmodernism*, Ihab Hassan (Hassan, 1987) has compiled a "postmodern checklist" consisting of a dual listing of "modern" phenomena presented with their postmodern counterparts. In this list we find four pairs of contrasting concepts with a definite relevance to the situation experienced by the watcher of *Hyperland:*

Modernism	*Postmodernism*
Purpose	Play
Design	Chance
Centering	Dispersal
Hierarchy	Anarchy

This set of contradictions can easily be found to be contained within the practice of hypertextual structures.

Although the idea behind hypertext is based on a very strong sense of *purpose*, the *Hyperland* film ends up with a strong emphasis on the *playfulness* of the medium, with a tour-de-force presentation of virtual reality "goggles." In the sequence referred to, the user clearly falls prey to playful curiosity as the beckoning micons pop up, one after another.

Play and games are central components of the computer culture as such, as a visit to any computer store and a look at any BBS files list should bear witness to. The counterpart to the purpose-oriented "computer programmer" is the play-oriented "hacker."

This contradiction, between purpose and play, spills over into the next pair of concepts. In authoring languages and systems for interactive multimedia, an area of application where hypertext holds a central position, purposeful *design* is what textbooks and courses propagate. Although the interface with the user should appear as ·"friendly" as possible, presenting the user with what seems to be a wide choice of options, the program in the background is specifically designed in order to fulfil a stated purpose behind the program, usually didactically defined.

At every hypertext node this design is challenged by *chance* in the form of possible "wrong" choices of links or paths. A critical part of multimedia design is therefore to minimize chances of "wrong" decisions, at the same time keeping up the appearance of presenting "real" choices.

A first glance at a design chart for a hypertext program can thus easily give the false impression of an information flow that lead in all directions, seemingly at random. This impression of information *dispersal* is in turn contrasted with the previously mentioned *centering* represented by the many pointers imbedded in the program design aimed at leading the user through a presumed meaningful discourse. The implied *hierarchy* of instructional design is made as a defense against the playful *anarchy* that is the didactic lure of computer-assisted learning programs.

These four major contradictions within the concept of hypertext-based learning programs all point to the contested ground of *space* in the ongoing debate on modernity and post-modernity, and lead to a detour to the field of architecture and urban geography.

Getting lost in postmodern hyperspace

The case for the modern conception of orientation in space is perhaps best made by Kevin Lynch in his classic study from 1960, *The Image of the City*. This book is especially interesting in our context because some of Lynch's key concepts for city geography bear close resemblance to important principles of hypertext. Lynch defines five types of elements pertaining to the physical form of the city: *paths, nodes, landmarks, districts, and edges*.

These elements are crucial in our perception of the city, as they help us define the *legibility* of the urban environment. *Paths* are the routes of frequent travel, and are invariably related to the concept of *nodes* defined as strategic junction points and, according to Lynch, a dominant feature in the individual's image of the city. *Landmarks* are reference points, usually in some form of physical shape, like monuments of buildings that facilitates navigation in the city landscape. *Districts* are areas with a common identity, and *edges* are linear structures representing the boundaries between areas (Lynch, 1960: 46-49).

All of these five elements can and have been transferred to hypertext, where concepts like nodes and paths (links) are part of any definition of the concept, like the one made by McKnight, Dillon, and Richardson in their book *Hypertext in Context*: "Simply stated, hypertext consists of *nodes* (or "chunks") of information and *links* between them" (McKnight, Dillon, Richardson, 1991: 2).

Further on in that book, the authors make extensive use of the geography analogy in order to cast light over the problem of *navigation* in hypertext. Referring to several empirical studies of learning efficiency in hypertext programs as compared to linear text presentation of the same subject matter, the authors conclude that hypertextual presentation is no guarantee of better performance, and emphasize the problem of navigation:

Interestingly, these studies seem to suggest that the hypertext structure places an extra burden on the reader in terms of navigation and consequently leads to poorer performance (p. 62). And: With the advent of hypertext it has become widely accepted that the departure from the so-called "linear" structure of paper increases the likelihood of readers or users of getting lost (p. 65).

Lynch frequently points to the *horror* of getting lost in his book:

> To become completely lost is perhaps a rather rare experience for most people in the modern city. We are supported by the presence of others and by special way-finding devices: maps, street numbers, route signs, bus placards. But let the mishap of disorientation once occur, and the sense of anxiety and even terror that accompanies it reveals to us how closely it is linked to our sense of balance and well-being. The very word "lost" in our language means much more than geographical uncertainty; it carries overtones of utter disaster.   (*Lynch*, 1960: 4).

This danger of getting lost is underscored by the authors of *Hypertext in Context*, who devote an entire chapter to the problem of navigation in hypertextual space, based on the (surprisingly scant, according to the authors) research done in the psychology of navigation with an emphasis on the development of *cognitive mapping*.

Cognitive mapping: A counter strategy to hyperspace

The question of cognitive mapping is also prominent in the work of Fredric Jameson on postmodernism. In his 1991 book on the subject, he elaborates on the points of view set forth in his 1984 article, where he places the post-modern phenomenon in a wider social and cultural context. Unlike other theoreticians with a Marxist background who have rejected the postmodern argumentation (for example, Callinicos, 1989), Jameson has set out to "historize" a concept that appears to be ahistorical. Postmodernism, Jameson contends, is the cultural logic of late capitalism, representative for an epoch where capital expands truly *multinationally*, not only imperialistically. It is the period when the last pre-capitalist enclaves in modern time — nature and the unconscious — are invaded by omnipresent multinational capital. Instead of viewing postmodernism as something that transcends the ideology of capitalism, Jameson sees postmodernism as the cultural logic of "late capitalism" as defined by the Marxist economist Ernest Mandel.

Jameson turns to architecture to illustrate his point and uses John Portman's Westin Bonaventure Hotel in Los Angeles as an analysis example. This building, prominent among its large number of siblings all over the industrialized world, sticks out in the city landscape with its rejective glass facade (Jameson uses the word "repulsive"), signaling itself as a self-contained world. Which it in a way is, with its combination of habitation (hotel) and consumption (restaurants and shopping arcades).

The visitor, when entering the building through one of its inconspicuous entrances, is sucked into a shopping, eating, and living machine where orientation becomes almost impossible with its multitude of levels and panorama elevators, and criss-crossing escalators combine to elicit what Jameson calls *postmodern hyperspace*. And he sees in this spatial disorientation a metaphor for postmodernism as such:

So I come finally to my principal point here, that this latest mutation in space — postmodern hyperspace — has finally succeeded in transcending the capacities of the individual to locate itself, to organise its immediate surroundings perceptually, and cognitively to map its position in a mappable external world. It may now be suggested that this alarming disjunction point between body and its built environment ... can itself stand as the symbol and analogon of that even sharper dilemma which is the incapacity of our minds ... to map the great global multinational and decentered communicational network in which we find ourselves caught as individual subjects.

(Jameson, 1991: 44).

It is interesting to note that Jameson uses the word "alarming" in this context, thus echoing the horror of getting lost expressed by Kevin Lynch, and he has followed this up in his 1988 article *Cognitive Mapping* (Jameson, 1988) by suggesting a counter strategy of cognitive mapping based on acceptance of the idea of a *social totality*. This is where Jameson departs from other theoreticians of the postmodern (like Lyotard and Baudrillard) for whom the rejection of any social totality is one of the very hallmarks of the postmodern condition.

A similar strategy, underscoring the historical importance of mapping, is proposed by David Harvey in his book, *The Condition of Postmodernity*. Harvey points out how the accessibility, appropriation, domination, and production of space has been crucial in the development of modern society from the first, primitive stages of capitalism and up to today's "flexible accumulation," which is his more precise definition of Jameson's "late capitalism."

Linking the growth of capitalism with the concept of spatial control, Harvey shows that, historically, the fragmentation and pulverization of space was a major factor in achieving this, and that the development of accurate maps was one of the tools facilitating this. ("Space can be conquered only through the production of space.")

During the last hundred years, this development has, quite literally, been "speeded up," mainly as a result of the development in communication, represented by the now so-trite metaphor about "the shrinking world" or, as Harvey put it, the annihilation of space through time. This time-space compression has resulted in the "great global multinational and decentered communicational network" that Jameson points to, which has given rise to a cultural homogenization that Harvey describes this way: "Extraordinary decentralization and proliferation of industrial production ends up putting Bennetton or Laura Ashley in almost every serially produced shopping mall in the advanced capitalist world" (Harvey, 1989: 296).

Loss of place-identity

One obvious effect of this is what Harvey terms as a "loss of place-identity" — the inability of the individual to identify his or her world geographically — and there seem to be two distinct reactions to this in contemporary thinking. One reaction, emanating from what could be termed "postmodern ideology," is to view this as a positive phenomenon, where the individual ought to take advantage of this new cultural pluralism, freed from the shackles of the old hierarchic, moralistic, place-bound, and static culture.

An early manifestation of this view is to be found in one of the seminal texts of postmodern theory, *Learning from Las Vegas*, by Robert Venturi, Denise Scott Brown, and Steven Izenour. This book on architecture was published in 1972 and proposed an architecture of the "ugly and ordinary" by using popular and commercial building styles as examples for an architecture in opposition to the dominating modern and functionalist architecture.

The authors suggested that by drawing lessons from the way urban architecture in America had developed on its own, outside the world of sys-
temised and institutionalized modern architecture, an alternative position to
modernist architecture could be developed. The geographical expression of
this is *the urban sprawl,* as it has grown organically in the automobile oriented culture of the United States. The counterpart and identified enemy to
this expression of popular, "low culture" and commercial city non-planning,
in *Learning from Las Vegas,* is the planned, elitist, "high culture," modern
city planning tradition identified as *megastructure.*

Using a contrasting table very much like Hassan's modern/postmodern
"checklist," the authors go through a list of how urban sprawl and megastructure differ fundamentally: ugly and ordinary vs. heroic and original,
mixed media vs. pure architecture, popular life-style, vs. "correct" life-style,
vital mess vs. "Total Design," building for men (markets) vs. building for
Man, to name a few of the 30 pairs in question. (Venturi, Brown, and Izenour,
1972: 84). The aim is clearly to "rehabilitate" the "vital mess" of urban
sprawl, pointing to Los Angeles and Las Vegas as the Rome and Florence for
future generations of architects. For the postmodern architects, loss of place-
identity is no great loss.

For the other view, we can return to Kevin Lynch and his description of
the urban sprawl of Jersey City as it appeared through interviews with inhabitants: "In studying the individual sketches and interviews, it became apparent that none of the respondents had anything like a comprehensive view
of the city they had lived in for many years. The maps were often fragmented, with large, blank areas" (Lynch, 1960: 29).

Jersey City is made into a negative example by Lynch by the very lack of
place-identity that it elicits, and Lynch is absolutely clear on the alternative
to this in his conclusion: "By appearing as a remarkable and well-knit *place,*
the city could provide a ground for the clustering and organization of ...
meanings and associations. Such a sense of place in itself enhances every
human activity that occurs there"(p. 119).

Harvey points out that the apparently liberating function of antiauthoritar-
ian, anti-structural "organic" growth has some sinister overtones. The accel-
erating speed of time-space compression is not matched by a similar speedily
reorientation of our mental maps and this loss of place-awareness may have
serious political implications. One such implication that Harvey suggests, the
retreat into geopolitical fragmentation, has been strongly emphasized by recent developments (winter of 1992) in the former Soviet Union and
Yugoslavia.

Another negative aspect to this loss of space pertains to the experience of
space as a reality. During the Gulf War of 1991, the television audience of

the world was bombarded by high-tech images from the war, to an extent that it was referred to as *the Nintendo effect*. This metaphor very revealingly points to a loss of reality in perception — reality extended to the level where the borders between play and physical reality becomes obscure, the realm of postmodern *hyperreality*.

Going off on an ice-lolly: The digression as master

In *Hyperland* an exasperated Douglas Adams finally asks his "guide": "Where were we before we went off on this — what do you call it?" Guide: "You can call it anything you like." "What if I call it an ice-lolly?" "Very good!" "So what happened when we went off on this ice-lolly?"

And since the field of hypertext is an uncharted one, with numerous nameless concepts yet to be mapped and named, let us appropriate Douglas Adams' new word into the hyperspeak vocabulary and look closer at the "ice-lolly" as a hypertext phenomenon.

In ordinary conversation the ice-lolly is known as a *digression*, the situation where two partners engage in a conversation on one topic and end up on a completely different topic.

The digression in turn, has relevance to the *coherence* of the text. Coherence, recent work in text linguistics suggests (for example, Agar and Hobbs, 1982), comes in three versions that act together. *Thematic coherence* refers to our ability to relate a proposition to an explicit theme. It is the quality that enables us to recognize what a certain text "is about." Closely connected to this, is *local coherence* where one sentence is obviously linked to the next, virtually "pointing" at it, without necessarily referring to the thematic coherence. The footnote is a typical example of local coherence. Thematic coherence and local coherence are participating in building a third kind of encompassing coherence that enables us to perceive series of isolated propositions as a whole — a *global coherence*.

What happens in the *Hyperland* example is that local coherence becomes dominant at the cost of thematic and global coherence and we feel the need to retrace the path to find our bearings. Local coherence is the stuff that digressions are made of.

The rapidly expanding field of hypertext theory take diverging views on the dangers of digression, and these views fall roughly along the separating lines of the followers and adversaries of postmodern ideology referred to above. One clear contradiction seems to follow the purpose/play dichotomy set forth by Hassan, with George P. Landow as a stern defender of purpose and global coherence.

In the article *The Rhetoric of Hypermedia: Some Rules for Authors*, Landow also invokes the navigation metaphor, noting that any user of a hypertext will assume that links represent useful and interesting relationships, hence Landow's first and third rules (of altogether nineteen) for hypertext authors:

Rule 1.　The very existence of links in hypermedia conditions the reader to expect useful, important relationships between linked materials.

Rule 3.　Since Hypermedia systems predispose users to expect such significant relationships among documents, those documents that disappoint these expectations appear particularly incoherent and nonsignificant.

Landow treats hypertext as the modern learning-efficient tool that Bush and Nelson expected it to be, and his set of rules contributes to this. His 19 rules construct a useful set of concepts for those wanting to map and structure the seemingly chaotic field of hypertext. In fact, what Landow does is provide the hypertext authors with rules that help them create maps for the users to navigate by in the "urban sprawl" of multi-linear hypertext.

In his Rule 6, Landow echoes Lynch's ideas of an imaginable city:

Rule 6.　Devices of orientation permit readers (a) to determine their present location, (b) to have some idea of that location's relation to other materials, (c) to return to their starting, and (d) to explore material not directly linked to those in which they presently find themselves.

Another and different stance on the question of digression and lack of coherence in hypertext is taken by Terence Harpold, who puts the phenomenon of digression into a psychoanalytic context (Harpold, 1991). Turning to the French psychoanalytic tradition from Lacan, Harpold delivers a "defense" for the digression in hypertext that is strongly reminiscent of psychoanalytically oriented film theory.

The common concept here is what Jacques-Alain Millar named *suture* literally the "sewing together" of the "cut" or "gap" in the signifying chain, representing the death of the subject. In Lacanian and Althusserian inspired film theory, *suture* is used to explain how the "seamless" narrative techniques of the Hollywood film is able to elicit pleasure in the viewer by representing a "whole" subject, a world where all the uncomfortable gaps have been "sewn together."

For Harpold, *suture* similarly represents "knots" that tie together the unwanted gaps in hypertext links, the gaps that open to innumerable other nar-
rations. When these knots are loosened it has the effect of erasing subjectiv-
ity:

> These loopings and the knots that bind them are the traces of collective structures
> enclosing and obscuring the gap of subjectivity. What distinguishes hypertexts as
> collaborative forms of textuality-as-detour is that they concretize in a social form the
> significance of the structures of gap and erasure in narrative digression.
>
> (*Harpold*, 1991: 178).

Thus digression becomes a revealing agent in the process of de-centering the
subject, and hypertext appears to be an ideal medium for making this more
visible. Instead of being an anarchic detour into meaninglessness and
nothingness, the digression actually allows for greater insight.

Stewart Moulthorpe takes this view even further, when he suggests hypertext as an answer to Jameson's scepticism about the possibility of a politically relevant postmodern art (Aarseth, 1991: 81).

Knowing where you are, or getting lost and enjoying it

In this chapter I have pointed out how some of the crucial aspects of hypertext and hypermedia tie in with the continuing controversy around postmodern thought. Popularly it can be stated as a controversy between upholding
the modernist vision of "knowing where you are" or succumbing to the
temptation of the postmodern position of "getting lost and enjoying it."

From the debate in architecture between modern and postmodern, represented by the views of Lynch and Venturi et al., this contradiction can be
said to crystallize between the "imaginable city" of Lynch and the "urban
sprawl" of Venturi, with the first emphasizing the need for *knowledge and
control* and the latter pointing to the *enjoyment* aspect of popular culture.

These two stances can be viewed as representing the same dialectics conveyed by the selected pairs from Hassan's postmodern "checklist" — pur-
pose/play, design/chance, centering/dispersal, and hierarchy/anarchy, where
special consideration should be given to the first pair, that of purpose *versus*
play.

When we look to hypertextual practices in the present and in the near future, it is quite obvious that this debate does not easily resolve into an ei-
ther/or. In the established field of interactive hypermedia (mainly interactive
video learning programs), the question of "correct" navigation and securely
structured pathways is and will definitely be the main concern, clearly signalling a bias toward "purpose." "Interactive design" has for several years

existed as an academic discipline at American universities, adjusting and improving the purpose-related hypertext tools of interactive authoring systems.

On the other hand, development in hypertextual literary systems seems to have developed a duality. In addition to normative work on the rhetoric of hypertext, such as Landow's, there is also a marked emphasis on the "playful," in theory as well as in practice, as the examples cited from Harpold and Moulthorpe suggest.

In certain areas of hypertextual practices, the "play" side seems to be totally dominating. In a recent master's thesis, Espen Aarseth focuses on the practices of *MUDs* — multi-user dungeons — which has developed into a sub-culture within the on-line community. Admittedly, the practices of on-line role-playing in a constantly changing cybernetic environment stretches the hypertext concept to its outer limit, but Aarseth maintains that "if we can study the games within a text, then why not study the texts within a game?" (Aarseth, 1991: 84-85).

This raises the question where to place the latest technological innovation related with hypertext — *virtual reality* where the postmodern simulacrae described by Baudrillard and others is taken to the extreme. With the help of a pair of "goggles" connected to a powerful three-dimensional graphic computer, the "reader" can enter the text pseudo-physically, seemingly without having to resort to representing devices like film, TV, or a book. At the bottom of this experience (or really pseudo-experience) lies a hypertext design with links and nodes that only differ from "ordinary" hypertext in its computational complexity.

According to recent rumors, commercial versions of virtual reality programs are expected to be available as the next generation of video games in the near future. We will then have an extraordinary example illustrating the paradox of "the postmodern condition" in the fact that large, centralized entertainment corporations, with the help of tightly, hierarchically designed virtual reality programs, will provide the public with pseudo-realities invoking playful multiplicity and chance.

This result does definitely not confirm with the utopian views of Bush and Nelson, and it hardly conforms with the implicit promise of "subversive hypertext" set forth by the theoreticians of postmodern hypertext. However, it points to an interdependent duality between modern and postmodern expressions in hypertextual practice that seems to belie the seemingly unbridgeable gap that theory has constructed.

Could it be that we are looking at two sides of the same coin?

Bibliography

AARSETH, E. (1991). *Texts of Change. Towards a Poetics of Nonlinearity.* Unpublished M.A. thesis. Bergen: Department of Comparative Literature, University of Bergen, Norway.

AGAR, M., HOBBS, J. (1982). Interpreting discourse. In *Discourse Processes*, 5 pp.1-32.

BUSH, V. (1945). As We May Think. *Atlantic Monthly* 176, July 1945, pp.101-108.

CALLINICOS, A. (1989). *Against Postmodernism.* Cambridge: Polity Press.

DELANY, P., LANDOW, G. (1991). *Hypermedia and Literary Studies.* Cambridge, Mass.: The MIT Press.

EVENSEN, L. (1988). Lokal og global koherens i elevers skriving. In *TRANS — Trondheim Papers in Applied Linguistics*, IV.

HARPOLD, T. (1991). Threnody: Psychoanalytic Digressions on the Subject of Hypertext. In *Hypermedia and Literary Studies*, eds. Delaney, Landow, pp.171-181. Cambridge, Mass.: The MIT Press.

HARVEY, D. (1989). *The Condition of Postmodernity.* Oxford: Basil Blackwell.

HASSAN, I. (1987). *The postmodern turn.* Ohio: Ohio State University Press.

JAMESON, F. (1988). Cognitive Mapping. In *Marxism and the Interpretation of Culture*, eds. Nelson, G., Grossberg, L. Chicago: University of Illinois Press.

JAMESON, F. (1991). *Postmodernism, or The Cultural Logic of Late Capitalism.* London: Verso.

LANDOW, G. (1991). The Rhetoric of Hypermedia: Some Rules for Authors. In *Hypermedia and Literary Studies*, eds. Delaney, Landow, pp.81-103. Cambridge, Mass.: The MIT Press.

LYNCH, K. (1960). *The Image of the City.* Cambridge, Mass.: The MIT Press.

MCKNIGHT, C., DILLON, A., RICHARDSON, J. (1991). *Hypertext in Context.* Cambridge: Cambridge University Press.

MOULTHORP, S. (1991). Reading from the Map: Metonymy and Metaphor in the Fiction of Working Paths. In *Hypermedia and Literary Studies*, eds. Delaney, Landow, pp.119-132. Cambridge, Mass.: The MIT Press.

NELSON, T.H. (1965). A File Structure for the Complex, The Changing and the Indeterminate. In *Association for Computing Macinery Proceedings of the 20th National Conference*, pp.84-100.

NELSON, T.H. (1987a). *Computer Lib.* Redmond: Microsoft Press.

NELSON, T.H. (1987b) *Dream Machines.* Redmond: Microsoft Press.

VENTURI, R., BROWN, D. S., IZENOUR, S. (1972). *Learning from Las Vegas.* Cambridge, Mass.: The MIT Press.

Index